Fodor's

ESSENTIAL TURKEY

Welcome to Essential Turkey

In modern Turkey, the legacy of centuries of history coexists with progressive and contemporary culture. Its exciting capital, Istanbul, spans Europe and Asia: here, upscale eateries and swanky nightclubs are squeezed between Byzantine and Ottoman structures, with calls-to-prayer from city mosques sounding above the city. The Aegean and Mediterranean coasts mix ancient Roman ruins with stunning beaches and resorts. Still, the real cultural lessons come from the Turkish people, always welcoming and eager to share their homeland's fascinating past and present.

TOP REASONS TO GO

★ **Istanbul:** The Aya Sofya, Blue Mosque, Topkapı Palace, plus fabulous food and shopping.

★ **History:** Greco-Roman ruins such as Ephesus, Ottoman palaces, World War I battlefields.

★ **Local Eats:** Kebabs and meze are essential, along with regional and cutting-edge fare.

★ **Natural Wonders:** Cappadocia's fairytale rock formations, Pamukkale's travertine pools.

★ **Shopping:** Markets and bazaars brim with treasures from carpets to fragrant spices.

★ **Seaside Serenity:** Beautiful beaches, charming coastal towns, memorable Blue Cruises.

Contents

Fodor's Features

MAPS

Chapter 1

EXPERIENCE TURKEY

25 ULTIMATE EXPERIENCES

Turkey offers terrific experiences that should be on every traveler's list. Here are Fodor's top picks for a memorable trip.

1 The Masterful Sülemaniye Mosque

Mimar Sinan was the greatest Ottoman architect, and the Sülemaniye Camii in Istanbul's Fatih district is one of his masterpieces. It offers architectural harmoniousness and scope, with a massive, light-filled central dome. The peaceful gardens have a spectacular and much-photographed view of the Golden Horn. *(Ch. 3)*

2 Trekking the Lycian Way

The 540-mile Lycian Way, which winds along and above the Mediterranean coast from Fethiye to Antalya, is still Turkey's most popular hiking route, including dozens of easy day hikes if you aren't a hardcore trekker. *(Ch. 6)*

3 A Feast of Meze and Fish

A night at a *meyhane* is an unmissable part of any trip to Turkey. Start with a table full of *meze* (small plates) before moving on to a perfectly grilled fish and glasses of anise-flavored *rakı* mixed with water and ice. *(Ch. 3, 4, 5, 6)*

4 Exploring Ancient Ani

Once the capital of a 10th-century Armenian empire and an important crossroads of trade before invasions and a devastating earthquake provoked its decline, Ani is hauntingly beautiful. *(Ch. 8)*

5 Windsurfing in Alaçatı

With its broad, shallow bay, steady winds, and sparkling sea, the Aegean town of Alaçatı is renowned among windsurfers, and even complete beginners can feel the wind in their hair in no time. (Ch. 5)

6 Exploring Topkapı Palace

The Topkapı Palace was once accessible only to the privileged few, but today everyone can experience the grandeur of one of the world's most powerful empires, including the sultan's private harem. *(Ch. 3)*

7 Oil Wresting in Edirne

Men wearing only leather trousers and a thick coating of olive oil still gather to grapple on a grassy field in Kırkpınar to take part in Turkey's national sport, a competition that began in 1346. *(Ch. 3)*

8 Climbing to the Top of Kaçkar Dağı

The highest point in the rugged Kaçkar Mountains range, 3,900-meter (12,900-foot) Kaçkar Dağı, can be reached in a single day in late summer with a guide. *(Ch. 8)*

9 The Magnificent Aya Sofya

Byzantine church, Ottoman mosque, and now world-famous museum, the Aya Sofya is topped by a towering golden dome—built in the 6th century—that appears to float high above the building's marble floor. *(Ch. 3)*

10 Camel Wrestling

Each January in Selçuk, pairs of wrestling camels, massive beasts decked out in colorful, banner-adorned saddle blankets, lumber at each other in the ring until one asserts its dominance. (Ch. 5)

11 Seeing Sacred Sights in Antakya

Antakya (Antioch) was an important center of early Christianity, where St. Peter preached in a cave (now a church). Don't miss the majestic Roman-era mosaics on display at the Hatay Müzesi. *(Ch. 6)*

12 Beautiful Aphrodias

This 1st-century BC city was built to honor Aphrodite, the Greek goddess of beauty and love. It's surely one of the beautiful archaeological sites in Turkey and includes a fascinating museum. *(Ch 5)*

13 Visiting an Underground City

A visit to ancient Derinkuyu or Kaymaklı— underground cities believed to have sheltered thousands of people each—has been a highlight of a visit to Cappadocia since the 5th century BC. *(Ch. 7)*

14 Remote Akdamar Monastery

Lake Van is Turkey's largest lake, and its highlight is a visit to the uninhabited islet of Akdamar and its 10th-century Armenian monastery, reached by ferry. *(Ch. 8)*

15 Dramatic Rock Tombs

More than 2,000 years ago, the kings of the Pontic Empire carved tombs in their capital, Amasya. The ancient Lycians created tombs of their own in Fethiye and Myra, near Demre. *(Ch. 6)*

16 Shopping in Weekly Markets

Despite the increasing prominence of malls, for many Turks there's still no better place to shop than the weekly local *pazar*, which sells everything from olives to underwear, plus great street foods. *(Ch. 3–8)*

17 Ancient Troy

Troy is best known through Homer's *The Iliad*, but archaeologists have uncovered nine layers of civilization dated back 5,000 years; a brand-new museum at the site brings it all to life. *(Ch. 4)*

18 Sampling Black Sea Culture

In the mountains above the Black Sea coast, the yayla (highland pastures) have a distinctive culture all their own. Charming Çamlıhemşin is a good jumping-off point for sampling yayla life. *(Ch. 8)*

19 Walking through Ephesus

The heavy hitter among Turkey's wealth of archaeological sites, Ephesus offers the Library of Celsus; a giant outdoor theater; and the lavish "terrace houses." *(Ch. 5)*

20 Sailing on a Blue Cruise

Whether you swim, snorkel, curl up with a book, or lay for a sunny snooze, a chartered sailing trip along Turkey's Mediterranean Coast, stopping in pristine, uninhabited coves is a quintessential Turkish experience. *(Ch. 5, 6)*

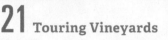

21 Touring Vineyards

Viniculture in Turkey dates back some 7,000 years. Increasingly, enterprising vintners, particularly in Urla and Thrace, offer wine routes and Napa Valley-like views without the crowds. *(Ch. 4, 5)*

22 The Turquoise Riviera

Whether you base yourself in sleepy Patara or Dalyan or in busier Kaş, you'll be within easy striking distance of two of the best beaches—Patara and İztuzu—both on Turkey's popular Turquoise Coast. *(Ch. 6)*

23 Paying Your Respects to Modern Turkey's Founder

Eighty years after his death, Mustafa Kemal Atatürk still casts a long shadow over Turkish politics and society. His massive mausoleum, in Ankara is the best place to get a sense of how monumental he was. *(Ch. 7)*

24 Getting Lost in Istanbul's Grand Bazaar

Often described as the world's oldest mall, Istanbul's Grand Bazaar offers thousands of vendors. It's overwhelming and unbearably touristy, but still quite fun. *(Ch. 3)*

25 Flying High above Cappadocia

The sight of dozens of colorful hot-air balloons floating above the fantastical volcanic-rock formations (known as "fairy chimneys") of Cappadocia has become an iconic image of Turkey. *(Ch. 7)*

WHAT'S WHERE

1 Istanbul. Straddling Europe and Asia, Istanbul is the undisputed cultural, economic, and historical capital of Turkey. There are enough monuments and attractions, as well as enticing restaurants, shops, and museums, to keep you busy for days.

2 The Sea of Marmara and the North Aegean. The battlefields of Gallipoli are one of the main reasons travelers visit this part of Turkey, but the area is also a destination for beach lovers and those looking for pleasant places to hike. The archaeological sites of ancient Troy and Pergamum are here, too.

3 The Central and Southern Aegean Coast. he heart of what was once known by the ancient Greeks as Asia Minor, this area has been drawing visitors since the time of, well, Homer. The heavyweight attraction these days is the Roman city of Ephesus but there are also many beach destinations, ranging from glitzy to relaxed.

4 The Turquoise Coast. The beaches along Turkey's Mediterranean shores—dubbed the Turquoise Coast—are some of the best in the country, and the ruins here are spectacular. With unspoiled seaside villages and charming hotels and *pansiyons*, this is very close to paradise. Steer clear of the megaresorts though, which have invaded many towns, particularly around Antalya and Marmaris.

5 Cappadocia and Central Turkey. In magical Cappadocia, wind and rain have shaped soft volcanic rock into a fairy-tale landscape, where conical outcroppings were centuries ago turned into churches and homes. Southwest of Cappadocia is Konya, home to a museum and tomb dedicated to the 13th-century poet and mystic Rumi, founder of the whirling dervishes. Ankara, Turkey's capital, is also here.

BLACK SEA

Inebolu
Sinope
Gerze
765
Kastamonu
Bafra
Samsun
Terme
010
100
İskilip
Merzifon
Ünye
Ordu
Görele
Trabzon
010
Çankırı
Amasya
Niksar
Giresun
Rize
785
Turhal
Kırıkkale
Zile
Suşehri
950
Kars
Ani
ARMENIA
957
Kaman
200
Sivas
Erzincan
Erzurum
100
Iğdır
YEREVAN
260
Divriği
100
Mt. Ararat
Ağrı
Doğubeyazıt
IRAN
5
Göreme
Kayseri
Elazığ
957
Uchisar
Ürgüp
300
6
750
Afsin
300
Lake Van
Van
805
965
076
Ereğli
Kahramanmaraş
Sıvarek
Tarsus
Adana
Osmaniye
950
Mersin
Dörtyol
Şanlıurfa
Mardin
İskenderun
IRAQ
Antakya
(Antioch)
SYRIA
Mosul
Samadağı

GEORGIA

TBILISI

6 The Black Sea Coast and Lake Van. It may not have the resorts, boutique hotels, and upscale restaurants of western Turkey, but there are impressive sites—both natural and man-made—including picturesque mountain villages; historic monasteries and churches; the ancient city of Ani; Lake Van; and the towering Mt. Ararat (believed by some to be the resting place of Noah's Ark). In all these places, you're certain to get a taste of a different and rewarding Turkey.

What to Eat and Drink in Turkey

MEZE

Meze are small dishes that emphasize fresh vegetables usually in oil. Sample *patlıcan salatası*, a smoky eggplant puree; *giritezmesi*, a mix of crumbly cheese, pistachios, and herbs; or *atom*, thick yogurt laced with blazing hot dried red peppers. Restaurants often rotate their meze offerings.

MANTI

Every culture has their take on dumplings, and the Turkish version is particularly satisfying. Small pockets of minced meat are doused in garlicky yogurt and topped with melted butter or oil and a dusting of mint and red pepper flakes. Various regions offer different varieties; most famous are the tiny mantı from the city of Kayseri and the larger delicate mantı from the Black Sea city of Sinop.

SAHLEP

Only available during the colder winter months, *sahlep* is a sweet, creamy drink made from the root of an orchid. Topped with cinnamon, it's an excellent non-caffeinated beverage to warm your hands and soul during the grayer months. Keep an eye out for *hakiki sahlep*, which is the real deal.

KAHVALTI

There's breakfast, and then there's Turkish breakfast, a spread that splays out across the table. It often includes oily olives, cucumber and tomatoes, thick white cheese, homemade jams, sizzling sunny-side-up eggs, *tahin pekmez* (a sweet mix of tahini and grape molasses), and crunchy bread, served with tea.

RAKI

Turkey's national drink isn't just a beverage—it's an experience. Like Greek *ouzo* and French *pastis*, rakı is a clear anise liquor that turns milky white when diluted with water (it is sometimes referred to as "lion's milk"). It is served chilled and meant to be sipped slowly over a large feast, generally of meze and fish. The rakı table is where people come together, tell stories, and break bread.

SIMIT

Sold on every Istanbul street corner, *simit* is the ideal snack on the go. A bready circle encrusted with sesame seed, it's crunchy on the outside and soft on the inside and delivered fresh to vendors throughout the day. For a real treat, track down a simit bakery and get a hot, fresh one.

MIDYE DOLMA

One of the most satisfying of Istanbul's street snacks is *midye dolma*, rice-stuffed mussels served with a spritz of lemon juice. Some restaurants specialize in midye dolma, but there's something about eating them streetside that adds to the experience.

LAHMACUN

Sometimes in Turkey, it's the simple food that packs the bigger punch. *Lahmacun* is deceptively simple, with spicy minced lamb spread over a crispy thin dough. But roll it up with some parsley, a squeeze of lemon, and a dusting of sumac, and you have a perfect low-key Turkish meal.

ÇAY

Black tea is the fuel on which Turkey runs. Grown in its lush northeastern corner and consumed in tiny tulip-shaped tea cups, Turkish çay is omnipresent, often offered upon entering a shop, boarding a ferry, or visiting someone's house. While Turkish coffee is popular after meals, and third-wave coffee shops pop up faster and faster, they can't replace the nationwide love for a hot cup of çay.

AŞURE

This dessert is named for the Muslim holiday of *aşure* and traditionally served at that time of year (the tenth day of the first month of the Islamic calendar), but it's also available and enjoyed all year-round. A porridge with a base of grains and nuts, aşure can contain many ingredients, including dried fruits, pomegranate seeds, chickpeas, beans, and rose water.

What to Buy in Turkey

POTTERY

Intricately painted earthenware is produced all over Turkey, but the tiles and other ceramics made in İznik, a town in northwestern Turkey, are the most famous. You can find pieces with a more traditional Ottoman aesthetic as well as unique designs created by individual artisans' families.

JEWELRY

Jewelry design has long been an important and well-regarded trade in Turkey, dating back to the Ottoman era. Today it is still one of Turkey's leading handicrafts, and many stone inlaying techniques were originally conceived in the Ottoman court nearly 500 years ago. Knock-offs and cheap costume jewelry can be found in abundance, but unique designs and precious stones are abundant as well.

MEERSCHAUM

Hydrated magnesium silicate, meerschaum is more elegantly known as "sea foam." It's a white, ivory-like substance found in the Black Sea region, most often used to make carved pipes. You can also find jewelry and other accessories made from it. Raw meerschaum exportation is banned in Turkey, so this is one of the few places in the world you can still find the real thing.

FOOD AND SPICES

You can't leave Istanbul without picking up some Turkish delight, otherwise known as *lokum*. Spices, dried fruits, and nuts (particularly hazelnuts) are other Turkish staples, as well as coffee and special teas. For something with a kick, look for *rakı*, the popular Turkish anise liqueur.

ANTIQUES

Quality antiques are widely available in Istanbul at fair prices. Trade routes from the Far East and West have passed through the city for hundreds of years, leaving a fascinating stockpile of goods from all over the world. Some of the most valuable and interesting may not be Turkish, but look for pieces of Ottoman metalwork.

Calligraphy Prints

BOUTIQUE WARES

Istanbul is bursting with small boutiques selling contemporary handmade goods. Karaköy and Galata are the areas to peruse interesting shops and explore the tiny alleyways in some of the city's oldest neighborhoods. Nearby Nişantaşı showcases international and Turkish fashion designers.

TEXTILES

Embroidery, gold silk thread, and hand painting (known as *yazma*) are all prominent in Turkish textiles that can be bought as is or made into beautiful scarves, dresses, pillows, and other housewares. Cotton, wool, brocade, and çatma, similar to velvet, can also be wonderful.

TOWELS

Turkish towels, also known as *peştemal*, are used in Turkish hammam baths and are handwoven with domestic cotton, a particularly sturdy and high-quality fiber. Much thinner than terry cloth towels, the fabric is highly absorbent and dries quickly. They're also easy to carry home.

RUGS

Intricate, meticulously hand-knotted Turkish pile rugs are often woven with silk thread, and Turkey is known for its Holbein carpet design, a unique pattern developed under the Ottomans. Kilim rugs, produced in Turkey's rural areas, employ simpler geometric designs.

CALLIGRAPHY PRINTS

Some of the most beautiful decorations in Istanbul's mosques and palaces are the elaborate calligraphic writings etched into the wall, many of which are quotes from the Quran or the impossibly intricate signatures of the sultans. Under the Ottomans, new styles of Arabic calligraphy were developed and have since become an important part of Turkey's handicraft tradition.

10 Best Beaches of Turkey

PATARA BEACH
Patara's beach is the longest and most beautiful stretches of sand in Turkey, and it abuts some extensive Lycian ruins. Patara is also one of the nesting grounds for protected Caretta Caretta turtles, which doesn't diminish its beauty but does limit where you can place your umbrellas. *(Ch. 6)*

CLEOPATRA BEACH
Alanya is one of southwestern Turkey's most visited vacation destinations, and Cleopatra Beach is its crown jewel. Adjacent to the city center, it's also one of the easiest to access. Many beachside cafés and restaurants are spread along the shore. Water sports vendors are numerous. *(Ch. 6)*

OVABÜKÜ PLAJI
This quiet beach on the *Datça* peninsula feels like an escape from it all. The rolling landscape of pine-crowned hills and olive groves gives way to the deep blue waters of the Aegean Sea. If you make it all the way here, be sure to go the additional 38 km (24 miles) west to visit the Knidos ruins. *(Ch. 6)*

KAPUTAŞ BEACH
Tucked between two dramatic cliffs off the road between Kalkan and Kaş, Kaputaş Beach feels like stepping inside a photograph. With turquoise Mediterranean water, this beach is small but very popular, thanks to its convenient location near a major road. Because the beach it situated at the bottom of deep cliffs (hence lots of stairs going down), the noise from the road is a distant memory as you wade in the water. *(Ch. 6)*

OLYMPOS
Perfect for laid-back travelers who want to stay in a tucked-away, rustic treehouse (at Şaban Tree Houses), the beach at Olympos is relaxed and lovely. The cove contains calm water, and the sandy beach gives way to sprawling ruins nestled in dense forests. Olympos is located on the Lycian Way, so there is ample hiking in the area for those who want to do some more extensive exploring. *(Ch. 6)*

ÖLÜDENIZ
This beautiful a short ride outside the city of Fethiye is one of Turkey's most iconic beaches. The long bend of sandy white beach against azure waters has been deemed the blue lagoon (which actually refers to the lagoon that's mostly enclosed by the sandbar at the northern tip of the beach (it's part of Ölüdeniz Natural Park). The long, beautiful beach and the near-constant winds have made Ölüdeniz a popular destination for both vacationers and

Kaputaş Beach (Kas)

paragliders, who take in the views of the beach from above. (Ch. 6)

İZTUZU BEACH

Known as a nesting area for Caretta Caretta turtles in June and July, İztuzu Beach is located on a narrow strip of land that separates the Mediterranean from the Dalyan River. In order to protect the turtles, the beach is closed to night swimming, but by day it's a calm cove for a cool dip. (Ch. 6)

LIMANAĞZI

This tiny bay across from the main harbor in Kaş is only accessible by boat (or by hiking), which makes it the perfect retreat from the bustle of the city center. On the small beach, you can rent chairs and buy a drink from small bar. Limanağzı is a perfect spot for a casual swim during a long, relaxing day. (Ch. 6)

ALAÇATI

Nestled in the Çeşme peninsula west of İzmir, Alaçatı beach is best known for windsurfing and kite-surfing. Adventure seekers flock here to take advantage of the constant gusts blowing from the Aegean Sea. There are plenty of beach clubs, as well as calmer bays where you can lounge by the clear water. The town of Alaçatı is cobblestoned and charming, with blooming bougainvillea. (Ch. 6)

BUTTERFLY VALLEY

Only accessible by boat or a treacherous climb down a cliff, the beach at the Butterfly Valley is situated in the bottom of a wide valley (a protected nature preserve) beneath the village of Faralya. Clear turquoise waters and lush nature attract a laid-back crowd. Boats depart daily from Ölüdeniz. (Ch. 6)

Islam

ISLAM AND MUHAMMAD

Islam is an Abrahamic religion—one of the three largest (and somewhat interrelated) monotheistic religions in the world. The prophet Muhammad is believed to be descended from Ishmael, son of Abraham, through a union with his wife Sarah's handmaiden, Hagar. Abraham also sired Isaac, who was one of the patriarchs of Judaism and Christianity. Thus, many of the prominent figures in Judaism and Christianity—Adam, Moses, and Jesus—are also revered as prophets in Islam.

Muhammad was born in Mecca on the Arabian Peninsula (near the Red Sea in present-day Saudi Arabia). He became a religious figure in 610 AD when, according to Islamic tradition, while meditating in solitude he began to receive visions from the angel Gabriel. The words of these visitations became the *shuras* (verses) of the Koran, the holy book of Islam. When Muhammad first began preaching the new religion he was met with hostility by pagan tribesmen and forced to flee to Medina (also in Saudi Arabia) in 622 AD.

After converting the people of Medina to Islam, Muhammad returned to Mecca and converted his hometown, and by the end of the 6th century, Islam was the dominant religion in Arabia. In the subsequent centuries Muslim armies would sweep across North Africa and into Spain, throughout the Levant and eastward into Central Asia and Persia. Turkic peoples were converted to Islam sometime during their journey across Asia, and when the Seljuks swept through Byzantine territory in Asia Minor, they brought Islam with them. After the rise of the Ottoman Empire, Muslims crossed the Dardanelles into Eastern Europe, where the Turks conquered as far as Vienna. Today there are 1.8 billion Muslims throughout the world.

ISLAM TODAY

Islam is a comprehensive religion and its tenets touch all aspects of life. Devout Muslims pray five times a day: at sunrise, midday, in the afternoon, at sunset, and in the early evening—exact times are determined by the sun's passage. One of the first things visitors to Istanbul notice is the sound of the call to prayer—called the *ezan*—wafting from the minarets of local mosques. The focal point of Muslim prayer is the Sacred Mosque in Mecca, at the center of which is the Kabaa, a shrine said to have been built by Abraham and rebuilt by Muhammad. One duty of able-bodied Muslims is to make the pilgrimage, or *hajj*, to Mecca at least once in their lifetime.

Many modern Turks have a relaxed approach to their religion. Some drink alcohol and many smoke cigarettes—both of which are forbidden by strict interpretations of Islam. They typically don't, however, eat pork. While the Koran expressly forbids eating all carnivores and omnivores, pigs are especially abhorrent. Turkish men can be shameless flirts and modern women often dress in contemporary and revealing couture, though such behavior is not in keeping with Islamic ideas of modesty. There are, however, a great many conservative folks, too, and in modern Turkey, the role of religion in society is hotly debated, as is the ongoing relevance of Atatürk's definition of secularism.

RAMADAN

The Islamic holy month of Ramadan, called "Ramazan" in Turkish, lasts for 30 days and is an especially pious time. During it, observant Muslims abstain from eating, drinking, smoking, and sexual relations, from dawn to sunset; this self-denial teaches restraint and humility and is meant to bring one closer to God. Those who are fasting start each day with a predawn meal called *sahur*. At sundown, the fast is broken with a meal called *iftar*, which traditionally includes dates, soup and bread, olives, and other foods. Many restaurants offer special iftar fixed menus during Ramadan. In small towns and conservative parts of Turkey it may be hard to find restaurants open during the day during Ramadan, but in most cities and tourist areas it's not an issue. Though it's understood that non-Muslims will not be fasting, it's respectful to avoid eating in public (such as on the street or on public transportation) during Ramadan. You should also be prepared for the fact that in some places, even touristy areas like Sultanahmet in Istanbul, it's still customary for drummers to walk around in the wee hours of the morning to wake people for the sahur—which can make for a rather startling, and early, awakening. The end of Ramadan is celebrated with a three-day holiday called Ramazan Bayramı or *Şeker Bayramı* ("sugar holiday"), during which people visit family and friends and plentifully consume sweets.

Another festival, *Kurban Bayramı* (feast of the sacrifice), requires Muslims to sacrifice an animal—typically a sheep or a cow—for their faith, honoring Abraham's willingness to sacrifice his firstborn son to God and God's last-minute substitution of a ram for the boy. Today, many Turks purchase vouchers that empower a professional butcher to make the kill in their name. Ramazan Bayramı and Kurban Bayramı are national holidays, and schools and many businesses are closed for the duration; museums and other attractions generally close only for the first day of the holiday.

MOSQUE ETIQUETTE

The Turks are quite lenient about tourists visiting mosques and most are open to the public during the day, but there are some rules of etiquette. It's best not to enter a mosque during the five daily prayer sessions, especially at midday on Friday, when attendances are higher; it's also considered offensive for a non-Muslin to sit down in a mosque. Immodest clothing is not allowed but an attendant by the door will lend you a robe if he feels you aren't dressed appropriately. For women, bare arms and legs aren't acceptable, and men should avoid wearing shorts. Women should cover their heads before entering a mosque.

Shoes must be removed before entering a mosque; there's usually an attendant who watches over them, or you can put them in your backpack or handbag, or use the plastic bags often provided near the entrance. Don't take photographs inside the mosque, particularly of people praying, and it's advisable to show respect by talking only in whispers.

A small donation is usually requested for the upkeep of the mosque.

What to Read and Watch Before Your Trip

As you explore this list, you'll find that these works bite: even the most light-hearted of these titles has a deep soul, and carries with it a certain amount of political commentary, weighty history, and heartbreaking beauty specific to Turkey.

DOCUMENTARY: *KEDI*

This 2017 documentary begins about cats, a staple of Istanbul street life for thousands of years. The film ends up as a beautiful walkabout of Istanbul's sights and streets, touching enough to convert even the most stubborn dog-lover. The visual portrayal of the city is lovely, as is the time getting to know the citizens and shopkeepers whose lives cross with these four-legged creatures.

MOVIE: *WINTER SLEEP*

Adapted from Chekhov's short story "The Wife," this 2014 movie takes place in Cappadocia, Central Turkey, where the protagonist Aydin—a writer, landlord, and former actor—accidentally gets too close one of his tenants (and the intricacies of his financial and legal difficulties); his wife is Nihal. The movie is a glance into the complicated economic and class boundaries of contemporary Turkey, set in a fascinating landscape of ancient mountains and high plateaus.

MOVIE: *THE TWO FACES OF JANUARY*

Viggo Mortensen and Kirsten Dunst star in this racy crime thriller from 2014, adapted from the 1964 novel by Patricia Highsmith (author of *The Talented Mr. Ripley*). The film revolves around a 1960s couple, their sketchy pursuits, and fatal mistakes, while touring Greece (and eventually landing in Istanbul). Beautiful scenes later on in the thick of the movie show Istanbul and the Grand Bazaar.

MOVIE: *ONCE UPON A TIME IN ANATOLIA*

This dark, soulful film from 2011 tours the Anatolian countryside in Turkey's Western Asian peninsula, as a group of men from a small town search for a dead body. Most of the movie involves this search, making for a film of lovely, long desert scenes and lengthy conversations on a variety of topics between the men.

MOVIE: *GALLIPOLI*

Directed by Peter Weir and starring Mel Gibson, this 1981 flick centers around an Australian army sent during World War I to Gallipoli, in the southern part of East Thrace. The film depicts a somewhat fictionalized version of the battle of Nek that took place there, when Australians were badly defeated by the Ottoman Empire. If you can get past some of its historical inaccuracies, it's a gut-wrenching anti-war film.

MOVIE: *MIDNIGHT EXPRESS*

This story became the stuff that travel nightmares are made of: when a young American man gets thrown into a Turkish prison for life, with no signs of aid from the United States. The 1978 film is such a classic that it's almost cliche now, and hard to remember that it's based on the true story of Billy Hayes, who was caught smuggling hashish out of Turkey, and then improbably escaped a Turkish prison to return home.

BOOK: *MY NAME IS RED*
BY ORHAN PAMUK

Narrators in this 1998 postmodern novel represent a wide, alternating range of characters, most of them miniature painters, a noble group of artists in the 16th-century Ottoman Empire, who created finely detailed manuscript illustrations. A book that is at once many things culminates as a beautiful novel about love, art, and mystery. Pamuk's other books, *Istanbul: Memories and the City* and *Museum of Innocence* also focus on the Istanbul he calls home.

BOOK: *THE BASTARD OF ISTANBUL* **BY ELIF ŞAFAK**

This full, if somewhat messy 2006 novel that greatly displeased the Turkish government jumps time spans, geographic locations, and the lives of its interconnected characters. Aside from its political and historical delving, especially into the Armenian Massacre of 1915, the descriptions of Istanbul and Turkey as a homeland are some of the book's best features.

BOOK: *FIVE SISTERS: A MODERN NOVEL OF KURDISH WOMEN* **BY KIT ANDERSON**

This 2012 book follows the lives of women, all from the same mountain village, and all of Kurdish descent, as their stories diverge. The novel is based on true stories Anderson gathered while living among the Kurdish (a traditional ethnic group that makes up about twenty percent of Turkish population) in Eastern Turkey for eight years.

BOOK: *THE OTHER SIDE OF THE MOUNTAIN* **BY ERENDIZ ATASÜ**

The feminist and activist author creates a rich, multigenerational tale of different characters and perspectives throughout Turkey (and jumping around several time periods), making the 2000 novel a complex (if not sometimes confusing) portrayal of Turkey and of Turkish women, through generations dating back to the Ottoman Empire.

BOOK: *DEAR SHAMELESS DEATH* **BY LATIFE TEKIN**

Political activist and best-selling author Latife Tekin pens a vivid portrayal of growing up as a woman in Turkey, based on her own experiences. The novel, while rooted in realistic, contemporary Turkey, maintains an element of magical realism in its portrayal of the small towns and big cities of the country, and the juxtaposition between contrasting ways of life.

Turkey Today

Though the lands it now contains have a history going back thousands of years, the modern Turkish Republic is less than a century old. Formed in 1923 after the defeat of the Ottoman Empire in World War I, the country has experienced its share of growing pains and continues to wrestle with political and economic challenges. It remains, however, a vibrant, fascinating place with an important global role.

POLITICS

The conservative Justice and Development Party (AKP) has led Turkey since its first election victory in 2002, and its Prime Minister-turned-President Recep Tayyip Erdoğan has become the dominant figure in Turkish politics, drawing equally passionate responses from supporters and detractors alike. Most elections, no matter who is on the ballot, are seen as a referendum on Erdoğan, whose efforts to consolidate and hang on to power have become increasingly controversial. From the start, the AKP has sparked alarm among diehard secularists who assert that the party seeks to erode the secular legacy of Mustafa Kemal Atatürk. Some even contend that the AKP seeks to impose Sharia (strict Islamic day-to-day religious law) on the country, pointing to its removal of restrictions on headscarf wearing and Erdoğan's conservative social pronouncements and vocal opposition to alcohol and tobacco use, though party leadership denies this.

Under the AKP, Turkey moved toward greater political and economic engagement with the Arab world, as well as with developing countries in other regions, as interest in joining the EU appeared to take a back seat. Though the country is still a candidate for membership, there are some strong opponents to Turkey's accession, and the talks have made only halting progress as Turkey faces criticism on several other issues. Continued Turkish occupation of Northern Cyprus (which only Turkey recognizes as a sovereign nation) is one major stumbling block; another is the Turkish government's refusal to label the deaths of hundreds of thousands of Armenians during World War I as genocide. Domestically, critics cite criminal laws that punish anyone found guilty of insulting "Turkishness" (amended in 2008 to insulting the Turkish nation) and pressures on the media, judiciary, and political opposition as further obstructions.

Simmering tensions between the AKP and its critics boiled over in the summer of 2013, when the heavy-handed police response to a peaceful sit-in at a central Istanbul park sparked weeks of anti-government protests in Istanbul, Ankara, and elsewhere around the country. Parliamentary elections in June 2015 saw a Kurdish party cross the 10% threshold for parliamentary representation for the first time and the AKP lose its majority, but only for a short time. The subsequent three years were tumultuous ones for Turkey, which endured a wave of terrorist attacks blamed on both ISIS and the militant Kurdistan Workers' Party (PKK); a failed military coup in July 2016 and a subsequent crackdown on civil society, opposition politicians, and other groups; and four additional elections, including a 2017 referendum on a powerful new presidential system.

The most recent parliamentary election in June 2018 saw the AKP hold on to its majority thanks to an alliance with the far-right Nationalist Movement Party (MHP) that already appears shaky. More uncertainty is likely ahead for a country already troubled by economic downturn, political polarization, and regional conflicts.

THE ECONOMY

The rosy outlook for the Turkish economy in the early 2000s now seems a distant memory, as the country hailed as an up-and-coming powerhouse suffered from a currency collapse in 2018 that brought the lira's value against the dollar to an all-time low. Turkey still enjoys a diverse economy: self-sufficient levels of agricultural production, a massive textile industry, and a growing electronics sector, plus its tourism industry appears to have rebounded after a bad few years. But following nearly a decade of strong annual GDP growth, considerable foreign investment, and reduced inflation, these trends started to reverse in the early 2010s due to regional turmoil, domestic political instability, and a general slowdown among the world's emerging markets. Concerns about increasingly authoritarian politics, large amounts of foreign-currency debt, and soaring inflation have all contributed to the growing perception that the country's economy is in an increasingly fragile position.

RELIGION

In Istanbul they sell a T-shirt with the name of the city spelled using a crescent, a cross, and a Star of David a testament to how Turks have traditionally prided themselves on their tolerance of other religions, a legacy of the Ottoman Empire, which governed people of all faiths. While Turkey is a secular republic, the population is overwhelmingly (99%) comprised of Muslims; the remaining 1% are Christians (mostly Greek Orthodox and Armenian Apostolic) and Jews. One reason for the relative harmony between people of different faiths may be the more relaxed approach toward religion found in much of Turkey. Many Turks drink alcohol and smoke cigarettes, and on any given day in Istanbul you're as liable to find as many scantily clad fashionistas walking down the street as women wearing headscarves (many of whom are plenty stylish themselves).

THE ARTS

Turkey has made many recent contributions to the art world—no surprise from a country that boasts such stunning antiquity. The Istanbul Film Festival will be in its 38th year as of 2019: held every April, the festival awards prizes for both Turkish and international films. The organization behind it, the Istanbul Foundation for Culture and Arts (İKSV), also puts on a well-regarded art biennial and design biennial, held in the fall in alternating years. The country's most well-known creative mind may still be novelist Orhan Pamuk, who garnered Turkey's first Nobel Prize in 2006 for his dreamy yet historical novels, though the stars of other authors—as well as filmmakers, designers, and musicians—are on the rise as well. Turkish film director Nuri Bilge Ceylan, for example, has received numerous honors at the Cannes Film Festival, including its highest award, the Palme d'Or, in 2014 for his "Winter Sleep." Additionally, Turkey's status as a large textile exporter has helped ensure the nation a place in fashion design, and Istanbul's Nişantaşı district is a maze of small boutiques selling imported and Turkish clothing. In the visual arts, Turkey is most famous for its ceramics and porcelain, especially handmade Kütahya and İznik tiles.

SPORTS

Turkey is a diehard soccer nation (they call it football), and heated rivalries run strong. Turkey's clubs boast lots of homegrown talent along with some players imported from Europe and South America. The Turkish national football team has enjoyed sporadic success in international play. In the last decade, the team reached the semifinals in the 2002 World Cup and 2008 European Cup. The Atatürk Olympic Stadium in Istanbul, home ground for the national team, will host the UEFA Champions League final in 2020. Basketball is also an increasingly popular sport in Turkey, which hosted the 2010 FIBA World Championship—and cheered its national team of "12 giant men" to a second-place finish. In the Olympics, Turkey has won the majority of its medals in wrestling, followed by weightlifting and taekwondo. Western-style gyms are increasingly common in big cities such as Istanbul, and though you still won't see many people running on city streets, there's been a huge growth in the number of running events, particularly trail races in scenic parts of the country.

MEDIA

Press freedom has become an increasingly urgent issue in Turkey, where some 150 journalists and media workers are behind bars and 174 media outlets have been closed by the government in recent years, according to numbers collected by human-rights organizations. Most are accused of "supporting terrorism," a vague charge that has often been applied broadly and without credible evidence. Frequent shutdowns of popular Internet sites, most prominently YouTube, Twitter, and Wikipedia, have added to concerns about freedom of speech, as has the consolidation of media properties in the hands of business interests allied with the government. Media self-censorship is also growing along with political pressure. Despite these controversies, there are still many small opposition newspapers and websites, as well as press-freedom organizations, trying to keep a diversity of voices alive.

TURKEY THROUGH THE AGES

According to an ancient saying, "Turkey is a man running West on a ship heading East." Today this adage is more apt than ever; amid growing tensions over the current government's Islamic leanings, the nation is still seeking EU membership. The ambivalence here underscores the country's age-old search for identity. Few can deny that Turkey is once again trying to remake itself.

Situated at the point where the continents of Europe and Asia come together, Turkey has served as the stomping ground for sundry migrations of mankind. Hittites, Persians, the armies of Alexander the Great, Romans, Byzantines, and Ottomans all have their place in the intriguing history of this land, whose early inhabitants, living on the vast Anatolian plain, created many of civilization's most enduring myths. Ancient Troy, immortalized in Homer's *Iliad*, is located on Turkey's Aegean coast, while in Phrygia, it is said, Alexander the Great split the Gordian knot with his sword, fulfilling the prophecy that this feat would make him king of Asia. These colorful legends are no match for the plain facts of history, but together they make Turkey one of the most fascinating places on earth.

TIMELINE

| 25,000 BC Paleolithic humans inhabit Karain Cave in Anatolia | 7000 BC Anatolians begin to grow crops and raise livestock | 6500 BC Çatal Höyük thrives as the world's earliest urban settlement |

PREHISTORY   7000 BC   6000 BC   5000 BC

Top: Archaeologist discovers obsidian objects in a Çatal Höyük house.
Right: Entrance to Karain Cave, Antalya.
Far right: Statues from Hacılar.

The Earliest Cultures

25,000 BC–3000 BC

The history of the lands that comprise modern Turkey began to unfold as long as 25,000 years ago, on the plains of Anatolia (Asia Minor), where bones, teeth, and other evidence of early humans have been unearthed in the Karain Cave near Antalya. Some of the most fascinating finds include Göbekli Tepe (in southeast Turkey), the world's oldest known shrine, whose monolithic pillars and templelike structures were erected by hunter-gathers around 9500 BC. Then there are the first signs of agricultural life, from about 7000 BC, which have been found at Hacılar, near Burdur. And by 6500 BC, Çatal Höyük, (near Konya)—often considered the world's first city—was at its height; evidence suggests that as many as 8,000 inhabitants lived in flat-roofed, one-story mud-brick houses, grew crops, and fashioned clay figurines representing a mother goddess. By 3000 BC the residents of many such Anatolian settlements were wielding tools and creating figurines hammered from gold, silver, and copper, and trading them with Mesopotamians to the east and Mediterranean cultures to the west.

■ Sights to see: Karain Cave, Antalya (⇨ Ch.6). Çatal Höyük (⇨ Ch.7).

The Hittites

2000 BC–1200 BC

Ushering in the Bronze Age, the Hittites arrived from lands north of the Black Sea around 2000 BC to establish a powerful empire that flourished for almost 800 years. They expanded their holdings as far east as Syria and, c.1258 BC, made an accord with Egypt's great Pharaoh Ramses II—the world's first recorded peace treaty. The Hittites adopted a form of hieroglyphics, developed a pantheon of deities, established a complex civil code, and built shrines and fortifications, many of which have been unearthed at such sites as Alacahöyük, Hattuşa and Kültepe.

Left: Lycian rock tombs, Right: Roman ruin, Phaselis, Anatolia.

During this time, colonies were settled on the west coast of modern-day Turkey by Achaeans and Mycenaeans from Greece, who went on to wage a famous war against the Anatolians in Troy (c. 1200 BC), later immortalized by Homer in *The Iliad*. After their victory, not all Achaeans rushed back home.

■ Sights to see:
Troy (⇨ *Ch.4*).
Museum of Anatolian Civilizations, Ankara (⇨ *Ch.7*).

1200 BC–600 BC

Invaders & Home-grown Kingdoms

▬ With the passage of time, the Hittite society began to fall to encroaching civilizations. Lycians, Mycenaens, and other early Greeks sailed across the Aegean to establish Ephesus, Smyrna, and other so-called Ionian cities on the shores of Anatolia. The Phrygians also migrated to Anatolia from Thrace, flourishing for a mere century or so, until 690 BC—though long enough to leave the legends of kings Gordias and Midas: Gordias, of the intricate knot that could not be unraveled until Alexander the Great slashed through it with a bold stroke of his sword, and Midas, of the

touch that turned everything to gold. The Lydians emerged as a power in the 7th century BC by introducing the world's first coinage. With their vast gold deposits, they became so wealthy that the last of the Lydian kings has forever since been evoked with the term "rich as Croesus."

■ Sights to see:
Lycian tombs at Fethiye and Carian tombs at Dalyan (⇨ *Ch.6*). Greek ruins at Phaselis (⇨ *Ch.6*).

Far left: Alexander the Great, King of Macedon, fighting, at Battle of Issus, mosaic, circa 100 BC.
Top: Arch at Ephesus.
Left: Temple of Trajan, built to honor Trajan, the Roman Emperor (98-117).

Persians & Alexander the Great

550 BC–50 BC

The Persians invaded Anatolia in 546 BC and controlled the area for two centuries, until Alexander the Great swept across Asia. The young warrior's kingdom died with him in 323 BC, and Anatolia entered the Hellenistic Age. Greek and Anatolian cultures mixed liberally amid far-flung trading empires. None of these kingdoms were more powerful than Pergamum (present-day Bergama). Adorned with great sculptures such as the Laocoön and an acropolis modeled after that of Athens, it was one of the most beautiful cities of the ancient world.

■ Sights to see: Pergamum (⇨ Ch.4).

Romans & Early Christians

100 BC–AD 100

By the middle of the 1st century BC, Roman legions had conquered Anatolia, and Ephesus had become the capital of the Roman province of Asia Minor. As Christianity spread through the empire, it was especially well received in Anatolia. Saint John is said to have come to Ephesus, bringing Mary with him, and both are allegedly buried nearby. Saint Paul, a Jew from Tarsus (on Turkey's coast), traveled through Anatolia and the rest of the empire spreading the Christian word for 30 years, until his martyrdom in Rome in AD 67.

■ Sights to see: Ephesus (⇨ Ch.5).

The Rise of Constantinople

306–563

Constantine the Great became Roman emperor in 306 and made two momentous moves: he embraced Christianity and re-established ancient Byzantium as the capital of the increasingly unwieldy Roman empire. With the fall of Rome in AD 476, the Byzantine Empire ruled much of the Western world from its newly named capital Constantinople. The Byzantines reached their height under Justinian I (527–563), whose accomplishments include the Justinian Code (a compilation of Roman law), and such architectural monuments as the Aya Sofya.

■ Sights to see: Aya Sofya, Istanbul (⇨ Ch.3).

527 Byzantine Empire flourishes under Emperor Justinian	1071 Seljuks defeat the Byzantines	1300 Ottoman Empire established	1520 Ottoman Empire enters Golden Age
650 AD	**950 AD**	**1250 AD**	**1550 AD**

In Focus | TURKEY THROUGH THE AGES

Top left: Map of Constantinople.
Above: Wall tiles, Topkapı Palace, Istanbul.
Bottom left: Byzantine mosaic of Jesus, Aya Sophia, Istanbul.
Left: Süleyman the Magnificent

The First Turks

1071–1300

Around the 8th century, the nomadic Turkish Seljuks rose to power in Persia and began making inroads into Byzantine lands. The defeat of the Byzantine army in 1071 ushered in the Great Seljuk Empire and Seljuks converted their new subjects to Islam. In turn, Pope Urban II launched the First Crusade to reclaim Byzantium in 1097. Armies from Western Europe clashed with Seljuk forces for the next two centuries. The Mongols, under Genghis Khan, swept down from the north and put an end to the weakening Seljuks.

■ Sights to see:
Mevlana Museum, Konya
(⇨ *Ch.7*).

The Rise of the Ottomans

1300–1500

By 1300, the Seljuk lands had been divided into independent states, known as the ghazi emirates. Osman I was one of the leaders, and began to expand what would come to be known as the Ottoman Empire, establishing a capital at Bursa. By the 14th century the Ottomans had extended their rule over most of the eastern Mediterranean. Constantinople, the last Byzantine holdout, fell in 1453 and became the new Ottoman capital, which it would remain until the founding of modern Turkey.

■ Sights to See:
Topkapı Palace, Istanbul
(⇨ *Ch.3*).

The Golden Age of the Ottomans

1520–1566

By the time of the reign of Süleyman the Magnificent, the Ottomans controlled lands stretching east into Persia, through Mecca and Medina (Islam's holiest cities), south into Egypt and west into central Europe. The empire entered its Golden Age under Süleyman, himself a poet and author of civil laws. Literature, music, and craftsmanship thrived, while Süleyman's architect, Sinan, built beautiful shrines such as the Süleymaniye Mosque in Istanbul.

■ Sights to see:
Süleymaniye Mosque, Istanbul
(⇨ *Ch.3*). Blue Mosque, Istanbul (⇨ *Ch.3*).

1571–EARLY 1900S

The Long Decline

The defeat of the Ottoman navy in 1571 by a coalition of European forces at the Battle of Lepanto, off the western coast of Greece, heralded the end of Ottoman supremacy in the Mediterranean. Incompetent leadership plagued the empire almost continually over the next several centuries, and the empire shrank. Abdülhamid II supported liberal reforms when he became Sultan in 1876, and effectively Westernized many aspects of public works, education, and the economy. He also turned his energies to reinvigorating Islamic identity, aiming to unite the increasingly restive ethnic groups of the empire. Most infamously, he surpressed Armenian revolutionary groups and an estimated 300,000 Armenians were killed under his regime. A movement of revolutionary societies grew throughout the country and one in particular, the so-called Young Turks, rose up in revolution in 1908, deposing the Sultan. By the early 20th century, the days of the once great empire—now known as the "Sick Man of Europe"—were clearly numbered.

■ Sights to see: Dolmabahçe Palace, Istanbul (⇨ *Ch.3*)

WWI–1938

The Birth of the Republic

World War I, during which the Ottomans sided with the Axis powers, put an end to what was left of the Ottoman Empire. In a key battle in 1915, the Allies landed at Gallipoli but were eventually repulsed with heavy losses. In 1920, the Treaty of Sèvres turned Ottoman lands over to France, Italy, Greece, and other victors, but a nationalist hero had come onto the scene: Mustafa Kemal formed the first Turkish Grand National Assembly in Ankara and led the forces that routed Greek armies, pushing across Anatolia to reclaim lands once part of the Byzantine Empire. In

Top left, opposite: Battle of Lepanto.
Bottom left, opposite: Süleymaniye Mosque.
Bottom right, opposite: Sultan Abdülhamid II.
Left: Mustafa Kemal Atatürk
Above: Pera Palas Hotel, Istanbul, Turkey: Atatürk's bedroom preserved as a museum.

1923 the Treaty of Lausanne banished foreign powers and established the boundaries of a Turkish state with its capital in Ankara. Kemal—who took the name Atatürk (literally "Father of the Turks")—reinvented Turkey as a modern nation. Turkey embraced secularism and instituted widespread reforms that replaced religious law with secular jurisprudence, advanced education, implemented universal suffrage, and introduced a Western style of dress, abolishing the fez as a symbol of Ottoman backwardness.

■ Sights to see:
Gallipoli (⇨ Ch.4).

1938–PRESENT

After Atatürk

Turkey has largely allied itself with the West since Atatürk's death in 1938, though the balance between secularization and the religious right has at times been precarious, with the military often stepping in to ensure the country's Western leanings. A military coup in 1960 removed a Democratic Party government that had reinstituted the call for prayer in Arabic and instituted other right-wing reforms. The military seized control in two other coups, in 1971 and 1980, while the government of Turgut Özal from 1983 to 1993 ushered in widespread legal and economic reforms. First

elected in 2002, the Islamic-rooted AKP deftly led the country through the first years of the new millennium, reinvigorating the economy, reinvigorating Turkey's candidacy for EU membership, and forging economic and political relationships with once-contentious neighbors. But the future looks a bit less rosy as EU talks have stalled, fresh conflicts have broken out in the region, the economy has weakened.

■ Sights to see:
The Anıtkabir (Atatürk's Mausoleum), Ankara (⇨ Ch.7).

Chapter 2

TRAVEL SMART TURKEY

★ **CAPITAL:**
Ankara

👥 **POPULATION:**
75,627,384

💬 **LANGUAGE:**
Turkich

€ **CURRENCY:**
Turkish lira (TL)

☎ **COUNTRY CODE:**
90

⚠ **EMERGENCIES:**
155

🚗 **DRIVING:**
On the right

⚡ **ELECTRICITY:**
200v/50 cycles; electrical
plugs have two round prongs

🕐 **TIME:**
Seven hours ahead of
New York

🌐 **WEB RESOURCES:**
www.goturkey.com
www.evisa.gov.tr
www.turkeytravelplanner.com

BULGARIA

GREECE

BLACK SEA

○ Istanbul

GEORGIA

ANKARA ✪

ARMENIA

TURKEY

IRAN

GREECE

CYPRUS

SYRIA

IRAQ

13 Things You Need to Know Before You Go to Turkey

TURKEY IS A BIG, DIVERSE COUNTRY
Visited by nearly 38 million people a year, Turkey is one of the world's top 10 tourism destinations, and for good reason. Actually, make that many reasons: history, nature, food, culture, hospitality. And it's a lot bigger than people often expect. Nearly twice the size of California (at 300,000 square miles), Turkey has mountains and deserts, forests and farmland, traditional rural villages and the vibrant mega-city of Istanbul. Justifiably famous for its ancient ruins, scenic coastlines, and the fantastical landscapes of Cappadocia, Turkey still holds plenty of surprises. Outdoor-lovers will thrill to hiking in the rugged Kaçkar range or on the Lycian Way above the sparkling Mediterranean Sea, while foodies can enjoy fine dining in Istanbul or delicious regional home cooking and a warm welcome in no-frills *lokantas* (restaurants).

TURKEY IS A DESTINATION FOR ALL SEASONS
Summer is the busiest and most expensive time to visit Istanbul, Cappadocia, and the coast; cooler temperatures can be found along the Black Sea Coast and in the mountains. Winter can be wet and dreary, but you'll find good deals on hotels and shorter lines. There's often snow in Cappadocia and the far north and east, and some beach hotels and restaurants close for the season. Istanbul's cultural calendar is busiest in spring and fall, and lines will still be shorter. Cappadocia's valleys are especially beautiful once the wildflowers start blooming in spring. Fall is a great time to hike, sightsee, and even sunbathe along the coasts, when the water is warmer than in spring.

BUSES GO JUST ABOUT EVERYWHERE
Rapid growth in the number of regional airports in Turkey makes it easy, and often quite inexpensive, to get around the country by plane. But if you have the time for a more immersive experience, join the locals traveling by bus. Large, comfortable coaches with seat-back TVs and snack and beverage service connect most cities. Minibuses (sometimes called a *dolmuş*) generally serve even rather remote destinations at least once a day, often bringing along deliveries as well as passengers (payment is in cash).

THE MUSEUM PASS IS YOUR GOLDEN TICKET INTO HISTORY
The Museum Pass Istanbul (sold at any major sight) is 185 TL and is good for five consecutive days of admission to a dozen can't-miss attractions, as well as discounts at many other places. Pass holders get to skip the ticket lines, too. Similar passes cover sights in other parts of the country, including the Aegean, Mediterranean and Cappadocia. For the really ambitious, the Museum Pass Turkey offers admission into 300 sights all across the country over a 15-day period.

DRINKING TEA IS A NATIONAL PASTIME
You've probably heard more about Turkish coffee, but tea is what really powers the country—endless tiny tulip-shaped cups of strong black tea, usually with a cube (or a few) of sugar added. Turks drink more tea per capita than any other country in the world (ask for yours *açık* if you want it light). An offer of tea is a very common overture of hospitality; in rural places or small towns, especially, it would be easy to spend all day drinking tea with the people you come across.

SULTANAHMET ISN'T THE ONLY (OR EVEN THE BEST) PLACE TO STAY IN ISTANBUL
Istanbul's historic peninsula is chock-full of hotels within easy walking distance of the city's most famous sights. But you'll get a better sense of the lively, complicated,

modern city by staying outside of its tourist district—and better food and nightlife too. Bustling Beyoğlu just across the Golden Horn is perhaps the most appealing option, but boutique hotels in character-filled neighborhoods like Galata and Karaköy are just as good, and the sights of Sultanahmet are just a short tram ride away. Hotels in tony Nişantaşı, lively Kadıköy on the city's Asian side, and along the shores of the Bosphorus aren't as convenient for sightseeing but have their own appeal.

THE 'EVIL EYE' IS ACTUALLY MEANT TO PROTECT YOU

That ubiquitous blue eye-shaped amulet, known as *nazar boncuğu* in Turkish, is popularly referred to as an "evil eye bead," but rather than casting a nasty spell, it's meant to protect against them. Tiny versions are customarily pinned to the clothing of an infant, while larger ones are displayed inside a house.

THERE'S A PHRASE FOR EVERYTHING IN TURKISH

Turkish isn't an easy language to learn—though not as tough as Arabic or Japanese. Consequently, many Turks (especially in Istanbul and in the travel industry) speak some English, though people in smaller towns may not. But your attempts to speak it will be rewarded. Turks are generally very appreciative of foreign visitors trying to speak their language, and indulgent with their

mistakes. So learning a few words is likely to provoke smiles, extra helpfulness, and invitations to tea.

TURKS DON'T SHY AWAY FROM PERSONAL QUESTIONS

Once you get a conversation going, it often won't take long for the questions to start to coming. Be ready to field (or gently deflect) inquiries about your marital status, plans to have children, what hotel you're staying at, how much you paid for it, and the cost of living back home. Turks can also be doting with strangers' children, from playing peek-a-boo with a baby on the subway to tsk-tsking a "wayward" parent who's brought their child outdoors without bundling them up in what's deemed a sufficient amount of clothes. People may also want to take photos with you or your child. It's OK to say no politely, keeping in mind that no harm is likely intended.

BUT POLITICS CAN BE A TRICKY SUBJECT

Talking politics is a popular pastime in Turkey, and locals may try to press you for your opinion on what's going on in your country, or theirs. Unless you know the person well, it's best to avoid any direct criticism of Turkey, including its politicians, political parties, and religion. Many people will have an opinion about the U.S. and its politics, especially its foreign policy, and won't be shy about sharing it, though most recognize that individual travelers

are not responsible for the actions of politicians.

HOW TO PROTECT YOUR HEALTH WHILE TRAVELING

No immunizations are required to enter Turkey as a tourist, though the CDC recommends that all travelers be vaccinated against Hepatitis A, and that those who will be visiting rural areas get the typhoid vaccine as well.

HOW TO GET A VISA

All foreign travelers to Turkey must have a passport valid for at least 60 days, and preferably six months, after the end of their trip. U.S. citizens must obtain an electronic visa online before their trip. The process is quick and simple, and costs $20 for a visa valid for a stay not exceeding 90 days within a 180-day period. Print out your e-visa or have it ready on your phone to display at immigration control.

WHAT TO DO IF YOU RUN INTO TROUBLE

Should you need assistance from the U.S. government, there is a U.S. Consulate General in the İstinye neighborhood of Istanbul, and a U.S. Embassy in the Kavaklıdere neighborhood of Ankara. There is also a consulate in the southern city of Adana.

Getting Here and Around

Istanbul remains the major gateway to Turkey, served by two airports (Europeans can still get to popular package-tour destinations by direct flights). Once you are in the country, buses are still a very common way to get around Turkey, for both Turks and tourists, though the rapidly growing number of provincial airports and cheap domestic flights are making air travel an increasingly appealing alternative. If you don't mind the long ride, the extremely popular night buses that connect the major cities inland and on the coast are comfortable and inexpensive, but faster train service has cut the time it takes to get to Ankara from Istanbul, though limited options make trains only a partial solution at best. Once you've arrived at your destination, you can get around by taxi, minibus, dolmuş (shared taxi), or rented car. A car gives you more freedom to explore on your own but is more costly and the experience can be a bit stressful at times.

✈ Air Travel

Flying time to Istanbul is 10-11 hours from New York, Washington, D.C., Boston, or Chicago; 12-13 hours from Houston, Miami, or Atlanta; and 13-14 hours from Los Angeles or San Francisco, all destinations served by nonstop flights on Turkish Airlines. Flights from Toronto to Istanbul take 10-11 hours. London to Istanbul is a 4-hour flight. In Turkey, security checks for travelers to the United States mean that you need to be at the airport at least two hours before takeoff regardless of which airline you are flying, though lines for check-in at Turkish Airlines are generally long no matter what.

THY/Turkish Airlines operates nonstop flights from U.S. and European gateways, though an international carrier based in your home country is more likely to have better connections to your hometown. Third-country carriers (foreign carriers based in a country other than your own or Turkey) such as Air France, British Airways, KLM, and Lufthansa often have well-priced flights from the United States to Istanbul via their hubs in Paris, London, Amsterdam and Frankfurt. In addition to the more common connections, one-stop carriers also include Air Europa (via Madrid), TAP (via Lisbon), Ukraine Air (via Kiev), Aeroflot (via Moscow), Alitalia (via Milan Malpensa), Egypt Air (via Cairo), Emirates (via Dubai), Qatar Air (via Doha). Popular low-cost carriers like Atlasglobal, Pegasus, and SunExpress offer cheap flights throughout Turkey and to/from European cities. Turkish Airlines operates an extensive domestic network, with more than two dozen flights daily on weekdays between Istanbul and Ankara alone.

AIRPORTS

Turkey's major international airport is the new **Istanbul Airport**, about 50 km (31 miles) north of central Istanbul, which opened in March 2019, replacing Istanbul Atatürk Airport. Sabiha Gökçen Airport serves the Asian part of Istanbul and offers an increasing number of flights to European destinations along with international charters and domestic flights.

Adana, Alanya, Ankara, Antakya (Hatay), Antalya, Bodrum, Bursa, Çanakkale, İzmir, Kars, Konya, Sinop, Trabzon, and Van all have domestic airports, as do more than two dozen other smaller destinations. Turkey is a large country so to save travel time, it's always worth checking to see if a convenient domestic flight is an option.

GROUND TRANSPORTATION FROM AIRPORTS

In many destinations the Havaş company operates shuttle buses to the airports. (In Istanbul, this service is provided by the similarly named, but separately run Havabüs.) These run at regular intervals in the major cities and in the provinces are timed to coincide with incoming and outgoing flights. An alternative is to take a taxi. From the smaller airports, it is sometimes possible to negotiate with a taxi driver for less than the metered fare. Many hotels will arrange for a driver to collect you from the airport and for someone to take you to the airport. In Cappadocia and other popular tourist regions, it is not unusual for hotels to offer this transportation free of charge, although the driver will still appreciate being tipped 5 or 10 TL.

TRANSFERS BETWEEN AIRPORTS

If you have a connection between an international flight and a domestic flight in Istanbul, try to ensure that they both use the same airport, which will most likely be Istanbul Airport. While domestic flights to Sabiha Gökçen Airport are usually cheaper than flights into Istanbul Airport (although prices to the latter vary considerably according to the time of day), if you have a connecting international flight from Istanbul Airport, any savings will be more than offset by the time and expense of transferring between airports by taxi—the trip could easily take two to three hours at a busy time of day.

✪ Boat and Ferry Travel

In the greater Istanbul area, ferries can be the most efficient (and pleasant) means of getting around. On the Aegean and Mediterranean coasts, boats are used mostly for leisurely sightseeing and yachting.

Şehir Hatları, a subsidiary of Istanbul Metropolitan Municipality, and private companies Dentur Avrasya and Turyol provide regular ferryboat services within Istanbul, while İDO offers boats to Yalova and Bandırma (both in the Marmara region) and to Bursa, as well as a sea bus to Istanbul's Princes' Islands. From Bodrum and other Aegean resorts, ferries make frequent runs between Turkey and the Greek islands in the summer.

✪ Bus Travel

In Turkey, buses are generally faster than most trains and provide inexpensive service almost around the clock between all cities and towns, and they're usually quite comfortable. Most offer complimentary tea, Nescafé, soda, and packaged crackers or cookies, though with smaller companies you will want to bring your own water in case beverages are not available. All are run by private firms, each of which has its own fixed fares for different routes and, usually more significantly, its own standards of comfort. Larger bus companies, such as Ulusoy, Kamil Koç, and Pamukkale, which go between major cities and resort areas, can be counted on for comfortable air-conditioned service with snacks. Most of the larger companies have their own terminals and in larger cities run shuttles from locations around the city to the main terminal. Note that *ekspres* buses running between major cities are significantly faster and more comfortable than local buses. By law, all buses are nonsmoking.

Buses traveling the Istanbul–Ankara route depart either city at least once an hour, and cost about 75 TL for a one-way trip. The Istanbul–İzmir fare ranges from about 90 TL to 100 TL. All buses make periodic rest stops along the way.

Getting Here and Around

The larger companies have their own sales offices as well as websites and call centers offering e-tickets, though travelers without a Turkish ID number will likely have to purchase their tickets in person. For smaller companies, tickets are sold at stands in a town's *otogar* (central bus terminal); the usual procedure is to go to the bus station and shop around for the best route and price. All seats are reserved. ■TIP→ **When buying your ticket, tell the ticket agent that you would like to sit on the shady side of the bus; even on air-conditioned buses the sun can feel oppressive on a long trip.**

🚗 Car Travel

In Turkey a driver's license issued in most foreign countries is acceptable. While Turkey still has a high car accident rate, especially over busy holiday travel periods, driving is an excellent way to explore regions outside the major cities and having a car allows you the freedom that traveling by bus, train, or plane does not. Turkey has 67,000 km (41,600 miles) of paved and generally well-maintained highways, but off the intercity highways, surfaces are often poor and potholes frequent. A system of four-lane toll roads is now in place around Istanbul, Ankara, and İzmir, but most major highways are two lanes, and cars overtake with some frequency. ■TIP→ **Sometimes roads have a third lane meant for passing; although the lane is usually labeled with which direction of traffic is meant to use it, drivers don't always follow this rule, so be extremely careful when passing.** In general, always expect the unexpected. Don't, for example, assume that one-way streets are one-way in practice or that because you wouldn't do something, such as trying to pass in a dangerous situation, the other driver wouldn't either.

In major cities it's possible to hire a driver along with a car. In some remote places, a driver may be included in the package with the rental car and will either be the owner of the car or an employee of the agency. If you're particularly happy with the service you may wish to give a tip in addition to the price you pay to the agency. Around 20 to 30 TL for a day's driving is reasonable.

■TIP→ **Driving in Istanbul and other major cities is best avoided.** Urban streets and highways are frequently jammed with vehicles operated by high-speed lunatics as well as otherwise sane drivers who constantly honk their horns. In Istanbul, especially, just because a street is marked one-way, you never know when someone is going to barrel down it in the wrong direction. Parking is also a problem in cities and larger towns. In these places it's best to leave your car in a garage and use public transportation or take taxis.

■TIP→ **If possible, avoid driving on highways after dusk. Drivers often don't use their lights and vehicles may be stopped on the roads in complete darkness. Carts and other farm vehicles are often not equipped with lights.**

Highways are numbered or specified by direction (e.g., the route to Antalya). Trans-European highways have a European number as well as a Turkish number (European Route E80 is also known as Turkish Route O-3, O-7, O-4, and D100 as it passes through Turkey, for example). ■TIP→ **Note, though, that route numbers may be inconsistent from map to map.** Archaeological and historic sites are indicated by brown signposts.

GASOLINE
Gas costs about 7 TL per liter, making Turkey one of the most expensive places in the world to fuel up. Many of the gas stations on the main highways stay open

around the clock, others generally from 6 am to 10 pm. Almost all Turkish gas stations provide full service and have unleaded gas. Many attendants will clean your windows while the car's tank is being filled. Tipping is not obligatory though not uncommon if the attendant has been attentive—a few TL is usually enough. There may be long distances between gas stations in rural areas, so if you're heading off the beaten track, don't allow the tank to run too low. Most gas stations in towns and major highways take credit cards, though you may need cash in rural areas. Many gas stations also have small shops, or just a cooler, where you can buy snacks and chilled drinks.

RENTING A CAR

In many places, such as Cappadocia and the Turquoise Coast, you may want to rent a car so you can explore on your own. When traveling long distances, however, you may find it easier to take public transportation (either a bus or plane)—unless you plan on sightseeing en route—and renting a car at your destination.

Car rental rates begin at about 160 TL ($30) a day and TL 950 ($170) a week for an economy car with unlimited mileage. The majority of rental cars are equipped with manual transmission, though it's possible to get an automatic (usually for a higher price). Car seats for children are not compulsory and are often difficult to find, although offices of the multinational firms in larger cities may be able to provide them. A wide variety of mostly European car makes are available, ranging from the locally manufactured Tofaş (the Turkish licensee to build Fiat models) to Renault and Mercedes.

Check the websites of the major multinational companies to see if they have offices at your destination. Many reliable local agencies also operate throughout Turkey. *Only the contacts for the major companies are listed below. Some local car rental agencies are listed in the relevant chapters of this book.*

Hotels often rent cars or have a relationship with a local agency—the local agency is usually anxious to keep the hotel happy by providing a good service, and it's not unusual for the owner of the agency to be a relative of someone at the hotel. The rates for deals done through the hotel, which will include insurance, etc., are often much lower than rates charged by multinational firms.

The rental agency will usually tell you what to do if you have a breakdown or accident and will provide a contact number—often the personal cell number of someone working at the agency—if they don't, ask for one. It's worth remembering that in the case of an accident, Turkish insurance companies usually refuse to pay until they have seen a police report. It is particularly important to obtain a police report if another vehicle is involved, as the driver will need to submit the report when filing a claim with his or her insurance company or with your rental agency. In such a situation, call the contact number for your rental agency and allow a representative to handle all the procedures.

Most likely, agencies will ask you to contact them before attempting to have any repairs done and will usually bring you a replacement car. Most major car manufacturers in Turkey (for example, Renault, Tofaş, and Opel/General Motors) also have roaming 24-hour services and rental agencies may ask you to contact one of them.

Getting Here and Around

RULES OF THE ROAD

Driving is on the right and passing on the left. Seat belts are required for front-seat passengers and should be used by those in back as well. Using a cell phone while driving is prohibited—but this law is seldom obeyed. Turning right on a red light is not permitted, but it is legal to proceed through a flashing red light provided no traffic is coming the other way. Speeding and other traffic violations are subject to on-the-spot fines. Fines for driving under the influence of alcohol are steep and are often accompanied by imprisonment. Most rental companies do not allow you to cross international borders in a rented car.

Throughout rural Turkey, roads are often not well marked, lighting is scarce, and roads are sometimes rough. City traffic is generally chaotic. The top speed limit of 120 kph (about 75 mph) is rarely enforced on major highways, although it is not unusual for the Turkish police to set speed traps on other roads. Drive carefully and relatively slowly. Be prepared for sudden changes in road conditions and be alert to the behavior of other drivers.

🚘 Taxi Travel

Taxis in Turkey are yellow and easy to spot. Fares in Istanbul are about 2.5 TL for 1 km (about ½ mile) with a starting flat rate of 4 TL; the former difference between the day and night rates has been abolished. Prices in other large cities are similar. Be aware that taxi drivers in tourist areas sometimes doctor their meters to charge more; don't ride in a taxi in which the meter doesn't work. Before setting out, ask at your hotel about how much a ride should cost and have a sense of what direction you should be traveling in. Note that saying

the word *direkt* (direct) after giving your destination may help prevent you from getting an unplanned grand tour of town. In cities it's fairly easy to flag down a taxi, but it's recommended to instead go to a taxi stand where drivers wait for fares. In Istanbul and Ankara many of the larger hotels will find a cab for you, usually with drivers or companies they know and trust. The website Online Taksi (⊕ *www.onlinetaksi.com*) lists taxi companies all around Istanbul, Ankara, and İzmir, while BiTaksi lets you call and pay for a taxi in Istanbul and Ankara using its mobile app, and Taksiyle lets you estimate fares for point-to-point trips in major cities. Uber established a popular presence in Istanbul and some major resort towns, but its legal status in Turkey is now uncertain following an uproar by taxi drivers that resulted in fines being levied on both Uber drivers and passengers.

Drivers will round the fare up to the next lira; no further tip is necessary. There are no extra charges for luggage. In Istanbul, if you cross one of the Bosphorus bridges, you will be expected to add the cost of the toll (8.75 TL for each of the first two bridges, 13.35 TL for the third) to the bill regardless of which direction you are going (vehicles only pay going from west to east—the theory is that even if he does not have to pay to take you across, the taxi driver will have to pay to go back). Particularly in Istanbul and Ankara, taxi drivers are often recent arrivals to the country, with a very limited knowledge of the city and will have to ask bystanders or other taxi drivers for directions.

Dolmuşes (shared taxis) are generally minibuses (often bright yellow, blue, or green in Istanbul) that run along various routes. You can often hail a dolmuş on the street, at bus stops, or at dolmuş stands marked by the signs "D." The destination is shown either on a roof sign or a card in the front window. The savings over a private taxi are significant. A trip by dolmuş is often just as fast as by taxi, and service extends through the wee hours of the morning. Although dolmuşes only run along specific routes, they generally go to tourist destinations, as well as nightlife hot spots. If you're not familiar with your destination, tell the driver where you are going when you get in; he will usually try to drop you as close to your destination as possible.

It is not customary to tip dolmuş drivers, and they will probably be confused if you try to hand them something extra.

🚆 Train Travel

Train routes in Turkey are relatively limited and tend to meander, meaning that train travel is usually much slower than bus travel—sometimes twice as long. With a few exceptions, the term *ekspres tren* (express train) is essentially a misnomer in Turkey. One of those exceptions is the high-speed rail line that now connects Istanbul and Ankara (stopping in Eskişehir), reducing the travel time between the two cities to about four hours. For now, though, the Istanbul terminus is in Pendik, far from the city center. A fast train also runs between Ankara and Konya, from where travelers can switch to a regular train onward to Adana. Eskişehir is a transfer point for regular trains to İzmir. Note that ongoing work expanding the Marmaray rail system has heavily disrupted service between Istanbul and Edirne, as well as to Bulgaria and Greece, with buses filling in for part of the route. Train services in Istanbul are expected to resume from the central Haydarpaşa and Sirkeci train stations (on the Asian and European sides of the city, respectively) in 2019, but check for the latest updates before booking.

Dining cars on trains between major cities usually have waiter service and offer decent and inexpensive food. Overnight express trains have sleeping cars and bunk beds. The popular Ankara—Kars run (the *Doğu Ekspresi*), for example, costs about 50 TL for a berth in a two-bed room; although advance reservations are a must, cancellations are frequent, so you can often get a space at the last minute.

Fares are generally lower for trains than for buses, and round-trip train fares cost less than two one-way tickets. Student discounts are 20%. Ticket windows in railroad stations are marked *gişeleri*. Some post offices and authorized travel agencies also sell train tickets. It's advisable to book in advance, in person, for seats on the best trains and for sleeping quarters.

Long-distance trains offer a number of accommodation options, such as Pullman (first-class type, reclining seats), compartments with six or eight seats, reclining or not, couchette (shared four-bunk compartments), and sleeper (private one- or two-bed compartments). In Turkish, Pullman is *pulman*, compartment is *kompartımanlı*, couchette is *kuşetli*, and sleeper is *yataklı*.

Most train stations do not accept credit cards, foreign money, or traveler's checks, so be prepared to pay in Turkish lira.

Turkish State Railways (*Türkiye Cumhuriyeti Devlet Demiryolları*) operates train service throughout the country. The website is helpful (when its English-language version is not being revamped) and provides information on how to buy tickets online or at the station as well as schedules and maps. ⊕ *Seat61.com* is another useful website about train travel in Europe and Turkey. Both Eurail and Interrail passes can be used in Turkey.

Before You Go

Visa

All U.S. citizens, even infants, need a valid passport and a visa to enter Turkey for stays of up to 90 days. Visas must be obtained prior to arrival by filling out an application via ⊕ *www.evisa.gov.tr.* The cost is $20. Even though visas are multiple entry and usually valid for 90 days out of a 180-day period, they cannot be issued for periods longer than the validity of the passport you present. If your passport has less than a month to run, or does not have enough blank space for entry and exit stamps, you may not be given a visa at all. Turkish officials may impose stiff fines for an overstay on your visa. You should also print out a copy of your e-visa for presentation to immigration officials on arrival.

Immunizations

There are no immunization requirements for visitors traveling to Turkey for tourism. However, vaccinations for hepatitis A and typhoid are recommended.

Embassies

The U.S. Embassy is in Ankara. There are consulates in Istanbul and Adana.

Packing

Standards of dress differ across the country, so you'll want to consider your destinations and activities when packing. The urban garb you'd wear in any big city will fit in fine in Istanbul, while casual and conservative is best in small towns. The Aegean and Mediterranean coasts tolerate skimpy clothes, though female visitors should err on the sedate side, especially if traveling alone, in order to avoid unwanted attention.

Women must cover their heads, legs, and shoulders in mosques. Standards for men are less rigid, though they should also avoid wearing shorts or tank tops (and may be denied entry if they do) when visiting mosques (both are OK if hiking). All visitors must remove their shoes to enter mosques, and it's polite and expected to do the same if you are invited into a private home.

Sunscreen and sunglasses will come in handy everywhere. It's a good idea to carry toilet paper and hand sanitizer, especially outside the bigger cities and resort areas. You'll need mosquito repellent from March through October, a flashlight for exploring caves in Cappadocia, and perhaps soap if you're staying in inexpensive hotels.

When to Go

HIGH SEASON $$$$
July and August are the busiest, hottest, and priciest months to visit Turkey. The Aegean and Mediterranean will be packed with beachgoers, but it's a good time to explore the often-rainy Black Sea.

LOW SEASON $
Prices and crowds are significantly reduced in winter, which is wet and gray in Istanbul and can be brutally cold in central and eastern Turkey. The Mediterranean coast and southeast Turkey stay relatively mild, though beach towns partially shut down.

VALUE SEASON $$
Spring and fall are pleasant and lively in Istanbul, though it can be rainy into April. Eastern Turkey won't fully thaw out until May or June, but the Mediterranean stays warm well into October.

Essentials

🛏 Lodging

Accommodations in Turkey range from international luxury chain hotels to charming inns in historic Ottoman mansions and *kervansarays* to comfortable but basic family-run *pansiyons* (guesthouses). It's advisable to plan ahead if you'll be traveling in the peak season (April–October), when resort hotels are often booked by tour companies, or during the two main religious holidays, *Şeker Bayramı* (at the end of the Ramadan fasting period) and *Kurban Bayramı*.

Note that reservations should be confirmed more than once, particularly at hotels in popular destinations. Phone reservations are not always honored, so it's a good idea to email the hotel and get written confirmation of your reservation, as well as to confirm again before you arrive.

Our local writers vet every hotel to recommend the best overnights in each price category, from budget to luxury. Unless otherwise specified, you can expect private bath, phone, and TV in your room. We specify whether or not meals are included in each review. Prices in the reviews are the lowest cost of a standard double room in high season.
■ TIP→ **In the low season you should be able to negotiate discounts of at least 20% off the rack rate; it never hurts to try.**

HOTELS

Hotels are officially classified in seven categories in Turkey: one to five stars, "special class," and "boutique hotel." ("Special class" is for hotels that are unique but don't meet certain requirements of being a "boutique hotel.") There are also many *pansiyons*—guesthouses—outside this system. The star classifications can be misleading, however, as they're based on the number of facilities rather than the quality of the service and interior design,

and the lack of a restaurant or lounge automatically relegates the establishment to the bottom of the ratings. In practice, a lower-grade hotel may actually be far more charming and comfortable than one with a higher rating.

Though luxury accommodations can be found in many places in Turkey, the standard Turkish hotel room, which you will encounter throughout the country, has bare walls, low wood-frame beds (usually twin beds, often pushed together in lieu of a double bed), and industrial carpeting or kilims on the floor. Less expensive properties will probably have plumbing and furnishings that leave something to be desired.

These are some Turkish words that will come in handy when you're making reservations: "air-conditioning" is *klima,* "private bath" is *banyo,* "tub" is *banyo küveti,* "shower" is *duş,* "double bed" is *iki kişilik yatak,* and "twin beds" is *iki tane tek kişilik yataklar* ("separate" is *ayrı;* "pushed together" is *beraber*). There is no Turkish word for "queen bed" but they will probably use the English (a direct translation is *kraliçe yatağı*). The same is true for "king bed" (they will probably use the English, though a direct translation is *kral yatağı*). Noise-sensitive travelers should ask for a quiet room, *sessiz bir oda.*

Wherever you stay, keep the following money-saving tips in mind:

High-end chains catering to businesspeople are often busy only on weekdays and drop rates dramatically on weekends to fill up rooms. Ask when rates go down.

Watch out for hidden costs, including resort fees, energy surcharges, fees to use the hotel's Wi-Fi (usually only an issue at luxury hotels), in-room safes, or air-conditioning (usually only at the cheapest

Essentials

beach resorts), and "convenience" fees for such extras as unlimited local phone service you won't use and a free newspaper written in a language you can't read.

Always verify whether local hotel taxes are or are not included in the rates you are quoted, so that you'll know the real price of your stay. In some places, taxes can add 20% or more to your bill.

If you're trying to book a stay right before or after Turkey's high season (April–October), you might save considerably by changing your dates by a week or two. Many properties charge peak-season rates for your entire stay, even if your travel dates straddle peak and nonpeak seasons.

PANSIYONS

Outside the cities and resort areas, these small, family-run establishments are generally the most common option. They range from charming old homes decorated with antiques to tiny, utilitarian rooms done in basic modern style. As a rule, they are inexpensive and scrupulously clean. Private baths are common, though they are rudimentary—stall showers, toilets with sensitive plumbing. A simple breakfast is typically included; other meals may be available upon request for an extra charge, particularly if the location is remote. A stay in a *pansiyon* is a comfortable money-saver, especially if you plan on spending most of your time out and about.

🍴 Dining

The restaurants we list are the best in each price category. A small service or "cover" (*kuver* in Turkish) charge of a few liras per person (a charge just for sitting at the table, the bread, the water, etc.) is often added to the bill, especially in *meyhane*-style restaurants, but you should tip 10% on top of this unless a service (*servis*) charge is already listed. If a restaurant's menu has no prices listed, ask before you order, especially for fresh fish and seafood—you'll avoid a surprise when the bill comes. *For information on food-related health issues, see Health below.*

MEALS AND MEALTIMES

Breakfast, usually eaten at your hotel, typically consists of *beyaz peynir* (soft white cheese, made from cow, sheep, or goat's milk), sliced tomatoes, cucumbers, olives, jams, honey, and fresh fruit, with a side order of fresh bread, perhaps a hard-boiled egg or basic omelet, and tea or Nescafé; the menu varies little, whether you stay in a simple *pansiyon* or an upscale hotel.

Breakfast typically starts by 8 am. Lunch is generally eaten between noon and 2 pm, dinner from 8 to 10 pm, with restaurants staying open latest in Istanbul and coastal resorts. You can find restaurants or cafés open almost any time of the day or night in cities; in villages getting a meal at odd hours can be a problem. Many Turks fast during daylight hours during the Islamic holy month of Ramadan. If you're visiting during Ramadan, be sensitive to locals and avoid eating on public transportation or other places where you might make mouths water. During Ramadan, many restaurants, particularly smaller ones outside the major cities, close during the day and open at dusk.

Unless otherwise noted, the restaurants listed are open daily for lunch and dinner.

PAYING

Most relatively upscale restaurants, particularly those in western Turkey, take major credit cards. Smaller eateries will often accept only cash.

For guidelines on tipping, see Tipping below.

RESERVATIONS AND DRESS

It's a good idea to make a reservation at popular restaurants. We mention when reservations are essential (there's no other way you'll ever get a table) or when they are not accepted. We mention dress only for the very rare places where men are required to wear a jacket or a jacket and tie.

✪ Health and Safety

To avoid problems at customs, diabetics and other persons who carry needles and syringes for medical reasons should have a letter from their physician confirming their need for injections. Rabies can be a problem in Turkey, occasionally even in the large cities. If bitten or scratched by a dog or cat about which you have suspicions, go to the nearest pharmacy and ask for assistance. If you need a rabies shot, you'll likely need to go to a state hospital (devlet hastanesi), but the pharmacist can advise on this.

Especially along the coasts, you'll want to use something to ward off mosquitoes. All pharmacies and some corner stores and supermarkets stock a variety of oils and/or tablets to keep mosquitoes at bay, as well as sprays and creams you can apply to exposed skin; it's generally easy to identify these products as the packaging usually includes a picture of a mosquito. If you can't find what you want, try asking using the Turkish word for mosquito: sivrisinek. It often seems as though mosquitoes favor foreigners, particularly the fair-skinned, so a Turk's assurances that mosquitoes in a particular place are "not bad" can be both sincere and misleading.

Given the high temperatures in summer, dehydration can be a problem, especially in southern and eastern Turkey. Remember to sip water throughout the day rather than waiting until you are very thirsty.

For minor problems, pharmacists can be helpful. Pharmacists at any eczane, or pharmacy, are well versed in common ailments and can prescribe some medications for common travelers' illnesses. Many of the same over-the-counter remedies available in Western countries can be found in Turkish pharmacies, which are usually well stocked. Even a Turkish pharmacist who doesn't speak English will often be able to recognize a specific remedy—particularly if you write the name down—and be able to find an appropriate alternative if that medication is not available.

Doctors and dentists abound in major cities and can be found in all but the smallest towns; many are women. There are also hastanes (hospitals) and kliniks (clinics, also called sağlık ocağı). Road signs marked with an "H" point the way to the nearest hospital. Even if doctors cannot converse fluently in English, most will have a working knowledge of English and French terminology for medical conditions. Turkish dentists, called diş hekimi, diş doktoru, or dişçi are highly regarded.

FOOD AND DRINK

Tap water is heavily chlorinated and supposedly safe to drink in cities and resorts. It's okay to wash fruits and vegetables in tap water, but it's best to play it safe and only drink şişe suyu (bottled still water) or maden suyu (bottled sparkling mineral water, also referred to simply as soda), which are better tasting and inexpensive. ■TIP→ Do not drink tap water in rural areas or in eastern Turkey. Turkish food is generally safe, though you should still be careful with some types of street food, such as chickpeas and

Essentials

rice (*nohutlu pilav*), grilled lamb intestines (*kokoreç*), and stuffed mussels (*midye dolması*), which can host a number of nasty bacteria.

SAFETY

Violent crime against strangers in Turkey has increased in recent years but, when compared with Western Europe or North America, is still relatively rare. You should, nevertheless, watch your valuables, as professional pickpockets do operate in the major cities and tourist areas. Women should be careful of the prospect of bag snatching both when walking and when sitting at open-air cafés and restaurants. Bear in mind that organized gangs often use children to snatch bags.

To be extra safe, distribute your cash, credit cards, IDs, and other valuables between a deep front pocket, an inside jacket or vest pocket, and a hidden money pouch. Don't reach for the money pouch once you're in public.

Istanbul and Ankara were hit by a series of terror attacks in 2015 and 2016 that rattled Turkey's two largest cities. The U.S. State Department has issued a Level 3 advisory for Turkey, but many people visit without incident. Whether you do will depend on your own tolerance for uncertainty. Things have been fairly quiet in Turkey since 2016, with no other major issues of terrorism, but it's still a good idea to keep your wits about you and be aware of potential exit strategies while in crowded places. Protests and demonstrations should always be avoided.

Violence has flared up again in recent years in southeastern Turkey, where the Kurdistan Workers Party (PKK) has waged an armed campaign against the Turkish military. Due to this, and the ongoing conflicts across the border in Syria and Iraq, the U.S. State Department recommends that travelers do not visit the region at this time. This area includes several popular tourist destinations including Diyarbakır, Mardan, Midyat, Hasankeyf, Gaziantep, Mt. Nemrut, and Urfa in the southeast.

Many U.S. actions in the Middle East have been deeply unpopular in Turkey, and Turks will often have little hesitation in letting you know how they feel. However, they will invariably distinguish between the actions of the U.S. government and individual Americans. For an up-to-date report on the situation, check with the State Department website.

LOCAL SCAMS

You should keep your credit cards within sight at all times to prevent them from being copied. In many restaurants waiters will swipe your card at the table. If a waiter takes the card away, you should either ensure that it remains within eyesight or ask to accompany the waiter to the POS terminal (you can manufacture an excuse, such as telling the waiter that your bank sometimes asks for a PIN).

There have been a few cases of tourists traveling alone being given drugged drinks and then being robbed. The doctored drinks are usually soft drinks such as sodas. Turks are naturally anxious to ply guests with food and drink, and in the vast majority of cases, there should be no cause for alarm. However, if, for example, you are traveling alone and someone is particularly insistent on you having a cold soft drink and comes back with one already poured into a glass, treat it with extreme caution. If the drink is drugged, the person giving it to you will probably be suspiciously insistent that you drink it. If you have any doubts, do not consume it. Someone who is being genuinely hospitable will probably be confused and maybe a little hurt; but both are better than your being robbed.

In crowded areas of large cities, particularly Istanbul, be aware of a common scam in which two men stage a fight or similar distraction while an accomplice picks the tourist's pocket. Single male travelers in particular should also be aware of another popular scam that starts with an innocent-seeming conversation on the street (sometimes initiated by being asked the time: "Saat kaç?"), continues with an invitation to go grab a beer, and ends with a preposterously large bill being presented to the unsuspecting foreigner. In extreme cases, the hapless visitor has been brought by force or threat to an ATM to withdraw enough money to pay the tab.

Less intimidating, but annoying, is the "shoe shine trick": an itinerant shoe shiner "accidentally" drops his brush as he walks past a foreigner, who helpfully calls out to him and picks up the brush. The shoeshine man feigns effusive gratitude, and insists on shining the shoes of the visitor—then overcharging, and sometimes refusing to clean the polish off until the price is paid.

Before taking a private taxi, it can be useful to ask the information desk at your hotel what route (i.e., past what landmarks) the driver will likely drive, how many minutes the ride usually is, and what the average cost is: this way you will avoid an unwanted, and often lengthy, tour of the city. Note that Turkish hospitality is such that if you need directions, someone will often insist on accompanying you part or all the way to your destination.

WOMEN IN TURKEY

Turkey is a generally safe destination for women traveling alone, though in heavily touristed areas such as Istanbul's Sultanahmet, Antalya, and Marmaris, women unaccompanied by men are

likely to be approached and sometimes followed. In rural towns, where visits from foreigners are less frequent, men are typically more respectful toward women traveling on their own. As in any other country in the world, the best course of action is simply to walk on if approached, and avoid potentially troublesome situations, such as walking in deserted neighborhoods at night.

Some Turkish men are genuinely curious about women from other lands and really do want only to "practice their English." Still, be forewarned that the willingness to converse can easily be misconstrued as something more meaningful. If you are uncomfortable, seek assistance from a Turkish woman or move to a place where other women are present; when it comes to harassment by males, there really is safety in female solidarity. If a man is acting inappropriately toward you, it is acceptable to be forward and tell him to go away. The phrase çok ayıp ("shame on you") will come in handy, as it will also attract attention from passersby. Another phrase, defol ("get lost") is more severe and should dispel any persistent men you may encounter. Women who are pregnant or have small children with them are generally treated with such respect as to be virtually immune from harassment.

Turkey, especially outside tourist areas and major cities, is not the place to sport clothing that is short, tight, or revealing. Longer skirts, and shirts and blouses with sleeves, are less likely to attract unwanted attention. Women are expected to cover their heads with scarves when entering mosques.

Many hotels, restaurants, and other eating spots identify themselves as being for an aile (family) clientele, and many restaurants have special sections for women and children. How comfortable

Essentials

you are with being alone will affect whether you like these areas, which are often away from the action—and you may prefer to take your chances in the main room (though some establishments will resist seating you there).

When traveling alone by intercity bus, you will almost certainly be seated next to another woman (and often refused a ticket if such a seat is not available). If a man sees that you are traveling alone, he will probably offer his own seat so that you may sit next to a woman.

$ Money

Turkey used to be the least expensive of the Mediterranean countries, but prices have risen in recent years. The plummeting value of the lira, however, means that there are plenty of bargains to be had for travelers with dollars, euros, or pounds despite the high levels of inflation. Istanbul hotels are still roughly equivalent to other cities in the Mediterranean in terms of cost, but in the countryside, and particularly away from the main tourist areas, prices are much lower—room and board are not likely to be much more than $50 per person per day, and can be far cheaper.

Coffee can range from about $1 to $2.50 a cup, depending on whether it's the less-expensive Turkish coffee or American-style coffee, and whether it's served in a luxury hotel, a café, or an outlet of a multinational chain such as Starbucks or Caffè Nero. Coffee lovers beware: outside of major urban and resort centers (and something even within them) much coffee listed on menus in a restaurant, unless specified otherwise (e.g., as *filtre kahve*, or "filter coffee"), is likely to be instant coffee (Nescafé). Tea will cost you about 25¢–50¢ a glass,

rising to 75¢–$1 for a cup (*fincan*), which is larger. Local beer will be about $2–$4, depending on the type of establishment; soft drinks, 75¢–$1; and a lamb shish kebab, $3–$5.

Prices *throughout this guide* are given for adults. Substantially reduced fees for transportation and admission fees are often available for children, students, and senior citizens. *For information on taxes, see Taxes.*

ATMS AND BANKS

ATMs can be found even in some of the smallest Turkish towns. Many accept international credit cards or bank cards (a strip of logos is usually displayed above the ATM). Almost all ATMs have a language key that enables you to read the instructions in English. To use your card in Turkey, your PIN must be four digits long.

In Turkey, as elsewhere, using an ATM is one of the easiest ways to get money. Generally the exchange rate is based on the Turkish Central Bank or the exchange rate according to your bank. Some ATMs in major destinations even output cash in lira, U.S. dollars, and euros.

CREDIT CARDS

Turkey largely uses the "chip and PIN" system for debit and credit-card payments, a more secure method than swipe-and-sign. (The chip in the card contains identifying information.) The card is inserted in the POS terminal, which reads the chip and sends the information down the line. The user is then asked to enter his/her PIN and this information is also sent down the wire; if everything matches, the transaction is completed. If you don't have a PIN, check with your bank to get one before you leave the United States.

It's a good idea to inform your credit-card company before you travel, especially if you don't travel internationally very often. Otherwise, the credit card company might put a hold on your card owing to unusual activity—not a good thing halfway through your trip. Record all your credit-card numbers—as well as the phone numbers to call if your cards are lost or stolen—in a safe place. If possible, you're better off calling the number of your issuing bank, which is sometimes printed on your card. Note that American Express is not commonly accepted in Turkey.

Although it's usually safer to use a credit card for large purchases (so you can cancel payments or be reimbursed if there's a problem), some credit-card companies and the banks that issue them add substantial percentages to all foreign transactions. Check on those fees before using your card.

Before you charge something, ask the merchant whether or not he or she plans to do a dynamic currency conversion (DCC). In such a transaction the credit-card *processor* (shop, restaurant, or hotel) converts the currency and charges you in dollars. In most cases you'll pay the merchant a 6% fee for this service in addition to any credit-card-company and issuing-bank foreign-transaction surcharges.

DCC programs are becoming increasingly widespread. Merchants who participate in them are supposed to ask whether you want to be charged in dollars or the local currency, but they don't always do so. And even if they do offer you a choice, they may well avoid mentioning the additional surcharges. The good news is that you *do* have a choice.

Credit cards are accepted throughout Turkey, especially in larger cities or towns, but many budget-oriented restaurants or hotels in rural areas do not accept them.

CURRENCY AND EXCHANGE
The Turkish lira is divided into 100 *kuruş*, and is issued in denominations of 5, 10, 20, 50, 100, and 200 TL notes; 5, 10, 25, 50 kuruş; and 1 TL coins.

Your bank will probably charge a fee for using an ATM abroad, and the Turkish bank may also charge a fee. Even so, you'll get a better rate than you will at currency exchanges or at some banks

Hotels and banks will change money, as will larger post offices, but in Turkey the rates are usually better at the foreign exchange booths (look for signs saying "foreign exchange" or "*döviz*"). Most are now connected online to the currency markets and there will be little difference between them.

Exchange bureaus are found only in big cities, usually in the center, so if you are heading to small towns make sure you change your money before leaving.

Bureaus in tourist areas often offer slightly less attractive rates—rarely more than 2%–3% difference—than bureaus in other places. Almost all foreign exchange bureaus are open Monday–Saturday. Hours vary but are typically 9:30 am to 6:30 pm. In tourist areas it is sometimes possible to find bureaus that are open later or on Sunday, but they will usually compensate for the inconvenience by offering a rate 2%–3% worse than during normal working hours.

İş Bankası (İş Bank) is Turkey's largest bank, with many branches in the cities and at least one in each town, usually in the center of town.

Essentials

TAXES

The value-added tax, in Turkey called Katma Değer Vergisi, or KDV, is 18% on most goods and services. Hotels typically combine it with a service charge of 10% to 15%, and restaurants may add a similar charge for service (look for a line labeled *servis* on your bill).

Value-added tax is nearly always included in quoted prices. Certain shops are authorized to refund the tax (but you must ask).

When making a purchase, ask for a VAT refund form and find out whether the merchant gives refunds—not all stores do, nor are they required to. Have the form stamped by customs officials when you leave the country. After you're through passport control, take the form to a refund-service counter for an on-the-spot refund (which is usually the quickest and easiest option), or mail it to the address on the form (or the envelope with it) after you arrive home—the processing time can be long, especially if you request a credit card adjustment.

Global Blue is a worldwide service with 300,000 affiliated stores and more than 700 refund counters at major airports and border crossings. Its refund form, called a Tax Free Check, is the most common across the European continent. The service issues refunds in the form of cash, check, or credit card adjustment.

Tipping

A 10%–15% charge may be added to the bill in restaurants (look for it under the label *servis*). In top establishments, waiters expect tips of 10%–15% in addition to the service charge. It's not always possible to include the tip with your credit card payment, and in any event, cash is always much appreciated.

In Turkey, taxi drivers will round off the fare to the nearest lira and may try to keep more, though you're well within your rights to ask for your change back. Dolmuş drivers do not get tipped. Hotel porters expect a few TL. At Turkish baths, staff members who attend to you expect to share a tip of 30%–35% of the bill: don't worry about missing them—they'll be lined up expectantly on your departure.

Tour guides often expect a tip. Offer as much or (as little) as you feel the person deserves, usually around 10 percent of the tour price if you were happy with the guide. If you've been with the guide for a number of days, tip more. Crews on chartered boats also expect tips.

Restroom attendants will not expect a tip in addition to the charge (usually 1 to 1.50 TL) for using their facilities.

Contacts

✈ Air Travel

AIRPORTS
Istanbul Airport. ☎ 212/601–4100 ⊕ www.igairport.com/en. **Sabiha Gökçen Airport.** ☎ 216/588–8888 ⊕ www.sgairport.com.

AIRPORT TRANSFERS
Havaş. ☎ 850/222–0487 ⊕ www.havas.com.tr. **Havabüs.** ☎ 444–2656 (no area code required in Turkey) ⊕ www.havabus.com.

🚌 Bus Travel

Kamil Koç. ☎ 444–0562 (no area code required in Turkey) ⊕ www.kamilkoc.com.tr. **Pamukkale.** ☎ 850/333–3535 ⊕ www.pamukkale.com.tr. **Truva Turizm.** ☎ 444–0017 (no area code required in Turkey) ⊕ www.truvaturizm.com. **Ulusoy.** ☎ 850/811–1888 ⊕ www.ulusoy.com.tr.

🚗 Car Travel

CAR RENTALS
Avis. ☎ 800/633–3469 in U.S., 444–2847 in Turkey; use 216 area code if dialing from outside of Turkey ⊕ www.avis.com.tr. **Budget.** ☎ 800/472–3325 in U.S., 444–4722 in Turkey; use 216 area code if dialing from outside of Turkey ⊕ www.budget.com.tr. **Enterprise.** ☎ 444–4937 in Turkey ⊕ www.enterprise.com.tr. **Europcar.** ☎ 850/377–0377 ⊕ www.europcar.com.tr. **Hertz.** ☎ 800/654–3001 in U.S., 444–0227 in Turkey ⊕ www.hertz.com.tr.

🚆 Train Travel

Turkish State Railways (Türkiye Cumhuriyeti Devlet Demiryolları). ☎ 444–8233 (no area code required in Turkey) ⊕ www.tcdd.gov.tr.

$ Tax Refunds

Global Blue. ☎ 866/706–6090 in U.S. ⊕ www.globalblue.com.

📍 Visitor Information

Turkish Culture and Tourism Office. ⊕ www.goturkeytourism.com.

Helpful Phrases in Turkish

BASICS

Hello	Merhaba	mer-**hab**-a
Yes/no	Evet/hayır	**lewt**-vet/**hi**-yer
Please	Lütfen	**lewt**-fen
Thank you	Teşekkür ederim	tay-shake-**kur** eh-day-**reem**
You're welcome	Rica ederim/ Bir şey değil	ree-**jah** eh-day-**reem**/beer shay **day**-eel
Sorry	Özür dilerim	oh-**zewr** deel-air-eem
Sorry	Pardon	**pahr**-dohn
Good morning	Günaydın	goon-eye-**den**
Good day	İyi günler	ee-yee gewn-**lair**
Good evening	İyi akşamlar	ee-yee ahk-shahm-**lar**
Goodbye	Allahaısmarladık/ Güle güle	**allah**-aw-ees-mar-law-deck/ **gew**-leh **gew**-leh
Mr. (Sir)	Bey	by, bay
Mrs./Miss	Hanım	ha-nem
Pleased to meet you	Memnun oldum	**mam**-noon ohl-doom
How are you?	Nasılsınız?	**nah**-suhl-suh-nuhz

NUMBERS

one	bir	beer
two	iki	ee-**kee**
three	üç	ooch
four	dört	doort
five	beş	besh
six	altı	ahl-tuh
seven	yedi	yed-dee
eight	sekiz	sek-**keez**
nine	dokuz	doh-**kooz**
ten	on	**ohn**
eleven	onbir	**ohn**-beer
twelve	oniki	**ohn**-ee-kee
thirteen	onüç	**ohn**-ooch
fourteen	ondört	**ohn**-doort
fifteen	onbeş	**ohn**-besh
sixteen	onaltı	**ohn**-ahl-tuh
seventeen	onyedi	**ohn**-yed-dy
eighteen	onsekiz	**ohn**-sek-**keez**
nineteen	ondokuz	**ohn**-doh-**kooz**
twenty	yirmi	yeer-mee
twenty-one	yirmibir	**yeer**-mee-beer
thirty	otuz	oh-**tooz**
forty	kırk	kerk
fifty	elli	ehl-lee
sixty	altmış	**alt**-muhsh
seventy	yetmiş	**yeht**-meesh
eighty	seksen	sehk-san
ninety	doksan	dohk-**san**

one hundred	yüz	yewz
one thousand	bin	bean
one million	milyon	**mill**-ee-on

COLORS

black	siyah	**see**-yah
blue	mavi	**mah**-vee
brown	kahverengi	**kah**-vay-**rain**-gee
green	yeşil	yay-sheel
orange	portakal rengi	poor-tah-kahl rain-gee
red	kırmızı	ker-muz-uh
white	beyaz	**bay**-ahz
yellow	sarı	sah-**ruh**

DAYS OF THE WEEK

Sunday	Pazar	pahz-**ahr**
Monday	Pazartesi	pahz-**ahr**-teh-see
Tuesday	Salı	sa-**luh**
Wednesday	Çarşamba	char-shahm-bah
Thursday	Perşembe	pair-shem-beh
Friday	Cuma	joom-**ah**
Saturday	Cumartesi	joom-**ahr**-teh-see

MONTHS

January	Ocak	oh-**jahk**
February	Şubat	shoo-**baht**
March	Mart	mart
April	Nisan	nee-**sahn**
May	Mayıs	my-us
June	Haziran	hah-zee-**rahn**
July	Temmuz	**tehm**-mooz
August	Ağustos	ah-oos-tohs
September	Eylül	ey-**lewl**
October	Ekim	eh-**keem**
November	Kasım	kah-suhm
December	Aralık	ah-rah-**luhk**

USEFUL WORDS AND PHRASES

Do you speak English?	İngilizce biliyor musunuz?	in-**gee-leez**-jay bee-lee-**yohr** moo-soo-nooz
I don't speak Turkish.	Türkçe bilmiyorum.	**tewrk**-cheh **beel**-mee-yohr-um
I don't understand.	Anlamıyorum	ahn-**lah**-muh-yohr-um
I understand.	Anlıyorum	ahn-**luh**-yohr-um
I don't know.	Bilmiyorum	**beel**-meeh-yohr-um
I'm American.	Amerikalıyım	ahm-ay-**ree**-kah-luh-yuhm
I'm British.	İngilizim	**een**-gee-leez-eem
What's your name?	İsminiz nedir?	ees-mee-niz nay-deer
My name is . . .	Benim adım . . .	bay-**neem** ah-duhm
What time is it?	Saat kaç?	sah-aht **kahch**
How?	Nasıl?	**nah**-suhl
When?	Ne zaman?	**nay** zah-mahn

Yesterday	Dün	dewn
Today	Bugün	boo-goon
Tomorrow	Yarın	yah-ruhn
This morning/ afternoon	Bu sabah/ öğleden sonra	boo sah-bah/ol-lay-den sohn-rah
Tonight	Bu gece	boo ge-jeh
What?	Efendim?/Ne?	eh-fan-deem/neh
What is it?	Nedir?	neh-deer
Why?	Neden/Niçin?	neh-den/nee-chin
Who?	Kim?	keem
Where is . . .	Nerede . . .	nayr-deh
. . . the train station?	. . . tren istasyonu?	tee-rehn ees-tah-syohn-oo
. . . the subway station?	. . . metro durağı?	metro doo-raw-uh
. . . the bus stop?	. . . otobüs durağı?	oh-toh-bewse doo-raw-uh
. . . the terminal? (airport)	. . . hava alanı?	hah-vah-ah-lah-nuh
. . . the post office?	. . . postane?	post-ahn-eh
. . . the bank?	. . . banka?	bahn-kuh
. . . the hotel?	. . . oteli?	oh-tel-lee
. . . the museum?	. . . müzesi?	mew-zay-see
. . . the hospital?	. . . hastane?	hahs-tah-neh
. . . the elevator?	. . . asansör?	ah-san-sewr
Where are the restrooms?	Tuvalet nerede?	twah-let nayr-deh
Here/there	Burası/Orası	boo-rah-suh/ ohr-rah-suh
Left/right	sag/sol	sah-ah/sohl
Is it near/ far?	Yakın mı?/ Uzak mı?	yah-kuhn muh/ ooz-ahkmuh
I'd like . . .	istiyorum . . .	ees-tee-yohr-ruhm
. . . a room	Bir oda. . .	beer oh-dah
. . . the key	Anahtarı. . .	ahn-ah-tahr-uh
. . . a newspaper	Bir gazete. . .	beer gahz-teh
. . . a stamp	Pul. . .	pool
I'd like to buy . . .	almak istiyorum . . .	ahl-mahk ees-tee-your-ruhm
. . . city map	Şehir planı. . .	shay-heer plah-nuh
. . . road map	Karayolları haritası. . .	kah-rah-yoh-lahr-uh hah-ree-tah-suh
. . . magazine	Dergi. . .	dair-gee
. . . envelopes	Zarf. . .	zahrf
. . . writing paper	Mektup kagıdı. . .	make-toop kah-uh-duh
. . . postcard	Kartpostal. . .	cart-poh-stahl
. . . ticket	Bilet. . .	bee-let
How much is it?	Fiyatı ne kadar?	fee-yaht-uh neh kah-dahr
It's expensive/ cheap	pahalı/ucuz	pah-hah-luh/ oo-jooz
A little/a lot	Az/çok	ahz/choke
More/less	daha çok/ daha az	da-ha choke/ da-ha ahz

Enough/too (much)	Yeter/çok fazla	yay-tehr/choke fahz-lah
I am ill/sick	Hastayım	hahs-tah-yum
Call a doctor	Doktor çağırın	dohk-toor chah-uh-run
Help!	İmdat!	eem-daht
Stop!	Durun!	doo-roon

DINING OUT

A bottle of . . .	bir şişe . . .	beer shee-shay
A cup of . . .	bir fincan . . .	beer feen-jahn
A glass of . . .	bir bardak . . .	beer bar-dahk
Beer	bira	bee-ra
Bill/check	hesap	heh-sahp
Bread	ekmek	ekmek
Breakfast	kahvaltı	kah-vahl-tuh
Butter	tereyağı	tay-reh-yah-uh
Cocktail/aperitif	kokteyl, içki	cocktail, each-key
Coffee	kahve	kah-veh
Dinner	akşam yemegi	ehk-shluhm yee-may-ee
Fixed-price menu	fiks menü	feex menu
Fork	çatal	chah-tahl
I am a vegetarian/ I don't eat meat	vejeteryenim/ et yemem	vegeterian-eem/ eht yeh-mem
I cannot eat . . .	yiyemem . . .	yee yay-mem
I'd like to order . . .	Ismarlamak isterim . . .	us-mahr-lah-mahk ee-stair-eem
I'd like . . .	. . . isterim	ee-stair-em
I'm hungry/thirsty	acıktım/susadım	ah-juck-tum/ soo-sah-dum
Is service/the tip included?	servis fiyatı dahil mi?	sehr-vees fee-yah-tah dah-heel-mee
It's good/bad	güzel/güzel degil	gew-zell/gew-zell day-eel
It's hot/cold	sıcak/soguk	suh-jack/soh-uk
Knife	bıçak	buh-chahk
Lunch	ögle yemegi	oi-leh yeh-may-ee
Menu	menü	meh-noo
Napkin	peçete	peh-cheh-teh
Pepper	karabiber	kah-rah-bee-behr
Plate	tabak	tah-bahk
Please give me . . .	lutfen bana . . . verirmisiniz	luut-fan bah-nah vair-eer-mee-see-niz
Salt	tuz	tooz
Spoon	kaşık	kah-shuhk
Tea	çay	chai
Water	su	soo
Wine	şarap	shah-rahp

Great Itineraries

How to See Istanbul in Three Days

Spread over two continents bisected by the Bosphorus Strait and bursting with history and culture, Istanbul is never boring. Explore ancient basilicas and Byzantine churches, modern art galleries, the palaces of Sultans, and lively markets as you weave your way through the city. Three days is just enough to get a taste of a place that never seems to stop moving.

DAY 1

Begin your day bright and early in the old city of Sultanahmet. Visit the splendid Aya Sofya, a rose-colored Byzantine church that became an imperial mosque when the Ottomans conquered Constantinople, and made a final transformation into a museum soon after the founding of the Turkish Republic in the beginning of the 20th century. Admire the gold-speckled mosaics that decorate the walls. Afterwards, make your way across the street to the Basilica Cistern, where you can descend into the cool dim-lit depths of the Byzantine-era waterway. Nearby is Topkapı Palace, the seat of the Ottoman Empire until the 19th century, where the Sultan maintained his court and harem. Spend time admiring the intricate tile work in the Harem and the ornate rooms with wide views of the Bosphorus.

Pause for lunch at Tarihi Sultanahmet Köftecisi, a historical no-frills shop in the heart of Sultanahmet that serves perfectly crafted meatballs, to fuel up for the afternoon.

Hop on the tram and ride it two stops to Beyazit, where you'll find the entrance to the Grand Bazaar. Filled with twisting, labyrinthine pathways and bursting with shops selling everything from leather goods to colorful carpets to pocket watches, the Grand Bazaar is an ideal place to let yourself get lost. Shop owners will often invite you in for a tea while you haggle prices; this a place to shop at a leisurely pace.

When you've found your perfect souvenirs and emerged from the bazaar, walk a short distance to Süleymaniye Mosque, where you can soak in views of the city from one of the most renowned mosques in the city.

Go for dinner at Hamdi Restaurant, a kebab house with stunning terrace views of the Golden Horn.

DAY 2

Fill up with a hearty full-spread breakfast at one of the many kahvaltı places in the city such as Van Kahvaltı Evi (⊠ *Kılıçali Paşa Mahallesi, Defterdar Ykş. 52/A, Beyoğlu*) before you set out to explore the other side of European Istanbul in Beyoğlu. This is the lively cultural center of the city, where Istanbul's art scene flourishes. Visit the Istanbul Modern temporary space in Asmalımescit, where the museum has relocated while its usual building on the shores of the Bosphorus is rebuilt. Then delve into the independent gallery scene nearby, with favorites like Galerist (⊠ *Meşrutiyet Cd. 67/1*), DEPO (⊠ *Lüleci Hendek Caddesi No.12*), and Zilberman Gallery (⊠ *İstiklal Cad. No.16*), all offering innovative exhibitions of local and international artists.

Beyoğlu's cosmopolitan vibe is rooted in its late-Ottoman history, when the neighborhood was primarily home to Greeks, Jews, Armenians, and other Ottoman minorities. Learn about the Jewish history of Turkey at the Jewish Museum, which has comprehensive exhibitions about the Jewish residents who called Istanbul home.

Stroll down İstiklal Caddesi, the main pedestrian boulevard, towards Taksim Square; from there, descend via funicular to the shore road, where you'll find Dolmabahçe Palace. This was the imperial "European"-style residence that the Ottoman sultans relocated to in the 19th century, and you can tour the luxurious, decadent interiors.

For dinner, you can choose to dine at a meyhane like Sıdıka in Beşiktaş (near Dolmabahçe Palace), which specializes in freshly made Aegean meze and seasonal fish. Or, make your way to Ahesta in Beyoglu, where the stylish and innovative contemporary menu draws from Persian, Arabic, and Turkish influences.

DAY 3

After two days exploring Istanbul's European side, board a transcontinental commuter ferry and set off for the varied textures of Asia. Sip a Turkish tea on the 20-minute ride and enjoy the views of the city from the water. You'll disembark in Kadıköy, a vibrant and trendy neighborhood on the Sea of Marmara and the Bosphorus. Wander through the twisting tree-lined streets of the neighborhood, and notice the colorful murals that cover many of the buildings. Eventually, make your way to the Kadıköy fish market, where vendors hawk their fresh catch along with a cornucopia of fruits and vegetables, silky olives, hunks of white cheese, sharp sour pickles, and more.

Head to Çiya for lunch, where the ever-rotating daily menu utilizes seasonal produce to make regional recipes from the country's southeast.

Hop in a cab or dolmuş and take a short ride to Üsküdar, a more conservative neighborhood. This is where you can spot some splendid Ottoman-era mosques and experience a different side of Istanbul's Asian side. Mihrimah Sultan Mosque and Yeni Valide Mosque are both central and easy to visit.

Afterwards, continue along the coast to Beylerbeyi Palace, a former Ottoman summer palace that sits just under the Bosphorus Bridge. It's a fairly short (15 minutes) drive or long (one-hour) walk. The modern and historical twist and mesh, with the mighty modern bridge shadowing the Ottoman palace. Sit in the tea garden by the water and enjoy a moment of quiet in this city in motion.

Great Itineraries

Best of Turkey, 8 days

A week in Turkey will only give you a taste of what the large and varied country has to offer, from the big-city buzz of Istanbul to the surreal natural landscape of Cappadocia. Regardless, this busy itinerary makes sure you hit the big sights and whets your appetite for a return visit.

DAYS 1–3: ISTANBUL

Arrive in Istanbul and check into a hotel in Sultanahmet, the neighborhood close to most major sights, or one of the newer areas of Istanbul, which will be equally convenient and give you a better sense of the city today. If you have time, visit the Aya Sofya, the Blue Mosque, and the Basilica Cistern, all within a stone's throw of each other. The Aya Sofya is one of the world's largest and most important religious monuments, as well as one of the most widely regarded examples of Byzantine architecture. The Blue Mosque and its 20,000 shimmering blue-green İznik tiles showcase the grandeur of Ottoman architecture while the Basilica Cistern is a stunning example of an ancient underground waterway and a quiet place to relax amid the chaos of the city above.

Start your second day with a visit to Topkapı Palace, home to the Ottoman sultans for nearly 400 years, and explore the gorgeously tiled rooms of the Harem and the palace collections of weaponry, religious artifacts, and jaw-dropping jewels. In the afternoon, cross the Galata Bridge and head up to the art museum Istanbul Modern, where you can browse artwork from both local and international contemporary artists. Continue your journey into the city's contemporary culture at the numerous art galleries and other exhibition spaces along nearby

İstiklal Caddesi, winding up at one of Beyoğlu's many meyhanes for a dinner of meze and rakı.

On your last day, spend your morning taking a guided tour of the Dolmabahçe Palace in Beşiktaş, on the banks of the Bosphorus. After the Ottoman sultans left Topkapı, they moved the court to this new palace built in the mid-19th century. Then hop on a tram and head back to the famous Grand Bazaar to try your hand at haggling and pick up some classic Turkish souvenirs.

DAY 4: EPHESUS

Take an early flight from Istanbul to İzmir (roughly one hour) and rent a car at the airport to drive the 84 km (52 miles) to Ephesus, a well-preserved ancient Roman city that is one of the most popular tourist attractions in Turkey. Explore the marble-paved streets and partially reconstructed buildings and monuments. Depending on your forward travel schedule, you can either return to İzmir for the night or stay near Ephesus in the town of Selçuk or the attractive mountain village of Şirince, 10 km (6 miles) away from the ruins. Either way, if you have an extra day, detour to the Çeşme Peninsula on your way back to İzmir for some quality beach time.

DAY 5: ANKARA

Take an early flight from İzmir to Ankara, Turkey's capital city, where you won't want to miss the Museum of Anatolian Civilizations, with its ancient treasures going back nearly 10 millennia, and Anıtkabir, the mausoleum of Mustafa Kemal Atatürk, the revered founder of the modern Turkish Republic.

DAYS 6 AND 7: CAPPADOCIA

Rent a car or buy a bus ticket for the approximately 4½-hour drive to Göreme, the most convenient base for a short visit in Cappadocia. Stay at

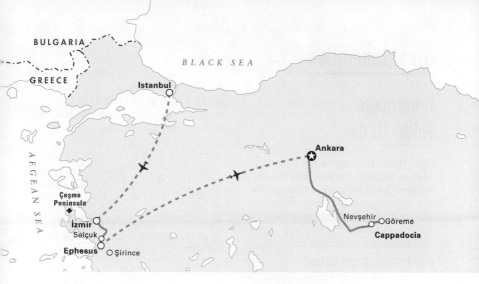

one of the comfortable boutique hotels fashioned out of the area's many old cave homes and spend the afternoon exploring the Göreme Open-Air Museum, a breathtaking complex of cave monasteries and rock-cut churches full of brightly colored frescoes.

Greet the sunrise on your second day in Cappadocia from an early morning hot-air balloon ride, one of the most popular ways to take in the area's fantastical rock formations. In the afternoon, visit the Kaymaklı or Derinkuyu underground city, both mazes of rooms descending deep into the earth that once sheltered up to 20,000 people. Close out your trip with a meal and some local wine at one of the growing number of fine restaurants in nearby Ürgüp.

DAY 8: RETURN TO ISTANBUL
You can fly back to Istanbul from Nevşehir, about a 30-minute bus ride away. If your flight is later in the day, go for a morning hike in the Rose Valley before departing Göreme.

Tips

In order to see Dolmabahçe Palace, you'll need a timed ticket so you can join an organized tour (they do sell out, especially in the busy seasons), so you may wish to book one online as soon as your plans are solidified.

As you decide which museums and archaeological sites you want to see, consider if it's worthwhile to purchase a Museum Pass Turkey for 315 TL, which gives you admission to all sites operated by the Ministry of Culture and Tourism (but not Dolmabahçe Palace). It also allows you to skip lines, which can be long in the busy seasons.

Do make hotel reservations as you plan your trip. Particularly in the busy summer season, it's hard to find good lodgings on the fly.

Great Itineraries

Crossroads of Faith, 10 days

Once home to powerful Christian and Muslim empires, the area that makes up modern Turkey has played a crucial role in the development of both religions. This tour takes you to some of the most important religious sites in Turkey, places that still poignantly convey spirituality.

DAYS 1 AND 2: ISTANBUL

Arrive in Istanbul and check into a hotel in Sultanahmet. If you have time, visit two of the quintessential Istanbul sights: the Aya Sofya and the nearby Blue Mosque.

Start your second day with a visit to the Süleymaniye Mosque, one of the greatest achievements of Mimar Sinan, the Ottomans' favorite architect. Then head to the western edge of Istanbul's old city walls, where you'll find the Kariye Museum in what was the Byzantine Chora Church. It's filled with glittering mosaics and beautiful frescoes that are considered among the finest in the world. End your day in Eyüp Camii, a historic mosque complex on the Golden Horn that is one of the holiest areas in Istanbul.

DAY 3: KONYA

Take a morning flight from Istanbul to Konya and pick up a rental car at the airport. In Konya you'll see the magnificent Mevlâna Museum and tomb, dedicated to the life and teachings of Rumi Celaleddin, the 13th-century mystic who founded the order of the whirling dervishes. The city's 13th-century Alaaddin Mosque is also worth a visit. In the evening, catch a live dervish performance at the cultural center behind the museum if they're performing.

DAYS 4 AND 5: CAPPADOCIA

After Konya, head east toward the lunar landscape of Cappadocia, where the volcanic rock outcroppings and cliffs were used by local Christians centuries ago as churches, monasteries, and homes. One of the best places to see these unique structures is in the village of Göreme. Spend the night in one of the hotels built into the stone caves. Ürgüp has what is regarded by some as the best collection of boutique hotels in Turkey.

The attractions in Cappadocia are above ground and below it. Under siege from Arab invaders in the 7th through 10th centuries, local Christians built a series of underground cities—some going down 20 stories and capable of holding 20,000 people—where they sought refuge. The ruins in Kaymaklı and Derinkuyu are marvels of ancient engineering. Get an early start if you want to beat the summer crowds, and bring a flashlight.

If you have time, consider a visit to the Ihlara Valley, a deep gorge that has numerous monasteries and churches cut into its cliffs and a lovely green river running through it.

DAYS 6 AND 7: CAPPADOCIA TO TRABZON

Have a hearty breakfast in Cappadocia to fuel up for a long day of travel. First head northwest to the Turkish capital city of Ankara, 302 km (188 miles) away. Break your journey here with a visit to Ankara's Museum of Anatolian Civilizations, featuring artifacts from all around Turkey dating back to 7000 BC. If time allows, trek up to the historic citadel for grand views of the city and have a meal before heading to Ankara Esenboğa Airport for your evening flight to Trabzon.

The next day, head to the Sümela Monastery (scheduled to reopen in

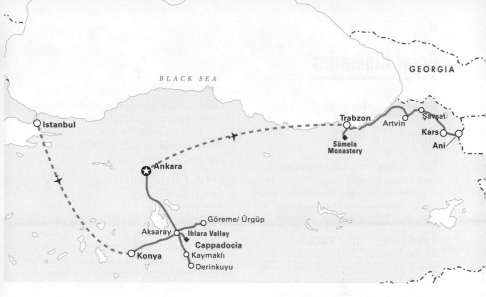

May 2019 after restorations), which clings dramatically to a cliff side in the mountains above Trabzon. Founded by Greek Orthodox monks in the 5th century, the monastery remained in use until 1922 and still contains impressive 14th- to 18th-century frescoes. You can visit either in your own vehicle or on a day tour from Trabzon. Back in town, pop in to the 13th-century Aya Sofya, a well-preserved Byzantine church that has been converted into a mosque, and then settle in for a fish dinner at Fevzi Hoca or grab a quick bite at Çardak Pide before calling it a night.

DAY 8: TRABZON TO KARS

Hit the road early for the 443 km (269 miles) trip to Kars, first heading east along the Black Sea coast and then up into the mountains. Break the occasionally harrowing drive with a stop in the mountain outpost of Artvin, or (taking a slightly longer route) in the beautiful valley town of Şavşat. If your schedule allows, book in at one of the simple accommodations in either town and spend an extra day exploring the area's stunning natural landscape, which shelters numerous abandoned Georgian churches and monasteries, some of them dating to the 9th century. (A local guide can be useful for helping find them.)

DAY 9: KARS AND ANI

The sprawling ruins of Ani, located 46 km (28.5 miles) outside of Kars along the closed border with Armenia, are one of Turkey's most remote attractions, but also among its most picturesque. The capital of a medieval Armenian kingdom, Ani was once known as "the city of 1,001 churches." Though only a handful of these buildings are still visible today, ruined structures like the massive cathedral dating to 1001 are important examples of the religious architecture of their time—and all the more striking for their forlorn setting. Back in town for the evening, dine on roasted Kars goose (kaz), a local specialty, at Oçakbaşı Restoran or Kamer Cafe & Restaurant.

DAY 10: KARS AND RETURN TO ISTANBUL

If you have an afternoon flight back to Istanbul from Kars, take some time in the morning to visit Kars' picturesque castle, interesting small museum, and the Kümbet Cami, originally built in the 10th century as the Armenian Church of the Twelve Apostles, and now a mosque.

Great Itineraries

Best Beaches and Ruins, 10 days

This itinerary covers the best of both the beaches and archaeological sites, along the two major coastlines. Adding a couple of days in Istanbul at the beginning or end makes a perfect trip.

DAYS 1 AND 2: ISTANBUL

Arrive in Istanbul and head to one of the charming small hotels in Sultanahmet (the Hotel Empress Zoë and the Sarı Konak Hotel are two good options). If you have time, go to see the awe-inspiring Aya Sofya and the nearby Blue Mosque.

The next day, visit Topkapı Sarayı to get a sense of how the Ottoman sultans lived (make sure to take a tour of the Harem). From there, go to the nearby Archaeological Museums complex, displaying Roman and Greek artifacts that come from many of the sites that you'll soon be visiting. In the evening, head by taxi to one of the little neighborhoods along the Bosphorus, such as Ortaköy or Arnavutköy, for a fish dinner by the waterside (if you time it right, you can take one of the limited Bosphorus commuter ferry services there, though none go back down to the Beyoğlu or Sultanahmet areas at night).

DAY 3: EPHESUS

On the morning of Day 3, take the roughly one-hour flight to İzmir and rent a car at the airport to make the quick 84-km (52-mile) drive down to the ancient Roman city of Ephesus. If you get an early flight out, you should be here by lunch. The buildings and monuments are remarkably well preserved and easily give you the sense of what life must have been like in this important trading city 2,000 years ago. After Ephesus, visit the nearby Meryem Ana Evi, where the Virgin Mary is believed to have spent her final years. You can spend the night in Selçuk, which is right on the doorstep of Ephesus, but better yet, head 8 km (5 miles) into the mountains above Selçuk and stay in the tranquil village of Şirince.

DAY 4: PRIENE, MILETUS, AND DIDYMA

Start off your day with a visit to Priene, an ancient Greek city that sits on a steep hill looking out on a valley below—it's about 65 km (40 miles) from Şirince. From there continue 22 km (14 miles) south to Miletus, another Greek city, where a spectacular theater is the main example of its former glory. Twenty kilometers (12 miles) south of here is Didyma and its magnificent Temple of Apollo, its scale as grand as the Parthenon, with 124 well-preserved columns. To keep yourself from burning out on ruins, continue another 5 km (3 miles) to the white-sand beach of Altınkum (this is not the same as the similarly named beach near Çeşme) and take a dip in the warm water, then have a meal at one of the numerous fish restaurants lining the shore. Drive back to the busy seaside resort town of Kuşadası, where there are several hotels and *pansiyons* at which you can spend the night.

DAY 5: APHRODISIAS

Get an early start for the drive to the ruins of Aphrodisias, a Roman goddess of love, Aphrodite, which has a spectacular setting and as much to offer as Ephesus, although with significantly fewer crowds. From here work your way down to the coast and the quiet town of Dalyan, where you can spend the next two nights in one of several riverside *pansiyons*.

DAY 6: DALYAN, İZTUZU BEACH, AND THE ROCK TOMBS OF KAUNOS

At Dalyan's riverside quay, you can hire a boat to take you to the ruins of ancient Kaunos, a city dating back to the 9th

century BC and famous for its collection of cliff tombs. Watch for the herons and storks idling in the river's reeds. Continue your day cruise to the famed İztuzu Beach, a 5-km (3-mile) stretch of undeveloped sand that's also a nesting ground for sea turtles. There are a few snack bars at the beach, but you might want to consider packing a lunch.

DAY 7: LETOON, PATARA, AND KAŞ

The mountainous coastal region south of Dalyan is the home of ancient Lycia. The Lycians built a series of impressive cities whose ruins are sprinkled throughout the area. To see one, drive from Dalyan to Letoon, a UNESCO World Heritage site with three fascinating temples dating back to the 2nd century BC. From here continue to Patara, another Lycian ruin that has the added bonus of being right next to one of Turkey's finest and longest beaches. You can spend the night in the relaxing little seaside town of Kaş, which has several good lodging and eating options.

DAY 8: OLYMPOS

On your eighth day, drive to the Lycian ruins of Olympos, which have a small river running through them that ends at a beautiful crescent beach backed by mountains. Stay in the little village of

Çıralı, a good spot for an evening visit to the legendary Chimaera, small flames of ignited gas that shoot out of the rocks of a nearby mountain.

DAY 9: ANTALYA/TERMESSOS (OR ASPENDOS)

Spend your last night in the rapidly growing resort city of Antalya, but first visit the dramatic site of Termessos, an impregnable city that both Alexander the Great and the Romans decided not to attack. (Alternatively, continue 48 km [30 miles] past Antalya to visit Aspendos, a spectacular Roman theater that is still in use today.) Return to Antalya in the afternoon and stay in one of the renovated old Ottoman houses in the Kaleiçi, the city's charming old town.

DAY 10: RETURN TO ISTANBUL

If you have time before your flight back to Istanbul, use the morning to walk around the narrow streets of the Kaleiçi and then visit the city's large Archaeological Museum. If you need to stock up on souvenirs before your return, head to Antalya's bazaar before going to the airport.

Recommended Tours

Tours aren't for everyone, but they can be convenient and help you reach parts of the country you might not find on your own, especially if you don't want to drive. Plus, a package tour to Turkey can be less expensive than independent travel and you'll be spared the trouble of arranging everything yourself. There are, of course, cons, too, one disadvantage being that you'll have less flexibility in being able to choose your hotels and restaurants (and you will have to live by a schedule you might not otherwise keep).

GENERAL TOURS

Euphrates Tours. Offers 10-day to two-week tours of Turkey's highlights, as well as off-the-beaten-path destinations; single- and multi-day tours of Cappadocia, Ephesus, and Gallipoli; and specialty trips including tours of Biblical sites, wine-tasting trips, and ski packages. ☎ 384/341–7485 in Turkey ⊕ www.cappadociatours.com.

Credo Tours. Custom trips with a focus on archaeology, culture, and history, including a six-day tour of Istanbul through the lens of contemporary and classical art; a 10-day tour of the historical sites of Western Turkey; and a 10-day gastronomic tour taking in Istanbul, Cappadocia, İzmir, and Bodrum. Also gives single-day tours of Istanbul. ☎ 212/254–8175 in Turkey ⊕ www.credotours.com.

Heritage Tours. New York–based Heritage Tours is highly recommended as a higher-end, full-service travel company. Heritage can design a trip start to finish, including great hotels, private drivers, and tour guides. ☎ 800/378–4555 toll-free in U.S. and Canada, 212/206–8400 in New York ⊕ www.heritagetours.com.

Istanbul Life. Specializes in cultural experiences in Istanbul, including calligraphy lessons, cooking courses, and tours of the city's religious sites. Also offers tours to Gallipoli, Cappadocia, Ephesus, and Pamukkale. ☎ 533/738–5862 in Turkey ⊕ www.istanbullife.org.

SPECIAL-INTEREST TOURS

Birdwatch Turkey. Birdwatch Turkey organizes a number of tours that vary in length and region, all geared toward learning about Turkey's indigenous bird species. ⊕ birdwatchturkey.com.

Journey Anatolia. Journey Anatolia leads photography tours of Istanbul's historic neighborhoods, Bodrum's village markets, and the mountainous Black Sea region, and arranges sailing and beach holidays. ⊕ www.journeyanatolia.com.

Kirkit Voyage. Kirkit Voyage has tours ranging all over the country, with a special focus on hiking and horseback riding trips in Cappadocia. ☎ 212/518–2282 in Istanbul, 384/511–3259 in Cappadocia ⊕ www.kirkit.com.

Middle Earth Travel. Middle Earth Travel organizes trekking, mountaineering, and other outdoor-adventure trips, including walking tours along the scenic Lycian Way hiking trail and biking tours in Cappadocia. ☎ 384/271–2559 in Turkey ⊕ www.middleearthtravel.com.

Peter Sommer Travels. Peter Sommer Travels is a U.K.–based company that provides academic, yet friendly, guided archaeological tours of Turkey, many of them on *gulet* (wooden sailing boat) cruises. ☎ 855/443–3027 in U.S., toll free ⊕ www.petersommer.com.

Runner Tourism and Travel. Runner Tourism and Travel offers archaeological, botanical, culinary, and photography tours, in addition to organizing gulet cruises. ☎ 242/237–9842 in Turkey ⊕ www.runnertourism.com.

Chapter 3

ISTANBUL

Updated by
Katie Nawdorny

⬤ Sights	🍴 Restaurants	🛏 Hotels	🛍 Shopping	🍸 Nightlife
★★★★☆	★★★★★	★★★★☆	★★★☆☆	★★★☆☆

WELCOME TO ISTANBUL

TOP REASONS TO GO

★ **Change continents:**
Spend the morning in Europe and the afternoon in Asia, with just a ferry ride in between; how cosmopolitan is that?

★ **Cruise the Bosphorus:**
Taking a boat ride up the strait, past scenic waterfront neighborhoods, forested slopes, and fortresses, is quintessentially Istanbul.

★ **Haggle in the bazaars:**
Bargain like the locals do as you make your way through the Grand Bazaar and Spice Bazaar—these markets may be touristy, but it's still fun.

★ **Marvel at ancient domes:**
From the stunning Aya Sofya to the graceful Süleymaniye Mosque, the city's greatest works of imperial architecture never cease to impress, especially from the inside as you look up.

★ **Ogle at opulence:** With their sumptuous decor and fascinating harem quarters, the Topkapı and Dolmabahçe palaces offer a glimpse of the splendor of the Ottoman Empire.

The Bosphorus divides Istanbul between Europe and Asia.

1 Sultanahmet. Many of the city's major attractions are in this historic area.

2 The Bazaar Quarter and Environs. Known for Istanbul's major markets and several mosques.

3 The Western Districts. Includes historically Greek and Jewish neighborhoods of Fener and Balat.

4 Beyoğlu. The so-called "new town" is focused on Taksim Square and İstiklal Caddesi.

5 Galata and Karaköy. These timeworn, rapidly gentrifying neighborhoods are home to both historic sites and new attractions.

6 Beşiktaş and Nişantaşı. Dolmabahçe Palace is the main attraction here.

7 The Bosphorus. Hop on a ferry and zigzag back and forth between Asia and Europe.

8 The Asian Shore. The pleasant neighborhoods on Istanbul's Asian side have fewer "sights" but much atmosphere.

9 Princes' Islands. This nine-island archipelago can be visited by ferry.

ISTANBUL STREET FOOD

As much as Turkish people love to sit down for a leisurely dinner, they're also serious snackers, day and night, so finding a quick bite to eat is never a problem. The only challenge is choosing among the numerous tempting options.

Street food is not an afterthought in Turkey. Turks are quite demanding when it comes to eating on the run, expecting what is served to be fresh and made with care. Although McDonald's and other chains have made inroads in Turkey, many people still prefer their country's original "fast food," which sometimes is not so fast at all. Rather, some of Turkey's most popular street food dishes require some tender loving care in preparation, and frequently will be cooked or assembled right before your eyes, though there are also simple things like roasted chestnuts available.

In Istanbul and other large cities, snack bars and food stalls are open from early morning until late into the night. Look for the crowded places: chances are they're the local favorites.

FOR THE ADVENTUROUS

To make *kokoreç*, seasoned lamb intestines are wound up into a long, fat loaf, grilled over charcoal, and then chopped up with tomatoes and spices and served on a half loaf of crusty bread. *Işkembe* is a soup made out of tripe—cow stomach—and flavored with garlic and vinegar. It's usually sold in small eateries that serve nothing but this soup, said to be the ultimate way to prevent a hangover. Both are popular with late-night revelers in Turkey's big cities.

BÖREK

In the windows of *börek* shops, you can see long coils of rolled-up filo dough stuffed with ground meat, potato, spinach, or cheese and baked until golden brown. *Su böreği* is a börek made of buttery egg noodles layered over crumbles of tangy white cheese and baked in a deep dish.

DÖNER

This cheap and filling sandwich *(below)* is Turkey's most popular street food. Meat, usually lamb or chicken, is grilled on a rotating vertical spit, shaved off in paper-thin slices, and served in either crusty bread or *pide*, or rolled up in a tortilla-like flatbread into a wrap called a *dürüm*. For many Turks, a döner sandwich, downed with a glass of refreshing *ayran* (a drink made of salted, watered-down yogurt), is a meal in itself.

KUMPIR

Think of this as a baked potato on steroids. At *kumpir* stands, massive spuds are taken hot out of the oven, split open, and filled with an almost overwhelming assortment of toppings. Options include everything from grated cheese to chopped pickles, olives, and hot dog bits. It's not unusual for people to ask for six or more ingredients. The kumpir-maker then mixes it

all up into a glorious mess and puts it back in the potato skin.

MIDYE

In Turkey, mussels *(above)* truly deserve to be called street food. They're usually sold by roving vendors carrying big baskets filled with glistening black shells that have been stuffed with a combination of mussels, rice, and herbs and spices, and they are commonly eaten from these vendors. If you are concerned, err on the safe side and eat *midye* only at snack bars or restaurants, where there are higher standards of hygiene. Some specialty snack bars serve mussels coated in batter and deep-fried, in addition to the stuffed form.

SIMIT

Sort of the Turkish answer to the bagel, or a New York street pretzel, these humble sesame-coated bread rings are found all over Turkey. They're the ultimate street food: cheap, satisfying, and—when fresh from the oven—delicious. And they're available all day long, from pushcarts found on almost every street corner. The *simit* has gone slightly upscale in recent years, with the appearance in Istanbul and other Turkish cities of several chains that serve simits and other baked goods.

The only city in the world that can lay claim to straddling two continents, Istanbul—once known as Constantinople, capital of the Byzantine and then the Ottoman Empire—has for centuries been a bustling metropolis with one foot in Europe and the other in Asia. Istanbul embraces this enviable position with both a certain chaos and inventiveness, ever evolving as one of the world's most cosmopolitan crossroads.

It's often said that Istanbul is the meeting point of East and West, but visitors to this city built over the former capital of two great empires are likely to be just as impressed by the juxtaposition of old and new. Office towers creep up behind historic palaces, women in chic designer outfits pass others wearing long skirts and head coverings (sometimes chic and designer as well), peddlers' pushcarts vie with battered old Fiats and shiny BMWs for dominance of the noisy, narrow streets, and the Grand Bazaar competes with modern shopping malls. At dawn, when the muezzin's call to prayer resounds from ancient minarets, there are inevitably a few hearty revelers still making their way home from nightclubs and bars.

Most visitors to this sprawling city of more than 14 million will first set foot in the relatively compact Old City, where the legacy of the Byzantine and Ottoman empires can be seen in monumental works of architecture like the brilliant Aya Sofya and the beautifully proportioned mosques built by the great architect Sinan. Though it would be easy to spend days, if not weeks, exploring the wealth of attractions in the historical peninsula, visitors should make sure also to venture elsewhere in order to experience the vibrancy of contemporary Istanbul. With a lively nightlife propelled by its young population and an exciting arts scene that's increasingly on the international radar, Istanbul is truly a city that never sleeps. It's also a place where visitors will feel welcome: Istanbul may be on the Bosphorus, but at heart it's a Mediterranean city, whose friendly inhabitants are effusively social and eager to share what they love most about it.

Planning

WHEN TO GO
Summer in Istanbul is hot and humid. Winter usually hits around November or December and lasts until March or so, bringing with it a fair amount of rain. All

the surrounding water generally keeps the temperature above freezing, but a cold wind blows off the frozen Balkans and there's an occasional dusting of snow, typically in January or February. May and September are pleasant and the most comfortable times for exploring.

FESTIVALS
Istanbul Film Festival
Every April for two weeks, the Istanbul Film Festival presents films from Turkey and around the world, giving film buffs a great opportunity to see contemporary Turkish cinema subtitled in English. Screenings are held mainly in Beyoğlu, as well as in Nişantaşı and Kadıköy. Make sure to purchase tickets in advance, as seats are reserved and the festival is extremely popular. ⊕ *film.iksv.org/en.*

April also sees Istanbul's **Tulip Festival**, when parks all over the city become a riot of color.

The well-regarded **Istanbul Music Festival**, held during several weeks in June, features mostly classical music performed by world-class musicians.

The **Istanbul Jazz Festival** is generally held in the first two weeks of July and brings in major names, new and old, from Turkey and around the world.

In the fall, the **Istanbul Biennial** is held in odd-number years, while the Istanbul Design Biennial is held in even-number years; both showcase cutting-edge work in venues around the city.

Istanbul Foundation for Culture and Arts
Tickets for all of these events (other than the Tulip Festival, which is free and open to the public) can be ordered online through Biletix (www.biletix.com) or by contacting the Istanbul Foundation for Culture and Arts (İKSV). ⊠ *Istanbul Kültür Sanat Vakfı, Sadi Konuralp Cad. 5, Şişhane* ☎ *212/334–0700* ⊕ *www.iksv. org/en.*

PLANNING YOUR TIME
Istanbul is one of the most unique cities in the world and with two continents of treasures, three days will hardly do it justice. A week will give you time to enjoy the sights, sounds, and smells with a little leisure. Make sure to see the main sites like Topkapı, Aya Sofya, the Blue Mosque, Dolmabahçe Palace, other palaces, and the bazaars, then seek out more of what you like: there are plenty more Ottoman mosques and Byzantine monuments. Or you can just chill out, *çay* (tea) in hand, by the waters of the Bosphorus.

Check opening days when you plan your outings. Most museums in Istanbul are closed Monday, with a few exceptions: Topkapı Palace is closed Tuesday, and Dolmabahçe Palace is closed Monday. The military museum is closed both Monday and Tuesday.

If you want to see the Bosphorus but don't have a whole day, either take a short, privately run cruise, or take an evening commuter ferry to relax after a hard day's sightseeing.

The **Museum Pass Istanbul** (⊕ *www. muze.gov.tr*) allows single entry into 12 state-run museums over a period of five days; the most significant of which are the Aya Sofya, Topkapı Palace (including the Harem), the Istanbul Archaeological Museums, the Museum of Turkish and Islamic Arts, and the Kariye Müzesi. At 125 TL, it's a significant savings over the cost of paying for all these museums individually, and it also includes discounts off entrance fees at numerous private museums (including the Pera, Rahmi M. Koç and Sabancı) and 10% off purchases at many of these museums' gift shops. The other advantage of the museum pass is it allows you to bypass entrance lines, which will save time—a commodity you'll certainly need if you're going to pack in so many museums in just a few days.

3

Istanbul PLANNING

A boon for traveling parents in need of a helping hand, Hotel Momcierge offers comprehensive family travel concierge service: arranges experienced English-speaking babysitters so mom and dad can have a romantic night out; rents cribs, strollers, baby bath seats, and other child-care equipment to enable lighter travel; and organizes airport transfers with car seats. Complimentary tips about activities to do with kids in Istanbul are also provided.

CONTACTS Hotel Momcierge. ☎ *531/777–4580* ⊕ *www.hotelmomcierge.com.*

GETTING HERE AND AROUND
AIR TRAVEL
Most international and domestic flights arrive at Istanbul Airport, a new third airport that opened in March 2019. An increasing number of both domestic and international flights on low-cost carriers fly into the newer Sabiha Gökçen Airport on the Asian side of the city.

Regular shuttle service will connect central neighborhoods to the new airport, with the price dependent on the distance traveled. A metro connection to the new airport is anticipated, but not until sometime in 2020. There is no rail link to Sabiha Gökçen Airport, so you'll need to take a Havabus shuttle bus (18 TL to Taksim) or a taxi (⊕ *www.havatas.com*).

BOAT TRAVEL
It's no surprise that Istanbul is well served by ferries. With the exception of the leisure-oriented Bosphorus cruises, ferries are most useful for crossing the Bosphorus (rather than going up and down it) and for getting to the Princes' Islands. The main docks on the European side are at Eminönü and Karaköy (on either side of the Galata Bridge), while Üsküdar and Kadıköy are the most important docks on the Asian side. Traditional large ferryboats operated by Şehir Hatları (⊕ *www.sehirhatlari.com.tr*), as well as smaller, somewhat faster-moving ferries run by two private companies (Turyol and

Dentur Avrasya), crisscross the Bosphorus day and night, and cost about the same as land-based public transport. The Princes' Islands are served both by Şehir Hatları and by İDO on weekdays. İDO operates "sea bus" catamarans from Kabataş that are faster, sleeker, and completely enclosed (⊕ *www.ido.com.tr*).

Taking a ferry is also one of the best ways to get in and out of Istanbul. "Fast ferries," some of which carry cars, leave from Yenikapı, which is south of Aksaray and a short taxi ride from Sultanahmet, to various ports on the southern side of the Sea of Marmara. The most useful routes are the ferries to Yalova, Bursa, and Bandırma, for travelers heading to İznik, Bursa, and Çanakkale, respectively.

BUS TRAVEL
Bus service within Istanbul is frequent, and drivers and riders tend to be helpful, so you should be able to navigate your way to major tourist stops like Eminönü, Taksim, and Beşiktaş. You must have an İstanbulkart *(see İstanbulkart section below)* to board, and the fare is 2.60 TL.

For travel around the country, Turkey has an extensive system of intercity buses, and Istanbul's large, chaotic Esenler Otogar is the heart of it. Esenler itself is a bit out of the way, though easily accessible by metro from Taksim (via Yenikapı). Alternatively, most of the major bus companies have offices located near the top of İnönü Caddesi (which winds down from Taksim Square to Kabataş), from which they operate shuttle buses, known as a *servis*. These take passengers either to Esenler or to their own ministations on the main freeway, allowing you to avoid making the trek out to Esenler via public transport.

A second, smaller bus station, at Harem on the waterfront on the Asian side of the Bosphorus, is easily accessible by ferry from Eminönü.

CAR TRAVEL

If you're entering or leaving Istanbul by car, E80 runs from the Bulgarian border and through Turkish Thrace to Istanbul, continuing on to central Anatolia in the east; this toll road is the best of several alternatives. Getting out of the city by car can be challenging, as the signs aren't always clear. It's always useful to have a driving map.

Istanbul is notorious for congested traffic, a cavalier attitude to traffic regulations, poor signposting, and a shortage of parking spaces. In short, don't even think about renting a car for travel in the city.

CRUISE TRAVEL

Ships dock at Karaköy, in the shadow of the famous Galata Tower. It's a short walk to the Karaköy tram stop at the start of the Galata Bridge, which connects to Sultanahmet's main sites within about 10 minutes, and to the Karaköy entrance of the Tünel, a historic funicular that plies the steep hill up to İstiklal Caddesi. Taxis also wait at the pier for the 10-minute ride into Sultanahmet.

DOLMUŞ TRAVEL

A dolmuş, or shared taxi, is a cross between a taxi and a bus: they run set routes, leave when full, and make fewer stops than a bus, so they're faster. Most dolmuşes are bright yellow minibuses. Dolmuş stands are marked by signs (look for a large "D") but you can also hail one on the street; the destination is shown on a roof sign or a card in the front window. Dolmuşes mostly head out to the suburbs, but visitors may find a few routes useful, including those that go from Taksim to Beşiktaş and from Taksim to Nişantaşı/Teşvikiye (for both routes, dolmuşes leave from the top of İnönü Caddesi near Taksim Square, and the fare is 2.75 TL). Dolmuşes also run between Taksim and the Kadıköy neighborhood (7 TL) on the Asian side, which is useful if you are coming back at night after the last boat.

FOOT TRAVEL

Istanbul is a walker's city, and the best way to experience it is to wander, inevitably getting lost—even with a good map, it's easy to lose your way in the winding streets and alleyways. When in doubt, just ask. Particularly in the old part of the city, most of the main sites are within a short distance of each other, and the easiest way to get to them is on foot.

FUNICULAR AND METRO TRAVEL

Istanbul's two short underground funiculars are convenient for avoiding the steep, uphill walk from the Bosphorus and Golden Horn waterfront to Beyoğlu; each takes less than two minutes to ascend. The historic Tünel, in operation since 1875, connects Karaköy and Tünel Square. The ultramodern funicular from Kabataş (the end of the tram line) to Taksim is also convenient. The city has two main underground metro lines of use to visitors, which connect at Yenikapı: one passes through Şişhane (near Tünel) and Taksim before continuing north to the business districts, while the other runs through Aksaray, west of Sultanahmet and Esenler Otogar. Fares for each line are 2.60 TL with an İstanbulkart (see İstanbulkart section below).

THE İSTANBULKART

The İstanbulkart is a prepaid "smart card" that you can swipe to pay for buses, trams, the funiculars and metro, and most ferries. The 6-TL nonrefundable fee for the card may not be worth paying if you're only in town briefly, but it can save you money if you plan to take public transportation a fair bit (especially if you're in a group, as up to five people can use the same card). With an İstanbulkart, fares are 2.60 TL, and there is a discount on transfers within a two-hour period. The İstanbulkart can be purchased at major transit stops such as Taksim and Eminönü and reloaded at most stops. Most newsstands are able to upload credit as well. The municipality eventually plans for cardholders to pay for taxi rides and museum entrance fees with the card but so far, aside from transport, it can only be used to pay for some public toilets.

MARMARAY TRAVEL

The long-awaited and much-delayed Marmaray—a 13.3-km-long (8½-mile-long) rail tunnel extending under the Bosphorus from Sirkeci on the European side to Üsküdar on the Asian side—finally opened on October 23, 2013, the 90th anniversary of the Turkish Republic. The Marmaray will eventually revolutionize transport in Istanbul, linking up with new and existing rail lines to create a 76-km (47-mile) commuter rail line connecting the city's farthest-flung suburbs and allowing passengers to cross under the Bosphorus in just four minutes. But high-speed trains still don't come into Sirkeci; you have to travel to the Asian side to get those.

TAXI TRAVEL

Taxis are metered and relatively cheap—a ride from Sultanahmet to Taksim is about 17 to 20 TL. Many drivers don't speak English, so it may be helpful to write your destination on a piece of paper, and to bring the business card of your hotel with you so you don't have problems getting back later. Ask your hotel to call a taxi or find a stand in front of a hotel—you'll be more likely to get a driver who won't take you the long way around.

TRAIN TRAVEL

Istanbul has two main train stations: Sirkeci, near the Eminönü waterfront in Old Istanbul, and Haydarpaşa, on the Asian side of the Bosphorus, both of which are out of service for an extended period due to major work to extend the Marmaray and build high-speed rail lines. One of these high-speed lines, connecting Istanbul with Ankara and Konya, is now operational, but travelers must board in Pendik, far from the city center, making this much less of a convenient option than it should be. Travelers seeking to take the train from Istanbul to Bulgaria or Greece are likewise being bused from Sirkeci to a train station farther west.

TRAM TRAVEL

There are several tram lines in Istanbul, but the one most useful to visitors runs from Kabataş (below Taksim) along the Bosphorus to Karaköy, across the Galata Bridge to Eminönü, and then to Sultanahmet and Beyazıt/the Grand Bazaar before heading out to the western part of the city. The fare is 2.60 TL with an İstanbulkart, and trams run from around 6 in the morning to just before midnight. There is also a slow but atmospheric historic tram that runs along İstiklal Caddesi between Tünel and Taksim.

HOTELS

With the number of visitors to Turkey increasing every year, Istanbul's hoteliers are busy keeping up with the growing demand. New lodgings, from five-star hotels to smaller boutique inns, are opening all the time, while older establishments are busy renovating and expanding. This means there are plenty more options than there were in the past, but because Istanbul is such a popular destination, it's not the travel bargain it used to be. Hotels in Istanbul tend to quote their rates in U.S. dollars or euros, depending on which currency has a more advantageous exchange rate. Most lodgings, save four- and five-star hotels, include a full Turkish breakfast with the room rate. Sultanahmet has a large number of smaller hotels, but high-rise luxury hotels are more prevalent near Taksim Square and along the coveted strip of the Bosphorus between Beşiktaş and Ortaköy.

For the most luxurious, indulgent accommodations, stay in one of the large, modern, high-end hotels that are mostly clustered in the upscale neighborhood of Nişantaşı and along the coveted strip of the Bosphorus between Beşiktaş and Ortaköy. You'll pay considerably more to stay in these digs but the perks can include incredible waterfront views, swimming pools and top-notch fitness facilities, and sophisticated dining options. Wherever you stay, you may notice that hoteliers are starting to embrace traditional Turkish styles and motifs; one new trend is to design hotel bathrooms like hammams. Though the setup may be less familiar than a traditional shower or bath, these bathrooms can be quite luxurious, with marble-lined tubs and heated floors.

Hotel reviews have been shortened. For full information, visit Fodors.com.

What It Costs in Turkish Lira

	$	$$	$$$	$$$$
HOTELS				
	under $150	$150–$250	$251–$350	over $350

NIGHTLIFE

As Istanbul's reputation as a hip city continues to grow, the quality of the live acts that come to town has risen, too. Established and up-and-coming performers now frequently include Istanbul on their European tours, and the city has become a good place to catch a show for far less than what you might pay in Paris, London, or New York. Note that many live-performance venues close for part or all of the summer, when school is out and the city's elite departs for vacation.

To experience Istanbul's most high-end nightlife, head to the neighborhoods along the Bosphorus, where chic (and pricey) nightclubs play host to Istanbul's rich and famous and those who want to rub shoulders with them. The vibrant dance club scene here, as well as at a few places in Beyoğlu, is not for the faint of heart. Things typically get rolling at around midnight and go until 4 or 5 in the morning. The city's most upscale clubs tend to be expensive—admission fees can be steep on summer weekends—and there are no guarantees

Nargiles ◉

Nargiles (also known as hookahs) and the billowy smoke they produce have been an integral part of Istanbul's coffeehouses for centuries. Once associated with older men who would spend their days smoking, sipping strong Turkish coffee, and playing backgammon, the nargile is experiencing renewed popularity among younger Istanbullus. They are often used with a variety of flavored tobaccos, such as apple or strawberry. Because the smoke is filtered through water, it's cool and smooth, though it can make you light-headed if you're not used to it.

you'll get past the doorman, whose job it is to make sure only Istanbul's best dressed get in.

Sultanahmet isn't known for its nightlife, but in summer, the strip of tourist-oriented restaurants and dive bars at the end of Akbıyık Sokak close to the Aya Sofya can be quite lively, with a young crowd that fills the sidewalk tables.

PERFORMING ARTS

For upcoming events, reviews, and other information about what to do in Istanbul, visit the expat-run website Yabangee (⊕ www.yabangee.com) or pick up a copy of the monthly *Time Out Istanbul* or the bimonthly *The Guide*, both of which are English-language publications with listings of restaurants, bars, and events, as well as features about Istanbul. The English-language *Hürriyet Daily News* is also a good resource for listings and for keeping abreast of what's happening in Istanbul and in Turkish politics.

WHIRLING DERVISHES

The Mevlevi, a Sufi brotherhood originally founded in Konya, are best known around the world as the whirling dervishes, mystics who believe ritual spinning will bring them closer to God. If you can't make it to Konya to see the *sema* ceremony in the place where it all began, there are a couple of places to see them in Istanbul. It should be noted that these ceremonies—at least in Istanbul—have essentially turned into performances staged for tourists, lacking much religious context. Nonetheless, seeing the dervishes whirl tends to entrance even the least spiritual of people, and gives a window onto a unique aspect of traditional Turkish culture.

RESTAURANTS

This city is a food lover's town and restaurants abound, from humble kebab joints to fancy fish venues, with a variety of excellent options in between. Owing to its location on the Bosphorus, which connects the Black Sea to the Sea of Marmara, Istanbul is famous for its seafood. A classic Istanbul meal, usually eaten at one of the city's rollicking *meyhanes* (literally "drinking places"), starts off with a wide selection of tapas-style cold appetizers called meze, then a hot starter or two, and then moves on to a main course of grilled fish, all of it accompanied by the anise-flavored spirit *rakı*, Turkey's national drink. The waiter will generally bring a tray over to your table to show off the day's meze and you simply point to what you'd like. Note that the portions you get are often larger than the samples shown on the tray, so don't over-order; you can always select a second—or third—round later. When it comes to the main course, fish can be expensive, so check prices and ask what's in season before ordering. In Istanbul, fall and winter are the best seasons for seafood.

Istanbul's dining scene, though diverse, was once mostly limited to Turkish cooking, but a new generation of chefs is successfully fusing local dishes with more international flavors and preparations. Some are trained in the United States and Europe and bring home the contemporary culinary techniques they've learned abroad, and the result is a kind of nouvelle Turkish cuisine. Interest in little-known specialty foods and regional dishes from around Turkey is also taking hold, as chefs increasingly look at home, rather than abroad, for inspiration. Over the past few years, a handful of restaurants have opened where the chef-owner defines the vision and personality of the venue—though this may be old hat in Europe or North America, it represents an exciting new trend in Istanbul.

Istanbullus take their eating seriously, holding establishments to a very high standard; they expect their food to be fresh and well prepared at even the most basic of eateries, and are likely to feel that few places can hold a candle to "Mom's cooking." That said, at restaurants catering to a trendier, more upscale crowd, style sometimes seems to pass for substance, and consistency can be elusive; the fanciest venues may not necessarily offer the best food.

Since Istanbullus love to go out, reservations are essential at most of the city's better restaurants. In summer, many establishments move their dining areas outdoors, and reservations become even more important if you want to snag a coveted outside table. For the most part, dining is casual, although locals enjoy dressing smartly when they're out. You may feel terribly underdressed if you show up in a restaurant dressed in shorts and a T-shirt, even in summer.

Alcohol, beer, wine, and the local spirit *rakı* are widely available, but alcoholic drinks—particularly anything imported—tend to be considerably more expensive than in North America or Europe. The national lager Efes is the most widely available beer; venues may carry two or three other domestic and international labels, but don't expect a wide selection. Yeni Rakı, a state-run monopoly until not long ago, remains the most popular *rakı* brand. Wine consumption in Turkey has traditionally lagged far behind, but that's been slowly changing in recent years as the quality of local wines has started to improve. There are some very drinkable domestic wines on the market, most priced at only a fraction of what you'd pay for an imported label. Turkish wines are made from foreign grapes as well as indigenous varietals, of which the most noteworthy are the reds Öküzgözü, Boğazkere, and Kalecik Karası and the whites Emir and Narince.

During the Islamic holy month of Ramadan, when Muslims fast from sun-up to sundown, restaurants that cater primarily to tourists, and most venues in cosmopolitan parts of Istanbul such as Beyoğlu, continue to operate normally. In more traditional neighborhoods some restaurants close altogether or change their hours of operation. In recent years, it has become increasingly popular to go to restaurants for *iftar*—the evening meal that breaks the daily fast—instead of having it in the home, as was traditionally done.

What it Costs in Turkish Lira

$	$$	$$$	$$$$
RESTAURANTS			
under 20 TL	21 TL–35 TL	36 TL–50 TL	over 51 TL

SHOPPING

Istanbul has been a shopper's town for, well, centuries—the sprawling Grand Bazaar, open since 1461, could easily be called the world's oldest shopping mall—but this is not to say that the city is stuck in the past. Along with its colorful bazaars and outdoor markets, Istanbul also has a wide range of modern shopping options, from the enormous new malls that seem to be sprouting up everywhere to small independent boutiques. Either way, it's almost impossible to leave Istanbul without buying something and some say you haven't

truly experienced the city until you take a whirl through the Grand Bazaar or Spice Bazaar. Whether you're looking for trinkets and souvenirs, kilims and carpets, brass and silverware, jewelry, leather goods, old books, prints, and maps, or furnishings and clothes (Turkish textiles are among the best in the world), you can find them in this city. Shopping in Istanbul also provides a snapshot of the city's contrasts and contradictions: migrants from rural Turkey haggle with tourists and sell their wares on the streets while wealthy shoppers browse the designer goods found in plush, upscale Western-style department stores.

İstiklal Caddesi is a pedestrian-only boulevard with everything from global brands like Levi's and big-name Turkish companies like Mavi to small bookshops and old school shoe stores—though, sadly, increasingly high rent prices mean there are fewer and fewer independent local stores located on İstiklal these days. Down the hill from İstiklal, Çukurcuma Caddesi is home to a miscellany of antiques dealers carrying everything from small, Ottoman-era knickknacks to enormous antique marble tubs. Meanwhile, the character-filled Galata and Karaköy neighborhoods are becoming the places to find independent boutiques and intriguing shops selling clothing, jewelry, housewares, and objets d'art created by up-and-coming local designers.

Istanbul is also a good place to buy jewelry, as Turkey has a long tradition of jewelry making, and many jewelers are skilled at working with both gold and silver. While local brands often tend to copy European designs in their collections, recently there has been a trend towards creating beautiful pieces with a local flavor, using traditional motifs or taking Ottoman-era charms and setting them in silver or gold. The jewelry sold in the Grand Bazaar and in high-end boutiques in Nişantaşı tends to be fairly classic and high quality; if you're looking for something a bit more unusual or easier on the wallet, try the smaller-scale boutiques in Beyoğlu or Galata.

TOURS

An increasing number of tours offer the chance to explore Istanbul through the lens of history, food, art, or other specialty pursuits. Companies offering general tours and their itineraries change frequently so it's best just to make arrangements through a travel agency or your hotel; the offerings are all pretty similar. If you join a group, a "classic tour" of the Aya Sofya, Blue Mosque, Hippodrome, and Grand Bazaar will cost at least 120 TL for a half day. For a full-day tour that also includes the Topkapı Palace and Süleymaniye Camii, as well as lunch, expect to pay 225 TL and up. Bosphorus tours include a cruise and excursions to sights like Rumeli Hisarı and the Dolmabahçe or Beylerbeyi palaces. Rates for private tours with a guide and driver are higher, and more cost-effective if you have a large party; for two people, expect to pay at least 300 TL per person for a full day, and about a third less per person if you have four or more people. Keep in mind that admission fees and meals are generally not included in private tour rates, so this alternative ends up being considerably more costly.

Artwalk Istanbul

SPECIAL-INTEREST | Walking tours of galleries and artists' studios offer an insider's look into Istanbul's booming contemporary art scene. Private walks start at €100. ☎ 537/797–7525 ⊕ www. artwalkistanbul.com.

Context Travel

SPECIAL-INTEREST | Private and small group "walking seminars" led by art historians, archaeologists, and other local experts include close looks at Ottoman mosque architecture and the cosmopolitan heritage of the neighborhoods around İstiklal Caddesi. From $50 per person and $242 for a private tour. ⊕ www.contexttravel. com/city/Istanbul.

Culinary Backstreets

WALKING TOURS | Friendly, small-scale (maximum group size seven) walking tours of Istanbul neighborhoods focus on food—and plenty of it—with lots of local culture and atmosphere along the way. Most tours are $125 per person. ⊕ www. culinarybackstreets.com/culinary-walks/ istanbul.

Istanbul On Bike

BICYCLE TOURS | Cycling in chaotic, traffic-clogged Istanbul may seem like a daunting prospect, but these young guides make it fun (and safe). Tours cover classic sightseeing routes as well as the lesser-visited Asian side of Istanbul and Golden Horn waterfront. They also offer rent-a-bike service including helmet, lock, and reflective vest. Tours price vary; available upon request. ☎ 553/440–5544 ⊕ www.istanbulonbike.com.

VISITOR INFORMATION

There are several tourism information offices in Istanbul run by the Turkish Ministry of Culture and Tourism, including at both airports, in Sultanahmet (Divanyolu Cad. 3 ☎ 212/518–1802), just outside the entrance to the Sirkeci train station, near Eminönü (☎ 212/511–5888), and across from Gezi Park in Taksim (Mete Cad. 6, ☎ 212/233–0592). They are open every day from 9 to 6 in summer and 9 to 5 in winter.

Sultanahmet

Sultanahmet is the heart of Old Istanbul, where many of the city's must-see attractions are located: an incredible concentration of art and architecture spanning millennia is packed into its narrow, winding streets. At the eastern edge of the Old City, Topkapı Palace—the center of Ottoman power and the residence of sultans for centuries—sits perched on the promontory overlooking the Bosphorus and the mouth of the Golden Horn. Behind the palace rise the imposing domes and soaring minarets of the Blue Mosque and Aya Sofya, two of Istanbul's most famous landmarks.

As you walk through the Hippodrome, explore the underground Basilica Cistern, and view the Byzantine mosaics displayed in the Mosaic Museum, you'll also get a feel for what the city of Constantinople looked like more than a thousand years ago, well before the Turks conquered it in 1453. The three buildings that compose the Istanbul Archaeological Museums showcase an incredible collection of artifacts going back even further in time, left by ancient civilizations that once thrived in Anatolia and around the region. When the call to prayer echoes from Sultanahmet's great mosques, pause for a moment to soak up the atmosphere here; nowhere else in Istanbul do you get such a rich feel for the magic of this ancient and mysterious city.

👁 Sights

Many of Istanbul's most famous historic sights are found in Sultanahmet near Sultanahmet Square. The area is busy and very walkable.

★ **Aya Sofya** (*Hagia Sophia, Church of the Holy Wisdom*)
RELIGIOUS SITE | This soaring edifice is perhaps the greatest work of Byzantine architecture and for almost a thousand years, starting from its completion in 537, it was the world's largest and most important religious monument. As Emperor Justinian may well have intended, the impression that will stay with you longest, years after a visit, is the sight of the dome. As you enter, the half domes trick you before the great space opens up with the immense dome, almost 18 stories high and more than 100 feet across, towering above—look up into it and you'll see the spectacle of thousands of gold tiles glittering in the light of 40 windows. Only Saint Peter's

---

A Column of Lucky Charms 👁

The marble-and-brass **Sacred Column**, in the north aisle of Aya Sofya, to the left as you enter through the main door, is laden with legends. It's thought that the column weeps water that can work miracles, and over the centuries believers have worn a hole as they caress the column to come in contact with the miraculous moisture. It's also believed that if you place your thumb in the hole and turn your hand 360 degrees, any wish you make while doing so will come true.

---

in Rome, not completed until the 17th century, surpasses Hagia Sophia in size and grandeur. It was the cathedral of Constantinople, the heart of the city's spiritual life, and the scene of imperial coronations.

When Mehmet II conquered the city in 1453, he famously sprinkled dirt on his head before entering the church after the conquest as a sign of humility. His first order was for Hagia Sophia to be turned into a mosque and, in keeping with the Islamic proscription against figural images, mosaics were plastered over. Successive sultans added the four minarets, *mihrab* (prayer niche), and *minbar* (pulpit for the *imam*) that visitors see today, as well as the large black medallions inscribed in Arabic with the names of Allah, Muhammad, and the early caliphs. In 1935, Atatürk turned Hagia Sophia into a museum and a project of restoration, including the uncovering of mosaics, began.

Recent restoration efforts have, among other things, uncovered four large, beautifully preserved mosaics of seraphim,

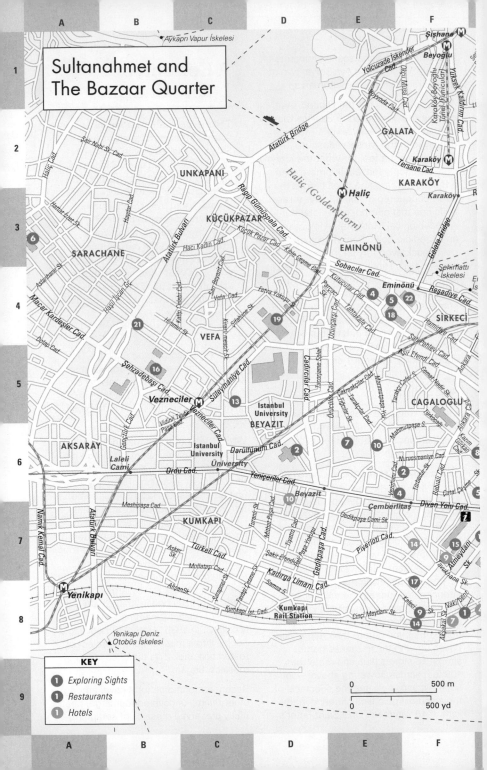

Sultanahmet and The Bazaar Quarter

KEY

- 1 Exploring Sights
- 1 Restaurants
- 1 Hotels

0   500 m
0   500 yd

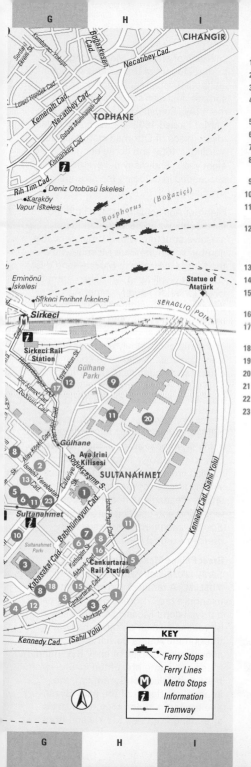

Sights ▼

1 Aya Sofya G6
2 Beyazıt Camii D6
3 Blue Mosque G7
4 Column of
  Constantine F6
5 Eminönü E4
6 Fatih Camii A3
7 Grand Bazaar E6
8 Great Palace Mosaic
  Museum G8
9 Gülhane Parkı H5
10 Hippodrome G7
11 Istanbul Archaelogy
   Museums H5
12 Istanbul Museum of
   the History of Science
   and Technology
   in Islam G5
13 Istanbul University C5
14 Küçük Aya Sofya F8
15 Museum of Turkish and
   Islamic Arts F7
16 Şehzade Camii B5
17 Šokollu Mehmet
   Paşa Camii F8
18 Spice Bazaar E4
19 Süleymaniye Camii D4
20 Topkapı Palace H5
21 Valens Aqueduct B4
22 Yeni Cami F4
23 Yerebatan Sarnıcı G7

Restaurants ▼

1 Doy-Doy F8
2 Fes Café F6
3 Giritli Restoran H8
4 Hamdi Restaurant E4
5 Khorasani G6
6 Mozaik G7
7 Seasons Restaurant H7
8 Sultanahnamet
  Fish House G6
9 Tarihi Çeşme
  Restaurant F8
10 Tarhi Subaşı
   Lokantası E6
11 Tarihi Sultanahmet
   Köftecisi G7

Hotels ▼

1 Armada Istanbul
  Old City Hotel H8
2 Celal Sultan Hotel G6
3 Darussaade Hotel
  Istanbul G8
4 Dersaadet Hotel
  Istanbul G8
5 Esans Hotel H7
6 Four Seasons Hotel
  Istanbul
  at Sultanahmet G7
7 Hotel Amira Istanbul F8
8 Hotel Empress Zoë H7
9 Hotel Ibrahim Pasha F7
10 Hotel Niles Istanbul D6
11 Hotel Peninsula H7
12 Hotel Tashkonak
   Istanbul G8
13 Kybele Hotel G6
14 Muyan Suites F7
15 Sarı Konak Hotel G8
16 Şebnem Hotel H7
17 Sirkeci Mansion G5
18 Sultanahmet Palace ... G8

or six-winged angels, in the pendentive of the dome, which had been plastered over 160 years earlier.

The upstairs galleries are where the most intricate of the mosaics are to be found. At the far end of the south gallery are several imperial portraits, including, on the left, the Empress Zoe, whose husband's face and name were clearly changed as she went through three of them. On the right is Emperor John Comnenus II with his Hungarian wife Irene and their son, Alexius, on the perpendicular wall. Also in the upper level is the great 13th-century Deesis mosaic of Christ flanked by the Virgin and John the Baptist, breathing the life of the early Renaissance that Byzantine artists would carry west to Italy after the fall of the city to the Turks—note how the shadows match the true light source to the left. The central gallery was used by female worshippers. The north gallery is famous for its graffiti, ranging from Nordic runes to a complete Byzantine galley under sail. On your way out of the church, through the "vestibule of the warriors," a mirror reminds you to look back at the mosaic of Justinian and Constantine presenting Hagia Sophia and Constantinople, respectively, to the Virgin Mary.

The tombs of various sultans and princes can be visited for free through a separate entrance around the back of Aya Sofya (daily 9–6). ✉ *Aya Sofya Sq., Sultanahmet* ☎ *212/522–1750* ⊕ *www.ayasofyamuzesi.gov.tr/en* 🎫 *60 TL.*

★ **Blue Mosque** (*Sultan Ahmet Camii*)
RELIGIOUS SITE | Only after you enter the Blue Mosque do you understand the name. The inside is covered with 20,000 shimmering blue-green İznik tiles interspersed with 260 stained-glass windows; calligraphy and intricate floral patterns are painted on the ceiling. After the dark corners and stern faces of the Byzantine mosaics in Aya Sofya, this mosque feels gloriously airy and full of light. Indeed, this favorable comparison was the

intention of architect Mehmet Ağa (a former student of the famous Ottoman architect Sinan), whose goal was to surpass Justinian's crowning achievement (Aya Sofya). At the behest of Sultan Ahmet I (ruled 1603–17), he created this masterpiece of Ottoman craftsmanship, starting in 1609 and completing it in just eight years, and many believe he indeed succeeded in outdoing the splendor of Aya Sofya.

Mehmet Ağa actually went a little too far though, when he surrounded the massive structure with six minarets: this number linked the Blue Mosque with the Masjid al-Haram in Mecca—and this could not be allowed. So Sultan Ahmet I was forced to send Mehmet Ağa down to the Holy City to build a seventh minaret for al-Haram and reestablish the eminence of that mosque. Sultan Ahmet and some of his family are interred in the *türbe* (mausoleum) at a corner of the complex, although as of this writing, the tombs are closed for renovations and are scheduled to reopen sometime in 2016.

From outside of the Blue Mosque you can see the genius of Mehmet Ağa, who didn't attempt to surpass the massive dome of Aya Sofya across the way, but instead created a secession of domes of varying sizes to cover the huge interior space, creating an effect that is both whimsical and uplifting. ✉ *Sultanahmet Sq., Sultanahmet* ⊕ *www.sultanahmetcamii.org* 🎫 *Free.*

Great Palace Mosaic Museum (*Büyük Saray Mozaikleri Müzesi*)
MUSEUM | A tantalizing glimpse into Istanbul's pre-Ottoman past, the small but well-done Mosaic Museum can be reached via an entrance halfway through the Arasta Bazaar and houses a fascinating display of early Byzantine mosaics—some presented in situ—from the Great Palace of Byzantium, the imperial residence of the early Byzantine emperors when they ruled lands stretching from Iran to Italy and from

Hammams

A favorite pastime in Istanbul is to spend time in one of the city's hammams, or Turkish baths, some of which are in exquisite buildings more than 500 years old. Hammams were born out of necessity—this was how people kept clean before there was home plumbing—but they also became an important part of Ottoman social life, particularly for women. Men had the coffeehouse and women the hammam as a place to gossip and relax. Now that people bathe at home, hammams have become much less central in Turkish life. There are still bathhouses dotted throughout Istanbul, but many wouldn't survive without steady tourist traffic.

Most hammams have separate facilities for men and women. Each has a *camekan*, a large, domed room with small cubicles where you can undress, wrap yourself in a thin cloth called a *peştemal*, and put on slippers or wooden sandals—all provided. Then you'll continue through a pair of increasingly hotter rooms. The first, known as the *soğukluk*, has showers and toilets and is used for cooling down at the end of your session. The centerpiece of the bath is the *hararet*, also known as the *sıcaklık*, a steamy, softly lit room with marble washbasins along the sides, where you can douse yourself by scooping water up from one of the basins with a copper bowl. In the middle of the room is the *göbektaşı*, a marble platform heated by furnaces below and usually covered with reclining bodies. This is where, if you decide to take your chances, a traditional Turkish massage will be "administered."

The masseur or masseuse (who traditionally has always been of the same gender as the person receiving the massage, although in some tourist-oriented hammams this is not the case) will first scrub you down with a rough, loofa-like sponge known as a *kese*. Be prepared to lose several layers of dead skin. Once you're scrubbed, you will be soaped up into a lather, rinsed off, and then given what will probably be the most vigorous massage you'll ever receive. Speak up if you want a lighter hand.

After you've been worked over, you can relax (and recover) on the göbektaşı or head back to your changing cubicle, where you'll be wrapped in fresh towels and perhaps massaged a bit more, this time with soothing oils. Most cubicles have small beds where you can lie down and sip tea or juice brought by an attendant. Before you leave, it's good etiquette to tip your masseur or masseuse.

the Caucasus to North Africa. Only scant ruins remained by 1935, when archaeologists began uncovering what is thought to have been the floor of a palace courtyard, covered with some of the most elaborate and delightful mosaics to survive from the era, most dating to the 6th century. They include images of animals, flowers, hunting scenes, and mythological characters—idylls far removed from the pomp and elaborate ritual of the imperial court. As you walk the streets of Sultanahmet you'll see many fragments of masonry and brickwork that were once part of the palace, and several cisterns have been found under hotels and carpet shops, some of which are open to visitors.⊠ *Torun Sok., Sultanahmet* ✛ *Alongside the Arasta Bazaar* ☎ *212/518–1205* 🎫 *20 TL.*

Gülhane Parkı

GARDEN | FAMILY | Central Istanbul has precious few public green spaces, which makes this park—once the private gardens of the adjacent Topkapı Palace—particularly inviting. Shaded by tall plane trees, the paved walkways, grassy areas, gazebos, and flower beds make this a relaxing escape from the nearby bustle of Sultanahmet. Walk all the way to the end of the park for excellent views of the Bosphorus and Sea of Marmara. The Istanbul Museum of the History of Science and Technology in Islam is inside the park, as are a municipal-run café and a couple of places serving tea and snacks. ⊠ Alemdar Cad., Sultanahmet.

Hippodrome (At Meydanı)

ARCHAEOLOGICAL SITE | It takes a bit of imagination to appreciate the Hippodrome—once a Byzantine stadium for chariot racing with seating for 100,000—since there isn't much here anymore. Notably absent are the rows of seats that once surrounded the track and the life-size bronze sculpture of four horses that once adorned the stadium—the Venetians looted the statue during the Fourth Crusade. You can, however, see several other monuments that once decorated the central podium. The **Dikilitaş** (Egyptian Obelisk) probably marked the finish line. The very partial **Yılanlı Sütun** (Serpentine Column) was taken from the Temple of Apollo at Delphi in Greece, where it was dedicated after the Greek victory over the invading Persians in the 5th century BC. The **Örme Sütun** (Column of Constantine Porphyrogenitus) was once entirely covered with gilt bronze, which was stripped off by vandals during the Fourth Crusade. Closer to the tram stop is a much more recent addition: a neo-Byzantine fountain that was a gift from the German government in 1901, commemorating Kaiser Wilhelm II's visit to Istanbul three years earlier. ⊠ Atmeydanı, Sultanahmet 🖭 Free.

★ Istanbul Archaeology Museums (İstanbul Arkeoloji Müzeleri)

MUSEUM | FAMILY | Step into this vast repository of spectacular finds, housed in a three-building complex in a forecourt of Topkapı Palace, to get a head-spinning look at the civilizations that have thrived for thousands of years in and around Turkey. The main museum was established in 1891, when forward-thinking archaeologist and painter Osman Hamdi Bey campaigned to keep native antiquities and some items from the former countries of the Ottoman Empire in Turkish hands. The most stunning pieces are sarcophagi that include the so-called Alexander Sarcophagus, found in Lebanon, carved with scenes from Alexander the Great's battles, and once believed, wrongly, to be his final resting place. A fascinating exhibit on Istanbul through the ages has artifacts and fragments brought from historical sites around the city that shed light on its complex past, from prehistory through the Byzantine period.

Exhibits on Anatolia include a display of some of the artifacts found in excavations at Troy, including a smattering of gold jewelry. Though the museum's holdings are impressive, the facility is showing its age; parts of the main building are currently undergoing much-needed renovation, leaving some halls closed off to visitors.

Don't miss a visit to the **Çinili Köşk** (Tiled Pavilion), one of the most visually pleasing sights in all of Istanbul—a bright profusion of colored tiles covers this onetime hunting lodge of Mehmet the Conqueror, built in 1472. Inside are ceramics from the early Seljuk and Ottoman empires, as well as brilliant tiles from İznik, the city that produced perhaps the finest ceramics in the world during the 16th and 17th centuries.

In summer, you can mull over these glimpses into the distant past as you sip coffee or tea at the café in the garden, surrounded by fragments of ancient sculptures.

Safety Concerns

Istanbul is, for a city of at least 14 million, very safe, especially in the areas frequented by tourists. The political situation in Turkey has, however, become somewhat more volatile in recent years, with street protests occurring more frequently and being more roughly dispersed by police. Most protests that tourists might encounter occur around İstiklal Caddesi in Beyoğlu and, to a lesser degree, in the *çarşı* (market) areas of Beşiktaş and Kadıköy; avoid such demonstrations when possible.

Remaining alert while amid large crowds or traveling on public transportation is always a good idea. Like any other big city that attracts hordes of travelers, Istanbul also has its share of unscrupulous touts and shills, as well as taxi drivers infamous for trying to inflate the fare by any means necessary. The busy and crowded areas around Aya Sofya and Taksim Square seem to especially attract potential scammers. Shoeshine boys sometimes drop their brushes when walking past helpful tourists, then try to massively overcharge for a quick clean. In Sultanahmet, most of the touts who approach you want no more than to steer you toward a harmless carpet shop where they will earn a commission, but the odd few might be less well intentioned. The nightclub ruse—in which a small group of friends offer to show a single tourist (usually male) a night on the town, then disappear, sticking their guest with a huge bill—tends to happen most often in the nightlife area of Beyoğlu. It can be hard to see through this scam because Turks are by nature exceedingly friendly and will go out of their way to help you—once you approach them. The key is to watch out for those who approach you first and seem a little too eager to help, and whose English is just a little too polished. Use your judgment, but don't be embarrassed to say no politely and move on if you feel accosted. You will certainly make many new friends during a visit to Turkey—just make sure you do it on your terms.

The **Eski Şark Eserleri Müzesi** (Museum of the Ancient Orient) transports visitors to even earlier times: The vast majority of the panels, mosaics, obelisks, and other artifacts here, from Anatolia, Mesopotamia, and elsewhere in the Arab world, date from the pre-Christian centuries. One of the most significant pieces in the collection is a 13th-century BC tablet on which is recorded the Treaty of Kadesh, perhaps the world's earliest known peace treaty, an accord between the Hittite king Hattusili III and the Egyptian pharaoh Ramses II. Also noteworthy are reliefs from the ancient city of Babylon, dating to the era of the famous king Nebuchadnezzar II. ⊠ *Alemdar Cad., Osman Hamdi Bey Yokuşu, Sultanahmet* ✚ *Inside Gülhane Park, next to Topkapı Palace* ☎ *212/520-7740* ⊕ *www.istanbularkeoloji.gov.tr* ☉ *30 TL* ☉ *Closed Mon.*

Istanbul Museum of the History of Science and Technology in Islam (*İstanbul İslam Bilim ve Teknoloji Tarihi Müzesi*)

MUSEUM | On the western side of Gülhane Parkı, this museum, located in the former stables of Topkapı Palace, chronicles the significant role played by medieval Muslim scientists, inventors, and physicians in advancing scientific knowledge and technology while Europe was still in the Dark Ages. Exhibits cover subjects such as astronomy, navigation, mathematics, physics, warfare, and medical expertise. Unfortunately, almost none of the items on display are actual historical artifacts, but the models and reproductions built especially for the museum are interesting nevertheless.☒ *Gülhane Parkı, Sultanahmet* ☎ *212/528–8065* ⊕ *www. ibttm.org* ⊉ *10 TL.*

Küçük Aya Sofya (*Little Aya Sofya*)
RELIGIOUS SITE | Built by Justinian as the Church of Sergius and Bacchus (patron saints of the Roman army), this church is commonly known as the "Little Aya Sofya" due to its resemblance to the great church up the hill. In fact, it was built just before Aya Sofya, in the 530s, and the architects explored here many of the same ideas of the larger church but on a smaller scale. The church was converted to a mosque around the year 1500 by Hüseyin Ağa, Beyazıt II's chief eunuch. Though the mosaics are long gone, a Greek inscription dedicated to Justinian, his wife Theodora, and the saints can still be seen running along the cornice of the colonnade. The marble and verd antique columns with their delicate, ornate capitals are also quite impressive, and you can climb the stairway to the upper-level gallery for a closer look. A shaded park alongside holds some small cafés and shops.☒ *Küçük Aya Sofya Cad., Sultanahmet.*

★ **Museum of Turkish and Islamic Arts** (*Türk ve İslam Eserleri Müzesi*)
MUSEUM | Süleyman the Magnificent commissioned Sinan to build this grandiose stone palace overlooking the Hippodrome in about 1520 for his brother-in-law, the grand vizier Ibrahim Pasha, and today it is one of the most important surviving examples of secular Ottoman architecture from its time. It now houses the Museum of Turkish and Islamic Arts, which has an exceptional collection of Islamic art and artifacts dating from the 7th through 20th century, including lavishly illustrated Qurans and other calligraphic manuscripts; intricate metalwork; wood and stone carvings;

an astrolabe from the 1200s; colorful ceramics; religious relics and artifacts, including an elaborate hajj certificate and device for determining the direction of Mecca; and one of the world's most highly regarded troves of antique carpets.☒ *Atmeydanı 46, Sultanahmet* ☎ *212/518–1805* ⊉ *35 TL.*

Sokollu Mehmet Paşa Camii (*Mosque of Sokollu Mehmet Pasha*)
RELIGIOUS SITE | Built in 1571 for Sokollu Mehmet Pasha, a grand vizier to three successive sultans, this small mosque is not as grand as the Süleymaniye Camii, but many consider it to be among the most beautiful of the mosques built by master Ottoman architect Sinan. Here, Sinan chose not to dazzle with size but to create a graceful, harmonious whole, from the courtyard and porticoes outside to the interior, where floral-motif stained-glass windows and gorgeous, well-preserved İznik tiles with both floral patterns and calligraphic inscriptions are set off by white stone walls. Inside, the *minbar* (pulpit), delicately carved in white marble and crowned with a tiled conical cap, is particularly noteworthy. ☒ *Şehit Mehmet Paşa Yokuşu, Kadırga, Sultanahmet.*

★ **Topkapı Palace** (*Topkapı Sarayı*)
CASTLE/PALACE | This vast palace on Sarayburnu ("Seraglio Point") was the residence of sultans and their harems, in addition to being the seat of Ottoman rule from the 1460s until the mid-19th century, when Sultan Abdülmecid I moved his court to Dolmabahçe Palace. Sultan Mehmet II built the original Topkapı Palace between 1459 and 1465, shortly after his conquest of Constantinople. Over the centuries it grew to include four courtyards and quarters for some 5,000 full-time residents. The main entrance, or Imperial Gate, leads to the **Court of the Janissaries,** also known as the First Courtyard. The modestly beautiful **Aya Irini** (Church of St. Irene) is believed to stand on the site of the first

church of Byzantium (separate admission). You will begin to experience the grandeur of the palace when you pass through the **Bab-üs Selam** (Gate of Salutation). Enter the **Harem** (separate admission) on the other side of the Divan from the Outer Treasury. The **Treasury** contains the popular jewels, including the 86-carat Spoonmaker's Diamond, the emerald-studded Topkapı Dagger, and two uncut emeralds, each weighing about 8 pounds(!). Save time by using a Museum Pass or booking a timed ticket online in advance. ✉ *Gülhane Parkı, Babıhümayun Cad., Sultanahmet* ✢ *Near Sultanahmet Sq.* ☎ *212/512–0480* 🌐 *www.topkapisarayi.gov.tr* 🎫 *Palace 60 TL, Harem 35 TL, Aya Irini 30 TL.*

★ **Yerebatan Sarnıcı** (*Basilica Cistern*)

ARCHAEOLOGICAL SITE | **FAMILY** | The major problem with the site of Byzantium was the lack of fresh water, and so for the city to grow, a great system of aqueducts and cisterns was built, the most famous of which is the Basilica Cistern, whose present form dates to the reign of Justinian in the 6th century. A journey through this ancient underground waterway takes you along dimly lit walkways that weave around 336 marble columns rising 26 feet to support Byzantine arches and domes, from which water drips unceasingly. The two most famous columns feature upturned Medusa heads. The cistern was always kept full as a precaution against long sieges, and fish, presumably descendants of those that arrived in Byzantine times, still flit through the dark waters. A hauntingly beautiful oasis of cool, shadowed, cathedral-like stillness (with Turkish instrumental music playing softly in the background), the cistern is a particularly relaxing place to get away from the hubbub of the Old City. Come early to avoid the long lines and have a more peaceful visit. ✉ *Yerebatan Cad. at Divan Yolu, Sultanahmet* ☎ *212/512–1570* 🌐 *www.yerebatan.com* 🎫 *20 TL.*

🍴 Restaurants

Sultanahmet might have most of the city's major sights and many hotels, but sadly, these places cater mostly to tourists and are the ones most likely to let their standards slip. Save for a few standouts, the area is sorely lacking in good dining options, though you can find some good food if you follow the locals to the no-frills eateries lining Gedik Paşa Caddesi (near the Beyazıt tram stop, across Yeniçeriler Caddesi from the entrance to the Grand Bazaar) or to Hoca Paşa Sokak near the Sirkeci train station.

Doy-Doy

$ | **TURKISH** | Doy-doy serves a fairly standard array of kebabs and *pide*—a type of Turkish pizza baked in a wood-burning oven—with different toppings, but at lunchtime, local workers come for the cheap daily specials, such as meat-and-vegetable stew or baked beans (displayed on the steam table to the left of the entrance). The two-level rooftop terrace, open in summer, has fine views of the area—but don't expect to savor them with a drink in hand, as no alcohol is served. **Known for:** cozy atmosphere; traditional Turkish food; Blue Mosque and Sea of Marmara views. [$] *Average main: 30 TL* ✉ *Şifa Hamamı Sok. 13, Sultanahmet* ☎ *212/517–1588.*

★ **Giritli Restoran**

$$$$ | **SEAFOOD** | Popular with locals and visitors alike, Giritli offers a prix-fixe multicourse dinner menu of well-prepared Cretan specialties that includes unlimited local alcoholic drinks (wine or rakı). At least 15 different cold meze—such as sea bass ceviche, herb-covered cubes of feta cheese with walnuts and olives, and various uncommon wild greens—are followed by hot starters like fried calamari in olive oil; the main course is a choice among several grilled fish, followed by dessert. **Known for:** oasis-like garden setting; innovative meze on prix-fixe menu;

Continued on page 102

TOPKAPI
SHOWPLACE OF THE SULTANS

Like Russia's Kremlin, France's Versailles, and China's Forbidden City, Istanbul's Topkapı Sarayı is not simply a spectacular palace but an entire universe unto itself. Treasure house of Islamic art, power hub of the Ottoman Empire, home to more than twenty sultans, and site of the sultry Seraglio, the legendary Topkapı remains a world of wonders.

Astride the promontory of Sarayburnu ("Seraglio Point")—"the very tip of Europe"—Topkapı Sarayı has lorded over Istanbul for more than 5 centuries. As much a self-contained town-within-a-town as a gigantic palace, this sprawling complex perches over the Bosphorus and was the residence and center of bloodshed and drama for the Ottoman rulers from the 1460s to the 1850s. At one time home to some 5,000 residents—including a veritable army of slaves and concubines—Topkapı was also the treasure house to which marauding sultans brought back marvels from centuries of conquest, ranging from the world's seventh-largest diamond to the greatly revered Mantle of the Prophet Muhammad.

Today's visitors are captivated by the beauty of Topkapı's setting but are even more bewitched by visions of the days of ruby wine and roses, when long-ago sultans walked hand-in-hand with courtesans amid gardens lit by lanterns fastened to the backs of wandering giant tortoises. As privileged as it was, however, Topkapı was rarely peaceful. Historians now recount horrifying tales of strangled princes, enslaved harem women, and power-mad eunuchs. Just in front of the main Gate of Salutation (from which decapitated heads were displayed centuries ago) stands the Fountain of the Executioner—a finely carved bit of onyx stonework where mighty vassals once washed the blood of victims from their hands in rose-petaled water. It is history as much as beauty that rivets the attention of thousands of sightseers who stream through Topkapı.

When you've had your fill of the palace's bloody yet beautiful past, venture to one of its marble-paved terraces overlooking the Bosphorus. Islands, mosques, domes, crescents shining in the sun, boats sailing near the strand: here shimmer the waters of the strait, a wonderland as seen by a thousand romantic 19th-century travelers—the Constantinople, at last, of our dreams.

Left: Imperial Hall in Harem

FOUR CENTURIES OF BLOOD & POWER

Stretching through times of tragedy and triumph, the story of Topkapı is a saga worthy of Scheherazade. Built between 1459 and 1465 by Sultan Mehmet II, the palace was envisioned as a vast array of satellite pavilions, many topped with cupolas and domes (Turkish architectural conservatism liked to perpetuate the tents of the nomadic past in stone). Over the centuries, sultan after sultan added ever more elaborate architectural frills, until the palace acquired a bewildering conglomeration of buildings extending over four successive courtyards, each more exclusionary than the last.

Sultan Mehmet II

MANSION OR MAUSOLEUM?

While Topkapı became the power center of the Ottoman Empire—it grew to contain the **state mint, the arsenal**, and the *divan* (chamber of the judicial council)—its most fearsome aspect was the **sultan's court**. Many of its inhabitants lived their entire adult lives behind the palace walls, and it was often the scene of intrigue and treachery as members of the sultan's entourage plotted and schemed, sometimes even deposing and assassinating the sultan himself.

A SURFEIT OF SULTANS

Set with stained-glass windows and mother-of-pearl decorations the "**Gilded Cage**" was where the crown prices lived in strict confinement—at least after the old custom of murdering all possible rivals was abandoned in the 17th century (the greatest number of victims—19 brothers—were strangled in 1595 by order of the mother of Mehmet III; seven of his father's pregnant concubines were drowned, to boot). House arrest in this golden suite kept the internal peace but deprived the heirs to the throne of interacting with the real world. After Süleyman II spent 39 years in the Gilded Cage he proved so fearful that, in 1687, he nearly refused the sultanate. Indeed, many sultans who ascended the throne were, in effect, ruled by their mothers, the all-powerful *Valide Sultans* (Queen Mothers). The most notorious was Kösem, whose rule over two sultan sons ended in 1651 when she was strangled upon orders of a vengeful daughter-in-law. As much to escape this blood-stained past as to please visiting European royalty, Topkapı was finally abandoned in 1856 when Abdülmecid I moved his court to Dolmabahçe Palace.

Procession of Constantinople in the Hippodrome (detail)

- 🌐 Babihümayun Caddesi, Gülhane Park, near Sultanahmet Sq.
- ☎ 212/512-0480
- 🌐 www.topkapisarayi.gov.tr
- 🎫 Palace 60 TL; Harem: 35 TL; Aya Irini 30 TL.
- 🕐 Palace: Wed.–Mon. 9–7 from April to Oct., 9–5 from Nov. to March (last entry one hour before closing time). Harem: Wed.–Mon. 9–6 from April to Oct., 9–4 from Nov. to March

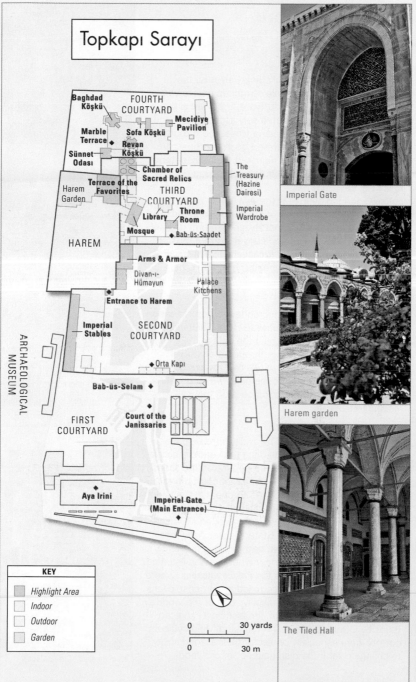

Topkapı Sarayı

Baghdad Köşkü

FOURTH COURTYARD

Mecidiye Pavilion

Marble Terrace

Sofa Köşkü

Revan Köşkü

Sünnet Odası

Chamber of Sacred Relics

The Treasury (Hazine Dairesi)

Harem Garden

Terrace of the Favorites

THIRD COURTYARD

Imperial Wardrobe

Throne Room

Library

Mosque

Bab-üs-Saadet

HAREM

Arms & Armor

Divan-ı-Hümayun

Palace Kitchens

Entrance to Harem

Imperial Stables

SECOND COURTYARD

Orta Kapı

ARCHAEOLOGICAL MUSEUM

Bab-üs-Selam

FIRST COURTYARD

Court of the Janissaries

Aya Irini

Imperial Gate (Main Entrance)

KEY

Highlight Area

Indoor

Outdoor

Garden

0 — 30 yards

0 — 30 m

Imperial Gate

Harem garden

The Tiled Hall

OF RICHES UNTOLD: TOPKAPI HIGHLIGHTS

THE FIRST COURTYARD

Upon arriving from Istanbul's noisy streets, the magic city of an Oriental tale stretches before you. Also known as the First Courtyard, the **Court of the Janissaries** has always been freely accessible to the public. In the shade of its plane trees, the turbulent Janissaries—the sultan's armed guard—prepared their meals and famously indicated their discontent by overturning their soup kettles: a dreaded protest followed, several times, by the murder of the reigning sultan. Looming over all is the **Aya Irini** church, dating from the time of Justinian; it's believed to stand on the site of the first church of Byzantium but, uniquely for Istanbul, has never been converted to a mosque. To the left is the imposing **Archaeological Museum,** housing treasures from Ephesus, Troy, and other ancient sites.

Archaeological Museum

GATE OF SALUTATION

You begin to experience the grandeur of Topkapı when you pass through **Bab-üs-Selam** (Gate of Salutation). Süleyman the Magnificent built the gate in 1524; only a sultan was allowed to pass through it on horseback. Prisoners were kept in the gate's two towers before they were executed next to the nearby Executioner's Fountain. The palace's ticket office is on the walkway leading to this gate.

Gate of Salutation

THE SECOND COURTYARD

A vast rose garden shaded by cypress trees, the second, or **Divan**, courtyard was once the veritable administrative hub of the Ottoman empire, often the scene of great pageantry when thousands of court officials would gather before the sultan's throne. On the far left is the entrance to the Harem. Also on the left is the **Divan-ı-Hümayun**, the strikingly ornate open-air Assembly Room of the Council of State. Occasionally the sultan would sit behind a latticed window, hidden by a curtain, so no one would know when he was listening. On the right of the yard are the **Palace Kitchens**, where more than 1,000 cooks once toiled at immense ovens. The cavernous space now displays one of the world's best collections of porcelain, amassed over the centuries by Ottoman rulers. The Yuan and Ming celadon pottery were especially prized for their alleged ability to change color if the dish held poisonous foods.

Gate to the Divan

Kitchen area of the palace

THE THIRD COURTYARD

As you walk through the **Bab-üs-Saadet**, or **Gate of Felicity**, consider yourself privileged, because only the sultan and grand vizier were allowed to pass through this gate. It leads to the palace's inner sanctum, the Third Courtyard, site of some of the most ornate of the palace pavilions. Most visitors here only got as far as the **Arz Odası**, the Audience Hall, or Throne Room, where foreign ambassadors once groveled before the sultan. Here, too, is the fabled **Treasury (Hazine Dairesi)**.

'Iznik tiles

CHAMBER OF SACRED RELICS

On the courtyard's left side is the Hasoda Koğuşu, housing the Chamber of Sacred Relics (1578), which comprises five domed rooms containing some of the holiest relics of Islam. Pride of place goes to the Mantle of the Prophet Muhammad, kept in a gold casket (exhibited behind shatter proof glass). Nearby are the Prophet's Standard, or flag; hairs from his beard; his sword; a cast of his footprint; and teeth. Other relics, including the "staff of Moses" and the "cooking pot of Abraham," are also on view.

Dome atop Gate of Felicity

THE IMPERIAL WARDROBE

An impressive collection of imperial robes, spanning many generations of the Ottoman dynasty, is displayed in a hall on the right side of the Third Courtyard. The sultans' oversized caftans and other garments, and the tiny costumes worn by the crown princes, are made of splendid silks and brocades and are stiff with gold and silver thread, tooled leather, and even jewels.

THE FOURTH COURTYARD

More of an open terrace, this courtyard was the private realm of the sultan, and small, elegant pavilions are scattered amid tulip gardens overlooking the Bosphorus and Golden Horn. The loveliest of the pavilions, the **Baghdad Kiosk** (covered with 'Iznik tiles), was built by Murat IV in 1638 after his conquest of Baghdad. Off the wishing-well terrace is the **Circumcision Room (Sünnet Odası)**, also famed for its lavish tiling.

Interior Baghdad Kiosk

On the right side of the courtyard are steps leading to the 19th-century rococo-style Mecidiye Pavilion, now **Konyalı Restaurant** (open Wed.—Mon., 10:30 to 7), which serves excellent Turkish food and has a magnificent vista of the Sea of Marmara. On a terrace below is an outdoor café with an even better view. Go early or reserve a table to beat the tour-group crush.

Circumcision Room colonnade

PLEASURE DOMES: THE HAREM

Evoking the exoticism and mystery of the Ottoman Empire, the Harem is a maze of 400 terraces, wings, and apartments. These were the quarters of the sultan's courtesans, mostly Circassian women from the Caucasus (Muslim women were forbidden to be concubines).

Seeing the forty rooms that have been opened to the public reminds us that the Harem (the term means "forbidden" in Arabic) was as much about confinement as it was about luxury. Of the 1,000 women housed in the harem, many finished their days here as servants to other concubines.

Built around grand reception salons—including the Imperial Hall, the Crown Prince's Pavilions, and the Dining Room of Ahmet III—the Harem was studded with fountains, whose splashes made it hard to eavesdrop on royal conversations.

Imperial Hall

WOMEN'S QUARTERS

Adjacent to the Courtyard of the Black Eunuchs (most of whom hailed from Africa's Sudan), the first Harem compound housed about 200 lesser concubines in tiny cubicles, like those in a monastery. As you move deeper into the Harem, the rooms become larger and more opulent; the four chief wives lived in grand suites around a shared courtyard.

Ornate ceiling in Harem

Most concubines were trained in music and poetry, but only those who achieved the highest status were given access to the sultan.

APARTMENTS OF THE SULTANS

The sultan's own apartments are, not surprisingly, a riot of brocades, murals, colored marble, wildly ornate furniture, gold leaf, fine carvings, and, of course, the most perfect İznik tiles. Nearby is the Gilded Cage, where the crown princes were kept under lock and key until they were needed.

Dining Room of Ahmet III

APARTMENTS OF THE VALIDE SULTAN

The true ruler of the Harem was the *Valide Sultan*, the sultan's mother, and her lavish apartments lay at the heart of the Harem complex. For the young women of the Harem, the road to the sultan, quite literally (using a hallway known as the "Golden Way") ran through his mother.

DO YOU LOVE EMERALDS?
DON'T MISS TOPKAPI'S TREASURY

If you love jewels, you're in luck—at the **Topkapı Treasury (Hazine Dairesi)** you can admire three of the world's most wondrous emeralds, which are embedded in the hilt of the fabulous Topkapı Dagger. Crafted in 1747, it was meant as a gift for the Shah of Persia; he could well have used it but it arrived too late—he was assassinated as the dagger was en route to him. Here also are two of the world's largest extant emeralds: uncut, they each weigh about eight pounds. Now displayed behind glass, they were originally hung from the ceiling as spectacular "lamps." Amazingly, even these mammoth gems were outshone by the 86-carat Spoonmaker's Diamond which, according to legend, was found by an Istanbul pauper glad to trade it for three wooden spoons. These are but six of the many jewels found here.

A true cave of Aladdin spilling over four rooms, the treasury is filled with a hoard of opulent objects and possessions, either lavish gifts bestowed upon generations of sultans, or spoils garnered from centuries of war. The largest objects are four imperial thrones, including the gold-plated Bayram throne given to Sultan Murat III by the Khedive of Egypt in 1574. Also on display is the throne sent to Istanbul by the same unfortunate shah for whom the Topkapı Dagger was intended. All is enhanced by the beautiful display of turban crests and jewel-studded armor, with every possible weapon encrusted with diamonds and pearls—all giving testimony to the fact that, before the 18th century, it was the man, not the woman, who glittered like a peacock.

There are trinkets, chalices, reliquaries, and jewels, jewels, jewels. Ladies, be sure to hide your engagement rings— they will be overwhelmed in comparison!

Sultan headgear

Spoonmaker's Diamond

ROCK STARS

The most glamorous jewel heist film ever, *Topkapi* (1964) is director Jules Dassin's dazzling homage to Istanbul, diamonds, and his famous *Never on Sunday* blonde (and wife), Melina Mercouri. Playing jet-set mastermind Elizabeth Lipp, she seduces a troupe of thieves into attempting to steal the Topkapı Dagger. Rooftop high jinks, a script scintillating with wit, the Oscar-winning performance by Peter Ustinov, and an eye-popping credit sequence make for a film almost as intoxicating as a visit to the Treasury itself.

Topkapı dagger

in a quiet neighborhood. $ *Average main: 160 TL* ✉ *Keresteci Hakkı Sok., Cankurtaran/Ahırkapı, Sultanahmet* ☎ *212/458–2270* ⊕ *www.giritlirestoran.com.*

Khorasani

$$$ | **TURKISH** | One of Sultanahmet's most outstanding restaurants emphasizes the Arab- and Kurdish-influenced cuisine of southeastern Turkey, including meze like hummus, *muhammara* (hot pepper and walnut spread), and thyme salad, as well as tasty kebabs like the lamb shish. Interesting non-kebab main dishes on offer are chicken stew, which has chunks of meat in a thick sauce of onions, mushrooms, and sweet pumpkin. **Known for:** sidewalk seating; serves wine and beer; kebabs cooked on a charcoal grill. $ *Average main: 55 TL* ✉ *Ticarethane Sok. 9, Sultanahmet* ☎ *212/512–1227.*

Mozaik

$$$ | **INTERNATIONAL** | This restored late-19th-century house with small, sun-dappled dining rooms, cozy furniture, and creaky wooden floors is a delightful refuge in the midst of the busy Sultanahmet neighborhood. But it's not just the setting that's noteworthy; the vast menu at this friendly venue ranges from a variety of kebabs and other Turkish specialties to salads, pastas, steaks, schnitzel, and other international fare. **Known for:** outdoor seating in the summer; attentive service; cozy atmosphere. $ *Average main: 58 TL* ✉ *İncili Çavuş Sok. 1, Sultanahmet* ☎ *212/512–4177.*

Seasons Restaurant

$$$$ | **TURKISH** | A delightful gazebo-like glass pavilion in the middle of the manicured garden courtyard of the Four Seasons is the ritziest restaurant in Sultanahmet (and also the most expensive). The menu highlights traditional Anatolian dishes—made with ingredients sourced locally from around the country—ranging from cold and hot meze to grilled meats and fish, including a boneless lamb shank cooked for eight hours. **Known for:** extensive rakı and wine menu; international

Museum Timing 👁

Check opening days when you plan your outings. Most museums in Istanbul are closed Monday, with a few exceptions: Topkapı Palace is closed Tuesday, and the military museum is closed both Monday and Tuesday.

and Anatolian cuisine; Sunday brunch buffet. $ *Average main: 110 TL* ✉ *Four Seasons Istanbul at Sultanahmet, Tevkifhane Sok. 1, Sultanahmet* ☎ *212/402–3150* ⊕ *www.fourseasons.com.*

Sultanahmet Fish House

$$ | **SEAFOOD** | There are no obsequious waiters at Sultanahmet Fish House and no fancy dress code—just a friendly, cozy atmosphere with well-prepared seafood, including sardines, octopus, and mackerel in olive oil, a range of fish, and a few kebabs. The fish preparations go beyond the standard grilling and frying: sea bass with saffron, cooked in a terra-cotta casserole, is a particular standout. **Known for:** sidewalk seating; cozy atmosphere with colorful textiles and antique lamps; innovative seafood menu. $ *Average main: 50 TL* ✉ *Prof. İsmail Gürkan Cad. 14, Sultanahmet* ☎ *212/527–4441* ⊕ *www.sultanahmetfishhouse.com.*

Tarihi Çeşme Restaurant

$ | **TURKISH** | Just a short walk from the area's major tourist attractions, Tarihi Çeşme is a rare find in Sultanahmet, offering good food at very reasonable prices, genuinely friendly service, and a congenial atmosphere that appeals to both visitors and local residents. The menu includes a fairly typical range of meze and kebabs, as well as *pide*, or flatbread baked with different toppings—the Turkish version of pizza. **Known for:** vine-shaded front patio; quiet location; traditional cuisine. $ *Average main: 30 TL* ✉ *Kadırga Liman Cad., Küçük Ayasofya Camii Sok. 1, Sultanahmet* ☎ *212/516–3580* 🌐 *www.tarihicesmerestaurant.com.*

Tarihi Sultanahmet Köftecisi

$ | **TURKISH** | Like pizza for New Yorkers, humble *köfte* (grilled meatballs) inspire countless arguments among Istanbullus about who makes the best. Tarihi Sultanahmet Köftecisi wins with a simple menu—meatballs, lamb kebab, lentil soup, *piyaz* (boiled white beans in olive oil), rice, and salad—that has remained virtually unchanged since 1920. **Known for:** historic central location; affordable menu; traditional köfte. $ *Average main: 22 TL* ✉ *Divanyolu Cad. 12, Sultanahmet* ☎ *212/520–0566* 🌐 *www.sultanahmetkoftesi.com* 💳 *No credit cards.*

Hotels

Many visitors to Istanbul stay in the Sultanahmet area, where they are conveniently within walking distance to most of the city's major sights, including Aya Sofya, the Blue Mosque, Topkapı Palace, and the bazaars. Sultanahmet has a good selection of hotels, smaller family-run guesthouses, and some charmingly stylish inns, many of which are decorated in typical Turkish style, with traditional touches like kilim carpets or old-fashioned furnishings. The rooms here generally tend to be on the small side, and bathrooms often only have showers, but what's lacking in space tends to be more than made up for in character and atmosphere. The downside of staying in Sultanahmet is that at the height of the season, the area is overrun not only with tourists but touts who will approach you at every turn. On the upside, stiff competition in the area means that Sultanahmet usually has the best deals in town; some hotels even offer a 5% to 10% discount for payment in cash, or a complimentary airport transfer if you stay three or more nights.

Armada Istanbul Old City Hotel

$$ | **HOTEL** | These comfortable accommodations are a 10-minute walk from Istanbul's main tourist sites, and most rooms look out either to the sea or over the Old City—although one of the best views is at night from the hotel's rooftop Armada Terrace restaurant, where you can see Aya Sofya and the Blue Mosque. **Pros:** amazing views of the water; professional service; in quiet area. **Cons:** somewhat steep uphill walk from hotel to the sights of Sultanahmet; smallish rooms, and those on ground floor can be dark; no fitness facilities. $ *Rooms from: €80* ✉ *Ahırkapı Sok. 24, Sultanahmet* ☎ *212/455–4455* 🌐 *www.armadahotel.com.tr* 🛏 *108 rooms* 🍴 *Free Breakfast.*

Celal Sultan Hotel

$$ | **HOTEL** | Three conjoined, restored town houses make up this comfortable, well-maintained hotel that has new furnishings designed to look old-fashioned, and an inviting lobby with a cozy bar decorated with colorful Turkish rugs and kilims. **Pros:** hotel is on a quiet street; personable staff; rooftop terrace. **Cons:** standard rooms and bathrooms are small; some guests report poor sound insulation in rooms; rather high rates. $ *Rooms from: €85* ✉ *Salkımsöğüt Sok. 16, Yerebatan Cad., Sultanahmet* ☎ *212/520–9323* 🌐 *www.celalsultan.com* 🛏 *55 rooms* 🍴 *Free Breakfast.*

Darussaade Hotel Istanbul

$$ | **HOTEL** | Two adjoining 19th-century houses offer old-world charm and comfortable rooms close to Sultanahmet's main sights. **Pros:** comfortable, nicely furnished accommodations; very helpful staff; rooms receive lots of natural light. **Cons:** some small rooms; most rooms don't have views; old building. $ *Rooms from: €100* ✉ *Akbıyık Cad. 90, Sultanahmet* ☎ *212/518–3636* 🌐 *www.darussaade.com* 🛏 *23 rooms* 🍴 *Free Breakfast.*

★ Dersaadet Hotel Istanbul

$$ | **B&B/INN** | Dersaadet means "place of happiness" in Ottoman Turkish and this small, cozy hotel lives up to its name—rooms have an elegant, even plush, feel, with colorful rugs on the floor, antique furniture, and ceilings hand-painted with traditional motifs. **Pros:** extraordinary level of service; lovely terrace; good value. **Cons:** some rooms are on the small side; no view from rooms on lower floors; walls are thin. [$] *Rooms from: €76* ✉ *Küçükayasofya Cad. Kapıağası Sok. 5, Sultanahmet* ☎ *212/458–0760* 🌐 *www.dersaadethotel.com* 🛏 *17 rooms* 🍴 *Free Breakfast.*

★ Esans Hotel

$$ | **B&B/INN** | The emphasis at this delightful family-run bed-and-breakfast is on guest satisfaction, and the ten rooms in the restored wooden house are decorated with thoughtful attention to detail, like lovely Ottoman-Victorian-style wallpaper, upholstery, and linens, real wooden floors and ceilings, and old-fashioned furniture. **Pros:** good value; located on quiet street; staff go out of their way to assist. **Cons:** no elevator; lack of soundproofing can be an issue; some rooms are small. [$] *Rooms from: €75* ✉ *Yeni Saraçhane Sok. 4, Sultanahmet* ☎ *212/516–1902* 🌐 *www.esanshotel.com* 🛏 *10 rooms* 🍴 *Free Breakfast.*

★ Four Seasons Hotel Istanbul at Sultanahmet

$$$$ | **HOTEL** | What a rehabilitation success story: a former prison just steps from Topkapı Palace and Aya Sofya is now one of Istanbul's premier accommodations, where rooms and suites are luxuriously outfitted and overlook the Sea of Marmara, the Old City, or a manicured interior courtyard. **Pros:** historic building surrounded by major tourist attractions; luxurious accommodations; exceptional service. **Cons:** limited fitness facilities; no view from rooms on lower floors; expensive rates and food. [$] *Rooms from: €420* ✉ *Tevkifhane Sok. 1, Sultanahmet* ☎ *212/402–3000* 🌐 *www.fourseasons.com/istanbul* 🛏 *55 rooms* 🍴 *No meals.*

★ Hotel Amira Istanbul

$$ | **HOTEL** | An attractive atrium between two wings houses the lobby, and well-appointed rooms are furnished in an eclectic mix of Turkish and contemporary styles, from ornate Ottoman ceiling patterns and metal lampshades evoking the Istanbul skyline to modern rugs and plush upholstery. **Pros:** extraordinarily helpful staff; good value; guests feel pampered. **Cons:** some rooms not accessible by elevator; located on somewhat noisy corner; basement-level rooms can be dark. [$] *Rooms from: €120* ✉ *Mustafa Paşa Sok. 43, Sultanahmet* ☎ *212/516–1640* 🌐 *www.hotelamira.com* 🛏 *32 rooms* 🍴 *Free Breakfast.*

Hotel Empress Zoë

$$ | **HOTEL** | At what is now a Sultanahmet institution, rooms and suites are varied and charming—standard rooms, with colorfully canopied four-posters, nomad textiles, and dark woods, have an almost rustic feel, while suites are more fully furnished, and some have marble-lined bathrooms done up to look like mini hammams. **Pros:** quirky, bohemian atmosphere; location just steps from major sights; lovely garden oasis. **Cons:** no elevator; narrow spiral staircase and labyrinthine layout require a fair bit of climbing; some rooms and bathrooms small and basic. [$] *Rooms from: €80* ✉ *Akbıyık Cad. 10, Sultanahmet* ☎ *212/518–2504* 🌐 *www.emzoe.com* 🛏 *22 rooms* 🍴 *Free Breakfast.*

★ Hotel İbrahim Pasha

$$ | **HOTEL** | What was once the home of an extended Armenian family offers comfortable, stylishly decorated rooms with vintage-looking wood and leather furniture, colorfully patterned Turkish carpets and textiles, and contemporary Middle Eastern touches. **Pros:** location just off Hippodrome; personable staff; inviting public areas and roof terrace.

Cons: standard rooms can be cramped; most rooms don't have a view; not all rooms are wheelchair-accessible. [$] *Rooms from: €79* ✉ *Terzihane Sok. 7, Sultanahmet* ☎ *212/518–0394* 🌐 *www.ibrahimpasha.com* 🛏 *24 rooms* 🍴 *No meals.*

Hotel Niles Istanbul

$ | **HOTEL** | The elaborate lobby—with its carved wooden columns and ceilings, plush antique furniture, chandeliers, and marble floors with Oriental rugs—could well be a film set, while the standard rooms have been recently redone in a sleeker, more contemporary style that retains some vintage elements as design accents. **Pros:** great value; close to Grand Bazaar and tram stop; small on-site gym. **Cons:** a little ways from other main sights; small bathrooms in standard rooms; a bit hard to locate amid somewhat unsightly nearby streets. [$] *Rooms from: €50* ✉ *Dibekli Cami Sok. 13, Beyazıt, Sultanahmet* ☎ *212/517–3239* 🌐 *www.hotelniles.com* 🛏 *39 rooms* 🍴 *Free Breakfast.*

Hotel Peninsula

$ | **B&B/INN** | One of the best values in Sultanahmet, the well-located Hotel Peninsula offers comfortable and clean rooms, with nice decorative touches that include mirrors, small artworks, kilims, and gauzy draped fabric; three rooms have a partial sea view. **Pros:** great value; convenient location near major sights; service is genuinely friendly and accommodating. **Cons:** no elevator; loud call to prayer from mosque directly behind hotel; bathrooms a bit small and basic. [$] *Rooms from: €48* ✉ *Akbıyık Cad., Adliye Sok. 6, Sultanahmet* ☎ *212/458–6850* 🌐 *www.hotelpeninsula.com* 🛏 *12 rooms* 🍴 *Free Breakfast.*

Hotel Tashkonak Istanbul

$ | **HOTEL** | Occupying two adjacent Ottoman-style wooden houses on a quiet side street, Hotel Tashkonak has appealing rooms, friendly service, and a spacious, leafy garden patio that provides a calming oasis in busy Sultanahmet. **Pros:** on quiet street; lovely secluded garden is a gem; good value. **Cons:** rather small rooms; no elevator and lots of stairs; walls are thin. [$] *Rooms from: €50* ✉ *Küçük Ayasofya Cad., Tomurcuk Sok. 5, Sultanahmet* ☎ *212/518–2882* 🌐 *www.hoteltashkonak.com* 🛏 *30 rooms* 🍴 *Free Breakfast.*

Kybele Hotel

$$ | **B&B/INN** | Named after an ancient Anatolian fertility goddess, this charming little inn is best known for the incredible profusion of antique lamps—4,000 at last count—that hang from the ceilings in the ornate, parlor-like lobby and small but imaginatively decorated rooms. **Pros:** unique decor and quirky charm; warm, friendly staff; cozy restaurant. **Cons:** no terrace, elevator, or TVs in most rooms; breakfast served in somewhat dim underground level; rooms are small and heavily ornamented style may not appeal to everyone. [$] *Rooms from: €50* ✉ *Yerebatan Cad. 23, Sultanahmet* ☎ *212/511–7766* 🌐 *www.kybelehotel.com* 🛏 *16 rooms* 🍴 *Free Breakfast.*

Muyan Suites

$$ | **B&B/INN** | **FAMILY** | The large rooms and suites at this cozy hotel on a quiet backstreet not far from the Çemberlitaş tram stop are attractively if a bit eclectically decorated, with brocade satin upholstery in Ottoman patterns, hanging Middle Eastern–style brass and cloth lamps, ornate mirrors, and kilims on parquet floors. **Pros:** good for families; very friendly, attentive staff; excellent breakfast. **Cons:** thin walls; some bathrooms showing wear and tear; no roof terrace or any area with views. [$] *Rooms from: €50* ✉ *Dizdariye Medresesi Sok. 13, Sultanahmet* ☎ *212/518–6061* 🌐 *www.muyansuites.com* 🛏 *11 rooms* 🍴 *Free Breakfast.*

Sarı Konak Hotel

$$ | **HOTEL** | These bright, well-maintained accommodations in a converted Ottoman mansion have mainly modern

furniture, though the decor also includes Turkish and period accents like brass lamps, antique mirrors, and Ottoman-era etchings; some rooms have original tiled floors. **Pros:** cozy, intimate feel; good value; rooftop terrace with a view. **Cons:** standard rooms a bit small; no views from rooms; no elevator. [$] *Rooms from: €70* ✉ *Mimar Mehmet Ağa Cad. 26, Sultanahmet* ☎ *212/638–6258* 🌐 *www.istanbulhotelsarikonak.com* 🛏 *23 rooms* 🍴 *Free Breakfast.*

Şebnem Hotel

$ | **B&B/INN** | This lovely little inn near the main sights of Sultanahmet has bright, clean, and attractively decorated rooms—with dark wooden floors, burgundy curtains, and a few four-post beds that have embroidered canopies—and a pleasantly laid-back vibe. **Pros:** extraordinarily friendly staff; outstanding breakfast; lovely terrace. **Cons:** rather small rooms; no elevator; no safes in rooms. [$] *Rooms from: €39* ✉ *Adliye Sok. 1, Sultanahmet* ☎ *212/517–6623* 🌐 *sebnem.inistanbulhotels.com* 🛏 *15 rooms* 🍴 *Free Breakfast.*

Sirkeci Mansion

$$ | **HOTEL** | The comfortable and inviting room decor emphasizes local character, while the bustling, ornate lobby and warm, helpful staff convey feelings of refined luxury. **Pros:** staff especially eager to please; excellent facilities; Gülhane tram station just steps away. **Cons:** lower-level rooms have lackluster views; poor soundproofing of rooms; some rooms are small. [$] *Rooms from: €127* ✉ *Taya Hatun Sok. 5, Sirkeci, Sultanahmet* ☎ *212/528–4344* 🌐 *www.sirkecimansion.com* 🛏 *52 rooms* 🍴 *Free Breakfast.*

Sultanahmet Palace

$$ | **HOTEL** | The sultans meet Las Vegas in this glitzy re-creation of an Ottoman palace, where grand marble stairways, columns, Greek statues, and fountains grace the public spaces, and rooms have touches like ornate ceiling mouldings, arched windows, and cushioned divans for reclining and gazing out the windows. **Pros:** prime location just behind Blue Mosque; elegant decor and feel; great views from restaurant. **Cons:** some small rooms; setup of hammam-style bathrooms can be awkward; no elevator. [$] *Rooms from: €90* ✉ *Torun Sok. 19, Sultanahmet* ☎ *212/458–0460* 🛏 *45 rooms* 🍴 *Free Breakfast.*

Nightlife

Surviving strictly on the tourist trade, Istanbul's nightclub shows include everything from folk dancers to jugglers, acrobats, belly dancers, and singers. Rather than being authentically Turkish, the shows are a kitschy attempt to provide tourists with something exotic and Oriental. Typically, dinner is served at about 8, and floor shows start at around 10. Be aware that these are not inexpensive once you've totaled up drink, food, and cover. Reservations are a good idea; be sure to specify whether you're coming for dinner as well as the show or just for drinks.

A'ya Lounge

BARS/PUBS | Sultanahmet doesn't have many noteworthy nightlife spots, but the open-air rooftop lounge at the Four Seasons Sultanahmet is an inviting place to have a drink. Relax on the comfortable deck furniture as you take in the spectacular views of the Aya Sofya and Blue Mosque lit up at night. The lounge closes at 11 pm. ✉ *Four Seasons Hotel Istanbul at Sultanahmet, Tevkifhane Sok. 1, Sultanahmet* ☎ *212/402–3000* 🌐 *www.fourseasons.com/istanbul.*

Shopping

BOOKS

Galeri Kayseri

BOOKS/STATIONERY | If you're looking for books about Turkey, this is the place to visit. The two Galeri Kayseri shops (the storefronts simply say "Bookshop") are across the street from one another, and between them you'll find an outstanding collection of nonfiction books about Turkey in a variety of subject areas, as well as a selection of Turkish and Turkey-related novels and elegant coffee-table books on Islamic art, architecture, and culture. Number 58 is the main store, No. 11 is across the street. ✉ *Divanyolu Cad. 58, Sultanahmet* ☎ *212/516–3366* ⊕ *www. galerikayseri.com.*

CARPETS
Gallery Aydın
HOUSEHOLD ITEMS/FURNITURE | The collection at Gallery Aydın includes high-end antique Turkish, Persian, Georgian, and Caucasian carpets dating back to as early as the 16th century. Dealer Adnan Aydın seriously knows his rugs, and also specializes in repairing and restoring antique pieces. ✉ *Küçükayasofya Cad. 5/B, Sultanahmet* ☎ *212/513–6921.*

CERAMICS
Magnaura Palace Ceramics
CERAMICS/GLASSWARE | Shoppers swear by the service and prices at this Sultanahmet gift shop that specializes in various ceramics. Offerings include items from all over Turkey, including Iznik ware. The store will also pack and ship your purchases home. ✉ *Binbirdirek Meydani Sokak no 3/A, Sultanahmet* ☎ *538/250-6880* ⊕ *www.treeoflifeistanbul.com.*

HANDICRAFTS
Meerschaum Pipes
CRAFTS | You can find carved meerschaum pipes in many shops in the Grand Bazaar, as well as in many antique shops, but the extensive collection here, in a shop founded by Bilal Donmez (and now run by his son, Bulent Donmez), has a very helpful staff and reliably good wares, as well as other high-quality handicrafts. ✉ *Arasta Carsisi, No. 63, Sultanahmet* ☎ *212/516–4142.*

MARKETS
Arasta Bazaar
OUTDOOR/FLEA/GREEN MARKETS | Just behind the Blue Mosque, the Arasta Bazaar is a walkway lined with shops selling items similar to those you'll find at the Grand Bazaar (primarily carpets, ceramics, textiles, jewelry, and other handicrafts), at sometimes lower prices. The atmosphere is also considerably calmer and, unlike the Grand Bazaar, the Arasta is open on Sunday and stays open later (until about 9 pm). ✉ *Arasta Çarşısı, Sultanahmet* ⊕ *www.arastabazaar.com.*

SPAS
★ Ayasofya Hürrem Sultan Hamamı
SPA/BEAUTY | This hammam, which reopened in 2011 following a several-year, $10-million restoration after decades of disuse, is the sleekest and most luxurious in the Old City. It has a prestigious history, having been built by Ottoman architect Sinan in 1556 on the order of Sultan Süleyman the Magnificent, in honor of his wife Roxelana (Hürrem). The setup here is more like that of a modern spa: there is no self-service option, reservations are strongly encouraged, and you'll certainly feel pampered (particularly by the redbud-scented bath amenities). The prices are on par with this level of service—the cheapest treatment is a whopping €80 (about 550 TL). In addition to traditional hammam services, more modern treatments such as aromatherapy massage are offered. ✉ *Ayasofya Meydanı 2, Sultanahmet* ☎ *212/517–3535* ⊕ *www.ayasofyahamami.com.*

Cağaloğlu Hamamı
SPA/BEAUTY | Housed in a magnificent building dating to 1741, the Cağaloğlu Hamamı has long been considered one of the best in Istanbul. Florence Nightingale and Kaiser Wilhelm II once steamed here, and the clientele has remained generally upscale. Prices are on the high side, starting at about €30 (about 194 TL) for a self-service visit; if you want both a scrub and a massage from an attendant, it'll cost you about €50 (about 323 TL). Unfortunately, in recent years the Cağaloğlu has become fairly overrun by tourists and service has gone downhill; guests complain of quick,

3

Istanbul SULTANAHMET

perfunctory massages by attendants and persistent demands for tips. If you want to experience this famous hammam, consider going the self-service route, so you can relax at your own pace. ⊠ *Prof. Kazım İsmail Gürkan Cad. 24, Cağaloğlu, Sultanahmet* ☎ *212/522–2424* ⊕ *www. cagalogluhamami.com.tr.*

Çemberlitaş Hamamı

SPA/BEAUTY | Built in 1584, Çemberlitaş Hamamı is famous for its beautiful architectural design and has long been a favorite hammam with visitors, as it's one of the city's most atmospheric. However, it's become so heavily trafficked that service can be somewhat rushed and attendants can be aggressive in asking for tips. Fees for scrubbing by an attendant start at 355 TL. The self-service option, which gives you the chance to linger longer, is €20 (about 130 TL). Avoid going between 4 and 8 pm, which is the busiest time. ⊠ *Vezirhan Cad. 8, Çemberlitaş, Sultanahmet* ☎ *212/522–7974* ⊕ *www.cemberlitashamami.com.*

Gedikpaşa Hamamı

SPA/BEAUTY | In operation since 1475, this hammam is unique in that both the men's and women's sections have small indoor plunge pools and saunas added in modern times. The atmosphere here is somewhat less touristy than at other hammams, but standards of cleanliness seem a little less stringent than they are at more expensive baths. The surrounding neighborhood is a bit scruffy, but this is the most affordable of the hammams in the area. Gedikpaşa charges around 80 TL for self-service and about 120 TL for a professional scrub. ⊠ *Emin Sinan Hamamı Sok. 65–67, Beyazıt, Sultanahmet* ☎ *212/517–8956* ⊕ *www.gedikpasa-hamami.com.*

Süleymaniye Hamamı

SPA/BEAUTY | Part of the complex of buildings around the Süleymaniye Camii, and built, like the mosque, by Sinan in the 1550s, the Süleymaniye Hamamı is unique in being the only coed hammam in the Old City. It caters specifically to couples and families—in fact, single travelers and single-sex groups cannot visit. Some may find the coed arrangement (with no nudity) preferable to going to a sex-segregated hammam, but it's no less touristy than the rest and women should note that there are only male masseurs. Rates are about €40 (about 255 TL) per person. ⊠ *Mimar Sinan Cad. 20, Süleymaniye, Sultanahmet* ☎ *212/519–5569* ⊕ *www.suleymaniyehamami.com.tr.*

TEXTILES

Jennifer's Hamam

TEXTILES/SEWING | If you are looking for handwoven *pestamels* (thin, flat-woven towels), blankets, bedpsreads, curtains, or upholstery material, you'd be hard-pressed to find a better source than this inviting shop in the Arasta Bazaar behind the Blue Mosque. There's a larger showroom nearby Ogul Sok. No: 20 ⊠ *Arasta Carsisi, No. 135, Sultanahmet* ☎ *212/516–3022* ⊕ *www.jennifershamam.com.*

The Bazaar Quarter and Environs

The area between the Grand Bazaar and the Spice Bazaar was historically the city's center of business and trade, and the streets here still teem with tradespeople and shoppers. You could easily spend hours exploring the Grand Bazaar, and the Spice Bazaar also has its charms. But take time to wander outside them, too, whether along Nuruosmaniye Caddesi with its upmarket jewelry, antiques, and carpet boutiques, or through the narrow, somewhat run-down streets—lined with stores and stalls selling all manner of everyday items at bargain prices, primarily to locals—that lead from the Grand Bazaar down toward the Golden Horn.

Even though most of the old Byzantine and Ottoman buildings have long disappeared, the area gives an impression of what the city must have been like when it was the bustling capital of a vast empire. The beautiful Süleymaniye Mosque, one of the architect Sinan's masterpieces, is grandly situated on a hilltop just a stone's throw from the Grand Bazaar and is worth a detour. When exploring this area, it's a good idea to start at the Grand Bazaar and work your way downhill to Eminönü—it's a rather stiff climb the other way.

⊙ Sights

Beyazıt Camii
RELIGIOUS SITE | Inspired by Aya Sofya and completed in 1506, this domed mosque holds the distinction of being the oldest of the Ottoman imperial mosques still standing in the city. Though the inside is somewhat dark, it has an impressively carved mihrab and the large courtyard has 20 columns made of verd antique, red granite, and porphyry that were taken from ancient buildings. Most sections of the mosque, except for a small area open for worship, will be closed for the forseeable future for an extensive, multi-year restoration project. ⊠ *Beyazıt Meyd., Beyazıt, The Bazaar Quarter and Environs.*

Column of Constantine (*Çemberlitaş*)
BUILDING | This column stood at the center of what was a large circular marketplace or forum where Constantine formally rededicated the city on AD May 11, 330. Carved out of blocks of a reddish-purple stone called porphyry that was especially prized by the ancient Romans, the column is 115 feet high and was once topped by a golden statue of Apollo, to which Constantine added his own head. Constantine was said to have placed various relics under the column, including an ax used by Noah to make the ark, a piece of the True Cross, and some of the leftover bread from the miracle of the loaves and fishes. ⊠ *Yeniçeriler Cad. and Vezirhan Cad., The Bazaar Quarter and Environs.*

Eminönü
NEIGHBORHOOD | The transportation hub of Old Istanbul, Eminönü teems with activity. There are docks for traditional ferryboats (including both short and daylong Bosphorus cruises) and faster "sea bus" catamarans that cross the Bosphorus, as well as the Eminönü tram stop, the Sirkeci train station, and the departure area for buses headed to Istanbul's western districts. Thousands of people and vehicles rush through this bustling, frenetic neighborhood by the hour, and the many street traders here do a quick business selling everything from trinkets to designer knockoffs. From Eminönü, you can cross the Galata Bridge on foot or via the tramway to Karaköy, the quick way to the "new town." ⊠ *The Bazaar Quarter and Environs.*

Fatih Camii (*Fatih Mosque*)
RELIGIOUS SITE | This complex consisting of a mosque, religious schools, and other buildings of a pious nature was the largest in the Ottoman empire, and is still one of the most culturally important mosques in the city. Today it remains the heart of Fatih, one of Istanbul's most religiously conservative neighborhoods. The original mosque, which was destroyed by an earthquake in 1766, was built from 1463 to 1470 by Mehmet the Conqueror on the site of the demolished Church of the Twelve Apostles, the burial church of Byzantine emperors from Constantine on. The 18th-century replacement, which recently underwent a complete restoration, is quite attractive—particularly the extensive stained-glass windows—though probably very little of what you're seeing is original. Behind the mosque is the reconstructed baroque-style tomb of the Conqueror himself, along with the far plainer tomb of his wife Gülbahar. It's best to avoid visiting the mosque at prayer times. ⊠ *Fevzi Paşa Cad., Fatih, The Bazaar Quarter and Environs.*

★ **Grand Bazaar** (*Kapalı Çarşı*)

MARKET | Take a deep breath and plunge into this maze of 65 winding, covered streets crammed with 4,000 tiny shops, cafés, restaurants, mosques, and court-yards. It's said that this early version of a shopping mall is the largest concentration of stores under one roof anywhere in the world, and that's easy to believe. Some of the most aggressive salesmanship in the world takes place here, so take that deep breath and put up your guard before entering. Oddly enough, though, the sales pitches, the crowds, and the sheer volume of junky trinkets on offer can be hypnotizing. Originally built by Mehmet II (the Conqueror) in 1461 over the main Byzantine shopping streets, the Grand Bazaar was rebuilt after fires in both 1943 and 1954. Just drink a glass of tea while you browse through leather goods, carpets, fabric, clothing, furniture, ceramics, and gold and silver jewelry. Remember, whether you're bargaining for a pair of shoes or an antique carpet, the best prices are offered when the would-be seller thinks you are about to slip away.⊠ *Yeniçeriler Cad. and Çadırcılar Cad., The Bazaar Quarter and Environs* ☎ *212/519–1248* ⊕ *www.kapalicarsi.com.tr* ۞ *Closed Sun.*

Istanbul University

COLLEGE | The main campus of Turkey's oldest institution of higher learning originally served as the Ottoman war ministry—hence the magnificent gateway arch facing Beyazıt Square and the grandiose, martial style of the main buildings, which surround a long greensward filled with giant plane trees. The stone 279-foot **Beyazıt Tower,** built in 1828 by Mahmud II as a fire-watch station, is the tallest structure in the Old City and is still one of the most recognizable landmarks in the area. At night, it is lit up with LED lights in different colors indicating weather conditions. Though it can no longer be climbed, it's worth seeing up close. Because of its history as a nexus of political activism over the past several

decades, the campus is not very publicly accessible, though in theory tourists are allowed entrance from 10 am to 3 pm on weekdays during the school year and until about 4 pm during the summer. Proceed along the main drive and past the rectorate building to the garden behind it, from which there is a stunning view overlooking the Süleymaniye Camii. ⊠ *Fuat Paşa Cad., Beyazıt, The Bazaar Quarter and Environs*.

Şehzade Camii

RELIGIOUS SITE | The medium-sized Şehzade Camii was built for Süleyman the Magnificent's eldest son, Prince Mehmet, who died of smallpox in 1543 at age 22. This was the great Ottoman architect Sinan's first imperial mosque and he called it his "apprentice work." The result is quite attractive, although less spectacular than the nearby Süleymaniye. The tranquil gardens contain several imperial tombs—including that of Prince Mehmet, decorated with some of the best İznik tiles in Istanbul. ⊠ *Şehzadebaşı Cad., Fatih, The Bazaar Quarter and Environs*.

Spice Bazaar (*Mısır Çarşısı*)

MARKET | The enticing Spice Bazaar, also known as the Egyptian Bazaar, is much smaller than the Grand Bazaar but more colorful—though not as colorful, perhaps, as it was in the 17th century, when it was built to generate rental income to pay for the upkeep of the Yeni Cami (New Mosque) next door. In those earlier days the bazaar was a vast pharmacy filled with burlap bags overflowing with herbs and spices fresh off the ships from Egypt and the Spice Islands. Today, although an increasing number of souvenir shops have opened up in the bazaar, you can still wander past numerous stalls chock-ablock with sacks of spices (including highly sought-after Iranian saffron), bags full of dried fruit and nuts, and delicacies including *lokum* (Turkish delight), caviar, and Turkish coffee and tea. The maze of narrow streets around the back of the bazaar is filled with open-air booths and shops selling similar foodstuffs at generally cheaper prices—as well as everything from household items to medicinal leeches. ⊠ *Yeni Cami Meydanı, The Bazaar Quarter and Environs* ☎ *212/513–6597* ⊘ *Closed Sun. in Summer.*

★ **Süleymaniye Camii** (*Mosque of Süleyman*)

RELIGIOUS SITE | Perched on a hilltop opposite Istanbul University, this is one of the most magnificent mosques in Istanbul and is considered one of the architect Sinan's masterpieces. The architectural thrill of the mosque, which was built between 1550 and 1557, is the enormous dome, the highest of any Ottoman mosque. Supported by four square columns and arches, as well as exterior walls with smaller domes on either side, the soaring space gives the impression that it's held up principally by divine cooperation. Except for around the mihrab (prayer niche), there is little in the way of tile work—though the intricate stained-glass windows and baroque decorations painted on the domes more than make up for that. A full restoration was completed in late 2010. The tomb of Sinan is just outside the walls, on the northern corner, while those of his patron, Süleyman the Magnificent, and the sultan's wife, Roxelana, are housed in the adjacent cemetery. Take a stroll around the beautiful grounds and don't miss the wonderful views of the Golden Horn.⊠ *Süleymaniye Cad., near Istanbul University's north gate, The Bazaar Quarter and Environs.*

Valens Aqueduct

ARCHAEOLOGICAL SITE | A Roman city needed its aqueduct, and Constantinople, which seriously lacked drinking water, finally got one in 375 under Emperor Valens. The aqueduct, which was just one element of a well-engineered water distribution system that extended for miles, was restored in the 16th century by the Ottoman architect Sinan and continued to function well into the Ottoman era. The best and most dramatic surviving section is that near Şehzade Mosque, where Atatürk Bulvarı, a major urban thoroughfare, passes through the great arches of the aqueduct—still one of Istanbul's most significant landmarks. ⊠ *The Bazaar Quarter and Environs.*

Yeni Cami (*New Mosque*)

RELIGIOUS SITE | A dominant feature of the Istanbul skyline, thanks to its prime spot on the Eminönü waterfront, the "new mosque" is known as much for its history as its architecture. Its location, rising out of the Golden Horn, presented formidable engineering challenges to the former apprentice to Sinan, who laid the waterlogged foundations in 1597. Due to sultans' deaths and complicated harem politics, the project wasn't completed until 1663 by the queen mother at the time, Turhan Hatice. The entrance to the courtyard from the main square offers a marvelous view of the small domes and semidomes that appear to cascade down around the main dome, flanked by two minarets. Inside, almost every square inch of the interior is decorated—from the elaborate, multicolored İznik tiles to the intricately painted domes and gilded minbar—while numerous windows, including in the wall of the mihrab, fill the mosque with light. The mosque is undergoing renovations but remains open to the public.⊠ *Eminönü waterfront, The Bazaar Quarter and Environs.*

🍴 Restaurants

Fes Café

$ | **CAFÉ** | Squeezed into a former market stall in the heart of the Grand Bazaar, the small kitchen at Fes Café turns out simple sandwiches, salads, excellent fresh lemonade and fruit juices, homemade desserts, and other American-style fare. A second, larger branch just outside the Bazaar on Ali Baba Türbe Sokak (No. 15/A) offers a fuller menu that includes salads, pastas, and meat dishes, and also

Word of Mouth

"Wandering the streets of Sultanahmet, with the Blue Mosque in the background, we came across this juice vendor in traditional costume. With the heat of the day the juice was very refreshing!" —photo by Maureen Barber, Fodors. com member

houses a small boutique selling products by sister company Abdulla. **Known for:** good quick-bite option in the bazaar; good views inside the Grand Bazaar; housewares and jewelry from young Turkish designers. $ *Average main: 23 TL* ✉ *Halıcılar Cad. 58–62, Grand Bazaar, The Bazaar Quarter and Environs* ☎ *212/528–1613* ⊕ *www.fescafe.com* ⊘ *Closed Sun. No dinner.*

Hamdi Restaurant

$$ | TURKISH | This longtime grill house is an Istanbul institution, with its huge selection of kebabs, as well as appetizers like mini *lahmacun* (thin flatbread topped with spicy ground meat); although the food may not be too different from other kebab houses, Hamdi's three dining floors still tend to be packed with both tourists and locals. This makes for a lively, even boisterous, atmosphere, and service can be a bit harried; make sure that you get—and pay for—exactly what you order. **Known for:** terrace-level tables with views of the Golden Horn; wide kebab selection; bustling atmosphere. $ *Average main: 53 TL* ✉ *Kalçın Sok. 11, Eminönü, The Bazaar Quarter and Environs* ☎ *212/528–0390* ⊕ *www.hamdi.com.tr.*

Tarihi Subaşı Lokantası

$ | TURKISH | Hidden away down an unpromising-looking side street near the Sirkeci tram stop, this friendly *lokanta* (a hotel also offering food) has been serving up hearty home-cooked meals to local workers and businesspeople since 1959. Step up to the cafeteria-style counter and choose from the inexpensive daily selections, such as chicken with mushrooms or stewed meatballs and potatoes, to fuel up for the long afternoon of sightseeing ahead. **Known for:** unpretentious atmosphere; inexpensive Turkish cuisine; central location. $ *Average main: 32 TL* ✉ *Ankara Cad., Emirler Han Sok. 3, Sirkeci, The Bazaar Quarter and Environs* ☎ *212/512–0272* ⊘ *No dinner* ▭ *No credit cards.*

View from the Bridge 👁

The Galata Bridge, or Galata Köprüsü, connects Old Istanbul to the so-called "new town" on the other side of the Golden Horn. The bridge was finished in 1994, replacing the old pontoon bridge that had been around since about 1910, when horse-, ox-, and mule-drawn carriages rattled across it for a fee. The bridge itself isn't much to look at, but it offers a postcard-worthy view of the main sights of the Old City, and is a particularly nice vantage point from which to watch the sun set.

🎭 Performing Arts

WHIRLING DERVISHES

Hodjapasha Culture Center

ARTS CENTERS | Housed in a nicely restored 15th-century hammam, the Hodjapasha Culture Center hosts whirling dervish ceremonies most nights of the week. The hour-long event starts with a performance of classical Turkish music before the dervishes whirl. Though some are captivated by the whirling, others may find it excessively slow and hypnotic, so consider whether this sort of cultural experience is your cup of tea. Note that photography is not allowed during the *sema* ceremony. Hodjapasha also offers two different dance shows on alternating nights that are considerably more lively; one features traditional Turkish folk dancing and the other is a theatrical performance that combines traditional and modern dance. ✉ *Hocapaşa Hamamı Cad. 3/B, Sirkeci, The Bazaar Quarter and Environs* ☎ *212/511–4686* ⊕ *www.hodjapasha.com* ▭ *From US$20.*

3

İstanbul THE BAZAAR QUARTER AND ENVIRONS

⬤ Shopping

ANTIQUES

★ Sofa

ANTIQUES/COLLECTIBLES | One of Istanbul's most highly regarded antiques stores, Sofa is located on pedestrian-only Nuruosmaniye Caddesi. Two levels are filled with a fascinating collection of metalwork, original İznik and Kütahya ceramics, old maps and prints, calligraphy and miniatures, textiles, vintage jewelry, artwork, and assorted other treasures. ✉ *Nuruosmaniye Cad. 53/A, Cağaloğlu, The Bazaar Quarter and Environs* ☎ *212/520–2850* ⊕ *www.kashifsofa.com.*

BATH ACCESSORIES

Abdulla

CRAFTS | This delightful boutique sells high-quality towels, tablecloths, throw rugs, and other traditional Turkish home textiles with a simple, modern aesthetic. The immensely appealing and stylish collection also includes luscious, all-natural olive-oil soaps. Abdulla also has a small sales outlet inside the Fes Café branch on nearby Ali Baba Türbe Sokak. ✉ *Halıcılar Cad. 60, Grand Bazaar, The Bazaar Quarter and Environs* ☎ *212/526–3070* ⊕ *www.abdulla.com.*

Derviş

CRAFTS | At Derviş, the emphasis is on handcrafted towels, bathrobes, soaps, and traditional Turkish bath accessories, as well as antique and vintage kaftans and robes from Anatolia. There's a second shop inside the Bazaar's tucked-away Cebeci Han (at No. 10), just off Yağlıkçılar Sokak. ✉ *Halıcılar Sok. 51, Grand Bazaar, The Bazaar Quarter and Environs* ☎ *212/528–7883* ⊕ *www.dervis.com.*

BOOKS

Sahaflar Çarşısı

BOOKS/STATIONERY | Reached through a doorway just outside the Fesciler Kapısı (Fezmakers' Gate) at the western end of the Grand Bazaar, the Sahaflar Çarşısı is the traditional home of Istanbul's secondhand booksellers. The market now mainly houses bookshops selling new editions in Turkish, primarily school textbooks, though a handful of secondhand and rare book dealers carrying books in English and other languages, as well as prints and other ephemera, are still located here. The market is open every day. ✉ *The Bazaar Quarter and Environs.*

CARPETS

Adnan & Hasan

HOUSEHOLD ITEMS/FURNITURE | One of Istanbul's most reputable carpet dealers, Adnan & Hasan espouses a "hassle-free shopping" policy and is favored by the diplomatic community. The company and its friendly staff offer a large selection of antique, semi-antique, and new carpets and kilims, mainly from Anatolia. ✉ *Halıcılar Cad. 89–90–92, Grand Bazaar, The Bazaar Quarter and Environs* ☎ *212/527–9887* ⊕ *www.adnanandhasan.com.*

Dhoku

HOUSEHOLD ITEMS/FURNITURE | Design brand Dhoku stands out among the traditional carpet merchants of the Grand Bazaar for its radically different, contemporary styles, which include bold geometric designs and stylized floral patterns. The high-quality rugs are handmade near İzmir using organic handspun wool and natural dyes. Directly across the street is sister company Ethnicon (Takkeciler Cad. 49–51), which pieces together different-sized squares of colorful rug material to create carpets reminiscent of American-style quilts. Both stores offer fixed prices; at Dhoku, pricing is by the square meter. ✉ *Takkeciler Sok. 58–60 and 74–76, Grand Bazaar, The Bazaar Quarter and Environs* ☎ *212/527–6841* ⊕ *www.dhoku.com.*

Şengör

HOUSEHOLD ITEMS/FURNITURE | Established in 1918 and now run by the fourth generation of the Şengör family, this experienced and trustworthy dealer has a large inventory of carpets from different regions of Anatolia. ✉ *Takkeciler Sok. 65–83, Grand Bazaar, The Bazaar Quarter and Environs* ☎ *212/527–2192.*

HANDICRAFTS

Kaptan Bros

CRAFTS | This store specializes in hand-worked copper and brass pieces, both old and new; it's also full of stylish lanterns in traditional Middle Eastern and contemporary styles. ✉ *Terziler Sok. 30, Grand Bazaar, The Bazaar Quarter and Environs* ☎ *212/526–3650.*

Nick's Calligraphy Corner

CRAFTS | One of the most unusual stores in the Grand Bazaar—indeed, any-where—is Nick Merdenyan's tiny shop. The artist produces intricate calligraphic works and miniature paintings incorporating motifs and themes from major world religions, as well as universal nonreligious messages. Each small masterpiece is done on dried Dieffenbachia leaves, which he calls "Nick's missionary leaves of tolerance and peace." ✉ *Cevahir Bedesteni 24, Grand Bazaar, The Bazaar Quarter and Environs* ☎ *212/513–5473* ⊕ *www.nickscalligraphy.com.*

Özlem Tuna

JEWELRY/ACCESSORIES | This is more of an atelier and private showroom than a conventional store, but it's worth stopping in to check out designer Özlem Tuna's delightful collections of jewelry and delicate ceramic and metal tableware that put a contemporary twist on traditional Turkish designs and motifs. ✉ *Ankara Cad. 65, Nemlizade Han., Suite 23, 5th fl., The Bazaar Quarter and Environs* ☎ *212/527–9285* ⊕ *www.ozlemtuna.com.*

JEWELRY

Horasan

JEWELRY/ACCESSORIES | There are piles and piles of antique rings, bracelets, necklaces, and earrings from Central Asia at Horasan, as well as walls covered in strands of colorful beads made out of precious and semiprecious stones from which the staff will help you create your

own jewelry. Prices are fair. ✉ *Yorgancılar Cad. 22, Grand Bazaar, The Bazaar Quarter and Environs* ☎ *532/313–3874.*

MARKETS

Grand Bazaar

SHOPPING NEIGHBORHOODS | The Grand Bazaar is a neighborhood unto itself and a trove of all things Turkish—carpets, brass, copper, jewelry, textiles, and leather products. Many of the stores have resorted to selling cheap goods aimed at the tourist market, but the bazaar still holds many treasures. ✉ *Yeniçeriler Cad. and Çadırcılar Cad., The Bazaar Quarter and Environs* ☎ *212/519–1248.*

Nuruosmaniye Caddesi

SHOPPING NEIGHBORHOODS | One of the major streets leading to the Grand Bazaar, Nuruosmaniye Caddesi has a pedestrian boulevard section lined with some of the Old City's most stylish (and high-end) shops, with an emphasis on fine carpets, jewelry, and antiques. ✉ *The Bazaar Quarter and Environs.*

SPECIALTY FOODS

Kurukahveci Mehmet Efendi

FOOD/CANDY | On a backstreet just outside the western entrance of the Spice Market is the tiny flagship store of Kurukahveci Mehmet Efendi, Turkey's oldest coffee producer (founded 1871), whose finely ground coffee—which can be seen being ground on the premises—is legendary. Customers can purchase either whole beans or ground coffee, which makes a good souvenir of a trip to Turkey. ✉ *Tahmis Sok. 66, The Bazaar Quarter and Environs* ☎ *212/511–4262* ⊕ *www.mehmetefendi.com.*

Hayfene

FOOD/CANDY | Located in the back wing of the Spice Bazaar, Hayfene (previously known as Ucuzcular Baharat) not only has great prices, but it's also just about the friendliest and most hassle-free shop in the bazaar. It's run by the energetic Bilge Kadıoğlu, a U.S.–educated, fifth-generation spice purveyor who is the bazaar's first (and still only) female shop owner. Kadıoğlu prides herself on the shop's extremely fresh spices and specially prepared mixes—which she is happy to have you taste—as well as pure, alcohol-free essential oils and a variety of Turkish sweets. ⊠ *Mısır Çarşısı 51, The Bazaar Quarter and Environs* ☎ *212/444–8289* ⊕ *www.hayfene.com.*

TEXTILES

İgüs

JEWELRY/ACCESSORIES | With two shops in the Grand Bazaar, İgüs offers one of the widest selections of scarves and pashminas found anywhere in Turkey, along with reasonable prices. ⊠ *Yağlıkçılar Cad. 29 and 80, The Bazaar Quarter and Environs* ☎ *212/512–3528* ⊕ *www.igustekstil.com.*

Western Districts

The historical peninsula's western districts are farther off the beaten path than the heavily tourist-trod Sultanahmet and bazaar areas, but the rewards of visiting are a number of interesting sights and a more authentic atmosphere. Just inside the ancient city walls, the former Chora Church, now Kariye Müzesi, contains a wealth of gorgeous Byzantine mosaics and frescoes whose splendor surpasses those in the Aya Sofya. The Great Walls themselves, sections of which have been restored, give an idea of the scale of the ancient city and of how Constantinople successfully resisted so many sieges before finally falling to the Ottomans in 1453. Along the water, Fener and Balat—once predominantly Greek and Jewish neighborhoods, respectively—are home to several historic churches, including the Greek Orthodox Patriarchate, as well as the city's oldest synagogue. Farther up the Golden Horn, the Eyüp Sultan Mosque complex is an important Muslim pilgrimage site.

◉ Sights

Ahrida Synagogue

RELIGIOUS SITE | Located in Balat, the city's historically Jewish district, Istanbul's oldest synagogue is believed to date back to the 1430s, when it was founded by Jews from the town of Ohrid in what is today Macedonia. The synagogue was extensively restored in 1992 to the Ottoman baroque style of its last major reconstruction in the 17th century. The most interesting feature of this Sephardic place of worship is the boat-shape wooden *bimah* (reading platform), whose form is thought to represent either Noah's Ark or the ships that brought the Jews from the Iberian Peninsula to the Ottoman Empire in 1492. To visit, you must apply by email (preferred) or fax at least four business days in advance to the Chief Rabbinate (follow the directions on the website). ⊠ *Kürkçü Çeşmesi Sok. 7, Balat, Western Districts* ☎ *212/293–8794* ⊕ *www.turkya-hudileri.com.*

Ecumenical Orthodox Patriarchate

(*Church of St. George or Rum Ortodoks Patrikhanesi*)
RELIGIOUS SITE | After being kicked out of Aya Sofya after the Turkish conquest of the city, the Greek Orthodox Patriarchate wandered among several churches before settling here in the Church of St. George in 1601. Rebuilt after a fire in 1720, the church is a relatively simple basilica, though the (rather dark) interior has a refined atmosphere. Sarcophagi with the remains of some famous Byzantine saints, a Byzantine-era patriarchal throne, and two very old mosaic icons on the right side of the elaborate iconostasis are considered the most noteworthy features of the church. The main front gate of the compound has been welded shut ever since Sultan Mahmud II had Patriarch Gregory V hanged from it in 1821 as punishment for the Greek revolt. This small church is theoretically the center of the Orthodox world, though some Turks would like to claim that it serves only the

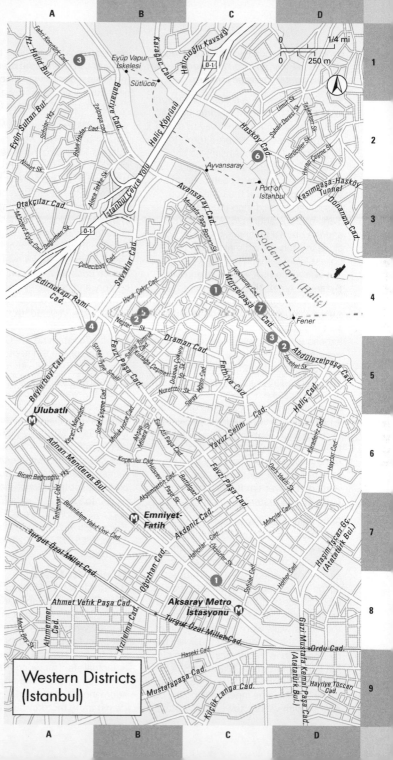

Sights ▼

1 Ahrida Synagogue . **C4**

2 Ecumenical Orthodox Patriarchate **D5**

3 Eyüp Sultan Camii **A1**

4 Great Walls of Con-stantinople.. **A4**

5 Kariye Müzesi **B4**

6 Rahmi M. Koç Museum **C2**

7 Sveti Stefan Bulgar Kilisesi **C4**

Restaurants ▼

1 Akdeniz Hatay Sofrası **C8**

2 Asitane...... **B4**

3 Forno **C5**

Western Districts (Istanbul)

dwindling community of Istanbul Greeks. ✉ *Dr. Sadık Ahmet Cad. 1, Fener, Western Districts* ⊕ *www.ec-patr.org.*

Eyüp Sultan Camii (*Eyüp Sultan Mosque*)
RELIGIOUS SITE | Muslim pilgrims from all over the world make their way to the brightly colored, tile-covered tomb of Eyüp Ensari (Ayyub al-Ansari)—a companion of the Prophet Muhammad who served as his standard-bearer—at this mosque complex on the Golden Horn. Ensari was killed during the first Arab siege of Constantinople (AD 674–78), and the eternal presence of a man so close to Muhammad makes this the holiest Islamic shrine in Turkey. His grave site was visited by Muslim pilgrims in Byzantine times and "rediscovered" during Mehmet the Conqueror's siege of Constantinople. After the conquest, Mehmet monumentalized the tomb and built a mosque, where investiture ceremonies were held for successive sultans; the mosque currently on the site was built after the original edifice was ruined in the 1766 earthquake. The plane-tree-shaded courtyards and large numbers of visitors imbue Eyüp Sultan Camii with a sense of peace and religious devotion not found in many other parts of this often frenetic city. A vast cemetery has grown up around the mosque. It's best to avoid visiting at prayer times. ✉ *Cami Kebir Cad., Eyüp, Western Districts.*

Great Walls of Constantinople
BUILDING | The walls of Constantinople were the greatest fortifications of the medieval age and, although they were severely damaged by Sultan Mehmet II's canon in the siege leading up to the Ottoman conquest of the city in 1453, large sections still stand more or less intact today. The walls were built in the 5th century after the city outgrew the walls built by Constantine, and they stretched 6½ km (4 miles) from the Marmara Sea to the Golden Horn. The "wall" was actually made up of a large inner and smaller outer wall, with various towers and gates, as well as a moat. Parts have been restored and you can even climb around on top; the easiest section on which to do this is near Edirnekapı, a short walk uphill from Chora Church. ✉ *Western Districts.*

★ **Kariye Müzesi** (*Kariye Museum or Church of the Holy Savior in Chora*)
MUSEUM | The dazzling mosaics and frescoes in the former Church of the Holy Savior in Chora are considered to be among the finest Byzantine artworks in the world. Most of the mosaics, in 50 panels, depict scenes from the New Testament and date from the 14th century. They are in splendid condition, having been plastered over when the church became a mosque in the 16th century and not uncovered until the 1940s. "Chora" comes from the Greek word for countryside; the original church here was outside the city walls that were built by Constantine the Great, but at the beginning of the 5th century AD Theodosius built new fortifications to expand the growing city, which brought the church inside the walls. The current edifice is believed to have been built in the 12th century. The easiest way to reach Kariye Müzesi is by taxi or by Edirnekapı-bound bus from Eminönu or Taksim Square. The tree-shaded café outside the church and Asitane Restaurant next door are both pleasant spots for lunch before you trek back into town. ✉ *Kariye Türbesi Sok., a short walk north of Fevzi Paşa Cad., near Edirnekapı in Old City walls, Western Districts* ☎ *212/631–9241* ⊕ *kariye.muze. gov.tr* ▦ *45 TL.*

Rahmi M. Koç Museum
MUSEUM | **FAMILY** | Housed on the grounds of an Ottoman-era shipyard on the shore of the Golden Horn, and in an adjacent foundry where anchors were cast for the Ottoman fleet, this museum complex was founded by one of Turkey's leading industrialists. The wonderful, eclectic collection includes aircraft, boats, a submarine, a tank, trucks, trains, a horse-drawn tram, motorcycles, antique cars,

Anastasis fresco, artist unknown, Kariye Müzesi

medieval telescopes, and every type of engine imaginable. Along with the many vehicles and machines, interactive displays on science and technology, as well as recreations of a sawmill and a 1920s olive oil factory, are of special appeal to children. There are several food and beverage venues on the premises, including Café du Levant, a Parisian-style bistro with Art Nouveau furnishings, and the waterfront Halat Restaurant. Take a Golden Horn ferry, a bus from Şişhane, or a taxi to get here. ⊠ *Hasköy Cad. 5, Hasköy, Western Districts* ☎ *212/369–6600* ⊕ *www.rmk-museum.org.tr* ⊠ *18 TL; additional fee for submarine and planetarium entry* ⊗ *Closed Mon.*

Sveti Stefan Bulgar Kilisesi (*Bulgarian Church of St. Stefan*)

RELIGIOUS SITE | One of the most remarkable and odd structures in Istanbul—and that's saying a lot—this small neo-Gothic church looks like it's covered with elaborate stone carvings but when you get up close, you realize that it's all cast iron. It was prefabricated in Vienna, shipped down the Danube on barges, and erected on the western shore of the Golden Horn in 1898. The then-flourishing Bulgarian Orthodox community in Istanbul was eager to have an impressive church of its own as a statement of its independence from the Greek Orthodox Patriarchate; the Ottoman Sultan had given the community permission to break away in 1870 but the first church built on the site had burned down. The Istanbul municipality announced in mid-2011 that the church—one of the few such surviving prefab cast-iron churches in the world—would undergo restoration. Whether or not you can get in, the building, set in neatly tended gardens by the waters of the Golden Horn, is an impressive structure to look at. ⊠ *Mürsel Paşa Cad. 10, Balat, Istanbul* ⊕ *www.svetistephan.com.*

🍴 Restaurants

Akdeniz Hatay Sofrası

$$ | TURKISH | Popular with locals, this restaurant specializes in the Arab-influenced cuisine of Hatay (originating near Turkey's border with Syria), which features delicious meze like hummus, baba ghanoush, *muhammara* (a spread of mashed chile peppers and walnuts), *kısır* (a spicy version of tabbouleh), and a wide range of uncommon kebabs. The venue's famous "meter kebab" serves several people and requires advance ordering, as does the salt-shell-baked chicken and lamb. **Known for:** lavish weekend breakfast spread; less common regional cuisine; tuzda tavuk, chicken encased in salt and set on fire. $ *Average main: 45 TL* ✉ *Ahmediye Cad. 44/A, Fatih, Western Districts* ☎ *212/444–7247* ⊕ *www. akdenizhataysofrasi.com.tr.*

Asitane

$$$ | **TURKISH** | One of Istanbul's most distinctive restaurants serves seasonally changing menus based on the traditional cuisine of the Ottoman court, which the venue's owners have carefully researched over the past two decades. Dishes feature unusual combinations of ingredients, such as eggplant stuffed with quail, baked melon with a pilaf and ground-meat filling, and stuffed grape leaves with sour cherries. **Known for:** shaded courtyard; elegant atmosphere; Ottoman-influenced menu. $ *Average main: 50 TL* ✉ *Kariye Camii Sok. 6, Edirnekapı, Western Districts* ☎ *212/635–7997* ⊕ *www.asitanerestaurant.com.*

Forno

$ | **TURKISH** | Part of a new wave of small cafés, craft shops, restaurants, and antiques dealers popping up in the atmospheric but long-neglected neighborhood of Balat, Forno distinguishes itself with owner Yona Grunberg's short, high-quality menu of freshly prepared *pides*, pizzas, salads, and soups. With its brightly colored geometric tiles, exposed-brick walls, and large wooden communal table, this is an equally pleasant place to just relax for a while over a coffee or tea, and the weekend breakfast gets raves. **Known for:** cozy, relaxing atmosphere; pizza and pide;

Turkish Coffee 🍴

Most teahouses serve Turkish coffee and espresso, although a more upscale café, which will probably use better coffee and take the time to prepare it properly. Well-made Turkish coffee should be thick and almost chocolaty, with espresso-like foam on top, and it's generally served after a meal. (If you are sitting down in a cafe for a pick-me-up, you will likely want to order espresso or an espresso drink.) Turks drink their coffee three ways: *sade* (plain), *az* (a little sweet), *orta* (medium sweet), and *şekerli* (extra sweet). It's usually served with a small glass of water and, frequently, a little piece of *lokum* (Turkish delight).

weekend breakfast. $ *Average main: 27 TL* ✉ *Fener Kireçhane Sok. 13, Balat, Western Districts* ☎ *212/521–2900* ⊕ *www.fornobalat.com* ⊘ *Closed Mon.* ▭ *No credit cards.*

Beyoğlu

Beyoğlu has traditionally been thought of as the "new town," and this is where you will feel the beating pulse of the modern city: the district is a major destination for eating and drinking, shopping, and arts and culture. "New" is of course a relative term in Istanbul, and many of the grand, European-style buildings you'll see on the hill above Galata date from the late 19th century, when this part of Beyoğlu—then known as Pera—was one of the city's most fashionable areas, home to large numbers of the city's non-Muslim minorities and the foreign diplomatic community. After a period of decline in the latter decades of the 20th century, Beyoğlu was revived around the turn of the millennium, as Istanbullus rediscovered the elegant old buildings and incredible views.

At the southern end of the neighborhood, Tünel Square marks the start of İstiklal Caddesi (Independence Avenue). Istanbul's main pedestrian street, İstiklal is lined with shops, cafés, and nightlife venues; allow some time to stroll along this bustling thoroughfare and simply take in the scene. İstiklal climbs gently uphill through Beyoğlu and across Galatasaray Meydanı (Galatasaray Square) to Taksim Square, the center of modern Istanbul. The Galata Mevlevihanesi (Galata dervish lodge), historic Fish Market, and private art museums and art galleries, including the Pera, are also in this area.

◉ Sights

Fish Market (Balık Pazarı)
MARKET | Located just off İstiklal Caddesi next to the entrance to the Çiçek Pasajı, the Balık Pazarı is a bustling labyrinth of streets filled with stands selling fish, produce, spices, sweets, and souvenirs, and there are a couple of eateries specializing in kokoreç, or grilled lamb intestines: it all makes for great street theater. The adjacent Second Empire–style arcade, known as **Çiçek Pasajı**, was one of Istanbul's grandest shopping venues when it was built in 1876. In the early 20th century, it was gradually taken over by flower shops run by White Russian émigrés—earning it the name "Flower Arcade." In later decades, the arcade became dominated by famously boisterous meyhanes, or tavernas. It now houses about a dozen rather touristy meyhane-style restaurants offering meze and fish. For a more authentic local vibe, continue toward the end of the Fish Market and turn right on narrow **Nevizade Sokak**, a lively strip of bars and meyhanes, all with tiny sidewalk tables packed with locals in summer. ✉ Sahne Sok., Beyoglu.

Galata Mevlevihanesi Müzesi (Galata Mevlevi Lodge Museum)
MUSEUM | Istanbul's oldest Mevlevi dervish lodge, which served as a meeting place and residence for "whirling dervishes" (followers of the Sufi mystic Celaleddin Rumi), was founded on this site in 1491 and rebuilt after a fire in 1765. Recently restored, it now houses a small but interesting museum with displays of dervish garments, handicrafts, and other artifacts, along with background information about the Mevlevi order and Sufism more generally. On the upstairs floor of the lodge's semahane (ceremonial hall) are additional exhibits of calligraphy, ebru (traditional marbling art), and musical instruments; the serene, leafy grounds contain a handful of tombs and a small cemetery. The biggest draw are the sema ceremonies (popularly known as whirling dervish ceremonies) that are performed by different Sufi groups at 5 pm each Sunday in the semahane. Tickets are sold in front of the museum on ceremony days only; it's best to buy them early in the day because performances can sell out. ✉ Galip Dede Cad. 15, southeast of Tünel Sq., off İstiklal Cad., Beyoglu ☎ 212/245–4141 ⊕ www.galatamevlevihanesimuzesi.gov.tr ✉ 10 TL, audio guide 5 TL, sema ceremonies 40 TL.

★ Istanbul Modern
MUSEUM | Currently housed in a temporary space while its usual home on the shore of the Bosphorus is rebuilt, the Istanbul Museum of Modern Art showcases modern and contemporary painting, sculpture, photography, and works in other media from Turkey and around the world. A top-notch program of temporary exhibitions features significant local and international contemporary artists. A private tour can be organized in English for groups of four or more (20 TL per person) and will give you a good introduction to the art scene in Turkey. The museum also has a small cinema, cafe, and design

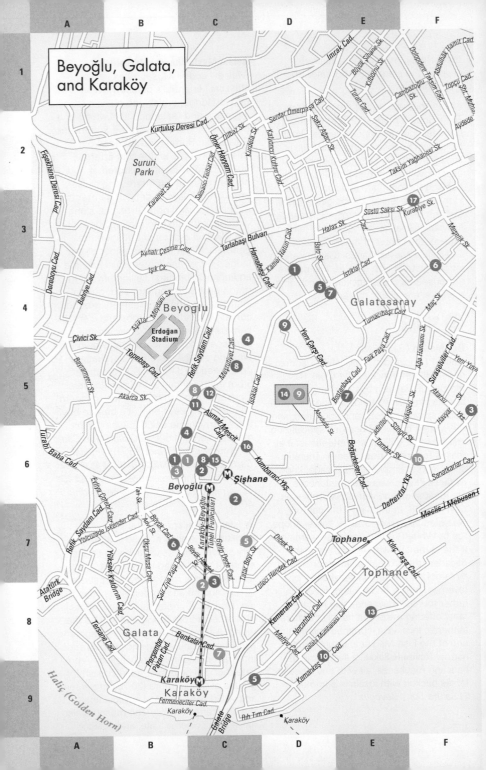

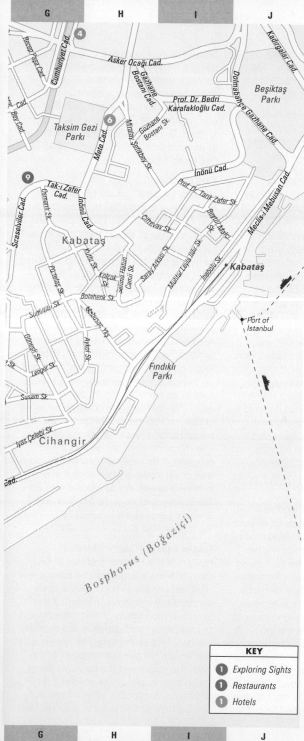

Sights ▼

Restaurants ▼

Hotels ▼

KEY

1 Exploring Sights

1 Restaurants

1 Hotels

store. ⊠ *Asmalımescit Mah., Meşruti-yet Cad. 99, Beyoglu* ☎ *212/334–7300* ⊕ *www.istanbulmodern.org* ☒ *55 TL; audio guide 15 TL* ⊙ *Closed Mon.*

İstiklal Caddesi (*Independence Avenue*)

NEIGHBORHOOD | Running for almost a mile between Taksim Square and Tünel Square, İstiklal Caddesi is the heart of modern Istanbul. The street was once known as "La Grande Rue de Péra," after the Pera neighborhood. In the 19th century, palatial European embassies were built here, away from the dirt and chaos of the Old City. The wealthy city folk soon followed, particularly after the short funicular called the Tünel—the first underground urban rail line in continental Europe—was built in 1875. The area was traditionally non-Muslim, and the Greek, Armenian, Catholic, and Protestant churches here are more prominent than the mosques. Today İstiklal is a lively pedestrian thoroughfare, filled with shops (an increasing number of them international chains), restaurants, cafés, and a handful of cinemas. Turks love to promenade here, and at times it can turn into one great flow of humanity; even in the wee hours of the morning it's still alive with people. This is the Istanbul that never sleeps. ⊠ *İstiklal Cad., Beyoglu.*

The Museum of Innocence (*Masumiyet Müzesi*)

MUSEUM | Nobel Prize–winning Turkish novelist Orhan Pamuk's Museum of Innocence is one of the most unusual museums in Istanbul—and, perhaps, in the world. Opened in 2012 in the gentrifying Çukurcuma neighborhood in a former town house dating to the late 19th century, it's based on Pamuk's eponymous novel chronicling a decades-long story of unrequited love. On display are thousands of everyday objects, from vintage silverware and clothing to lottery tickets and matchbooks—obsessively "collected" over the years by the novel's main character—that present a portrait of daily life in Istanbul over the second half of the 20th century. The quirky, intimate museum is a must-see for anyone familiar with Pamuk's work or interested in Turkish social history, though some may find it esoteric. Audio tours available in English offer context. ⊠ *Çukurcuma Cad., Dalgıç Çıkmazı 2, Beyoglu* ☎ *212/252–9738* ⊕ *www.masumiyetmuzesi.org* ☒ *40 TL* ⊙ *Closed Mon.*

Pera Museum

MUSEUM | A small private museum housed in a grand 1893 building (the former Bristol Hotel), the Pera showcases a diverse range of exhibits. It's best known for its permanent collection of Orientalist paintings by both European and Ottoman artists, dating from the 17th to 19th century and including panoramas of the city and court life; *The Tortoise Trainer* by Osman Hamdi Bey—a late-Ottoman painter who also founded the Istanbul Archaeological Museums—is particularly famous. Two smaller permanent exhibits focus on Kütahya ceramics and tiles, and on the history of Anatolian weights and measures from the Hittite period to the early 20th century. The upper three levels house well-conceived temporary exhibits featuring local and international artists. The museum also runs a regular film program in its basement screening room that often features international and subtitled selections. ⊠ *Meşrutiyet Cad. 65, Tepebaşı, Beyoglu* ☎ *212/334–9900* ⊕ *www.peramuzesi.org.tr* ☒ *20 TL (free Fri. nights after 6)* ⊙ *Closed Mon.*

Taksim Square (*Taksim Meydanı*)

PLAZA | At the north end of İstiklal Caddesi, Istanbul's largest public square was once essentially a chaotic traffic circle and public transportation hub, but the Istanbul municipality undertook a project to completely pedestrianize the area and create a true open plaza. The entrance to the Taksim Square station, from which both the metro and the funicular going down to Kabataş can be reached, is located in the square, so you'll probably end up here at one point or another. The

Gallery-Hopping Along İstiklal

Art-lovers can easily spend half a day, or even a full one, visiting the many galleries, art centers, and other exhibition spaces clustered along İstiklal Caddesi and on nearby streets.

For an overview of the city's vibrant contemporary-art scene, start at the **Mısır Apartmanı** (İstiklal Cad. 163), an early 20th-century Art Nouveau gem that's full of boundary-pushing galleries. Closer to Tünel is **ARTER** (İstiklal Cad. 211), housed in a beautifully restored mansion of similar vintage, and regularly presenting an adventurous lineup of individual and group shows. The brainy exhibits at **SALT Beyoğlu** (İstiklal Cad. 136) often most reward those with a knowledge of Turkish history and politics; the venue also hosts frequent film screenings and talks (sometimes in English)

and is home to the Robinson Crusoe bookstore.

Smaller spaces are worth visiting, too: the French (İstiklal Cad. 4), Greek (İstiklal Cad. 60), and Hungarian (İstiklal Cad. 213) cultural centers put on regular shows by artists from their respective countries, while nearby **Galerist** (Meşrutiyet Cd. 67/1) spotlights contemporary artists.

History buffs shouldn't miss the always-interesting exhibits, often featuring archival photography, at the **Koç University Research Center for Anatolian Civilizations** (İstiklal Cad. 181) and the **Istanbul Research Institute** (Meşrutiyet Cad. 47).

Admission to all galleries mentioned is free of charge; most are closed Sunday or Monday.

open area at the top of İstiklal is dominated by the Monument of the Republic, built in 1928 and featuring Atatürk and his revolutionary cohorts. Cumhuriyet Caddesi, the main street heading north from the square, is lined with travel agencies, currency-exchange offices, and airline ticket offices. Farther up Cumhuriyet, Vali Konağı Caddesi splits off from the avenue and veers right, taking you to Nişantaşı, the city's high-fashion district. ✉ Beyoglu.

🍴 Restaurants

The lively Beyoğlu district has everything from holes in the wall serving delicious home cooking to some of Istanbul's sleekest restaurants.

Aheste
$$$$ | ECLECTIC | A casual café by day and an inviting bistro venue by night, stylish Aheste (meaning "slowly" in

Persian) offers a small but appealing menu consisting mainly of hot and cold meze with some Persian, Ottoman, and Middle Eastern influences with contemporary twists; the sea beans with smoked yogurt and rose petals and the wild rice with currants and herbs are particularly tasty. Prices are a bit high, but the friendly, laid-back service and hip-yet-cozy atmosphere make up for it. **Known for:** innovative fusion cuisine; extensive wine and cocktail list; chef's tasting menu. $ Average main: 130 TL ✉ Mesrutiyet Cad. 107/F, Asmalımescit, Beyoglu ☎ 212/243–2633 ⊕ www. ahesterestaurant.com ☾ No dinner Sun. No lunch Mon.

Antiochia
$$ | TURKISH | This restaurant with exposed brick walls in the popular Tünel area of Beyoğlu offers specialties of Turkey's Arab-influenced southeastern Hatay province. The menu includes a variety of

Drinks with a View

In recent years, venues in Istanbul have been aiming high, literally, as an increasing number of savvy entrepreneurs take advantage of the city's greatest natural asset—its spectacular views. The proliferation of open rooftop dining and nightlife spots has been especially pronounced in the Beyoğlu neighborhood, which sits on a ridge overlooking the Bosphorus, the Golden Horn, and the sights of Sultanahmet.

With the notable exception of **Mikla,** an upscale restaurant and sophisticated roof bar at the top of the 18-story Marmara Pera Hotel that is one of the city's best, most of the venues offering panoramic views of the city tend to fall flat when it comes to food. But they make great places for a pre- or post-dinner drink—where else in the world can you gaze at two continents with a martini in hand?

In Beyoğlu, **Leb-i Derya** has an upper level where you can watch the sun set over the Bosphorus from a breezy, roofless terrace that's open in summer. **5. Kat** in Cihangir is a restaurant and lounge offering excellent views of the Bosphorus from both its indoor section and summer-only upper-level deck. Also in summer, the open-air terrace at **Balkon** in Asmalımescit houses a restaurant and bar with excellent views of the Golden Horn.

meze and kebabs with intense flavors and served with Antiochia's uncommonly tasty chile pepper–rubbed flatbread. **Known for:** regional cuisine; cozy interior; central location. [$] *Average main: 50 TL* ✉ *General Yazgan Sok. 3, Asmalımescit, Beyoglu* ☎ *212/292–1100* 🌐 *www.antiochiaconcept.com* 🕒 *Closed Sun.*

Demeti Meyhanesi

$$ | **TURKISH** | The cozy, homey atmosphere of Demeti, with its cabinets filled with antiques, opens up to a small balcony with an excellent view of the Bosphorus. The menu is meze-heavy, with the traditional small dishes prepared fresh every day, including such unique choices as *domates turşusu* (pickled tomatoes), pomegranate salad, and a börek filled with fish, eggplant, and cheese. **Known for:** outdoor seating with a view; home-cooked meze; daily fresh fish options. [$] *Average main: 40 TL* ✉ *Şimşirci Sok. 6/1, Beyoglu* ☎ *212/244–0628* 🌐 *demeti.com.tr.*

Fıccın

$ | **TURKISH** | Occupying a number of rooms and storefronts on both sides of narrow Kallavi Sokak, this down-to-earth restaurant is best known for Turkish standards and specialties of the Circassian kitchen, including the signature fıccın, a savory pastry filled with ground meat. The menu, which changes daily, always includes a range of mezes—many of them vegetarian—as well as a handful of simple meat and fish dishes, and prices are extremely reasonable. **Known for:** regional cuisine, including Circassian chicken; plentiful outdoor seating; seasonal meze. [$] *Average main: 37 TL* ✉ *Kallavi Sok. 7/1–13/1, Beyoglu* ☎ *212/293–3786* 🌐 *www.ficcin.com.*

Hala Mantı

$ | **TURKISH** | As its name suggests, this homey restaurant on a side street not far from İstiklal Caddesi specializes in ravioli-like *mantı* (small pockets of pasta filled with ground meat); *hingal* (a variation eaten in the Caucasus with a cheese-and-potato filling) is also served.

Beer in Turkey

🍴

For years, visitors to Turkey basically had one choice when ordering beer: Efes. These days, international brands are also brewed locally, and imports like Guinness, Leffe, Corona, and Heineken are available, too, though they are often very pricey. A handful of bars, including The United Pub in Beşiktaş and Zeplin Pub in Kadıköy pride themselves on having a broader-than-usual selection. Efes itself has branched out and now makes several different brews (including Efes Dark and Efes Light), and also brews the somewhat maltier Bomonti—Turkey's first beer, recently revived as a nostalgic brand. But if you want to drink local, look for Gara Güzü, a small new Muğla-based label that's making a splash despite its (so far) limited distribution; it makes a variety of beers, including a blonde ale and an amber one, which are both very good. Istanbul is also home to two brewpubs, the Bosphorus Brewing Company in the Gayrettepe district and the frankly inferior Taps on the Bosphorus, just north of Bebek.

Gözleme (a type of very thin flatbread filled with ingredients such as cheese and spinach) is cooked on a huge griddle as you watch and very good here; other options include tasty home-style soups and vegetable and meat dishes. **Known for:** fresh-made gözleme; simple and cozy atmosphere; hearty traditional cuisine. [$] *Average main: 24 TL* ✉ *Çukurlu Çeşme Sok. 14/A, Beyoglu* ☎ *212/293–7531.*

Hayvore

$ | TURKISH | This informal restaurant just off İstiklal Caddesi turns out hearty specialties of Turkey's Black Sea coast at very affordable prices. There's no menu, but the daily offerings (just point to what you want) usually include several items with anchovies—a mainstay of the region's cooking—as well as meat dishes like lamb stew and vegetarian alternatives made with chickpeas, baked beans, bulgur pilaf, and pickled vegetables. **Known for:** Black Sea cornbread; casual atmosphere; central location. [$] *Average main: 24 TL* ✉ *Turnacıbaşı Sok. 4, Beyoglu* ☎ *212/245–7501* 🌐 *www.hayvore.com.tr.*

Helvetia

$ | TURKISH | The menu at Helvetia changes daily, but there are always at least a dozen home-cooked dishes on offer at this very affordable restaurant, ranging from meat dishes to plentiful vegetarian options. The atmosphere is laid-back, and the easiest way to order is to simply point at what you want from the day's specials, which are displayed in front of the open kitchen; ask for a mixed plate if you'd like to try several small portions. **Known for:** seasonal, changing menu; casual, relaxed atmosphere; extensive vegetarian selections. [$] *Average main: 15 TL* ✉ *General Yazgan Sok. 8/A, Beyoglu* ☎ *212/245–8780* 🕒 *No lunch Sun.*

Kafe Ara

$$ | CONTEMPORARY | This popular, cozy hangout, named after famous Turkish photographer Ara Güler, whose black-and-white photographs of Istanbul line the walls, is a nice place for a light meal or cup of coffee. The menu includes several Turkish meat dishes along with more international fare, such as grilled entrecôte (sirloin) steak with pommes frites or tagliatelle with salmon. **Known for:** alfresco seating out front; wide variety of salads and pastas; warm and inviting atmosphere. [$] *Average main: 37 TL* ✉ *Tosbağı Sok. 2, Galatasaray, Beyoglu* ☎ *212/245–4105.*

Meze by Lemon Tree

$$$ | **TURKISH** | The meze selection in this trendy and attractive spot changes seasonally and even daily, and puts a clever international spin on traditional favorites—a gazpacho-like, basil-infused version of *acılı ezme* (red pepper spread) is served in a shot glass—while others, such as sea bream with chickpeas and mustard sauce, are friendly chef-owner Gençay Üçok's unique creations. Main dishes include standouts like lamb sirloin with baked potatoes and beets and a delicious variation on sea bass cooked in paper. **Known for:** varied seasonal meze; innovative presentations; hip atmosphere. [$] *Average main: 70 TL* ✉ *Meşrutiyet Cad. 83/B, Beyoglu* ☎ *212/252–8302* 🌐 *www.mezze.com.tr.*

★ **Mikla**

$$$$ | **CONTEMPORARY** | With sleek, contemporary decor and a stunning 360-degree view of Istanbul from the top floor of the 18-story Marmara Pera Hotel, Mikla is the dramatic setting for prestigious American-trained Turkish-Finnish chef Mehmet Gürs's modern Anatolian cuisine. Sophisticated dishes of domestically sourced ingredients offer unique flavor combinations rarely seen in traditional Turkish cuisine, such as grilled dentex (a Mediterranean fish) served with olives, charred red peppers, and pistachio puree, or a dessert of sour- cherry compote with bulgur wheat and *lor* cheese (similar to ricotta). **Known for:** prix-fixe menu and tasting menus only; extensive wine list of Turkish and international wines; sweeping views. [$] *Average main: 275 TL* ✉ *Marmara Pera Hotel, Meşrutiyet Cad. 15, Beyoglu* ☎ *212/293–5656* 🌐 *www.miklarestaurant.com* 🕒 *Closed Sun. No lunch.*

★ **Nicole**

$$$$ | **MEDITERRANEAN** | Young French-trained chefs Kaan Sakarya and Aylin Yazıcıoğlu have quickly earned a reputation as among the best in town since opening Nicole atop the Tomtom Suites. Their prix-fixe menu of what they describe as "Mediterranean flavors with modern presentation" changes every six weeks or so based on seasonal ingredients they find at local markets. **Known for:** stunning views; boutique Turkish wines; innovative cuisine. [$] *Average main: 300 TL* ✉ *Tomtom Suites, Boğazkesen Cad., Tomtom Kaptan Sok. 18, Beyoglu* ☎ *212/292–4467* 🌐 *www.nicole.com.tr* 🕒 *Closed Sun. and Mon. No lunch.*

Sofyalı 9

$$ | **TURKISH** | With Greek music playing in the background, photographs of old Istanbul on the walls, and friendly, laid-back surroundings on a lively backstreet in Beyoğlu's Asmalımescit area, the quaint atmosphere here elevates the classic meyhane food. The meze, whether from the regular menu or the daily specials, and the hot appetizers are more notable than the main dishes; try the zucchini with walnuts in yogurt, or the Albanian-style fried liver. **Known for:** central location; cozy, vintage atmosphere; wide selection of meze. [$] *Average main: 45 TL* ✉ *Sofyalı Sok. 9, Beyoglu* ☎ *212/252–3810* 🌐 *www.sofyali.com.tr* 🕒 *No lunch weekends.*

★ **Yeni Lokanta**

$$$ | **TURKISH** | Rising chef Civan Er puts a unique and contemporary twist on traditional Turkish dishes, using ingredients sourced from local producers in different regions of the country. The menu consists mainly of small plates that offer innovative flavor combinations, as in sweet-and-sour *kısır* (tabbouleh) made with a sour-cherry infusion, or spicy, rustic sucuk sausage with walnuts and served on top of a borlotti bean puree. **Known for:** contemporary vibe; dishes prepared in a wood-fired oven; tasting menu. [$] *Average main: 115 TL* ✉ *Kumbaracı Yokuşu 66, Beyoglu* ☎ *212/292–2550* 🌐 *www.yenilokanta.com* 🕒 *Closed Sun.*

Zübeyir Ocakbaşı

$$ | **TURKISH** | This *ocakbaşı*, or grill house, is popular for its delicious food, authentic

This Istanbul street vendor is selling freshly roasted chestnuts.

feel, and especially lively atmosphere. The wide variety of kebabs are cooked on a special grill over hardwood coals—part of the fun here is watching the chefs at work—and include some cuts of meat not found on the average kebab menu, such as *kaburga* (lamb ribs). **Known for:** tasty, unique meze; meat cooked on an open grill; bustling atmosphere. $ *Average main: 50 TL* ⊠ *Bekar Sok. 28, Beyoglu* ☎ *212/293–3951* ⊕ *www.zubeyirocakbasi.com.tr.*

🛏 Hotels

The Beyoğlu district, only a 15- or 20-minute tram ride or cab ride from the sights of Sultanahmet, has emerged as an attractive alternative to the Old City. Entrepreneurs have caught on to the tourism potential of the historic area and are restoring elegant, century-old buildings and giving them new life as hotels. Staying near Taksim Square or in one of Beyoğlu's trendy sub-neighborhoods— such as Şişhane/Tünel, Cihangir, Galata, or Karaköy—puts you closer to Istanbul's best restaurants and nightlife spots and also gives you a chance to stroll through the area's lively backstreets.

Adahan Istanbul

$$ | HOTEL | An elegant apartment building from 1874 has been lovingly restored by architect-owner Sedat Sırrı Aklan and turned into a charming boutique hotel where no two rooms are exactly alike. **Pros:** highly atmospheric public spaces; excellent homemade breakfast; very comfortable beds. **Cons:** staff is a little inexperienced and could speak better English; no real minibar or room service available; neighborhood can be noisy at night, especially on weekends. $ *Rooms from: €120* ⊠ *General Yazgan Sok. 14, Beyoglu* ☎ *212/243–8581* ⊕ *www.adahanistanbul. com* 🛏 *49 rooms* ⦿ *Free Breakfast.*

Ansen Suites

$$ | HOTEL | The roomy, open-plan "suites" in this stylish and hip early-20th-century building are arranged with separate sleeping and living areas and decorated in a smart, minimalist style, with slightly retro touches; a few on the upper floors

have excellent views of the Golden Horn. **Pros:** large, attractive accommodations; just steps from nightlife and entertainment; some rooms have Golden Horn views. **Cons:** though units are set up as apartments, they don't have kitchenettes; service, and staff's English, could be improved; area can be noisy at night. [$] *Rooms from: €70* ✉ *Meşrutiyet Cad. 70, Tepebaşı, Beyoglu* ☎ *212/245–8808* 🌐 *www.ansensuites.com* 🛏 *11 suites* 🍴 *Free Breakfast.*

Divan Istanbul

$$$$ | HOTEL | An Istanbul institution established in 1956 offers grand luxury that brings together authentic Turkish style and contemporary design elements, from the traditional Anatolian kilims and textiles in the rooms to the spectacular flowerlike chandeliers by American glass artist Robert DuGrenier in the lobby. **Pros:** first-class service; beautiful half-Olympic-size indoor pool; excellent breakfast (not included in all room rates). **Cons:** fairly uninteresting city views from most rooms; expensive food and beverages; surrounding area can be noisy. [$] *Rooms from: €150* ✉ *Asker Ocağı Cad. 1, Taksim* ☎ *212/315–5500* 🌐 *www.divan.com.tr* 🛏 *190 rooms* 🍴 *No meals.*

Gezi Hotel Bosphorus

$$$ | HOTEL | Contemporary, minimalist decor infuses a bit more personality than you'll find in most business-caliber hotels, and rooms in this 11-story building have views of the Bosphorus, the park, or the city. **Pros:** central location just across from Taksim's Gezi Parkı; classy atmosphere; helpful staff. **Cons:** most rooms and bathrooms are small; rooms on lower floors don't have much of a view; breakfast could be better. [$] *Rooms from: €120* ✉ *Mete Cad. 34, Taksim* ☎ *212/393–2700* 🌐 *www.gezibosphorus.com* 🛏 *67 rooms* 🍴 *Free Breakfast.*

★ Pera Palace Hotel

$$$$ | HOTEL | Extensive restoration has brought this Istanbul landmark—founded in 1892 to provide upscale accommodations for travelers arriving on the Orient Express—back to its former glory, with beautifully outfitted rooms and plenty of period decorations and antique furniture. **Pros:** historic venue; luxurious facilities; attentive staff. **Cons:** some rooms have small bathrooms; rooms on back side look onto street with lots of traffic; expensive food and drinks. [$] *Rooms from: €190* ✉ *Meşrutiyet Cad. 52, Tepebaşı, Beyoglu* ☎ *212/377–4000* 🌐 *www.perapalace.com* 🛏 *115 rooms* 🍴 *No meals.*

★ Tomtom Suites

$$$$ | HOTEL | A restored 1901 residence that once housed Franciscan nuns offers superb accommodations and authentic character, with guest rooms furnished with warm woods, textiles in natural colors, high ceilings, and original artwork. **Pros:** historic building with romantic ambience; on quiet street; helpful, welcoming staff. **Cons:** only upper room categories have sea views; reached via steep streets; rather high rates, especially considering lack of fitness facilities. [$] *Rooms from: €130* ✉ *Boğazkesen Cad., Tomtom Kaptan Sok. 18, Beyoglu* ☎ *212/292–4949* 🌐 *www.tomtomsuites.com* 🛏 *20 suites* 🍴 *Free Breakfast.*

Witt Istanbul Hotel

$$$ | HOTEL | All accommodations at this stylish boutique hotel in the popular Cihangir neighborhood are suites—essentially very large open-plan apartments with separate sleeping and living areas and (in most) "kitchenettes" with marble countertops—and the design is contemporary and überchic: hardwood floors, exposed concrete ceilings, neutral tones, and designer lamps and furniture. **Pros:** swanky design aesthetic; location in quiet residential neighborhood with trendy café scene; personalized service. **Cons:** steep uphill walk from nearby tram stop; venue is not that family-friendly; minimal public spaces. [$] *Rooms from: €175* ✉ *Defterdar Yokuşu 26, Beyoglu* ☎ *212/293–1500* 🌐 *www.wittistanbul.com* 🛏 *18* 🍴 *Breakfast.*

☻ Nightlife

Istanbul's nightlife still revolves, in many ways, around its *meyhanes*, the tavern-like restaurants where long nights are spent nibbling on meze and sipping the anise-flavored spirit *rakı*. The atmosphere at these places—mostly found in the lively Beyoğlu area—is jovial, friendly, and worth experiencing. But there are lots of other options, too, again mostly in Beyoğlu, which has everything from grungy American-style dive bars to sophisticated lounges, performance spaces that host world-class live acts, and dance clubs. In recent years, the trend in the neighborhood has been literally upward, with the opening of rooftop bars that offer stunning views and fresh breezes.

BARS AND LOUNGES
5. Kat

BARS/PUBS | A rather pricey restaurant that turns into a trendy lounge/bar later in the evening, 5. Kat is on the fifth floor of an unassuming building in the quiet Cihangir neighborhood and offers wonderful views of the Bosphorus—along with great cocktails. With its wooden furniture and potted plants, the upper-level terrace (open only in warm months) makes you feel like you're passing the time on somebody's roof deck. ⊠ *Soğancı Sok. 3, Cihangir, Beyoglu* ☎ *212/293-3774* ⊕ *www.5kat.com.*

Balkon

BARS/PUBS | A sixth-floor bar and lounge, Balkon has excellent views of the Golden Horn and a laid-back outdoor deck, now located atop the new By Murat Crown Hotel. Drink prices are reasonable compared to those at most other rooftop bars in the area. ⊠ *Şehbender Sok. 5, Beyoglu* ☎ *212/293-2052* ⊕ *www. balkonbeyoglu.com.*

★ Leb-i Derya

BARS/PUBS | The reward for finding this sixth-floor rooftop restaurant and bar—in an apartment building with only a small sign out front—is a magnificent view overlooking the Bosphorus and the Old City. The small venue is popular with an almost-too-hip crowd of locals and expats who come for the cocktails and the views, so you may have to wait for a table or stand by the bar if you show up without reservations. ⊠ *Kumbaracı Yokuşu 57/6, Beyoglu* ☎ *212/293-4989* ⊕ *www.lebiderya.com.*

Şahika

BARS/PUBS | On a narrow street lined with basic beer joints and meyhanes serving mostly identical food menus, Şahika offers something more unusual. The lively, multistory venue has a different concept and ambience on each level, ranging from a pub atmosphere on the street level, to casual lounge areas on the middle floors, to a clublike vibe on the terrace, which also has excellent views of the Golden Horn. ⊠ *Nevizade Sok. 5, Beyoglu* ☎ *212/249-6196* ⊕ *www.sahika.com.tr.*

JAZZ CLUBS
Nardis Jazz Club

MUSIC CLUBS | One of Istanbul's few dedicated jazz venues, the well-regarded Nardis Jazz Club hosts mainly Turkish musicians and the occasional big name from abroad. The cozy, intimate space only has room for 110, so reservations are strongly recommended. The club is closed Sundays and during the entire month of August. ⊠ *Kuledibi Sok. 14, Beyoglu* ☎ *212/244-6327* ⊕ *www.nardisjazz.com.*

MUSIC VENUES
★ Salon İKSV

MUSIC CLUBS | This top-notch performance space is housed in the headquarters and cultural center of the Istanbul Foundation for Culture and Arts (İKSV), one of the city's most important arts organizations. The concert lineup for this intimate venue features both local and international acts spanning a wide range of genres, including jazz, rock, alternative, and world music. ⊠ *Sadi Konuralp Cad. 5, Şişhane, Beyoglu* ☎ *212/334-0841 for ticket info and box office (Mon.–Sat. 10–6)* ⊕ *www. saloniksv.com* ☾ *Closed June–mid-Sept.*

🎟 Performing Arts

PERFORMANCE VENUES

Akbank Sanat

ARTS CENTERS | Sponsored by one of Turkey's largest private banks, the six-story, multipurpose Akbank Sanat (Akbank Art Center) hosts regular classical music and jazz concerts, including the Akbank Jazz Festival, held annually over several weeks in fall. More than 700 other events are held at the center each year, including modern dance performances, theater productions, film screenings, and art exhibitions. ⊠ İstiklal Cad. 8, Beyoglu ☎ 212/252–3500 ⊕ www.akbanksanat. com ⊙ Closed Aug.

Garajistanbul

CONCERTS | Located in the basement of a parking lot near Galatasaray Square, Garajistanbul is an experimental venue that hosts an eclectic array of concerts, as well as contemporary dance and theater, and literary and artistic events. ⊠ Yeni Çarşı Cad., Kaymakam Reşit Bey Sok. 11/A, Galatasaray, Beyoglu ☎ 212/244–4499 ⊕ www.garajistanbul. org ⊙ Closed June–Sept.

WHIRLING DERVISHES

Mevlâna Education and Culture Society

DANCE | The Mevlâna Education and Culture Society (MEKDER) is one of the local dervish groups and cultural associations that holds sema ceremonies at 5 pm each Sunday at the Galata Mevlevihanesi. The ceremonies last about an hour and include traditional Mevlevi music and ritual whirling. Tickets cost 90 TL. ⊠ Galata Mevlevihanesi, Galip Dede Cad. 15, Beyoglu ☎ 216/349–1114 ⊕ www. mekder.org.

🛍 Shopping

ANTIQUES

★ Alaturca

ANTIQUES/COLLECTIBLES | Styled more like a grand private mansion than a store, Alaturca has four floors that house a carefully selected—and very high-end—collection of antiques, including artwork, ceramics, metalwork, and Ottoman calligraphy. Just a small fraction of proprietor Erkal Aksoy's extensive collection of antique carpets and kilims is on display here. ⊠ Faik Paşa Cad. 4, Çukurcuma, Beyoglu ☎ 212/245–2933 ⊕ www. alaturcahouse.com.

Artrium

ANTIQUES/COLLECTIBLES | Artrium has a range of antique items, including a fascinating collection of old prints and paintings, as well as some interesting ceramics, jewelry, and other handicrafts and gift items. ⊠ Müellif Sok. 12, Beyoglu ☎ 212/251–4302 ⊕ www.artrium.com.tr.

Tombak

ANTIQUES/COLLECTIBLES | One of the area's longest-established antiques dealers stocks an eclectic collection of antique metal objects, tablewares, lamps, paintings, clocks, jewelry, and other interesting finds. ⊠ Çukurcuma Camii Sok. 7, Çukurcuma, Beyoglu ☎ 212/244–3681.

BOOKS

Denizler Kitabevi

BOOKS/STATIONERY | This shop has a selection of antiquarian books—primarily in English and French, focusing on Turkish history and nautical subjects—along with old maps, prints, and a small section of new books. ⊠ İstiklal Cad. 199/A, Beyoglu ☎ 212/249–8893 ⊕ www.denizlerkitabevi.com.

Homer Kitabevi

BOOKS/STATIONERY | One of Istanbul's best bookstores, Homer carries an impeccable selection of English-language books, especially ones dealing with the politics and history of Turkey and the Middle East. ⊠ Yeni Çarşı Caddesi No: 52, Galatasaray, Beyoglu ☎ 212/249–5902 ⊕ www.homerbooks.com.

Istanbul Kitapçısı

BOOKS/STATIONERY | This municipality-run bookshop near the Tünel funicular entrance just off İstiklal Caddesi carries

The centuries-old practice of smoking tobacco in a *nargile,* also known as a hookah or water pipe

a broad range of coffee-table books and other titles on Istanbul and Turkey, as well as arty and historical postcards and small gift items. There are also branches in the Taksim metro station and at the Kadıköy and Eminönü ferry docks. ⊠ *Tünel Meydanı, Beyoglu* ☎ *212/292–7692* ⊕ *www.istanbulkitapcisi.com.*

Pandora

BOOKS/STATIONERY | One of Turkey's premier booksellers for more than two decades, Pandora has an upstairs floor dedicated to English-language works and carries an impressive selection of books in all genres, with a particular emphasis on nonfiction. A second branch in Nişantaşı (Vali Konağı Cad. 5) also carries a good selection of English-language books, along with nice stationery and small gifts. ⊠ *Büyükparmakkapı Sok. 3/A, Beyoglu* ☎ *212/243–3503* ⊕ *www.pandora.com.tr.*

Robinson Crusoe

BOOKS/STATIONERY | This Beyoğlu institution, now associated with the local arts institution SALT, stocks a well-chosen

selection that includes fiction and nonfiction in English, with a focus on the arts, architecture, and urban culture. Specialty magazines and journals are also available. ⊠ *SALT Beyoğlu, İstiklal Cad. 136, 4th fl., Beyoglu* ☎ *212/293–6968* ⊕ *www.rob389.com.*

CLOTHING
Mavi

CLOTHING | Turkey's homegrown jean company, Mavi (which means "blue" in Turkish), has come a long way since its founding in 1991, with stores now in dozens of countries. The flagship Istanbul store near the top of İstiklal Caddesi (there are two other, smaller, branches farther down the avenue) carries the brand's signature jeans and casual wear, as well as a collection of hip Istanbul-themed T-shirts created by different guest designers. ⊠ *İstiklal Cad. 123/A, Beyoglu* ☎ *212/244–6255* ⊕ *www.mavi.com.*

HANDICRAFTS

Amorf

HOUSEHOLD ITEMS/FURNITURE | Rustic cutting boards, bowls, mortar-and-pestles, and other kitchen accessories handmade from olive and walnut wood are among the traveler-friendly offerings at this Çukurcuma workshop, which also produces unique wooden furniture. ⊠ *Ağa Hamamı Sok. 11/A, Çukurcuma, Beyoglu* ☎ *533/269–4168.*

Nahıl

LOCAL SPECIALTIES | Everything in this homey store near Taksim Square—handbags, necklaces, key chains, baby booties, sachets, cards, natural soaps, bath sets, coasters, ornaments, and more—is handcrafted by women from across Turkey. The NGO that runs the shop, which also has a selection of vintage clothing for sale in back, helps women in underdeveloped communities find a sustainable source of income through their handiwork. Profits support centers for women and children around the country. ⊠ *Bekar Sok. 17, Beyoglu* ☎ *212/251–9085* ⊕ *www.nahil.com.tr.*

Sır Çini

CERAMICS/GLASSWARE | Having relocated from Galata to Beyoğlu, Sır Çini is the workshop and showroom of Sadullah Çekmece, a craftsman and artist who makes both traditional and contemporary interpretations of İznik and Küthaya ceramics and sells them at reasonable prices. ⊠ *Tomtom Mahallesi, Örtme Altı Sk. No:20, Beyoglu* ☎ *212/293–3661* ⊕ *www.sircini.com.*

3rd Culture

HOUSEHOLD ITEMS/FURNITURE | Globe-trotting pair Zeynep and Emre Rende have devoted their design and photography talents to creating home accessories, gifts, furniture, and images "inspired by the world, created in Istanbul." West African fabrics adorn lamps and pillows made by local Turkish craftspeople, and Emre's global portraits feature in framed prints and on iPhone cases. ⊠ *Çukurcuma Cad. 38/2, Çukurcuma, Beyoglu* ☎ *543/732–3633* ⊕ *www.3rdcultureproject.com.*

JEWELRY

Mor

JEWELRY/ACCESSORIES | On a side street off İstiklal Caddesi, Mor displays the work of a brother-and-sister designer pair who make funky, bold jewelry that incorporates antique and ethnic elements into modern designs. The chunky pieces, mostly made using bronze and stones, are affordably priced. ⊠ *Turnacıbaşı Sok. 10/B, Beyoglu* ☎ *212/292–8817.*

SPECIALTY FOODS

Hacı Bekir

FOOD/CANDY | Ali Muhiddin Hacı Bekir founded his sweets business back in 1777 and is considered the inventor of Turkish delight. Today, the Hacı Bekir stores run by his descendants are still among the best places to buy the delicacy, which comes in a variety of different types—including such uncommon flavors as pomegranate with pistachios—and is sold fresh by the kilo or prepackaged. The original location is in Eminönü, on a backstreet just east of the Yeni Cami, and there is also a branch on İstiklal Caddesi. ⊠ *İstiklal Cad. 83/A, Beyoglu* ☎ *212/244–2804* ⊕ *www.hacibekir.com.tr.*

Galata and Karaköy

Just across the Galata Bridge from Eminönü, Karaköy was formerly a major port and its busy trading houses and banks made the neighborhood the economic hub of the late Ottoman Empire. Today, only ferryboats and cruise ships stop here, but the area still has a historic feel to it: Ottoman mosques line the waterfront, and Istanbul's Jewish Museum is also here. It's also home to the Istanbul Modern, which is being renovated and has temporarily relocated to a space in Beyoglu. In the last few years, Karaköy has started to become gentrified, with cafés, restaurants, art galleries, boutiques, and hotels elbowing out dingy hardware stores and import-export offices. Galataport, a massive redevelopment project slated for the area, is likely to further revitalize the shoreline but also erase much of its historic character.

Just uphill from Karaköy is Galata, one of Istanbul's oldest neighborhoods, dominated by the 14th-century Galata Tower about halfway up the slope. Like Karaköy, Galata has become increasingly popular and gentrified in recent years, though the neighborhood's long history is still palpable. Serdar-ı Ekrem, one of the main streets leading off the square around the Galata Tower, is lined with cafés and cutting-edge fashion designers' boutiques.

Sights

Galata Tower (*Galata Kulesi*)
BUILDING | The Galata area was a thriving Italian settlement both before and after the fall of Constantinople, and the Genoese built this tower as part of their fortifications in 1348, when they controlled the northern shore of the Golden Horn. The hillside location provided good defense, as well as a perch from which to monitor the comings and goings of vessels in the sea lanes below. The 220-foot tower later served at times as a jail and at others as a fire tower and now houses a restaurant at the top. The viewing gallery, which offers fabulous panoramic views of the city and across the Golden Horn and Sea of Marmara, is accessible by elevator and open during the day, for a rather steep fee—though it bears noting that similar views can be had at rooftop cafés and restaurants around the area. ✉ *Büyük Hendek Cad., Galata* ☎ *212/293–8180* 🎫 *25 TL.*

Jewish Museum of Turkey
MUSEUM | The history of the Jews in Turkey is much more extensive and colorful than the size of this small museum might suggest. Nevertheless, the museum provides a fascinating glimpse into the lives of Turkish Jews, whose presence in Anatolia is traced back to as early as the 4th century BC. In 1492, the Spanish Inquisition drove Sephardic Jews from Spain and Portugal, and Sultan Beyazıt II welcomed the refugees to the Ottoman Empire. A large Jewish population thrived here for centuries, and some older Turkish Jews still speak a dialect of medieval Spanish called Ladino, or Judeo-Spanish. Today, Turkey's Jewish community numbers about 23,000, most of whom live in Istanbul, which has 18 active synagogues (3 of which are on the Princes' Islands). The museum exhibits, most of them based on items donated by local Jewish families, include photographs, documents, and an ethnographic section with changing exhibits on subjects such as marriage traditions. There are also religious items brought from some very old (no longer active) synagogues in other parts of Turkey. ✉ *Bereketzade Mah., Büyük Hendek Cad. 39, Galata* ☎ *212/292–6333* 🌐 *www.muze500.com* 🎫 *10 TL* 🕒 *Closed Sat.*

Restaurants

Karaköy and Galata also have an increasing range of dining options, often at more favorable prices than across the bridge in Sultanahmet.

Gümrük Karaköy
$$$ | **MEDITERRANEAN** | Greek chef Stavrianni Zervakakou brings a skillful hand and a variety of Mediterranean influences to her menu at this Karaköy restaurant, where the impeccable service matches the top-notch food. Lighter fare such as a gourmet version of a classic Istanbul fish sandwich is available throughout the day, while dinner specials include adventurous preparations such as smoked sardine with melon or *keşkek* (a traditional wheat stew) with cinnamon and grilled kidney. **Known for:** beautiful, quirky decorations; innovative Mediterranean cuisine; sidewalk seating. $ *Average main: 45 TL*

Continued on page 146

SHOPPING IN ISTANBUL
The Grand Bazaar & the Spice Market

Istanbul, historically one of the most important stops on the Silk Road, which linked the East and West through commerce, is today still a fabulous place to shop. You can find everything from the quintessential woven carpet to cheap trinkets, from antique copper trays to faux Prada bags. At the center of it all is the sometimes chaotic Grand Bazaar, also known as the Kapalı Çarşı or "Covered Bazar," which in many ways can be considered the great-grandmother of the modern shopping mall: it's been around since the 15th century, has more than 20 entrances, covers about 65 streets, and is said to have some 4,000 shops. It can be a bit intense, but it's a must-see. The following pages will help you get oriented so the experience will be less daunting. For comparison, check out the Spice Market in Eminönü; it's also several centuries old but specializes in spices and food items and is much calmer. It's great place to find snack items and Turkish delicacies to take home (Turkish delight, anyone?).

THE GRAND BAZAAR

This behemoth of a shopping complex was built by Mehmet II (the Conqueror) in 1461 over several of the main Byzantine shopping streets and expanded over the years. Today it's almost a town unto itself, with its own restaurants, tea houses, mosques, banks, exchange bureaus, post office, police station, health clinic, and several bathrooms nestled among the myriad shops.

Streets in the bazaar are named after the tradespeople who traditionally had businesses there, with colorful names in Turkish like "slipper-makers street," "fez-makers street," and "mirror-makers street." Today, although there's little correspondence between street names and the shops now found on them, the bazaar is still organized roughly by type of merchandise: gold and silver jewelry shops line the prestigious main street, most of the leather stores are in their own wing, carpet shops are clustered primarily in the center, and souvenirs are found throughout. The amazingly polylingual sellers are all anxious to reassure you that you do not have to buy . . . just drink a glass of tea while you browse through leather goods, carpets, clothing (including counterfeit brand names), brass and copper items, furniture, ceramics, and gold and silver jewelry.

✉ Yeniçeriler Cad. and Çadırcılar Cad.
🕐 Mon.–Sat. 8:30–7

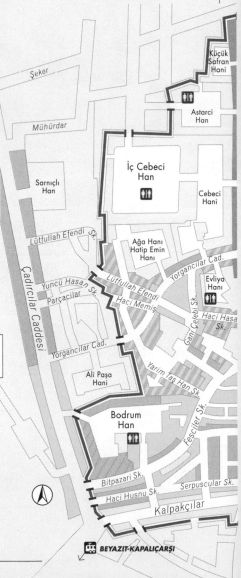

KEY	
▢ Gold	▢ Antiques
▢ Carpets	▢ Silver
▢ Denimwear	◀❙▶ Main Gates
▢ Copper	🚋 T1 Tram
▢ Fabric	🚻 Restroom
▢ Souvenirs	🍴 Restaurant
▢ Leather	

Grand Bazaar Shops

THE BEDESTEN

The domed *iç bedesten* (inner bazaar), aka the Cevahir Bedesteni, once a secure fortress in the heart of the market, is the oldest part of the bazaar and historically where the most valuable goods were kept. Today the *bedesten* is the place to find unique items: it's filled with tiny shops selling an array of antiques that are of generally better quality than the souvenirs sold in the rest of the bazaar. Here you can find anything from pocket watches to vintage cigarette tins, from jewelry to Armenian and Greek religious items. Look for the double-headed Byzantine eagle over the door and you'll know you've found the heart of the bazaar.

WHAT TO BUY

JEWELRY

There are over 370 jewelry shops in the bazaar, and you'll find as many locals in them as tourists. Gold and silver jewelry are sold by weight, based on the going market price plus extra for labor, so there's room for bargaining. Sterling silver pieces should have a hallmark. In terms of semiprecious stones, amber and turquoise are especially popular.

CERAMICS

Turkey's ceramics tradition goes back to Ottoman times. Today, the most important distinction is between İznik and Kütahya designs; traditional İznik designs, recognizable by the blue, red, and green colors on a white background, are more intricate and more expensive. You'll see gorgeous bowls and plates in both styles, but note that many are coated with lead glazes and are not safe for use with metal utensils or hot food. Medium-size bowls and plates go for between 50-100 TL. Decorative tiles can be made of either ceramic or quartz, with quartz tiles selling for two to three times more than ceramic tiles.

METALWARE (COPPER & BRASSWARE)

Turkey has a long tradition of metalworking, and you can find both new and antique copper and brass items engraved with elaborate designs. Round copper trays can run well into the hundreds of lira for large, intricately worked items if they're new, and into the thousands for antiques. Small serving trays can be acquired for around 100 TL. Most copper items are plated with tin to make them safe to eat from and therefore appear silver-gray in color. You can find pure copper items but these are suitable for decorative purposes only. Brass items like samovars and pitchers can be shiny if unoxidized or gray-black if oxidized. In general, brass costs more than copper because it's harder to work. Middle Eastern-style lanterns made of worked metal and glass are also neat to check out.

INLAID-WOOD ITEMS

You'll see a lot of wood items at the bazaar, beautifully inlaid with mother-of-pearl and different colored woods. Try to avoid imitation inlay: one clue that the inlay is fake is if the mother-of-pearl sections in the design are too uniform in color. You can also usually tell by weight and touch if a backgammon board is plastic. Price is also a dead giveaway: fake-inlay backgammon boards can be had for around 75 TL, whereas those made of walnut and real mother-of-pearl can go for 250-400 TL for a medium-size board. Prices vary based on the amount of inlay and intricacy.

LEATHER

Leather is a big industry in Turkey, and the Grand Bazaar has no shortage of stores selling leather jackets, bags, wallets, and, occasionally, shoes. When buying leather goods, look carefully at the quality of the workmanship, which can be assessed by examining seams, zippers, and linings. Imitation leather is, unfortunately, fairly widespread, and even dealers say they sometimes can't tell what's fake and what's not—one clue is that real leather is a bit softer than artificial leather. "Genuine fake" designer bags [i.e., imitation designer bags made with (supposedly) real leather] abound in the Bazaar and sell for around 250 TL.

SOUVENIRS AND GIFTS

The bazaar is chock-full of trinkets aimed at tourists—including ornaments featuring the ubiquitous evil-eye beads, Turkish tea sets, and fake designer clothing—but you can also find some nice souvenirs and gift items. Textiles like woven or embroidered pillow covers, and pashmina and silk scarves, are inexpensive (15-30 TL apiece) and come in many designs and patterns. Tiny jewelry boxes made of camel bone and decorated with Persian-miniature-style paintings sell for under 50 TL. Turkey is also famous for its meerschaum, a mineral that is used primarily to make pipes; prices range from about 75-250 TL based on the quality of the meerschaum and the intricacy of the carving.

■ TIP→ Exporting antiquities from Turkey is forbidden, and the ban is rigorously enforced. If you buy a carpet or other item that looks old, make sure you get certification from the seller that it's not an antiquity.

BUYING A CARPET

Carpet salesmen in the Grand Bazaar (Kapalı Çarşı)

It's almost impossible to visit Istanbul without making a detour into at least one rug shop, and you'll inevitably be poured a glass of tea (or several) while the salesman rolls out one carpet after another on the floor in front of you. Just remember, regardless of how many cups of tea you drink and how persistent the salesman, you are not obligated to buy anything.

The vivid colors and patterns of Turkish carpets and kilims, which are flat-woven rugs (without a pile), are hard to resist. Patterns and colors vary by region of origin, and in the case of kilims they often have symbolic meanings.

The Grand Bazaar is, without a doubt, the most convenient place in Istanbul to buy a rug, since the sheer number of rug dealers means there is a wide selection. That said, don't go to the Grand Bazaar looking for bargains—there are enough tourists coming through every day to keep prices on the high side.

When shopping for a carpet or kilim, the most important thing is to find a dealer you can trust. Avoid dealers who are pushy, and don't let anyone pressure you into buying something. It's best to look at merchandise at several different shops before buying anything, in order to get an idea of prices and see what's out there. Ask lots of questions, such as what a carpet is made of (wool or silk), what kind of dyes were used, and where it was made (many so-called Turkish carpets are now made in countries like Iran, India, and China). Note that silk carpets are considerably more expensive than wool ones, and kilims are generally less expensive than carpets because they involve less labor.

■TIP➔ The Arasta Bazaar, near the Blue Mosque, also has a number of good rug shops in a somewhat more relaxed environment.

GRAND BAZAAR TIPS

■ You may want to mentally prepare yourself for being aggressively pursued by merchants who are as shameless about making sales pitches as they are competitive over business; it can be overwhelming at first but underneath the hard sell most of the shop owners are quite friendly.

■ The Grand Bazaar is less crowded earlier on weekday mornings.

■ Once you're in the bazaar, spend some time getting your bearings and comparison shopping before you make any major purchases; this will help you get an idea of prices as well as narrow down what you'd like to buy.

■ Watch out for fakes, be they antique rugs, leather, or jewelry—if a dealer's price seems too good to be true, it probably is.

CARPET AND KILIM TIPS

■ Ask for a Certificate of Authenticity for rugs that are handmade or antique.

■ A new (non-antique) rug should sit flat on the floor when it's laid out, and the edges should be straight.

■ The number of knots per square inch is not the only thing to go by when choosing a carpet. A lower-knot carpet made with high-quality wool and dyes is worth more than a higher-knot carpet made with poor materials.

■ In Turkey, wool or wool on cotton warp carpets and kilims are your best bet. Silk carpets are traditionally made only in Hereke.

■ Try to buy a carpet directly from the store owner, not a third party.

■ If you have your rug shipped, get a receipt describing exactly what you bought (not just a serial number), and take a picture of the item.

BARGAINING AT THE BAZAAR

Prices at the Grand Bazaar can be high due to high rents and the never-ending stream of tourists, but the huge selection offered in the bazaar often makes it a good place to shop. Shop owners will expect you to bargain, so here are some tips.

■ Ask the price of several different items before focusing on the thing you really want, to get an idea of a store's prices and to make your intentions less obvious.

■ After the merchant quotes a price, make a counter-offer that's about two-thirds what they asked; then negotiate until you reach a price somewhere in the middle.

■ Do accept a shopkeeper's offer of tea. This gives you the chance to get familiar with the dealer. Accepting tea, however, does not obligate you to buy anything.

■ If you and the merchant can't reach a deal, starting to walk away often results in the merchant lowering the price.

■ The more items you buy from a merchant, the more you can bargain the price down.

Did You Know?

The Grand Bazaar was ravaged twice by fire in relatively recent years—once in 1954, when it was almost destroyed, and once in 1974, in a smaller conflagration. In both cases, the bazaar was quickly rebuilt in something resembling the original style, with arched passageways and brass-and-tile fountains at regular intervals.

THE SPICE MARKET

MISIR ÇARŞISI, OR
THE EGYPTIAN BAZAAR

The 17th-century Egyptian Bazaar, also known as the Spice Market, in Istanbul's Eminönü neighborhood, is a riot of colors and fragrances. Although some of the spice shops have recently given way to stalls selling tourist souvenirs like you'll find in the Grand Bazaar, the Spice Market, with its mounds of *lokum* (Turkish delight), bags of spices, and heaps of dried fruit and nuts, is still a wonderfully atmospheric place to shop for spices and other delicious edibles.

For the most part prices at the Spice Market are clearly marked. Unlike in the Grand Bazaar, bargaining is discouraged here—if you're buying a lot, you might get the seller to come down by 10%, but don't expect much more.

✉ Yeni Cami Meydanı, Eminönü
🕐 Mon.–Sat. 8:30–7, Sun. 9–6:30

WHAT TO BUY

Lokum, or **Turkish delight**, in a wide variety of flavors, including rosewater and fruit-essenced, stuffed with pistachios or walnuts, or chocolate-covered. Merchants will enthusiastically ply you with free samples.

Herbs and spices, including cumin, sumac, turmeric, nigella ("black sesame") seeds, many varieties of pepper, and curry mixes. The best saffron (safran) found here comes from neighboring Iran, and although it's still not cheap it's less expensive than in the United States.

Dried fruits, particularly figs, dates, and apricots.

Nuts, including domestically harvested pistachios and hazelnuts.

Essential oils, including attar of roses, of which Turkey is one of the world's leading producers.

Black and herbal **teas** and finely ground **Turkish coffee.**

Caviar is also sold here for less than in the U.S. or Europe due to Turkey's proximity to its source, the Caspian Sea. Considering the serious endangerment of sturgeon, however, you might think twice about buying it.

You'll also see a variety of rather questionable-looking concoctions being sold as natural aphrodisiacs or "Turkish Viagra." Draw your own conclusions about their reliability.

✉ *Gümrük Sok. 4, Karaköy* ☎ *212/244–2252* 🌐 *www.karakoygumruk.com.tr* 🕒 *Closed Sun.* 💳 *No credit cards.*

Karaköy Lokantası

$$ | **TURKISH** | This popular dual-format venue is a bustling daytime spot offering a changing menu of reasonably priced vegetable and meat dishes from the Turkish kitchen and a classy meyhane at night, serving an excellent variety of meze, including octopus salad and salted, dried mackerel. The gorgeous two-level dining room features a wrought-iron spiral staircase, blue and turquoise tiles, old-fashioned lamps, and long mirrors but doesn't allow children for dinner. **Known for:** varied meze; extensive wine list; stylish atmosphere. [$] *Average main: 46 TL* ✉ *Kemankeş Cad. 37/A, Karaköy* ☎ *212/292–4455* 🌐 *www.karakoylokantasi.com* 🕒 *No lunch Sun.*

Mürver

$$$$ | **TURKISH** | Seasonal Turkish cuisine is served here with a contemporary twist, from *cacık* with smoked yogurt, charred garlic, and pickles to tender octopus slow-cooked for hours to fresh fish—all artfully plated. It is not surprising that Mehmet Gürs, the famous chef behind Mikla, is a consultant to the restaurant. **Known for:** extensive wine list of local and international wines; locally sourced Anatolian ingredients; stylish atmosphere. [$] *Average main: 100 TL* ✉ *Novotel Istanbul Bosphorus Hotel, Kemankeş Cd. 57-59, Karaköy* ☎ *212/372–0750* 🌐 *www.murverrestaurant.com.*

Karaköy Fish Sandwiches 🍴

For a truly delicious, cheap snack, the no-frills sandwich known as *balık ekmek*—literally "fish in bread"—may be one of your most memorable seafood meals in Turkey. The recipe is simple: take a freshly grilled fillet of fish and serve it in a half loaf of crusty white bread, perhaps with onion and/or tomato slices. What makes balık ekmek, though, is the setting—in Istanbul, the best sandwiches are served alfresco from small boats that pull up to the atmospheric quays near the Galata Bridge, smoke billowing from their onboard grills.

🛏 Hotels

Anemon Galata

$ | **HOTEL** | An attractively renovated, century-old building so close to the 14th-century Galata Tower that you can almost reach out and touch it, the Anemon Galata provides plenty of old-world charm. **Pros:** historic neighborhood; professional service; rooftop restaurant. **Cons:** rooms facing the square can be noisy at night; some rooms small; reached on steep, winding streets. [$] *Rooms from: €80* ✉ *Büyükhendek Cad. 5, Galata* ☎ *212/293–2343* 🌐 *www.anemonhotels.com* 🛏 *27 rooms* 🍴 *Free Breakfast.*

Georges Hotel Galata

$$$$ | **HOTEL** | Housed in a restored late-19th-century apartment building on a street lined with fashion designers' boutiques, the classy Georges and its minimalist yet old-fashioned rooms exude chic—think high ceilings and plain white walls with elaborate moldings, teakwood furniture, and brass lamps. **Pros:** situated in a trendy yet historic neighborhood; attentive, personalized service; romantic setting away from the tourist fray. **Cons:** can be hard to find; unexciting views from some lower-category rooms; no on-site fitness facilities. [$] *Rooms from: €200* ✉ *Serdar-ı Ekrem Sok. 24, Galata* ☎ *212/244–2423* 🌐 *www.georges.com* 🛏 *20 rooms* 🍴 *Free Breakfast.*

The House Hotel Karaköy

$$$ | **HOTEL** | A mid-19th-century bank building near the Galata Bridge combines

historical accents and contemporary design in comfortable, attractive rooms spread over two separate buildings. **Pros:** very central location; stylish, comfortable accommodations; rooftop bar with views. **Cons:** some rooms are on the small side; very few rooms have views; can be noisy. [$] *Rooms from: €150* ✉ *Bankalar Cad. 5, Karaköy* ☎ *212/244–6434* 🌐 *www.thehousehotel.com* 🛏 *60 rooms* 🍴 *Free Breakfast* 💳 *No credit cards.*

Nightlife

BARS AND LOUNGES

Finn Karakoy

BARS/PUBS | This trendy restaurant-bar serves a wide variety of stylish cocktails to an eclectic crowd. There is an accompanying food menu, but the cocktails are the true focus here. There is often a DJ on weekends for a lively vibe. ✉ *Necatibey Cad. 8, Karaköy* ☎ *530/946–0888.*

Shopping

SPAS

Kılıç Ali Paşa Hamamı

SPA/BEAUTY | Reopened in 2012 after a meticulous seven-year restoration, this is the only major Ottoman-era hammam above the Golden Horn, located just steps from the Istanbul Modern, which is closed and under renovation (and temporarily relocated to Beyoğlu). Completed in 1583, it is one of Sinan's last significant works, with the second-largest dome of any hammam in Istanbul. The services at this beautiful bath don't come cheap—prices start at 270 TL for a professional scrubbing—but it tends to be less crowded than the tourist-oriented baths in the Old City (at least so far). Since there's just one bathing facility, there are separate visiting times for women (8–4) and men (4:30–11:30), and reservations are recommended. ✉ *Kemankeş Mah. Hamam Sok. 1, Karaköy* ☎ *212/393–8010* 🌐 *www.kilicalipasahamami.com.*

Beşiktaş and Nişantaşı

A short ways up the Bosphorus from Karaköy is one of Istanbul's most visited attractions outside the Old City: the stunning neoclassical Dolmabahçe Palace, each room more ornate and over-the-top than the last. Nearby Beşiktaş is home to attractions like Yıldız Parkı and the Naval Museum, which showcases an impressive collection of Ottoman artifacts in a specially designed venue overlooking the water. Most of Istanbul's luxurious Bosphorus-side hotels, including a couple that are housed in former Ottoman palaces, are likewise found in and around this area. A major transit hub, Beşiktaş is also the gateway to the Bosphorus neighborhoods to the north, and a departure point for ferries to Istanbul's Asian side.

Up the hill from Beşiktaş is Nişantaşı, the city's high-fashion district, home to the flagship stores of internationally known luxury brands as well as local talent; numerous contemporary-art galleries are also scattered amid the upscale hotels, restaurants, patisseries, and third-wave coffee shops here, which offer plenty of opportunities to take a break and enjoy some good people-watching. The Military Museum is just a short walk away on Cumhuriyet Caddesi, which then leads back to Taksim Square.

Sights

★ **Dolmabahçe Palace** (*Dolmabahçe Sarayı*)

CASTLE/PALACE | Abdülmecid I, whose free-spending lifestyle later bankrupted the empire, had this palace built from 1843 to 1856 as a symbol of Turkey's march toward European-style modernization. It's also where Atatürk died (and all clocks in the palace are turned to his time of death). Its name means "filled-in garden," inspired by the imperial garden planted here by Sultan Ahmet I (ruled 1603–17). Abdülmecid gave father

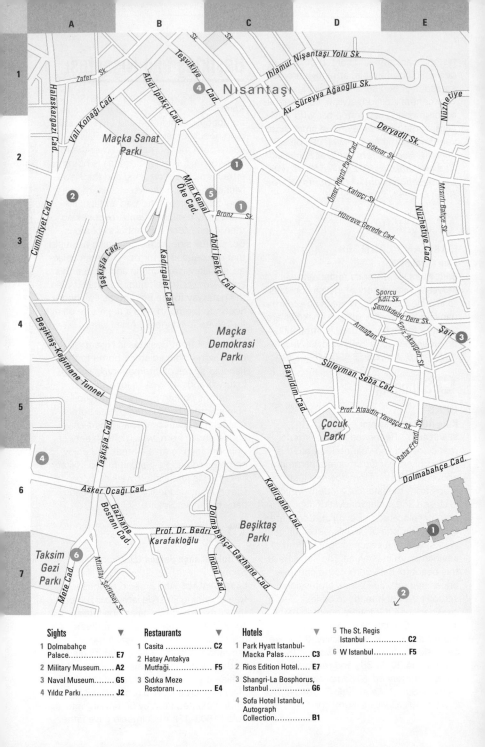

Sights ▼

1 Dolmabahçe
  Palace.................. **E7**
2 Military Museum...... **A2**
3 Naval Museum........ **G5**
4 Yıldız Parkı **J2**

Restaurants ▼

1 Casita **C2**
2 Hatay Antakya
  Mutfağı................ **F5**
3 Sıdıka Meze
  Restoranı **E4**

Hotels ▼

1 Park Hyatt Istanbul-
  Macka Palas **C3**
2 Rios Edition Hotel..... **E7**
3 Shangri-La Bosphorus,
  Istanbul **G6**
4 Sofa Hotel Istanbul,
  Autograph
  Collection.............. **B1**

5 The St. Regis
  Istanbul **C2**
6 W Istanbul............. **F5**

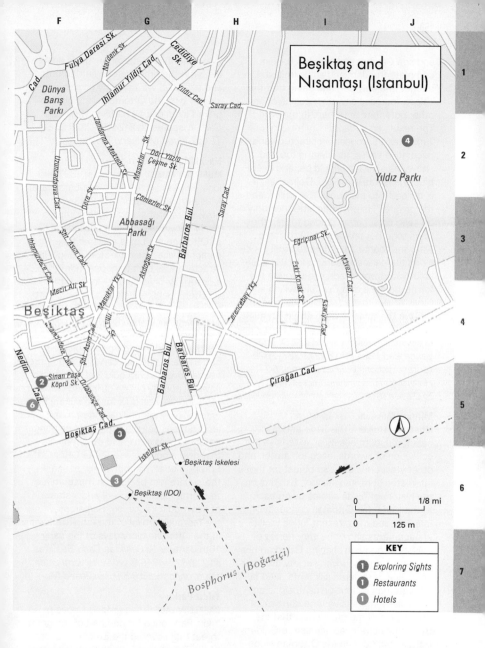

Beşiktaş and Nısantaşı (Istanbul)

Dünya Barış Parkı

Fulya Deresi Sk.

Naldenk Sk.

Cedidiye Sk.

Ihlamur Yıldız Cad.

Yıldız Cad.

Saray Cad.

Jandarma Mektebi Sk.

Masuki Sk.

Dört Yüzlü Çeşme Sk.

Cömezler Sk.

Abbasağı Parkı

Barbaros Bul.

Saray Cad.

Yıldız Parkı

Uzuncaova Cad.

Dere Sk.

Şht. Asım Cad.

Akdoğan Sk.

Egriçınar Sk.

Mevezzi Cad.

Ihlamurdere Cad.

Mecit Ali Sk.

Masuktar Ykş.

Ulu

Şht. Asım Cad.

Brencebey Ykş.

Eski Konak Sk.

Asariye Cad.

Beşiktaş

Nedim Cad.

Nanedere Cad.

Sinan Paşa Köprü Sk.

Orabakçe Cad.

Barbaros Bul.

Barbaros Bul.

Çırağan Cad.

Beşiktaş Cad.

İskelesi Sk.

Beşiktaş İskelesi

Beşiktaş (IDO)

Bosphorus (Boğaziçi)

0   1/8 mi

0   125 m

KEY	
❶	Exploring Sights
❶	Restaurants
❶	Hotels

and son Garabet and Nikoğos Balyan complete freedom and an unlimited budget, the only demand being that the palace "surpass any other palace of any other potentate anywhere in the world." The result, an extraordinary mixture of Turkish and European architectural and decorative styles, as over-the-top and showy as a palace should be, and every bit as garish as Versailles. Dolmabahçe is divided into the public "Selamlık" and the private "Harem" (the latter can only be seen on separate guided tours); the tours together take about 90 minutes. After the tour(s), take time to stroll along the palace's nearly ½-km (¼-mile)-long waterfront facade and through the formal gardens; the Crystal Pavilion and Clock Museum are found in the garden. ■ TIP→ The palace has a daily visitor quota, so call the reservation number at least a day in advance to reserve tickets. ⊠ Dolmabahçe Cad., Besiktas ☎ 212/327–2626 for reservations only ⌨ Selamlık 60 TL, Harem 40 TL, combined ticket 100 TL ☾ Closed Mon.

Military Museum (*Askeri Müze*)
MUSEUM | FAMILY | This large and fascinating museum boasts an extensive collection of swords, daggers, armor, and other weaponry, but it's not just for those interested in military history. Exhibits on the history of Turkic armies going back to the Huns, the Ottoman conquest of Istanbul, and more recent Turkish military engagements show the importance of military strength in shaping Ottoman history and modern Turkish society. Two gorgeously embroidered silk tents used by the Ottoman sultans on campaigns are particularly impressive. And don't miss the section of the great chain that the Byzantines stretched across the Golden Horn in 1453 during the Ottoman siege of the city. The highlight is the *Mehter*, or Janissary military band, which performs 17th- and 18th-century Ottoman military music in full period costume in a special auditorium at 3 pm when they're in town (most days when the museum is open).

Watching this 55-member-strong ensemble, with their thunderous kettledrums and cymbals, will certainly give you an idea of why the Ottoman army was so feared in its day. ⊠ Harbiye, Valikonağı Cad., Nisantasi ☎ 212/233–2720 ⌨ 8.5 TL ☾ Closed Mon. and Tues.

Naval Museum (*Deniz Müzesi*)
MUSEUM | FAMILY | Founded in 1897 and located here since 1961, Istanbul's Naval Museum reopened in late 2013 with a new, state-of-the-art wing that impressively showcases its large collection of Ottoman-era boats and maritime paraphernalia. The multistory, hangar-like structure was built to house more than a dozen *kayıks* (caiques)—long, slim wooden boats, rowed by oarsmen, that served as the primary mode of royal transportation in Istanbul for several hundred years. These graceful boats are decorated with gorgeous painted patterns and intricate carvings and figureheads covered with gold leaf; most also have an equally ornate curtained wooden pavilion that was built for the sultan, his wife, or his mother. The underground level houses several exhibits of paintings, naval coats of arms, and other objects that give a good sense of the Ottoman Empire's onetime supremacy at sea. In the square just beside the museum are the tomb (usually locked) and a statue of Hayreddin Pasha, or "Barbarossa," the famous admiral of the empire's fleet in the Ottoman glory days of the early 16th century. ⊠ Beşiktaş Cad., Besiktas ☎ 212/327–4346 ⊕ www.denizmuzeleri. tsk.tr/en/idmk ⌨ 8.5 TL ☾ Closed Mon.

Yıldız Parkı
CASTLE/PALACE | The wooded slopes of Yıldız Parkı once formed part of the great forest that covered the European shore of the Bosphorus from the Golden Horn to the Black Sea. In the waning years of the Ottoman Empire, the park was the private garden of the nearby Çırağan and Yıldız palaces, and the women of the harem would occasionally be allowed

to visit, secluded from prying eyes as they wandered among acacias, maples, and cypresses. Today the park is still beautiful, particularly in spring when the tulips and other flowers bloom, and in fall when the leaves of the deciduous trees change color.

At the top of the park (a 15- to 20-minute walk from the entrance) is the relatively modest (by Ottoman standards) **Yıldız Şale** (Yıldız Chalet), where the despotic Sultan Abdülhamid II (ruled 1876–1909) spent most of his time. It also served as a guesthouse for visiting heads of state, from Kaiser Wilhelm II to Charles de Gaulle and Margaret Thatcher. The chalet, which can be visited on a guided tour only (30–40 minutes), is often blissfully empty of other tourists, which makes a visit all the more pleasurable. From the ornate French-style furniture to the huge, gilded Rörstrand porcelain stoves, the European influence is perhaps more obvious here than at any other Ottoman imperial residence, yet the elaborate mother-of-pearl inlay work in the dining room and the enormous Hereke carpet in the Ceremonial Hall are distinctly Turkish. Also in the park is the **Malta Köşkü**, a late 19th-century Ottoman pavilion that now houses a restaurant with period decor and views of the Bosphorus. ✉ *Çırağan Cad., Besiktas* ☎ *212/261–8460 for park, 212/259–4570 for chalet* 🎫 *Chalet 10 TL.*

🍴 Restaurants

Casita

$$ | **TURKISH** | This charming little restaurant is best known for its *mantı*—a ravioli-like Turkish pasta traditionally stuffed with ground meat—and specifically *Feraye* (a name the restaurant has trademarked), a fried variation filled with cheese and spinach, potato and cheese, or chicken. The atmosphere is casual, and diners can either sit at sidewalk tables on a lively pedestrian side street lined with other restaurants and shops, or at tables looking onto a quiet garden in the back. **Known for:** outdoor seating; laid-back vibe; café food with a modern Turkish twist. [$] *Average main: 40 TL* ✉ *Abdi İpekçi Cad., Atiye Sok. 3, Nisantasi* ☎ *212/327–8293* 🌐 *www.casita.com.tr.*

Hatay Antakya Mutfağı

$ | **TURKISH** | This tiny restaurant turns out dishes with big flavors from Turkey's southeast: spicy kebabs (including regional specialities like *Arap kebabı*, ground meat cooked with onions, tomatoes, peppers, and parsley) and *lahmacun*, as well as assorted meze. Eat in the cheery, homey dining room or at one of the small tables arrayed streetside. **Known for:** regional Turkish cuisine; outdoor seating; laid-back atmosphere. [$] *Average main: 37 TL* ✉ *Şair Nedim Cad. 20, Akaretler, Besiktas* ☎ *212/236–3985* 🌐 *www.hatayantakyamutfagi.com* 💳 *No credit cards.*

Sıdıka Meze Restoranı

$$ | **TURKISH** | Sıdıka, with its cheerful, welcoming ambience, offers stellar Aegean-influenced starters and fish dishes at reasonable prices. Unique mezes include a delicious spread made from feta, pistachio, and garlic; seasonal daily specials could include artichoke hearts with fava bean puree; simple but tasty main-course fish dishes, such as grilled sea bass fillets wrapped in vine leaves, are especially recommendable. **Known for:** seasonal Aegean cuisine; cozy, casual atmosphere; wide selection of meze. [$] *Average main: 40 TL* ✉ *Şair Nedim Cad. 38, Besiktas* ☎ *212/259–7232* 🌐 *www.sidika.com.tr* ⏲ *Closed Sun.*

🛏 Hotels

Park Hyatt Istanbul–Maçka Palas

$$$$ | **HOTEL** | A restored Italian-style art deco 1922 apartment building offers spacious, elegant rooms decked out in sleek walnut with modern amenities alongside old-fashioned touches like period chandeliers and black-and-white photographs

of Istanbul. **Pros:** large rooms; located in upscale shopping and nightlife area; staff is friendly and efficient. **Cons:** most rooms have no view; spa rooms somewhat overwhelmed by their bathrooms; no restaurant. $ *Rooms from: €230* ✉ *Bronz Sok. 4, Nisantasi* ☎ *212/315–1234* ⊕ *www.istanbul.park.hyatt.com* ⌖ *89 rooms* ⦿ *Free Breakfast.*

★ **Rios Edition Hotel**
$$ | HOTEL | Soft, neutral tones, from sand-hued wing chairs to chocolate-brown silky drapes, and a tranquil, monochromatic vibe provide a welcome respite from the busy streets of the Levent business district. **Pros:** sophisticated, sleek design; spacious, luxurious rooms and bathrooms; elaborate spa facilities. **Cons:** at least 30 minutes from the Old City tourist attractions; main restaurant and nightclub closed in summer months; limited city views. $ *Rooms from: €115* ✉ *Buyukdere Cad. 136, Levent, Besiktas* ☎ *212/317–7700* ⊕ *www.rioseditionhotel. com* ⌖ *79 rooms* ⦿ *No meals.*

Shangri-La Bosphorus, Istanbul
$$$$ | HOTEL | Offering all the opulence and sophistication expected of this world-class brand, the Shangri-La Bosphorus overlooks the water, with a glittering lobby that features a two-story crystal chandelier, richly colored marble flooring, and gold-rimmed furniture. **Pros:** plush, spacious rooms; extraordinarily attentive service; next to ferry dock. **Cons:** overlooks Bosphorus but no open-air spaces or waterfront access for guests; location next to prime minister's offices can mean heavy security presence; box-style hotel architecture feels rather insular. $ *Rooms from: €340* ✉ *Hayrettin İskelesi Sok. 1, Besiktas* ☎ *212/275–8888* ⊕ *www.shangri-la.com* ⌖ *186 rooms* ⦿ *No meals.*

Sofa Hotel Istanbul, Autograph Collection
$$$$ | HOTEL | Design is the emphasis here, with large rooms that have attractive contemporary textiles and furniture in neutral tones, including

an eponymous trademark sofa. **Pros:** spacious, comfortable rooms; original design and hip feel; rooftop bar. **Cons:** rooms can be noisy due to rooftop restaurant and location on busy street; interior-facing rooms rather dim; wellness center is small. $ *Rooms from: €189* ✉ *Teşvikiye Cad. 41–41/A, Nisantasi* ☎ *212/368–1818* ⊕ *www.marriott.com* ⌖ *82 rooms* ⦿ *Free Breakfast.*

The St. Regis Istanbul
$$$$ | HOTEL | This ultrastylish recent addition to Istanbul's ever-growing array of luxury hotels has large, beautifully designed, art deco–tinged rooms and suites and a prime location in the heart of the Nişantaşı shopping district, overlooking the dense greenery of Maçka Park. **Pros:** plush, attractive rooms; extensive spa facilities; attentive service. **Cons:** location not the most convenient for sightseeing; limited public transportation options; small pools are meant for lounging, not swimming. $ *Rooms from: €300* ✉ *Mim Kemal Öke Cad. 35, Nisantasi* ☎ *212/368–0000* ⊕ *www.thestregisistanbul.com* ⌖ *120 rooms* ⦿ *No meals.*

W Istanbul
$$$ | HOTEL | An 1870s Ottoman block of row houses has been restored and enhanced with posh ultramodernity—sexy lighting, chic East-meets-West decor, and cool amenities like iPod docks and rain showers. **Pros:** cool, trendy atmosphere; ultracomfortable beds; some rooms have private gardens. **Cons:** dim, nightclub-like lighting in public spaces may not suit all tastes; gym and spa areas are small; service can be hit or miss. $ *Rooms from: €140* ✉ *Süleyman Seba Cad. 22, Akaretler, Besiktas* ☎ *212/381–2121* ⊕ *www.wistanbul.com. tr* ⌖ *140 rooms* ⦿ *No meals.*

ⓨ Nightlife

BARS AND LOUNGES

The W Lounge

BARS/PUBS | The stylish yet comfortable lounge/bar in the W Hotel has plush divans, low tables, and signature cocktails, drawing a sophisticated, trendy crowd. There is always a DJ on the decks, and the lounge frequently hosts after-parties for fashion-, music-, and design-related events around town. ⌧ *W Istanbul Hotel, Süleyman Seba Cad. 22, Akaretler, Besiktas* ☎ *212/381–2121* ⊕ *www.wistanbul.com.tr/en/wlounge.*

MUSIC VENUES

★ Babylon Bomonti

MUSIC CLUBS | Istanbul's top live-music space occupies an entertainment complex in Bomonti, which includes a hotel and the Populist brewery, on the other side of the Osmanbey metro stop from Nişantaşı. It hosts world-famous performers in genres ranging from jazz, indie pop, and rock to world music and electronica, along with pop-up events, alternative theater performances, and film screenings. The 500-person capacity venue has a top sound system and friendly crowds that take their music seriously. In summer, the action moves to Babylon Kilyos, on Istanbul's Black Sea coast, and Babylon Aya Yorgi in the beach town of Çeşme, near İzmir. ⌧ *Tarihi Bomonti Bira Fabrikası, Birahane Sok., Bomonti, Nişantaşi* ☎ *212/334–0100* ⊕ *www.babylon.com.tr.*

🎭 Performing Arts

PERFORMANCE VENUES

Cemal Reşit Rey Concert Hall

CONCERTS | Located near the Lütfi Kırdar Congress Center off Cumhuriyet Caddesi between Taksim and Nişantaşı, Cemal Reşit Rey Concert Hall is run by the Istanbul Municipality and hosts a wide variety of performances, from classical music, opera, and the occasional jazz and pop concert to ballet and flamenco. ⌧ *Gümüş*

Sok., Harbiye, Nisantasi ☎ *212/232–9830* ⊕ *www.crrkonsersalonu.org* ⊗ *Closed Jan. 1–15 and June–Sept.*

Zorlu Performing Arts Center

ARTS CENTERS | Turkey's largest performing-arts venue, located inside the Zorlu Center shopping mall, has a state-of-the-art 2,000-seat main theater that hosts everything from Broadway and West End musicals to rock concerts, international performance troupes to operas. The complex also contains a small "city stage" for free public shows by up-and-coming local performers, as well as exhibition spaces for contemporary visual art. Accessible by metro via the Gayrettepe station. ⌧ *Zorlu Center, Koru Sok. 2, Zincirlikuyu, Besitas* ☎ *850/222–6776* ⊕ *www.zorlucenterpsm.com.*

👜 Shopping

The high-fashion district is the upscale Nişantaşı neighborhood, 1 km (½ mile) north of İstiklal Caddesi. This is where you'll find the boutiques of established Turkish fashion designers, such as Özlem Süer, as well as the flagship stores of high-end international brands like Chanel, Prada, and Louis Vuitton—though because of high import taxes and unfavorable exchange rates, these labels are usually considerably more expensive in Turkey than they are in the United States.

CLOTHING

Beymen

CLOTHING | Istanbul's version of Bloomingdale's, Beymen has suited doormen and sells expensive, up-to-date fashions from well-known international brands and designers in its multistory flagship department store. The two underground levels house **Beymen Blender,** a hip store-within-a-store that carries youthful styles of clothing and shoes. The ground-floor **Beymen Brasserie** is a popular see-and-be-seen spot for lunch or an afternoon coffee. ⌧ *Abdi İpekçi Cad. 23, Nisantasi* ☎ *212/373–4800* ⊕ *www.beymen.com.*

★ **Gönül Paksoy**

CLOTHING | Longtime designer Gönül Paksoy is known for her elegant and stunning women's clothing that reinterprets Ottoman and tribal designs. Her museumlike store shows off beautiful pieces created with vintage textiles, as well as new garments handmade using all-natural fabrics and dyes. There is also a collection of more casual (and less pricey) items including jewelry, bags, shoes, and other accessories, all crafted in Paksoy's characteristic style. ⊠ *Atiye Sok. 1/3, Nisantasi* ☎ *212/236–0209* ⊕ *www.gonulpaksoy.com.*

★ **Vakko**

CLOTHING | One of Turkey's oldest and most elegant fashion houses, Vakko carries its own lines as well as clothing, shoes, and accessories from high-end international labels at its flagship department store in Nişantaşı. The company is particularly well-known for its collection of silk scarves and ties in a variety of traditional and modern designs. It also sells its own signature chocolates. A spin-off "concept store" next door, V2K Designers (Abdi İpekçi Cad. 31), sells hip men's and women's apparel by international names. ⊠ *Abdi İpekçi Cad. 33, Nisantasi* ☎ *212/248–5011* ⊕ *www.vakko.com.*

JEWELRY
Urart

JEWELRY/ACCESSORIES | One of Turkey's most established jewelry companies makes re-creations, and also chic interpretations, of ancient Anatolian designs and motifs; they've also branched out into home accessories along similar themes. There is an additional sales point in the Zorlu Center shopping mall near the Gayrettepe metro station. ⊠ *Abdi İpekçi Cad. 18/1, Nisantasi* ☎ *212/246–7194* ⊕ *www.urart.com.tr.*

The Bosphorus

Whether explored in person or seen from the vantage point of a boat on the water, the Bosphorus shores are home to some of the prettiest parts of the city. Both sides of the strait are dotted with palaces, fortresses, and waterfront neighborhoods lined with old wooden summer homes, called *yalıs* (waterside mansions), which were built for the city's wealthier residents in the Ottoman era. As you cruise up the Bosphorus, you'll have the chance to disembark at some of these waterside enclaves for a stroll.

👁 Sights

Arnavutköy

NEIGHBORHOOD | This picturesque European-side neighborhood just below Bebek is a pleasant place for a stroll. The waterfront is taken up by a row of beautiful 19th-century wooden yalıs, some of which now house fish restaurants. Up the hill from the water, narrow streets are lined with more old wooden houses, some with trailing vines. ⊠ *Bosphorus.*

Bebek

NEIGHBORHOOD | One of Istanbul's most fashionable suburbs, Bebek is especially popular with the affluent boating set, thanks to the area's pretty, natural harbor. The European-side neighborhood has a number of cafés and restaurants on both sides of the main coastal road and a few upscale boutiques selling clothing and jewelry; there's also a small, shaded public park on the waterfront. The stretches of coastline both north and south of Bebek are perfect for a promenade. Bebek is about 20 to 30 minutes by taxi from central Istanbul. ⊠ *Bosphorus.*

Borusan Contemporary

MUSEUM | Filled with office workers during the week, this distinctive building under the second Bosphorus Bridge on the European side turns into a gallery on weekends, with the public welcomed in

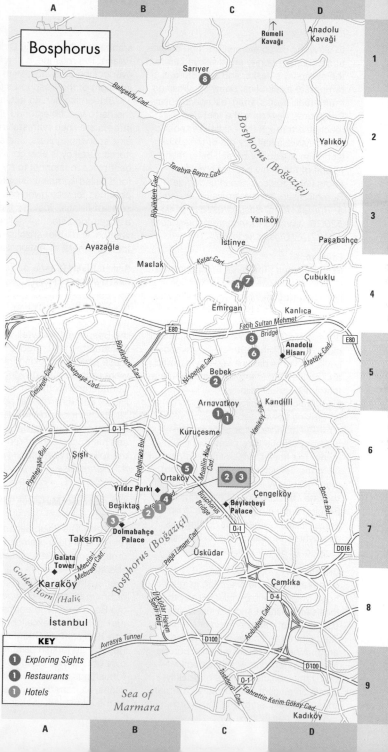

Bosphorus

KEY
1 Exploring Sights
1 Restaurants
1 Hotels

to view the corporate owners' fine collection of contemporary art, displayed amid the company's desks, and adventurous temporary exhibitions, many showcasing multimedia works. There's a spectacular Bosphorus view from the roof deck, reachable through the castle-like redbrick turret. Make a half day out of the excursion with a leisurely brunch beforehand at one of the many popular breakfast spots lining the coast road underneath Rumeli Hisarı. ⊠ *Baltalimanı Hisar Cad. 5, Rumeli Hisarı, Bosphorus* ☏ *212/393–5200* ⊕ *www.borusancontemporary.com* ⊡ *10 TL* ⊙ *Closed Mon.-Fri.*

Emirgan

NEIGHBORHOOD | The quiet European-side suburb of Emirgan is best known for its large, attractive public park, **Emirgan Korusu**—formerly an estate owned by the Khedive of Egypt—which has flower gardens, a small pond, walking paths, and picnic areas. Three 19th-century wooden pavilions in the park have been restored, and house restaurants and cafés. During Istanbul's annual Tulip Festival in April, visitors flock to Emirgan Korusu for its striking flower displays—each year, a million or more tulips of dozens of different varieties are planted in this park alone. The flower, which takes its name from the Turkish word *tülbend* (turban), was most likely introduced to Europe in the late 16th century via the Ottoman Empire, setting off the famous "tulip craze" in the Netherlands. Emirgan is also where the **Sakıp Sabancı Museum** is located. ⊠ *Bosphorus.*

Ortaköy

NEIGHBORHOOD | The charming neighborhood of Ortaköy is popular with both locals and visitors and is a lovely spot to spend a summer afternoon or evening. Restaurants and cafés are clustered around the small square on the European-side waterfront, which is dominated by the iconic silhouette of **Ortaköy Camii**, an elegant 19th-century Ottoman mosque designed by the same Armenian architects who built the Dolmabahçe Palace. The mosque is perched directly overlooking the water, with the imposing sight of the Bosphorus Bridge (built 1973) looming behind it. On Sundays, the narrow, cobblestoned surrounding streets are lined with stalls selling jewelry, scarves, trinkets, and small antique items. Ortaköy is also considered the best place in Istanbul to try the street food called *kumpir* (basically giant baked potatoes for which you can choose all sorts of fillings): look for the row of about a dozen food stands—selling kumpir, waffles, and other snacks—all competing for customers' attention. ⊠ *Bosphorus.*

Rumeli Hisarı (Castle of Europe)

CASTLE/PALACE | **FAMILY** | Built on a hill on the European side of the city overlooking the water, Rumeli Hisarı is the best preserved of all the fortresses on the Bosphorus and well worth a visit. Constructed in just four months in 1452, these eccentric-looking fortifications were ordered built by Mehmet the Conqueror directly across from Anadolu Hisarı, at the narrowest point of the strait. This allowed the Ottomans to take control of the waterway, and Mehmet and his troops conquered Constantinople the following year. ⊠ *Yahya Kemal Cad. 42, Rumelihisarı, Bosphorus* ☏ *212/263–5305* ⊡ *15 TL.*

Sakıp Sabancı Museum (Sakıp Sabancı Müzesi)

MUSEUM | The Sakıp Sabancı Museum is one of Istanbul's premier private museums, thanks to its world-class exhibits and stunning location in a historic villa overlooking the water in the leafy suburb of Emirgan, on the European shore of the Bosphorus. The permanent collection includes an excellent display of late-19th-century Orientalist and early Republican Turkish paintings, rare examples of Ottoman calligraphy, and antique furnishings such as exquisite Sèvres vases, all from the private collection of the industrialist Sabancı family. The

Planning a Bosphorus Day Cruise 👁

One of the most pleasant experiences in Istanbul—and an easy way to escape the chaos of the city—is a trip up the Bosphorus by ferry. If you want to go all the way to the mouth of the Black Sea, and have the time to make a day of it, you can take a "full Bosphorus cruise." These boats leave from Eminönü and zigzag up the Bosphorus with set stops, arriving in the middle of the day for a three-hour break at either **Rumeli Kavağı** (European side) or **Anadolu Kavağı** (Asian side), two fishing villages with fortresses at the opening to the Black Sea. Then they zigzag back down to Eminönü. Operated by Şehir Hatları, the ferries depart daily from the first quay on the Bosphorus side of the Galata Bridge (look for the sign that says "Boğaz İskelesi") at 10:35 and 1:35 in the summer months (approximately early June to mid-September) and at 10:35 in the winter. A one-way ticket is 15 TL, while the round-trip costs 25 TL. On Saturday nights in summer, a "Sunset Cruise" follows the same route, leaving Eminönü at 6:25 and returning around midnight (20 TL). The Dentur Avrasya company recently launched its own boat rides to Anadolu Kavağı from Kabataş (departing 11:15) and Beşiktaş (departing 11:30), for a round-trip fare of 30 TL.

If your time is more limited, you can take a short cruise with no stops, lasting two hours or less, which goes to the second Bosphorus bridge or a bit farther on to Emirgan or İstinye before turning around. Şehir Hatları runs one daily short tour (leaving Eminönü at 2:30; 12 TL), as does Dentur Avrasya (10:30 from Kabataş; 17.50 TL), while another private company, Turyol, on the Golden Horn side of Galata Bridge, offers them near-hourly (20 TL).

Alternatively, several commuter ferries leave from Boğaz İskelesi in Eminönü between around 5 and 7 pm every day (more frequently on weekdays than weekends) and zigzag up the Bosphorus for a mere 5 TL—but you'll have to catch a bus or taxi back later, as there are no return ferries until the morning. A number of buses run up and down both sides; most useful on the European side are the 25E (Kabataş to Sarıyer) and 25T (Taksim to Sarıyer). On the Asian side, several buses run from Üsküdar past Beylerbeyi, Anadolu Hisarı, and Kanlıca to Beykoz, from where the 15A continues up to Anadolu Kavağı.

---

biggest draws, though, are the temporary installations—of a caliber equal to that seen at top museums around the world—which range from retrospectives on major artists like Picasso and leading contemporary names such as Ai Weiwei to exhibits on Anatolian archaeology and masterpieces of Islamic art. The beautiful grounds, which boast 150-year-old monumental trees and a variety of rare plants from around the world, are perfect for a stroll after viewing the art. ✉ Sakıp Sabancı Cad. 42, Emirgan, Bosphorus ☎ 212/277–2200 ⊕ www. sakipsabancimuzesi.org 🎟 30 TL; free on Wed. ⊙ Closed Mon.

Sarıyer

NEIGHBORHOOD | One of the northernmost settlements on the European shore of the Bosphorus, Sarıyer, centered on a small harbor and backed by a row of seafood restaurants, still has the feel of a fishing village. As you stroll along the Bosphorus with the hustle of the big city at arm's length, you'll see majestic old *yalıs*—some of which are beautifully kept up, and others that have been abandoned and are in a sad state of deterioration. Sarıyer is one of the stops on the full Bosphorus cruises that leave from Eminönü, and is a nice place for a fish lunch. ✉ *Bosphorus.*

🍴 Restaurants

The small, charming neighborhoods along the Bosphorus are famous for their fish restaurants; while these establishments tend to be more upscale and expensive, there are some affordable options as well.

Adem Baba
$$ | **SEAFOOD** | This place is the Turkish version of a New England fish shack, with nets and crab traps hanging from the ceiling in two venues across the street from one other. Families and groups come here to enjoy simple, fresh, and well-prepared fish, at much less than what they would pay at some of the fancier seafood restaurants along the Bosphorus (it's cheaper in part because no alcohol is served). **Known for:** location in a scenic neighborhood on the water; various fish dishes, including a catch of the day; laid-back atmosphere. [$] *Average main: 35 TL* ✉ *Satış Meydanı Sok. 2, Arnavutköy, Bosphorus* ☎ *212/263–2933* 🌐 *www.adembaba.com.*

Çınaraltı
$$ | **TURKISH** | Named after the massive sycamore tree growing through the center of the restaurant and shading the upstairs terrace, unpretentious Çınaraltı ("under the sycamore") has been in business for three decades in the same spot on Ortaköy's waterfront square. The spring roll-like fish pastry (*balık böreği*) is a highlight among the wide but otherwise fairly standard selection of meze, while fish is mainly served grilled or fried (make sure the price quoted is per fish or serving, not per kilo). **Known for:** relaxed atmosphere; reasonable prices; traditional Turkish cuisine. [$] *Average main: 37 TL* ✉ *İskele Meydanı 28, Bosphorus* ☎ *212/261–4616* 🌐 *www.cinaralti.com.*

The House Café Ortaköy
$$ | **INTERNATIONAL** | The largest and one of the most popular branches of this local chain of chic eateries is directly on the waterfront, with stylish furnishings and two enormous open-air terraces. The international menu ranges from starters like Asian-style crispy chicken fingers and salmon ceviche to main-course salads, pastas, pizzas, steaks, and the signature House Burger. **Known for:** excellent cocktail list; views of the Bosphorus; lively atmosphere. [$] *Average main: 50 TL* ✉ *Salhane Sok. 1, Bosphorus* ☎ *212/227–2699 Ortaköy* 🌐 *www.thehousecafe.com.*

Tuğra Restaurant
$$$$ | **TURKISH** | Fitting for a restaurant housed in the Çırağan Palace, dinner here is a refined, luxurious affair, with formal service, rich Ottoman and Turkish specialties, and one of the most high-end wine lists in Turkey (Chateau Pétrus, anyone?). The quite pricey menu features a variety of cold and hot meze, and entrées emphasize fish and meat, such as in the restaurant's signature *külbastı*, lamb escalope served with pureed eggplant. **Known for:** alfresco seating with a Bosphorus view; elegant interior; luxurious Ottoman and Turkish cuisine. [$] *Average main: 145 TL* ✉ *Çırağan Palace Kempinski Istanbul, Çırağan Cad. 32, Bosphorus* ☎ *212/236–7333* 🌐 *www.kempinski-istanbul.com* 👔 *Jacket required.*

🛏 Hotels

★ Çırağan Palace Kempinski Istanbul
$$$$ | **HOTEL** | Once a residence for the Ottoman sultans, the late 19th-century Çırağan Palace (pronounced chi-rahn) is Istanbul's most luxurious hotel, with ornate public spaces that feel

absolutely decadent and a breathtaking setting right on the Bosphorus—the outdoor infinity pool seems to hover on the water's edge and most rooms, full of Ottoman-inspired wood furnishings and textiles in warm colors, have balconies overlooking the Bosphorus as well. **Pros:** grand setting in incredible Bosphorus-front location; over-the-top feeling of luxury; infinity pool. **Cons:** exorbitant price of food and drinks; high rates, especially for rooms that have no Bosphorus view; service can be slow. [$] *Rooms from: €360* ✉ *Çırağan Cad. 32, Bosphorus* ☎ *212/326–4646* 🌐 *www.kempinski.com/istanbul* 🛏 *312 rooms* 🍴 *No meals.*

Four Seasons Hotel Istanbul at the Bosphorus
$$$$ | HOTEL | This restored 19th-century Ottoman palace with two modern wings exudes luxury; rooms and suites, a quarter of which have Bosphorus views (others have garden and city views), are elegant yet understated, with soaring ceilings, muted tones, and Ottoman touches such as handcrafted mirrors. **Pros:** impeccable service; beautiful views and location; top-notch spa and fitness facilities. **Cons:** expensive food and drinks; underwhelming views from non-Bosphorus rooms, especially considering high rates; can be noisy. [$] *Rooms from: €450* ✉ *Çırağan Cad. 28, Bosphorus* ☎ *212/381–4000* 🌐 *www.fourseasons.com/bosphorus* 🛏 *170 rooms* 🍴 *No meals.*

Swissôtel The Bosphorus Istanbul
$$$$ | HOTEL | In a superb spot just above Dolmabahçe Palace, the Swissôtel offers excellent facilities and—from most of the comfortable, businesslike guest rooms—magnificent views of the Bosphorus that extend all the way to Topkapı Palace across the Golden Horn. **Pros:** first-class service; extensive dining options; huge, top-notch gym. **Cons:** expensive food, drinks, and Internet; hotel can only be reached by taxi (or on foot); fairly impersonal atmosphere. [$] *Rooms from: €150* ✉ *Bayıldım Cad. 2, Maçka, Bosphorus* ☎ *212/326–1100* 🌐 *www.swissotel.com/istanbul* 🛏 *566 rooms* 🍴 *Some meals.*

🍸 Nightlife

BARS AND LOUNGES

Bebek Bar
BARS/PUBS | With its masculine interior decor that brings to mind a private club, and a breezy terrace directly overlooking the Bosphorus, Bebek Bar attracts a dressed-up crowd. There is a particularly wide selection of liqueurs, Scotch, and other spirits, as well as classic cocktails, making it a perfect spot for a before- or after-dinner drink. ✉ *Bebek Hotel, Cevdet Paşa Cad. 34, Bebek, Bosphorus* ☎ *212/358–2000* 🌐 *www.bebekhotel.com.tr.*

DANCE CLUBS

Ruby
DANCE CLUBS | Overlooking the Ortaköy waterfront, Ruby (formerly known as Anjelique) offers a classy atmosphere and more intimate feel to partiers than the larger nightclubs farther up the Bosphorus. Dinner is served to a well-heeled crowd before the venue turns into a dance club. ✉ *Muallim Naci Cad., Salhane Sok. 5, Bosphorus* ☎ *212/327–2844* 🌐 *www.rubyistanbul.com.*

Sortie
DANCE CLUBS | If you want to mingle with Istanbul's rich and famous (and the paparazzi that await them), swanky Sortie is your place. In summer, a half dozen of Istanbul's trendiest restaurants open up locations here to serve dinner. If you're not dining at the venue, there's a steep entrance fee to get into the club on summer weekends. ✉ *Muallim Naci Cad. 54, Ortaköy, Bosphorus* ☎ *212/327–8585* 🌐 *www.sortie.com.tr.*

📛 Performing Arts

PERFORMANCE VENUES

UNIQ Istanbul

ARTS CENTERS | This complex in the Maslak business district is home to the Volkswagen Arena (formerly Black Box), a top-of-the-line concert venue that draws big-name touring acts like Bob Dylan and the Pixies; the bar-restaurant-café-lounge Tamirane, which hosts jazz concerts every Sunday afternoon; and an open-air theater, along with various shops, restaurants, and gallery exhibition spaces. The closest metro stop is İTÜ Ayazağa. ⊠ *Ayazağa Cad. 4, Maslak, Bosphorus* ☎ *212/286–0391* ⊕ *www. uniqistanbul.com.*

🛍 Shopping

CERAMICS

İznik Foundation

CERAMICS/GLASSWARE | In the upscale suburb of Etiler is the flagship showroom of the İznik Foundation, dedicated to reviving and preserving the classic art of İznik ceramic and tile work. Operating as a kind of design studio for İznik tiles, the foundation has lately worked mainly on large-scale institutional projects—ranging from metro stations and mosques in Istanbul to Hermès window displays in Paris—but also design tiles for private clients, and some individual pieces are for sale as well. Prices are high, but the quality is outstanding. ⊠ *Cengiz Topel Cad., Tuğcular Sok. 1/A, Etiler, Bosphorus* ☎ *212/287–3243* ⊕ *www.iznik.com.*

The Asian Shore

While some of the waterside enclaves on the Asian side of the Bosphorus are popular stops on day cruises, spread out along the Asian shoreline of the lower Bosphorus and the Sea of Marmara are also some large residential districts. They have few "sights" as such but offer a pleasant change of pace from the faster tempo of the European side—as well as a welcome escape from the tourist crowds. Üsküdar has several Ottoman imperial mosques and presents a slice of Istanbul life that is more traditional than what visitors generally see across the water. Farther down the coast, Kadıköy has a youthful, relaxed vibe; the pedestrian-only area off the waterfront and lively nightlife are among its top draws. From Kadıköy, a short taxi or dolmuş ride takes you to the beginning of Bağdat Caddesi, or "Baghdad Avenue," a 6-km-long (3.7-mile-long) boulevard that is the Asian side's ritziest avenue. Lined with elegant apartment buildings, upscale designer boutiques, and trendy restaurants, it gets increasingly posh as you get farther away from Kadıköy towards Suadiye.

👁 Sights

Anadolu Kavağı

TOWN | At the upper end of the Asian shore, Anadolu Kavağı is the final destination on the full Bosphorus cruises. A pretty little fishing village, it gets enough tourists to have a large number of seafood restaurants, waffle stands, and ice cream shops. The main attraction is the dramatically situated Byzantine Castle (aka Yoros Castle), a 15-minute walk uphill from the village. The hill was once the site of a temple to Zeus Ourios (god of the favoring winds), which dates back, legend has it, to the days when Jason passed by in search of the Golden Fleece. The castle, built by the Byzantines and expanded by their Genoese allies, is today in a fairly ruined state and as of this writing closed to visitors, but the climb up is still worth it for the spectacular views over the upper Bosphorus from the cafés and restaurants just below its walls. ⊠ *Bosphorus.*

Beylerbeyi Palace (*Beylerbeyi Sarayı*)

CASTLE/PALACE | Built as a summer residence for Sultan Abdülaziz in 1865, Beylerbeyi is a bit like a mini-Dolmabahçe

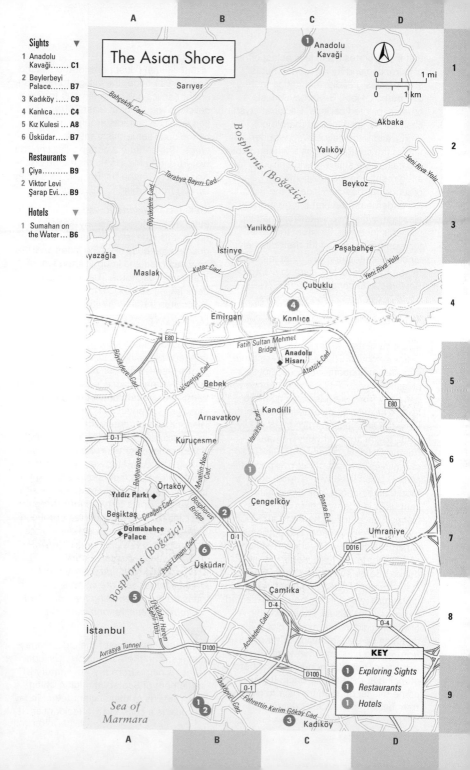

The Asian Shore

Anadolu Kavaği

Sarıyer

Bahçeköy Cad.

Bosphorus (Boğaziçi)

Akbaka

Yalıköy

Yeni Riva Yolu

Beykoz

Tarabya Bayırı Cad.

Büyükdere Cad.

Yaniköy

İstinye

Paşabahçe

ayazağa

Maslak

Katar Cad.

Yeni Riva Yolu

Çubuklu

Emirgan

Kanlıca

E80

Fatih Sultan Mehmet Bridge

Anadolu Hisarı

Atatürk Cad.

Bebek

Büyükdere Cad.

Nispetiye Cad.

Kandilli

E80

Arnavatköy

Yanıköy Cad.

Kuruçesme

O-1

Barbaros Bul.

Ortaköy

Çengelköy

Bosna Bul.

Yıldız Parkı ◆

Mütallim Naci Cad.

Beşiktaş

Çırağan Cad.

Bosphorus Bridge

Umraniye

Dolmabahçe Palace ◆

O-1

D016

Paşa Limanı Cad.

Üsküdar

Bosphorus (Boğaziçi)

Çamlika

O-4

İstanbul

Üsküdar Harem Şehir Yolu

O-4

Avrasya Tunnel

D100

Acıbadem Cad.

D100

O-1

Taşköprü Cad.

Fahrettin Kerim Gökay Cad.

Sea of Marmara

Kadıköy

KEY

Exploring Sights

Restaurants

Hotels

that incorporates a similarly eclectic mix of European and Turkish styles but is smaller, less grandiose, and has more of a personal feel. Beylerbeyi boasts ornately painted ceilings, Baccarat crystal chandeliers, gold-topped marble columns, and intricately carved wooden furniture; the central hall has a white-marble fountain and a stairway wide enough for a regiment. The magnolia-shaded palace grounds on the Asian side of the Bosphorus underneath the first bridge are also pleasant, while two waterfront bathing pavilions (one was for men, the other for women) stand out for their bizarrely fanciful architecture. You must join a tour to see the palace. ⊠ *Çayırbaşı Durağı, Beylerbeyi, Bosphorus* ☎ *216/321–9320* ⊛ *40 TL* ☾ *Closed Mon. and Thurs.*

Kadıköy

NEIGHBORHOOD | Though there's no visible evidence of its beginnings as the ancient Greek colony of Chalcedon, the relaxed, suburban neighborhood of Kadıköy is a pleasant area to explore on foot once you get away from the busy area near the ferry. Once you've disembarked from the ferry, the area just up from the Kadıköy dock, to the south of busy Söğütlü Çeşme Caddesi, is known as the Çarşı, or "market"—a grid of narrow, pedestrian-only lanes filled with a small open-air food market, shops, cafés, nightlife venues, and a few modern churches. Güneşlibahçe Sokak, home to an assortment of fish restaurants and some bars, is particularly lively. Several streets up and farther to the right, Kadife Sokak, dubbed Barlar Sokağı, or "bars street," is the center of Kadıköy's nightlife, lined with small, wooden rowhouses occupied by bars with a casual, laid-back vibe. A tiny, nostalgic tram runs in a clockwise direction up General Asım Gündüz, from where it loops down to the lovely waterfront neighborhood of Moda before stopping at the Kadıköy dock. If you've come this far on foot, it's nice to ride the tram back to the dock. ⊠ *Asian Side.*

Kanlıca

NEIGHBORHOOD | Just north of the second Bosphorus bridge, the village-turned-suburb of Kanlıca has been famous for its delicious yogurt for at least 300 years, and small restaurants around the square by the quay serve this treat. Nearby, white 19th-century wooden villas line the waterfront. Kanlıca is the first stop on the Asian shore on the full Bosphorus cruises leaving from Eminönü. ⊠ *Bosphorus.*

Kız Kulesi (*Maiden's Tower*)

BUILDING | Fortified since Byzantine times, this little islet off the Asian shore guarded the busy shipping lanes and, now, restored and lit up, it's the star of the lower Bosphorus. The name Leander's Tower, as it was known in antiquity, associates the island with the legend of Leander, who was said to have swum the strait each night guided by the lamp of his lover, Hero—though this myth in fact took place in the Dardanelles to the southwest. The Turkish name "Maiden's Tower" comes from a legend associated with several offshore castles: as the story goes, a princess is placed on an island after a prophecy that she will die of a snakebite, but it happens anyway, when a snake comes ashore in a basket of fruit. The current tower, which dates to the 18th century, now houses an expensive but not all that impressive café and restaurant. Boats ferry visitors at regular intervals from Kabataş on the European side and Salacak (near Üsküdar) on the Asian shore. ⊠ *Asian Side* ☎ *216/342–4747* ⊕ *www.kizkulesi.com.tr* ⊛ *25 TL for round-trip boat ride from Salacak or Kabataş for daytime visitors; boat transfers free in evening for restaurant customers (reservations essential).*

Üsküdar

NEIGHBORHOOD | One of the oldest inhabited areas on the Asian shore, Üsküdar takes its name from the 7th-century BC settlement of Scutari, though nothing now remains of that ancient town. Today, Üsküdar is a conservative residential district with a handful of noteworthy Ottoman mosques. Though still rather chaotic, the waterfront area has undergone substantial renovation to accommodate the late 2013 opening of the Marmaray, a rail tunnel under the Bosphorus that transports passengers from Üsküdar to Sirkeci in just four minutes. The ferry landing is dominated by Sinan's pretty, if somewhat dark, Mihrimah Sultan Camii, also known as the İskele Camii (built 1548). The large Yeni Valide Camii from 1710 and another Sinan mosque, the small, beautifully situated Şemsi Paşa Camii, are a short walk southwest along the waterfront. ✉ *Asian Side.*

🍴 Restaurants

★ Çiya

$$ | TURKISH | Chef-owner Musa Dağdeviren, who hails from the southeastern Turkish city of Gaziantep, is something of a culinary anthropologist, serving recipes from around Turkey that you're unlikely to find elsewhere in three no-frills branches on the same street. This restaurant is the original, Çiya Sofrası, known for its selection of seasonal and daily specials—both meat-based and vegetarian—featuring unusual flavor combinations. **Known for:** innovative cuisine from different regions of Turkey; seasonal ingredients; unique desserts, including candied olives, tomatoes, or eggplant. [$] *Average main: 45 TL* ✉ *Güneşlibahçe Sok. 43, Kadıköy, Asian Side* ☎ *216/330–3190* 🌐 *www.ciya.com.tr.*

Viktor Levi Şarap Evi (*Viktor Levi Wine House*)

$$ | INTERNATIONAL |The large, relaxing back garden is the star attraction at this restaurant-café-bar in the midst of bustling central Kadıköy. A broad mixed menu of Turkish and international fare has something for everyone: from salads and meze to fajitas and steak. **Known for:** large enclosed garden; selection of house wines; lively atmosphere. [$] *Average main: 50 TL* ✉ *Moda Cad., Damacı Sok. 4, Kadıköy, Asian Side* ✣ *Behind the Rexx Cinema* ☎ *216/449–9329* 🌐 *www.viktorlevimoda.com.*

🛏 Hotels

For a wider range of hotel options in somewhat less tourist-oriented neighborhoods, head across the Golden Horn.

★ Sumahan on the Water

$$$ | HOTEL | What was once a derelict distillery on the Asian waterfront of the Bosphorus is now one of Istanbul's most chic and original places to stay, with comfortable rooms and suites—all with incredible views of the water and decorated in a contemporary style with a few Turkish touches. **Pros:** stunning waterfront location; stylish and inviting public areas; secluded, romantic atmosphere. **Cons:** far from sights and commercial center; somewhat inconvenient to get to without the launch; not all rooms are wheelchair-accessible. [$] *Rooms from: €225* ✉ *Kuleli Cad. 43, Çengelköy, Asian Side* ☎ *216/422–8000* 🌐 *www.sumahan.com* 🛏 *13 rooms* 🍴 *Free Breakfast.*

🍸 Nightlife

BARS AND LOUNGES

Karga Bar

BARS/PUBS | The longest-established and most popular venue on Kadıköy's so-called "Barlar Sokağı" ("bars street"), Karga takes up several levels of an old wooden house, whose many small rooms and intimate niches provide a perfect laid-back hangout. There is often live music on weekends during the winter months and occasional art events. There's no sign out front but look for a building with a green facade and an emblem of a crow over the doorway (karga means "crow" in Turkish). ✉ *Kadife Sok. 16, Asian Side* ☎ *216/449–1725* 🌐 *www.karga.com.tr.*

Lâl

BARS/PUBS | The best thing about this low-key café/bar on Kadıköy's main nightlife street is the large courtyard in the back, where patrons can gather around tables and an old, distinctive tree. In cooler months, the rustic interior is a cozy place to chat. ⊠ *Kadife Sok. 19, Kadıköy, Asian Side* ☎ *216/346–5625* ⊕ *www.kadyagrup.com.tr.*

Side Trips to the Princes' Islands

20 km (12 miles) off the coast of Istanbul from Sultanahmet.

The Princes' Islands—a cluster of nine islands in the Sea of Marmara, known simply as "Adalar" in Turkish—are everything that Istanbul isn't: quiet, green, and car-less. They are primarily a relaxing getaway from the noise and traffic of the big city, though they can be quite crowded on weekends, particularly in summer. Restrictions on development and a ban on automobiles help maintain the charmingly old-fashioned and quiet atmosphere —transportation here is only by horse-drawn carriage or bicycle. There are few real "sights," per se; the main attraction is the laid-back ambience and natural beauty of the islands, which are hilly and mainly wooded, with a fresh breeze that is gently pine-scented. Thanks to frequent ferries from the mainland, an excursion to the islands makes a fun day trip, or a pleasant overnight getaway from the city.

The islands have served various purposes for the people of Istanbul over the years. Back in Byzantine times, religious undesirables and deposed members of the royal family sought refuge here, while during the Ottoman Empire, the islands likewise provided a convenient place to exile troublesome princes and other notables—hence the name. By the mid-19th century, well-heeled Istanbul businessmen had staked their claim and built many of the Victorian gingerbread–style houses that lend the islands their charm. The islands became especially popular as summer residences for Istanbul's non-Muslim communities (Jews, Armenians, and Greeks), and were known for their cosmopolitan way of life. For several years in the 1930s, Büyükada, the largest of the islands, was the home of the exiled Leon Trotsky; the islands were considered to be safer than Istanbul, with its 35,000 hostile White Russian refugees.

Of the nine islands, four have regular ferry service, but only the two largest, Büyükada and Heybeliada, are of real interest to the general traveler, offering a variety of places to eat and stay and a few small beaches and other attractions. Two of the other inhabited islands are Kınalıada, long popular with the city's Armenians, and Burgazada, which has traditionally been more Greek. From the ferry you can see the larger two of the uninhabited islands, known in Greek and Turkish as the "pointy" Oxia/Sivri and the "flat" Plati/Yassı. Sivri's main claim to fame is that in the 19th and early 20th centuries Istanbul's stray dogs would be occasionally rounded up and dumped there, while Yassı was the site of the trial and execution of Prime Minister Adnan Menderes after a 1960 military coup.

GETTING HERE AND AROUND

From Katabaş, near Taksim at the end of the tram line, and Eminönü, both atmospheric old ferryboats and more modern catamarans known as sea buses depart regularly for the islands, with more frequent service in summer. Ferries cost 5.20 TL with an İstanbulkart and take around 90 minutes (⊕ *www.sehirhatlari.com.tr/en*). On weekends in summer both the ferries and the islands themselves can be very crowded, so it's preferable to visit

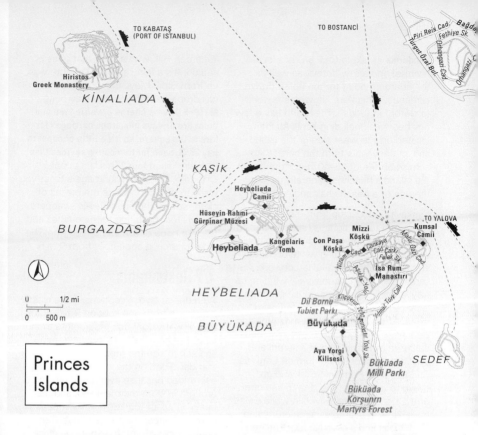

Princes Islands

during the week. If you're planning on staying the night, most hotels also have cheaper rates on weekdays.

No cars are allowed on the islands other than official/service vehicles, so you'll do most of your exploring on foot. The cost of horse-drawn carriage rides varies by distance. On Büyükada, a "short tour" (40–45 minutes) costs 67 TL and a "long tour" (70–75 minutes) is 79 TL, while a one-way ride to the Monastery of St. George is 29 TL. Fares on Heybeliada are 45 TL and 58 TL, respectively, for short and long tours. As there have been reports in the Turkish press lately about neglect of workhorses on the islands, look for a carriage whose animals seem well treated and well fed. Renting bicycles (15–20 TL per hour; about 30–50 TL for the day, with prices generally at the higher end of the price range on

Büyükada) from one of the numerous bike shops on Büyükada and Heybeliada is also a fun (and more strenuous) way to get around.

To get from one of the Princes' Islands to the other, hop aboard any of the several daily ferries or sea buses—though note that you'll pay the same fare for this short hop as you did to get out to the islands in the first place, unless you fall into the two-hour transfer window.

Büyükada

Büyükada is the largest of the Princes' Islands (about 5 square km, or 2 square miles) and generally the one with the most to offer visitors. Just by the ferry docks is the main commercial center, filled with restaurants, shops, bike rental places, ice-cream stands (**Roma**

Dondurma at İskele Cad. 5/C is a local favorite) and a few hotels, as well as the boarding point for the horse-drawn carriages, which are known as *fayton* (phaeton) in Turkish. The island has a few tiny beaches, including **Yörük Ali Plajı,** located on the west side of the island and an easy walk from the harbor. An admission fee of 35–40 TL for the day at the island's beaches generally includes the use of a beach chair and umbrella.

Çankaya Caddesi, up from the clock tower and to the right, is home to the island's most splendid old Victorian houses, painted in gleaming white or pastel colors and with beautiful latticework. The carriage tour passes this way, winding up hilly lanes lined with gardens filled with jasmine, mimosa, and imported palm trees. After all of Istanbul's mosques and palaces, the frilly gingerbread-style houses come as something of a surprise. If you're on foot or a bike, turn off Çankaya Caddesi onto Hamlacı Sokak and go down to the end of the lane to see one of the houses Trotsky lived in while exiled here. Now in shambles, with crumbling brick walls and a caved-in roof, the house can only be viewed from outside the locked gate, but offers an interesting glimpse into the past.

Working to preserve the islands' unique history is the **Museum of the Princes' Islands**, which hosts exhibitions on various topics, from local fishing traditions to the rich diversity of religious practices once represented here, at two permanent sites on Büyükada, the open-air Çınar Museum Grounds in the center of town and the St. Nicholas Hangar Museum Site along the island's eastern coast, as well as at pop-up displays elsewhere. The St. Nicholas Hangar Museum Site is open Tuesday–Sunday 9–7 (closes 6 pm in winter) and the admission fee is 5 TL.

The island's most significant attraction is the **Greek Monastery of St. George (Aya Yorgi),** a 19th-century church built on Byzantine foundations at the top of Yücetepe Hill, with a view that goes on and on. It's a fairly steep 20-minute walk up from Birlik Meydanı, where your driver will drop you off if you come by buggy. ■ **TIP→ Drivers charge a waiting fee and there are always numerous carriages for hire in the square, so it's a little cheaper to pay 29 TL each for two one-way rides than to do the "short tour."** This is a popular Orthodox Christian pilgrimage site; as you walk up the path, notice the pieces of cloth, string, and even plastic wrappers that visitors have tied to the bushes and trees in hope of a wish coming true. The small church is open daily from 9 to 6.

🍴 Restaurants

With one or two exceptions, there is little difference from one spot on Büyükada's row of waterfront fish restaurants to the next. The best bet is to look at a menu and ask to see the meze and fish on offer that day. Food on the island is generally overpriced because everything has to be brought in from the mainland, and the heavy influx of tourists means venues have little incentive to stand out. Generally, prices are more expensive closer to the docks; the side streets farther in have some cheaper cafés and eateries (Konak at Recep Koç Cad. 47 is one popular choice), as well as small groceries and bakeries where you can stock up on picnic supplies.

Altın Fıçı Mercan

$ | TURKISH | This cluster of small tables under a spreading tree not far from the ferry dock is a friendly place to have an inexpensive meal of grilled meat or fried seafood, or to while away some time people-watching while sipping a beer or a glass or wine or *rakı.* **Known for:** scenic location; close to the ferry; fresh seafood. $ *Average main: 39 TL ⊠ Recep Koç Cad. 17/E, Büyükada, Princes Islands* ☎ *216/382–3535 ▬ No credit cards.*

Secret Garden Restaurant
$$ | **TURKISH** | The meze, meatballs, salads, grilled fish, and other mainly Turkish fare are fresh and well prepared but the hospitable service and lovely, secluded setting are what really make this restaurant attached to the Ada Palas hotel stand out. Seating is in quaint greenhouse-style structure or the lush garden, where one outdoor table is romantically draped in a filmy canopy. **Known for:** garden seating; wide array of meze; seasonal fish selection. [$] *Average main: 50 TL* ✉ *Çiçekyalı Sok. 24, Büyükada, Princes Islands* ☎ *216/382–1444* 🌐 *www.secretgardenrestaurant.com.tr* 💳 *No credit cards.*

Hotels

Ada Palas Büyükada
$ | **B&B/INN** | Housed in a restored, late-19th-century building that was formerly a schoolhouse, this hotel and its dozen rooms are decorated in an old-fashioned Victorian style outfitted with modern lighting, bathrooms, and other conveniences. **Pros:** charming, intimate property; romantic garden; friendly staff goes out of their way to make guests feel at home. **Cons:** no views; rooms off the reception area may be noisy; style can be old-fashioned. [$] *Rooms from: €45* ✉ *Çiçekliyalı Sok. 24, Büyükada, Princes Islands* ☎ *216/382–1444* 🌐 *www.adapalas.com.tr* 🛏 *12 rooms* 🍴 *Free Breakfast.*

Splendid Palace Hotel
$$ | **HOTEL** | This charming turn-of-the-century hotel (built in 1908) is the grande dame of Büyükada, with old-fashioned furniture, large rooms—including those in the front with stunning sea views—and a blend of Ottoman and art nouveau styles. **Pros:** peaceful, romantic setting; waterfront views can't be beat; historic building. **Cons:** no air-conditioning; vintage ambience may not be to everyone's taste; no car access. [$] *Rooms from: €100* ✉ *23 Nisan Cad. 53, Büyükada, Princes Islands* ☎ *216/382–6950* 🌐 *www.splendidhotel.net* ⏲ *Closed Dec.–Mar.* 🛏 *69 rooms* 🍴 *Free Breakfast.*

Heybeliada

Heybeliada, the closest island to Büyükada and the archipelago's second largest, is similar in appeal, and the quiet, lovely surroundings attract similar boatloads of day-trippers in summer, some hoping to avoid the crowds on the "big island."

To the right of the dock are teahouses and cafés stretching along the waterfront; heading inland up İşgüzar Sokak, you'll find some tiny, charming shops selling locally made jams (Ev'den Reçel at İşgüzar Sok. 34/B), handicrafts (Luz Cafe & Shop at İşgüzar Sok. 36), and gift-worthy paper products (Ya Da at Zeybek 2 Sok. 3/1). You can take a leisurely carriage ride or rent a bike, stopping, if the mood strikes, at one of the island's several small, sandy beaches—the best are on the north shore on either side of Değirmen Burnu (Windmill Point). Some of these beaches now fall within the confines of **Değirmenburnu Tabiat Parkı**, a 30-acre natural park area (5 TL admission) that also includes picnic spots, BBQ pits, children's play areas, small cafés, bike-rental shops, and the ruins of a 19th-century windmill.

The big building to the left of the ferry dock is the **Deniz Lisesi** (Turkish Naval High School), founded in 1773. The island's most significant landmark is the **Haghia Triada Monastery**, built in the 19th century on Byzantine foundations and perched amid peaceful garden grounds at the top of Heybeliada's highest hill. The building, parts of which are now open to visitors from 8:30 to 4 daily (free admission), served as the Halki Seminary (Halki is the Greek name of the island), a theological school for Greek Orthodox priests, until it was shut down in 1971 by the Turkish government. That controversial move is still unresolved decades later despite diplomatic pressure from the United States and Europe. The island is also home to a modern Greek Orthodox church and a synagogue, though they are usually closed.

🍴 Restaurants

Heyamola Ada Lokantası
$$ | TURKISH | One of the best places to eat on any of the islands, Heyamola offers a daily selection of fresh vegetable and seafood meze (including affording mixed-plate options), salads, and seafood, including specialties of the house like a sardine casserole or *mezgit* (whiting) cooked with white wine and ginger. The charming indoor-outdoor garden has a relaxing Aegean air. **Known for:** garden seating; wide selection of meze; well-chosen Turkish wine list. $ *Average main: 44 TL* ✉ *Yalı Cad., Heybeliada, Princes Islands* ✛ *Across from the Mavi Marmara ferry pier* ☎ *216/351–1111* ⊕ *www.heyamolaadalokantasi.com.*

🛏 Hotels

Perili Köşk
$ | B&B/INN | Rooms in this tiny hotel tucked away near the entrance to Değirmenburnu park are simply but tastefully decorated, with old radios and furniture adding nostalgic charm; a top-floor king suite has a minibar, Jacuzzi tub, and terrace. **Pros:** peaceful location not far from ferry pier; attractive rooms; homey feeling. **Cons:** fairly simple accommodations; few facilities for guests; restaurant-bar downstairs can get noisy, especially when there's live music. $ *Rooms from: €45* ✉ *Ayyıldız Cad. 103, Heybeliada, Princes Islands* ☎ *216/351–8710* ⊕ *www.perilikosk.net* ↻ *7 rooms* ❍❙ *Free Breakfast* ⊟ *No credit cards.*

Chapter 4

THE SEA OF MARMARA AND THE NORTH AEGEAN

Updated by
Kevin Mataraci

4

⊙ Sights	🍴 Restaurants	🛏 Hotels	🛍 Shopping	🍸 Nightlife
★★★★☆	★★★☆☆	★★★☆☆	★★☆☆☆	★★☆☆☆

WELCOME TO THE SEA OF MARMARA AND THE NORTH AEGEAN

TOP REASONS TO GO

★ **Explore "Green Bursa":** Visit Yeşil Cami (Green Mosque), stroll the covered bazaar, and make sure to try the local kebab specialty, İskender kebap.

★ **Go back in time at Troy:** Visit the ruins of this 5,000-year-old city of Homer's Iliad, where more than nine layers of civilization have been uncovered.

★ **Pay respects at Gallipoli:** Tour the battlefields and memorials where one of the key campaigns of World War I was fought.

★ **Ramble through ancient Pergamum:** Explore this spectacular showcase of the classical period, second in Turkey only to Ephesus.

★ **Relax in Assos:** Enjoy the quiet of Behramkale village, marvel at the Greek ruins, and soak up the sun on nearby beaches.

★ **Shop for İznik tiles:** Watch craftswomen engrave the famous ceramics and buy some to take home.

A ferry ride across the Sea of Marmara from Istanbul will take you close to İznik, famed for its beautiful tiles, and the old Ottoman capital of Bursa. The historic World War I battlefields of the Gallipoli Peninsula are best visited from Çanakkale or Eceabat, on either side of the Dardanelles Strait; Çanakkale is also the jumping-off point for visits to the fabled ancient city of Troy. Farther down the Aegean coast you'll find a scenic hilltop village and ruins at Assos (Behramkale), the laid-back harbor town of Ayvalık and its nearby sandy beaches, and (a short distance inland) the ancient ruins of Bergama (Pergamum).

1 İznik. Located on a lake shore, it was an important center of early Christianity; today it's better known for its famous ceramic tiles.

2 Bursa. Once an Ottoman capital but now an important industrial center, it's particularly known for its many green-tiled buildings.

3 Gallipoli. Location of an infamous battle during World War I, where many ANZAC forces were killed, it's now known for its expansive military cemeteries.

4 Çanakkale. The largest city on Turkey's northern Aegean coast and a popular base for exploring the Gallipoli battlefields.

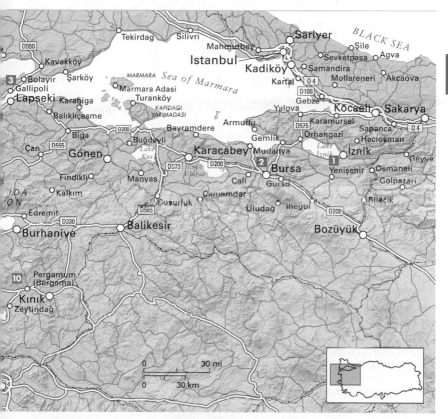

5 Eceabat. The closest town to the Gallipoli battlefields on the European side of the Dardanelles.

6 Troy. Ancient ruins of the city associated with the war depicted in the Iliad; a new museum opened in 2018.

7 Behramkale (Assos). A small but picturesque fishing village with nearby ruins of ancient Assos, an important Greek city.

8 Ayvalik. Beautiful former Greek outpost surrounded by little islands.

9 Cunda Island (Ali Bey Adasi). Once part of Greece; now a popular tourist resort.

10 Pergamum (Bergama). Among the most spectacular ancient ruins in Turkey and one of the world's greatest powers in its time.

The ruins of Pergamum, Troy, and Assos, along with the Gallipoli battlefields, are the main draws of the region, but leisurely exploration is also rewarded with fresh air, a cool sea, great food, and havens in the wilderness.

The North Aegean and the Sea of Marmara areas are rich in history, spanning many centuries and empires. Civilizations rose and fell at Troy for 5,000 years, and the ruins of Pergamum date from the time of Alexander the Great. The bustling city of Bursa was the first capital of the Ottoman Empire, before Istanbul. The battlefields of Gallipoli bear testament to the more recent past, World War I, while the backstreets of Ayvalık still echo with the footsteps of the Greeks who lived there until early in the 20th century.

The beaches in this region tend to be more pebbly (and the water a touch colder) than they are in other parts of Turkey, but they're also frequently less crowded. You can see the whole of the region in a week or, if you're based in Istanbul, on separate, shorter journeys. Spend at least one evening watching the sun go down over Homer's wine-dark sea, and you'll agree that the North Aegean has a little bit of everything—and a lot you won't find anywhere else.

MAJOR REGIONS

You can still feel the Ottoman spirit along the **Sea of Marmara,** where you'll find some of the best examples of early Ottoman architecture, faithfully restored thermal baths, the surviving arts of tile making and silk weaving, and wonderful old bazaars in İznik and Bursa.

The area north of the straits of Marmara—more popularly known as **The Dardanelles,** which connect the Aegean and Marmara seas—is full of moving historical sites marking one of the bloodiest campaigns of World War I. Beautifully tended cemeteries stretch along the 35-km (22-mile) Gallipoli Peninsula, where so many soldiers are buried. Çanakkale is south of Gallipoli. Escabat is where most soldiers are buried.

The combination of Greek heritage and Turkish rural life in the country's **North Aegean,** where you'll find an unspoiled natural setting of azure sea, curving coastline, and pine-clad hills, is perfect for unwinding. It's an area of both ruins and resorts, including Troy, Behramkale (Assos), Ayvalik, Cunda Island (Ali Bey Adasi), and Pergamum (Bergama).

Planning

WHEN TO GO

The Southern Marmara and the North Aegean region are considerably cooler than the South Aegean and Mediterranean coast, but summer is still very hot. In July and August, the national park at Uludağ, in Bursa, remains refreshingly cool; with its skiing opportunities, it's also an attraction in winter. If you're here in colder months, soaking in Bursa's thermal baths is a good antidote to the winter blues.

Travelers from New Zealand and Australia throng the Gallipoli Peninsula and nearby towns for the April 25 Anzac Day commemorations; other visitors may want to avoid the area at this busy time. Çanakkale, Gallipoli, Troy—which Homer referred to as a windy city—and Assos can all be gusty in late summer and fall.

PLANNING YOUR TIME
You can see a bit of the Sea of Marmara on a quick one- or two-day trip from Istanbul: you could do just a day in İznik (make sure you leave Istanbul early), but you'll want to spend a night, at least, in Bursa. The ferry from Istanbul's Yenikapı terminal to Yalova takes about an hour; from there, you can catch a bus to İznik or Bursa. There are also direct ferries to Bursa (Güzelyalı) from Yenikapı, though you should allow an hour to get between the ferry terminal and the city center by public transportation.

An optimal way to spend two days around the Sea of Marmara is to leave Istanbul by ferry early enough to be in Yalova by mid-morning, then catch a bus or drive to İznik and have lunch by the lake. Next, head into the center of town to visit the Saint Sophia, the Lefke Gate, and some of the famous tile workshops. If you leave İznik by late afternoon, you'll be in Bursa in the early evening. Spend the second day sightseeing in Bursa—don't miss Yeşil Cami, the covered bazaar, Ulu Cami, and the Muradiye Tombs. For lunch, make sure to try the *İskender kebap*. If you have time, you can take the gondola lift up Uludağ and enjoy the view from the mountain's pine-covered slopes. Head down to the Bursa ferry station in the early evening and catch the last boat back to Yenikapı terminal in Istanbul.

You can visit Gallipoli in a long, rushed day trip from Istanbul (as many tour operators do) but you're better off spending

the night in Çanakkale and seeing the ruins of Troy as well. If you have five or six days, you can pretty much see everything in the vicinity, visiting İznik, Bursa, and Çanakkale, then continuing on to Behramkale (Assos) and Ayvalık, with a visit to Cunda, Ayvalık's main island, and the ruins of Pergamum. Be warned, though: Once you get a taste of the area's natural beauty and relaxing vibe, you might want to stay longer.

GETTING HERE AND AROUND
AIR TRAVEL
There are several small airports in the area, but due to the proximity to Istanbul, there are few direct flights. From Balıkesir Koca Seyit Airport in Edremit, 50 km (31 miles) north of Ayvalık, Pegasus flies daily to and from Sabiha Gökçen. Both Bursa, the largest city in the region, and Çanakkale have an airport, but they are not served by direct flights from Istanbul.

BOAT AND FERRY TRAVEL
Ferries provide the quickest, most pleasant way to get to Bursa or İznik from Istanbul. İDO ferries operate daily between Istanbul's Yenikapı terminal and ports in Yalova and Bursa. The Yalova fast ferries accommodate vehicles and run more frequently, approximately every two hours between 7:30 am and 9:30 pm in summer, with fewer departures in winter; the journey takes just over an hour, and tickets start at around 20 TL each way for walk-on passengers and around 80 TL to 150 TL for a car (including a driver and one passenger). Ferries from Yenikapı to Bursa (Güzelyalı port) take about 90 minutes and cost somewhat more; some are fast car ferries, while others are passenger-only sea buses. (Check the latest times and fares at ⊕ www.ido.com.tr/en.) İDO also operates ferries daily between Yenikapı and Bandırma (two hours), a good point from which to make your way to Çanakkale, Assos, or Ayvalık.

If you're traveling without a vehicle, you can also take a BUDO sea bus from Istanbul's Eminönü/Sirkeci terminal to Bursa (Mudanya port). Sea buses operate about every two hours between early morning and midevening in summer, and less frequently in winter. Tickets cost about 34 TL each way. (Check ⊕ budo. burulas.com.tr for fares and schedules.)

BUS TRAVEL
Buses are a good form of transport in this region, though the frequent stops on some routes, such as between Çanakkale and Ayvalık, can be frustrating. Most bus companies have branches both in the terminals and in the town centers. Several buses make the trip from Istanbul's Esenler terminal to İznik or Bursa via the Yalova ferry (about four hours). The trip from Istanbul to Çanakkale is about six hours and costs 60 to 70 TL. The trip from Bursa to Çanakkale is five hours and costs about 40 TL. From Çanakkale buses run almost every hour to İzmir, passing Ezine, Ayvacık, Edremit, Ayvalık, and Bergama on the way. The fare is about 35 to 40 TL, depending on your destination.

CAR TRAVEL
The best way to explore this area is by car, especially if you want to travel off the beaten path and forgo organized tours of Gallipoli, which is very spread out. Roads are quite good and well marked. There are several options for getting to the region from Istanbul; one is to take the E80 headed for Ankara. At Gebze, take the O-5 across the İzmit Bay Bridge toward Bursa, then take Route 575 into the city.

TRAIN TRAVEL
Train travel in this region is not advisable: trains (and tracks) are old and painfully slow.

RESTAURANTS
Aegean cuisine is in many ways different from Turkish food elsewhere. The shared Turkish and Greek culture of the region's past, the climate and soil suitable for growing a wide range of vegetables, including tasty local greens and herbs, and the prevalence of olive trees and olive oil production have helped the region develop a much more varied way of eating that is healthier than in other Turkish regions. Olive oil replaces butter, and fish, rather than meat, is the star on most menus. The class of dishes generally called zeytinyağlı (literally "with olive oil") mostly comes from this region; these are usually comprised of tomatoes, onions, and other vegetables cooked in olive oil and served cold. Vegetarians will be in heaven.

HOTELS
From simple, family-run pansiyons (guesthouses) in rural Assos, to luxurious, well-established palaces in Bursa; from garden retreats in Bozcaada to Greek stone houses in Ayvalık and Bergama, the Marmara and North Aegean areas have an impressive range of lodging options. In general, however, smaller boutique hotels that make the most of the region's alluring natural beauty are what define the best accommodations here. Many can be found in Bozcaada, Assos, and Ayvalık; breakfasts are fresh and made with herbs, fruit, and vegetables that are often sourced in the hotels' own gardens and orchards. Hotels in more rural towns like Bergama or İznik can also be your best sources for information, as local tourist offices have inconsistent opening hours and sometimes lack resources. Room rates drop significantly in the off-season, and it is always a good idea to ask for a discount in quiet periods. As many of the destinations featured here are hubs for their rural hinterlands, weekends can fill up with wedding guests and other local visitors, so phone ahead to confirm that there are rooms. Advanced bookings are crucial if you are considering visiting the Gallipoli Peninsula or Çanakkale around

Anzac Day, and are advisable throughout the region in summer.

Hotel reviews have been shortened. For full information, visit Fodors.com

What It Costs in Turkish Lira

	$	$$	$$$	$$$$
RESTAURANTS				
	under 15 TL	16 TL–30 TL	31 TL–50 TL	over 50 TL
HOTELS				
	under $75	$76–$150	$151–$250	over $250

TOURS

If you have a car, you can tour the battlefields and memorials on your own, though a good guide can help bring the area's history to life. Hotels that run tours also often screen the feature film *Gallipoli* or the documentary *The Fatal Shore* in the evenings, to set the mood. Tours are conducted year-round out of Çanakkale and Eceabat, and typically run about 5½ hours, starting around noon, and include lunch. (Tour companies operating out of Çanakkale allow time to make the ferry trip to Eceabat before heading out on the peninsula.) Most half-day tours of Gallipoli focus on the ANZAC sites on the upper part of the peninsula, including Lone Pine Cemetery and Chunuk Bair; tours go to Cape Helles on the southern end less regularly, and may need to be arranged privately. Some companies also have day trips to Gallipoli from Istanbul, leaving around 6 am and returning around 10 pm, but these can make for a long and exhausting experience. For all tours, good walking shoes are advised and, in summer, a hat and water.

Crowded House Tours

GUIDED TOURS | Considered one of the best tour companies in Gallipoli, Crowded House Tours runs daily afternoon tours of the key ANZAC sites on the Gallipoli Peninsula. Guides include the legendary Bülent "Bill" Yılmaz Korkmaz, and groups are kept on the small side. The company also has morning tours to Troy and snorkeling excursions around the peninsula. ⊠ *Zübeyde Hanım Meydanı 28, Eceabat* ☎ *286/814–1565* ⊕ *www.crowdedhousegallipoli.com* ⊠ *Half-day tours from €29.*

Hassle Free Travel Agency

GUIDED TOURS | One of the area's longest-running and most professional tour companies, Hassle Free runs daily afternoon tours of the ANZAC battlefields and cemeteries and morning tours to Troy. The company also organizes boat trips around the beaches at Suvla Bay, which give a unique sense of the topography of the peninsula and the chance to snorkel. Customized private tours of the peninsula and overnight packages from Istanbul can be arranged as well. ⊠ *Cumhuriyet Meydanı 59, Çanakkale* ☎ *286/213–5969* ⊕ *www.anzachouse.com* ⊠ *Half-day Gallipoli tours from €45.*

TJ's Tours

GUIDED TOURS | Run by a Turkish and Australian couple, TJ's Tours has been operating out of Eceabat for about 20 years. The tour of the main Gallipoli battlefields includes a short visit to the Gallipoli Simulation Center. Daily tours to Troy, and snorkeling/diving excursions to shipwrecks around the Gallipoli Peninsula, are also available. ⊠ *Kemalpaşa Mah., Cumhuriyet Cad. 5/A, Eceabat* ☎ *286/814–3121* ⊕ *www.anzacgallipoli-tours.com* ⊠ *Half-day tours from €33.*

VISITOR INFORMATION

Each featured town in the region has a visitor information center, and although staffers are generally extremely helpful, the office opening hours vary depending on the number of tourists around and are unreliable. *Resources for self-guided tours in Gallipoli are detailed later in the chapter, but the new interpretive center*

The Sea of Marmara

at Kabatepe is worth visiting for more information. For much of the rest of the region, with the exception of Bursa, hotels serve as the primary sources of visitor information.

İznik

190 km (118 miles) from Istanbul.

Nature has been generous to İznik, which is beautifully situated around the east end of Lake İznik. You can swim (though the water can be chilly), picnic, or watch the sun set over the lake, and you can also soak in centuries of history and witness the city's legendary tile-making tradition, in full revival today.

An important city in early Christian history, İznik (known in ancient times as Nicaea) was the site of the First and Second Councils of Nicaea, which drew up the Nicene Creed that outlines the basic principles of Christianity and set the church's stance on iconography. The city was put on the map in 316 BC, when one of Alexander the Great's generals claimed it. The Seljuks made the city their capital for a brief period in the 11th century, and Byzantine emperors-in-exile did the same in the 13th century, when Constantinople was in the hands of Crusaders. The Ottomans captured the city in 1331, and İznik became famous for its production of colorful tiles, unequaled even today.

İznik's Tiled Beauty

İznik tile makers believe that their tiles have magical properties. There is one sound explanation for this (alongside any number of unsound ones): İznik tiles, made from soil that's found only in the area, have a high level of quartz, an element believed to have soothing effects. It's not just the level of quartz that makes İznik tiles unique, though. The original tiles also have distinctive patterns and colors: predominantly blue, then green and red, reflecting the colors of precious stones. The patterns are inspired by local flora—flowering trees or tulips. These days artists use different colors and designs as well as the traditional ones.

İznik became a center for the ceramics industry after the 15th-century Ottoman conquest of Istanbul. To upgrade the quality of native work, Sultan Selim I (ruled 1512–15) brought 500 potters over from Tabriz in Persia. The government-owned kilns were soon turning out exquisite tiles with intricate motifs of circles, stars, and floral and geometric patterns, in lush turquoise, green, blue, red, and white. Despite their costliness, the tiles' popularity spread through the Islamic world, until the industry went into decline in the late 17th century.

İznik tiles are expensive—more so than those produced in the rival ceramics center of Kütahya, 120 km (72 miles) farther south. Prices for real İznik tiles and plates, which should be at least 70% quartz, can run into the hundreds of lira. Because of their higher quartz content than ceramics made elsewhere, İznik tiles are heavier and more durable, making them ideal for decorating high-traffic spaces such as airports and mosques. They're all handmade, with no artificial colors, and the designs tend to be more intricate and elegant than those of their rivals. The tile-makers' street (Salim Demircan Sokak), near the city center, is lined with small shops and workshops where you can see the tiles being made and buy the famous wares.

GETTING HERE AND AROUND

If you're driving, İznik is 140 km (86 miles) from Istanbul via Route E80 and O-5 to the İzmit Bay Bridge and Route 130 followed by Route 595 to İznik. Or take the ferry from Istanbul's Yenikapı terminal to Yalova (one hour) and then get on Route 595.

In Istanbul, several buses (the 69A, YT-1, 70KY, and 70FY are the most frequent) run from Cumhuriyet Caddesi near Taksim Square to Yenikapı terminal. The M2 metro line, which passes through Taksim, terminates at Yenikapı, and leaves about a 10-minute walk to the terminal.

Once you arrive in Yalova by boat, if you don't have your own car, exit the ferry port, turn right, and walk about 50 yards past the police station to the minibus station. Destinations are clearly displayed in the bus windows, and you'll find the one to İznik near a series of buildings on your right. The trip from Yalova to İznik costs about 15 TL.

İznik is easy to navigate and the town's sights are all easily within reach on foot; you'll encounter the city's walls as you explore. The four main gates date back to Roman times, and the city's two main streets intersect each other and end at these gates. Running east–west is

4 — The Sea of Marmara and the North Aegean İZNİK

Kılıçaslan Caddesi; north–south is Atatürk Caddesi. Saint Sophia church is at the intersection of these streets.

VISITOR INFORMATION

CONTACTS Visitor Information. ✉ *Atatürk Cad. and Kılıçaslan Cad.*

Sights

Aya Sofya (*Saint Sophia, Aya Sofya Camii*)
RELIGIOUS SITE |. The primitive mosaic floor is believed to date from the church's construction in the 6th century, during the reign of Justinian; the church was later reconstructed in the 11th century, after an earthquake toppled the original edifice. A faded fresco of Jesus, Mary, and John the Baptist at ground level on the north wall and some rather poorly preserved frescoes in the domes on either side of the apse date to the Byzantine era. In a controversial move, authorities converted this former museum into a mosque in 2011. **■TIP→ Try to arrange your visit outside of prayer times, when you can explore the site freely and take photographs.** ✉ *Atatürk Cad. and Kılıçaslan Cad.* 🎟 *Free.*

Lefke Kapısı (*Lefke Gate*)
ARCHAEOLOGICAL SITE |. The eastern gate to the ancient city was built in honor of a visit by the Roman emperor Hadrian in AD 120 and is among the best-preserved remnants of the thick, sturdy fortifications that once encircled İznik. Some of the original inscriptions, marble reliefs, and friezes remain intact. Outside the gray stone and faded brick gate is a leafy graveyard and the city's small but technically impressive aqueduct. ✉ *At the eastern end of Kılıçaslan Cad.*

Tomb and Mosque of Abdülvahap
MEMORIAL | If you're looking for a good spot to watch the sunset over İznik Lake, the tomb of Abdülvahap Sultan Sancaktarı, a hero of the battle in which the Ottomans captured the city in 1331, is well worth the trip for its sweeping view. From this monument, on a clear evening the orange glow of sunset makes the surrounding mountains look like the backs of gigantic serpents sleeping in the lake. The spot—a short drive or a 30-minute walk (some of it uphill) from the city center—attracts couples young and old as well as extended families, many of whom bring dinner along to accentuate the experience. Take Kılıçaslan Caddesi east through Lefke Gate and then follow the ruins of the Roman aqueduct along the road on your right until you can see the large Turkish flag on the hilltop near the tomb. ✉ *East of İznik Orhangazi Yolu/Sansarak Yolu.*

Restaurants

Kenan Çorba & Izgara
$ | TURKISH | This popular spot just opposite the Aya Sofya serves soups, beans with sliced Turkish pastrami and rice, and typical home-style dishes. The *işkembe* (tripe soup) is probably best for those who are into experimenting—you'll either hate it or love it. **Known for:** home-style meals; central location; reasonable prices. [$] *Average main: 14 TL* ✉ *Atatürk Cad. 93/B* ☎ *224/757–0235* 🌐 *www.kenancorba.com.*

Köfteci Yusuf
$ | TURKISH | Turks love their *köfte* (meatballs), and almost every city in the country makes a claim to fame based on its own way of preparing them, including İznik. Locals fill the large, canteen-type tables of this casual bi-level eatery with both indoor and deck seating at almost all times of the day to enjoy İznik köfte, served with tomatoes, peppers, onions, and a mildly spicy red pepper sauce. **Known for:** large portions; künefe (a sweet, cheese-filled pastry soaked in syrup); excellent service. [$] *Average main: 15 TL* ✉ *Atatürk Cad. 73*

☎ *224/757–3597, 224/444–6162 main call center* 🌐 *www.kofteciyusuf.com.tr.*

Hotels

Çamlık Motel
$ | **HOTEL** | The simple, clean rooms of the oldest hotel in İznik are a bit on the dull side, but this quiet lakefront establishment is, after 30 years, still an excellent choice. **Pros:** nice location near the quietest part of the lake; good, reasonably priced restaurant. **Cons:** fairly basic accommodations; only four rooms face the lake; no elevator. [$] *Rooms from: $50* ✉ *Göl Sahil Yolu* ☎ *224/757–1362* 🌐 *www.iznik-camlikmotel.com* 🛏 *24 rooms* 🍴 *Free Breakfast.*

Grand Hotel Belekoma
$ | **HOTEL** | This welcome addition to Iznik's lodging options wins fans with its modern, spotless regular and family rooms, half of which face the lake, which is on the other side of a busy road. **Pros:** good location; rooms with views; very clean. **Cons:** limited English spoken; noise from wedding parties on the weekend; a bit impersonal. [$] *Rooms from: $65* ✉ *M. Kemalpasa Mh., Göl Sahil Yolu 8* ☎ *224/757–1407* 🌐 *www.iznikbelekomahotel.com* 🛏 *46 rooms* 🍴 *Free Breakfast.*

Hotel Zeytin Bahçesi
$ | **HOTEL** | İznik's newest lakefront hotel is relatively secluded from the main part of town. **Pros:** spotless, modern facilities; attractive pool; peaceful location. **Cons:** a long walk from center of town; breakfast could be better; weak Wi-Fi in some areas. [$] *Rooms from: 230 TL* ✉ *Selçuk Mah., Kutalmışoğlu Süleyman Şah Cad. 119* ☎ *224/757–2404* 🌐 *www.hotelzeytinbahcesi.com* 🛏 *39 rooms* 🍴 *Free Breakfast.*

Seyir Butik Pansiyon
$ | **B&B/INN** | Just steps from the waterfront at the end of İznik's main east–west thoroughfare, this family-run guesthouse opened in 2015 rents comfortable, affordable accommodations in a pleasant setting. **Pros:** friendly vibe and personal service; good value; great location. **Cons:** bathrooms somewhat basic; most rooms have no views; area can be noisy at night. [$] *Rooms from: €38* ✉ *M. Kemalpaşa Mah., Kılıçaslan Cad. 5* ☎ *224/757–7799, 505/505–2250 cell phone* 🌐 *www.seyirbutik.com* 🛏 *9 rooms* 🍴 *Free Breakfast.*

Bursa

240 km (150 miles) from Istanbul.

An important center since early Ottoman times, Bursa is today one of Turkey's more prosperous cities (due to its large automobile and textile industries) and is also a pleasing mix of bustling modernity, old stone buildings, mosques, thermal spas, and wealthy suburbs with vintage wood-frame Ottoman villas. Residents proudly call their city Yeşil Bursa (Green Bursa)—for the green İznik tiles decorating some of its most famous monuments, and also for its parks and gardens and the national forest surrounding nearby Uludağ, Turkey's most popular ski mountain.

Bursa became the first capital of the nascent Ottoman Empire after the city was captured in 1326 by Orhan Gazi. Although it was moved to Edirne in the 1360s and then to Istanbul in 1453, the city retained its spiritual importance for the Ottomans. Each of the first five sultans after Orhan Gazi built his own complex on five different hilltops, and each included a mosque, a *medrese* (theological school), a hammam, a soup kitchen, *kervansaray* (old-fashioned inn), and tombs. It was in Bursa that Ottoman architecture blossomed and the foundations laid for the more elaborate works in the later capitals. More than 125 mosques here are on the list of historical sites kept by the Turkish Historical Monuments Commission, and their minarets make for a grand skyline.

GETTING HERE AND AROUND

If you're driving, Bursa is 154 km (93 miles) from Istanbul via Route 100 or E80 to the İzmit Bay Bridge, O-5 toward Bursa, and Route 575 into the city. Bursa is 80 km (50 miles) from İznik. You can also get to Bursa by taking an İDO fast ferry from Istanbul's Yenikapı to Yalova or Bursa (Güzelyalı port).

From Istanbul, it's a four-hour bus trip to Bursa, including the ferry ride from Darıca to Yalova, and costs about 40 TL. A better option is to take a MUDO sea bus to Bursa (Mudanya port) from Istanbul's Kabataş dock for around 35 TL each way. From the Bursa ferry terminal, yellow city buses go to downtown Bursa; a faster alternative may be to take a city bus to Emek metro station, from which you can take the Bursaray metro the rest of the way downtown. The journey takes about an hour and costs around 5 TL.

Bursa is a large city, stretching out along an east–west axis. The town square, at the intersection of Atatürk Caddesi and İnönü Caddesi, is officially named Cumhuriyet Alanı (Republic Square), but is popularly called **Heykel** (Statue), after its imposing equestrian statue of Atatürk. East of Heykel is the Yeşil neighborhood, with Yeşil Cami and Yeşil Türbe. To the northwest is Çekirge, the thermal spa district, with the city's fanciest lodging options.

Buses from outside the city center converge on Heykel, from where you can reach most sites. Shared taxis with white destination signs on top regularly ply the route between Heykel and Çekirge; hop in or out at signs marked with a "D" (for *dolmuş*). The main bus routes run about every 15 minutes during the day and roughly every 30 minutes at night. There

Take the Waters ⊙

Bursa has been a spa town since Roman times. Rich in minerals, the waters are said to cure a variety of ills, from rheumatism to nervous complaints. The thermal springs run along the slopes of the Çekirge neighborhood, and mineral baths are an amenity at many hotels in this area. The historical **Eski Kaplıca Hamamı** is now affiliated with the Kervansaray Termal Hotel, but open to the public at reasonable rates for a soak, scrub, or massage. ☎ 224/233–9300 ⊕ www.kervansarayhotels.com.tr

are signs and posted schedules at most major stops.

VISITOR INFORMATION

CONTACTS Visitor Information. ✉ Atatürk Cad., Ulu Cami yanı,, Heykel ☎ 224/220–1848.

⊙ Sights

Bursa Kent Müzesi (*Bursa City Museum*) **MUSEUM** |. Right behind Heykel, this well-conceived museum is a showcase for local history and handicrafts. Among the exhibits are impressive re-creations of sections in a traditional bazaar—such as those for silk weavers, saddle makers, and metalsmiths—and clothing; household items; and dioramas of life at home, school, and in the hammam. Panels narrate the history of Bursa and the Ottoman Empire's first six sultans. Artifacts relating to the War of Independence are also on show. ■TIP→ **The exhibits are in Turkish, so get one of the English-language headsets at the entrance, though the audio does not provide full narration.** ✉ Atatürk

Cad. 8 ☎ *224/220–2626* ⊕ *www.bursakentmuzesi.com* ✉ *2 TL.*

Emir Sultan Camii (*Emir Sultan Mosque*)
RELIGIOUS SITE |. The daughter of Sultan Yıldırım Beyazıt built the Emir Sultan Camii in 1429 for her husband, Emir Sultan, and it sits amid cypresses and plane trees on a quiet hilltop overlooking the city. The single-domed mosque was badly damaged in the 1855 earthquake and almost totally rebuilt by Sultan Abdülaziz. The two cut-stone minarets are considered great examples of rococo, and the assemblage faces an attractive courtyard that houses the tombs of Emir Sultan, his wife, and their children. ✉ *Doyuran Cad.*

★ **Kapalı Çarşı** (*Covered Bazaar*)
MARKET |. The vast complex behind Ulu Cami comprises many adjoining *hans* (kervansarays, or inns for merchants) surrounding a *bedesten* (the central part of a covered bazaar, which is vaulted and fireproofed). Bursa sultans began building bazaars in the 14th century to finance the construction or maintenance of their schools, mosques, or soup kitchens. The precinct was soon topped with roofs, creating the earliest form of covered bazaar, and late in the century Yıldırım Beyazıt perfected the concept by building a *bedesten* with six parts connected by arches and topped by 14 domes. The complex was flattened by a massive earthquake in 1855, and sections were badly burned by fire in the 1950s, but the Kapalı Çarşı has been lovingly restored to provide a flavor of the past. Best buys here include gold jewelry, thick Turkish cotton towels (for which Bursa is famous), and silk goods. ✉ *Behind Ulu Cami, Between Atatürk Cad. and Cumhuriyet Cad.*

Kültür Parkı (*Culture Park*)
MUSEUM |. Refreshingly green, this park is laced with restaurants, tea gardens, a pond with paddleboats, and an amusement park. It's always crowded and

pleasantly animated, though it seems more like a busy public gathering spot than a place of refuge. Amid the lawns and walkways is Bursa's **Arkeoloji Müzesi** (Archaeology Museum), which displays a range of finds from the surrounding region, including coins and ceramics. ✉ *Çekirge Cad. and Stadyum Cad.* ☎ *224/234–4918 (museum)* ✉ *5 TL (museum).*

Muradiye Tombs
MEMORIAL | The complex around the Sultan Murat II Camii (built 1425–26) is probably the city's most serene resting place, with 12 tombs tucked amid a leafy park. Among those buried here are Murat (1404–51), the father of Mehmet the Conqueror, and Mustafa (1515–53), the eldest son of Süleyman the Magnificent, who was strangled in his father's tent. Murat's plain tomb was built in accordance with his will, with an open hole in the roof right above the tomb to let the rain in. The most decorated tombs are those of two grandsons of Murat, Çelebi Mehmet and Cem Sultan, which are kept locked most of the time—ask the caretaker to open them for you. The historical complex also included a nearby hammam, medrese (now the Uluumay Museum), and a soup kitchen for the poor (now Darüzziyafe restaurant). ✉ *Muradiye Mahallesi, Muradiye Cad.* ☎ *224/222–0868* ✉ *Free.*

Termal
HOT SPRINGS | A popular spa since Roman times, Termal is a good stop if you're en route from Yalova to either İznik or Bursa. The springs were used by the Ottomans, refurbished in 1900 by Sultan Abdül Hamid II, and regularly visited by Atatürk in the 1920s and 1930s. Termal is a self-contained resort with three hotels (Çamlık, Çınar, and Termal), exotic gardens, a huge swimming pool, and four historic bathhouses that have many options for soaking in the mineral-rich waters. The baths are open to non-hotel

guests, and private family bathing cabins can be reserved for an extra charge. Avoid summer weekends, when the place is absolutely packed and the crowds will probably outweigh the baths' relaxing properties. Besides, the hot baths are more appealing, and the rates cheaper, in other seasons. Also consider a walk in the pine forests, where you can enjoy a packed lunch. ✉ *Termal* ✛ *About 70 km (42 miles) west of İznik; 12 km (8 miles) southwest of Yalova on the way to Çınarcık* ☏ *226/675–7400* ⊕ *www. yalovatermal.com.*

Türk İslam Eserleri Müzesi (*Turkish Islamic Arts Museum*)

MUSEUM |. To the west of Yeşil Cami, this small museum in an attractive 15th-century medrese (theological school) is part of a complex that includes the mosque and Yeşil Türbe. Displayed in chambers around a shaded courtyard are inlaid wood, jewelry, calligraphy and manuscripts, Turkish shadow puppets, carpets, coins, weapons, İznik ceramics, and traditional clothes embellished with colorful embroidery. ✉ *Yeşil Cad.* ☏ *224/327–7679* ⊡ *5 TL.*

Ulu Cami (*Grand Mosque of Bursa*)

RELIGIOUS SITE |. Bursa's most important mosque dates from 1399, when Sultan Beyazıt had it constructed after vowing to build 20 mosques if he was victorious in the battle of Nicopolis in Macedonia; he settled for a compromise, this one huge mosque with 20 domes. The interior is decorated with an elegantly understated display of quotations from the Koran in fine calligraphy. The fountain, with taps on the sides for ritual washing before prayer, is inside the mosque rather than outside the entrance—an unusual feature. ■TIP→ **Ulu Cami draws huge crowds during prayer times, which are best to avoid.** ✉ *Atatürk Cad.*

Uludağ Milli Parkı (*Uludağ National Park*)

MOUNTAIN—SIGHT |. To fully appreciate why Bursa is called Green Bursa, visit lush Uludağ Milli Parkı. The 30-minute trip up the ultramodern *teleferik* (gondola)—one of the longest in the world—is worth it for the views alone. The first station, **Sarıalan point** (5,364 feet), is lively in summer, with restaurants and picnic areas. In winter, skiers and night-clubbers head to the mountain's 5,938-foot high **Oteller Bölgesi** (Hotels Zone), 7 km (4 miles) farther up. The teleferik departure station is a 15-minute ride from Heykel; board a dolmuş (shared taxi) just behind the Bursa Kent Müzesi for 2 TL or hail a cab. There are also various walking paths up the mountain between Bursa and Uludağ; the hike takes about three hours each way. ■TIP→ **Take a sweater or jacket, as temperatures fall dramatically as you climb, even when it's warm downtown.** ✉ *Piremir Mahallesi, Teleferik Teferrüç İstasyonu Yıldırım* ☏ *224/327–7400, 224/444–6345 call center* ⊕ *www. teleferik.com.tr/bursa* ⊡ *Round-trip teleferik ride: 38 TL to Sarıalan.*

Uluumay Müzesi (*Uluumay Ottoman Folk Costume and Jewelry Museum*)

MUSEUM |. A fine, albeit small, collection of traditional costumes from the lands of the Ottoman Empire, some dating back centuries, is on display in this museum opposite the Muradiye Tombs. Mannequins dressed in the costumes revolve to afford a thorough study of the colorful textiles and embroidery. There are also gorgeous antique silver jewelry pieces and accessories, along with some folkloric items. The building is a medrese (theological school) built in 1475 by Şair Ahmet Paşa, whose tomb is in the garden. ✉ *Muradiye Mahallesi, Murat Cad.* ☏ *224/222–7575* ⊕ *www.uluumay. com* ⊡ *10 TL.*

★ Yeşil Cami (*Green Mosque*)

RELIGIOUS SITE |. A juxtaposition of simple form, inspired stone carving, and

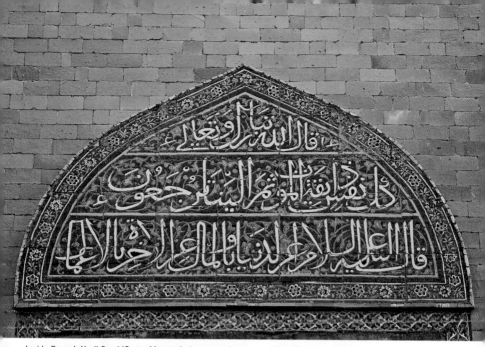

Inside Bursa's Yeşil Cami (Green Mosque), the array of green and blue tiles is mesmerizing.

spectacular tile work, this is among the finest mosques in Turkey. Work on the building was completed in 1420, during the reign of Mehmet I Çelebi (ruled 1413–21). Its beauty begins in the marble entryway, where complex feathery patterns and calligraphy are carved into the stone; inside is a sea of blue and green İznik tiles. The central hall rests under two shallow domes; in the one near the entrance an oculus sends down a beam of sunlight at midday, illuminating a fountain delicately carved from a single piece of marble. The *mihrab* (prayer niche) towers almost 50 feet, and is covered with stunning tiles and intricate carvings. On a level above the main doorway is the sultan's loge, lavishly decorated and tiled. ⊠ *Yeşil Cad.*

Yeşil Türbe (*Green Tomb*)

RELIGIOUS SITE |. The "Green Tomb," built in 1421, is the final resting place of Mehmet I Çelebi. It's actually covered in blue tiles, added after an earthquake damaged the originals in the 1800s, but inside are incredible original İznik tiles, including those sheathing Mehmet's immense sarcophagus—many of which are green and turquoise. The surrounding tombs belong to Mehmet's children. ⊠ *Yeşil Cad.*

🍽 Restaurants

Arap Şükrü Çetin

$$$ | TURKISH | The place to be on a busy Bursa weekend evening, this irrepressible *meyhane* is a local institution, serving a delectable selection of fresh fish from the open-air market on the corner. In the early 1930s, a veteran of the War of Independence nicknamed "Arab" Şükrü opened a fish restaurant here on Sakarya Caddesi, a narrow side street just south of Altıparmak Caddesi. **Known for:** live, table-side Turkish classical music; friendly and animated service; perfect spot for rakı-balık. Ⓢ *Average main: 48 TL* ⊠ *Sakarya Cad. 6, Arap Şükrü* ☎ *224/221–1453* ⊕ *www.*

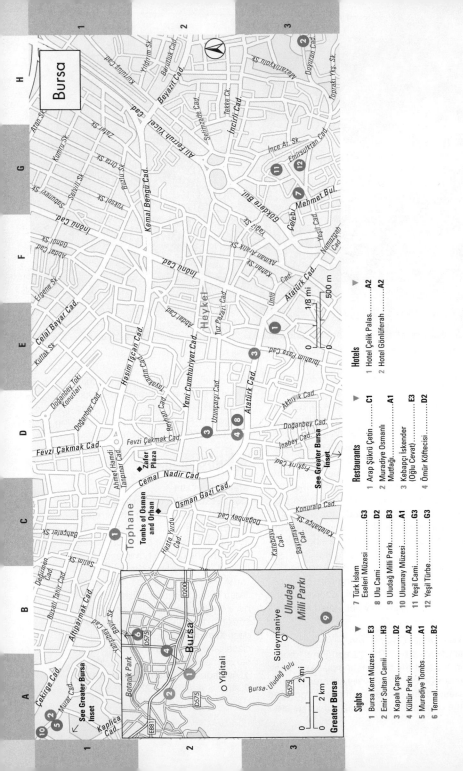

Bursa

Sights ▸

1 Bursa Kent Müzesi	E3
2 Emir Sultan Camii	H3
3 Kapalı Çarşı	D2
4 Kültür Parkı	A2
5 Muradiye Tombs	A1
6 Termal	B2
7 Türk Islam Eseleri Müzesi	G3
8 Ulu Cami	D2
9 Uludağ Milli Parkı	B3
10 Uluumay Müzesi	A1
11 Yeşil Cami	G3
12 Yeşil Türbe	G3

Restaurants ▸

1 Arap Şükrü Çetin	C1
2 Muradiye Osmanlı Mutfağı	A1
3 Kebapçı İskender (Oğlu Cevat)	E3
4 Ömür Köftecisi	D2

Hotels ▸

1 Hotel Çelik Palas	A2
2 Hotel Gönlüferah	A2

Greater Bursa

Local Flavors of Western Turkey 🍴

Most cities in Turkey claim some kind of fame for their köfte (meatballs), but *İnegöl köfte*—traditionally cooked over charcoal—are especially delicious and said to have been invented near Bursa. Another popular dish that has origins in Bursa is *İskender kebap*, tender shavings of lamb or beef on *pide* (soft flatbread), which is soaked in tomato sauce, drizzled with hot melted butter, and served with yogurt on the side. Even if you haven't liked İskender elsewhere in Turkey, try it in Bursa, where it's far superior.

The Aegean region is known for mezes made with wild herbs collected in the area and cooked or dressed in olive oil. Cunda Island in Ayvalık is particularly famous for its amazing range of seafood and fish mezes and main dishes, enriched by lesser-known Greek specialties and the restaurants' own creations.

arapsukrucetin.com ⏲ No lunch. Closed during Ramadan.

Kebapçı İskender (Oğlu Cevat)
$$ | TURKISH | Eager patrons line up outside this little white-and-blue house near the bazaar to enjoy heaping servings of meat, dished up by a grandson of Mehmet İskenderoğlu, who invented the *İskender kebap* back in 1867. (He's pictured on the wall, opposite Atatürk.) The kebab is tender, the portions filling, and the photograph-lined dining rooms quaint. The kitchen closes by 6:30 during the week and 8 on weekends, so go early. **Known for:** crowds of locals; best İskender kebab in Turkey; hefty portions. [$] *Average main: 32 TL ✉ Atatürk Cad. 60, at Orhan Sok., Heykel ☎ 224/221–1076 general management 🌐 www.iskender.com.tr.*

★ Muradiye Osmanlı Mutfağı
$$ | TURKISH | Across from the Muradiye Tombs, this soup kitchen built by Sultan Murat II in the 15th century to help feed the poor now houses a restaurant serving Ottoman and Turkish cuisine in wonderfully atmospheric surroundings. *Hünkar beğendi* (tender lamb on a bed of grilled-eggplant puree) literally means "the Sultan liked it," and it's impossible not to. The place is also known for its meat dishes as well as its Ottoman desserts. **Known for:** quiet and intimate feel; elegant decor; köfte. [$] *Average main: 28 TL ✉ 2. Murat Cad. 36, Muradiye ☎ 224/224–6439 🌐 www.muradiyeosmanlimutfagi.com ⏲ No lunch during Ramadan.*

Ömür Köftecisi
$$ | TURKISH | The location is charming, in the covered market by Ulu Cami, and köfte (meatballs) is the thing to order, served with grilled peppers and tomatoes. Among the salad options, *piyaz* (bean salad with vinegar) accompanies köfte best. **Known for:** excellent prices; quality and friendly service; various köfte dishes, including one filled with cheese. [$] *Average main: 20 TL ✉ Ulu Cami Cad. 7 ☎ 224/221–4524 ⏲ Closed Sun. and during Ramadan.*

🛏 Hotels

★ Hotel Çelik Palas

$$$ | HOTEL | The most venerable of the Çekirge spa hotels has gone glam with contemporary-style rooms, Las Vegas–worthy lounge areas, and an outdoor pool deck with a stunning view of the city. **Pros:** views; big rooms; luxurious spa area. **Cons:** pricey; not easy walking distance to most sights; some rooms smell like smoke. $ *Rooms from: €100* ✉ *Çekirge Cad. 79* 🕾 *224/233–3800* ⊕ *www.celikpalas.com* ☞ *164 rooms* ⑩ *Free Breakfast.*

Hotel Gönlüferah

$$$ | HOTEL | Claiming to have the city's best thermal baths, this hotel has rooms with several different design concepts, ranging from plush contemporary to sumptuous Ottoman style, complete with high beds, velvet curtains, and ornamental hanging lamps. **Pros:** big, well-decorated, light-filled rooms; attentive service; some rooms have excellent views. **Cons:** on the expensive side; far from sights; some bathrooms fairly small. $ *Rooms from: $120* ✉ *1. Murat Cad. 22, Çekirge* 🕾 *224/232–1890* ⊕ *www. gonluferah.com* ☞ *70 rooms* ⑩ *Free Breakfast.*

ⓨ Nightlife

Nightlife in Bursa is liveliest in winter, and the best place is out of town at the ski resort Uludağ, where Istanbul's elite fill the hotels on weekends and holidays. There's popular Turkish and Western music, and lots of dancing. The rest of the year, nightlife in Bursa either imitates the Uludağ scene or sticks to Ottoman tradition with Turkish *fasıl* music, which can be found in restaurants such as Konak 18 or Muradiye Osmanlı Mutfağı during weekend dinners. For nightclubs, try one of the places at the Kültür Parkı such as **Altın Ceylan.**

Jazz Bar, on the way to Uludağ, is a clubbing options among the liveliest in winter. Near the center, **Sakarya Caddesi** (aka Arap Şükrü) is a popular spot year-round for meyhane-style dining accompanied by roaming musicians; past the restaurants is **M Pub (Kafe Müsadenizle).** It doesn't look much like a pub, but its shiny lounge and large terrace are among the nicer places in town to have a few drinks, if you're not averse to Turkish pop music.

🛍 Shopping

Bursa's Kapalı Çarşı is the place to go if you want to shop in the traditional way but the city also has many modern stores. The Zafer Plaza mall at the east end of Atatürk Caddesi has many international brands, and instead of the tea gardens of the old bazaars you'll find a large Starbucks housed underneath a glass pyramid and a food court offering American and Turkish fast food.

Bursa has been a center of the silk industry since the coming of the Ottoman sultans and remains a good place to buy silk scarves, raw-silk fabric by the yard, and other silk products. The price of a silk scarf varies widely depending on design, brand, and quality, from as little as 5 TL to well over 100 TL; the same goes for the city's famed cotton towels, depending on their thickness and density. Bathrobes are a favorite souvenir, as they're high-quality and well-priced, but they might be a bit bulky to carry overseas.

Kapalı Çarşı (*Covered Bazaar*)

OUTDOOR/FLEA/GREEN MARKETS |. As is traditional, each section of the Kapalı Çarşı, behind the Ulu Cami, is dominated by a particular trade: jewelers, silk weavers, antique dealers. The Koza Han (Cocoon Kerrvansaray) section next to the Orhan Gazi Mosque by the east entrance is the center of the silk trade. It has a lovely courtyard with a tiny *mescit* (prayer room) and a 150-year-old linden

War and Peace

The Dardanelles have provided the world with many myths and heroes, romances and tragedies. The most recent, and the main reason that the region draws visitors today, was the Gallipoli campaign in World War I. In this offensive, Britain (with soldiers from Australia and New Zealand, then still British colonies) and France tried to breach Çanakkale's defenses in a campaign devised by the young Winston Churchill, at the time First Lord of the Admiralty. The goal was to capture Istanbul, control the entire waterway from the Aegean to the Black Sea, open up a supply channel to Russia, and pave the way for an attack on Germany from the south. After nine months of bloody fighting that left as many as 50,000 Allied and perhaps twice as many Turks dead, the Allies admitted defeat and evacuated, beaten by the superior strategy of Lieutenant-Colonel Mustafa Kemal—later called Atatürk.

Churchill lost his job as a result of the failure in the Dardanelles, and his career suffered until the next world war, two decades later. Mustafa Kemal, on the other hand, became a national hero. He had been an insignificant lieutenant, unpopular among the ruling Committee of Union and Progress, but the fame he earned in this war helped him start and lead the War of Independence against the occupying Allies. Soon his enemies were overthrown, and so were the Ottoman sultanate and caliphate. A few years after the Gallipoli campaign, the modern, secular republic of Turkey emerged with Atatürk as president.

For Australians and New Zealanders, World War I was their first real experience of war overseas, and the shocking losses they sustained left an indelible mark. For the Turks, it was an unexpected defensive victory. The Anzacs and the Turks came from opposite ends of the earth: there was no history of hostility, or even familiarity, between them, until they were told to kill one another, but in some ways the war marked the start of a friendship, and thousands of Anzac pilgrims come to visit the battlefields every spring. Atatürk's speech, engraved on a Turkish monument in Anzac Cove, seemed to foresee this:

"Those heroes that shed their blood and lost their lives! You are now lying in the soil of a friendly country, therefore rest in peace. There is no difference between the Johnnies and the Mehmets to us, where they lie side by side here in this country of ours. You, the mothers who sent their sons from far-away countries, wipe away your tears. Your sons are now lying in our bosom, and are at peace. After having lost their lives on this land, they have become our sons as well."

tree under which you can sip your tea. The Emir Han, behind the Ulu Cami, in the southwest section, is an interesting combination of jewelers and a religious book market, and also has a fountain and a courtyard tea garden. Antiques and souvenirs can be found in the small Eski Aynalı Carşı section of the bazaar, between Koza Han and Emir Han. Try *Karagöz* for traditional shadow puppets and other interesting items. ⊠ *Merkez, Ozmangazi Mh.*

Karagöz

ANTIQUES/COLLECTIBLES | This decades-old shop in the Eski Aynalı Çarşı sells Turkish Karagöz shadow puppets, traditional costumes, and other interesting antique and folkloric items. Owner Şinasi Çelik-kol has done much to keep the art of shadow-puppet theater alive in Bursa and may oblige visitors with a brief performance in his shop. ⊠ *Kapalı Çarşı, Eski Aynalı Çarşı 12* ☎ *224/221–8727* ⊕ *www. karagozshop.net.*

Gallipoli

310 km (192 miles) southwest of Istanbul.

The Gallipoli Peninsula lies to the north of the Dardanelles. Turks call it Gelibo-lu—there's also a town of the same name about 40 km (25 miles) north-east of Eceabat. Thirty-one beautifully tended military cemeteries of the Allied dead from World War I line the Gallipoli battlefields. The major battles were in two main areas along a 35-km (22-mile) stretch of the Gallipoli Peninsula—on the northern coast between Kabatepe and Suvla Bay, and at Cape Helles at the peninsula's southern tip, where the main Turkish memorial is located.

Most visitors come to this peaceful and scenic part of the country to pay their respects to the victims of the crucial World War I campaign in which ANZAC (Australian and New Zealand Army Corps), British, and French troops clashed with Turkish forces, with massive losses on both sides. Battles have been fought over the Dardanelles, the commercially and militarily strategic strait separating Europe from Asia and connecting the Aegean Sea to the Marmara Sea, since the 13th-century BC war between the Achaeans and Trojans.

Today, you can visit the region year-round if your intent is sightseeing, but spring may be the best time, when it's cool enough to walk comfortably around the sights, and when the area is at its most colorful, with wildflowers dotting the cemeteries and hillsides. Turks commemorate the battle for Gallipoli on March 18, and British, Australians, and New Zealanders on April 25. The second date, in particular, brings many travelers to the region for the emotional memorial services, but the mass influx requires that you make reservations for hotels and guided tours well in advance. It's probably best to avoid Gallipoli this time of year unless you wish to join the memorial.

Most visitors base themselves in Çanak-kale, on the south side of the straits, rather than in Eceabat on the European side of the Dardanelles. Even though the latter is actually closer to the battlefields, Çanakkale is livelier, has more options for accommodations and dining, and is where many of the guided tours start. Regular ferries make the short crossing in both directions.

GETTING HERE AND AROUND

From Çanakkale, take the car ferry to Eceabat and then head north along the coast from the ferry terminal, following Route D550/E87 as it turns westward to cut across the peninsula, where fruit stands and sunflower fields line the well-maintained road. It takes about 20–30 minutes to drive from Eceabat to the site entrance, where a well-signed loop road passes the main sights in the Kabatepe/Suvla Bay area, most of which have English-language explanatory texts. For a richer self-guided experience, the Australian Government Department of Veterans' Affairs (⊕ *www.anzacsite. gov.au*) has detailed instructions for an "Anzac Walk" and other tours, including historical information and free audio commentaries to download. The Commonwealth War Graves Commission

LONE PINE

(⊕ *www.cwgc.org*) publishes a free pamphlet, "The Gallipoli Campaign, 1915," that can be picked up at hotels in Çanakkale or Eceabat or downloaded from the website. It contains a map of the battlefields, a basic history of the campaign, and short descriptions of key points of interest.

◉ Sights

Cape Helles
MEMORIAL | On the southernmost tip of the Gallipoli Peninsula, the cape has a massive, four-pillared memorial to Turkey's World War I dead. No one knows how many fell in battle; estimates suggest there were around 250,000 Turkish casualties, including at least 85,000 deaths. If you take the ferry from Gallipoli to Çanakkale, look for the memorials to the campaign carved into the cliffs. The large one at Kilitbahır reads: "Stop, O passerby. This earth you tread unawares is where an age was lost. Bow and listen, for this quiet place is where the heart of a nation throbs." ✛ *Off D550.*

Chunuk Bair (*Çanak Bayırı*)
MEMORIAL |. The goal of the Allies was to occupy this strategic location overlooking the Gallipoli Peninsula. They failed, and Mustafa Kemal (Atatürk) became a hero and went on to establish the secular republic of Turkey. It was here that he told his soldiers, "I order you not just to fight, but to die." All the men of one of his regiments were wiped out, and he himself was saved miraculously when a bullet hit the pocket watch that was over his heart—a moment commemorated with a huge statue of Atatürk here—but the line held. The hilltop holds Turkish trenches, a cemetery, and the New Zealand national memorial and has good views of the peninsula and the Dardanelles Strait. ✉ *Gelibolu Tarihi Milli Parkı, Eceabat.*

Gallipoli Simulation Center (*Kabatepe Information Center*)
MUSEUM |. Letters from soldiers on both sides of the Gallipoli tragedy are among the most moving of the objects on display at this interpretive center, along with uniforms, weapons, and other findings from the battlefields. An 11-part, hour-long immersing simulation of the Gallipoli campaign—which some have criticized as being too focused on "entertainment"—completes the experience. ✉ *Gelibolu Tarihi Milli Parkı, Kabatepe Mevkii, Eceabat* ☎ *286/810–0050* ✉ *13 TL.*

★ Lone Pine Cemetery
CEMETERY | The stunningly situated memorial here bears the names of some 5,000 Australian and New Zealand soldiers with unknown graves killed at Gallipoli during the grueling eight-month World War I campaign to defeat the Ottoman forces. Savage hand-to-hand fighting took place on the battlefield where the cemetery was established—thousands were killed on both sides here in four days of fighting—and seven Victoria crosses, the highest award given by the British government for bravery and usually quite sparingly distributed, were awarded after the Battle of Lone Pine. This is the most affecting of all the ANZAC cemeteries, and the epitaphs on the tombstones are very moving. ✉ *Gelibolu Tarihi Milli Parkı, Eceabat.*

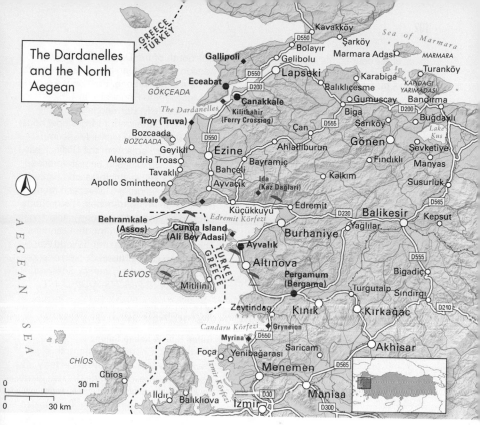

The Dardanelles and the North Aegean

Çanakkale

340 km (211 miles) southwest of Istanbul; 270 km (168 miles) from Bursa.

West of Bursa, on the southern shore of the Dardanelles, Çanakkale is the largest city on the North Aegean coast and makes a very pleasant base for visiting the memorials and battlefields of Gallipoli, a half-hour ferry journey across the straits.

The heart of Çanakkale is in the docks area, and you really don't need to go inland. An Ottoman clock tower is between the two halves of the dock. Head toward the sea from this tower and find the ferry that departs for the historic Gallipoli Peninsula. Hotels and restaurants are spread on either side of the docks, along the seafront; some of the most appealing lodging and dining options, as well as bars and nightlife, are located in the narrow streets behind the seafront to the left of the tower if you're facing the sea. A short ways on the waterfront past the clock tower in the other direction is the Trojan Horse that appeared in the 2004 movie *Troy*, later donated to the city of Çanakkale; there's also a nicely done model of the ancient city.

GETTING HERE AND AROUND

Flights arrive at Çanakkale Airport (⊕ *www.canakkale.dhmi.gov.tr*), just south of the city center.

By car from Bursa, Route 200 (which becomes E90) runs west toward Çanakkale; the trip is 270 km (168 miles) and takes about four hours. If you're heading for Çanakkale from Istanbul, take E80 west to Tekirdağ and then the E84, turning onto the E87 in Keşan to continue on to Eceabat's car ferry terminal. From Çanakkale, the E87 goes through Troy, Ezine, Ayvacık, Edremit, Ayvalık, and Bergama. Ezine is 50 km (31 miles) from Çanakkale, and from there you can take the coast road west to Geyikli, where ferries run to Bozcaada.

Since the Bandırma–Çanakkale road is normally less crowded than the Istanbul–Çanakkale road, when traveling to Gallipoli from Istanbul, you may want to take a boat to Bandırma and continue from there by car. Ferries operate daily from Istanbul's Yenikapı terminal to Bandırma in summer, but much less frequently in winter; there are special timetables for religious holidays (check 🌐 *www.ido.com.tr*). The journey takes two hours, and tickets start about 60 TL each way per passenger and about 175 for a car including a driver and one passenger. Reservations are essential during holidays and summer weekends and advisable generally anytime between June and August.

The bus trip from Istanbul to Çanakkale is about six hours and costs about 60 to 70 TL. From Bursa to Çanakkale, it's around five hours and costs about 40 TL. If the ride ends at the new bus terminal outside town, you can take a city bus or minibus to the port area in about 20 minutes for a fare of around 3 TL, or a taxi for about 30 TL.

VISITOR INFORMATION

CONTACTS Visitor Information. ✉ *İskele Meydanı 65* ☎ *286/217–1187.*

Sights

Çimenlik Fortress

MILITARY SITE | The main reason to come here is for the sweeping view of the mouth of the Dardanelles and the Aegean, but the long history and exhibits come a close second. Built on the orders of Mehmet the Conqueror in 1462 after he successfully stormed Istanbul, the impressive waterfront fortress now houses the **Deniz Müzesi** (Naval Museum), displaying artifacts from the Gallipoli battlefields and exhibits in English (proceed counterclockwise inside), accompanied by a Turkish-language, live-action reenactment of life in the trenches. The grounds contain all kinds of weaponry, including dozens of ancient and modern cannons. There's also a replica of the World War I–era **minelayer ship Nusret** docked offshore. ✉ *İsmetpaşa Mah., Çimenlik Sok. and Hanım Sok.* ☎ *286/213–1730* 🎫 *4 TL.*

🍴 Restaurants

Gülen Pide & Kebap Salonu

$ | TURKISH | Cheery and bright, this casual two-floor eatery near the ferry dock serves delicious *pide* (Turkish pizza), topped with minced meat, sausage, cheese, or any combination. There's also a wide variety of kebabs, *döner*, and other grilled meats, as well as the thin flatbread *lahmacun*, topped with minced meat, and a couple of traditional desserts. **Known for:** massive portions; great value; fındık lahmacun (smaller, saucer-sized pieces of lahmacun). [$] *Average main: 19 TL* ✉ *Cumhuriyet Meydanı 27/A* ☎ *286/212–8800.*

Sardunya Ev Yemekleri

$ | TURKISH | In a century-old former house on Fetvane Sokak, Sardunya serves home-style Turkish cooking at very reasonable prices. There's no menu; simply choose several items from the counter displaying that day's meat and vegetable dishes, which might include meatballs with potatoes, eggplant in a garlicky yogurt sauce, green beans cooked in olive oil, or saffron rice. **Known for:** excellent home-style cooking; friendly service; charming garden seating area. $ *Average main: 13 TL* ⊠ *Fetvane Sok. 11* ☎ *286/213–9899* ⊘ *Closed Sun.*

Yalova Restaurant

$$$ | TURKISH | At this decades-old Çanakkale establishment, take in views across the Dardanelles from the rooftop terrace as you enjoy such seafood mezes as grilled octopus in vinegar or sardines wrapped in vine leaves. Non-seafood mezes like fried eggplant with cheese are equally tasty. **Known for:** views of the water; best seafood mezes in Çanakkale; baby calamari and akuvadis (a type of local mussel). $ *Average main: 50 TL* ⊠ *Yalı Cad., Gümrük Sok. 7* ☎ *286/217–1045* ⊕ *www.yalovarostaurant.com.*

🛏 Hotels

Grand Anzac Hotel Çanakkale

$ | HOTEL | The compact rooms and somewhat uninspiring common areas of this centrally located hotel are more than made up for by the excellent service and extremely helpful English-speaking staff. **Pros:** especially helpful staff; on-site restaurant; good location. **Cons:** rather cramped rooms; noisy premises with poor soundproofing; difficult to reach with a car. $ *Rooms from: 180 TL* ⊠ *Kemalyeri Cad. 11* ☎ *286/217–7777* ⊕ *www.grandanzachotel.com* ↪ *37 rooms* �’❘ *Free Breakfast.*

Hotel des Etrangers

$$ | HOTEL | This charming bed-and-breakfast is located on the supposed former premises of the hotel where famed Troy archaeologist Heinrich Schliemann is said to have stayed. **Pros:** lovely atmosphere and design; personal service; central location. **Cons:** located on a street with noisy nightlife; no elevator; smallish bathrooms. $ *Rooms from: €60* ⊠ *Yalı Cad. 25-27* ☎ *286/214–2424* ⊕ *hoteldesetrangers.com.tr* ↪ *8 rooms* ❘◯❘ *Free Breakfast.*

Kervansaray Hotel

$ | HOTEL | This 1903 house near the clock tower has a traditional Ottoman style, with large bay windows, an elegant lobby, and small but comfortable rooms with wooden furniture, plush red curtains, and high ceilings. **Pros:** nice character; good location in the heart of the city; reasonable prices. **Cons:** small bathrooms, especially in the single rooms; somewhat dated facilities; no on-site parking. $ *Rooms from: 160 TL* ⊠ *Kemalpaşa Mah., Fetvane Sok. 13* ☎ *286/217–8192* ⊕ *www.canakkalekervansarayhotel.com* ↪ *20 rooms* ❘◯❘ *Free Breakfast.*

🌙 Nightlife

The parallel streets to the left of the clock tower if you're facing the sea—Fetvane, Yalı, and Eski Balıkhane—are the main bar streets, where you can choose from spacious open-air bars dominated by pop music, waterfront cafés, or small, dark dives. Narrow Matbaa Sokak between Fetvane and Rıhtım Caddesi has been converted into a mini version of Istanbul's Nevizade, with bars and restaurants packed in side by side. Some of the waterfront tea gardens north of the ferry terminal also serve beer.

Hayal Kahvesi Çanakkale

MUSIC CLUBS | The Çanakkale outpost of one of Istanbul's most successful performance venues has live music every night, mainly by local rock and pop bands. ⊠ *Fetvane Sok. 6* ☎ *286/217–0470* ⊕ *www.hayalkahvesicanakkale.com.*

Yalı Hanı

CAFES—NIGHTLIFE | The historic *han* (inn) near the end of Fetvane has a leafy, cobbled courtyard for smoking a *nargile* (water pipe) or having a low-key drink, with rock music or blues playing in the background. There's some additional seating upstairs. ⊠ *Fetvane Sok. 26–28.*

🛍 Shopping

Fetvane Sokak in the old city is lined with attractive old stone buildings, and some have been converted into bookstores or shops selling funky clothing, ceramics, and other locally made items. Follow Çarşı Caddesi southeast to see more and eventually come across Aynalı Çarşı, the Mirrored Bazaar.

Aynalı Çarşı
SHOPPING CENTERS/MALLS | The 19th-century Mirrored Bazaar remained unused for much of the last century after being seriously damaged by shelling in the Gallipoli campaign. It was renovated in the early 2000s to house about two dozen shops, mostly selling souvenirs. Its design is based on Istanbul's Mısır Çarşı (Spice Bazaar). ✉ *Çarşı Cad., Aynalı Çarşı, Kemalpaşa Mh.*

Eceabat

335 km (208 miles) southwest of Istanbul.

Eceabat, on the Gallipoli Peninsula, is the closest town to the most-visited battlefields and cemeteries. The town is small and most of the restaurants and hotels are along the waterfront. So is the Tarihe Saygı Parkı (Respect for History Park), which has maps, murals, and dioramas related to the Gallipoli campaign, with text in both English and Turkish. Unless you're planning on spending a lot of time at the battlefields, though, Eceabat is a much less appealing base than Çanakkale.

GETTING HERE AND AROUND

The Eceabat ferry puts you right in the middle of town. Car ferries make the 30-minute crossing from Çanakkale to Eceabat every hour from 7 am to midnight in both directions (and less often during the night). Taxis from Eceabat to other parts of the peninsula can be quite expensive.

🍴 Restaurants

Liman Balık Restaurant
$$ | **TURKISH** | Newer and shinier options on the peninsula have failed to tempt the Liman's loyal clientele away from this decades-old favorite, where large windows and a small covered patio draped in vines overlook a small park next to the sea. The fare includes a wide variety of mezes, along with fish and grilled meat; all are fresh and tasty. **Known for:** beautiful outdoor terrace with a view; best value in Eceabat; extensive wine list. [$] *Average main: 20 TL* ✉ *İstiklal Cad. 67* ☎ *286/814–2755.*

🛏 Hotels

The Gallipoli Houses
$$ | **B&B/INN** | Located in a small farming village between Eceabat and Kabatepe, The Gallipoli Houses provide a relaxed, intimate getaway, with large rustic and comfortable rooms, each with a terrace or balcony, and home cooking that includes a hearty breakfast and (for an extra charge) a delicious dinner. **Pros:** quiet, peaceful surroundings; lots of atmosphere; close to battlefields. **Cons:** remote location is hard to reach without a car; closed in winter; nothing to do outside the hotel in the immediate area. [$] *Rooms from: €70* ✉ *Kocadere Village* ☎ *286/814–2650* 🌐 *www.thegallipolihouses.com* 🕒 *Closed Nov. 15–Mar. 15* 🛏 *10 rooms* 🍴 *Free Breakfast.*

Troy (Truva)

32 km (20 miles) south of Çanakkale.

Troy, known as Truva to the Turks and Ilion to the Greeks, is one of the most evocative place names in literature. To bring this UNESCO World Heritage site more to life, the Turkish government named 2018 the Year of Troy and in October of that year opened the Troy Museum, which tells the story of Troy and display artifacts from the excavations.

GETTING HERE AND AROUND

Many tours to Troy operate out of Çanakkale, most leaving early in the morning and returning by noon. Independent travelers can also hop a minibus to the site, which takes about a half hour; these leave every hour on the half hour on weekdays—less often on weekends—and it's a good idea to inquire about the last return bus from Troy so you don't get stranded. If driving, the turnoff for Troy is about 30 km (19 miles) from the Çanakkale city center on Route E87 toward İzmir; the ruins are another 5 km (3 miles) farther south.

Though it's easy enough to get to Troy on your own, with or without a car, a good guide significantly enhances your visiting experience, as the ruins are, frankly, not much to look at without some knowledge of the city's history, both real and legendary. The knowledgeable and amiable Mustafa Aşkın of Hisarlık Hotel & Cafe & Restaurant near the site gives one- to two-hour tours of Troy; he grew up in the area, speaks excellent English, and has written books about the fabled city. His narrative will illuminate easily overlooked features of the ruins (☎ 542/243–9359).

◉ Sights

Bozcaada

ISLAND | Heading south from Troy, you'll pass through Ezine or Geyikli. In either case you'll see a signpost for Bozcaada, one of the two Aegean islands that belong to Turkey. If you have time, spare a day for this island (though you'll probably then want to spare another), with its unspoiled harbor town, beautiful old houses, pristine sandy beaches, and lovely countryside covered with vineyards. The local wine may be the best you'll taste in Turkey without having to spend a fortune.

Troy Museum (*Troia Müzesi*)

MUSEUM |. The brand-new Troy Museum sits at the entrance of the archeological site and was the government's primary initiative for 2018's Year of Troy. The impressive building, standing at the pre-excavation height of ancient Troy, brings to life more than 5,000 years of history in the region through seven different sections, which include "Troas Area Archeology," "The Iliad and Trojan War," and "Troas and Ilion in Antiquity." Some 2,000 archeological pieces are on display, ranging from gold jewelry to sarcophagi, weapons, tear bottles, and sculptures. It is an excellent place to start before journeying further into the Northern Aegean, putting into perspective the significance of the region with exhibits on the history of Assos and other nearby cities. ✉ 17100 Tevfikiye Köyü, Tevfikiye 🎫 35 TL.

★ Troy (*Troia*)

ARCHAEOLOGICAL SITE |. The wooden horse that stands outside the site is a modern addition, there to remind us of Homer's epics, but the city walls, layer upon layer of them, date back several millennia. Long thought to be a figment of the Greek poet Homer's imagination and written about in his epic *The Iliad*, Troy was excavated in the 1870s by Heinrich Schliemann.

What you see of Troy today depends on your imagination or the knowledge and linguistic abilities of your guide. You may find the site highly evocative, with its remnants of massive, rough-hewn walls and its strategic views over the coastal plains—where the battles of the Trojan War were supposedly fought—to the sea. Or you may consider it an unimpressive row of trenches with piles of earth

Homer's Story

Because *The Iliad* was written 500 years after the war—traditionally believed to have taken place around 1184 BC—it's hard to say how much of it is history and how much is invention. Nonetheless, it makes for a romantic tale: Paris, the son of King Priam, abducted the beautiful Helen, wife of King Menelaus of Sparta, and fled with her to Troy. Menelaus enlisted the aid of his brother, King Agamemnon, and launched a thousand ships to get her back. His siege lasted 10 years and involved such ancient notables as Achilles,

Hector, and the crafty Odysseus, king of Ithaca. It was Odysseus who ended the war, after ordering a huge wooden horse to be built and left outside Troy's gates. Then the Greeks retreated to their ships and pretended to sail away. The Trojans hauled the trophy into their walled city and celebrated their victory. Under cover of darkness, the Greek ships returned, the soldiers hidden inside the horse crept out and opened the city's gates, and the attackers at last gained entry to Troy. Hence the saying: "Beware of Greeks bearing gifts."

and stone. The city is surprisingly small; the best-preserved features are from the Roman city, with its **bouleuterion** (council chamber), the site's most complete structure, and small theater. A site plan shows the general layout and marks the beginning of a signposted path leading to key features from several historical periods. ⊠ *Tevfikiye Köyü, Tevfikiye* ✛ *Follow signs from Rte. E87* 🖾 *35 TL, parking 8 TL.*

🛏 Hotels

Hisarlık Hotel & Cafe & Restaurant

$ | B&B/INN | Run by local guide Mustafa Aşkın and his two brothers, this is the only lodging in the immediate vicinity of the Troy ruins (and is across from the site of the Troy Museum, opened in 2018). **Pros:** great location for touring Troy; unmatched hospitality for the region; nice breakfast. **Cons:** basic rooms and bathrooms; prices a bit high for what you get; facilities somewhat dated. $ *Rooms from: €40* ⊠ *Tevfikiye Köyü, Tevfikiye* 🕾 *286/283–0026* ⊕ *www.troyhisarlik.com* 🛏 *11 rooms* ⦿I *Free Breakfast.*

Behramkale (Assos)

65 km (40 miles) south of Troy; 17 km (11 miles) south of Ayvacık.

The port of Assos is a marvel, pressed against the sheer cliff walls. It's crammed with small hotels built of volcanic rock, a fleet of fishing boats, and a small rocky beach at each end. A short but steep drive up from the port, Behramkale village is home to the lofty ruins of ancient Assos—the Acropolis—which provide a panoramic view over the Aegean. It has blossomed in recent years and now surpasses the port area in terms of prices—and perhaps in charm as well. Nowadays, the name "Behramkale" is used for the village at the top and "Assos" for the port area.

Outside of June, July, August, and weekends the rest of the year, the area is less crowded and prices are likely to come down a bit, especially in the port. For more spacious and sandier beaches try Kadırga, on the way to Küçükkuyu.

The ruins at Troy are not as well preserved as others in Turkey, but are still atmospheric.

GETTING HERE AND AROUND

Buses from Çanakkale to the north and Ayvalık or İzmir to the south stop at Ayvacık, which is the closest (17 km/11 miles) town to Behramkale. From there, minibuses make the 20- to 30-minute trip to Behramkale about every hour for 7 TL, though less frequently out of high season. Make sure you get one that goes down to the port, if that's your final destination.

The minibus ride between the port and the village takes 10 minutes and costs 2.5 TL. The minibus also goes to Kadırga beach, a 15-minute ride, for 10 TL. If you're driving, as you approach, the road forks, with one route leading to the ancient, pretty village atop the hill and the other twisting precariously down to the tiny, charming harbor.

◉ Sights

Acropolis

ARCHAEOLOGICAL SITE | The hilltop Acropolis measures about five square city blocks. Founded about 1000 BC by Aeolian Greeks, the city was successively ruled by Lydians, Persians, Pergamenes, Romans, and Byzantines, until Sultan Orhan Gazi (ruled 1324–62) took it over for the Ottomans in 1330. Aristotle is said to have spent time here in the 4th century BC, and St. Paul stopped on route to Miletus in about AD 55. You're best off leaving your car on one of the wider streets and making your way on foot up the steep, cobbled lanes to the top, where you'll be rewarded with sensational views of the coastline and, in the distance, the Greek island of Lesbos, whose citizens were the original settlers of Assos. At the summit is the site of the **Temple of Athena** (circa 530 BC), which has splendid sea views but has been somewhat clumsily restored. A more modern addition, right before the entrance to the ruins, is the **Murad Hüdavendigâr Camii,** a mosque built in the late 14th century. ✉ *Behramkale* ✣ *At the top of Behramkale village* ☎ *286/721–7218* 🌐 *assosarchproject.com* 🎫 *15 TL.*

🍴 Restaurants

Assos Köyüm Restaurant

$$ | **TURKISH** | There's no menu at this friendly, family-run spot in Behramkale's tiny main square: Just pick from the selection of mezes on display (don't miss the crunchy, garlicky greens called *deniz börülcesi*) and let one of the young waiters tell you what meat dishes are available that day. The covered terrace looks over the village and down to the sea—it's a wonderful spot to watch the sun set—while a few seats out front allow diners to watch the comings and goings on the square. **Known for:** saç kavurma (a sizzling plate of diced lamb and onions); attentive staff; excellent views. [$] *Average main: 25 TL* ✉ *Behramkale village square, by çay bahçesi, Behramkale* ☎ *286/721–7424.*

Kale Restaurant

$$ | **TURKISH** | A few minutes' walk from the Acropolis, this casual eatery with stone tables and colorful flowerpots is a welcome stop on the way back from a visit to the ruins, especially on a hot day. The *ayran* (a salty yogurt drink) is thirst quenching and a great restorative. **Known for:** good value; relaxed decor; excellent Turkish coffee. [$] *Average main: 18 TL* ✉ *Acropolis road, Behramkale* ☎ *543/317–4969* 💳 *No credit cards* 🕒 *Closed weekdays Nov.–Feb.*

🛏 Hotels

★ Assos Alarga

$$ | **B&B/INN** | In two gorgeous old stone houses centered on a shady courtyard, Assos Alarga provides a serene and intimate stay in the quiet end of Behramkale village, and its small outdoor pool and garden ensure an idyllic getaway atmosphere. **Pros:** secluded swimming pool; extremely attentive owner and staff; excellent breakfast. **Cons:** bathrooms on the small side; steep driveway/walkway up to hotel; weak Wi-Fi in some areas. [$] *Rooms from: 380 TL* ✉ *Behramkale 88, Behramkale* ☎ *286/721–7260* 🌐 *www.assosalarga.com* 🛏 *5 rooms* 🍴 *Free Breakfast.*

Assos Kervansaray Otel

$$ | **HOTEL** | The best of the waterside hotels in Assos port has rooms in a variety of sizes and styles, some of which have terrific view of the Aegean. **Pros:** romantic setting near the Aegean; swimming in pools and sea; small private beach. **Cons:** the half-board arrangement may not be desirable; slightly impersonal atmosphere; no elevator. [$] *Rooms from: 650 TL* ✉ *Assos Liman (Assos Harbor), Behramkale* ☎ *286/721–7093, 286/721–7198* 🌐 *www.assoskervansaray.com* 🛏 *70 rooms* 🍴 *Free Breakfast.*

Assos Nar Konak

$$ | **B&B/INN** | In an old stone house perched on the Behramkale hillside not far from the Acropolis, Assos Nar Konak is run by an enthusiastic young Turkish-Argentine couple who treat guests more like friends. **Pros:** exceptional hosts; tranquil atmosphere; variety of room types. **Cons:** somewhat limited room amenities; no families with children allowed; poor or no Wi-Fi in rooms. [$] *Rooms from: €75* ✉ *Behramkale Köyü 62, Behramkale* ☎ *532/422–8052* 🌐 *www.assosnarkonak.com* 🕒 *Closed Jan. and/or Feb.* 🛏 *5 rooms* 🍴 *Free Breakfast.*

★ Biber Evi

$$ | **B&B/INN** | Beautiful rooms and the warmest of welcomes make this sublimely tranquil boutique hotel a top choice for a peaceful getaway. **Pros:** centrally located; wonderful common areas;

attractively decorated rooms. **Cons:** showers are not enclosed; some rooms can feel a bit cramped; no children allowed. *[$] Rooms from: 350 TL ✉ Behramkale Köyü 46, Behramkale ☎ 530/320–1017 🌐 www.biberevi.com 🛏 6 rooms 🍴 Free Breakfast.*

Ayvalık

48 km (30 miles) from Edremit; 117 km (73 miles) from Çanakkale.

Ayvalık is beautiful, stretching onto a peninsula and surrounded by islands, with many bays swirling in and out of its coastline. The bustling harbor town and Cunda Island across the way retain strong evidence of the Greek community that flourished here and prospered in the olive oil trade until being deported in the population exchange of 1923. Atmospheric backstreets are full of crumbling old Greek houses. A long, sandy beach is just a short minibus ride away and various pleasure boats stand ready to take visitors on swimming and snorkeling excursions.

Ayvalık has some of the finest 19th-century Greek-style architecture in Turkey, and recent restoration has begun to reverse decades of neglect. Unlike typical Ottoman houses (tall, narrow, and built of wood, with an overhanging bay window), Greek buildings are stone, with classic triangular pediments above a square box. The best way to explore is to turn your back to the Aegean and wander the tiny side streets leading up the hill into the heart of the old residential quarter (try Talatpaşa Caddesi or Gümrük Caddesi).

The town's historic churches have had different fates. Taksiyarhis Church was recently turned into a museum, but others were long ago converted into mosques. St. John's is now the **Saatli Cami** (Clock Mosque), bearing few traces of its past as a church. St. George's is now the **Çınarlı Cami** (Plane Tree Mosque). There are many mosques converted from churches in Turkey, but these are among the most striking—the elaborate style of Orthodox churches does not suit the plain minimalist style of mosques, and the unimpressive minaret erected later at the Çınarlı Mosque, along with the highly ornamented iconostasis inside, makes it look almost absurd. The **Hayrettin Paşa Camii** was also converted from a church. **Phaneromeni Church** (Ayazma Kilisesi) has beautiful stonework and was restored in 2018, while the former **Aya Triada**, which later served as a tobacco warehouse, is in a total state of ruin.

In summer, Sarımsaklı Plajı, the 10-km (6-mile) stretch of sandy beach 7 km (4½ miles) from the center of town, is popular, and easily and cheaply reached by minibuses that stop near the harbor. It's a crowded resort with a mess of concrete hotels right behind the seafront,

A Quick Trip to Greece

A trip to the Greek island of Lesbos will allow you to see another country and culture with a sea journey of little more than an hour. In summer months, ferries depart from Ayvalık pier for Lesbos daily at 9 am and return at 6 pm. In winter months, however, there are only a few sailings per week, meaning that tourists from Ayvalık may need to stay over a night or two in Lesbos. Ferry schedules change from year to year, so check before making plans. Fares are about $40 for the round-trip. Offices next to the port compete to sell tickets.

and traffic and parking can be a problem, but the beach and sea are lovely.

Day or evening cruises to the bays and islands of Ayvalık are enjoyable, and range from party-boat trips to lower-key swimming excursions to the Patriça Nature Reserve on the far side of Cunda Island. Hucksters on the docks will try to sell you a trip as you walk by the boats, and competition makes prices very reasonable—about 30 to 40 TL for a day trip including a fish meal. Diving trips are also available at a higher cost. The tours are available from May until the end of October.

Şeytan Sofrası ("the devil's dinner table"), a hilltop 9 km (5½ miles) from town, on a right turn on the road from Ayvalık to Sarımsaklı, is the place to get a panoramic view of the islands and the bays and enjoy a cup of tea or a snack at one of the cafés. It's particularly lovely at sunset, when minibuses make the return trip from town for about 5 TL.

GETTING HERE AND AROUND

There's a regular bus service from Çanakkale, a journey of about three hours; tickets cost about 45 TL one way. By road, it's just off E87.

VISITOR INFORMATION

CONTACTS Visitor Information. ✉ *In front of Tansaş supermarket, opposite harbor* ☎ *266/312–4494.*

Sights

Taksiyarhis Anıt Müzesi (*Taxiarchis Church Museum*)
MUSEUM |. This beautiful church, built in 1844 on the site of a 15th-century edifice that was the first church in Ayvalık, was carefully restored and reopened as a museum by the Turkish government in 2013. Along with the gorgeous frescoes and imitation marble panels, the elaborate pulpit with icons of saints and the marble bishop's seat with gold bird reliefs are particularly noteworthy. ✉ *Mareşal Çakmak Cad., 9. Sokak* ☎ *266/312–5328* 🎫 *6 TL.*

Restaurants

Fırat Lokantası
$$ | TURKISH | In the heart of Ayvalık, just north of Saatli Cami, this eatery serves up filling lunches to hardworking street traders; it's tiny but almost always full, so you may have to share one of the dozen or so tables. The Turkish home cooking—rice, beans, eggplant with minced meat, and lamb stew—is delicious and this is the perfect place for lunch when wandering the historic part of the town. **Known for:** crowds of locals; generous portions; excellent value. [$] *Average main: 18 TL* ✉ *Cumhuriyet Cad. 25/A* ☎ *266/312–1380* 🕒 *Closed Sun. No dinner.*

Şehir Kulübü Restaurant
$$$ | TURKISH | With excellent food, views of Cunda Island, and a prime location on the Ayvalık waterfront, this restaurant is worth walking down narrow backstreets to find. The mezes include local specialties made with Aegean herbs and greens, and some that you're unlikely to see elsewhere, such as *deniz mücver* (fried mussel patties) or sole marinated in a lemony mustard sauce. **Known for:** amazing views; first-rate service; wide selection of mezes. [$] *Average main: 50 TL* ✉ *Gazinocular Cad., Belediye arkası* ☎ *266/312–1519.*

Hotels

Sızma Han
$$ | HOTEL | This hotel's unrivaled setting on Ayvalık's serene waterfront allows you to enjoy a fortifying glass of wine by the glistening sea without having to leave the property. **Pros:** nice waterfront location; on-site restaurant; excellent breakfast. **Cons:** downstairs rooms by lobby can be noisy; no views from rooms; property a

bit hard to find. $ *Rooms from: 260 TL* ✉ *Gümrük Cad., 2. Sok. 49* ☎ *266/312–7700* ⊕ *www.butiksizmahan.com* ⌨ *10 rooms* ⦿❘ *Free Breakfast.*

ⓨ Nightlife

Ayvalık's Muhabbet Sokak, between Atatürk Boulevard and the waterfront in the area of the old Gümrük (Customs) building, has a selection of busy bars, with live blues, jazz, and rock on weekends. In Sarımsaklı, the beach area just outside of Ayvalık, are discos and clubs that play pop and electronic techno. Cunda has bars that play Turkish and Greek pop music.

Cunda Island (Ali Bey Adası)

Just off the coast of Ayvalık (connected by a causeway to mainland).

Like Ayvalık, Cunda Island was once predominantly Greek, and some Greek is still spoken here. The island has a mix of the two cultures in its food, music, and nightlife, and lately has been deliberately cultivating this, having realized the tourism potential. There's a growing number of cafés, bars, bakeries, and small restaurants in the charming cobbled backstreets away from the water, which are full of old Greek buildings in various states of repair. At the top of the hill, an attractive old windmill has been restored and the adjacent Panorama Café at the small Sevim and Necdet Kent Library is open 9:30 to 9:30 daily and has great views.

GETTING HERE AND AROUND

There are regular buses to Cunda from Ayvalık, but the best way to travel is by boat (8 TL one way); they run every hour each way from 10 am to midnight in summer (June 15–September 15), and dock at the quay right in the middle of the restaurant area in Cunda. In winter, buses and dolmuşes are the only option (3 TL).

◉ Sights

Ayvalık Rahmi M. Koç Museum (*Taxiarchis Church*)
MUSEUM | . In an unusual historical-preservation choice, Cunda's Taxiarchis Church, a landmark dating to 1873, has been wonderfully restored and reopened in 2014 as a museum that also houses an eclectic array of objects belonging to the collection of Turkish businessman and philanthropist Rahmi M. Koç. The restoration has saved the elegant neoclassical architecture and decor of the church and its religious iconography from disrepair. Unfortunately, the display of vintage cars and vehicles, ship anchors, nautical instruments, antique dolls and toys, and other curiosities overwhelms the space. ✉ *Namık Kemal Mah., Şeref Sok. 6/A, Cunda* ⊕ *www.rmk-museum.org.tr* ☐ *5 TL* ☾ *Closed Mon.*

ⓦ Restaurants

Cunda's restaurants lining the waterfront, although expensive, are among the best in Turkey. They're noted for their grilled *çipura* and *papalina* (small local fish) and for an amazing variety of other Turkish and Greek seafood dishes served grilled, fried, baked, or in cold salads. For casual eats, try Pizza Uno (not the American chain) in the center of town, a popular spot for kebabs, pasta, and *pide* (soft flatbread) as well as pizza.

Bay Nihat (*Lale Restaurant*)
$$$$ | SEAFOOD | . The most popular and probably the most expensive of the waterfront restaurants on Cunda serves a selection of mezes and prepared seafood that is a feast for the eyes as well as the stomach. Many options are original

creations based on Greek and Turkish cuisine—squid in saffron sauce, sole in yogurt, aquadis (a type of local mussel) in whiskey sauce, and cured fish *pastırma* are among the unusual specialties. **Known for:** huge selection of mezes; seating right on the water; exceptional presentation. [$] *Average main: 95 TL* ✉ *Sahil Boyu 21, Cunda* ☎ *266/327–1777* 🌐 *www.baynihat.com.tr.*

★ Lal Girit Mutfağı

$$$ | TURKISH | There's no grilled fish on the menu at this cozy, family-run restaurant—indeed, there's no menu, and most of the time only one entrée available: lamb cooked with thyme. But chef and owner Emine Elik makes some of the most delicious and inventive mezes on Cunda, which include several signature dishes. **Known for:** Girit lokumu (thick slices of eggplant topped with charred, caramelized walnuts); friendly and engaging owner; comfortable, homey atmosphere. [$] *Average main: 38 TL* ✉ *Namık Kemal Mah., Ayvalık Cad. 20, Cunda* ☎ *266/327–2834* 🕒 *No lunch July and Aug.*

Hotels

Cunda has become increasingly popular in recent years as a weekend escape, and boutique hotels and trendy restaurants have cropped up to meet demand. Most Cunda hotels are fairly expensive for what they offer,

★ Otel Sobe

$$$ | HOTEL | This charming small hotel has beautiful, spacious accommodations around an intimate atrium in a reconstructed stone building just a five-minute walk from Cunda's harbor area. **Pros:** peaceful, relaxing ambience; access to private beach; professional yet personal service. **Cons:** no views; rooms near reception may be a bit noisy; narrow streets make it difficult to access with a car. [$] *Rooms from: 600 TL* ✉ *Namık Kemal Mah., Hayat Cad. 5, Cunda* ☎ *266/327–3102* 🌐 *www.otelsobe.com* 🛏 *7 rooms* 🍴 *Free Breakfast.*

Zehra Teyze'nin Evi

$$ | B&B/INN | Hidden among the trees in the courtyard just next to the Taxiarchis Church Museum, this small guesthouse feels like a step back in time in comparison to its more upscale boutique-hotel neighbors. **Pros:** atmospheric location; casual and warm atmosphere; highly personalized service. **Cons:** standard rooms are quite small; rooms a bit dated and antique-cluttered; pricey for what you get. [$] *Rooms from: €75* ✉ *Namık Kemal Mah., Şeref Sok. 7, Cunda* ☎ *266/327–2285* 🌐 *www.cundaevi.com* 🛏 *7 rooms* 🍴 *Free Breakfast.*

Pergamum (Bergama)

62 km (39 miles) from Ayvalık.

The windswept ruins of Pergamum, which surround the modern town of Bergama, are among the most spectacular in Turkey. Pergamum was one of the world's major powers, though it had only a relatively brief moment of glory, notably under the rule of Eumenes II (197 BC–159 BC), who built the city's famous library. Of more lasting influence perhaps was the city's Asklepion, an ancient medical center that had its heyday under the renowned early physician, writer, and philosopher Galen (131 AD–210 AD). By then Pergamum was capital of the Roman province of Asia, which for centuries supplied the empire with great wealth. Bergama has not been heavily influenced by tourism, except perhaps for the carpet shops at the base of the Acropolis road. People still ride tractors, lead donkeys, and drive vegetable trucks through town, and a bus inching along behind a herd of sheep is not an uncommon sight.

GETTING HERE AND AROUND

If you're coming from Ayvalık, drive 51 km (32 miles) south on E87, then turn off following the signs to Bergama on Route 240 for another 11 km (7 miles). The bus from Ayvalık takes about an hour and a half and costs 15 TL. Frequent buses travel onward from Bergama to İzmir.

The Bergama bus terminal is 8 km (5 miles) out of the city center, but there's a free municipal shuttle service at least once an hour that stops near the post office and Red Basilica in the center of the old town. There's also minibus service for 3 TL. If a taxi driver tells you there's no bus service and tries to charge you 25 TL for the short trip, know that there are other options—or bargain with him. The last minibus back to Ayvalık is at 8:30 in summer, earlier in winter. If you find yourself stuck, take a minibus to nearby Dikili and change for Ayvalık.

There's no useful minibus service to the area's attractions. Thanks to the *teleferik* (gondola lift), the Acropolis is easily reachable on foot. If you want to hire a taxi to take you to all three of Bergama's main sites, expect to pay up to 100 TL for the driver to shuttle you around for a few hours.

VISITOR INFORMATION

CONTACTS Visitor Information. *EHükümet Konağı, B Blok, ground fl., Bergama* 232/631–2852.

Sights

Arkeoloji Müzesi (*Archaeology Museum*)
MUSEUM |. This small museum houses a substantial collection of statues, coins, jewelry, and other artifacts excavated from the ancient city and nearby sites. A relief from the Kızıl Avlu (Red Basilica) showing gladiators fighting bulls and bears and a Medusa mosaic from the Acropolis are particularly noteworthy. The well-preserved statue of Nymphe comes from the site of Allianoi, a Roman spa town now submerged under the waters of a dam in 2010. The ethnography section includes antique handwoven carpets, for which Bergama is well-known. ⊠ *Cumhuriyet Cad. 10, Bergama* 232/631–2884 TL 6.

Asklepion

ARCHAEOLOGICAL SITE | This is believed to have been one of the world's first full-service health clinics. The name is a reference to Asklepios, god of medicine and recovery, whose snake and staff are now the symbol of modern medicine. In the center's heyday in the 2nd century AD, patients were prescribed such treatments as fasting, colonic irrigation, and running barefoot in cold weather. The entrance to the complex is at the column-lined **Saorod Wuy,** once the main street connecting the Asklepion to Pergamum's Acropolis. Follow it for about a city block into a small square and through what was once the main gate to the temple precinct. Immediately to the right is the **library,** a branch of the one at the Acropolis. Nearby are pools that were used for mud and sacred water baths, fed by several sacred springs. A subterranean passageway leads down to the cellar of the **Temple of Telesphorus,** where the devout would pray themselves into a trance and record their dreams upon waking; later, a resident priest would interpret the dreams to determine the nature of the treatment the patient required. ⊠ *Bahçelievler Mah., Asklepion Cad., Bergama* ✛ *Follow Cumhuriyet Cad. west to Rte. E87; near tourist information office, follow sign pointing off to right 1½ km (1 mile)* 232/631–2886 30 TL, parking 8 TL.

Kızıl Avlu (*Red Basilica*)

ARCHAEOLOGICAL SITE |. The Red Basilica is named for the red bricks from which it's constructed. You can't miss it on the road to and from the Acropolis—it's right at the bottom of the hill, in the old

part of the city. This was the last pagan temple constructed in Pergamum before Christianity was declared the state religion in the 4th century, when it was converted into a basilica dedicated to St. John. Egyptian deities were worshipped here, and an 27-foot cult statue of the lion-headed goddess Sekhmet has recently been reconstructed. The main building—whose walls remain, but not the roof—is fenced off for restoration, but you can still walk around the site and see the "before" and "after" of the work in progress. One of the two towers has also been restored and has some displays inside; the other tower is used as a mosque. ✉ *Kurtuluş Mah., Kınık Cad., Bergama* ☎ *232/631–2885* 🎫 *6 TL.*

★ **Pergamum Acropolis**
ARCHAEOLOGICAL SITE | The most dramatic of the remains of Pergamum are at the Acropolis. Take a smooth, 15-minute ride on the teleferik, which includes sweeping views on its way up the hill, or follow signs pointing the way to the 6-km (4-mile) road to the top, where you can park. After entering through the Royal Gate, bear right and proceed counterclockwise around the site. At the summit, the partially restored 2nd-century AD **Temple of Trajan** is the very picture of an ancient ruin, with burnished white-marble pillars high above the valley of the Bergama Çayı (Selinus River). Nearby are the ruins of the famous **library**, built by Eumenes II (197 BC–159 BC) and containing 200,000 scrolls. On the terrace below, you can see the scant remains of the **Temple of Athena**. Climb down through a stone tunnel to get to the **Great Theater,** carved into the steep slope west of the terrace that holds the Temple of Athena. On a nearby terrace, the **Altar of Zeus** was once among the grandest monuments in the Greek world. If you're prepared for a long and rather steep descent, there's more to see on the slope leading down toward the town. ✉ *Akropol Cad., Bergama* ☎ *232/631–0778* 🎫 *35 TL, parking 8 TL; gondola 15 TL round-trip, 10 TL one-way.*

🍴 Restaurants

Akropol (*Ticaret Odası Sosyal Tesisleri*)
$$ | **TURKISH** |. The best thing about this restaurant, in a 150-year-old Greek building, is the setting and the estate-like grounds in a tranquil part of town. The food is nothing spectacular, but the large outdoor terrace area has views of the Acropolis and Red Basilica, making it a romantic spot for an evening meal. **Known for:** amazing views of the city; perfect spot for a drink; lamb dishes. [$] *Average main: 30 TL* ✉ *Ulucami Mah., İttihati Terraki Cad. 47, Bergama* ☎ *232/632–7722.*

Arzu Pide and Çorba Salonu
$ | **TURKISH** | In the heart of town, Arzu has inexpensive, simple, and satisfying Turkish fare that is popular with the locals, especially at lunchtime. The *pide*, *lahmacun*, and lentil soup are particularly tasty and the staff is friendly. **Known for:** Mercimek Çorba (lentil soup); simple decor; kuşbaşılı-peynirli pide (with minced meat, finely chopped vegetables, and cheese). [$] *Average main: 15 TL* ✉ *İstiklal Meydanı 35, Bergama* ☎ *232/631–1187.*

Bergama Sofrası
$ | **TURKISH** | Alongside a 16th-century hammam in downtown Bergama, this casual room serves around 20 dishes—stews, casseroles, grilled meats, and soups (fewer options are available at dinnertime). Try the *kadın budu köfte* (ground meat mixed with rice and parsley and lightly fried in egg batter) and the *kemalpaşa*, a traditional sweet served with *kaymak* (clotted cream) and tahini, for dessert. **Known for:** çığırtma, a local dish similar to moussaka; excellent value; vegetarian options. [$] *Average main:*

15 TL ✉ Bankalar Cad. 44, Bergama ☎ 232/631–5131 ⏲ No dinner in winter.

Kybele Restaurant

$$ | **TURKISH** | The restaurant at Les Pergamon, a small hotel in a mid-19th-century former Greek boys' school, draws nonguests for its splendid views of Bergama, romantic ambience, and food that's well above other options in town. Main courses include a variety of salads, pastas, and grilled meats, and desserts like the limoncello trifle are also excellent. **Known for:** Bergama çığırtması (a local specialty of fried eggplants cooked with tomatoes in a terra-cotta casserole); historic atmosphere; friendly and attentive service. [$] *Average main: 32 TL ✉ Kurtuluş Mah., Taksim Cad. 35, Bergama ☎ 232/632–3935.*

Hotels

Akropolis Guest House

$ | **B&B/INN** | This quiet, family-run hotel at the edge of town near the Kızıl Avlu (Red Basilica) is a reliable choice for its good value and pleasant atmosphere. **Pros:** near Red Basilica and Acropolis; owner and his family go out of their way to assist guests; excellent breakfast served in picturesque garden. **Cons:** downstairs rooms may get noise from pool and common areas; not many parking places; staff speaks limited English. [$] *Rooms from: €40 ✉ Kurtuluş Mah., Kayalık Sok. 3, Bergama ☎ 232/631–2621 🌐 www.akropolisguesthouse.com 🛏 12 rooms 🍴 Free Breakfast.*

★ Hera Hotel

$$ | **HOTEL** | Bergama's most attractive lodging is a favorite with couples on romantic retreats as well as visiting archaeologists, and all are made equally welcome by multilingual owner Mehibe, a mine of local information. **Pros:** serene location; beautiful rooms; good hospitality. **Cons:** neighborhood can be noisy at night; hotel reached on steep, narrow road; bathrooms a little dated. [$] *Rooms from: $70 ✉ Talatpaşa Mah., Tabak Köprü Cad. 21, Bergama ☎ 232/631–0634 🌐 www.hotelhera.com 🛏 10 rooms 🍴 Free Breakfast.*

Red Basilica

$ | **B&B/INN** | Located directly across from the Red Basilica, one of Bergama's newest accommodations provides quality service and good-value rooms furnished in a contemporary style, with dabs of local color, such as kilims on the floor. **Pros:** central location; restaurant serving alcohol; hospitable owners. **Cons:** no common areas besides restaurant; some bathrooms small and lack privacy; limited English among staff. [$] *Rooms from: $45 ✉ Kınık Cad. 77/B, Bergama ☎ 232/632–7601 🌐 www.redbasilica.com 🛏 8 rooms 🍴 Free Breakfast.*

Chapter 5

THE CENTRAL AND SOUTHERN AEGEAN COAST

Updated by
Jennifer Hattam

👁 Sights	🍴 Restaurants	🛏 Hotels	🛍 Shopping	🍸 Nightlife
★★★★★	★★★★★	★★★★★	★★★★★	★★☆☆☆

WELCOME TO THE CENTRAL AND SOUTHERN AEGEAN COAST

TOP REASONS TO GO

★ **Visit Ephesus:** For a glimpse into the Hellenistic, Roman, and Byzantine periods, take a walk through the ruins of Ephesus, lined with the remains of temples, houses, shops, and the famed Library of Celsus.

★ **Feast on local seafood and fresh meze:** Enjoy a relaxing meal, preferably on a terrace overlooking the sea or countryside.

★ **Swim, windsurf, and scuba dive:** Some of the brightest and bluest waters in the Aegean region surround the attractive coastal towns of Çeşme and Bodrum.

★ **Take a Blue Cruise:** A gulet, or wooden boat, is the perfect vehicle for exploring the Aegean coast, visiting secluded coves sprinkled along pristine clear waters.

★ **Wander through Şirince:** This picturesque wine-making village is full of lovely restored houses; the hills are great for hiking.

In addition to gorgeous white-sand and pebble beaches, crystal-clear waters, and a variety of water sports and nightlife, the central and southern Aegean regions of Turkey have some of the country's most captivating historical sites, including the ruins of Ephesus, Aphrodisias, and the travertine cliffs of Pamukkale. You'll never lack for delicious local food; the soil yields bumper crops of figs, peaches, olives, vegetables, and citrus fruits.

1 İzmir. Lively waterfront city rich in history and culture.

2 Çeşme. Idyllic beaches, seaside villages, and fine dining.

3 Selçuk. Small town set amidst a wealth of archaeological treasures.

4 Ephesus. Magnificent, well-preserved ruins of a grand ancient city.

5 Şirince. Rural hillside escape known for cozy boutique hotels and local fruit wines.

6 Kuşadası. Busy cruise-ship port with easy access to sights and nature.

7 Pamukkale. Surreal travertine cliffs, hot springs, and the ruins of a Roman spa city.

8 Aphrodisias. Evocative ruins of the city of Aphrodite, an ancient sculpture center.

9 Priene, Miletus, and Didyma. Fascinating trio of ancient archaeological sites.

10 Bodrum. Booming resort town in a beautiful setting, with restaurants and nightlife aplenty.

11 Bitez. Mandarin groves, olive trees, and a mile-long beach.

12 Göl-Türkbükü. Glitzy seaside getaway for the socialite set.

13 Turgutreis. Gateway to Greek isles and host to a popular classical music festival.

14 Gümüşlük. Charming seaside village with romantic sunsets and a bohemian vibe.

15 Yalıkavak. Windsurfing, luxury shopping, and a popular street market.

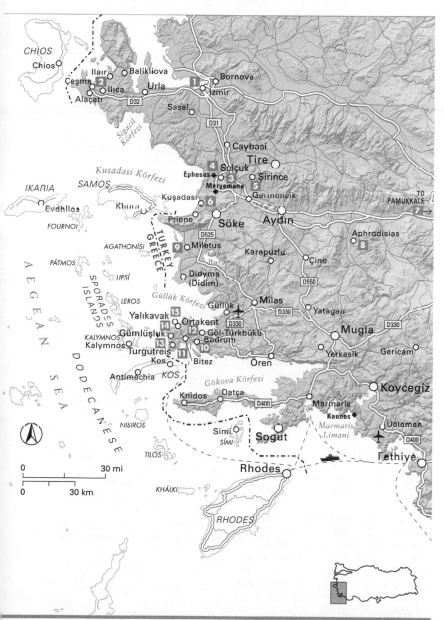

The Aegean is one of Turkey's most visited and most developed regions, for good reason: the area is home to some of Turkey's most captivating treasures, from gorgeous white-sand beaches to the ancient ruins of Ephesus.

The Roman city of Ephesus is the big draw for sightseers, and rightfully so. Bodrum and its surrounding beach towns attract sunseekers from around the world and spoil them with sophisticated hotels, a buzzing nightlife scene, and remarkably unspoiled historic sites. Even İzmir, Turkey's third-largest city and no stranger to concrete sprawl, will surprise travelers with a nice collection of museums, bustling bazaars, and lively seaside promenades. Then there are the many places in between these major stops: pretty little hill towns like Şirince; the otherworldly white cliffs and thermal springs at Pamukkale; the seaside charms of laid-back Gümüşlük village, near snazzy Bodrum; the ancient cities of Priene, Miletus, and Laodicea; and long, sandy beaches at Altınkum and elsewhere along the coast.

MAJOR REGIONS
The port city of **İzmir** (ancient Smyrna) is the third-largest city in Turkey, with enough sights and glimpses into everyday Turkish life to keep you well occupied for a day or two. Nearby **Çeşme,** a dry peninsula at the western tip of the region, has some of the region's most pristine waters. Some of the best beaches are Altınkum and Pırlanta, both southwest of Çeşme—the names literally mean "golden sand" and "sparkling." For the trendy beach clubs, head to Ayayorgi Bay and for restaurants, shopping, and nightlife, go to Alaçatı.

Selçuk is the town nearest to the archaeological ruins at **Ephesus** and a charmer; it's also well worth the extra 15-minute drive to see the lovely hill village of **Şirince**.

These days, **Kuşadası** is an overdeveloped cruise port, with passengers disembarking for day trips to Ephesus, but there's stunning nature nearby in Dilek Peninsula National Park. Within driving distance are several more sites well worth visiting: the layered limestone-travertine terraces and hot springs of **Pamukkale,** the ancient Roman city of **Aphrodisias,** and the ruins of **Didyma, Miletus, and Priene** are notable stops as you work your way south.

Throbbing resort life has descended upon the coves and bays of the stylish **Bodrum Peninsula** on the southern Aegean coast over the years, but each town still has its own charms. Bodrum itself is the booming gateway; **Bitez** is known for its mandarin oranges; **Göl-Türkbükü** is the most glamorous destination on the peninsula; **Turgutreis** is busy and touristy; **Gümüşlük** is a more authentic village without high-rise hotels; and **Yalıkavak** is an increasingly bustling (and expensive) town with good windsurfing.

Planning

WHEN TO GO

July and August are the high season, and Ephesus gets lots of tourists, especially those coming in from the cruise ship port at Kuşadası. In June and September you'll have the beaches mostly to yourself, though the water is cooler. If you want to visit the historical sights in mild weather, plan your trip between October and May—traveling at this time also guarantees fewer crowds and more affordable accommodations. The winter months can be rainy, but if you don't mind a chill in the air, it's an off-season treat to stroll through windy, deserted ancient monuments, then duck into a toasty kebab restaurant for lunch. Some hotels and restaurants close for the winter, and local bus services become less frequent, but almost all sights and museums stay open.

GETTING HERE AND AROUND
AIR TRAVEL

The quickest way to get to the central and southern Aegean coast is by plane. Daily flights connect Istanbul with airports in İzmir and Bodrum. Depending on the season, there are direct flights to İzmir and Bodrum from Ankara and Adana as well. İzmir is also a hub for Sun-Express, a joint venture of Turkish Airlines and Lufthansa, which offers an increasing number of flights to the Aegean city from European destinations.

AIRPORT TRANSFERS Bodrum Airport Taksi (Milas-Bodrum Airport). ⊠ *Bodrum Airport, Bodrum* ☎ *252/523–0024* ⊕ *www.bodrumairporttaxi.com* **Bodrum Tour (Bodrum airport transfers).** ⊠ *Bodrum Airport Exit 1, Gulluk Junction, BP Petrol Station, Bodrum* ☎ *252/313–3668 office, 530/391–9616 mobile* ✉ *bodrum@ bodrumtour.com* ⊕ *www.bodrumtour. com/bodrum-airport-transfer.html* **Havaalanı Taksi (İzmir airport taxi).** ⊠ *Adnan Menderes Hava Limanı, Izmir* ☎ *232/274– 2075* ⊕ *www.izmirhavaalanitaksi.com*

Havaş (İzmir and Bodrum airport bus). ☎ *850/222–0487 call center* ⊕ *www. havas.net.*

BUS TRAVEL

A number of bus lines serve the Aegean coast—Kamil Koç, Pamukkale, and Ulusoy are among the bigger ones, with a range of perks such as air-conditioning, free snacks, and reserved seats. However, bus travel is not always time efficient, and can be tiring, especially with kids. Websites have online booking in English, but telephone reservations are in Turkish only, and travelers without a Turkish ID number will likely have to purchase their tickets in person anyway. The ride from Istanbul to İzmir takes around 9 hours, and from Istanbul to Bodrum about 12. There are bus lines, often operated by smaller local companies, linking İzmir, Selçuk, Kuşadası, Didyma, and Bodrum, too. Typical travel times are: İzmir to Bodrum, 3½ hours; İzmir to Çeşme, 1 hour; İzmir to Selçuk, 1½ hours; İzmir to Kuşadası, 1¼ hours; and Çeşme to Bodrum, 4½ hours.

CONTACTS Kamil Koç. ☎ *444–0562 reservations; press 2 to buy tickets (toll-free in Turkey)* ⊕ *www.kamilkoc.com.tr.* **Pamukkale.** ☎ *850/333–3535 call center (24/7)* ⊕ *www.pamukkale.com.tr.* **Ulusoy.** ☎ *850/811–1888 reservations; press 1 to buy tickets* ⊕ *www.ulusoy.com.tr.*

CAR TRAVEL

A car will give you more freedom to explore this region, especially off the beaten path. Major roads and modern highways are in good condition and clearly marked, so driving from İzmir to Ephesus (in Selçuk) is quite easy; navigating the small winding roads around the towns of the Bodrum Peninsula can be trickier. Portions of the highway that run along the Aegean coast are quite beautiful, especially as you approach Çeşme and Bodrum. For an idea of distances: İzmir to Ephesus/Selçuk, 80 km (50 miles); İzmir to Çeşme, 85 km (53 miles); İzmir to Kuşadası, 100 km (62 miles); İzmir to Bodrum, 240 km (150 miles); and Ephesus to Bodrum, 170 km (105 miles).

TAXI AND DOLMUŞ TRAVEL

Taxis are metered and can be hailed on the street, though going to a taxi stand is usually the most reliable choice. There are flat rates for traveling between towns, but bargaining is appropriate. Traveling by *dolmuş* (shared minibus) is a more economical way to travel in and around the resort towns. To get dropped off along the driver's route, use the phrase "*inecek var*" (Ee-neh-jeck var), which means "I want to get off." Be sure to speak loudly and clearly—drop one sound by accident and you'll find yourself announcing "*inek var*," which is Turkish for "there is a cow!"

HOTELS

Hotels along the Aegean coast range from international-standard luxury properties and city-center corporate options to artsy or historic boutique hotels, and from rather stark lodgings for local business travelers to warm family-run bed-and-breakfasts or *pansiyons* (guesthouses). Almost everywhere offers free Wi-Fi and air-conditioning (but check before booking), and most include breakfast in the price—at least a basic spread, usually consisting of cucumbers and tomatoes, tea, instant coffee, eggs, feta cheese, bread with jam and butter, and watermelon in summer. The Bodrum and Çeşme peninsulas are infamous for A-list hotel prices to match their swanky clientele, with world-class resorts frequented by international glitterati, especially around Bodrum. İzmir has luxury options, too, mostly a bit more sedate. If you don't care about certain amenities (pool, spa, interior design), decent and reasonably central budget options are almost always available, even in the fanciest destinations.

Lodging in small towns like Selçuk and Pamukkale tends to be less expensive, and often has more local flavor. To get the best deal, check prices on the hotel's website or a third-party booking site, then call or email the hotel in advance to see if they'll quote you a better rate. Hotels listed here are generally honest, helpful, and hospitable, and many will gladly offer advice on visiting local sights. Always ensure that a hotel's location suits your requirements: central for walkable sightseeing or remote for pure relaxation. If you're arriving by public transportation, ask in advance how best to travel from the bus station to the hotel. You'll need your passport to check in, so if you think a day trip might turn into an overnight stay, take it along.

Hotel reviews have been shortened. For full information, visit Fodors.com.

What It Costs in Turkish Lira			
$	$$	$$$	$$$$
RESTAURANTS			
Under 25 TL	26 TL– 40 TL	41 TL– 60 TL	over 60 TL
HOTELS			
Under 200 TL	201 TL– 450 TL	451 TL– 800 TL	over 800 TL

RESTAURANTS

Dining out along the Aegean coast is a pleasure, especially if you enjoy seafood and fresh produce. There are countless seafood restaurants at all price ranges. A typical meal includes an assortment of hot and cold meze (appetizers), a mixed salad, and the catch of the day, capped off with a Turkish dessert. To make it authentic, accompany your meal with *rakı* (a spirit similar in taste to oúzo). Some of the more common fish you'll find along the Aegean coast are *levrek* (sea bass), *çipura* (sea bream), *barbunya* (red mullet), and *palamut* (bonito), as well as tasty smaller fish like *sardalya* (sardines). Note that most fish restaurants charge per kilogram for whole fish, and the prices often aren't listed; ask before ordering to avoid receiving an unexpectedly large bill at the end of an otherwise pleasant meal. Of course, there are plenty of meat and kebab restaurants around, too, if that's what you're craving.

For dessert, try local *dondurma* (Turkish ice cream, often thickened with orchid root or mastic resin), as well as milk puddings (*muhallebi*) and baklava. It's often better to avoid hotel restaurants at lunch and dinner—you can frequently find better and less expensive food a short walk away—but luxury and boutique hotels might be an exception as they are often firm favorites on the local restaurant scene. And don't forget street snacks! In season, you can grab fat local Smyrna figs; a cup of icy, dark berry *şerbet* (think of it as Ottoman Gatorade); or a sesame-studded bun stuffed with feta and tomato slices, each for less than a dollar in central İzmir. *Simit*, the classic Turkish bagel-like street snack, is called *gevrek* in the İzmir region, and often purchased along with a piece of *tulum peyniri* (goat's milk cheese) and a hard-boiled egg, following an old Sephardic culinary custom.

For more about the fish you'll find on the menu in Turkey, see the "Seafood on the Turkish Coast" food spotlight in Chapter 5.

BLUE CRUISES

Blue Cruises started in the 1970s as inexpensive boat tours catering to the Turkish bohemian set, and they're still an enjoyable and relaxing way to explore the secluded coves of the Aegean coastline. Of course, nothing is that inexpensive anymore, and there are plenty of luxury options. A typical Blue Voyage cruise lasts about seven days, but can be shorter or longer—there's not much to do other than reading, swimming, and relaxing, so many find that three or four days is optimal. April through October is the best time for a cruise; prices vary according to the month, the type of boat, and whether you opt for full board. You can arrange your trip before you leave home, or when you get to the docks. On the Aegean coast, Bodrum marina is the best place to hire a boat, with the most options. ⇨ *See the "Blue Cruising" box in Chapter 5 for more information.*

Era Yachting

One of the oldest yacht charter agencies in Bodrum, Era organizes weeklong tours around the Gulf of Gokova, the Gulf of Hisaronu, and out to the Greek Dodecanese islands. From €260 per person. ⊠ *Neyzen Tevfik Cad. 120/2, Bodrum* ☎ *252/316–2310* ⊕ *www.erayachting.com.*

Motif Yachting

Motif's charters of three days to a week or even longer take Blue Cruisers along Turkey's Turquoise Coast. Inquire about pricing. ⊠ *Caferpaşa Cad. 11/A, Bodrum* ☎ *532/233–3057, 252/316–2309 harbor office* ⊕ *www.motifyachting.com.*

Neyzen Tours

Neyzen's luxury charters of the Bodrum coast, Gökova Gulf, Hisaronu Gulf, and the Greek Dodecanese Islands offer onboard perks such as flat-screen TVs, air-conditioning, and free Wi-Fi. From €820 (5,080 TL) per person, all-inclusive, for a one-week cruise. ⊠ *Kibris Şehitleri Cad. 34, Bodrum* ☎ *252/316–7204* ⊕ *www.neyzenyachting.com.*

ScicSailing

Offering regular Blue Cruises as well as themed ones centered around activities such as art, archaeology, or cuisine, Dutch/English-run ScicSailing prides itself on sailing (instead of motoring) as much as the winds allow. From €940 (5,820 TL) per person, all-inclusive, for a one-week cruise. ☎ *758/300–1766 in the U.K., 62/906–3180 in the Netherlands* ⊕ *www.scicsailing.eu.*

True Horizon Travel

Organizes Blue Cruises of the Gulf of Gokova departing from Bodrum on small *gulets* (wooden sailing boats) that range from simple and affordable to luxurious. From €38 (235 TL) per person, per night. Private charters also available. ☎ *320/296–5757 in Italy, 533/451–7712 in Turkey* ⊕ *www.truehorizontravel.com.*

VISITOR INFORMATION

Visitor information offices are generally open daily 8:30–12:30 and 1:30–5, though you may not find much of use inside other than a few brochures and the odd map. *See city listings below for contact information.*

İzmir

565 km (351 miles) south of Istanbul.

Once a vital trading port, though often ravaged by wars and earthquakes, Turkey's third-largest city (formerly known as Smyrna) may today seem modern and harsh at first glance—even the beautiful setting, between the Gulf of İzmir and the mountains, doesn't soften some of the starkness of industrial districts and sprawling concrete suburbs. Spend a few days here, though, either on your way to other parts of the south Aegean, or as a base for visiting Ephesus and the surrounding area, and you'll find an extremely pleasant, progressive city with 7,000 years of history. Homer, the legendary Greek poet, is said by some to have been born in Old Smyrna sometime around 850 BC. Alexander the Great ousted the Persians and rebuilt the city at the foothills of what is today called Kadifekale in 333 BC. The city was an important religious center during the Byzantine Empire and was a battlefield during the Crusades, passing back and forth between Muslim and Christian powers. After World War I, it was occupied by the Greek army until 1922, when it was reclaimed by Atatürk. Shortly thereafter a fire destroyed three-fourths of the city and was quickly rebuilt under a modern urban plan. Like its name, much of the city center dates from the 1920s, with wide boulevards lined with palm trees, office buildings, and apartment houses painted in bright white or soft pastels.

As a modern visitor, the key is to make a beeline for the waterfront. An attractively refurbished promenade known as the Kordon follows the Gulf of Smyrna for almost 3 km (2 miles), chockablock with cafés and restaurants along most of its length. A short walk inland, a refreshing wealth of landmarks include the Kemeraltı outdoor bazaar and a collection of interesting museums, while the ancient Kadifekale fortress crowns a hill of the same name. The waterside Konak district is at the heart of İzmir life, with shops, restaurants, and clubs that are continually moving farther afield along the waterfront into the narrow lanes of the old Alsancak and Pasaport neighborhoods. You can take in the scene on a walk along Pasaport pier, past a restored customs house originally built by Gustave Eiffel, or on the Asansör (elevator), an early-20th-century relic that connects the slopes of Karataş, a Jewish enclave that is one more piece of this cosmopolitan city that will delight you with its richness. The relaxed, largely residential neighborhoods of Karşıyaka and Bostanlı are a pleasant ferry ride across the harbor. There's a developing gallery and restaurant scene in the Bayraklı business district, situated between Alsancak and Karşıyaka, and lively bars catering to a young crowd in Bornova (especially around the old train station there), where many İzmir universities are located.

The International İzmir Festival, held annually in early summer, brings in both Turkish and international musicians to perform classical, traditional, and contemporary works of music, ballet, theater, and opera.

GETTING HERE AND AROUND

While in İzmir, you can travel around by bus, the expanding metro and tram system, *dolmuş*, or taxi. For bus, metro, and tram travel, buy a 6 TL İzmir Kent Kartı at any metro ticket booth or kiosks around town and load it up to pay your fares (around 3 TL per ride with free transfers within a generous time period). There's also a bikeshare system called

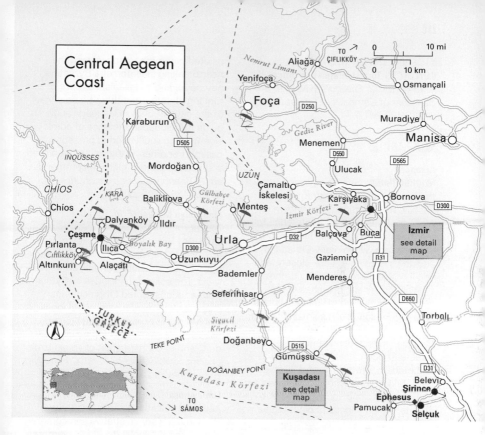

Central Aegean
Coast

Risim with rental points along the waterfront; membership cards can be obtained at the Konak ferry pier. From the İzmir airport, the most comfortable and economical way to get downtown is via Havaş shuttle bus (about 11 TL one way). If you're arriving by intercity bus at the main İzmir bus station (otogar), most major bus companies offer a free shuttle service to the city center. Most taxi drivers do not speak much, if any, English, so you're better off having your hotel call a taxi for you (and write your destination on a piece of paper).

TOURS
Çittur
GUIDED TOURS | This Turkish tour company can arrange private English-language tours on various themes, including visits to lesser-known archaeological sites in the İzmir area and tours of the Urla

vineyards. ⊠ Gaziosmanpaşa Blv. 10/1-B, Pasaport ☎ 232/446–4400 ✉ bilgi@cittur. com ⊕ www.cittur.com.

Culinary Backstreets
WALKING TOURS | These popular food walks have branched out from Istanbul to sample İzmir's culture and cuisine—from Sephardic savory pastries to poached sheep's head—one bite at a time. From $125 per person. ⊕ www.culinarybackstreets.com.

İzmir Jewish Heritage
SPECIAL-INTEREST | Explore İzmir's rich Jewish heritage on day tours of the city, as well as longer trips around the region. The website also offers helpful information for visiting İzmir's synagogues, some of which are newly restored and reopened to the public, and other Jewish sites on your own. ⊠ Gaziosmanpaşa Blv. 10/1-B, Pasaport ☎ 232/446–4400 ⊕ www.izmirjewishheritage.com.

VISITOR INFORMATION

CONTACTS Tourist Information Office.
✉ *1344 Sok. 2, Pasaport* ✛ *Next to the Chamber of Commerce (Ticaret Odası)* ☎ *232/483–5117.*

Sights

Alsancak

NEIGHBORHOOD | Stretching inland from the breezy Kordon waterfront, the trendy, upscale neighborhood now known as Alsancak ("red banner," a reference to the Turkish flag) was called Punta in the Ottoman era, when many Christians and Jews lived here. Look closely, and you'll notice there are still a number of synagogues and churches in the area. Pedestrianized main street Kibris Şehitler Caddesi is like a smaller version of Istanbul's İstiklal Caddesi, with lively bars, cafés, and restaurants filling its side streets. Though Alsancak is mostly slick and modern, pretty two- and three-story Levantine houses with bay windows are tucked away along some of the back-streets, which perk up at night with an influx of young İzmirians. ✉ *İzmir.*

Arkas Art Center

HOUSE | This late-19th-century mansion has been beautifully restored into a small museum, featuring rotating exhibits of painting, glass and textile art, and the like, usually with a historical bent. ✉ *1380 Sok. 1, Konak* ☎ *232/464–6600* ⊕ *www.arkassanatmerkezi.com.*

Arkeoloji Müzesi (*Archaeology Museum*)

MUSEUM | Though badly in need of refurbishing, İzmir's showplace for archaeology holds some notable treasures. Look over the railing in the lobby, down at what must have once been a spectacular classical mosaic of lions, peacocks, and other brightly colored creatures, then wander down haunting (but pitiably lit) halls of statuary, which include a front-row Hellenistic theater seat carved with griffins, and evocative Roman faces. Upstairs you'll find unusual painted ceramic sarcophagi (and the heartbreaking skeleton of a Byzantine newborn), and a Hellenistic bronze of a running athlete—and there's a neat view of the city. An English-language audio guide is included in the price of admission (though you'll need to present your passport or other ID to borrow the player and headset) and is highly recommended. ✉ *Bahribaba Parkı, Cumhuriyet Bul.* ☎ *232/489–0796* 💲 *12 TL.*

Etnoğrafya Müzesi (*Ethnography Museum*)

MUSEUM | This delightfully hokey museum, across the street from the Archaeology Museum, focuses on folk art and daily life. The collection includes everything from a reconstructed Ottoman bridal chamber (the mannequin groom looks like he's had second thoughts) to camel-wrestling gear, 19th-century embroidery, and a reconstruction of an old İzmir pharmacy. ✉ *Bahribaba Parkı, Cumhuriyet Bul., Konak* ☎ *232/489–0796* 💲 *Free.*

Izmir Agora

ARCHAEOLOGICAL SITE | This was the Roman city's administrative and commercial center; if it looks decidedly unimpressive from the entrance, that's because the best-preserved bit is underground: the basilica basement, separated into four galleries covered by dozens of stone arches. Alas, much of the rest of the site has been closed off for excavations, though there are still some other ruins to satisfy classical history buffs, and an interesting collection of Ottoman gravestones and Roman capitals near the entrance of the grassy, open site, surrounded by ancient columns and brick foundations. There is decent signage in English. ✉ *920 Sok.* ✛ *Off Eşrefpaşa Cad* 💲 *12 TL.*

★ Kemeraltı

MARKET | Konak Meydanı marks the start of this energetic marketplace, encircled by Anafartalar Caddesi, that spills into a maze of tiny streets, filled with shops and covered stalls. In the smaller side streets, you'll find tiny districts dedicated to musical instruments, leather, costume jewelry, and accessories, among other things. Begin at a restored Ottoman *kervansaray*, the **Kızlarağası Hanı,** completed around 1745. Downstairs, its vaulted shops mostly sell cheesy souvenirs, while the quieter upper floor, where some artisans still have their workshops, is a peaceful spot for a cup of tea or for poking through the antique dealers' old books and records. The nearby, late-16th-century **Hisar Camii** (one of the largest and oldest in İzmir) is worth a peek, and is surrounded by kebab joints shaded by large trees. Go farther into Kemeraltı and you'll wind up at **Havra Sokağı,** an outdoor market full of stalls selling spices, fruits, and other foodstuffs. Among this labyrinth of streets you'll also find the crumbling remains of numerous old synagogues, some of which are being restored. ⊠ *Konak.*

Konak Meydanı (*Konak Square*)
PLAZA | At the water's edge, this vast space is one of the city's two main squares (the other, Cumhuriyet Meydanı, or Republic Square, is to the north along Atatürk Caddesi), and is a good place to pick up a cheap street snack from roving vendors. The **Saat Kulesi** (clock tower), the city's icon, stands out at the center of the plaza, with its ornate, late-Ottoman design. The tower was built in 1901, in honor of Sultan Abdulhamid's 25th year on the imperial throne, and the clock itself was sent as a gift from Kaiser Wilhelm II. The small, 18th-century single-domed **Yalı Camii** (sometimes known as Konak Mosque), set back from the clock tower, is decorated with colorful tiles and was originally built by Mehmet Paşa's daughter, Ayşe. Just to the north is Konak Pier. ⊠ *İzmir.*

★ Kordon
PROMENADE | FAMILY | The lively and pleasant waterfront promenade is the most popular section of town and is perfect for a summer stroll; many locals use the sea breeze to fly kites. It starts at the Pasaport ferry pier and stretches north to Alsancak. Along the grassy, waterfront strip are several excellent seafood restaurants and cafés, all with outdoor seating overlooking the Aegean sea. It's fun to tour the area by *fayton* (horse-drawn carriage); they are stationed in the Cumhuriyet Meydanı, steps from the beginning of the Kordon (be sure to agree to a fair price in advance). ⊠ *İzmir.*

Kültürpark İzmir
MUSEUM | İzmir's vast, central park and fairgrounds has approximately 8,000 trees to stroll under, as well as an open-air theater, a culture center, a sports arena, a swimming pool, tennis courts, a shaded walking/running path, and the Tarih ve Sanat Müzesi (History and Art Museum). The museum compound ($) showcases Hellenistic and Roman-era statues and reliefs—including larger-than-life carved gods and goddesses recovered from İzmir's Agora and nearby sites. ⊠ *İzmir* ⊕ *www.kulturparkizmir.org.*

🍽 Restaurants

Alsancak Dostlar Fırını
$ | TURKISH | This very popular bakery in hip Alsancak serves up probably the broadest selection you'll find of *boyoz,* a flaky pastry with Sephardic roots that's these days almost unique to İzmir. Get yours savory or sweet, or perhaps with a hard-boiled egg on the side in traditional style. **Known for:** sweet boyoz filled with tahini; savory boyoz filled with mixed Aegean herbs; savory boyoz filled with eggplant. ⑨ *Average main: 5 TL* ⊠ *Kıbrıs Şehitleri Cad. 120, Alsancak* ☎ *232/421–9202* ⊕ *alsancakdostlarfirini.com* ⊗ *No lunch or dinner* ⊟ *No credit cards.*

Ayşa Boşnak Börekçisi
$ | TURKISH | Fresh, delicious food at reasonable prices in atmospheric surroundings—this is a real find tucked away inside an peaceful stone-walled courtyard amidst the chaotic energy of Kemeraltı bazaar.

Take a horse-drawn carriage ride along İzmir's Kordon, the waterfront promenade.

Make your own plate (cost is by weight) from the colorful variety of lovingly displayed salads, vegetarian dishes, savory pastries, and other home-cooked dishes for a bargain lunch. **Known for:** assorted börek (savory pastries); yaprak sarma (stuffed vine leaves); stuffed peppers. $ *Average main: 12 TL* ✉ *Alsancak Mahallesi, 1437. Sk. 11/A, Konak* ☎ *232/421–7085* ⏱ *Closed Sun. No dinner.*

Balıkçı Hasan

$$$ | SEAFOOD | There are many popular seafood restaurants along the Kordon waterfront in Alsancak but this one, with indoor and outdoor seating areas and a relaxed feel, is especially busy. It features a good selection of appetizers, including the decadent *sütlü karides* (shrimp sautéed in butter, then topped with béchamel and mozzarella), as well as the usual seasonal seafood choices. **Known for:** fried calamari; seafood pasta; shrimp sauteed with cream and chard. $ *Average main: 50 TL* ✉ *Kordon, Atatürk Cad. 186/A, Konak* ☎ *232/464–1354* 🌐 *www. balikcihasan.com.tr.*

Cafe La Cigale

$$$ | MEDITERRANEAN | Hidden away on a side street off busy Cumhuriyet Bulvarı, this peaceful garden oasis attached to the French Cultural Center offers a range of well-prepared Mediterranean dishes, including fresh, flavorful salads, pastas, and grilled meats. There's a winter garden for cold-weather days and regular live jazz, generally on Wednesday and Friday nights. **Known for:** risottos; salmon pasta; seafood pizza. $ *Average main: 45 TL* ✉ *Fransız Kültür Merkezi, Cumhuriyet Bul. 152, Alsancak* ☎ *232/421–4780* ⏱ *Closed Sun.*

Can Döner

$$ | TURKISH | Not far from the clock tower at the entrance of Kemeraltı, this small local favorite has served traditional İskender kebabı (and only İskender kebabı) from the city of Bursa since 1981. The spit-roasted meat is sliced thin and topped with melted butter and tomato sauce. **Known for:** ayran (a salted yogurt drink); no alcohol; closes early (by 6:30 or sometimes sooner). $ *Average* *main: 35 TL* ✉ *Milli Kütüphane Cad. 6/B* ☎ *232/484–1313* 🌐 *www.candoner.com* 🕑 *Closed Sun. No dinner.*

Deniz Restoran

$$$ | **SEAFOOD** | Deniz means "sea" in Turkish, an appropriate name for this popular, pricey seafood eatery on the Kordon waterfront, whose tables spill out of the ground floor of the İzmir Palas Hotel. It's buzzing with local notables, travelers, and a swanky business crowd, who come to splurge on exceptional fish and meze, including samphire with garlicky yogurt. **Known for:** sütlü balık (fish slow-cooked in béchamel sauce); sea bass in creamy basil sauce; sea bass in salt crust. [$] *Average main: 55 TL* ✉ *İzmir Palas Hotel, Atatürk Cad. 188/B, Alsancak* ☎ *232/464–4499, 533/145–8199 reservations* 🌐 *www.denizrestaurant.com.tr.*

★ İsabey Bağevi

$$$ | **INTERNATIONAL** | The owners of Sevilen, one of Turkey's best-known wine brands, have renovated and opened their family home to visitors as a fine-dining restaurant in a bucolic setting near İzmir airport. Summertime meals are served under a 300-year-old plane tree that provides cooling shade on a hot day. **Known for:** dry-aged steaks; rack of lamb; beef carpaccio. [$] *Average main: 70 TL* ✉ *Gölcükler Mah., İstasyon Mevkii, 901 Sok. 38, Menderes* ☎ *232/782–4959* 🌐 *isabey.com.tr.*

Reyhan Patisserie

$ | **CAFÉ** | **FAMILY** | With a huge variety of baked goods and dessert, including some intricate confections, and excellent house-made ice cream and chocolates, this pastry shop has been popular for decades. This branch of the legendary patisserie, in the heart of trendy Alsancak, is also a sit-down café serving coffee and Turkish-style breakfast. **Known for:** strawberry cheese-cake; profiteroles; sütlaç (creamy rice pudding). [$] *Average main: 15 TL* ✉ *Dr. Mustafa Enver Bey Cad. 24, Alsancak* ☎ *232/422–2802* 🌐 *www.reyhan.com.tr* 🕑 *No lunch or dinner.*

Sakız Alsancak

$$$ | **TURKISH** | By day a popular spot for a fast, fresh lunch, this homey restaurant on the waterfront by the Pasaport pier (it used to be in Alsancak, hence the name) turns into a lively *meyhane*-style eating and drinking establishment at night. A heaping mixed plate of vegetarian-friendly dishes like stuffed mushrooms, falafel, and fried cauliflower with yogurt is an affordable way to fill up midday; the evening set menu is equally delicious and a good value. **Known for:** sea bass roll with halloumi cheese; smoked octopus; sea bass with Aegean milk thistle. [$] *Average main: 48 TL* ✉ *Kordon, Atatürk Cad. 158/A, Konak* ☎ *232/464–1103* 🌐 *www.sakizalsancak.com.*

Servet (*Servet'in Yeri*)

$$ | **TURKISH** | The specialty of the house at this lively casual restaurant is *çöp şiş*, small pieces of skewered grilled lamb interspersed with delectable morsels of lamb fat. The grilled meats come with warm pillowy flatbread, soft cheese, spicy arugula, and grilled onions—nearly a meal in themselves. **Known for:** köfte (meat-balls); ciğer (liver); kuzu tandır (roasted lamb). [$] *Average main: 30 TL* ✉ *Şehit Fethi Bey Cad. 78/C, Pasaport* ☎ *232/484–0453* 🌐 *www.servetcopsis.com.*

Villa Levante

$$$ | **MEDITERRANEAN** | Fine Turkish and international cuisine served in an attractive secluded gazebo and courtyard make this hotel restaurant in the Bornova suburb worth the 8-km (5-mile) trek from the waterfront for a romantic meal. Villa Levante makes its own wine, best enjoyed with one of the popular cheese and charcuterie platters. **Known for:** house-made wine; cheese plates; charcuterie platters. [$] *Average main: 45 TL* ✉ *Erzene Mah., 80. Sok. 25, Bornova* ☎ *232/343–1888* 🌐 *www.hotelvillalevante.com.*

Yudumla

$ | **CAFÉ** | On a hot, hectic day in the Kemeraltı bazaar, you'll be happy to stumble on this little *şerbet* stall that's

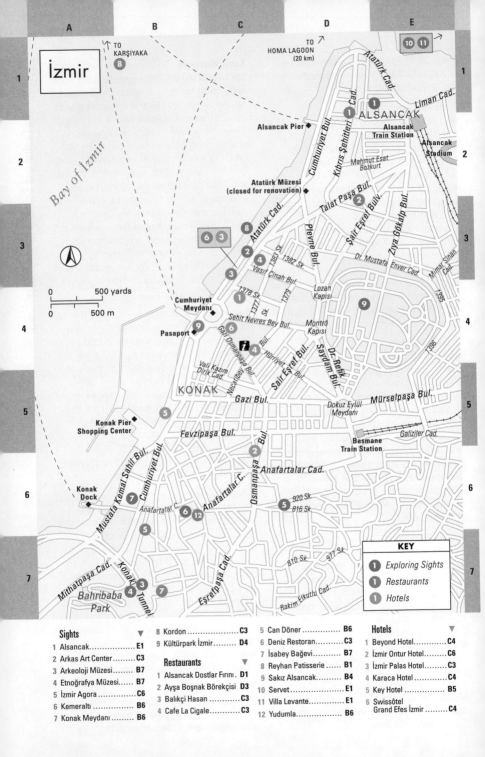

İzmir

TO KARŞIYAKA

TO HOMA LAGOON (20 km)

Bay of İzmir

0   500 yards
0   500 m

Alsancak Pier

ALSANCAK

Alsancak Train Station

Alsancak Stadium

Liman Cad.

Atatürk Cad.

Cumhuriyet Bul.

Kıbrıs Şehitleri Cad.

Mahmut Esat Bozkurt

Atatürk Müzesi (closed for renovation)

Talar Paşa Bul.

Şair Eşref Bulv.

Ziya Gökalp Bul.

Dr. Mustafa Enver Cad.

Mimar Sinan Cad.

Atatürk Cad.

Plevne Bul.

1383 Sk.

1382 Sk.

Vasıf Çınah Bul.

Lozan Kapısı

1378 Sk.

1379

1377 Sk.

Cumhuriyet Meydanı

Pasaport

Şehit Nevres Bey Bul.

Gazi Osmanpaşa Bul.

Montrö Kapısı

Hürriyet Bul.

Şair Eşref Bul.

Dr. Refik Saydam Bul.

1395

1396

KONAK

Vali Kazım Dirik Cad.

Necatibey Bul.

Gazi Bul.

Dokuz Eylül Meydanı

Mürselpaşa Bul.

Konak Pier Shopping Center

Fevzipaşa Bul.

Osmanpaşa Bul.

Basmane Train Station

Galiziler Cad.

Konak Dock

Anafartalar Cad.

Anafartalar C.

920 Sk.

816 Sk.

Mustafa Kemal Sahil Bul.

Cumhuriyet Bul.

Anafartalar C.

810 Sk.

977 Sk.

Mithatpaşa Cad.

Konak Tünel

Bahribaba Park

Eşrefpaşa Cad.

Rakım Elkutlu Cad.

KEY

- **1** Exploring Sights
- **1** Restaurants
- **1** Hotels

Sights ▼

1	Alsancak	**E1**
2	Arkas Art Center	**C3**
3	Arkeoloji Müzesi	**B7**
4	Etnoğrafya Müzesi	**B7**
5	İzmir Agora	**C6**
6	Kemeraltı	**B6**
7	Konak Meydanı	**B6**
8	Kordon	**C3**
9	Kültürpark İzmir	**D4**

Restaurants ▼

1	Alsancak Dostlar Fırını	**D1**
2	Ayşa Boşnak Börekçisi	**D3**
3	Balıkçı Hasan	**C3**
4	Cafe La Cigale	**C3**
5	Can Döner	**B6**
6	Deniz Restoran	**C3**
7	İsabey Bağevi	**B7**
8	Reyhan Patisserie	**B1**
9	Sakız Alsancak	**B4**
10	Servet	**E1**
11	Villa Levante	**E1**
12	Yudumla	**B6**

Hotels ▼

1	Beyond Hotel	**C4**
2	İzmir Ontur Hotel	**C6**
3	İzmir Palas Hotel	**C3**
4	Karaca Hotel	**C4**
5	Key Hotel	**B5**
6	Swissôtel Grand Efes İzmir	**C4**

been selling ice-cold and very delicious fruit juices and nectars since 1971. Buy a cup to drink on the spot, or a bottle to take home. **Known for:** black mulberry juice; blueberry juice; red currant juice. *[$] Average main: 4 TL ✉ Kemeraltı, Kestelli Cad. 2, Off Anafartalar Cad., Konak ☎ 232/472–2549 💳 No credit cards.*

Hotels

Beyond Hotel

$$ | HOTEL | This solid midrange choice not far from the water has a sleek, modern look with some softer touches, and attentive service befitting its boutique concept. **Pros:** attractive rooms with comfortable beds and Jacuzzi tubs; good central location; helpful staff. **Cons:** no views and few windows; small fitness area; no other recreational facilities. *[$] Rooms from: 375 TL ✉ Kızılay Sok. 5, Alsancak ☎ 232/463–0585 🌐 www.hotelbeyond.com 🛏 60 rooms 🍴 Free Breakfast.*

İzmir Ontur Hotel

$$ | HOTEL | The city hotel of a well-established local İzmir brand offers attractive, modern accommodations at an excellent price in a central location just outside Kültürpark. **Pros:** spacious, comfortable rooms; small indoor pool, gym, and sauna; good breakfast buffet with lots of options. **Cons:** no views; not on waterfront; not much local character. *[$] Rooms from: 250 TL ✉ Gazi Bul. 130, Konak ☎ 232/425–8181 🌐 izmir.onturhotels.com 🛏 80 rooms 🍴 Free Breakfast.*

İzmir Palas Hotel

$$$ | HOTEL | One of the first modern hotels in İzmir when it opened in 1927, this Kordon waterfront property has full sea views from half of its relaxing, attractive rooms. **Pros:** great location; nice buffet breakfast with a view; classic İzmir seafood restaurant Deniz is on ground floor. **Cons:** rather nondescript rooms; some rooms are small; no pool. *[$] Rooms from: 460 TL ✉ Atatürk Cad., Vasıf Çınar Bul. 2, Pasaport ☎ 232/465–0030 🌐 www.izmirpalas.com.tr 🛏 148 rooms 🍴 Free Breakfast.*

Karaca Hotel

$$ | HOTEL | FAMILY | In an appealing location on a palm-lined street, this friendly hotel is a good-value option for families—it includes free tickets to the next-door movie theater (closed in summer months), a generous buffet breakfast, and free airport shuttle for guests. **Pros:** spacious rooms and bathrooms; five minutes from the Kordon waterfront; welcoming atmosphere. **Cons:** decor could use an update; bland restaurant; tiny gym and spa area. *[$] Rooms from: 350 TL ✉ Şevket Özçelik Sok. 55, Alsancak ☎ 232/489–1940 🌐 www.otelkaraca.com.tr 🛏 72 rooms 🍴 Free Breakfast.*

★ Key Hotel

$$$ | HOTEL | If James Bond came to İzmir, he'd stay here—the city's sleekest, most chic hotel, where scrupulous attention to detail paired with up-to-the-minute technology draws a grown-up crowd, from major politicians to honeymooners. **Pros:** superlative service; beautifully designed rooms, many overlooking the sea; excellent bar and restaurant. **Cons:** very small exercise area; not all rooms have sea views; some rooms subject to traffic noise from busy main road. *[$] Rooms from: 600 TL ✉ Mimar Kemalettin Cad. 1, Konak ☎ 232/482–1111 🌐 www.keyhotel.com 🛏 31 rooms, 3 suites 🍴 Free Breakfast.*

Swissôtel Grand Efes İzmir

$$$ | HOTEL | FAMILY | An İzmir institution since the '60s, now under clockwork Swiss management, this swish business hotel is a serene place to recharge, with most rooms overlooking İzmir Bay or the lush gardens and outdoor pool. **Pros:** state-of-the-art spa and wellness center; centrally located steps from the Kordon waterfront promenade; kid-friendly resort feel. **Cons:** in its own world apart from the neighborhood; often hosts large trade conventions; pricey restaurants. *[$] Rooms from: 615 TL ✉ Gaziosmanpaşa*

Bul. 1, Alsancak ☎ *232/414–0000* ⊕ *www.swissotel.com/hotels/izmir* ⊷ *402 rooms* ⦿ *Free Breakfast.*

ⓨ Nightlife

Varuna Gezgin Cafe (*Café del Mundo*)
BARS/PUBS | Decorated with walls full of books and colorful souvenirs of the owners' global wanderings, this hip "travelers' café" and bar in Alsancak—now part of a popular Turkish chain—has made a name for itself with a keenly priced international menu (from Turkish breakfast to pad Thai to steak with oyster sauce) and a merry round of theme nights, quiz nights, and happy hours, with a wide range of cocktails on offer. ✉ *Muzaffer İzgü Sok. 13, Alsancak* ✛ *Off Kıbrıs Şehitleri Cad.* ☎ *232/421–0584* ⊕ *www. delmundocafe.com.*

Eko Pub
BARS/PUBS | By day a restaurant, open from 8 am, and by night a pub, open until 2 am, that's popular with expats and a mixed crowd of buisinesspeople and students. ✉ *Plevne Bul. 1, Alsancak* ☎ *232/421–4459.*

Sardunya Café & Bar
BARS/PUBS | A semi-alternative crowd hangs out at this bar on one of Alsancak's popular nightlife streets, taking in live jazz and alternative music events, and ordering off the international menu in the family-friendly café area. ✉ *Muzaffer İzgü Sok. 11, Alsancak* ✛ *Off Kıbrıs Şehitleri Cad.* ☎ *232/464–4665* ⊕ *www.sardunyabar.com.*

ⓣ Performing Arts

Atatürk Açık Hava Tiyatrosu
CONCERTS | For outdoor concerts of classical and Turkish pop and rock music, along with dance and other stage performances, see what's scheduled at the open-air theater in Kültürpark. Open May to September. ✉ *Kültür Parkı* ☎ *232/293–1705* ⊕ *www.kulturparkizmir.org.*

State Opera and Ballet House
DANCE | Ballet performances, classical music concerts, and opera (generally in the original language) are staged here, and tickets can often be purchased at the theater on the day of the performance. ✉ *Milli Kütüphane Cad. 33* ☎ *232/484–6445* ⊕ *www.operabale.gov.tr.*

ⓐ Activities

BIRD-WATCHING
İzmir Kuş Cenneti (*Gediz Delta*)
BIRD WATCHING | FAMILY | An excellent day trip out of the city, this natural reserve on the north shore of İzmir Bay near Çamaltı is best known as İzmir's *kuş cenneti* (bird heaven). The delta's lagoons, mudflats, salt marshes, reed beds, and farmland provide diverse habitats to more than 300 species of birds, mammals, reptiles, and fish. Tours of the lagoon can be taken by car or on foot: all tours start at the visitor center and are free. Only a few of the staff members speak English. You'll need a car to get here, or you can hire a taxi for the trip; it's 24 km (16 miles) from Karşıyaka neighborhood in İzmir. ✉ *İzmir* ☎ *232/482–1213* ⧆ *Free.*

HIKING
The most popular region for hiking (and skiing) near İzmir is the 120-km (75-mile) stretch between the Gediz and Küçük Menderes rivers.

Trails on the slopes of **Mount Bozdağ,** 110 km (68 miles) from İzmir, are also a welcome refuge from the city's sometimes suffocating heat. At Gölcük, trails climb gentle hills that cradle a lake, which is ideal for a picnic. Several tour companies organize daily trips to the area from İzmir.

With dozens of routes accessible nearly year-round, the area around Kaynaklar village in İzmir's Buca district (about 30 km [18 miles] inland from Konak) is an increasingly popular bouldering and rock-climbing destination. There's a campsite in the vicinity and a climbing festival organized each spring.

🛍 Shopping

For high-end, brand-name, and designer clothing, the Alsancak neighborhood has it all. Konak Pier shopping center is also full of glossy global brands, in addition to restaurants, a movie theater, and Remzi Kitabevi, a bookstore with English-language titles and maps. Head to Kemeraltı bazaar or Karşıyaka, or to Alsancak during the Sunday street market, for local color and edible souvenirs.

Bubobubom

CRAFTS | Designer Okşan Fındık's tiny shop in the Kemeraltı bazaar is full of delightfully whimsical decorative items— wooden ornaments and display stands, mini-chalkboards, crocheted bowls and pouches, and silver jewelry. ✉ *Kızlarağası Hanı No. 122, 2nd fl.* 📞 *542/344-0000.* ⊕ *www.bubobubom.com.*

Bostanlı pazar (Bostanlı market)

OUTDOOR/FLEA/GREEN MARKETS | The open-air street market held on Wednesday in the Bostanlı neighborhood of Karşıyaka features the usual array of fruit and vegetable vendors but is also known for its good-quality, inexpensive apparel: the earlier you go, the better the selection. ✉ *Bostanlı, Karsiyaka.*

Konak Pier

STORE/MALL | On the waterfront an easy stroll north from Konak Meydanı (turn right if you're facing the water), this 19th-century pier is now an updated shopping mall with several restaurants, a movie theater, and a bookstore with some English-language options, and fabulous views. It was originally designed as a customs house by the famous French architect Gustave Eiffel. ✉ *Waterfront.*

Çeşme

85 km (53 miles) west of İzmir.

Known for its hot springs and beaches, Çeşme has always been a summer resort for İzmirians, but in recent years the gorgeous sands have been luring Istanbullus and an international crowd, too. Despite rapid and often unsightly development, the towns and villages on the Çeşme Peninsula retain their provincial charm, and the area is still more off the beaten path than the resorts of the Bodrum Peninsula. The real lures, understandably, are the beaches that span 29 km (18 miles) of coastline.

Çeşme has a large marina, but for sandy beaches and crystal-clear waters, head to one of the nearby seaside villages. Ilıca, with its deluxe hotels, is closest and the most popular, with a long sandy beach. Dalyanköy is on the northern tip of the bay and is quite quiet and peaceful, known more for its fish restaurants than its swimming. The most beautiful beaches, Altınkum and Pırlanta, are in or near Çiftlikköy. Alaçatı, with its almost constant wind, is a windsurfer's paradise and has become extremely popular, to the point of overcrowding in high season, with upscale Turkish tourists for its restaurants and old stone houses converted into boutique hotels. Boyalık Bay and Ayayorgi attract a hip crowd. The villages are close enough that you can move around by car or public transportation quite easily, though some routes are more frequently served by *dolmuş* than others.

Public beaches are generally crowded and don't have amenities, so if you're planning more than a quick dip, you'll do well to spend the cash (typically 50 TL to 80 TL) to secure a spot at a beach club with chaise longues, umbrellas, towel service, and often a restaurant and bar. The swimming season starts in April and continues until mid-November—high season is July and August.

If you are driving from Izmir to Çeşme, most visitors zip by the towns of Urla and Seferihisar, but both are worth a stop for an afternoon or more, especially for anyone interested in food and wine. Urla's pretty harbor area has some good restaurants and cafés. Its Zafer Caddesi is known as "Art Street" (Sanat Sokağı) for its galleries and Saturday antiques market and art events. Farther inland, six wineries on the "Urla Bağ Yolu" (Urla Vineyard Route) offer tours, tastings, and meals amongst the vines; one of them, Urla Şarapçılık, has its own exclusive boutique hotel, with just two luxurious rooms. Seferihisar, Turkey's first "slow city" within the Slow Food movement, is known its Sunday market, featuring locally made handicrafts and food products, which fills the narrow streets of its historic Sığacık district. Many of the charming old buildings there are being converted into small B&B-style accommodations. The atmospheric ruins of ancient Teos, noted in Roman times for its wine, are nearby. Both Seferihisar and Urla are reachable by *dolmuş* from Izmir's Üçkuyular bus stop.

GETTING HERE AND AROUND

The peninsular villages are quite close together so getting around by taxi, *dolmuş*, or rental car is quite easy. Bus service is limited. From Çeşme proper, Alaçatı is 10 km (just over 6 miles), Dalyanköy is 5 km (3 miles), Ilıca is 6 km (nearly 4 miles), and Çiftlikköy is 5 km (3 miles).

Çeşme Seyahat Bus Company provides the only bus service between Izmir and Çeşme. In summer, buses shuttle between Çeşme's main bus station (*otogar*) and Izmir's main bus terminal, stopping at the old Üçkuyular bus station in Izmir's suburbs (take the metro to the Fahrettin Altay station and follow the signs for "terminal"), every 15 minutes, between 7 am and 8 pm. Reservations are highly recommended. The one-way cost is around 18 TL per passenger and the ride takes about 45 minutes.

In high season, the Havaş airport bus also runs direct services every hour between Izmir airport and the Çeşme otogar. The one-way fare is 27 TL per passenger for the approximately 90-minute ride.

For a quick hop to a Greek Island, head to Chios (or Sakız Adası, literally "gum mastic island," in Turkish), about a 45-minute boat ride away, or 20 minutes by fast catamaran. Several tour companies near the Çeşme docks offer excursions, as well as car rental on Chios; boat fares are typically quoted in euros and are about € 25 to € 35 (150 to 210 TL) per person. Chios town has nice waterfront dining options; rent a car or join a tour to see the picturesque medieval villages where mastic is produced, and the island's UNESCO-listed Nea Moni monastery can be found.

BUS INFORMATION Çeşme Seyahat Bus Company. ☎ *232/712–6499 Çeşme bus station, 533/593–1498 Izmir/Üçkuyular bus stop, 232/716–6191 Alaçatı bus stop* ⊕ *www.cesmeseyahat.com.*

⊙ Sights

Alaçatı

TOWN | Known for its windmills, trendy cafés, boutiques, and gourmet restaurants, this pretty village has become wildly popular of late. On summer evenings, the main strip of Alaçatı bustles with hip crowds; to avoid the hubbub come in the afternoon, when the crowd is mostly locals and store owners, although it can get very hot and many restaurants don't open until later in the day. Wander the backstreets to see picturesque Greek houses (many turned into boutique hotels) and the Greek church-turned-mosque (*Pazaryeri Camii*), where a curtain hides 19th-century Orthodox icons at prayer times. Tiny outdoor cafés selling tea, lemonade, plum juice (*erik suyu*), and mastic-infused Turkish coffee cluster under the windmills overlooking town, a popular spot for wedding photos. ⊠ *Alaçatı* ✛ *9.1 km (5.6 miles) southeast of Çeşme.*

Ayios Haralambos

RELIGIOUS SITE | Named for St. Charalambos (also known as Haralambos), a local bishop martyred at the age of 113, and whose skull is still venerated in Greece, this large, early-19th-century Greek basilica church is a relic of Çeşme's former Greek Orthodox inhabitants, and was restored by the municipality in 2012. The space is now used as a cultural center that hosts art exhibitions and handicrafts bazaars. If it's open for one of these events, it's worth taking a peek inside as you stroll down the main street of Çeşme's shopping district; look up to see painted saints peering down at you from the ceiling. ⊠ *Inkilap Cad. 26.*

★ Çeşme Kalesi

CASTLE/PALACE | **FAMILY** | Constructed during the reign of Sultan Bayezid II (ruled 1401–1512) to defend the port, this castle is very picturesque, with its stone walls often lined with sun-basking lizards and tortoises. The keep is often deep in wildflowers. The castle houses a small Archaeology Museum, displaying weaponry from the glory days of the Ottoman Empire, cannons from 18th-century sea skirmishes with the Russians, and a modest collection of ancient artifacts. Clamber around the towers for sweeping views of the sea and the city; keep close watch on kids around the less-than-secure railings. ⊠ *Çesme* 🗓 *12 TL.*

① Beaches

★ Alaçatı Beach

BEACH—SIGHT | The sandy beach at Alaçatı, about 6 km (nearly 4 miles) south of town, is ideal for windsurfing, with strong winds and few waves. Unfortunately, there is only a small public beach here, but many of the comfortable private beach clubs and hotels with private beaches allow nonguests for a day rate. The water is cooler at Alaçatı than it is at other beaches, and stunningly blue over the pale, fine sand. In addition to windsurfing, water sports like waterskiing,

banana boat rides, and kitesurfing are available here. **Amenities:** food and drink; toilets; showers; water sports. **Best for:** windsurfing. ⊠ *Alaçatı Plajı, Alaçati.*

Altınkum Beach

BEACH—SIGHT | **FAMILY** | The name is Turkish for "golden sand," and this beach has crystal-clear and calm water lapping the silky sand. The area has yet to undergo a huge development boom and there are many private and public beaches to choose from, most with shallow waters. You can rent a beach chair and umbrella at many points along the beach for a very reasonable price compared to trendier beach clubs. **Amenities:** food and drink; parking; showers; toilets; water sports. **Best for:** swimming; walking. ⊠ *About 10 km (6 miles) east of Çeşme off Hulusi Ortan Cad., Şehit Mehmet Yolu.*

Ayayorgi Bay (Ayayorgi Koyu)

BEACH—SIGHT | The most sheltered water and trendiest spot for a dip is at this dazzling turquoise bay named after St. George, Turkey's legendary dragon-slayer. A quick drive from Çeşme center, near Boyalık Bay, Ayayorgi Bay's beach clubs and restaurants are ever-popular with hip İzmirians and Istanbullus. There's no public beach, so plan to hang out at one of the swanky beach clubs (Paparazzi is a snazzy favorite, while Kafe Pi has a more youthful vibe), which metamorphose into beach bars as the sun goes down, often with live music. **Amenities:** food and drink; parking (fee); showers; toilets; water sports. **Best for:** partiers; swimming. ⊠ *Off Ayayorgi Yolu.*

Boyalık Bay

BEACH—SIGHT | Just west of Ilıca, Boyalık Bay has a 5-km (3-mile) beachfront of warm turquoise waters and pale, smooth sand. Boyalık Bay has many private and public beaches and hotels, as well as a campground. You may have to walk between summer residences to reach the sea. But once you reach the shore, you will find clear, relatively calm waters over smooth, almost milky-colored sand, with umbrellas and beach chairs available to rent. Boyalık Bay is getting better known, but its relaxing waters are not yet as crowded as Ilıca beach. **Amenities:** food and drink; toilets. **Best for:** swimming. ⊠ *Off Altinyunus Cad.*

Ilıca

BEACH—SIGHT | FAMILY | Still a summer retreat for Izmir's wealthy, Ilıca fronts one of the peninsula's most popular beaches, with many hotels lined up along the seafront and unusually warm, crystal-clear water and white sand. The public beach here is large, and has lots of waves, but gets crowded on weekends. There's no kitesurfing at Ilıca beach in summer, but it's allowed in winter, though you'll have to bring your own gear. Jet Skis and banana boats are available. **Amenities:** food and drink; showers; toilets; water sports. **Best for:** swimming; walking. ⊠ *Ilıca Plajı, Ilıca.*

★ Pırlanta Beach

BEACH—SIGHT | FAMILY | The name means "brilliant" or "diamond" and this beach outside Çiftlikköy certainly has seawater that's as clear as glass, gentle and shallow (you can sit in the water and read a book!). The waters are warmer here than at nearby beaches such as Altınkum, and mercifully free of seaweed or sea urchins. The pale, fine sand is usually clean, the beach peaceful, and there are changing rooms. You can snorkel, but kitesurfing is prohibited. If you want shade, you'll have to rent a beach chair and umbrella from the snack shack. There are many motels and pensions near this area, as well as a campground. **Amenities:** food and drink; parking; toilets. **Best for:** sunbathing; swimming; walking. ⊠ *About 9 km (5½ miles) from Çesme, Pırlanta Plajı, Çiftlikköy.*

🍴 Restaurants

Alaçatı Tatlıcısı İmren

$ | CAFÉ | FAMILY | For dessert, try this local favorite, where ice cream comes

---

Mastic: A Taste 🍴 of the Trees

New Englanders have maple syrup; the inhabitants of Çeşme have their own iconic tree sap: mastic resin, or *sakız* in Turkish. This piney, aromatic resin of the small evergreen, *Pistacia lentiscus*, is typically imported from nearby Chios island (known by Turks as *Sakız Adası*), though increasing efforts are being made to grow the trees in the Çeşme area, particularly around Çiftlikköy. It is used to flavor *sakızlı* ice cream, milk pudding, Turkish delight, and other dishes.

in many different flavors, and is served in a homemade waffle cone. *Sakızlı muhallebi*, a local specialty, is Turkish milk pudding flavored with gum mastic, the aromatic resin of the mastic tree. A beloved local brand, İmren has opened a casual Turkish restaurant on the same street (Kemalpaşa Cad. 70), as well as an Alaçatı hotel. **Known for:** black forest cake; mastic cookies; semolina cake with ice cream. $ *Average main: 14 TL* ⊠ *Tokoğlu Mah., Kemalpaşa Cad. 65 and 72, Alaçati* ☎ *232/716–8356* ⊕ *www.alacatitatli-cisiimren.com* ♡ *No lunch or dinner.*

★ Agrilia Restaurant

$$$ | MEDITERRANEAN | This Mediterranean restaurant was around (in a different location) long before the rest of Alaçatı's trendy dining options came on the scene, and remains one of the best and most stylish in town. The deliciously inventive food, and romantic garden courtyard atmosphere make Agrilia a local favorite. **Known for:** smoked beef; liver with grapefruit and sweet potatoes; chicken confit over einkorn risotto. $ *Average main: 65 TL* ⊠ *Kemalpaşa Cad. 86, Alaçati* ☎ *232/716–8594* ⊕ *www.*

agriliarestaurant.com ⏲ *Closed weekdays Nov.–Jun. No lunch summer.*

Asma Yaprağı

$$ | **TURKISH** | This small and romantic garden restaurant is widely regarded as one of Alaçatı's best, with chef Ayşe Nur Mıhçı famed for her fresh renditions of Aegean cooking using seasonal, local produce, especially the region's wealth of wild herbs and greens. There's no menu, but the staff will help you select from the options on display in the kitchen. **Known for:** roasted pumpkin meze; slow-roasted lamb; stuffed squash blossoms. [$] *Average main: 55 TL* ✉ *1005 Sok. 50, Alaçati* ☎ *232/716–0178* 🌐 *www.asmayapragi.com.tr.*

Avrasya Lokantası

$$ | **TURKISH** | **FAMILY** | Hearty traditional Turkish soups, stews, and meat and vegetable dishes are arrayed buffet-style at this cheery *lokanta*, which is always bustling at lunchtime. At the top of Alaçatı village near the minibus stop, it offers a reasonably priced and reliable alternative to the increasingly expensive fare found farther into town. **Known for:** meatballs with pureed potato; mücver (zucchini fritters) with homemade yogurt; lamb and golden thistle stew. [$] *Average main: 25 TL* ✉ *Tokoğlu Mah., Uğur Mumcu Cad. 22, Alaçati* ☎ *232/716–9144* 🌐 *www.avrasyalokantasi.com.*

Babushka Alaçatı

$$ | **TURKISH** | Chef Olga Irez's intimate restaurant takes a farm-to-table approach to the food traditions of her and her husband's Russian and Turkish grandmothers. There are many vegetarian options among the always-fresh meze and appetizer selections, which change throughout the year to spotlight seasonal produce. **Known for:** pelmeni (Russian dumplings); spicy beef liver; stuffed squash blossoms. [$] *Average main: 40 TL* ✉ *3000 Sok. 38, Alaçati* ☎ *232/716–0070* ⏲ *Closed most weekdays in winter. No lunch.*

★ **Dalyan Restaurant "Cevat'ın Yeri"**

$$$ | **SEAFOOD** | This outdoor terrace overlooking the waterfront is an ideal spot in Dalyanköy for a splurgy seafood dinner. Everything here is prepared with great attention to taste and presentation, and the service is impeccably gracious. **Known for:** deniz börülcesi (samphire) meze; tuzda balık (fish baked in salt); sakızlı muhallebi (creamy traditional milk pudding flavored with gum mastic). [$] *Average main: 55 TL* ✉ *Dalyan Mah., 4226 Sok. 45/A, Dalyanköy* ☎ *232/724–7045.*

Dost Pide & Pizza

$$ | **TURKISH** | **FAMILY** | Stopping here for *pide* (Turkish-style pizza or *calzones,* piled with a variety of ingredients that can include cheese, spinach, meat, or egg) is a highlight of a trip to Ilıca and a great choice for a quick lunch, or even breakfast, though on the pricey side compared to similar fare elsewhere. The menu also includes kebabs, soup, pizza, and traditional Turkish desserts. **Known for:** kıymalı (mincemeat) pide; döner kebab; meatballs with cheese. [$] *Average main: 35 TL* ✉ *5152 Sok. 27, Ilica* ☎ *232/723–2059* 🌐 *www.dostpidepizza.com.*

Hanimeli Restaurant

$ | **TURKISH** | **FAMILY** | This home-style restaurant just off the main street in downtown Çeşme may look a little bland from the front. But there's a lush, inviting garden out back fully shaded by fruit trees where you can fill up on affordable Turkish dishes like silky *kuru fasulye* (white beans in a tomato-based broth) or flavorful chicken with peppers and onions. **Known for:** Turkish breakfast; artichoke soup (in season); mücver (zucchini fritters). [$] *Average main: 18 TL* ✉ *16 Eylül Mah., 3001 Sok. 7/A* ☎ *232/712–2200* 🌐 *www.hanimelirestaurant.net* 💳 *No credit cards.*

Kapha

$$$$ | **FUSION** | Fusion fine-dining is offered in a sleek contemporary setting that's as stylishly well-designed as the plates that come out of chef Sedat Arslan's kitchen.

Make a meal out of the seafood-focused starters, which are more adventurous than main dishes such as beef ribs or *moules marinières*. **Known for:** baked octopus with smoked pepper cream and garlic butter; shrimp mantı (dumplings) with squid-ink sauce; duck mousse with pear chutney. [$] *Average main: 125 TL* ✉ *Cumhuriyet Cad. 13, Alaçati* ☎ *532/253–5715* 🌐 *www.kaphaalacati.com* 🕓 *Closed Oct.–Mar.*

Karina

$$$ | SEAFOOD | Tables spill out of the small courtyard into the cobblestone alley at this fish and meze restaurant in central Alaçatı. The service is on the ball and the innovative house specialties include a delicious dish of octopus cooked with mushrooms, onions, and soy sauce, and for dessert, apple baklava. **Known for:** sütlü balık (fish in béchamel sauce); grilled calamari; semolina cheese dessert. [$] *Average main: 55 TL* ✉ *Yenimecidiye Mah., 3002 Sok. 6, Alaçati* ☎ *232/716–9155* 🌐 *www.karinaalacati.com.tr.*

Kumrucu Şevki

$ | TURKISH | FAMILY | Ilıca is known for *kumru*—Turkish-style panini prepared with special sesame-seed rolls and stuffed with salami, *sucuk* (beef spicy sausage), cheese, tomatoes, and pickles—and this place serves the best in town. Pair your sandwich with a glass of *ayran*, a refreshing yogurt drink. **Known for:** Turkish breakfast; omelets; kumpir (stuffed baked potatoes). [$] *Average main: 15 TL* ✉ *5066 Sok. 2, Ilica* ☎ *232/723–2392 Ilıca waterfront branch* 🌐 *www.kumrucusevki.com.*

Rumeli Pastanesi

$ | CAFÉ | FAMILY | Since 1945, the Rumeli bakery has been *the* place in Çeşme to scoop up treats like thick, chewy Turkish-style mastic ice cream (*sakızlı dondurma*) in flavors such as black mulberry (*karadut*) and cinammon (*tarçın*) as well as jams, sweet mastic paste, and other traditional goodies. It's on the main shopping street, not far from Ayios Haralambos church. **Known for:** sakızlı muhallebi (mastic-flavored pudding); balbadem (honey and almond) ice cream; mastic cookies. [$] *Average main: 10 TL* ✉ *İnkilap Cad. 46/A* ☎ *232/712–6759* 🌐 *www.rumelidondurma.com* 🕓 *No lunch or dinner.*

Tuval Restaurant

$$$ | TURKISH | This seafood and grill restaurant at Çeşme Marina has a menu of international and Turkish dishes, including meze, pasta, fajitas, grilled lamb chops, and more inventive fare, as well as a respectable, if pricey, selection of wines and cocktails. The waterside location is lovely, with views of the castle; the winking lights far across the water are from the Greek island of Chios. **Known for:** shrimp with hummus; slow-cooked veal ribs; baked peaches with hazelnut-amaretto biscuits. [$] *Average main: 65 TL* ✉ *Çeşme Marina, 1016 Sok. 2, Suite 21-B* ☎ *530/824–8383.*

Hotels

Alaçatı Beach Resort & Spa

$$$$ | RESORT | FAMILY | Right on the beach and built of attractive Alaçatı stone, this resort is a fabulous getaway, with most of its well-appointed rooms opening to sea-facing balconies. **Pros:** large seawater pool and full spa facilities; hotel has its own windsurfing and kiteboarding school; kids club with activities for children. **Cons:** 10 to 15 minutes by car or dolmuş to Alaçatı center; the hotel's on-site nightclubs can get noisy; pricey drinks and food. [$] *Rooms from: 1400 TL* ✉ *Çark Plajı, Liman Mevkii, Alaçati* ☎ *232/716–6161* 🌐 *www.alacati.com* 🛏 *45 rooms* 🍴 *Free Breakfast.*

Alaçatı Marina Palace

$$$ | HOTEL | Rustic stone walls and charmingly decorated interiors with a nautical feel offer comfortable and atmospheric surroundings at this peaceful boutique hotel, only a short drive from antiquing, dining, and nightlife in picturesque Alaçatı. **Pros:** close to the nightlife at Port Alaçatı Marina; free admission to nearby beach club; on-site restaurant. **Cons:** need private transportation or dolmuş to reach downtown Alaçatı; 15-minute walk to beach; some bathrooms are small and could use a little refurbishing. [$] *Rooms from: 680 TL* ✉ *Liman Mevkii, Alaçati* ☎ *232/716–0740* 🌐 *www.alacatimarina.com* 🛏 *12 rooms* 🍴 *Free Breakfast.*

Asma Han
$$ | **B&B/INN** | This charming country house with nicely appointed rooms and a beautiful porch and garden feels peacefully secluded from Alaçatı's hubbub despite its central location. **Pros:** beautiful, intimate setting; excellent hospitality; rich and delicious breakfast. **Cons:** design of some bathrooms doesn't afford much privacy for couples sharing a room; location is a little tricky to find; minimal facilities. [$] *Rooms from: 360 TL* ✉ *Atatürk Bul., 3068 Sok. 11, Alaçati* ☎ *232/716–7642* 🌐 *www.asmahanotel.com* 🛏 *9 rooms* 🍴 *Free Breakfast.*

Dalyan Residence & Suites
$$ | **RESORT** | **FAMILY** | A private waterfront lounge deck, pool, restaurant, and outdoor bar ensure that you never need to leave this family-friendly resort, where the well-equipped rooms are full of light. **Pros:** spacious rooms; ample sunbathing areas; right on the beach. **Cons:** without a car, it'll be difficult to travel to the other coves; simple rooms are a bit old-fashioned; some guests say service could be improved. [$] *Rooms from: 360 TL* ✉ *Dalyanköy, 4227 Sok. 26* ☎ *232/724–8000* 🌐 *www.dalyanresidence.com* 🛏 *16 suites* 🍴 *Free Breakfast.*

Gaia Alaçatı
$$ | **B&B/INN** | Soothing earth tones, natural textiles, and wicker hanging lamps soften the sleek, contemporary rooms at this exclusive-feeling small boutique hotel in Alaçatı. **Pros:** central but still peaceful location; attractive, comfortable rooms; attentive service. **Cons:** dim lighting in rooms; poor Wi-Fi signal in rooms; minimal facilities. [$] *Rooms from: 600 TL* ✉ *13002 Sok. 11, Alaçati* ☎ *232/729–7777* 🌐 *gaiaalacati.com* 🛏 *10 rooms* 🍴 *Free Breakfast.*

Ilıca Spa & Wellness Thermal Resort
$$$$ | **RESORT** | **FAMILY** | Elegant, attractive rooms and bungalows, many with sea views and some spreading over two levels, provide a perfect getaway, while lots of on-site amenities make this luxurious resort a great place for families. **Pros:** kid-friendly; private beach and sunbathing platforms that extend out over the sea; spa and several thermal pools. **Cons:** long walk to Ilıca's nightlife and shopping area; service can be inconsistent; can get crowded in high summer. [$] *Rooms from: 1220 TL* ✉ *Boyalık Mevkii, Ilıca* ☎ *232/723–3131* 🌐 *www.ilicahotel.com* 🛏 *310 rooms* 🍴 *Free Breakfast.*

★ **Kapari Otel**
$$$$ | **HOTEL** | **FAMILY** | This stylish, serene boutique hotel near the Alaçatı Marina has spacious, well-appointed rooms—many with balconies or cozy window seats—and a large, well-tended pool and lawn area. **Pros:** lovely, peaceful surroundings; beautifully designed rooms and grounds; good service. **Cons:** need own transportation or dolmuş to reach Alaçatı's restaurants, bars, and shops; not on the beach; minimal on-site facilities. [$] *Rooms from: 625 TL* ✉ *Alaçatı Marina Mevkii, 8024 Sok. 4, Alaçati* ☎ *232/716–0674* 🌐 *www.alacatikapariotel.com* 🛏 *22 rooms* 🍴 *Free Breakfast.*

Pasifik Otel
$ | **HOTEL** | **FAMILY** | A good option for families, this waterfront hotel at the edge of Çeşme town sits above a small public beach and is just a 10-minute walk from the main square—though far enough away to ensure peace and quiet at nighttime. **Pros:** nice quiet location; family friendly; easy beach access. **Cons:** simple rooms and amenities; adjacent beaches get crowded during the day; no pool.

$ Rooms from: 160 TL ⊠ 16 Eylül Mah., 3254 Sok. 16 ☎ 232/712–2700 ⊕ pasifiko-tel.com ⮡ 17 rooms ¶◎¶ Free Breakfast.

Sheraton Çeşme Hotel, Resort & Spa

$$$$ | RESORT | FAMILY | Spacious, well-appointed rooms, many with expansive sea views from their balconies, are a highlight at this deluxe seaside resort in Ilıca. **Pros:** beautiful and peaceful private beach; sundeck extending into the sea; on-site spa and lots of water sports. **Cons:** expensive and meal-inclusive rates compulsory in high season; service can be inconsistent; need private transportation. $ Rooms from: 1250 TL ⊠ Şifne Cad. 35, Ilıca ☎ 232/750–0000 ⊕ www.sheratoncesme.com ⮡ 398 rooms ¶◎¶ Free Breakfast.

Villa Fanti

$$ | B&B/INN | A tiny place that's big on hospitality, this family-run hotel in central Çeşme is a fine choice for singles or couples looking for a peaceful place to lay their heads at the end of the day. **Pros:** great location near the water; excellent breakfast; attractively decorated rooms. **Cons:** some rooms are small; limited facilities; multiple sets of stairs and no elevator. $ Rooms from: 350 TL ⊠ 16 Eylul Mah., 3047 Sok. 1/A ☎ 232/712–6696 ⊕ www.villafanti.com.tr ⮡ 12 rooms ¶◎¶ Free Breakfast.

Villa Vongole Hotel

$$ | HOTEL | Accommodating staff and a prime waterfront spot in central Çeşme elevate this small family-run hotel from simple guesthouse to cozy home-away-from-home. **Pros:** central location; friendly and welcoming; excellent breakfast. **Cons:** most rooms are small; Wi-Fi signal is weak; limited facilities. $ Rooms from: 250 TL ⊠ 16 Eylul Mah., 3053 Sok. 14 ☎ 232/712–0205 ⊕ www.villavongole.com ⮡ 9 rooms ¶◎¶ Free Breakfast.

▼ Nightlife

Çeşme Açık Hava Tiyatrosu

CONCERTS | Çeşme's open-air theater hosts a series of concerts by Turkish and international acts in summer. ⊠ Adnan Menderes Cad., 2053 Sok.

Paparazzi

DANCE CLUBS | The DJs at this popular, if pricey, beach club spin music from the 1970s through the '90s, which is appropriate because this place has been around for 30 years. Partying goes 'til the wee hours of the morning, with live music acts featured a couple of nights a week. The food isn't bad, either. ⊠ Ayayorgi Bay, Ayayorgi Mevki 11 ☎ 232/712–6767 ⊕ paparazzi.com.tr.

Take Five

MUSIC CLUBS | This intimate coffee shop in Alaçatı's Haçımemiş neighborhood hosts top-notch local jazz performers for nighttime concerts on summer weekends. Wine, cocktails (try the espresso martini), and small bites are also available in the evenings. ⊠ Hacımemiş Mah., 12001 Sok. 30, Alaçati ☎ 541/689–8969.

⛷ Activities

BOAT TOURS

During high season, daily boat tours to coves along the coastline leave from the main harbors in Çeşme and Ilıca. The cost varies, depending on whether lunch and beverages are served. One of the most popular stops is Donkey Island (Eşek Adası). Be warned that in high season the boats tend to be crowded and play loud music, so consider renting a boat privately.

KITESURFING AND WINDSURFING

Bu Bi Surf School (Bu Bi Sörf Okulu)

WINDSURFING | Windsurfing and kitesurfing lessons for beginners on up—as well as windsurfing equipment rental—are available at this surf school right on Alaçatı Beach, from 250 TL per person for one lesson. ⊠ Liman Mevkii, Alaçati ☎ 232/716–6876 ⊕ www.bubisurf.com.

Kite-Turkey Kitesurf Centers

WINDSURFING | Kitesurfers of all experience levels can rent equipment or receive instruction at the Kite-Turkey center on Alaçatı Bay, known for its strong, steady winds, or catch a lift to Urla, another popular kitesurfing destination on the Çeşme Peninsula, about 29 km (18 miles) away. ⊠ *Alaçatı Beach* ☎ *538/381–5686 in Turkey, 207/193–1829 in the U.K.* ⊕ *www.kite-turkey.com.*

💼 Shopping

Pedestrianized İnkılap Caddesi (2001 Sokak), which runs through Çeşme from the bus stop near Cumhuriyet Meydanı to the harbor, has many gift shops selling trinkets and souvenirs, beachwear, carpets, and leather items. There are also many jewelry stores selling silver and gold; bargaining is acceptable and expected. Çeşme Marina has many higher-end chain shops. Downtown Alaçatı is also great for shopping, and small upscale boutiques selling jewelry, clothing, and decorative items occupy stone houses along the narrow lanes. The antiques shops are treasure troves of interesting trinkets, and sometimes more.

Chitra Alaçatı

CLOTHING | Designer Selin Bozkurt's lovely little shop right on the main street in central Alaçatı sells a range of women's linen and cotton beachwear and home textiles adorned with beautiful woodblock prints in abstract or playful patterns, many inspired by the creatures and plants of the sea. ⊠ *Kemalpaşa Cad. 35/1A, Alaçatı* ☎ *232/431–0413* ⊕ *www.chitra.com.tr.*

Eski Tütün Dükkanı

CRAFTS | Colorful and often quirky jewelry, sculptures, plates, lamps, and other objects by Turkish designers fill this stone-walled shop in Alaçatı's popular Hacımemiş neighborhood. Like many other small boutiques in town, you may find it closed during the daytime and open late into the evening, when the most people are out and about. ⊠ *Hacımemiş Mah., 12000 Sok. 24, Alaçatı* ☎ *532/351–6644.*

Gemici Alaçatı

FOOD/CANDY | A huge variety of locally produced and nicely packaged herbs, jams, wines, and other culinary treats, along with small housewares like olivewood coasters, are for sale at this big, bright store on the main street leading into central Alaçatı. Prices are surprisingly good considering its prime location in this expensive town. ⊠ *Uğur Mumcu Cad. 16/C, Alaçatı* ☎ *232/716–6785.*

Terracotta Ceramic Art

CERAMICS/GLASSWARE | Sleek bowls and elaborately detailed cups are among the many kinds of handmade ceramic housewares and decorations you'll find in this airy shop in Alaçatı. Designer Gül Alper and her team can even make ceramics to your own design in their on-site workshop. ⊠ *12015 Sok. 5/1, Alaçatı* ☎ *554/407–9140.*

Selçuk

79 km (49 miles) south of İzmir.

Selçuk, the closest city to Ephesus, lies beneath the ancient **Fortress of Ayasuluk** and is unfortunately often overlooked. The former farming village has interesting sights of its own to offer—St. John the Evangelist is said to have been buried here, just below the medieval fortress, and the city has one of the oldest mosques in western Turkey, the lovely **İsa Bey Camii**. On her visit over half a century ago, the renowned explorer Freya Stark rhapsodized over the historical treasures of the small city of Selçuk: "All are tightly clustered together," Stark wrote in her book *Ionia: A Quest,* "like the landscape in a medieval book of hours. And that is indeed what it is, though the hours are centuries, and the book written on the transformations of earth." Selçuk is easy to navigate on foot (keep an eye out for small gems of Seljuk and Ottoman architecture scattered across town), and there are many good casual restaurants along the main square and along side streets where you can eat outside. Rather pricey shops selling carpets and jewelry cater to souvenir seekers. The town hosts an annual camel-wrestling festival every third weekend in January. Lesser-known excursions from Selçuk include the archaeological ruins of Klaros, once an important ancient Greek shrine to the god Apollo (about 40 minutes northwest along highway D515 with your own car), and the farming town of Tire (easily reachable on a day trip by *dolmuş*), known for its felt makers, its attractive old center, and its lively market on Tuesdays and Fridays.

GETTING HERE AND AROUND

By car, Selçuk is about one hour from İzmir on Route E87, following the well-marked *otoyol* (toll highway) toward Aydın. The Selçuk exit is well marked. If driving from Selçuk to Ephesus, look for brown signs with its Turkish name, Efes.

Alternatively, if you do not want to rent a car, you can take a train to Selçuk from İzmir. The Denizli-bound *bölgesel seferler* (regional services) depart from the Basmane station in central İzmir roughly every two hours and travel time to Selçuk is about 1½ hours; for schedules and online tickets, visit ⊕ *www.tcdd.gov.tr.* İzmir's suburban rail line, the İzban, now extends to Selçuk, with about a dozen trains daily in each direction. Local bus companies also offer minibus service to Selçuk, with departures from the main bus terminal in İzmir.

Travelers flying to İzmir can take the Havaş shuttle to Kuşadası (27 TL), which stops in Selçuk upon request.

CONTACTS Kamil Koç. ⊠ *Selçuk Bus Terminal (Otogar)* ☎ *444–0562 call center (no area code needed in Turkey), 232/892–6263 Selçuk office* ⊕ *www. kamilkoc.com.tr.*

VISITOR INFORMATION

CONTACTS Tourist Information Office. ⊠ *Uğur Mumcu Sevgi Yolu 37* ✛ *Across the street from the museum* ☎ *232/892–6328.*

◉ Sights

★ **Ephesus Müzesi** (*Ephesus Museum*)
MUSEUM | This small museum has one of the best collections of Roman and Greek artifacts found anywhere in Turkey. The well-displayed and labeled holdings date from the neolithic to Ottoman periods and include fine sculptures, friezes, mosaics, and reliefs. The elaborately carved white statues of Artemis are particularly notable, while the exhibit of jewelry, cosmetics, medical instruments, and housewares from Ephesus's terrace houses gives an intimate glimpse into day-to-day life in the ancient city. ⊠ *Uğur Mumcu Sevgi Yolu* ✛ *Opposite the Selçuk Tourist Information Center* ☎ *232/892–6010* 🎫 *15 TL.*

İsa Bey Camii (*İsa Bey Mosque*)
RELIGIOUS SITE | Lovely and evocative, this is one of the most ancient mosques in western Turkey, dating from 1375. The jumble of architectural styles suggests a transition between Seljuk and Ottoman design: like later-day Ottoman mosques, this one has a large courtyard, though the interior is plain (in the 19th century, it doubled as a kervansaray). The structure is built out of *spolia*, or "borrowed" stone: marble blocks with Latin inscriptions, Corinthian columns, black-granite columns from the baths at Ephesus, and pieces from the altar of the Temple of Artemis. Don't miss it if you're visiting the St. John Basilica—it's a three-minute walk downhill as you turn right out of the gate. ⊠ *Corner of St. Jean Cad. and 2040 Sok.*

Meryem Ana Evi (*Virgin Mary's House*)
RELIGIOUS SITE | This wooded complex in the hills above Selçuk draws pilgrims to the small stone house where the Virgin Mary is said to have spent the last days

of her life. A nearby "wishing wall" is covered with notes written by visitors on scraps of paper and cloth. The setting is beautiful, but a trip here may be of limited interest to nonbelievers as there's not all that much to see. ⊠ Selçuk ✛ Off Rte. E87, 5 km (3 miles) southwest of Ephesus ☎ 530/469–0844 ⌂ 25 TL.

See the highlighted Ephesus feature in this chapter for more information.

★ **St. John Basilica & Fortress of Ayasuluk**
(*St. Jean Anıtı*)
ARCHAEOLOGICAL SITE | Step through the impressive, pre-Justinianic marble portal (its huge blocks likely plundered from the nearby Temple of Artemis) to approach the basilica, which sits below the crenellated walls of the Fortress of Ayasuluk, likely covering the site of the most ancient settlement in Selçuk. In the 6th century AD, after earthquakes destroyed the modest church believed to mark the grave of St. John the Evange-list, Byzantine Emperor Justinian and his wife Theodora commanded that a grand marble basilica be erected over the site on Ayasuluk Hill, its eleven domes grand enough to rival the imperial pair's other legendary building project, Hagia Sophia. The basilica's barrel-vaulted roof col-lapsed after another long-ago earthquake, but the ruined church is still an incredibly evocative sight, with its labyrinth of halls and marble courtyards, and occasional mosaic fragments. Both the basilica and the fortress, the work of Byzantine, Seljuk, and Ottoman builders, provide stunning views of the Plain of Ephesus and the İsa Bey Mosque. Come by in the early morning or late afternoon when there are rarely crowds; if arriving later in the day, be sure to visit the fortress first—it closes earlier than the basilica area. ⊠ Selçuk ✛ Off St. Jean Cad., just east of Isa Bey Camii ⌂ 15 TL.

Temple of Artemis (*Artemis Tapınağı*)
ARCHAEOLOGICAL SITE | Today a lone column towering over a scattering of fallen stones in a marshy lowland on the

Selçuk–Ephesus road is all that remains of a temple that was once four times larger than the Parthenon in Athens, one of the Seven Wonders of the Ancient World. Fragments of the temple are on display at İsa Bey Mosque. Begun in the 7th century BC, greatly expanded by the wealthy Lydian king Croesus, and redone in marble in the 6th century BC, the temple was torched by a disgruntled worshipper in 356 BC. Rebuilt by Alexander the Great, it was captured by Goths in AD 263 and later stripped for materials to build Istanbul's Aya Sofya and Selçuk's St. John Basilica. As goddess of the hunt and wild creatures, Artemis might well approve of the temple's new inhabitants: lizards, frogs, storks, and dozens of other birds. The temple is an easy 10-minute walk along a tree-lined road from Selçuk center, and more evocative if you visit it on your own. ⊠ Dr. Sabri Yayla Bul. ⌂ Free.

🍴 Restaurants

Agora Restaurant
$$ | TURKISH | This large Turkish restaurant near the Ephesus Museum has an equally large menu, focusing on grilled meats, but also including *pide*, meze, salads, break-fast, and some specialty desserts. There are also some daily specials, such as roasted lamb on Fridays. **Known for:** pirzola (lamb chops); çökertme kebabı (meatballs on top of shoestring fries with yogurt and tomato sauce); mixed grill. $ *Average main: 35 TL* ⊠ *Agora Çarşısı 2* ☎ *232/892–3053* ⊕ *www.agora-restaurant.com.*

Ayasoluk Restaurant
$$ | TURKISH | The Ayasoluk Hotel's res-taurant offers meals in a pleasant dining room and romantic courtyard, both with a bucolic sunset view, and features local and organic ingredients for a light, fresh take on Turkish favorites. One of the more intimate and sophisticated dining options in town, with a good wine list, too. **Known for:** lamb shank with rice; fish baked in parchment paper; homemade soups. $ *Average*

main: 40 TL ✉ *Ayasoluk Hotel, 1051 Sokak 12* ☎ *232/892–3336* 🌐 *www.ayasolukhotel.com.*

★ Ejder Restaurant

$$ | TURKISH | FAMILY | This popular spot overlooking the Selçuk aqueduct is run by a friendly family team—husband, wife, and son—and offers a menu that includes such traditional vegetarian dishes as exemplary stuffed peppers and fried eggplant. It may sometimes take a while for the generous, juicy lamb and chicken kebabs to cook in the small hearth, but it's worth the wait. **Known for:** pirzola (lamb chops); kanat şiş (chicken wings); kuzu beyti (lamb rolls). [$] *Average main: 35 TL* ✉ *Cengiz Topel Cad. 9/E* ☎ *232/892–3296* 🌐 *www.ejderselcuk.com.*

Eski Ev

$$ | TURKISH | The Ottoman motifs seem a bit touristy, but the place is done up nicely, in the peaceful, open-air courtyard of an old house, shaded by a towering grapefruit tree. Eski Ev ("old house" in Turkish) serves a wide selection of Turkish meze (appetizers) and main dishes, including some nice choices for vegetarians. **Known for:** Old House special (lamb with vegetables and rice); lamb kebabs; steak. [$] *Average main: 30 TL* ✉ *1005 Sok. 1/A* ✥ *Off Cengiz Topel Cad.* ☎ *232/892–9357.*

Kahvecin

$ | CAFÉ | Popular with a young local crowd, this cute and friendly little café serves up assorted coffee drinks, including flavored ones mixed with Italian syrups, and Western-style cakes and other desserts. Most seating is street-side, on a central corner near the aqueduct, and it stays open late. **Known for:** frappes; milkshakes; cheesecake. [$] *Average main: 10 TL* ✉ *Namık Kemal Cad. 11* ☎ *232/785–4589* 🌐 *www.kahvecin.com.tr* ⏲ *No lunch or dinner.*

Selçuk Pidecisi

$ | TURKISH | FAMILY | Blissfully lacking the touts trying to lure tourists into the restaurants around Cengiz Topel Caddesi, this tiny, friendly *pide* shop is conveniently located near the Selçuk Museum. In addition to the crisp, tasty *pide* offerings, there is also a selection of *güveç* (casserole) dishes on the menu. **Known for:** vegetarian-friendly pide toppings such as spinach and mushrooms; lahmacun (flatbread with spicy minced meat topping); tahini-topped pide for dessert. [$] *Average main: 15 TL* ✉ *Atatürk Mah., Uğur Mumcu Sevgi Yolu 12/A* ☎ *232/892–1434* 💳 *No credit cards.*

Hotels

Akanthus Hotel

$$$ | B&B/INN | The amply sized, elegant rooms at this intimate boutique hotel, which opened in early 2018, are in two traditional stone houses on either side of a small courtyard with a small pool. **Pros:** attractive, good-sized rooms with lots of light; attentive, personal service; good breakfast with lots of local ingredients. **Cons:** bathrooms are on the small side; location feels a bit out of the way; no restaurant. [$] *Rooms from: 540 TL* ✉ *1064 Sok. 11* ☎ *232/892–9212* 🌐 *www.akanthushotel.com* 🛏 *12 rooms* 🍴 *Free Breakfast.*

★ Ayasoluk Hotel

$$ | HOTEL | The young Turkish and American owners have combined elements of traditional style with modern comforts in well-appointed rooms around an elegant patio area with a small pool and a lovely sunset view over the surrounding countryside. **Pros:** comfortable rooms with all the modern amenities; fine on-site restaurant; attentive service. **Cons:** some rooms are quite small; some lower-level rooms have windows opening right onto the street; some hall noise through thin walls. [$] *Rooms from: 450 TL* ✉ *1051 Sok. 12* ☎ *232/892–3334* 🌐 *www.ayasolukhotel.com* 🛏 *17 rooms* 🍴 *Free Breakfast.*

Camel Wrestling

While Americans are busy stuffing turkeys and stocking up on Christmas trees, Turkish camels and their owners prepare for an intense season of travel, confrontation, and competition. Every year, around 150 male camels and their owners tour the Marmara, Mediterranean, and Aegean regions to compete in more than 30 camel-wrestling festivals.

There are different theories about camel wrestling's origins, although many argue it was a nomadic practice and part of a competition between caravan owners. Nomadic or not, these festivals have become a deep-rooted cultural pastime in Turkey. Their primary motivation: get the girl. Camels will wrestle only during their mating season, which lasts from November to March, and a female camel is paraded around to provoke them into these contests. The camels' mouths are tied during the match so that they can't do real harm to each other, and among the judges, separators (urgancı), and commentators (cazgır), are 21 officials (not including the camel owners) moderating the events.

The camels begin their wrestling "career" at age four, when many are purchased from Iran. They train for the next four years and spend years 8 through 10 coming of age and developing their own strategies. Their rite of passage, much like that of Turkish boys, occurs at this age, when the camels receive their havut, a decorative cloth with their name and the word maşallah (may God protect him) sewn on the inside. According to camel owners and those familiar with the sport, wrestling is not a foreign, inhumane practice being imposed on the camels. On the contrary, these

dayluk (as they're called until age 7, when they become tüylü, or hairy) begin wrestling naturally in the wild during their first years out of the womb, and if trained, can continue until age 25.

Celebratory events actually begin the day before the match, during halı gecesi, or carpet night, when camels are flaunted around to percussive music, their bells jingling as they amble along. The camel owners, who often get to know one another during the pre-festivities, are also dolled up in cornered caps, traditional neck scarves, and accordion-like boots.

To prevent wearing out the camels, the matches last no more than 10 minutes, and camels compete only once a day. The victor, the camel who gets the most points for outsmarting his rival by swiftly maneuvering and having the most control over the match (which might simply mean not running away), can win anywhere from 5,000 TL to 50,000 TL depending on the competition. There's usually a wrestling World Cup of sorts at the culmination of the festivals, in which the top camels compete.

The exact dates, times, and locations of the festivals change from year to year, but competitions are always held every Sunday between mid-November and March. The central and southern Aegean cities of Selçuk, İzmir, Bodrum, and Kuşadası are among those that host camel-wrestling festivals. Local tourism offices will have specific information about that year's festivals. Tickets are sometimes free, and typically no more than around 15 TL per match, and can be purchased on-site.

Boomerang Guesthouse

$ | **B&B/INN** | This friendly, cozy spot by the Ephesus Museum is popular with budget travelers and families, and offers a rooftop terrace and shady garden along with simple but tidy rooms. **Pros:** central location; friendly, helpful staff; very good value. **Cons:** small, basic rooms; limited amenities; some rooms have shared bathrooms. [$] *Rooms from: 120 TL* ✉ *Atatürk Mah., Uğur Mumcu Sevgi Yolu, 1047 Sok. 10* ☎ *232/892–4879* 🌐 *www.ephesusboomerangguesthouse.com* 🛏 *10 rooms* 🍴 *Free Breakfast.*

Hotel Bella

$$ | **HOTEL** | One of the first boutique hotels in Selçuk, this quaint establishment, which reopened in Spring 2019 after a major renovation, has a spacious terrace overlooking the St. John Basilica next door (and a stork nest in season) that makes a fine setting for breakfast. **Pros:** great location near sights and restaurants; large and inviting outdoor terrace; free shuttle service to Ephesus. **Cons:** some rooms are small and dark; bathrooms are cramped; not the best place for kids. [$] *Rooms from: 250 TL* ✉ *St. Jean Cad. 7* ☎ *232/892–3944* 🌐 *www.hotelbella.com* 🛏 *10 rooms* 🍴 *Free Breakfast.*

Kalehan

$$ | **HOTEL** | **FAMILY** | The lodging itself is in a century-old farmhouse, decorated in traditional Anatolian style, with antique furniture and dark timber beams, and there's a large landscaped garden with a pool that's very welcome after a day of sightseeing. **Pros:** refreshing pool and garden; family-friendly; good on-site restaurant. **Cons:** inconvenient location outside the center of town; aging, if atmospheric, facilities; rooms near road can be noisy. [$] *Rooms from: 440 TL* ✉ *Atatürk Cad. 98* ☎ *232/892–6154* 🌐 *www.kalehan.com* 🛏 *46 rooms* 🍴 *Free Breakfast.*

Livia Hotel Ephesus

$$ | **B&B/INN** | This tiny family-run hotel charms visitors with its plush rooms, intimate atmosphere, and helpful staff. **Pros:** good-sized, comfortable rooms; personal service; high-quality breakfast. **Cons:** mythology-themed décor can come off a bit kitschy; limited facilities; no restaurant. [$] *Rooms from: 420 TL* ✉ *1045 Sok. 25* ☎ *546/883–7001, 232/892–9299* 🌐 *www.liviaotel.com* 🛏 *7 rooms* 🍴 *Free Breakfast.*

Shopping

Selçuk's weekly bazaar is held on Saturday in the main square from 9 to 6. There's also a daily market by the İsa Bey Camii that sells souvenirs and Turkish-themed touristy gifts. Unscrupulous dealers in dubious "antiquities" cluster around the gates to the St. John Basilica; they should be ignored.

Ephesus

4 km (2½ miles) west of Selçuk.

Ephesus (*Efes* in Turkish), the showpiece of Aegean archaeology, is probably the most evocative ancient city in the eastern Mediterranean, and one of the grandest reconstructed ancient sites in the world. The remarkably preserved ruins were rediscovered in the late 1800s and excavations have been going on for nearly a century. The site is a pleasure to explore: marble-paved streets with grooves made by chariot wheels lead past partially reconstructed buildings and monuments. The remains are especially appealing off-season, when the place can seem deserted. In the summer it's packed with tourists, many of whom pour off the ships that cruise the Aegean and call at Kuşadası, 20 km (12 miles) to the south. (Cruise ships have been known to organize rather campy "historical" shows inside

Ephesus itself, complete with polyester togas and fake trumpets.) Go early or late in the day, if possible. ■TIP→ **Guides are available at the trinket stands ringing the parking lot, but be sure to gauge their qualifications and English before you strike a deal. Many travelers find the portable audio guide available inside the site (40 TL) a convenient, inexpensive, and definitely reliable substitute—it even comes with a map. Alternatively, join a tour from Selçuk, Kuşadası, or İzmir.**

Ancient Ephesus grew from a seaside settlement to a powerful trading port and sacred center for the cult of Artemis. Its fame drew the attention of a series of conquerors, among them Croesus of Lydia and 6th century BC Cyrus of Persia. After a Greek uprising against the Persians failed, the people of Ephesus, exercising effective diplomacy, managed to avoid conflict by appeasing each side, both of which took turns controlling the city until Hellenistic times. The city was visited by powerful leaders such as Alexander the Great, who aided the city in its efforts to rebuild.

Like most Ionian cities in Asia Minor, Ephesus was conquered by the Romans, and eventually became Christian. St. Paul is believed to have written some of his Epistles here, and was later driven out by the city's silversmiths for preaching that their models of the goddess Diana (the Greek Artemis) were not divine. The artisans were "full of wrath, and cried out, saying 'Great is Diana of the Ephesians'" (Acts 19:24–40). St. John visited Ephesus between AD 37 and 48, perhaps with the Virgin Mary, and again in 95, when he ostensibly wrote his gospel and then died. In 431 Ephesus was the scene of the Third Ecumenical Council, during which Mary was proclaimed the Mother of God; the ruins of the basilica that housed the Council are near the Lower Gate of the site.

Ephesus was doomed by the silting in of its harbor. By the 6th century the port had become useless, and the population had shifted to what is now Selçuk; today Ephesus is 5 km (about 3 miles) from the sea. The new city, then known as Ayasuluk or Ayasuluğ, was surrounded by ramparts, and a citadel was built on the mound still known as Ayasuluk Hill. In the year 1000, Crusaders came from the west, Turks from the east. The first Seljuk invaders were fought off in 1090, and the Byzantines held out until 1304. The town was incorporated into the Ottoman Empire at the beginning of the 15th century.

TOURS
Several travel agencies in Selçuk can arrange daily tours to Ephesus and other nearby attractions. Some offer small, private tours as well as group tours. *Below are a few of the most reliable agencies:*

No Frills Ephesus Tours
A cheerful Turkish-Australian couple run this well-liked agency, whose reasonably priced tours focus exclusively on the sights, with zero stops at tourist flooring carpet factories. From €55 per person. ⊠ *Atatürk Mah., St. Jean Cad. 3/A, Selçuk* ☎ *232/892–8828* ⊕ *www. ephesus.co.*

Apasas Travel
The company offers daily tours taking in Ephesus, Şirince, and the other main sights around town, as well as tours to Pamukkale and the Priene-Miletus-Didyma circuit of archaeological sites. From €40 per person. ⊠ *1006 Sok. 4, Selçuk* ☎ *232/892–9547* ⊕ *apasastravel.com.*

◉ Sights

Cave of the Seven Sleepers
RELIGIOUS SITE | According to the legend attached to the Cave of the Seven Sleepers, seven young Christian men hid in a cave to avoid persecution by the Romans in the 3rd century AD; the story

Continued on page 248

EPHESUS
CITY OF THE GODS

One might naturally think that the greatest Roman ruins are to be found in Italy. Not so fast! With an ancient arena that dwarfs the one in Pompeii, and a lofty library that rivals any structure in the Roman Forum, Ephesus—once the most important Greco-Roman city of the Eastern Mediterranean—is among the best-preserved ancient sites in the world. Set on a strategic trade route, it first won fame as a cultural and religious crossroads. Here, shrines honored Artemis, the ancient goddess of fertility, St. Paul did some serious soul-searching, and—legend has it—the Virgin Mary lived out her last days. Today, modern travelers can trace the fault lines of ancient civilizations in Ephesus's spectacular land-scape of ruined temples, the-aters, and colonnaded streets.

240

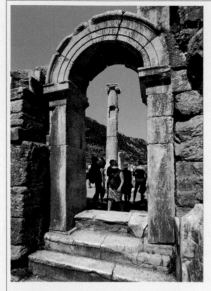

THE AWESTRUCK ADMIRERS who disembark from cruise ships and tour buses to wander through the largest Roman ruins of the Eastern Mediterranean are not really out of sync with ancient times, since Ephesus was a bustling port of call in the pre-Christian era. Home to upwards of 500,000 people at its height, Efes drew visitors from near and far with its promise of urbane and sybaritic pleasures, including baths, brothels, theaters, temples, public latrines, and one of the world's largest libraries. Even then, visitors approaching from the harbor (which has since silted up) could wander under the marble porticos of the Arcadian Way—the ancient world's Rodeo Drive—and visit shops laden with goods from throughout the Mediterranean world.

- ✉ Efes (Ephesus), 4 km (2.5 mi) west of Selçuk on Selçuk-Ephesus Rd.
- ☎ 0232/892-6010 (this is the museum's number; ask to be connected to the site. no official Web site)
- 🎫 60TL; terraced houses, 30TL; parking: 10TL
- ⏲ Apr.—Oct., daily 8—7; Nov.—Mar., daily 8—5.

SPIRIT & THE FLESH

Ephesus in pre-Hellenic times was the cult center of Cybele, the Anatolian goddess of fertility. When seafaring Ionians arrived in the 10th century BC they promptly recast her as Artemis, maiden goddess of the hunt. With her three tiers of breasts, this symbol of mother nature was, in turn, both fruitful and barren, according to the season; as such, she was also worshipped by thousands as the goddess of chastity. The riches of her shrines, however, awoke greed; in the 6th century BC, Croesus, king of Lydia, captured Ephesus, but was himself defeated by Persia's Cyrus. The wily Ephesians managed to keep on good terms with everyone by playing up to both sides of any conflict but by the 2nd century BC, Ephesus had become capital of the Roman province of Asia and Artemis had been renamed Diana. Today, the virgin reverenced here is called Mary.

THE GOSPEL TRUTH?

As with other Roman cities, Ephesus eventually became Christian, though not without a struggle. The Gospel of Luke recounts how the city's silversmiths drove St. Paul out of Ephesus for fear that his pronouncements—"there are no gods made with hands"—would lessen the sale of their silver statues. After Paul addressed a gathering of townsfolk in the amphitheater, the craftsmen rioted, but he succeeded in founding an early congregation here thanks to his celebrated "Epistle to the Ephesians." Another tourist to the city was St. John, who visited between 37 and 48 AD (he died here in AD 95 shortly after completing his Gospel); tradition has it he was accompanied by Mary, whom he brought to fulfill a pledge he had made to Jesus to protect her. Whether or not this is true, Ephesus's House of the Virgin Mary—where Mary is reputed to have breathed her last—draws pilgrims from across the world.

Top, Gateway to Odeon; Right, The Arcadian Way

Did You Know?

When Ephesus became a Roman capital in the 2nd century B.C., numerous shrines were erected to the ancient gods, including Hercules (figure at left). But by the 4th century, the early Christians had plundered Ephesus's classical temples for the building of numerous churches.

PRECIOUS STONES: WHAT'S WHERE

"Is there a greater city than Ephesus?" asked St. Paul. "Is there a more beautiful city?" Those who dig ruins can only agree with the saint. Ephesus is the best preserved Greco–Roman city of the Eastern Mediterranean.

1 Temple of Domitian. One of the largest temples in the city was dedicated to the first-century Roman emperor.

2 Odeon. At this intimate theater, an audience of about 1,500 sat on a semicircle of stone seats to enjoy theatricals and music recitals.

3 Prytaneion. One of the most important buildings in town was dedicated to Hestia, goddess of hearth and home. Priests kept vigil to ensure her sacred flame was never extinguished.

4 Curetes Street. One of the main thoroughfares cuts a diagonal swath through the ancient city and was a processional route leading to the Temple of Artemis; "curetes" are priests of Artemis.

5 Temple of Hadrian. Elegant friezes and graceful columns surround the porch and main chamber of this monument to the 2nd-century Roman emperor. A frieze, probably Medusa, guards the entrance to ward off evil spirits; in another, the

Christian Emperor Theodosius is surrounded by classical gods—a sign that worldly Ephesus was a tolerant place.

6 Terrace Houses. The luxurious homes of well-to-do Ephesians of the 1st to 7th centuries climb the slopes of Mount Koressos. Liberally decorated with frescoes and mosaics, this enclave is evocative of life in the ancient town.

7 Library of Celsus. One of the most spectacular extant ruins of antiquity, this remarkable two-storied building was commissioned in the 2nd century and was destined for double duty—as a mausoleum for Julius Celsus, Roman governor of the province of Asia minor and as a reading room stocked with more than 12,000 scrolls.

8 Brothel. Footsteps etched into the marble paving stones along Curetes Street led the way to one of the busiest businesses in town.

9 Theater. St. Paul preached to the Ephesians in this magnificent space.

One of the largest outdoor theaters of the ancient world was carved out of the flanks of Mount Pion over the course of 60 years and seats as many as 40,000 spectators.

10 Arcadian Way (Harbour Street). The grandest street in town was flanked by mosaic-floored porticos that were lined with elegant shops and—a luxury afforded by few ancient cities—torch-lit at night. This is where Cleopatra paraded in triumph.

11 Stadium. This 1st-century BC structure accommodated more than 70,000 spectators, who enjoyed such entertainments as chariot races and gladiatorial spectacles.

12 Temple of Artemis. A lone column rising from a swamp is all that remains of one of the Seven Wonders of the Ancient World. The largest building in the ancient Mediterranean, once surrounded by 127 columns, was a shrine to the goddess of fertility, abundance, and womanly concerns.

Top Left, Temple of Hadrian; Center, Library of Celsus; Top Right, Odeon

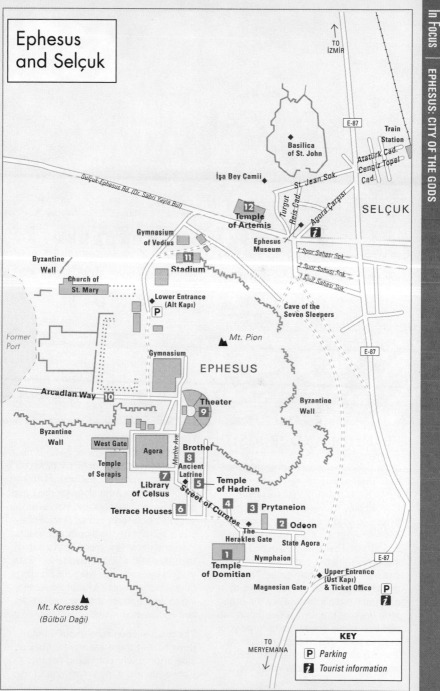

Ephesus and Selçuk

TO
İZMİR

E-87

Train
Station

Basilica
of St. John

Atatürk Cad.
Cengiz Topel
Cad.

İşa Bey Camii

Selçuk-Ephesus Rd. (Dr. Sabri Yayla Bul)

St. Jean Sok.

Turgut Reis Cad.

Agora Çarşısı

SELÇUK

12
Temple
of Artemis

Gymnasium
of Vedius

Ephesus
Museum

1. Spor Sahası Sok.

2. Spor Sahası Sok.

3. Spor Sahası Sok.

Byzantine
Wall

11
Stadium

Church of
St. Mary

Lower Entrance
(Alt Kapı)

P

Cave of the
Seven Sleepers

▲ Mt. Pion

E-87

Former
Port

Gymnasium

EPHESUS

Arcadian Way
10

Theater
9

Byzantine
Wall

Byzantine
Wall

West Gate

Agora

Marble Ave.

Brothel
8
Ancient
Latrine

Temple
of Serapis

7

5 Temple
of Hadrian

Library
of Celsus

Street of Curetes

Terrace Houses **6**

4

3 Prytaneion

2 Odeon

The
Herakles Gate

State Agora

E-87

1
Temple
of Domitian

Nymphaion

Magnesian Gate

Upper Entrance
(Üst Kapı)
& Ticket Office

P

▲
Mt. Koressos
(Bülbül Dağı)

TO
MERYEMANA
↓

Top, Amphitheater

PLANNING YOUR VISIT

Most people who tour Ephesus (Efes) base themselves in nearby Selçuk, a much nicer choice than Kuşadası. If arriving by car, take the road from Selçuk toward Kuşadası, turning left and following the signs to the archaeological site. There are two public parking lots, at the top and bottom of the site near the two main gates. Note that if you arrive by car you'll have to backtrack the hill one way or the other after walking the site (or opt for an cab ride back). It may be best to forgo your car and take taxis to and from Selçuk. There is also a *dolmuş* (shared taxi) that connects the lower gate with Selçuk.

TIPS FOR TOURING

The main entrance (Lower Gate) is near the turnoff to Selçuk; this is where you'll arrive by *dolmuş*. For the upper Magnesian Gate, follow the signs for the Cave of the Seven Sleepers and House of the Virgin Mary (Meryemana). Since Ephesus is laid out on the slopes of Mounts Pion and Koressos, many opt to begin their tour at the upper Magnesian Gate, visiting the state and religious buildings on the higher reaches before descending to where most of the public arenas and agoras are located.

The main avenue runs about a mile downhill but there are any number of side streets with intriguing detours. Consequently, a minimum visit of two

EPHESUS GUIDES

Perhaps the easiest way to see all the sights is to take a guided bus tour, which allows you to travel between the Ephesus site, the Ephesus Museum, the House of the Virgin Mary, and the Basilica of St. John stress-free. The day trip (lunch included) usually costs $75–$90. Tour agencies can be found in Izmir and Kuşadası, although the most convenient are located in Selçuk. Here are two recommended outfitters:

■ **No Frills Ephesus.** (⊠ Atatürk Mah. St. Jean Caddesi 3/A, Selçuk ☎ 232/892-8828 ⊕ www.nofrillsephesustours.com).

■ **Apasa Travel.** (⊠ Atatürk Mah. 1006 Sokak 4, Selçuk ☎ 232/892-9547 ⊕ www.apasastravel.com).

The guides who flock around the entrance gates to the main site are not particularly knowledgeable, and they usually charge around $50 for a two-hour tour. The best option—in addition to consulting one of the handy site guidebooks—is to rent the excellent one-hour audio guides (40TL)

hours can easily stretch to four, not including an hour in the museum and an hour or two at nearby sites like the Cave of the Seven Sleepers and Meryemana.

You'll better appreciate the treasures of Ephesus Museum if you tour the ancient city first—knowing where the statuary, mosaics, and other artifacts were located raises them from the dust to life when you visit the museum. As for timing, a visit in early morning or late afternoon might help you skirt the heaviest of the cruise ship crowds from Kuşadası. In summer you'll want to avoid the midday heat and sun. Be sure to bring water and a light snack—there are no concessions beyond the gate.

Above, Library of Celsus

246

WHO'S WHO IN ANCIENT EPHESUS

ALEXANDER THE GREAT

Upon entering Ephesus in triumph after defeating the Persians in 333 BC, Alexander saw the reconstruction efforts of the temple to Artemis underway and offered to pay for the new edifice with the proviso that his name be inscribed over the entrance. The Ephesians, not wanting to offend their goddess, diplomatically informed the noble warrior and mighty king that it would not be right for one divine being to so honor another.

ANDROKLOS

Banished from Athens upon the death of his father, King Kadros, in the 10th century BC, Androklos arrived at the shores of Asia Minor. The oracle at Delphi had told the prince that a fish and a boar would guide him on his way. A fish that Androklos was roasting on the beach leapt from the flames into the bush, and the commotion routed out a wild boar who led him to a fertile valley: the future Ephesus. Androklos went on to unite the twelve cities of Asia Minor as the Ionian League.

HEROSTRATUS

Stories of all great cities include at least one villain, and in Ephesus the most infamous is Herostratus. One night in 356 BC, the deranged young man burned the most important building in town, the Temple to Artemis. As fate would have it, Alexander the Great was born the same night. The Roman historian Plutarch later observed that the goddess was "too busy taking care of the birth of Alexander to send help to her threatened temple." Ephesian authorities executed Herostratus and tried to condemn him to obscurity by forbidding the mention of his name, but this obviously didn't work.

ST. PAUL

The well-traveled missionary stopped twice in Ephesus, of which he wrote in 1 Corinthians 16, "a great door and effectual is opened unto me, and there are many adversaries." Among them were local merchants, who were infuriated by Paul's proclamation that they should stop selling images of Artemis, lest the practice encourage the worship of pagan idols. Paul may have written his "Epistle to the Ephesians" while being held prisoner in Rome, before his execution in AD 67.

ST. JOHN

Legend has it that the author of the Fourth Gospel arrived in Ephesus with the Virgin Mary and died at age 98. He had his followers dig a square grave, proclaimed "You have called me to your feast," and expired, or so people thought: dust could be seen moving above his grave as if he still drew breath. Emperor Justinian's cathedral—it would be the seventh-largest in the world if reconstructed—was built directly over St. John's grave.

Center, Silver tetradrachm issued by Erythrai ca. 200–180 BC, obverse: Alexander the Great as Herakles wearing the lion skin.
Above, Tomb of St John in Mezrai, St. John's basilica in Selçuk

BEYOND THE RUINS: OTHER SIGHTS

House of the Virgin Mary

Cave of the Seven Sleepers

THE HOUSE OF THE VIRGIN MARY (MERYEMANA)

Legend has it that the Virgin Mary traveled to Ephesus with St. John and spent her last days in this modest stone dwelling. Such claims were given a boost of credulity in the 19th century when a bedridden German nun had a vision that enabled her to describe the house in precise detail. A hallowed place of pilgrimage, the house and adjoining sacred spring have been visited by three popes. John is allegedly buried nearby beneath the now-ruined Basilica of St. John in Selçuk. Surrounded by a national park, Mary's house is 7 km (4 mi) southwest of Selçuk, near the entrance to ancient Ephesus. There are regular religious services. ⊠ Off Rte. E87 ☎ 232/894–1012 ☎ 15TL/person, 8TL/car ⊙ Daily 8–6 (Closes earlier in winter.)

EPHESUS MUSEUM

While many of the finds from Ephesus were carted off to the British Museum in London and the Ephesus Museum in Vienna, some treasures remain in Selçuk. Among the mosaics, coins, and other artifacts are dozens of images of Artemis, including the famous statue of the fertility goddess with several rows of egg-shaped breasts. ⊠ Agora Çarşısı opposite visitor center in Selçuk ☎ 232/892–6010 ☎ 5TL △ Closed for renovations as of presstime.

CAVE OF THE SEVEN SLEEPERS

Ephesus is awash in legend, but the story associated with this hillside cavern takes the prize. It's said that during persecutions ordered by the Roman Emperor Decius in the 2nd century, seven young Christian men were sealed into a cave and left to die. Two centuries later, when Christianity had become the state religion, a farmer happened to unseal the cave and found the men, now aged, in deep slumber. On awakening, they wandered into Ephesus, as shocked at the affixed to churches as the townsfolk were confused by the sight of these archaically clothed characters who offered two-centuries-old coinage to buy food. After their deaths, a church was erected in their honor. The story has found its way into works as diverse as the Koran and the *Golden Legend*, the chronicle of the lives of the saints. ⊠ South of Sor Sahası Sok. 3 ☎ Free.

Fertility Goddess, Ephesus Museum

was immortalized in a poem by Goethe. They fell into a sleep that lasted 200 years, waking only after the Byzantine Empire had made Christianity the official state religion. When they died, they were buried here, and a large church and monastery complex was built over them. The site has unfortunately been closed off due to the collapse of much of the cave but it's still interesting to peek through the fence at the ruins or look down at them from the adjacent hillside. ⊠ Selçuk ✛ Off of 1079 Sok., near the Lower Gate to Ephesus.

★ Ephesus Archaeological Site

ARCHAEOLOGICAL SITE | The ruins of Ephesus, once the most important Greco-Roman city of the eastern Mediterranean, is one of the best preserved ancient sites in the world. Today, modern travelers can trace the splendor and collapse of ancient civilizations in Ephesus's spectacular landscape of ruined temples, theaters, and colonnaded streets. There are two entrances to the site, which is on a hill: one at the top of the site (Üst Kapı, or Upper Gate) and one at the bottom (Alt Kapı, or Lower Gate—this is where to find the public dolmuş stop). The main avenue is about a mile long but there are a number of intriguing detours, so a minimum visit of two hours can easily stretch to four. Buy water and a light snack in Selçuk town, before you head for Ephesus. In summer, when shade is at a premium, a hat is a very good idea. Highlights of the site include the spectacular **theater,** backed by the western slope of Mt. Pion, which once seated an estimated 25,000 to 40,000 spectators; the beautiful, two-story **Library of Celsus**; and the **terrace houses,** the multistoried houses of the nobility, with terraces and courtyards (which have a separate entrance fee). ⊠ Selçuk ✛ Site entry 4 km (2½ miles) west of Selçuk on Selçuk–Ephesus Rd. ☎ 232/892–6010 (Ephesus Museum; ask to be connected to the site) ⊠ 60 TL; 90 TL for combo ticket including terrace houses.

The Ionian Legend 👁

According to legend, the Delphic oracle, who led the Ionian Greeks to this region, advised Androkles, the Ionian leader, to follow a boar, while claiming that "the new town will be shown … by a fish." Androkles and his men came across some people ready to cook a fish that suddenly jumped and knocked embers into nearby brush. The fire spread, and Androkles followed a boar fleeing the flames to Mt. Koressos, later called Bülbül Dağı, or Nightingale Mountain. This is where the Ionians settled.

Şirince

8 km (5 miles) east of Selçuk; 12 km (7½ miles) from Ephesus.

Once upon a time, villagers of this picturesque little hilltop aerie christened their town Çirkince (Turkish for "rather ugly"), allegedly to keep outsiders from discovering its charms. Now renamed Şirince (appropriately, the name means "cute" or "quaint"), this lovely cluster of shops, traditional Greek houses, and restaurants is set on a lush hill; the rows of houses have decorative eaves with nature motifs. A former Greek enclave, Şirince has two restored 19th-century churches and a small museum of local history (mostly in Turkish), but the main attraction is the town itself. Long a favorite destination for day-trippers, Şirince is increasingly popular as an overnight base for travelers visiting the nearby historical sites. Village shops cater to them with quality handicrafts, including beautiful felt, or keçe at Kırkınca Keçe and other stores in the village center, and jewelry, embroidery, and other handicrafts at local boutiques, as well as the famous locally produced fruit wines (the villagers also grow olives, peaches, figs, apples, and walnuts and the approach road is lined with tempting farm stands). Hiking around Şirince is quite pleasant, as the hills are a bit cooler than the lowlands. In winter, Turkish visitors come for local wine by a roaring fireplace, as the cold rain readies the valley for spring.

GETTING HERE AND AROUND

A well-marked road connects Selçuk and Şirince. The road is narrow and winding, so it is best to travel during daylight hours, and with strong nerves. You can also take the *dolmuş* (shared minibuses) that depart every 20 minutes or so from the central Selçuk bus depot (otogar) between 8:30 and 5 (until around 7 in the summer). The last minibus usually leaves Şirince around 6, somewhat later in the summer months.

🍴 Restaurants

★ Arşipel Restaurant

$$ | TURKISH | FAMILY | Summer and winter, the dining room at the Kırkınca Houses Boutique Hotel is the best in town, overlooking the lovely landscape and serving delicious and authentic dishes prepared with oil produced from olives harvested in the garden. You can accompany your meal with wines produced in Şirince, and the sound of mellow live music on Friday and Saturday nights. **Known for:** şevketi bostanı (a root vegetable cooked with tender pieces of lamb); creamy eggplant soup; erişte (homemade pasta, served in a light cream and almond sauce). [$] *Average main: 30 TL ✉ Şirince Köyü ☎ 232/898–3133 🌐 www.kirkinca.com/arsipel-restaurant.*

Sedir Mantı & Börek Evi

$$ | TURKISH | Simple but delicious home-cooked dishes are served on a secluded patio at this friendly little restaurant just off Şirince's bustling main street. There are plenty of vegetarian options, and a cozy dining room with a fireplace for winter meals. **Known for:** mantı (Turkish "ravioli" with garlicky yogurt); kiremitte köfte (meatballs baked in tomato sauce); assorted börek (savory pastries). [$] *Average main: 25 TL ✉ 4 Sok. 2 ✣ Across from the Sağlık Ocağı (health clinic) ☎ 535/480–9873 💳 No credit cards.*

Şirincem Restaurant

$$ | TURKISH | FAMILY | Attached to a *pansiyon* of the same name near the entrance to town, this casual restaurant offers an assortment of grilled meats and home-cooked dishes as well as meze and *gözleme* (Turkish-style crepes). Meals are served in a pleasantly tree-shaded, plant-filled courtyard decorated with hanging lamps, some made out of dried gourds. **Known for:** saç kavurma (finely chopped meat and vegetables sautéed on an iron plate); kuru fasulye (white bean stew); köy kahvaltısı (village breakfast). [$] *Average main: 30 TL ✉ Şirince Köyü İç Yölü ☎ 537/831–8297 🌐 www.sirincem-pansiyon.com.*

Üzüm Cafe

$$ | INTERNATIONAL | This attractive garden café is a relaxing place to take an afternoon break over a cappuccino and dessert, or to nibble on a sandwich or other light fare, accompanied by a glass of Lamin Cabernet Sauvignon, Üzüm's own house wine. A bit on the pricey side, but very pleasant. **Known for:** assorted cakes; house-made lemonade; charcuterie plates. [$] *Average main: 35 TL ✉ 7 Sok. 7 ✣ Uphill from the village square towards the church ☎ 232/898–3024 🌐 www.uzumcafe.com.*

🛏 Hotels

Güllü Konakları

$$$$ | B&B/INN | Secluded on the edge of town, the old stone houses that make up the Güllü Konakları have plush rooms set amid a lush landscape with its own olive grove, rose garden, and vegetable garden. **Pros:** beautiful setting and views;

comfortable, well-appointed rooms; lots of pleasant common areas. **Cons:** fussy, flower-themed decor won't be to everyone's taste; rooms can be stuffy; prices are relatively high. $ *Rooms from: 760 TL* ⊠ *Şirince Köyü 44* 🕾 *232/898–3225* ⊕ *www.marti.com.tr/gullukonak* ⊗ *Closed Jan.* ⇆ *12 rooms* |○| *Free Breakfast.*

Kayserkaya Dağ Evleri (*Kayserkaya Mountain Cottages*)
$$ | **B&B/INN** | **FAMILY** | This bohemian place is a complex of rustically furnished little cottages, some with working fireplaces and private terraces, and the mountainside setting near Şirince makes this an excellent getaway for couples or families. **Pros:** peaceful and bucolic setting; lovely green views; swimming pool. **Cons:** need transportation to Şirince village dining options; cottage cooking facilities minimal; can be chilly in winter. $ *Rooms from: 300 TL* ⊠ *Kayserdağı Mevkii* ⊹ *Next to Nesin Matematik Köyü* 🕾 *232/898–3133* ⊕ *www.kayserkaya.com* ⇆ *11 units* |○| *Free Breakfast.*

Kırkınca Houses Boutique Hotel (*Kırkınca Evleri*)
$$ | **B&B/INN** | **FAMILY** | Peaceful in summer, cozy in winter, and always atmospheric, these three historic Greek houses in the village center are individually decorated in rustic style and share a delightful, vine-shaded terrace. **Pros:** friendly owners; unique, attractive decor; cozy fireplaces in some rooms. **Cons:** some rooms quite small; not all rooms have views, and those without can be dark; not the most modern furnishings. $ *Rooms from: 440 TL* ⊠ *Şirince Köyü* 🕾 *232/898–3133* ⊕ *www.kirkinca.com* ⇆ *11 rooms* |○| *Free Breakfast.*

Nişanyan Houses Hotel
$$ | **B&B/INN** | **FAMILY** | One of Şirince's oldest lodging options is also one of its most character-filled, a mini-village all its own with quaint, lovely rooms in the antique-filled main house and stand-alone cottages, some with shared kitchens,

scattered around a rambling estate. **Pros:** atmospheric setting; charmingly decorated rooms; peaceful and private. **Cons:** a bit of a hike from town; restaurant is on the pricey side; some rooms are small and/or dark. $ *Rooms from: 450 TL* ⊠ *Şirince Köyü İç Yolu, Selçuk* 🕾 *232/898–3208* ⊕ *nisanyan.com* ⇆ *20 rooms* |○| *Free Breakfast.*

Kuşadası

22 km (13½ miles) southwest of Selçuk on Rte. 515.

A small fishing village up until the 1970s, Kuşadası is now a sprawling, hyperactive town with a year-round population of around 110,000, rising to about half a million in season with the influx of tourists—mostly cruise ship passengers disembarking to make a mad dash to Ephesus—and Turks with vacation homes. Though the town has lost most of its local charm to invasive, sterile buildings and tacky souvenir shops and tourist restaurants, its long waterfront is lively and pleasant, with lots of ice cream stands, simple cafes, and a small public beach that's well-used by locals.

GETTING HERE AND AROUND
Kuşadası is 80 km (50 miles) from Adnan Menderes Airport in İzmir and 22 km (13½ miles) from Selçuk. Several local bus companies provide service between İzmir and Kuşadası, while you can travel between Selçuk and Kuşadası by taxi or *dolmuş.* You can also travel around Kuşadası town and reach the nearest beach, Kadınlar Plajı, by dolmuş. Between April and October, ferry excursions to the Greek island of Samos depart most days from Kuşadası; the journey takes about 1½ hours and costs from € 35 to € 45 (240 TL to 310 TL) per person for the round trip. Samos is most popular for its beaches, but also offers numerous hiking and climbing routes. The capital city of Vathi is a lively port; boats to

The hot springs at Pamukkale are rumored to be able to cure a variety of ailments, attracting visitors from all over the world.

Phythagorion will get travelers closer to the UNESCO-designated ruins of the Temple of Hera.

VISITOR INFORMATION
CONTACTS Visitor Information. ✉ *Near cruise ship dock, Mahmut Esat Bozkurt Cad. 7* ☎ *256/614–1103.*

◉ Sights

★ **Dilek Peninsula National Park** (*Dilek Yarımadası Milli Parkı*)
BEACH—SIGHT | FAMILY | If you're looking for beaches, either head north from Kuşadası to Pamucak or travel 33 km (20 miles) south to this lovely national park, which has good hiking trails through woods and canyons and several quiet stretches of sand. The İçmeler beach, closest to the entrance, is also the most crowded. Travel 15 minutes to Karaburun for a more low-key atmosphere. The beaches are clean, with nearby picnic tables, toilets, changing cabins, and outdoor showers, but you should bring your own food and drink. (Note that the park is only open to a limited number of private vehicles a day.) You can catch a Güzelçamlı-bound *dolmuş*/minibus from Kuşadası or nearby transport hub Söke that will take visitors into the park and make a circuit of some of the most popular beaches. The park also contains the so-called "Cave of Zeus," and an archaeological site from when the peninsula was known as Mycale. ✉ *Güzelçamli* ✛ *To get to the park, take the coast road, marked Güzelçamlı or Davutlar, for about 10 km (6 miles) south of Kuşadası.* ☎ *256/646–1079* ⊕ *www.dilekyarimadasi.gov.tr* ▧ *5 TL; 15 TL to enter with a car.*

Güvercin Adası (*Genoese Castle*)
CASTLE/PALACE | FAMILY | There aren't many sights in Kuşadası proper, but the causeway just south of the harbor connects the town to an old Genoese castle on Güvercin Adası (Pigeon Island). Once home to three infamous Turkish pirate brothers in the 16th century, the fortress has been restored and opened to visitors, with its tree-studded grounds providing a lovely space for strolling, relaxing, and

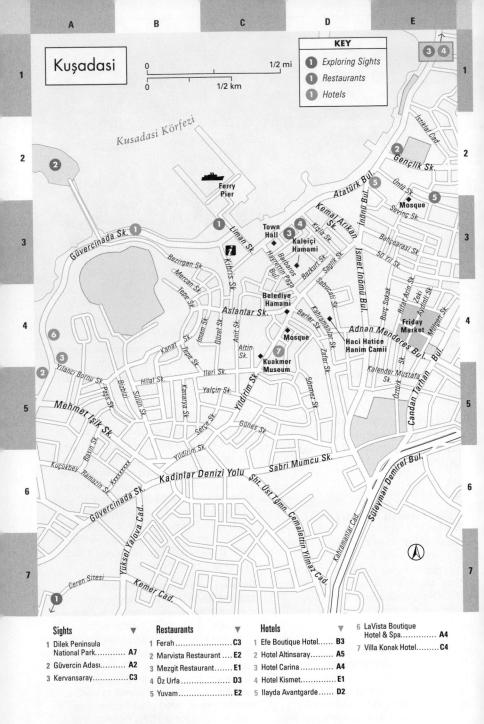

Kuşadası

KEY
- ① Exploring Sights
- ① Restaurants
- ① Hotels

Kusadasi Körfezi

Ferry Pier

Sights ▼

1 Dilek Peninsula National Park............ **A7**
2 Güvercin Adası.......... **A2**
3 Kervansaray.............. **C3**

Restaurants ▼

1 Ferah **C3**
2 Marvista Restaurant **E2**
3 Mezgit Restaurant....... **E1**
4 Öz Urfa **D3**
5 Yuvam..................... **E2**

Hotels ▼

1 Efe Boutique Hotel...... **B3**
2 Hotel Altınsaray.......... **A5**
3 Hotel Carina **A4**
4 Hotel Kismet.............. **E1**
5 Ilayda Avantgarde **D2**
6 LaVista Boutique Hotel & Spa.............. **A4**
7 Villa Konak Hotel......... **C4**

taking in the sea and city vistas. To the right of the castle entrance, there's a swimming platform well-used by locals in summer (despite the proximity to the city center, the water appears quite clean) and a casual café serving reasonably priced snacks and drinks with a million-dollar view. ⊠ Off Güvercin Cad. 🖱 Free.

Kervansaray (Caravanserai)
BUILDING | Kuşadası's 300-year-old cara-vanserai is a short stroll from the cruise ship dock; its central courtyard is open to the public during the day but there's not much to see. Previously a hotel, there are now plans to turn the building into a city museum. ⊠ Atatürk Bul. 1.

🍴 Restaurants

Ferah
$$$ | SEAFOOD | This unpretentiously upscale waterfront seafood restaurant is a favorite with locals, who spill out from the stone walls and onto the terrace with its lovely view. The menu features excellent meze, including grated zucchini with yogurt and toasted walnuts and grilled eggplant with a punchy white sauce, and fish either simply grilled or cooked with béchamel or tomatoes. **Known for:** fried calamari; shrimp casserole; oven-baked halvah with ice cream. Ⓢ Average main: 55 TL ⊠ Güvercinada Cad. 10 ☎ 256/614–1281.

Marvista Restaurant
$$ | INTERNATIONAL | This cheery, casual bistro-style restaurant on the ground floor of the Hotel Ilayda is popular with visitors for its broad international menu, ranging from pasta dishes to fajitas to traditional Turkish grills. Prices are reasonable, portions hearty, and alcohol served. **Known for:** burgers; steaks; Chinese noodles. Ⓢ Average main: 30 TL ⊠ Hotel Ilayda, Atatürk Bul. 46 ☎ 256/614–3807.

Mezgit Restaurant
$$ | TURKISH | Laid-back but still pleasantly lively, this fish restaurant across from the marina has indoor-outdoor dining and less

of a touristy vibe than those around the cruise ship port. Meze, hot starters, and fresh whole fish are all well prepared and the service is efficient. **Known for:** roasted octopus; stuffed calamari; fried red mullet. Ⓢ Average main: 40 TL ⊠ Atatürk Bul. 104 ☎ 256/618–2808 ⊕ www.mezgitkus-adasi.com.

Öz Urfa
$$ | TURKISH | FAMILY | The name means "pure Urfa" (Urfa is a city famed for its sizzling grilled meats), and the focus at this causal, 50-year-old spot is on kebabs and other meaty Turkish dishes, at slightly high but still reasonable prices. Though the crowd is mostly tourists (the helpful staff speaks a variety of languages), the food is happily still tasty and authentic enough to please locals. **Known for:** mixed grill; lamb kebab; pide. Ⓢ Average main: 35 TL ⊠ Cephane Sok. 9 ☎ 256/612–9881.

Yuvam (Ada Yuvam Restaurant)
$ | TURKISH | FAMILY | On a small side street in Kuşadası's main bazaar area, "My Nest/Home" truly lives up to its name, offering the kind of food you'd find in a Turkish home. It's open only at lunch, and items can sell out quickly, so get there early to enjoy daily specials such as meatballs in sour sauce, baked chicken with rice, or bamya (okra) in a tomato-olive oil sauce. **Known for:** soups and stews; vegetarian dishes; casseroles. Ⓢ Average main: 15 TL ⊠ 7 Eylül Sok. 4/A ☎ 256/613 3334 🕙 Closed Sun. No dinner.

🛏 Hotels

Efe Boutique Hotel
$$ | HOTEL | Casually stylish with a sea view from every room, the Efe has two lively bar/restaurants downstairs and a good central location. **Pros:** modern rooms, many with balconies; right in the middle of town; good views. **Cons:** downstairs bars can be noisy, especially on weekends; some fixtures could

use updating; no pool or spa. $ *Rooms from: 450 TL* ✉ *Güvercinada Cad. 37* ☎ *256/614–3661* ⊕ *efeboutiquehotel.com* ⏴ *40 rooms* ⧠ *Free Breakfast.*

Hotel Altınsaray

$ | HOTEL | FAMILY | This Ottoman-styled hotel has a bright yellow façade (the name mean "Golden Palace") and simple rooms with bay windows around a central courtyard. **Pros:** family-friendly atmosphere; pool, sauna, and hammam; hotel has its own beach. **Cons:** rooms are fairly simple and a bit worn in spots; bathrooms are quite small; a bit of a trek from town. $ *Rooms from: 200 TL* ✉ *Güvercinada Cad.* ✛ *Near Yılancı Burnu Sok.* ☎ *256/612–7144* ⊕ *www.hotelalt-insaray.com* ⊙ *Closed Nov.–Mar.* ⏴ *45 rooms* ⧠ *Free Breakfast.*

Hotel Carina

$$$ | HOTEL | FAMILY | On a hill overlooking the sea outside the city center, these rooms are spacious and decorated with soft creamy tones and a smattering of reproduction-antique furnishings, and most have views of the large pool and sea beyond. **Pros:** lovely views; nice big pool area; large, comfortable rooms. **Cons:** some fixtures could use updating; nearby nightclubs can be noisy; a bit of a trek to town or beaches. $ *Rooms from: 410 TL* ✉ *Güvercinada Cad., Yılancı Burnu Sok. 1* ☎ *256/612–4021* ⊕ *www.hotelcarina.com.tr* ⊙ *Closed Nov.–Apr.* ⏴ *59 rooms* ⧠ *Free Breakfast.*

Hotel Kısmet

$$$ | HOTEL | FAMILY | This venerable boutique hotel is one of Turkey's classic getaways, on a private peninsula amidst attractive gardens and overlooking the marina on one side and the Aegean on the other. **Pros:** grand views of harbor and sea; pleasant grounds and facilities; spacious rooms. **Cons:** bathrooms are basic; pool is part of a separate beach club; remote setting. $ *Rooms from: 460 TL* ✉ *Gazi Beğendi Bul. 1* ☎ *256/618–1291* ⊕ *www.kismet.com.tr* ⊙ *Closed mid-Nov.-late Mar.* ⏴ *100 rooms* ⧠ *Free Breakfast.*

Ilayda Avantgarde

$$$ | HOTEL | A sleek, modern option in the middle of Kuşadası gets high marks for its comfortable rooms and attentive service. **Pros:** stylish, good-sized rooms; professional service; central location. **Cons:** small bathrooms; no gym or sauna; not much local character. $ *Rooms from: 495 TL* ✉ *Atatürk Bul. 42* ☎ *256/614–4967* ⊕ *www.ilaydaavantgarde.com* ⏴ *85 rooms* ⧠ *Free Breakfast.*

LaVista Boutique Hotel & Spa

$$$ | HOTEL | A luxurious getaway overlooking the Aegean caters to an upscale adult crowd looking for a relaxing escape. **Pros:** large, attractive pool and lounge area; spacious rooms; rooms all have sea views. **Cons:** a bit of a trek to town or beaches; French Provençal style of rooms can come off a bit kitschy; mediocre Wi-Fi. $ *Rooms from: 610 TL* ✉ *Güvercinada Cad.* ✛ *Near Yılancı Burnu Sok.* ☎ *256/614–1235* ⊕ *www.lavista-hotel.net* ⊙ *Closed mid-Nov.–Feb.* ⏴ *39 rooms* ⧠ *Free Breakfast.*

★ Villa Konak Hotel

$$ | B&B/INN | On a quiet street uphill from the town center, the tastefully decorated rooms at this welcoming, family-run hotel are set around an attractive garden. **Pros:** peaceful setting; spacious, attractive rooms; free coffee and tea throughout the day. **Cons:** some bathroom fixtures a bit dated; weak Wi-Fi signal in some areas; walk up from town is a bit steep. $ *Rooms from: 335 TL* ✉ *Yıldırım Cad. 55* ☎ *256/614–6318* ⊕ *www.villakonakhotel.com* ⏴ *17 rooms* ⧠ *Free Breakfast.*

🍸 Nightlife

There are several Irish- and British-style pubs as well as other noisy drinking establishments along "Barlar Sokak" (Bar Street), not far from the harbor. A more sophisticated, and much less touristy, option for an evening drink is the grouping of restaurants and bars at the "Old Town Tanneries" (*Eski Tabakhane*

Binaları) complex across from the marina shopping center and behind the Doubletree Hotel.

🏃 Activities

New walking, hiking, and cycling routes outlined by the Kuşadası municipality in a series of brochures aim to help change the town's tacky-tourism reputation and get visitors to explore the local surroundings in more depth rather than just passing through en route to Ephesus. Maps and descriptions of the routes, which are also available in English online, take travelers to rural villages, lesser-known archaeological sites, local attractions like an olive-oil museum, and the wooded hills at the edge of Dilek Peninsula National Park. More information is available at ⊕ *www.kusadasirotalari.com*.

🛍 Shopping

The Old Town area is full of indistinguishable storefronts selling unremarkable souvenirs and other wares aimed at tourists, though there are a few little shops on the shaded little alley Cephane Sokak with more distinctive offerings, such as the charming ceramics at Atölye Marika (No. 24). The women's cooperative KUŞAKK has a small selection of handmade bags, tea towels, and other craft items, many screen-printed with lovely bird designs—Kuşadası means "bird island" in Turkish—for sale at its workshop/office at Yıldırım Caddesi No. 22. The shopping mall at the marina has outlets of numerous popular midrange Turkish brands, plus helpful amenities like a grocery store and a Turkcell outlet.

The central and southern Aegean is among the most developed parts of Turkey, and the rolling hills, mountains surrounded by clear blue seas, and glorious white-sand beaches are just a few of the reasons why. Wandering through historic ruins, boating, scuba diving, basking in the Anatolian sun, and eating fresh fish are just some of the ways you can fill your day here. Kuşadası itself is the most developed resort along the coast, with its tiny, atmospheric Old Town now surrounded by brash, modern development catering to tourists, but the city's attractive waterfront and newly restored Genoese castle are pleasant places to join the locals for a stroll. Nearby, Dilek Peninsula National Park has stunning nature and serene beaches, while new walking and cycling routes created by the Kuşadası municipality guide visitors around the surrounding area's villages and countryside. Kuşadası is also a stepping-stone to some of Turkey's most important ancient sites, including Ephesus and Meryem Ana Evi.

Pamukkale (Hierapolis)

190 km (118 miles) from Selçuk or Kuşadası.

Pamukkale (pronounced pam-ook-ka lay), which means "cotton castle" in Turkish, first appears as an enormous, chalky white cliff rising 330 feet from the plains. Mineral-rich volcanic spring water cascades over basins and natural terraces, crystallizing into travertines—white curtains of what looks like solidified white water, seemingly suspended in air. The hot springs at Pamukkale are believed to cure rheumatism and other ailments and have attracted visitors for millennia, as illustrated by the ruins of the Roman spa city of Hierapolis, whose well-preserved theater and necropolis lie within sight of Pamukkale.

In the mid-1990s, the diversion of water from the springs to fill thermal pools in nearby luxury hotels in the adjacent spa village of Karahayıt reduced the volume of water reaching Pamukkale. This, combined with a huge increase in the number of visitors, discolored the water's once-pristine whiteness. As a result, wearing shoes in the water is prohibited to protect the deposits, and the travertines can only be entered from designated areas. Although Pamukkale is not quite as dramatic as it once was, for first-time visitors the white cliffs are still an impressive sight. Parts of the site are now blocked off, as the authorities strive to conserve and restore a striking natural wonder to its former magnificence. However, you can still venture down the white cliffs and soak in the water: the rock can be prickly and slippery by turns, so remember to watch your step, no matter how enthralled you are.

If you have time, spend the night in Pamukkale, as the one-day bus tours from the coast are exhausting and limiting: you'll end up spending more time on the bus than you do at the actual site. A full day at Pamukkale will give you enough time to enjoy the water and the ruins. The site is large, but you can easily navigate it without a guide, if you want the freedom to swim, wade, and explore at your own pace. If you have more time, the area around Pamukkale is dotted with interesting geological formations and archaeological sites, including the nearby ruins of Laodicea and the newly excavated site of Tripolis; the "crying rock waterfall"(Ağlayan Kaya Şelalesi) near the town of Sakızcılar (about 28 km [17 miles] away; follow signs for Irlıganlı, and then the waterfall); and the springs of Karahayıt. It also makes a good base for a visit to Aphrodisias.

The town of Pamukkale itself is small and still very rural, with tractors sharing the streets with tour buses. Perhaps surprisingly for such a touristy place, the overall standard of hotels here isn't as high as on the coast, and though there's plenty of selection, booking in advance will help you brush off the pushy touts who await the arrival of tourists in the main square.

GETTING HERE AND AROUND

Pamukkale is approximately a three- to four-hour drive from İzmir, Selçuk, Kuşa-dası, or Bodrum on Route E87 (follow road signs after Sarayköy). There are daily bus tours from all of these towns to Pamukkale during the high season. You can also fly into Denizli airport, about an hour's drive away.

If you don't have your own car, a local travel agency can be very helpful, though in such a touristy town, rip-offs and pressure tactics are not uncommon. Seek recommendations from your hotel or fellow travelers. Guided tours of the travertines and ruins, often including a visit to Karahayıt, are generally offered daily, starting at around € 20 (140 TL) per person; trips to Laodicea, Aphrodisias, and other nearby sites can be arranged on request.

◉ Sights

Hierapolis

ARCHAEOLOGICAL SITE | The sprawling, well-maintained site of Hierapolis is lovely proof of how long the magical springs of Pamukkale have drawn eager travelers and pilgrims to partake of the waters' supposed healing powers. The ruins that can be seen today date from the time of the Roman Empire, but there are references to a settlement here as far back as the 5th century BC. Because the ruins are spread over nearly 3 km (2 miles), prepare for some walking—or hop on the mini-van shuttle ($), which runs between the North Gate and the Sacred Pool every 30 minutes. The main points of interest are well marked along the path and include a vast and beautiful necropolis (cemetery) with more than 1,000 cut-stone sarcophagi spilling all the way down to the base of the hill; the ruins of a Temple of Apollo and a bulky Byzantine church; a monumental fountain known as the Nymphaeum, just north of the Apollo Temple; and the Ploutonion, built over a cave that leaks poisonous fumes from the bowels of the earth, so deadly that the Romans revered and feared it as a portal to the Underworld. Below the theater, near the Sacred Pool,

the stone building that enclosed Hierapolis's public baths is now the **Pamukkale Müzesi** (museum) with a fine display of impressive carved sarcophagi and marble reliefs, statues, and funerary stelae found at the site. ⊠ *Pamukkale ✛ South Gate within easy walking distance of town; North Gate requires a shuttle (5 TL)* ☎ *258/272–2077 visitor center (for information), 258/272–2034 museum* 🖃 *50 TL (does not include admission to Sacred Pool); 7 TL extra for museum entry.*

Karahayıt
SPA—SIGHT | Only 7 km (4 miles) from Pamukkale, this down-to-earth village attracts visitors for its "red springs," where the warm mineral water and gooey mud are popular for their supposed health-giving properties. A small section of the springs is open to the public and flanked by inexpensive restaurants—mud baths and dead-skin-nibbling "doctor fish" pools are also available for a fee. Locals will tell you that drinking the springwater is good for digestion, and those with a strong stomach may want to put this to the test. There's regular *dolmuş* service from Pamukkale to Karahayıt, which also has a busy covered market area with lots of small local eateries and cafes. ⊠ *Karahayit.*

Laodicea (*Laodikeia*)
ARCHAEOLOGICAL SITE | On a hill overlooking the white travertines of Pamukkale about 10 km (6 miles) to the north, the relatively little-visited ruins of the ancient city of Laodicea on the Lycus are perfect for an atmospheric ramble down colonnaded streets, or (with care) down the crumbling slopes of two poetically lovely ancient theaters. Founded in the 3rd century BC, Laodicea passed into Pergamene, then Roman hands, and was a prosperous trading city, known for its black wool. Luxurious public buildings, including baths and a temple to an unknown divinity testify to its wealth. Roman Laodicea's relatively large Jewish population (in the thousands) likely

contributed to the early adoption of Christianity in the city, and the basilica, with its extensive geometric mosaics, was one of the "Seven Churches of Asia" in the Book of Revelation. You can join a tour or catch a Denizli-bound *dolmuş* from Pamukkale center. (The *dolmuş* drops you off on the main road about a 10-minute walk away from the archaeological site.) ⊕ *laodikeia.pau.edu.tr* 🖃 *15 TL.*

Pamukkale Natural Park
CITY PARK | **FAMILY** | At the very foot of the white travertines, this delightful park with grassy lawns entertains local families and visitors alike, with fantastically shaped pedal boats on the pond, ducks and geese to feed, private swimming pools, a cheery open-air café that stays open into the night, and ice cream stands. It's free to enter; the pools and boats cost extra. Nowhere in town has better views. ⊠ *Mehmet Akif Ersoy Bul., Pamukkale* ☎ *258/272–2244* ⊕ *www.pamukkalenaturalpark.com.tr.*

Sacred Pool of Hierapolis
ARCHAEOLOGICAL SITE | **FAMILY** | There are several reasons visitors flock to the thermal waters of the Sacred Pool at Hierapolis: the bathtub-warm water (a relatively constant 95 degrees Fahrenheit), the reputed therapeutic properties of the mineral-rich water (Cleopatra supposedly used it as toner), and the atmospheric marble columns and ancient stone carvings scattered about. The lushly landscaped complex has changing rooms, lock boxes (5 TL) to store your stuff, souvenir shops, and (overpriced) snack bars. Entry to the pools is expensive (you need to pay to get into Hierapolis as well) but floating over ancient ruins in hot, faintly effervescent mineral water is more fun than it sounds. If you don't want to spend the time/money, you can relax in one of the shaded seating areas with a beverage instead. The pool gets crowded in the summer months so plan your visit for early morning or after the tour buses depart. The pool closes earlier in winter

months but it's also much less crowded during the day. Consider bringing your own towel. Locals line up to collect spring water from the on-site faucets, but unless you have a strong stomach, it's probably best to avoid joining them. ✉ *Hierapolis, Pamukkale* 🚗 *50 TL.*

🍴 Restaurants

Asian Kitchen & Cafe
$$$ | ASIAN | Travelers craving a change from the usual Turkish fare will be happy to find this establishment right smack in the middle of Pammukale. Catering to the growing number of Asian tourists in the area, it turns out surprisingly authentic versions of mostly Chinese, Taiwanese, and Korean specialties, including noodle dishes, soups, and stir-fries. Service can be slow and there's not much in the way of decor. **Known for:** hot pot (winter only); Korean mixed-rice dish bibimbap; Taiwanese beef noodle soup. $ *Average main: 38 TL* ✉ *Pamukkale Mah., Cumhuriyet Meydanı 14/A, Pamukkale* ☎ *544/388–5666.*

Kayaş Restaurant & Bar
$$ | TURKISH | FAMILY | This cheery traveler favorite just off Pamukkale's main square serves up better-than-average grilled meats, *güveç* (casserole), and other traditional Turkish dishes (plus international staples like omelets and pasta) on an outdoor patio under a thick canopy of grapevines. Portions are on the small side, but nicely presented, and there's a full bar, a wine list, and a surprisingly good selection of bottled beers. **Known for:** mixed grill; karnıyarık (stuffed eggplant); sautéed beef with mushrooms. $ *Average main: 30 TL* ✉ *Ataturk Cad. 3, Pamukkale* ☎ *534/561–1080.*

Tıkır Pide Salonu & Grill House
$ | TURKISH | A no-frills spot to grab a quick bite en route to the travertines, there's more of a Turkish clientele here than at most Pamukkale eateries. Wind chimes, strands of dried peppers, and a couple of chatty pet birds liven up the simple patio seating. **Known for:** assorted pide (Turkish flatbread); pirzola (lamb chops); grilled chicken. $ *Average main: 20 TL* ✉ *Atatürk Cad., Pamukkale.*

🛏 Hotels

Ayapam Hotel
$$ | HOTEL | FAMILY | Simple but spacious rooms open onto balconies overlooking the swimming pool, while upper-floor rooms have views of the travertines. **Pros:** large outdoor pool; friendly atmosphere; elevator. **Cons:** basic rooms and amenities; poor-quality breakfast; building and furnishings could use some upkeep. $ *Rooms from: 150 TL* ✉ *Kale Mah., Bahçe Sok. 2/1, Pamukkale* ☎ *258/272–2203* ⊕ *www.ayapamhotel.com* 🛏 *20 rooms* 🍴 *Free Breakfast.*

Hal-Tur Hotel
$$ | HOTEL | FAMILY | Most of the clean, fresh rooms at this distinctive pale-stone hotel have balconies overlooking the white travertines, and one large family room has its own Jacuzzi and vast terrace. **Pros:** staff are knowledgeable and helpful; full view of the travertines from breakfast area and many rooms; midsize, kid-friendly pool. **Cons:** a bit expensive given the fairly basic comforts; not all rooms have views; some rooms are small. $ *Rooms from: 350 TL* ✉ *Mehmet Akif Ersoy Bul. 71, Pamukkale* ☎ *258/272–2723* ⊕ *www.haltur.net* 🛏 *11 rooms* 🍴 *Free Breakfast.*

Melrose Viewpoint Hotel
$ | HOTEL | FAMILY | The good-sized rooms are bright and clean, and the service warm and friendly at this newish family-run budget hotel not far from Pamukkale town center. **Pros:** spacious rooms; helpful staff; relaxed atmosphere. **Cons:** no elevator; only top-floor rooms have views; pool is small. $ *Rooms from: 150 TL* ✉ *Kadıoğlu Cad., Çay Sok. 7, Pamukkale* ☎ *258/272–3120* ⊕ *www.melroseviewpoint.com* 🛏 *16 rooms* 🍴 *Free Breakfast.*

Venus Hotel

$ | **B&B/INN** | Friendly and full of character, the cozy rooms here have wooden ceilings and Ottoman-accented decor. **Pros:** attractive rooms with lots of character; nice shared pool and garden area; friendly service. **Cons:** nearly 1 km (½ mile) from the town center; some fixtures could use updating; some rooms are small. [$] *Rooms from: 200 TL* ✉ *Pamuk Mah., Hasan Tahsin Cad. 16, Pamukkale* ☎ *258/272–2152* 🌐 *www.venushotel.net* 🛏 *15 rooms* 🍴 *Free Breakfast* 💳 *No credit cards.*

Aphrodisias

80 km (50 miles) from Pamukkale.

Aphrodisias, the city of Aphrodite, goddess of love, is one of the largest and best-preserved archaeological sites in Turkey, so although it's a bit of a detour, it's quite rewarding. You'll need a few hours to get a true taste of the site. The excavations here have led archaeologists to surmise that Aphrodisias was a thriving sculpture center, with patrons beyond the borders of the city—statues and fragments with signatures of Aphrodisian artists have shown up as far away as Greece and Italy. A number of surviving masterworks are on display in the on-site Aphrodisias Museum.

GETTING HERE AND AROUND

Aphrodisias is off the E87—turn south on Route 585 and head for the town of Geyre. If you'll be driving from Pamukkale to Selçuk, İzmir, or Kuşadası, or vice versa, it is most convenient to follow the example of most bus tours and visit Aphrodisias en route. You will save much time and energy if you rent a car and visit this and the other nearby ancient sites on your own because a private tour can eliminate backtracking. If there's enough demand (typically a minimum of four or five passengers), a local driver in Pamukkale takes visitors to the site and back daily for around 80 TL per person; it's not a tour per se, but you'll have a few hours to explore the site on your own. Inquire at any Pamukkale hotel or travel agency for details.

Sights

★ **Aphrodisias**

ARCHAEOLOGICAL SITE | FAMILY | Though most of what you see today dates from the 1st and 2nd century AD, archaeological evidence indicates that the local dedication to Aphrodite follows a long history of veneration of pre-Hellenic goddesses, such as the Anatolian mother goddess and the Babylonian god Ishtar. Only about half of the site has been excavated. It's much less crowded than Ephesus, and enough remains to conjure the ancient city. Once you reach the pretty, rural site, you'll take a short, bumpy ride on an open-air shuttle from the parking area to the main gate. The lovely **Tetrapylon** gateway has four rows of columns and some of the better remaining friezes. Behind it, the vast **Temple of Aphrodite** was built in the 1st century BC on the model of the great temples at Ephesus, and later transformed into a basilica church. Its gate and many of its columns are still standing. The impressive, well-preserved 1st century AD **stadium** could seat up to 30,000 spectators to watch footraces, boxing and wrestling matches. You'll also find the once-magnificent ruined residence, the fine **Odeon** (also known as the Bouleuterion, or Council House); an intimate, semicircular concert hall and public meeting room; towering **public baths**; and the sprawling **agora**. The 7,000 white-marble seats of the city's **theater**, built into the side of a small hill, are simply dazzling on a bright day. The adjacent **School of Philosophy** has a colonnaded courtyard with chambers lining both sides.

In the **museum**, just before the ticket booth, Aphrodisias bursts back into life in vivid friezes and sculptures that seem almost about to draw breath. The museum's collection includes dozens of impressive statues and reliefs from the site, including Aphrodite herself, with excellent labeling (particularly in the grand display in the Sevgi Gönül Salonu) explaining their significance and symbolism. ⊠ *Geyre* ⊕ *www.aphrodisias. org* ⊠ *20 TL; audio guide 10 TL.*

Priene, Miletus, and Didyma

Priene is 40 km (25 miles) from Kuşadası; from Priene it's 22 km (14 miles) to Miletus; from Miletus it's 22 km (14 miles) to Didyma; Didyma is 116 km (72 miles) from Bodrum.

The three towns of Priene, Miletus, and Didyma make up part of Ancient Ionia, homeland of many of the ancient world's greatest artistic and scientific minds, and each endowed with haunting ruins. They're all within 40 km (25 miles) of each other, and if you get an early enough start, you can visit them all in one day, either with a car or on a PDM (Priene, Miletus, Didyma) tour with a local agency. If you decide to spend a night in the area, you'll find the most hotels in and around Didyma (Didim in Turkish), where the modern town extends into the overbuilt seaside resort of Altınkum, but you're better off pressing on to the more agreeable offerings of Bodrum or Selçuk.

Famous for its magnificent Temple of Apollo, **Didyma** was an important ancient site connected to Miletus by a sacred road lined with statues, now opened as a 17 km (10 mile) waking path (the "Kutsal Yol").

Before the harbor silted over, **Miletus** was one of the greatest commercial centers of the Greek world, and the Milesians were renowned for their quick wits and courage. The first settlers were Minoan Greeks from Crete who arrived between 1400 BC and 1200 BC. The Ionians, who arrived 200 years later, slaughtered the male population and married the widows. Like the other Ionian cities, Miletus was passed from one ruling empire to another and was successively governed by Alexander's generals Antigonus and Lysimachus and Pergamum's Attalids, among others. Under the Romans the town finally regained some control over its own affairs and shared in the prosperity of the region. St. Paul preached here at least twice in the 1st century.

Dating from about 350 BC, the present-day remnants of once-wealthy **Priene** were still under construction in 334, when Alexander the Great liberated the Ionian settlements from Persian rule. At that time, it was a thriving port, but as in Ephesus, the harbor silted over, so commerce moved to neighboring Miletus, and the city's prosperity waned. As a result, the Romans never rebuilt Priene and the simpler Greek style predominates as in few other ancient cities in Turkey.

GETTING HERE AND AROUND

Tours to these towns can be arranged from İzmir, Selçuk, Kuşadası, and Bodrum (plan on around €50 to €60 per person). Pamukkale Turizm and other bus companies offer service from İzmir to Didyma (Didim), and minibuses departing Didyma stop near Priene and Miletus, though traveling this way entails multiple transfers and potentially much waiting about. To reach Miletus by public transportation, take a dolmuş to Söke, and another from Söke to Akköy, 5 km (3 miles) from the site. Take a taxi or dolmuş from Akköy to the ruins. For Priene, you can travel by dolmuş from Kuşadası or Selçuk to Söke, and from Söke to Güllübahçe, the small town at the foot of the ruins, and hike up to the site. For all these destinations, a car or tour will be much more efficient, especially if you are visiting two or more of the towns.

Sights

Altınkum

BEACH—SIGHT | FAMILY | For a break after all the history, continue another 5 km (3 miles) from Didyma south to Altınkum, popular for its pale-sand beach. The sand stretches for a bit less than 1 km (½ mile) and is bordered by a row of bars, restaurants, and hotels, all facing the water. At peak times, a lifeguard watches over the 500-yard, Blue Flag–designated public beach (*halk plajı*), which quickly gets crowded in summertime. There are some Jet Skis and pedal boats for rent at either end of the *halk plajı*. **Amenities:** food and drink; lifeguards; showers; toilets; water sports. **Best for:** swimming. ⊠ *At the end of Atatürk Bul., Didim.*

Didyma (*Didim*)

ARCHAEOLOGICAL SITE | As grand in scale as the Parthenon—measuring 623 feet by 167 feet—Didyma's **Temple of Apollo** has 124 well-preserved columns, some still supporting their architraves. Started in 300 BC and under construction for nearly five centuries, the temple was never completed, and some of the columns remain unfluted. The oracle here rivaled the one at Delphi, and beneath the courtyard is a network of underground corridors used by temple priests for their oracular consultations. The corridor walls would throw the oracle's voice into deep and ghostly echoes, which the priests would interpret. The tradition of seeking advice from a sacred oracle here probably started long before the arrival of the Greeks, who in all likelihood converted an older Anatolian cult based at the site into their own religion. The Greek oracle had a good track record, and at the birth of Alexander the Great (356 BC) predicted that he would be victorious over the Persians, that his general Seleucus would later become king, and that Trajan would become an emperor. Around AD 385, the popularity of the oracle dwindled with the rise of Christianity. The temple was later excavated by French and German archaeologists, and its statues are long gone, hauled back to England by Sir Charles Newton in 1858. Fragments of bas-reliefs on display by the entrance to the site include a gigantic head of Medusa (twin of the one in Istanbul's underground cistern, across from Hagia Sophia) and a small statue of Poseidon and his wife, Amphitrite. ■**TIP→ You can rent a combined Miletus and Didyma audio guide for 15 TL.** ⊠ *Didim ✛ 22 km (14 miles) south of Priene on Rte. 09–55* 🔳 *15 TL; audio guide 10 TL.*

Miletus

ARCHAEOLOGICAL SITE | The Miletus archaeological site is sprawled out along a desolate plain, and laced with well-marked trails. The parking lot is right outside the city's most magnificent building the **Great Theater**, a remarkably intact 15,000-seat, freestanding amphitheater built by the Ionians and maintained by the Romans. The fabulous *vomitoria*, huge vaulted passages leading to the seats, have the feel of a modern sporting arena. Climb to the top of the theater for a look at the walls of the defensive fortress built atop it by the Byzantines, and a view across the ancient city. To see the rest of the ruins, follow the dirt track down from the right of the theater. A row of buildings marks what was once a broad processional avenue. The series begins with the **Delphinion**, a sanctuary of Apollo; a **stoa** (colonnaded porch) with several reerected Ionic columns; the foundations and remaining walls and arches of a **Roman bath** and **gymnasium**; and the first story of the **Nymphaeum**, all that remains of the once highly ornate three-story structure, resembling the Library of Celsus at Ephesus, that once distributed water to the rest of the city. A three-minute drive outside the gates of the site, the small **Milet Müzesi** presents interesting artifacts from the site and the surrounding area with panache. Their bright displays will help you conjure a vision of ancient Miletus and its world. Ask your tour guide in advance if you can make at least a short stop here. If driving, ask the guards to point you in the right direction as you exit the Miletus archaeological site. ✉ *Didim* ✣ *22 km (14 miles) south of Didyma on Rte. 09–55* ☎ *256/875–5206 museum* 🎫 *12 TL (site and museum); audio guide 10 TL.*

Priene

ARCHAEOLOGICAL SITE | Spectacularly sited, the remains of Priene are on the top a steep hill above the flat valley of the Büyük Menderes Nehri . First excavated by British archaeologists in 1868–69, the site is smaller than Ephesus and far quieter and less grandiose. One of the most prominent ruins is the **Temple of Athena**, the work of Pytheos, architect of the Mausoleum at Halicarnassus (one of the Seven Wonders of the Ancient World) and the design was repeatedly copied at other sites in the Greek empire. Alexander apparently chipped in on construction costs. Between the columns, look on the marble floor for a small circle, criss-crossed with lines like a pizza—a secret symbol of Ionia's ancient Christians. Walk north and then east along the track that leads to the well-preserved little **theater**, sheltered on all sides by pine trees. Enter through the stage door into the orchestra section and note the five front-row VIP seats, carved thrones with lions' feet. If you scramble up a steep cliff known as Samsun Dağı (behind the theater and to your left as you face the seats), you will find the sparse remains of the **Sanctuary of Demeter,** goddess of the harvest; only a few remnants of the columns and walls remain, as well as a big hole through which blood of sacrificial victims was poured as a gift to the deities of the underworld. Since few people make it up here, it is an incredibly peaceful spot with a terrific view over Priene and the plains. Beyond are the remnants of a Hellenistic fortress. (Check safety conditions before you climb.) ✉ *Güllübahçe* ✣ *40 km (25 miles) from Kuşadası, southeast on Rte. 515, south on Rte. 525, west on Rte. 09–55 (follow signs)* 🎫 *6 TL.*

🍴 Restaurants

Didim Şehir Lokantası

$$ | **TURKISH** | **FAMILY** | The quality and price of the offerings here—primarily grills, *pide*, and home-style meat and vegetable dishes—make the trip out to this residential neighborhood (sometimes still known by its old name "Yenihisar Mahallesi") well worth the effort. Alcohol is served, despite the mosque across the street. **Known for:** İskender kebap; patlıcan (eggplant) kebap; good soups. [$] *Average main: 25 TL* ✉ *Çarşı İçi, 830 Sok., Didim* ☎ *256/811–4488* 🌐 *www.didimsehirlokantasi.com.*

🛏 Hotels

Orion Beach Hotel

$$ | **HOTEL** | **FAMILY** | On its own beach in Altınkum, this resortlike getaway has bright and airy guest rooms, all with balconies and most with sea views. **Pros:** good value; pleasant atmosphere; beach and pool. **Cons:** fairly simple rooms; nearby bars can be a bit noisy; dinner-inclusive room rates required. [$] *Rooms from: 300 TL* ✉ *Yalı Cad. 73, Altınkum, Didim* ☎ *256/813–5550* 🌐 *www.orionhoteldidim.com* 🕓 *Closed Nov.–Mar.* 🔑 *78 rooms* 🍴 *Free Breakfast.*

Bodrum

710 km (440 miles) from Istanbul; 236 km (146 miles) from İzmir; 153 km (95 miles) from Kuşadası; 116 km (72 miles) from Didyma.

Until the mid-20th century, the Bodrum Peninsula was little known, and its gorgeous coastline was home to fishermen and sponge divers. Then a bohemian set (artists, writers, and painters) discovered Bodrum and put the place on the map. Today, Bodrum is booming—a year-round getaway for Turks and foreigners alike. You'll be in the center of the action in Bodrum town, the busiest spot on the peninsula, but a stay in one of the smaller villages nearby will reveal the region's quieter charms and its landscape of mandarin orchards and stone windmills. The lovely, mysterious stone domes that dot the landscape are old water cisterns.

On the southern shores of a broad peninsula that stretches along two crescent-shape bays, Bodrum has for years been the favorite haunt of the Turkish upper classes. Today, thousands of foreign visitors come here, too. The town is throbbing with cafés, restaurants, and discos. Bodrum is decidedly not the quaint village it once was, but it's still beautiful, with gleaming whitewashed buildings covered in bougainvillea and unfettered vistas of sparkling bays. Each October, it hosts the Bodrum Cup, a five-day international yacht regatta.

The area's numerous music festivals are an additional draw in the summer months. The Gümüşluk Classical Music Festival, held annually for more than a decade, brings both classical and jazz acts to the seaside village between July and August, with some concerts being held in historical settings. Turgutreis has its own classical music festival held around the same time, when Bodrum also hosts a long-running ballet festival. The newer Chill-Out festival in July brings DJs and live indie and electronica acts to Xuma Beach in Yalıkavak.

Each municipality and its surrounding villages have their own style, charm, and ambience, so where you decide to stay will be based on your personal preferences. You can catch a dolmuş(minibus) to almost any town in the peninsula from the central Bodrum bus station (otogar) for 7 TL or less per person. You may have to return to Bodrum to transfer between other towns.

Outside the high summer season of July and August, things really slow (and even shut) down in smaller towns like Gümüşlük and Göltürkbükü, but there will be places to stay and eat year-round in Bodrum city center.

GETTING HERE AND AROUND

The Bodrum Ferryboat Association has ferry service from Bodrum to Kos and Rhodes, in Greece, and in Turkey, to Datça, a beachy peninsula between the Mediterranean and Aegean seas. It also operates ferries from Turgutreis on the Bodrum Peninsula to Kos, Kalymnos, and Leros, also in Greece. The Bodrum Express Lines has ferry and hydrofoil service from Bodrum to Kos and Rhodes, and from Turgutreis to Kos, Kalymnos, and Leros. Thanks to millennia of shared history, these Greek islands retain striking harmonies with the Turkish mainland, but are different enough to merit an excursion, if you have time. Make sure you bring your passport if traveling to Greece, and brace yourself for less-than-efficient passport control lines at the border.

Renting a car is a good idea if you wish to venture beyond Bodrum proper. Taxis are widely available, though pricey, and dolmuşes(inexpensive shared-ride minibuses) ply the route up and down the peninsula, departing from Bodrum's central otogar (bus station). Look for the name of your destination in the window of the dolmuş, and note that services usually run more frequently (around every 30 minutes) to/from Bodrum Ptogar and other towns than they do between smaller towns (usually once an hour).

CONTACTS Bodrum Express Lines. ✉ Barış Meydanı 18 ☎ 252/316–1087 ⊕ www. bodrumexpresslines.com. **Bodrum Ferryboat Association.** ✉ Barış Meydanı 30 ☎ 252/316–0882 ⊕ www.bodrumferryboat.com.

TOURS

Akustik Tourism Center

Organizes day trips around the peninsula, visits to local villages, and tours to historical attractions both locally and as far afield as Ephesus, Pamukkale, and

Bodrum Peninsula

Küçük Tavsan Island

Güllük Korfezi

Türkbükü
Gündoğan
Göl-Türkbükü
İkiz Island
Yalıkavak

Geriş
Torba Bay
Torba

Pazar Mountain
390
KEY
 Beaches

B O D R U M   P E N I N S U L A

Karakaya
Ortakent
Yahşi
Gümüşlük
Agaclı
Bitez
Gümbet
Bodrum
Kadikalesi
Yalıçiftlik

Kargi Bay
Turgutreis

Bagla Bay
Karaincir
İc Ada Island
Akyarlar
Karaincir Bay
Bodrum Korfezi
Kara Ada Island

Koca Point
Akyar Point

TO KOS, GREECE
TO DATÇA
TO KORMEN

0   2 mi
0   2 km

Pergamon. ⊠ *Neyzen Tevfik Cad. 146* ☎ *444–0848 toll-free in Turkey* ⊕ *www. akustik.tc.*

Neyzen Travel
In addition to luxury "blue cruise" charters of Turkey's Turquoise Coast and the Greek Dodecanese Islands, Neyzen also organizes private land tours of Bodrum's highlights, and trips around Turkey. ⊠ *Kıbris Şehitleri Cad. 34* ☎ *252/316–7204* ⊕ *www.neyzen.com.tr.*

◉ Sights

Ancient Theater (*Antik Tiyatro*)
ARCHAEOLOGICAL SITE | Construction of the magnificent, 5,000-seat ancient theater began during the 4th century BC reign of King Mausolus, back when Bodrum was known as Halicarnassus of Caria. The Hellenistic theater was used and updated

through the Roman era, and remains one of the ancient city's best-preserved monuments; it is still used for concerts and other performances. The view of Bodrum and the Aegean sea is breathtaking from this high, hillside vantage point, though the outlook is marred by the loud, busy highway that runs alongside the theater. ⊠ *Yeniköy Mah., Kıbris Şehitleri Cad.* ⊞ *Free.*

★ Bodrum Castle and Museum of Underwater Archaeology (*Petronion*)
CASTLE/PALACE | **FAMILY** | Built in the early 15th century by the Knights Hospitaller (Knights of St. John), the **Petronion**, better known as Bodrum Castle or the Castle of St. Peter, rises between Bodrum's twin harbors like an illustration from a fairy tale. With German knight-architect Heinrich Schlegelholt at the helm, the knightly builders plundered the **Mausoleum at**

Halicarnassus for green volcanic stone, marble columns, and reliefs to create this showpiece of late-medieval architecture, whose walls are studded with 249 coats of arms, including the crests of the Plantagenets and d'Aubussons. The castle's towers and gardens are visible from many parts of town, and the name "Bodrum" itself likely derives from the word *Petronion*. Some of the castle's towers are named after the homelands of the knights who built them: France, Germany, Italy, and England (the English Tower, embellished with a relief of a lion, is known as the Lion Tower, and contains a replica of a medieval hall). The castle now houses the fascinating **Museum of Underwater Archaeology**, where displays include the world's oldest excavated shipwreck (*Uluburun*), the tomb of the so-called "Carian Princess," and the sunken cargoes of many ancient and medieval ships that sank off the treacherous Aegean coast. The castle and museum are scheduled to reopen in June 2019 after a two-year restoration. ⊠ *Kale Cad.* ☏ *252/214–1261* ⌧ *30 TL; audio guide 15 TL.*

Bodrum Maritime Museum (*Bodrum Deniz Müzesi*)

MUSEUM | FAMILY | This small museum makes for an interesting break from the summer heat, with models of famous boats on the ground floor and a massive collection of seashells of all shapes, sizes, and colors, upstairs. Don't miss the old black-and-white photos of sponge divers and sponges being delivered from Bodrum harbor—it's what the town was known for in its pre-tourism days. ⊠ *Çarşı Mah., Nazım Hikmet Sok. 4/1* ☏ *252/316– 3310* ⊕ *bodrumdenizmuzesi.org* ⌧ *10 TL* ☟ *Closed Mon.*

Dibeklihan

ARTS VENUE | In the olive tree-covered hills above Bodrum, the "culture and arts village" of Dibeklihan is a pretty complex of traditional stone buildings holding artist studios, galleries, boutiques, and a couple of cafes and restaurants. It's a pleasant place for shopping or dinner, and there is sometimes live music on summer evenings. It's close to Yakaköy village on the outskirts of Ortakent, and best reached with your own transportation. ⊠ *Yakaköy, Çilek Cad. 46/2, Ortakent* ☏ *532/527–7649 for dinner reservations* ⊕ *dibeklihan.com* ☟ *Closed Nov.–Apr.*

Mausoleum of Halicarnassus

ARCHAEOLOGICAL SITE | Little remains of the extravagant white-marble tomb of King Mausolos, one of the Seven Wonders of the Ancient World—and the source of the word *mausoleum*. During the 4th century, Bodrum (then called Halicarnassus) was governed by King Mausolos. Upon his death in 353 BC, Queen Artemisia, his wife and sister, ordered the construction of the great white-marble tomb. At almost 150 feet in height, it must have been quite a sight—a towering rectangular base topped by Ionic columns and friezes of spectacular relief sculpture, surmounted by a pyramidal roof, and crowned with a massive statue of Mausolus and Artemisia, riding a chariot into eternity. The Mausoleum stood for over a millennium, but the 15th-century Knights of St. John plundered its stones to build the Petronion, while 19th-century Brits carted many of the surviving sculptures off to the British Museum. Admission price is relatively high for what little you'll see, but it does offer a rare opportunity to reflect on how a Wonder of the World has been reduced to fallen masonry and broken columns. The site also contains a bare but interesting earlier underground burial chamber. ⊠ *Turgutreis Cad.* ⌧ *12 TL* ☟ *Closed Mon.*

Pedasa

ARCHAEOLOGICAL SITE | On a spectacular perch high above Bodrum, the little-visited ruins of the ancient city of Pedasa date back some 2,500 years, when members of the Leleges civilization built a temple to the goddess Athena here. The site, parts of which are still under excavation, has an acropolis and a necropolis in addition to the temple—and the sweeping views. The archaeological site is located along a new cross-peninsula trekking route, the *Leleg Yolu* (Leleges Way) that will eventually include 88 km (55 miles) of marked paths. A scenic hike of around 6 or 7 km (4 miles) leads from the side of the motorway in Torba, a short *dolmuş* ride from Bodrum city center, to Pedasa; the trailhead is a bit tricky to find, but the rest is well marked. From Pedasa, it's about 3 km (2 miles) down a paved road to the town of Konacık, which while overdeveloped and unlovely, offers two good reasons to stop by: a hearty and well-priced meal at the popular lunchtime *lokanta* Kısmet, and coffee afterwards in the lush gardens of Zai Bodrum, a beautifully designed and art-bedecked library and cultural center. ⊠ *Pedasa Antik Kenti.*

Zeki Müren Arts Museum

MUSEUM | The modest home of one of Turkey's most famous and beloved singers, Zeki Müren, was turned into a museum after his death in 1996. There's not much signage in English, but the period furniture and personal effects, performance photos, elaborate Liberace-style stage costumes, and Müren's own paintings speak for themselves. His music plays throughout the building and there's a vending machine of quirky souvenirs by the reception desk. ⊠ *Kumbahçe Mah., Zeki Müren Cad. 11* ⊹ *Off İçmeler Yolu* ☏ *252/316–1939* 🎫 *6 TL* ⊘ *Closed Mon.*

🍴 Restaurants

Bitez Dondurma

$ | **CAFÉ** | **FAMILY** | Bitez Dondurma's creamy concoctions full of fresh fruit have proved so popular that the ice cream shop now has branches all over the Bodrum Peninsula, and as far away as Istanbul. The waterfront branch in Bodrum's town center is a convenient spot to grab a scoop or two as you stroll along the promenade. **Known for:** mandalina (mandarin) ice cream; balbadem (honey and almond) ice cream; nar (pomegranate) ice cream. ⓢ *Average main: 6 TL* ⊠ *Neyzen Teyfik Cad. 76* ☏ *252/313–3629* ⊕ *www.bitezdondurma.com* ⊘ *No lunch or dinner.*

Denizhan Et Lokantası

$$$ | **TURKISH** | Famed for its kebabs and other meat dishes, Denizhan also serves up very good meze and appetizers, including *lahmacun* (Turkish-style whisper-thin flatbread topped with spices and minced meat) and vegetable dishes such as mustard greens salad. The restaurant has a prime location on the Bodrum waterfront and an extensive wine list. **Known for:** Adana kebab; mixed grill; kuzu pirzola (lamb chops). ⓢ *Average main: 55 TL* ⊠ *Neyzen Teyfik Cad. 182/C* ☏ *252/313–2728* ⊕ *www.denizhan.com.tr.*

Dükkan

$$ | **TURKISH** | This tiny, colorful eatery serving up Greek and Turkish fare is an increasingly rare find in ever more chichi Bodrum—a homey place that's both low-key and relatively affordable. Choose from meze like smoked fish or roasted eggplant with tahini sauce, followed by fresh fish , ending perhaps with a cream-topped candied mandarin for dessert. **Known for:** grilled squid; fried calamari; mixed plate of six meze. ⓢ *Average main: 35 TL* ⊠ *Çarşı Mah., Adliye Sok. 5* ☏ *530/341–6620* ⊘ *Closed Sun. No lunch.*

Gemibaşı

$$$$ | **TURKISH** | For almost half a century, this popular presence near the marina has been serving the freshest seafood in town, in no-frills indoor and outdoor surroundings that are always packed during the season, often with locals. House specialties include fish soup and octopus with pilaf, and their fried calamari has been voted one of the best versions in Turkey. **Known for:** balık köfte (fish "meatball"); seafood börek (savory pastry); shrimp on a bed of pureed eggplant. ⓢ *Average main: 60 TL* ⊠ *Neyzen Teyvfik Cad. 176* ☏ *252/316–1220.*

Daily boat cruises from the marina in Bodrum's city center will take you to nearby coves and bays for a day of swimming and sunbathing.

★ Kalamare

$$$ | SEAFOOD | Down a quiet, pretty alley just a two-minute stroll from the waterfront, the white, candlelit tables at this seafood restaurant quickly fill with hungry locals. Accompany a heaping plate of fried local calamari (probably the most generous in town) with a tasting plate of up to four vegetable meze with toasted bread, and, if you're still hungry, order grilled fish and (more) *rakı* . **Known for:** grilled octopus; calamari stuffed with shrimp and cheese; köpoğlu (garlicky eggplant meze). [$] *Average main: 38 TL* ✉ *Çarşı Mah., Sanat Okulu Cad. 9* ☎ *252/316–7076.*

Köfteci Bilal'ın Yeri

$ | TURKISH | Turkish grilled meatballs and home-style cuisine, served at just a few tables in a no-frills setting, have been a hit for more than half a century and are especially popular at lunch. Accompany any dish you order with homemade plain yogurt. **Known for:** stewed okra; stuffed peppers; rice pilaf. [$] *Average main: 22 TL* ✉ *Yeni Çarşı 2. Sok. 11* ☎ *252/316–3666* ⏲ *Closed Sun.*

Körfez

$$$ | TURKISH | This long-standing, family-run fish house overlooks the harbor and is especially noted for a wide selection of Cretan dishes and seafood appetizers that include delectable shrimp cooked in butter, garlic, and seaweed. A local institution with courteous waitstaff, Körfez also serves some meat dishes, as well as brunch. **Known for:** fried calamari; barbun (red mullet), in season; fish soup. [$] *Average main: 50 TL* ✉ *Neyzen Tevfik Cad. 2* ☎ *252/313–8248* 🌐 *www.korfez-restaurant.com.tr.*

Musto

$$$ | INTERNATIONAL | This always-hopping waterfront bistro draws a local and tourist crowd with its broad Turkish-international menu of pastas, salads, bar snacks, and grilled meats. Some good local wines are available, along with a full bar menu. **Known for:** steaks; burgers; fried calamari. [$] *Average main: 55 TL* ✉ *Neyzen Tevfik Cad. 130* ☎ *252/313–3394* 🌐 *www.mustobistro.com.*

Sugar & Salt

$$ | INTERNATIONAL | Settle in under the shady trees and vines covering and cooling this relaxed garden café just off the waterfront, where the eclectic menu includes a wide range of starters (from hummus to orange-infused chicken liver pate), salads, pastas, and mains. Be sure to save room for the dessert of the day. **Known for:** Thai-style green curry; thin-crust pizzas; house-made cakes. $ *Average main: 40 TL* ⊠ *Eskiçeşme Mah., Danacı Sok. No 4/1-2* ☎ *252/316–8100, 530/170–4104* ⊕ *bodrumsugarandsalt.com.*

Sünger Pizza

$$ | ITALIAN | FAMILY | Italian-inspired pizzas, pastas, and salads are served alongside traditional Turkish chicken and beef dishes, and breakfast until 2 pm, on a large and cheery summer terrace. It's always packed with local families and tourists sitting back at wooden tables groaning under the enormous portions. **Known for:** calzones; garlic bread with cheese; Sünger special pizza with tuna and shrimp. $ *Average main: 40 TL* ⊠ *Neyzen Tevfik Cad. 160* ☎ *252/316–0854.*

Tarihi Yunuslar Karadeniz Unlu Mamüller

Stop by this incredibly popular bakery on Bodrum's main pedestrian shopping street for classic puddings, cheesecakes, pastries, and luxurious fruit-and-cream parfaits. The wide range of savory pastries make good on-the-go snacks, too. $ *Average main:* ⊠ *Çarşı Mah., Cumhuriyet Cad. 13* ☎ *252/316–4137* ▭ *No credit cards.*

🛏 Hotels

El Vino Hotel & Suites

$$$ | HOTEL | The surrounding neighborhood may be a bit gritty, but you wouldn't know it from inside this peaceful, beautifully designed small oasis where the gardens are full of flowers and surround a pool. **Pros:** beautiful surroundings; attractive, well-appointed rooms; attentive service.

Cons: not the most appealing or central location; bathrooms are on the small side; not all rooms have views. $ *Rooms from: 750 TL* ⊠ *Omurça Mah., Pamili Sok.* ☎ *252/313–8770* ⊕ *www.elvinobodrum. com* ⇌ *31 rooms* ⎟◯⎟ *Free Breakfast.*

Eskiceshme Hotel

$$$ | HOTEL | This stylishly designed and modern boutique hotel in the city center offers spacious rooms equipped with balconies and Nespresso machines. **Pros:** attractive, comfortable rooms; convenient location; free parking. **Cons:** no views from rooms; minimal facilities; no elevator. $ *Rooms from: 720 TL* ⊠ *Eskiçeşme Mah., Poyraz Sok. 10* ☎ *252/316-2500, 554/242–5884* ⊕ *www.eskiceshme.com* ⇌ *38 rooms* ⎟◯⎟ *Free Breakfast.*

★ Kempinski Hotel Barbaros Bay

$$$$ | RESORT | FAMILY | This is by far one of the most beautiful deluxe hotel properties in all of Bodrum, and its location on a private bay in secluded Yalıçiftlik makes it a preferred choice for international clientele seeking to avoid the paparazzi in luxurious comfort. **Pros:** luxurious splendor; two fine-dining and two casual restaurants (also open to non-guests); world-class infinity pool and spa. **Cons:** on-site restaurants predictably pricey; 20-minute ride to Bodrum city center (bus and private transfers available); some guests say service could be improved. $ *Rooms from: 1850 TL* ⊠ *Yalı Mah., Hacıgiden Cad. 33/1, Yalıçiftlik* ✛ *14 km (9 miles) from Bodrum* ☎ *252/311–0303* ⊕ *www. kempinski.com* ◉ *Closed Nov.–Mar.* ⇌ *173 rooms* ⎟◯⎟ *Free Breakfast.*

Manastır Hotel & Suites

$$$ | HOTEL | Few other hotels in Bodrum city center can match the serene surroundings and sublime views of this former monastery (*manastır* in Turkish), on a glorious perch overlooking Bodrum Bay, and all of the spacious rooms and suites have airy balconies. **Pros:** unique building amid lovely surroundings; exquisite sea views; peaceful. **Cons:** quite a trek from town; decor and some fixtures could

use updating; not all rooms have sea views. $ *Rooms from: 450 TL* ⊠ *Kumbahçe Mah., Mustafa Kemal Cad. 37* ☏ *252/316–2854, 252/480–0577 for info and reservations* ⊕ *www.manastirhotel.com* ⌖ *74 rooms* ⦿ *Free Breakfast.*

Marina Vista
$$$$ | **HOTEL** | With its large, pretty pool, sauna, steam room, and small gym and spa, this convenient in-town lodging with bright, stylish rooms feels like a resort. **Pros:** great location across from the marina; big pool and lounge area; comfortable rooms, many with sea or pool views. **Cons:** most rooms don't face the sea; can be noisy; some bathrooms are on the small side. $ *Rooms from: 750 TL* ⊠ *Neyzen Tevfik Cad. 168* ☏ *252/313–0350* ⊕ *www.hotelmarinavista.com* ⌖ *87 rooms* ⦿ *Free Breakfast.*

The Marmara Bodrum
$$$$ | **HOTEL** | Most of the elegant rooms at this hilltop aerie enjoy views of Bodrum and the sea from balconies and terraces, while a free shuttle to a private beach club in Göltürkbükü puts the seaside within easy reach. **Pros:** nicely decorated and appointed rooms; beautiful surroundings; luxury hotel with a boutique feel. **Cons:** a bit of a distance from the city center; bathrooms a bit dated; not on the beach. $ *Rooms from: 1400 TL* ⊠ *Yokuşbaşı Mah., Sulu Hasan Cad. 18* ☏ *252/313–8130* ⊕ *bodrum.themarmarahotels.com* ⌖ *95 rooms* ⦿ *Free Breakfast.*

★ Su Otel
$$$ | **HOTEL** | **FAMILY** | Cheery and colorful, this centrally located spot has good-sized rooms set around a lush garden and pool area, and a welcoming vibe. **Pros:** simple but attractive rooms; nice pool and lounge areas; central location that's still peaceful. **Cons:** no views; breakfast is ample but just average; noise from pool and other common areas can be heard in some rooms. $ *Rooms from: 500 TL* ⊠ *Turgutreis Cad., 1201 Sok.* ☏ *252/316–6906* ⊕ *www.bodrumsuhotel.com* ⌖ *25 rooms* ⦿ *Free Breakfast.*

ⓨ Nightlife

Körfez Bar
BARS/PUBS | Rock classics are the soundtrack at this small but popular bar in Bodrum's central market area. It's been around since 1992 and shows no signs of stopping. ⊠ *Çarşı Mah., Cumhuriyet Cad. 2* ✛ *Corner of Uslu Sok* ☏ *252/316–5966* ⊕ *korfezbar.com.*

Küba Bar & Restaurant
BARS/PUBS | With top-notch food and music, Küba is always crowded, especially on weekends. ⊠ *Neyzen Tevfik Cad. 60* ☏ *252/313–4450* ⊕ *kubabar.com.*

Mandalin
MUSIC CLUBS | Live blues, funk, jazz, and Latin acts frequently take the stage in this two-story waterfront bar, which has less of a meat-market reputation than some of the other Barlar Sokağı ("Bar Street") establishments. There are also '80s nights and salsa nights. ⊠ *Çarşı Mah., Dr. Alimbey Cad., 1025 Sok.* ☏ *549/226–4848* ⊕ *www.mandalinsound.com.*

★ Marina Yacht Club
CAFES—NIGHTLIFE | Surrounded by a forest of sailboat masts, this is the first place both Bodrum locals and Turkish tourists will recommend for a night out. The good live music (jazz, classical, etc.) is as diverse as the age groups that come to listen. The dining area on the second floor has a long bar with a terrific view of the marina. ⊠ *Bodrum Marina, Neyzen Tevfik Cad. 5* ☏ *252/316–1228* ⊕ *www.marinayachtclub.com.*

Mavi Bar
MUSIC CLUBS | A Bodrum institution, the small and quaint "Blue Bar" occupies century-old premises and features live Turkish music—some of Turkey's most prominent rock stars have appeared here. ⊠ *Cumhuriyet Cad. 175* ☏ *252/316–3932.*

🏃 Activities

DIVING

The sea around Bodrum provides some of the best diving in the Aegean, with more than a dozen dive spots and at least 10 schools that are registered with PADI, the worldwide diving organization.

Aegean Pro Dive Centre

SCUBA DIVING | Located in the next bay over from Bodrum in Gümbet, this is one of the most reliable PADI-certified dive operators in the area. ⊠ Adnan Menderes Cad. 63, Gümbet ☎ 252/316–0737 ⊕ www.aegeanprodive.com.

Erman Dive Center

SCUBA DIVING | This PADI-certified outfitter has three locations in the Yalıçiftlik area east of Bodrum: this one at the Kempinski Hotel Barbaros Bay; another at the Hapimag Resort Sea Garden; and the third at the Club Med Palmiye. ⊠ Kempinski Hotel Barbaros Bay, Yalı Mah., Hacıgiden Cad. 33/1, Yalıçiftlik ✛ 14 km (9 miles) from Bodrum ☎ 532/213–5989 ⊕ www.ermandive.com ⊘ Closed Nov.–Apr.

HORSEBACK RIDING

Gündoğan is the best place for horseback riding, with nice forest trails; Ortakent and Turgutreis are good alternatives.

Countryranch Atlı Spor Klübü (Countryranch Equestrian Sports Club)

HORSEBACK RIDING | The stables here offer tuition for all ages, pony-trekking for children, and horseback safaris for adults. ⊠ Piren Cad. 30, İslamhaneleri, Turgutreis ✛ Off the D330 hwy. ☎ 252/400–0567 ⊕ www.countryranch.com.

Yahşi Batı At Çiftliği (Yahşi Batı Horse Ranch)

HORSEBACK RIDING | Offers riding lessons to people of all age groups, including complete novices, as well as short horseback safaris on trails and by the seaside. ⊠ Kocataş Cad. 78, Ortakent ☎ 541/784–7800 ⊕ www.yahsibatiatciftligi.com.

WINDSURFING

Bitez, Yalıkavak, and Fener, near Turgutreis, are ideal for windsurfing.

Fener Windsurf Club

WINDSURFING | If you would like to try your hand at windsurfing, try this club on Fener Beach in Akyarlar, about 6.5 km (4 miles) from Turgutreis and 25 km (15 miles) from the Bodrum city center. Instructors speak English, and they also rent equipment to those already experienced. Open mid-April to mid-November. ⊠ Fener Plajı, Akyarlar ✛ Next to the Armonia Hotel ☎ 252/393–8414 beach phone, daytime only, 532/633–7079 office mobile ⊕ www.fenerwindsurf.com.

🛍 Shopping

There is an open-air bazaar every day of the week in Bodrum and in the surrounding towns. You will find fruits and vegetables and other foodstuffs, household goods, clothing, shoes, handbags, souvenirs, and, at some, high-quality jewelry and rugs. The Yalıkavak market is considered among the best. The schedule of the bazaars is: Türkbükü on Monday; Bodrum (no food), Yalıkavak (food only), and Gölköy on Tuesday; Ortakent, Gümüşlük, and Gündoğan on Wednesday; Yalıkavak (textiles and housewares) and Akyarlar on Thursday; Bodrum (fruits, vegetables, and other foodstuffs, on the second floor of the otogar) on Friday; Turgutreis on Saturday; and Gümbet and Mumcular on Sunday.

Atölye 4D

JEWELRY/ACCESSORIES | Artful jewelry is offered by a trio of Turkish designers who take their inspiration from natural shapes such as fish, coral, and olive leaves and branches, as well as ancient symbols. Prices are surprisingly reasonable, especially considering the prime waterfront Bodrum location. ⊠ Neyzen Tevfik Cad. 60C ☎ 533/638–3303 ⊕ www.atolye4d.com.

Çamur Bodrum
CERAMICS/GLASSWARE | Striking jewelry pieces; pretty plates, bowls, and mugs; and quirky sculptures, all made out of clay, are on display and for sale at this small ceramic workshop and store. ✉ *Çarşı Mah., Gerence Sok. 6.*

Sur Sandalet
SHOES/LUGGAGE/LEATHER GOODS | Bodrum's handmade leather sandals are renowned, and this family-run workshop has been turning them out, in both basic and decorative styles, since 1967. Lightweight and made from specially worked leather, they're very comfortable for the Mediterranean summer, and aesthetically pleasing as well. ✉ *Çarşı Mah., Cumhuriyet Cad. 56* ☎ *252/316–3021* 🌐 *www.sursandalet.com.*

Bitez

The beach in the inland village of Bitez is the longest on the peninsula, with most of the 2-km (1-mile) stretch of sand in this semicircle cove covered by chaises or plush pillows set up in little enclaves. A pedestrian walkway divides the cafés and hotels from the shore. There's a small windsurfing school at the western end of the cove, next to the Sarnıç Beach Club. Inland from the water, the stone houses in the village were built right on the road to make room for mandarin trees in the backyard. Until several decades ago, residents picked and packed the mandarins onto camels, which then carried them to the nearby ports. Walk along the back roads of Bitez to take in the fresh, citric scent of the mandarins, intermingled with 500-year-old olive trees. Though the beachfront area caters to foreign tourists, there's a bit of a trendy Turkish scene developing inland, with clubby restaurants and serene breakfast gardens interspersed among the groves of trees, and hipster spots like a raw juice bar and a vegan cafe in sedate Bitez village up the hill.

🍴 Restaurants

Bağarası
$$$ | TURKISH | Tables are tucked into a lovely hidden garden in summer and in cooler weather service is in a quaint, Bodrum-style, one-story house. The Mediterranean cuisine includes some local favorites. **Known for:** çıtır mantı (crispy fried Turkish-style ravioli); lokum pilav (rice prepared with local herbs and spices); girit köfte (Crete-style meatballs). [$] *Average main: 55 TL* ✉ *Pınarlı Cad. 59* ☎ *252/363–7693.*

Bitez Köftecisi
$$ | TURKISH | A pleasantly old-fashioned place popular with locals, this cozy, casual restaurant a short walk back from the beachfront offers a range of Turkish-style grilled meats, plus a smaller selection of appetizers and meze. Portions are small, but quality high. **Known for:** köfte (meatballs); pirzola (lamb chops); ciğer (liver). [$] *Average main: 30 TL* ✉ *Şah Cad. 31* ☎ *252/363–8215.*

Lemon Tree
$$$ | INTERNATIONAL | With a big menu of both Turkish and international fare, including pizza, pasta, salads, and grilled meats, this popular spot sits right on the beach in Bitez, with a lovely view of the cove. Service is friendly but can be a bit harried when it's busy. **Known for:** burgers; steaks; çökertme kebab (sliced beef served with green peppers and potatoes). [$] *Average main: 45 TL* ✉ *Çokertme Cad. 82* ☎ *252/363–9543* 💳 *No credit cards.*

🛏 Hotels

Doria Hotel Bodrum
$$$$ | RESORT | FAMILY | This modern hilltop haven overlooking Bitez Bay may not be right on the beach, but there's a complimentary shuttle to the hotel's hedonistic private beach club nearby. **Pros:** spacious rooms; glorious views; glamorous bar and restaurant. **Cons:** up a steep hill from town; high prices for food and drink;

beach shuttle only runs Jun.–mid-Sept. [$] *Rooms from: 840 TL* ✉ *Gündönümü Mevkii, 1410 Sok.* ☎ *252/311–1020* 🌐 *www.doriahotelbodrum.com* 🛏 *92 rooms* 🍴 *Free Breakfast.*

Yalı Han Hotel

$$ | **HOTEL** | **FAMILY** | This friendly spot right next to the beach has crisp, simple rooms and an attractive, well-kept pool area. **Pros:** nice pool; friendly atmosphere; good waterfront location. **Cons:** rooms and amenities are fairly simple; some rooms can be dark; pool is on the small side. [$] *Rooms from: 400 TL* ✉ *Şah Cad. 14* ☎ *252/363–7772* 🌐 *www.yalihanotel.com* 🛏 *16 rooms* 🍴 *Free Breakfast.*

Toloman Hotel

$$ | **HOTEL** | **FAMILY** | Right on the beachfront, these bright, airy accommodations overlook the water from balconies. **Pros:** central location; nice pool and grounds; good value. **Cons:** fairly simple rooms; only upstairs rooms have sea views; no gym or spa. [$] *Rooms from: 270 TL* ✉ *Çökertme Cad.* ☎ *252/363–7751* 🌐 *www.toloman.com* 🛏 *33 rooms.*

Göl-Türkbükü

The two adjacent coastal towns of Gölköy and Türkbükü merged a decade ago to become Göl-Türkbükü, the most glamorous part of the Bodrum Peninsula. Türkbükü, which has been aptly called the "St. Tropez of Turkey," is the summer playground of jet-setting, high-society Turks and foreigners, and its coastline is pleasantly packed with bars, cafés, restaurants, and boutiques. Gölköy has a slower pace and more stretches of undeveloped waterfront; Türkbükü is the see-and-be-seen hot spot for socializing, partying, and dining, though the season is short, and you may find it quiet outside of July and August, with many establishments nearly empty or closed altogether. Note that there's not much more to do in Gölköy besides sunbathe. Neither of its two beaches has sand, but the water is accessible from wooden decks. Private motorboats splash between the two bays; the local dolmuş is more prosaic, but a lot cheaper.

🍴 Restaurants

Atılay Balık

$$$ | **SEAFOOD** | With fishnets on the ceiling and simple tables under strands of small lights outside, this laid-back fish restaurant on the waterfront in Türkbükü has a nautical vibe. Start your meal with a selection of seafood or vegetable meze, and save room for the house special dessert, *helva sarma* (phyllo-dough rolls filled with tahini paste, flavored with cinnamon, and served with ice cream and chocolate sauce). **Known for:** levrek lokum (sea bass morsels); grilled octopus; lakerda (salt-cured bonito). [$] *Average main: 55 TL* ✉ *Yalı Mevkii, Liman Cad. 81/B, Göltürkbükü* ☎ *252/377–5095* 💳 *No credit cards.*

★ **Garo's**

$$$ | **MEDITERRANEAN** | The peripatetic Turkish-Armenian maestro Garo heads the kitchen at this enduringly popular stone cottage–turned–waterfront restaurant in Türkbükü with a comfy Greek-taverna feel, friendly staff, and an outdoor terrace with blue-and-white checkered tablecloths. Not in the mood for seafood and meze? **Known for:** grilled octopus; smoked salmon rolls; veal cheek. [$] *Average main: 55 TL* ✉ *Menemene Mah., 83 Sok. 9, Göltürkbükü* ☎ *252/377–6171* 🌐 *www.garosturkbuku.com* 🕓 *Closed Oct.–Apr.*

Hoca'nın Yeri

$ | **TURKISH** | **FAMILY** | The specialty of the house at this simple eatery on the boardwalk in Türkbükü is large, rather greasy portions of *çiğ böreği*, a Crimean dish brought to Turkey that consists of flat, fried pastry stuffed with ground beef, onion, and spices. One of the few unpretentious (and relatively inexpensive) places left on the Türkbükü shoreline, this place has a beach-hut vibe, its own little patch of sand, and a family clientele. **Known for:** baked or fried mantı (tiny Turkish "ravioli," stuffed with minced meat); gözleme (Turkish savory crepes with various fillings); Turkish breakfast. $ *Average main: 30 TL* ✉ *Yalı Mevkii, Liman Cad. 77, Göltürkbükü* ☎ *252/377–5907* ⊗ *Closed Oct.–Apr.*

Miam

$$$$ | **SEAFOOD** | Wonderfully prepared seafood is served with polish, as are the meat and pasta dishes. Meals are accompanied by soothing sea views from their terrace on the Türkbükü waterfront in summertime; after midnight, there are often DJs at the garden bar. **Known for:** sea bass medallions; rack of lamb; calamari salad. $ *Average main: 70 TL* ✉ *Atatürk Cad. 51, Göltürkbükü* ☎ *252/377–5612.*

 ## Hotels

★ Amanruya

$$$$ | **HOTEL** | Perched above the Aegean Sea is a 36-room retreat whose name is aptly translated to "peace" and "dream," offering guests the tranquil sense that they are all alone, even when every villa is occupied. **Pros:** beautiful setting and facilities; personalized service; private beach, fitness center, and spa. **Cons:** not all the pools are heated; water in the outdoor showers tends to be tepid; remote from any town. $ *Rooms from: 6670 TL* ✉ *Demir Mevkii, Bülent Ecevit Cad., Göltürkbükü* ☎ *252/311–1212* ⊕ *www. aman.com/resorts/amanruya* 🛏 *36 cottages* ⦿ *No meals.*

★ Flamm

$$$$ | **HOTEL** | A chilled-out retreat in Gölköy with a low-key eco-design flair that utilizes natural materials inside and out—a carved piece of driftwood for a towel rail, for instance—plus an Olympic pool and a pergola-shaded beach sundeck. **Pros:** effortlessly glam, without the

intensity of the Türkbükü scene; stylish comfort steps from the water; lovely private grounds. **Cons:** few other restaurants and no shops nearby; not all rooms have sea views; outdoor eating/drinking areas unprotected from wind. $ *Rooms from: 1500 TL* ✉ *Yalı Mah., 30. Sok. 3, Göltürkbükü* ☎ *252/357–7600* ⊕ *www. flammbodrum.com* ⊗ *Closed mid-Oct.– mid-May* 🛏 *14 rooms* ⦿ *Free Breakfast.*

Karianda Boutique Hotel

$$$ | **B&B/INN** | **FAMILY** | Overlooking a large, well-tended beach, and with lovely gardens (and pet chickens), this is a perfect place for families. **Pros:** cozy feel; excellent food; big, relaxed outdoor area. **Cons:** rooms and fixtures fairly simple; not all rooms have views; some rooms quite small. $ *Rooms from: 470 TL* ✉ *Atatürk Cad. 134, Göltürkbuku* ☎ *252/357–7303 hotel, 533/221–2131 owner's cell* ⊕ *www.karianda.com* ⊗ *Closed mid-Oct.–mid-May* 🛏 *25 rooms* ⦿ *Free Breakfast.*

Maça Kızı Boutique Hotel & Restaurant

$$$$ | **HOTEL** | You'll be in sophisticated company and away from the crowds in the elegantly decorated rooms at the "Queen of Spades," nestled on a hillside in a secluded bay at the tip of the Türkbükü waterfront. **Pros:** private pontoon swimming/sunbathing deck; sophisticated and secluded surroundings; top-class service. **Cons:** large mark-ups on food, drinks, and other items; meal-inclusive rates required; hefty deposit and cancellation fees. $ *Rooms from: 4630 TL* ✉ *Kesire Mevkii, Narçiçeği Sok., Göltürkbükü* ☎ *252/311–2400* ⊕ *www. macakizi.com* ⊗ *Closed mid-Oct.–Apr.* 🛏 *74 rooms* ⦿ *Free Breakfast.*

Hotel Mandalya Beach

$$$ | **HOTEL** | **FAMILY** | This relaxed, modest, waterfront establishment in Gölköy caters to families at reasonable prices. **Pros:** peaceful location with beach and pool; friendly vibe; accommodating to families with children and pets. **Cons:** simple rooms and amenities; small

bathrooms; no room service, gym, or spa. [$] *Rooms from: 500 TL* ✉ *Akdeniz Cad. 56, Göltürkbükü* ☎ *252/357–7017* 🌐 *www.mandalyahotel.com.tr* 🕓 *Closed Nov.–Apr.* 🛏 *20 rooms* 🍴 *Free Breakfast.*

Nightlife

Sahne Istanbul

MUSIC CLUBS | This popular Istanbul nightclub now hosts live Turkish acts in the summer months at a venue in Türkbükü. ✉ *Yalı Mevkii, Liman Cad., Göltürkbükü* ☎ *252/358–5858.*

Shopping

Hatice Teyze Doğal Ürünler (*Hatice Teyze Natural Products*)

FOOD/CANDY | This large shop on a residential street a few blocks back from the Türkbükü shorefront is filled with all kinds of natural, often regional, products: jams, olive oils, dried fruits and vegetables, sauces, soaps, gift baskets, and more. Good for a taste of Turkey to take home. ✉ *85 Sok. 5, Suite 6, Göltürkbükü* ☎ *252/377–5857, 850/582–1196* 🌐 *www.haticeteyze.com.*

İpekçe

JEWELRY/ACCESSORIES | All of the colorful linens, beachwear, jewelry, bags, and household accessories at this small boutique on Türkbükü's main waterfront road are designed by owner İpek Özdoğu and her team. They also have a shop in Alaçatı. ✉ *Yalı Mevkii, Liman Cad. 63, Göltürkbükü* ☎ *252/377–6308* 🌐 *www.ipekceturkbuku.com.*

Turgutreis

Named for an Ottoman admiral (some say pirate), Turgutreis lies due west on the opposite side of the peninsula from Bodrum. The second-largest town on the peninsula, it has a more developed coast, and a popular and lively (if very touristy) bazaar, along with a marina shopping complex that's less high-end than the one in Yalıkavak. Venues at the marina and in nearby Şevket Sabancı Park host most of the classical concerts in the Bodrum Music Festival held each summer. A large city-run gallery, part of the Şevket Sabancı Kültür Merkezi, puts on well-displayed shows by local artists. Turgutreis has a long, pleasant waterfront with a stretch of biking/running path, and 2½ km (1½ miles) of sandy beach, mostly lined by hotels. The more picturesque beaches around Akyarlar and Karaincir, two adjacent bays to the south, are easily reachable via a 30-minute *dolmuş*ride from Turgutreis. Accomodation options here mostly consist of large resorts, apart hotels, and simple lodgings.

Restaurants

Mavi Park Restaurant

$$ | **TURKISH** | This waterfront spot in green and pleasant Şevket Sabancı Park, just outside Turgutreis city center, offers grand views of the sea along with a nice selection of Turkish and international dishes (though, perhaps surprisingly given the location, no fish). Alcohol is served; reservations advisable in high season. **Known for:** kebabs; patlıcan sarması (eggplant rolls); Turkish breakfast. [$] *Average main: 45 TL* ✉ *Şevket Sabancı Parkı, Gazi Mustafa Kemal Bul.* ☎ *252/382–2608* 🌐 *www.maviparkrestaurant.com.*

Fatma Bacının Yeri

$ | **TURKISH** | Simple, hearty dishes are what's on offer at this casual restaurant in the middle of Turgutreis's bazaar. Choose from traditional Turkish favorites or get an omelet at any time of the day. **Known for:** mantı (Turkish-style ravioli in garlicky yogurt sauce); çiğ börek (deep-fried savory pastry); gözleme (Turkish-style savory crepes). [$] *Average main: 20 TL* ✉ *Plaj 2 Sok. 15* ☎ *252/382–5615.*

Hotels

Kortan Otel

$$ | HOTEL | Right by the beach in the middle of Turgutreis, this family-run seaside escape has simple but tasteful furnishings and offers good value for its prime location. **Pros:** nice seaside terrace with view for sunbathing; on the beach; on-site bar and restaurant. **Cons:** on the main stretch, so not totally private or quiet; fairly simple rooms and fixtures; bar can get noisy. [$] *Rooms from: 270 TL* ⊠ *Atatürk Meydanı, Sabancı Cad. 14* ☎ *252/382–2932* ⊕ *www.kortanotel.com* ➪ *25 rooms* ⦿ *Free Breakfast.*

Shopping

Atolye Begonvil

CRAFTS | This charming shop in the center of Turgutreis sells handicrafts and other homemade wares by the members of a local women's cooperative: jams, jewelry, textiles, wood decorations, stained-glass artworks, and more. ⊠ *Gazi Mustafa Kemal Bul. 3* ☎ *252/382–0426* ⊕ *www. atolyebegonvil.com.*

Sabuncakiz's Hamam

SPA/BEAUTY | A scented wonderland of beautiful hand-made soaps, Turkish bath towels, bath accessories, and other textiles, including beach towels and shawls. Choose from olive oil soaps like basil-citronella, apricot, or green tea, and towels in a huge range of colors, patterns, and styles. The owner has an Etsy shop, too. ⊠ *Plaj 2 Cad. 9/A* ☎ *555/355–5541.*

Gümüşlük

Charming Gümüşlük (named for its ancient silver mines) is built on the ancient ruins of Myndos. It is one of the peninsula's more authentic, slower-paced, less-developed villages—no high-rises or large hotels are allowed, so the bulk of lodging options are small aparthotels and pensions.

This bewitching little town is a popular excursion for residents and visitors staying all over the peninsula, who come to Gümüşlük to enjoy its romantic sunsets, fish restaurants, and "village breakfasts" on the water; it also has a Blue Flag public beach. The water is often shallow enough to wade over to Tavşan Adası (Rabbit Island), though the island's pre-Roman ruins, visible from the water, are off-limits to all but archaeologists. Much of the Myndos ruins are submerged underwater, and land excavations of the ancient city—where a drainage system dating to Myndos's Roman civilization period was previously discovered—have been long stalled. Gümüşlük hosts a popular summertime classical music festival, with concerts in and around town. If you have the time, and a car, you can make the trip up to Karakaya, a village of stone houses perched above Gümüşlük and surrounded with cactus and other foliage. In winter, the local population is augmented by writers and artists, drawn by the inspiring serenity and the off-season prices.

Restaurants

★ **Aquarium**

$$$ | SEAFOOD | FAMILY | At this waterfront restaurant, begin a meal with stuffed zucchini flowers, roasted eggplant with *tulum* cheese, and octopus salad—you may want to just keep working your way through the starters, a meal in themselves. Or let the owner, Cengiz Bey, help you select the best local fish for the grill. **Known for:** grilled prawns; Aquarium special (shrimp and octopus cooked with garlic, butter, and flame-roasted peppers and eggplant); laos (grouper), in season. [$] *Average main: 60 TL* ⊠ *Yalı Mevkii 54* ☎ *252/394–3682* ⊕ *www. akvaryumbodrum.com.*

★ **Gümüşcafé Fish Restaurant**

$$$ | TURKISH | This lovely restaurant on the waterfront specializes not only in fresh fish, seafood, and meze but also serves a princely summer brunch. Tables are only a few feet from the peaceful waters of the bay, with a truly romantic view of the ancient ruins of Rabbit Island, often with a soft breeze. **Known for:** prawns cooked with butter, garlic, mushrooms, and pepper; levrek (sea bass) wrapped in vine leaves; stuffed zucchini flowers. $ *Average main: 50 TL* ✉ *Gümüşlük Yalısı, 1120 Sok. 82* ☎ *252/394–4234* ⊕ *www.gumuscafe. com* ⊗ *Closed Nov.–Apr.*

Limon Cafe

$$$ | TURKISH | Settle into a lovely, fig-scented garden about 2 km (1 mile) outside town, overlooking citrus trees, the sea, and the ancient city of Myndos and enjoy a meal in these rural surroundings. A late-risers' breakfast is served until 3 pm daily; better still, come for the sunset while savoring one of the house-specialty cocktails. **Known for:** Turkish breakfast; fried calamari; homemade mantı (Turkish-style ravioli). $ *Average main: 45 TL* ✉ *Kardak Cad. 7* ☎ *252/394–4044* ⊕ *http://limongumusluk. com/* ⊗ *Closed Oct.–Apr.*

🛏 Hotels

Otel Gümüşlük

$$$ | HOTEL | FAMILY | Set amid pretty orchards near the Gümüşlük beachfront, these homey, simply appointed rooms surround a pool, garden, lawn area, and a bar/restaurant with an ocean view. **Pros:** good location in a pleasant setting; nice pool and garden area; excellent breakfast. **Cons:** fairly simple accommodations; nearby bars/restaurants can be noisy; ground-floor rooms don't have much privacy. $ *Rooms from: 410 TL* ✉ *Yalı Mevkii 28* ☎ *252/394–4828* ⊕ *www.otelgumusluk.com* ⇥ *36 rooms* ⊠ *Free Breakfast.*

ⓨ Nightlife

At the far end of the beach, Jazz Cafe has been a fixture on the Gümüşlük waterfront for a decade. Other venues are often changing but currently popular bar/club/restaurants include Off Gümüşlük (which hosts Turkish music concerts) and Club Gümüşlük, both of which have their own beaches. Tucked into the hillside back from the sea, colorful café/bar Hayat sprawls over a series of outdoor terraces, and serves food that gets good reviews. Don't expect much nightlife in Gümüşlük in the off season; if there is any, it will only be on weekends.

🛍 Shopping

The town's handicrafts markets, a line of open-air stalls by the bus stop, offers a nicer-than-usual selection of jewelry, bags, gourd lamps, and other products. The small Gümüşlük Sanat Evi near the water hosts exhibitions by local artists and artisans.

Gümüş Kediler

TEXTILES/SEWING | Designer Şükran Uyar, a longtime fixture at the Gümüşlük handicrafts market, now has her own shop selling cotton beachwear and other textile goods, mostly with colorful block-printed designs. ✉ *Muhtar Niyazi Sok. 1/11* ⊹ *Corner of Atatürk Cad.* ☎ *533/214–9045.*

Kikkula

CRAFTS | This charming, airy shop is filled with beautiful objects—lamps, bowls, notebooks, jewelry—made from paper by a friendly and talented husband-and-wife team. Graphic designer Tuna and former art teacher Uta are happy to chat about their work; they also sell some paintings, sculptures, and other pieces by other artists, but, they say, "only things we like looking at ourselves." Open year-round except when they're traveling to buy more unique papers from all over the world. ✉ *Atatürk Cad. 74* ☎ *544/650– 1407* ⊕ *kikkula.com.*

Yalıkavak

This town on the northwestern tip of the Bodrum Peninsula is surrounded by mandarin orchards and olive groves and easily identified by the beautiful windmills atop its hill. Once a tiny sponge-divers' village, Yalıkavak is a lot less quiet than it used to be since the opening of a large marina complex that includes a luxury hotel and mall. There are still some good local restaurants in the older part of town as well as many fine beaches ringing the surrounding coves. Xuma Beach Club and Dodo Beach Club, both about 4 km (2½ miles) north of town, are among the most popular; the latter is more family-friendly. Strong wind also makes Yalıkavak ideal for windsurfing.

🍴 Restaurants

Çardaklı Restaurant

$$$ | TURKISH | Bedecked with blossoms, this waterfront restaurant has a classic Aegean air and wide selection of meze, including stuffed zucchini flowers and yogurt with hot red peppers, as well as grilled fish and meat. In high season, the outside tables are usually full with Turks and foreign visitors alike. **Known for:** grilled octopus; vine-leaf-wrapped levrek (sea bass); levrek marin (marinated sea bass). [$] *Average main: 45 TL* ✉ *Merkez Mah., İskele Cad. 13* ☎ *252/385–2444.*

Kavaklı Köfteci

$ | TURKISH | FAMILY | *Köfte* (Turkish-style meatballs) is the mainstay of this popular, no-frills eatery, and you can enjoy these delectable morsels as a sandwich or with a side of *piyaz* (navy bean salad, with or without onions), homemade bread, and *ayran* (salted yogurt drink). The only other dish on the menu is *çöp şiş*, small pieces of skewered grilled lamb. **Known for:** good köfte; piyaz (navy bean salad); çöp şiş (skewered, grilled lamb). [$] *Average main: 25 TL* ✉ *Merkez Çarşı İçi* ☎ *252/385–4748* 🌐 *www.kavaklikofteci.com* 💳 *No credit cards* ☞ *Cash only.*

Minör Restaurant

$$$ | STEAKHOUSE | Popular with the yachting crowd and holidaymakers from Istanbul, this friendly steak house has live music—jazz, Latin, flamenco, Turkish, and pop—every night. The broad menu also includes chicken, fish, and other meat dishes, along with salads and assorted meze. **Known for:** steak in pepper sauce; surf and turf; king prawns in butter and garlic. [$] *Average main: 65 TL* ✉ *Çökertme Cad. 17* ☎ *252/385–3863.*

Zeytinlina Restaurant

$$ | INTERNATIONAL | A broad, mostly reasonably priced menu of well-executed dishes—both Turkish and international—is offered in a setting that encourages leisurely lingering over a meal or drinks (there's a full bar). Tables are scattered throughout a peaceful, beautifully landscaped garden with sea views, and there's a beach, too, if you want to cool off. **Known for:** Turkish breakfast; pizzas; steaks. [$] *Average main: 35 TL* ✉ *Plaj Cad. 64/1* ☎ *252/385–5758* 🌐 *zeytinlina.com.*

🛏 Hotels

Boho

$$$ | HOTEL | Spacious accommodations decked out in serene earth tones—just five rooms in all—share a private swimming and sunbathing pier out over the water at this tiny boutique hotel. **Pros:** waterfront location and views; stylish modern rooms; serene and private. **Cons:** kitchen and bar only open in summer; no pool or spa; extra charge for some items at breakfast. [$] *Rooms from: 750 TL* ✉ *Plaj Cad. 7* ☎ *252/385–2545* 🌐 *boho.com.tr* 🛏 *5 rooms* 🍴 *Free Breakfast.*

★ 4reasons hotel + bistro

$$$$ | HOTEL | FAMILY | Opportunities for relaxation abound at this hilltop retreat overlooking Yalıkavak, where the spacious grounds include a pool and sunbathing deck, a "chill-out zone" for reading and yoga, and private cabanas for outdoor massage. **Pros:** beautiful, relaxing setting; ample and lovely public spaces; excellent service. **Cons:** a fair trek from town or beaches without your own car; not all rooms have air-conditioning or fans; beach club access in high summer season only. [$] *Rooms from: 1200 TL* ✉ *Tilkicik Mavkii, Bakan Cad. 2* ☎ *252/385–3212* 🌐 *www.4reasonshotel.com* 🕓 *Closed Feb.* 🛏 *20 rooms* 🍴 *Free Breakfast.*

La Maison
$$$$ | **HOTEL** | At the quieter end of the Yalıkavak waterfront, this simple but charming small hotel consists of gleaming-white two-story buildings set around a nicely landscaped pool area, where thatch-roof cabanas provide shade. **Pros:** central location; relaxed atmosphere; has its own small beach. **Cons:** fairly basic rooms and amenities; expensive for what it is; bar/restaurant is pricey. [$] *Rooms from: 1100 TL* ✉ *Plaj Cad. 22* ☎ *252/385–2685* 🌐 *www.lamaison.com.tr* 🛏 *14 rooms* 🍴 *Free Breakfast.*

Yalıkavak Marina Beach Hotel
$$$$ | **HOTEL** | All of the large, attractive rooms are done in an appealingly minimalist style, face the water, and have their own decks with lounge chairs. **Pros:** beautiful waterfront setting; large and attractive beach and beach club; comfortable, spacious rooms. **Cons:** beach club music can be loud; rooms can get hot and stuffy due to sun exposure; no pool. [$] *Rooms from: 1100 TL* ✉ *Yalıkavak Marina, Çökertme Cad. 6* ☎ *252/385–3484* 🌐 *yalikavakhotels.com.tr/beach-hotel* 🛏 *15 suites* 🍴 *Free Breakfast.*

Shopping

Yalıkavak is known for its fabulous weekly market, which draws locals, tourists, and even visitors from the nearby Greek islands to stop at hundreds of stalls. It has proved so popular it's now split in two: local produce and edible delicacies on Tuesday, and textiles, housewares, and handicrafts on Thursday. The mall-like Yalıkavak Marina complex on the waterfront is full of higher-end restaurants and shops, including well-known Turkish brands like Beymen, Vakko, and Yargıcı (clothing), Misela (handbags), and Haremlique (fine towels and linens). An increasing number of smaller design boutiques and art galleries are also setting up shop nearby.

Chapter 6

THE TURQUOISE COAST

6

Updated by
Paul Osterlund

👁 **Sights**
★★★★★

🍴 **Restaurants**
★★★★☆

🛏 **Hotels**
★★★★★

🛍 **Shopping**
★★★☆☆

🍸 **Nightlife**
★★★★☆

WELCOME TO
THE TURQUOISE COAST

TOP REASONS TO GO

★ **Relax on beaches:** Some of the Mediterranean's most blissful beaches are here; lie on your sun bed or dive in from a floating platform.

★ **Sleep in one-of-a-kind lodgings:** Bed down in an Ottoman mansion-turned-hotel on the Datça Peninsula, an old stone house in the winding streets of Antalya's Kaleiçi, or a beachside cabin in Çıralı.

★ **See spectacular ruins:** Explore remains of ancient cities—from mountaintop Termessos and overgrown Olympos to the extraordinarily intact Roman theater at Aspendos.

★ **Take a Blue Cruise:** Sail away on your own chartered yacht, perhaps dropping anchor en route to take a swim or catch a fish for dinner.

★ **Trek the Lycian Way:** Choose a one-day or multiday hike along the legendary trail that runs parallel to much of the Turquoise Coast.

The area known as the Turquoise Coast extends along the Mediterranean from the wild Datça Peninsula on Turkey's southwestern tip to the resort hotels springing up along the Antalya-Alanya strip. The fir-clad mountains rising behind the water are dotted with the ruins of splendid ancient cities, through which passed the likes of Alexander the Great, Julius Caesar, and St. Paul.

1 **Datça**

2 **Eski Datça and Reşadiye**

3 **Knidos**

4 **Marmaris**

5 **Dalyan**

6 **Göcek**

7 **Fethiye**

8 **Kayaköy**

9 **Ölüdeniz**

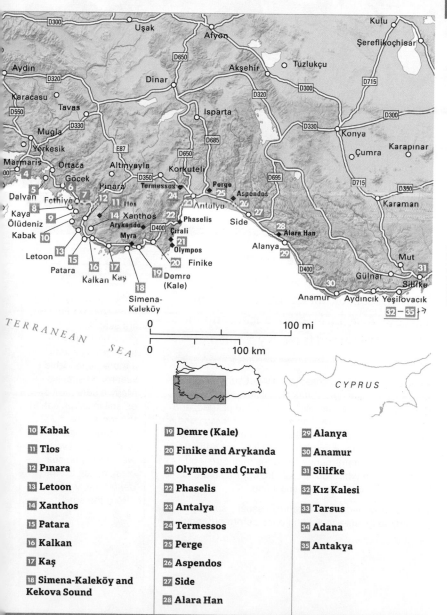

10 Kabak	19 Demre (Kale)	29 Alanya
11 Tlos	20 Finike and Arykanda	30 Anamur
12 Pınara	21 Olympos and Çıralı	31 Silifke
13 Letoon	22 Phaselis	32 Kız Kalesi
14 Xanthos	23 Antalya	33 Tarsus
15 Patara	24 Termessos	34 Adana
16 Kalkan	25 Perge	35 Antakya
17 Kaş	26 Aspendos	
18 Simena-Kaleköy and Kekova Sound	27 Side	
	28 Alara Han	

SEAFOOD ON THE TURKISH COAST

The kebab might be the first thing that comes to mind when you think about Turkish food, but in Istanbul and along Turkey's Aegean, Mediterranean, and Black seas, fresh seafood is readily available.

Considering the long coastline, it's not surprising that fish is an integral part of Turkish cuisine, and locals eat it at lunch or dinner, usually either grilled or fried, and served with little more than a squeeze of lemon and a side of fresh arugula or slices of raw onion. In winter, hearty fish soups—similar to chowder—are added to many restaurant menus. Varieties might be a bit different from what you're used to, but these are some of the more common ones you'll find.

Fresh fish served in restaurants is usually sold by weight, so be sure to ask the price before ordering.

WILD VS. FARMED

Although many of the fish served in Turkey are seasonal, the growth of aquaculture here has led to a more dependable year-round supply. Many diners, however, still insist on eating the more flavorful (and more expensive) wild variety. If you want the open-sea version, ask for the *deniz* type, which is "from the sea."

BARBUNYA

The tasty small red mullet is a top choice in Turkey. As the name implies, its skin is speckled with glistening reddish spots. Mild-tasting *barbunya*, usually only a few inches long, are typically panfried whole; an order can easily be shared. The prime season for them is spring through early summer.

ÇIPURA

Gilt-head bream is the most popular fish caught in the Aegean area. Like *levrek,* it's mild tasting with white, flaky meat, usually grilled whole and served unadorned. Fish farms now supply much of the *çipura* sold in restaurants, but the wild variety, known as *deniz çipurasi* is also available.

HAMSI

The finger-length anchovy is often referred to in Turkey as the "little prince" of fishes. In the Black Sea area, where *hamsi* are caught, they are used in numerous dishes and form an important part of the local economy. Hamsi typically comes fried in a light coating of cornmeal, but hamsi *pilav*—a rice-and-anchovy dish infused with an aromatic mix of herbs and spices—is also common. Hamsi season is fall and winter.

LEVREK

Sea bass, one of the most popular types of fish in Turkey, is prized for its delicate, almost sweet taste and firm white meat. Levrek is usually charcoal grilled whole and served with a drizzle of oil and a squeeze of lemon. Or a whole levrek might be encased in sea salt and baked in the oven. Many eateries serve the cheaper, smaller, farmed variety. Wild levrek is called *deniz levreği.* Both are available all year.

LÜFER

This is the general name for bluefish, which are generally tastier than the U.S. varieties. Bluefish is common enough that the different sizes have their own names: small bluefish are *çinekop,* large bluefish are *kofana,* and medium bluefish are *sarıkanat.*

PALAMUT

Also known as bonito, *palamut* is related to tuna. Unlike levrek and çipura, it's a strong-tasting, oily fish, similar to mackerel. Palamut fillets are often grilled, but another popular—and perhaps tastier—way they are prepared is baked in the oven with an onion and tomato sauce. Palamut appear in Turkish waters fall through winter.

The Turquoise Coast is just as stunning as its name suggests. Luminous blue waves in that signature shade (the word "turquoise" actually comes from the French for "Turkish") lap at isolated coves and some of the country's most iconic beaches—including Ölüdeniz, Patara, and İztuzu. Since the region has been inhabited for millennia, spectacular archaeological ruins of Greek, Roman, and Byzantine origin are never far away. Termessos is said to have defied Alexander the Great because he was daunted by its height, and the antique theater in Aspendos rivals the Colosseum in Rome.

To the northwest is the Datça Peninsula, a Mediterranean landscape of rolling hills, with almond and olive trees looking out on a sea dotted with Greek islands. East of Marmaris, a more-touristy town, you'll find the Lycian coast with its rich mix of ruins and camera-ready beaches. Each Lycian coast destination has a distinct feel: crowded Ölüdeniz with its lovely lagoon; laid-back, alternative Kabak; low-key Patara; upscale, ex-pat haven Kalkan; lively Kaş; and the green and relaxed Olympos area. Antalya, the biggest city on this stretch, has long beaches lined with resorts and an often tourist-free historic center, Kaleiçi,

filled with historic mansions (many now converted into boutique hotels). Antalya also has the coast's best museum and archaeological sites, Aspendos among them. East of the resort towns of Side and Alanya, the region becomes rugged, tourists rare, and prices much lower. Ruins, castles, and beaches remain plentiful, however, and the taste of "real Turkey" becomes more pronounced.

MAJOR REGIONS

Chartering a yacht in Marmaris or Bodrum is the best way to view the craggy hills and sublime coves of **The Datça Peninsula** From Datça to Eski Datça and Reşadiye to Knidos to Marmara, it's one of Turkey's most unspoiled stretches of shoreline.

To explore **The Lycian Coast,** rent a car and take time to explore the charming ports, quiet beaches, and ancient ruins along this less developed coastal circuit, including Dalyan, Göcek, Fethiye, Kayaköy, Ölüdeniz, Kabak, Tlos, Pınara, Letoon, Xanthos, Patara, Kalkan, Kaş, Simena-Kaleköy and Kekova Sound, Demre (Kale), Finike and Arykanda, Olympos and Çıralı, and Phaselis.

Vibrant **Pamphylia** has everything—an old city, beaches, eateries, nightlife—plus it's a good base for visiting Antalya and the age-old sites of Termessos, Perge, Side, and Alara Han, and the resort town Alanya.

East of Alanya, leave the tour buses behind on a road trip that takes you to uncrowded towns and off-the-beaten-path ruins all the way to Anamur, Silifke, Kız Kalesi, Tarsus, Adana, and the old city of Antioch (now Antakya).

Planning

WHEN TO GO
The ideal months for trips to the Turquoise Coast are May, June, September, and October. Summers can be hot and humid, especially in July and August; that's also when beaches tend to be busiest and the waterfront discos pump out their most egregious levels of noise. Alanya and Side—which stay warmest longest—are best visited before or after the high season, when charter tourists are least likely to be about.

Along the Lycian coast, expect thunderstorms after late October and an average 12 days of rain per month in December and January; otherwise, while not swimsuit weather, it can be sunny enough for T-shirts. Snow graces mountain peaks well into May, a magnificent sight from towns like Antalya

and Fethiye. Although not a winter sun destination, it rarely drops below freezing on the coast. Some hotels stay open between mid-December and March, often with limited facilities.

PLANNING YOUR TIME
If you just have a weekend or so to spend on the Turquoise Coast and want to see historic sites, base yourself in Antalya's Kaleiçi section and drive out to nearby Termessos, Olympos, or Aspendos; they're some of the best preserved classical ruins in the country.

The Lycian coast is beautiful and filled with the remains of ancient cities like Xanthos, Patara, and Olympos. Motorists should count on about 10 hours of driving in total, starting in either Antalya or Dalaman. There are many unspoiled towns and lovely hotels en route. You could spend as few as three days here, but five to seven would be more relaxing and allow for some beach time. On a sample six-day tour you could spend the morning in Kaleiçi, then drive up to Termessos and cross the mountains to Fethiye, overnighting around Ölüdeniz. On Day 2, visit the gorgeous lagoon at Ölüdeniz, the ghost town of Kaya, or the pine-fringed beach at Kabak, returning to the same hotel as the previous night. On Day 3, visit the Lycian city of Tlos, then explore the Saklıkent canyon, Xanthos, and Letoon; cap the day with a swim in Patara before checking into a hotel in Patara, Kalkan, or Kaş. On Day 4, take an excursion boat from Kaş to Kekova, and return to Kaş for the night. On Day 5, visit St. Nicholas Basilica in Demre, have lunch in Finike, and visit Arykanda in the afternoon, overnighting in Çıralı so that you can see the burning Chimera. On Day 6, visit Olympos in the morning and and Phaselis on the drive back to Antalya.

GETTING HERE AND AROUND

AIR TRAVEL

It makes sense to fly to the Turquoise Coast if you're coming from Istanbul or elsewhere in Turkey. The main airports here are in Dalaman and Antalya. Antalya has one of the country's busiest international airports, serving the coast from Alanya to Kaş, including Side, Olympos, and Finike. Dalaman Airport is more convenient to the stretch between Kaş and Datça, including Kalkan, Fethiye, Göcek, Dalyan, and Marmaris. There are also airports in Adana and Antakya. Turkish Airlines frequently flies to all these airports, as do budget carriers like Pegasus.

Car rental concessions operate at all airports, and all international agencies are represented. Havaş airport buses also link the two largest airports to major towns. Many hotels and travel agencies will arrange airport shuttles as well (usually for a fee). Yellow airport taxis are pricier for individuals (though still cheap by Western standards), but are usually well regulated, with a clear legal pricing system prominently displayed; these are an especially good option if you're sharing.

Taking a bus from Antalya airport into Antalya costs about 12 TL; they're timed to meet all arriving flights and leave the city center hourly. You can catch a 45-minute Havaş bus to the airport from the 5M Migros AVM (a shopping center) on Atatürk Boulevard, about 3 miles from Kaleiçi, or take the Antray public tram from just outside Kaleiçi directly to the airport. A taxi to the airport from Kaleiçi, by comparison, costs about 70 TL, but is well worth the convenience if you can afford it.

From Dalaman Airport, airport buses will take airline passengers east via Göcek to the Fethiye intercity bus terminal (17.5 TL and takes about an hour) and west to the Marmaris intercity bus terminal (20 TL, about 90 minutes). Theoretically, the buses leave Marmaris 3 hours before any flight and Fethiye 2½ hours before. For more exact information, call the Havaş airport bus company.

CONTACTS Havaş. ☎ 850/222–0487 central Turkey call center ⊕ www.havas.net.

BOAT AND FERRY TRAVEL

A car ferry (just under two hours) links Bodrum with Datça's Körmen port—it is several kilometers on the other side of the peninsula, but a shuttle meets the ferry. From mid-June through October, the Bodrum–Datça boats run from both ports one to four times a day. In winter, schedules are reduced, so always check ahead of time. If you're taking a car along, make sure to reserve in advance. Datça, Marmaris, Fethiye, and Kaş have regular Greek Island departures, but only to the islands closest to each. Private boat rentals are available in all the major harbors, but prepare to spend hundreds of euros to rent one. In summer, a public ferry runs three times daily between Antalya's Kaleiçi yacht harbor and the nearby city of Kemer.

CONTACTS Antalya Deniz Otobüsleri. ⊹ On the right-hand side of the yacht harbor, Kaleiçi ☎ 242/244–4145 **Bodrum Ferryboat Association.** ☎ 252/316–0882 ⊕ www.bodrumferryboat.com/en. **Yeşil Marmaris.** ☎ 252/413–2323 ⊕ www.yesilmarmarislines.com.

BUS AND DOLMUŞ TRAVEL

Inexpensive intercity buses travel between major towns all over Turkey—it's about 110 TL one way for the 12-hour journey from Istanbul to Antalya. These days, though, that's only about half the price of flying.

Buses and minibuses (dolmuşes) run regularly between the main Turquoise Coast cities but rarely travel to remote archaeological sites, such as Tlos and Pinara. Every city has a bus terminal, and minibuses to smaller destinations usually set off from there, too. Major routes, such as Marmaris to Fethiye and

Fethiye to Antalya, have hourly buses into the early evening; fares are typically about 24 TL per person for every 100 km (62 miles) traveled. Minibus schedules depend on the popularity of the route and these buses generally stop anywhere along the route if asked to; announce "İnecek var," which translates to "there's someone who will get off," to let the driver know you've reached your stop. Most buses are designed to take people from the villages into the city rather than the other way around.

When the intercity bus terminal is outside the city center (as in Antalya), major companies usually provide a free minibus service from their downtown locations to the station: ask for a *servis* (minibus transfer service) when you book your ticket—otherwise, finding your own way to the terminal can be difficult and time-consuming. ■TIP→ Book bus tickets online yourself, or ask your hotel concierge for help. Unscrupulous tour agencies have been known to charge double the going rate to do in person or over the phone what you could do yourself.

CAR TRAVEL
Once here, you'll find renting a car allows you to get around with the most ease; many of the sights you'll want to see are off the main roads, and the area is filled with beautiful coastal drives.

Although the highways between towns are well maintained, smaller roads can be unpaved and rough, and the twisty coastal roads require concentration. To estimate driving times, figure on about 70 km (43 miles) per hour. Driving from Istanbul to Marmaris or Antalya is at least a 10-hour, 750-km (470-mile) trek. The speed limit is 90 kph (56 mph) on most country roads—120 kph (75 mph) on real highways—and for your own safety it's best to stick to it. The police have radar devices and they do use them.

All airports have several car rental agencies to choose from; many hotels can also arrange rentals. In general, the smaller and more remote the place, the cheaper the rental, but the more minimal the service.

CRUISE TRAVEL
A relaxing yacht charter in a *gulet*, a wooden motorboat or sailing boat, is the quintessential way to explore Turkey's coast on a so-called "blue cruise." For the full experience, plan a trip lasting at least four days or ideally a week, perhaps from Antalya to Fethiye, or along the Datça Peninsula from Marmaris. *For more information, see the Blue Cruising Close Up in this chapter.*

TAXI TRAVEL
Provincial taxis are somewhat expensive; fares generally work out to about 4 TL for every 1 km (½ mile) traveled. It's best to take a taxi from an established taxi stand, where you see several lined up, since the drivers there will be regulars and if you should have a dispute or lose something, it is much easier to retrace the car. It's normal, however, to hail taxis in the street. For longer journeys, you may wish to settle a price in advance, but within city limits, the taxi driver should automatically switch on the meter when you get in. As elsewhere, if he doesn't, insist upon it.

HOTELS
Swaths of this coveted coast have long been dominated by large, identical resorts inhabited by European package tourists often more interested in the beaches than the country. The fancier resorts range from the eccentrically over-the-top (revolving bedrooms, hotels shaped like the Kremlin and Topkapi Palace, etc.) to the tranquilly luxurious. The best have excellent facilities, and you can often find good deals if you want to add a few relaxing sun-and-sand days to your itinerary. There's also a tradition of simple family-run *pansiyons*; though basic in terms of amenities, these can

provide a more personal experience, better value, and a pleasant refuge from mass tourism. In recent years, a number of stylish smaller hotels have also appeared. These century-old houses have been restored and converted into high-caliber boutique hotels that offer the ultimate in character and charm. Most are found in Antalya's Kaleiçi neighborhood, where they come in a variety of sizes and prices; there are also several in Eski Datça and Alanya as well as farther east. *Hotel reviews have been shortened. For full information, visit Fodors.com.*

What it Costs in Turkish Lira

$	$$	$$$	$$$$
RESTAURANTS			
Under 15 TL	16 TL– 30 TL	31 TL– 50 TL	over 50 TL
HOTELS			
Under 150 TL	151– 300 TL	301– 500 TL	over 500 TL

RESTAURANTS

This coast has been serving tourists for a long time, and you will find a rich choice of restaurants to prove this. There's no shortage of older, established eateries, which dish out the standard national fare (think mezes, kebabs, assorted grilled meats, and fresh seafood). Simple—but often superb—spots are as popular with vacationing Turks as they are with foreigners. In recent years, the number of fine dining options has also increased, especially in larger cities and tourist centers. The top ones prepare creative dishes, combining high-quality local ingredients with international flair.

Regional specialties along the Turquoise Coast include mussels stuffed with rice, pine nuts, and currants; *ahtapot salatası,* a cold octopus salad, tossed in olive oil, vinegar, and parsley; and grilled fish. Most of Turkey's tomatoes, cucumbers, eggplants, zucchinis, and peppers are grown along the coast, so salads are fresh and delicious. In Lycia, a local home-cooking specialty is stewed eggplant with basil—wonderful if you're offered it. *Semiz otu* (purslane) is a refreshing appetizer in a garlic yogurt sauce.

TOURS

Trekking opportunities abound in this part of Turkey. For serious walkers, the 540-km (335-mile) Lycian Way is the standing challenge; it's a 29-day walk from end to end. There's also the Carian Trail, which opened in 2013 and covers the country's southwest corner, known to the ancients as Caria. As more trekkers discover the gorgeous Lycian Way, many tour agencies have begun to offer packages, many including rafting trips as well. The country's main rafting areas are around Fethiye and Ölüdeniz, in Köprülü National Park near Antalya, and along Alanya's Dimçay River. You'll pass through soaring canyons and under Roman bridges.

Bougainville Travel
ADVENTURE TOURS | A well-established agency in Kas, Bougainville specializes in adventure tourism (canyoning, paragliding, sea kayaking, trekking, mountain biking, and scuba diving) and Lycian Way trips. ⊠ *Kas* ☎ *242/836–3737* ⊕ *www.bougainville-turkey.com.*

★ Culture Routes Society
SPECIAL-INTEREST TOURS | Founded in 2012 by Kate Clow, creator of the Lycian Way, and run by some of Turkey's preeminent historians (and walkers), the Culture Routes Society protects, creates, and promotes culture routes—including the Lycian Way, Carian Trail, Evliya Çelebi Way, and many others—suitable for walking, horseback riding, and/or biking. If you're considering such a trek, their website is the most reliable online source for up-to-date information. They also organize regular guided tours along a variety of these spectacular trails. ⊠ *1297 Sk. No. 14, Antalya* ☎ *532/604–4487* ⊕ *www.cultureroutesinturkey.com.*

Middle Earth Travel

ADVENTURE TOURS | Though its headquarters are in faraway Cappadocia, Middle Earth Travel was one of the first tour agencies to organize Lycian Trail walks back in 2001. They still offer a variety of outdoor activities along the Turquoise Coast, including trekking, sailing, mountaineering, and camping. Their sister company **Biking in Turkey** (⊕ www.bikinginturkey.com) will help you organize long-distance coastal bicycle trips. ⊠ Göreme ☎ 384/271–2559 ⊕ www.middleearthtravel.com.

Mithra Travel

ADVENTURE TOURS | A popular choice since 1991 (especially with British and Dutch travelers), Mithra Travel organizes a variety of self-guided treks and easy walks along the Lycian Way and St. Paul Trail, including trekking in the Köprülü Canyon and archaeological, nature, cycling, and adventure tours near Antalya and throughout Lycia. ⊠ Antalya ☎ 242/248–7747 ⊕ www.mithratravel.com.

Pulse Tourism

ADVENTURE TOURS | **FAMILY** | This adventure tourism agency in central Kaş organizes a variety of outdoor day tours through the region's rugged terrain, with options for sea-kayaking, climbing, trekking, paragliding, diving, and mountain biking, as well as excursions to Saklikent Canyon. ⊠ Kas ☎ 242/836–3560 ⊕ www.pulsotourism.com.

Seven Capes

ADVENTURE TOURS | Run by friendly husband and wife Dean and Ayşe, Seven Capes is based in Kaş, where Ayşe offers traditional Turkish cookery workshops in her outdoor mountain kitchen, and Dean organizes paddleboarding excursions and a variety of walking tours including the Lycian Way, the Carian Trail, and the Bozburun Peninsula. They also organize sea kayaking trips along the gorgeous coastline of the Fethiye-Ölüdeniz area several days a week. ⊠ Kas ☎ 537/403–3779 ⊕ www.sevencapes.com ⊕ www.culinarykas.com.

Southwest Turkey Tours

ADVENTURE TOURS | Run by an English-speaking local archaeologist, Southwest Turkey Tours blend exceptionally well-informed sightseeing with hiking and/or sea kayaking, and can organize self-guided walking tours on the Lycian Way or Carian Trail. They also operate more archaeologically focused three-day tours: "Carian Treasures" (Köyceğiz to Bodrum, including a boat trip and turtle watching) and "Lycian Quest" (Arykanda to Tlos, with a boat trip at Kekova). ⊠ Antalya ☎ 530/468–0327 ⊕ www.swturkey.com/index.php/en.

Datça

76 km (47 miles) west of Marmaris; 167 km (104 miles) west of Dalaman on Rte. 400.

If you make it all the way to the Datça Peninsula, you may never want to leave the rugged landscape of dark olive and pale green almond trees, scrubby hills, pine forests in sheltered hollows, and stunning blue waters. Until about 20 years ago, this was one of the most inaccessible parts of Turkey, and driving along the thin neck of land between the Aegean Sea to the north and the Mediterranean to the south still feels like entering the gateway to another, older world. This is not somewhere to drop by for just a day or two: ideally, you'll have at least three days to savor the uncluttered joys of this unique destination. Far from the world of tour buses, it's a place with few pressures but with wide horizons and more than 50 little beaches for inner contemplation. The best time to visit is in spring, when the hills are carpeted in poppies, daisies, and wildflowers, and restaurants offer dishes concocted with wild thyme, rosemary, and other herbs that flourish in the hills and by the sea; in autumn, you can watch the locals harvest olives.

Datça is a small, easily walkable port with some characteristics of a larger resort. It's one of the most relaxed towns along

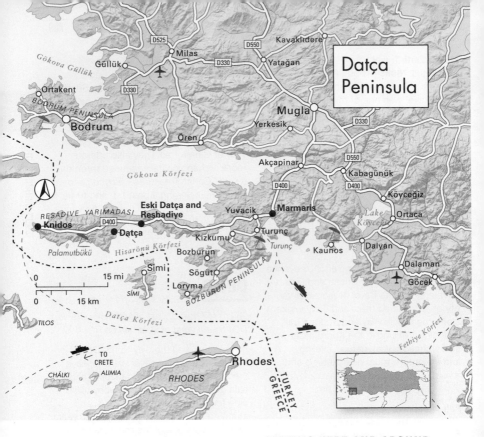

Datça
Peninsula

the whole coast. Nearby Eski Datça and Reşadiye with their timeless stone alleys are older with more personality, but no beaches. Even if you don't stay in Datça, spend an evening wandering around the harbor and sipping a drink at one of the quayside cafés. The weekly Saturday market sprawls up a long street near the harbor with its colorful parade of local produce, herbs, snacks, clothes, and housewares, all of which attract Greek islanders from nearby Symi. It's also the best place to arrange a boat trip to Knidos, whose ancient ruins constitute one of the loveliest and most evocative sites along the whole coast. A lovely day out and a meal at an unspoiled beach can also be had at Kargı Koyu, 3 km (2 miles) south of central Datça.

GETTING HERE AND AROUND

There are two ways to get to Datça: either fly to Dalaman Airport and make the three-hour drive west or, more pleasantly, fly to Bodrum Airport and then take a two-hour car-ferry ride from Bodrum to Datça's Körmen port. In the June–September season, boats run from both ports at 9 am and 5 pm. In winter they run only on Monday, Wednesday, and Friday at 9 am from Datça to Bodrum and at 5 pm from Bodrum to Datça. Regular buses go to Marmaris from the Pamukkale office in town, and in summer dolmuşes to Yazıköy continue to Knidos.
■ TIP→ Be aware that this is a small town, and boats don't necessarily run every day, even in summer.

Beaches

★ Ovabükü Plajl

BEACH—SIGHT | This quiet beach on the quiet Datça peninsula is the region's best and feels like an escape from it all. The rolling landscape of pine-crowned hills and olive groves gives way to the deep blue waters of the Aegean Sea. **Amenities:** Food and drink, parking (free). **Best for:** solitude, swimming, walking. ✉ *Datça* ✥ *20.4 km (12.6 miles) southwest of Datça.*

Restaurants

Culinarium

$$$ | TURKISH | On a terrace overlooking the harbor, this upscale, though expensive, option blends European style, atmosphere, and creativity with indigenous ingredients and flavors. The result is a refined low-key environment, with well-made food that provides an interesting variation on typical Turkish cuisine like zucchini flowers stuffed with local fish instead of the usual rice. **Known for:** boneless fish in lemon butter; ravioli; steak. [$] *Average main: 80 TL* ✉ *İskele Mahallesi, 64. Sk. No:20, Datça* ☎ *252/712–9770* 🌐 *www.culinarium-datca.com.*

Emek Restaurant

$$ | SEAFOOD | Everything is made on the premises of this excellent eatery overlooking Datça Yacht Harbor, where the menu includes seafood, Turkish grills, and various curries. Owner and chief chef Seyyar Kantarlı says her secret is all fresh ingredients. **Known for:** fried squid; grilled octopus; stuffed zucchini flowers. [$] *Average main: 40 TL* ✉ *Atatürk Cad., Datça* ✥ *1 street back from the western side of the yacht harbor* ☎ *252/712–3375.*

Yeşim Bar Restaurant

$ | TURKISH | FAMILY | One of only three buildings on the pleasant beach at Kargı Koyu, Yeşim has sun beds, umbrellas, and showers available all day for customers. A lawn out back, with trees shading the bar, makes a cool respite from the sun—especially with a glass of the fresh house lemonade. **Known for:** meze; pizza; çökertme kebabı (lamb kebab with yogurt). [$] *Average main: 30 TL* ✉ *İskele Mahallesi, Kargı Koyu, Datça* ✥ *Follow road south 3 km (2 miles) from Datça until you see the beach; it's the first building past parking lot* ☎ *252/712–8399* 🌐 *www.yesimbar.com.*

Hotels

★ Orcey Hotel

$$ | HOTEL | A delightful and stylish addition to the Datça lodging scene, this boutique hotel has its own postcard-worthy dock with lounge chairs, a small Blue Flag beach with gorgeous views, and a midsize pool; its bright, stylish rooms are spread out among a few buildings, including stone towers inspired by local windmills, with round beds inside. **Pros:** fabulous and overflowing local breakfast, complete with omelet chef; the dock is arguably the best spot in town for sunbathing and dining; helpful staff. **Cons:** not in the center of town; not all rooms have sea views; breakfast is by the pool, not the sea. [$] *Rooms from: 250 TL* ✉ *Iskele Mahallesi, 85. Sokak, No. 8, Datça* ☎ *252/712–9933* 🌐 *www.orceyhotel.com* 🛏 *45 rooms* 🍴 *Free Breakfast.*

Türk Evi

$$ | HOTEL | Built in the style of an Ottoman mansion and set in a pretty garden just south of the yacht harbor, this small boutique hotel is a relaxing place to stay **Pros:** comfortable and unpretentious; all rooms have balconies; excellent breakfast. **Cons:** rooms are on the small side; 15-minute walk or a short dolmuş ride to central Datça; no pool. [$] *Rooms from: 275 TL* ✉ *36 Sokak, No. 4, Iskele Mahallesi, Datça* ☎ *252/712–9212* 🌐 *www.datcaturkevi.com* 🕐 *Closed mid-Oct.–Apr.* 🛏 *8 rooms* 🍴 *Free Breakfast.*

★Villa Aşina

$$ | **HOTEL** | All rooms have a sea view at this pretty hotel that looks out over the Greek islands of Symi and Rhodes. **Pros:** lovely rooms; attentive host; the hotel is particularly proud of its food, which includes a hearty breakfast and free afternoon tea. **Cons:** a nine-minute drive south of Datça; no elevator; not right on the beach. [$] *Rooms from: 205 TL* ✉ *Datça* ✣ *From Datça harbor, head south along coast, following signs to Villa Aşina on left after large hill* ☎ *252/712–0443* 🌐 *www.villaasina.com* 🛏 *17 rooms* 🍴 *Free Breakfast.*

Villa Tokur

$$ | **HOTEL** | This family-run boutique hotel is a five-minute walk from the yacht harbor and its small but bright rooms all have large balconies overlooking either the garden or the water. **Pros:** good value; tranquil country location; very well run (co-owner Carina speaks excellent English). **Cons:** not in the center of town; furnishings are nice, but simple; steep hill on walk to hotel. [$] *Rooms from: 260 TL* ✉ *31. Sokak, No. 1, Iskele Mahallesi, Koru Mevkii, Datça* ☎ *252/712–8728* 🌐 *www.hoteltokur.com* ⏲ *Closed Nov.–Mar.* 🛏 *15 rooms* 🍴 *No meals.*

Eski Datça and Reşadiye

3 km (2 miles) inland from Datça harbor on the road to Reşadiye.

Turkish satirical poet and polemical left-wing social critic Can Yücel retired to a modest old stone house in Eski Datça, setting an artistic tone for this pretty backwater spot and for nearby Reşadiye. The formerly Greek-populated village is one of the few in Turkey that has survived intact. Fine restoration efforts have produced several lovely small houses, which vacationers can rent. Nobody hurries through the stone-paved alleys, which are a perfect spot to browse boutiques for local handicrafts, from jewelry to fabrics to home decor.

GETTING HERE AND AROUND

Eski Datça and Reşadiye are both just off the main Datça–Marmaris road, 3 km (2 miles) and 4 km (2½ miles) respectively. There is a regular bus service between Datça and both towns.

🍴 Restaurants

Datça Sofrası

$$ | **TURKISH** | This is an ideal lunch spot, with a terrace shaded by lush bougainvillea and grapevines, and traditional Turkish braised meats cooking under a brass-hooded charcoal brazier. The menu is exceptionally vegetarian friendly, with 20 meatless dishes and starters, many concocted from local wild herbs. **Known for:** bademli köfte(meatballs with chopped local almonds); mastic pudding; homemade lemonade. [$] *Average main: 25 TL* ✉ *Hurma Sokak, No. 16, Eski Datça, Datça* ☎ *252/712–4188.*

Leyla Restaurant

$$$ | **MEDITERRANEAN** | Even if you don't stay at the Mehmet Ali Ağa Konağı Mansion, consider soaking up the ambience for an evening at its restaurant, which was previously called Elaki. The seating is right beside the hotel (effectively the courtyard) and as you'd expect in such a stellar location, the food is a gourmet's delight, the service five-star, and the prices enthusiastically high. **Known for:** lamb chops; octopus carpaccio; cold almond soup. [$] *Average main: 80 TL* ✉ *Mehmet Ali Ağa Konağı, Kavak Meydanı, No. 1, Reşadiye, Datça* ☎ *252/712–9257* 🌐 *www.kocaev.com.*

🛏 Hotels

Eski Datça Evleri

$$ | **B&B/INN** | **FAMILY** | Scattered throughout the village, the Eski Datça Evleri (or Old Datça Houses) is a collection of spacious apartments in three traditional-style

stone homes, each with its own shared garden and plenty of true Turkish charm. **Pros:** good if you want to be self-sufficient; quiet, tree-shaded location in the heart of Eski Datça; welcoming hosts. **Cons:** need to walk to main house for breakfast; not all houses have Wi-Fi; a short drive to the beach. [$] *Rooms from: 300 TL* ✉ *D1 Sokak 26, on right as you enter village, Eski Datça, Datça* ☎ *252/712–2129* 🌐 *www.eskidatcaevleri.com* 🛏 *8 rooms* 🍴 *Free Breakfast.*

★ Mehmet Ali Ağa Konağı

$$$ | HOTEL | A stay in this restored mansion offers the unique chance to experience the lifestyle and surroundings of a 19th-century Ottoman country noble, in an idyllic rural setting. **Pros:** absolutely beautiful, with remarkable historical details and furnishings; delicious food; a well-kept pool, and transport to a private beach. **Cons:** small "cupboard" bathrooms in the mansion; pricey; Wi-Fi access only in the restaurant. [$] *Rooms from: 470 TL* ✉ *Kavak Meydanı, No. 1, Reşadiye, Datça* ☎ *252/712–9257* 🌐 *www.kocaev.com* 🕓 *Closed Nov.–mid-Apr.* 🛏 *18 rooms* 🍴 *Free Breakfast.*

Olive Farm Guest House

$$$ | B&B/INN | Retreat to this green and tranquil farmhouse and its elegant, unpretentious cottages, each with its own garden patio; be sure to experience the delicious food served in the on-site restaurant Olea. **Pros:** delicious restaurant incorporating produce from the farm; hammam and steam room; lovely, rustic flower garden with pool. **Cons:** isolated location; a short drive from the beach; slow Wi-Fi in some rooms. [$] *Rooms from: 480 TL* ✉ *Olive Farm, Türkiye Güller Dağı Çiftliği, Reşadiye Mah. No. 30, Datça* ☎ *252/712–4151* 🌐 *www.guesthouse.olivefarm.com.tr* 🕓 *Closed Nov.–Apr.* 🛏 *13 rooms* 🍴 *Free Breakfast.*

Yağhane Pansiyon

$$ | B&B/INN | If you're eager for inner reflection, this comfortable stone-built hotel with a fine English lawn out front (once the local olive oil press) specializes in weeklong courses of yoga, art, meditation, and Ayurvedic treatments. **Pros:** peaceful; tranquil garden, where you can pick your own vegetables; welcoming and helpful atmosphere. **Cons:** "alternative" feel may not suit all tastes; the sea is a short car or public minibus ride away; rooms are very simple. [$] *Rooms from: 175 TL* ✉ *Yaghane Sok. 4, Eski Datça, Datça* ☎ *252/712–2287* 🌐 *www.datcayaghane.com* 🛏 *8 rooms* 🍴 *Free Breakfast.*

Knidos

38 km (24 miles) west of Datça.

Windswept Knidos sits on a headland at the very end of the Datça Peninsula, at the point where the Aegean meets the Mediterranean. A primitive archaeological site, its ruins are scattered amid olive groves and a few hints of modern civilization. There is a small restaurant by the jetty where the tour boats arrive.

GETTING HERE AND AROUND

Knidos is most romantic when reached by sea, and in summer boats leave regularly from Datça; the trip takes three hours each way, with swimming stops en route. By car, you can reach Knidos from Datça in 40 minutes over bumpy roads. Dolmuşes to Yazıköy go on to the ruins in summer.

👁 Sights

Knidos

ARCHAEOLOGICAL SITE | FAMILY | Although a Greek-speaking city called Knidos has existed on the Datça Peninsula since at least the 7th century BC, the Knidos at this site was founded circa 360 BC and prospered because of its excellent location on shipping routes between Egypt, Rhodes, Ephesus, the Greek mainland, and other major ports. Enter the archaeological site near the large *agora* (the marketplace) down by the water and continue up the hill on the ancient main street, with its views over the water and the modern lighthouse. Pass the **Temple of Apollo** and then reach the ruins of a circular temple, which many believe stands on the site of Knidos' famed **Temple of Aphrodite**. Knidos's two ancient harbors are below; the Mediterranean laps the southern (left-hand) harbor while the waters of the northern (right-hand) harbor belong to the Aegean. Knidos was abandoned in Byzantine times (around the 8th century AD), which is part of why the site has remained as romantically unspoiled as it was when travelers first sketched it in the early 1800s; the only denizens you're likely to encounter are grazing goats. ⊠ *Yazı Köyü, Tekirburun Mevkii, Datça* ✛ *35.4 km (22 miles) west of Datça* ☞ *12 TL.*

Palamutbükü Beach

BEACH—SIGHT | Just before Knidos, a road heads south past many fishing villages and leads to the tiny Palamutbükü Beach, a nice place to stop and take a dip in the sparkling blue (but sometimes chilly) waters. Behind the beach are a number of restaurants, each serving their own zone of pebbled beach. **Amenities:** food and drink; parking (free); showers; toilets. **Best for:** swimming; walking. ⊠ *Palamutbükü* ✛ *4 km (2½ miles) south of Yakaköy on the Datça-Knidos road, 20 km (12 miles) from Datça.*

Marmaris

91 km (56 miles) west of Dalaman Airport.

This big, brash resort city has two faces, and they're hard to reconcile. From the sea, a line of hotels stretches around the northern edge of a great bay, the whole encircled by a magical necklace of pine-clad mountains. Behind those same hotels, however, the city has been overwhelmed by boxy concrete development and streets lined with a hundred generically named eateries. An annual horde of European tourists descends on these workaday establishments, but for the international traveler, there is little about Marmaris that can't be savored elsewhere in Turkey. Although it is a pretty spot—the lengthy seafront promenade is a redeeming feature—there isn't much reason to linger unless you are meeting a yacht, traveling on to the Greek island of Rhodes, or perhaps snapping up an unbeatable deal at one of the top resorts, some of which are spectacular worlds unto themselves. Marmaris Bay is home to some of Turkey's biggest and busiest marinas, and is one of the main bases from which sailing yachts and wooden *gulets* can be chartered for Blue Cruises. There are a number of easy options for day trips to natural beauty spots like Sedir/Cleopatra Island, Lake Köyeceğiz, and the resort of Turunç.

GETTING HERE AND AROUND

A series of color-coded minibuses run from the center of town for about 3 TL: light green goes to the bus station, orange to Içmeler, and pink to the "yacht marina." A 60-minute catamaran service to the Greek island of Rhodes leaves Marmaris harbor every day at 9 am, returning at 4 pm, with a single or day return ticket costing €70. It's worth spending the night in Rhodes, since Greek island life typically grinds to a halt during the midday hours.

VISITOR INFORMATION
CONTACTS Marmaris Tourist Office. ⊠ *İskele Meydanı 41. Sk. No. 2, Barbaros Cad., Tepe Mahallesi* ☎ *252/412–1035.*

◉ Sights

İçmeler Beach
BEACH—SIGHT | FAMILY | Marmaris has its own crowded beach, but many prefer to take a water taxi or minibus to this cleaner, somewhat quieter beach in the

nearby resort town of İçmeler, 8 km (5 miles) down the coast, and backed by high, tree-covered mountains. Rent a beach chair amongst the palm trees for only 20 TL or nab a spot at one of the many beachfront bars and restaurants. **Amenities:** food and drink; parking; toilets. **Best for:** swimming; walking. ⊠ İçmeler Plajı.

Marmaris Castle and Archaeological Museum

MUSEUM | A modest, crenellated 16th-century citadel near the Netsel Marina, this building is an example of the few historic sites within Marmaris. First built by Süleyman the Magnificent, then shelled to bits by the French in the First World War, it was rebuilt in the 1980s. There is a small museum inside, with the usual smattering of ancient sarcophagi and pottery (all found locally), with a small ethnographic collection of local textiles, tools, and handicrafts. ⊠ Marmaris Kalesi ✛ Near the tourist office and the seafront promenade, just off Barbaros Cad. ☎ 252/412-1459 ⊠ 12 TL.

Seafront Promenade

PROMENADE | The city's best achievement is a 10-km (7-mile) seafront promenade that stretches all the way from the easternmost marina known as Netsel, past the old fortress, along the palm-lined main boulevard of town, and then out between the beach and the fancy hotels that line the coast, all the way west to the outlying resort of İçmeler. Along the way there are any number of cafés and bars at which to pause for refreshment or to take in fine views of sea and mountains. For 15 TL, you can ride back on one of the deniz taksi (shared water taxis) that run up and down the coast in season (usually April–November). ⊠ Marmaris.

★ Sedir Island (Cleopatra Island)

BEACH—SIGHT | **FAMILY** | Harboring one of the most perfect beaches in the world, Sedir (Cedar) Island, also known as Cleopatra Island, is about a 30-minute

drive north of Marmaris, and then a boat ride into the Gulf of Gökova. Its sand is made of tiny egg-shaped pearls of luminous white, making the water brilliantly clear as you swim before the impressive escarpments of Mt. Kavak. Sand like this can only be found in Egypt and Turkey, and local tour guides will tell you that the sand was brought here by Marc Antony for Cleopatra. Various Marmaris-based tour operators run day trips here; prices run around 85 TL a head. Alternatively, drive to Çamlık and catch one of the 15 TL "dolmuş boats" that shuttle back and forth to the island. The island also features easily accessible ruins of ancient walls and a Roman theater. **Amenities:** food and drink; showers; toilets. **Best for:** swimming; walking. ⊠ Sedir Adası ⊠ 30 TL.

Turunç

TOWN | This pleasant resort town is only about 19 km (12 miles) from Marmaris. Come for the bustling Monday market where you can browse a combination of local produce and trinkets or lounge on the free sun beds of the pretty Blue Flag beach. A water taxi will take you here from the Marmaris seafront promenade and for the seasick or cash-strapped, a 10 TL dolmuş also runs from central Marmaris. ⊠ Turunç ⊕ www.myturunc.com.

🍴 Restaurants

Some city blocks in Marmaris appear to be made up entirely of restaurants with a pavement-to-pavement profusion of tables and menus that seem like a catalog of world food. The most striking views can be had from cafés where the seafront promenade curves into the bay around the citadel, and these attract the tourists. Locals, however, prefer the slightly better-prepared food in restaurants that look out onto the Netsel yacht marina just to the east.

Blue Cruising

The most charming way to visit the Turquoise Coast, or the Aegean coast, is by taking a Blue Cruise aboard a *gulet*—a wooden motor yacht or sailboat. Since time has done remarkably little to spoil the crystal-clear waters, wooded inlets, and limpid lagoons, this will be one of the most unforgettable holidays you've ever had. Some organization is, however, necessary.

How much will it cost? *Gulets* come in all shapes and sizes, the majority with between 4 and 12 two-person cabins. To hire your own boat, prices work out to between 600 TL to 800 TL per person per day in July and August, about half that in April or October. Most charter on terms that cover everything but food and drink. After a discussion with the boat's cook, you and a member of the crew go to the local supermarket and load up. Cabin charters—when you join a group of strangers—are generally on an all-inclusive basis, and start at about 2000 TL per week.

When to go? May is pretty, uncrowded, and charters are cheap, but the water is cooler. June is warm and still not too busy. July and August are hotter, busier, and more expensive. September and early October are often perfect at sea, but the mountainsides are less green.

Other things to consider are how long you have and which port is closest to the sites you want to see. Fethiye is a major jumping-off point, as are Bodrum, Marmaris, and Göcek. Ideally, two weeks are needed to see the whole coast from Bodrum to Antalya, but most travelers only take one.

Look for a boat with a large area for relaxing in the stern and a good flat space on the foredeck for sleeping outside in hot weather. Don't accept anything too squashed: eight cabins in a boat under 80 feet are too many. If you're out in July and August, look for air-conditioning—and enough power-generation capacity for it. Ask about extras like windsurfers or kayaks.

The captain is important, too. Make sure you can communicate, and if you're arranging the cruise from abroad, insist on a telephone conversation before sending your deposit. Look for someone who listens to your wishes, and be wary if you are met with a patronizing "leave-it-all-to-me" attitude. If you want to sail rather than motor, you need to be doubly sure you have the right vessel. When you get to the boat, check the captain's license, insist on seeing life vests, and test emergency equipment like radios.

If you're hiring a boat after you've arrived in Turkey, you can walk down the quayside and haggle, but this can be risky in high season. Most people book months ahead. Look for operators registered with both the Turkish Association of Travel Agencies (TURSAB) and the Chamber of Shipping.

There are websites for individual boats and large agencies operating from major ports. For Marmaris, try ⊕ www.yesilmarmaris.com. Fethiye is popular, with ⊕ www.albatrosyachting.com, ⊕ www.compassyachting.com, or ⊕ www.alestayachting.com. Antalya is served by ⊕ www.olymposyachting.com.

Pineapple

$$ | ECLECTIC | FAMILY | This restaurant on the Netsel marina has a lot more style and dignity than you would guess from the name, and it's a great escape from the mass tourism of Marmaris. The house specialty is tender Anatolian oven-cooked lamb; however, the chef also prepares octopus, pasta, pizza, steak, Turkish grills, and divine desserts. **Known for:** oven-cooked lamb; grilled calamari; steak in mushroom sauce. $ Average main: 50 TL ⊠ Netsel Marina ☎ 252/412–0976 ⊕ www.pineapple.com.tr.

Yat Marina Restaurant

$$ | TURKISH | Far from Marmaris's madding crowds, this is where to go for a taste of international yachting life (even if the decor is a bit hokey). The chefs don't go for the omnibus menus common in town, preferring to concentrate their considerable talents on getting favorite Turkish dishes just right. **Known for:** steak; grilled sea bass; jumbo prawns. $ Average main: 40 TL ⊠ Adaköy, Yalancı Boğaz Mevkii ⬧ Follow coast road 8 km (5 miles) east out of Marmaris and park outside the marina gate ☎ 252/422–0022 ⊕ www.yachtmarin.com.

🛏 Hotels

D-Resort Grand Azur

$$$$ | RESORT | FAMILY | The sleek, curving profile of this international resort overlooks lush tropical gardens and is a 15-minute walk to the city's restaurants and bars; if you're going to stay in central Marmaris, this is the best you'll find. **Pros:** nice private beach area; gorgeous views; exceptionally large indoor and outdoor pools; lots of recreation options, including tennis, waterskiing, and sailing. **Cons:** average rooms for the amount they cost; rooms and general style a bit impersonal; crowded during peak season. $ Rooms from: 900 TL ⊠ Cumhuriyet Bulvarı, No.17 ☎ 252/417–4050 ⊕ www.dresort-grandazur.com 🛌 363 rooms ❖ Free Breakfast.

🍸 Nightlife

Marmaris comes alive at night with a wide selection of bars and dance clubs. European charter tourists practice the art of serious drinking on garish Bar Street (aka 39 Sokak) in the old town and its four solid blocks of drinking establishments. The major clubs here offer seething dance floors, and it's generally an opportunity for (often rather overpriced) excess.

For more of a beach scene, drive 15 minutes out of Marmaris to İçmeler Beach, where bars, restaurants, dance clubs, and karaoke joints are open through the night.

Back Garden Club

DANCE CLUBS | All pumping pop music and flashing lights, the largest open-air club on Bar Street is Back Street Garden, at its liveliest in the wee hours of the night. ⊠ Old Town, near the Netsel Marina, 39 Sokak ☎ 532/485–8239.

Dalyan

25 km (16 miles) west of Dalaman Airport on Rte. 400 and local roads.

Dalyan is a lovely place for a short break, especially if you prefer a quiet destination that's been developed in a way that is sensitive to the natural surroundings and the native flora and fauna. The town sits on the winding Dalyan River, between the great expanse of Lake Köyceğiz and the lovely beach of İztuzu. Its Carian tombs, which are carved into the cliff that rises behind the 15-foot-high reeds fringing the undeveloped west bank, make an especially fine sight when floodlit at night. Boats lined up along the quayside in the center of town will take you on expeditions to the beach, to sulfur baths, to the ruins of ancient Kaunos, and to the pretty bay of Ekincik. If your hotel is on the river, the boatmen will pick you up there, too. (Note that all boats are part

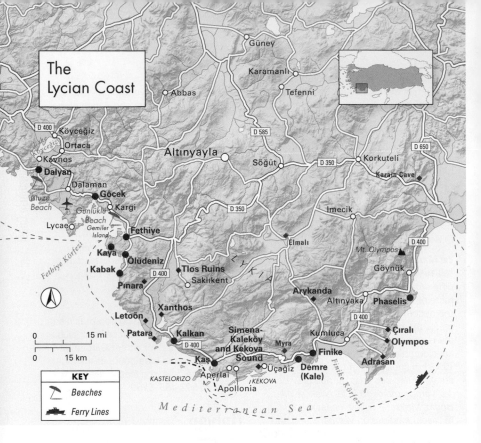

The Lycian Coast

of the Dalyan Kooperatifi; fares are regulated, so there is no bargaining unless many are idle.) Trekking and footpaths are developing fast, and include walks to Ekincik and elsewhere. Bird-watchers love the lake, where 180 species of bird have been logged. Local markets are also colorful: there's one in Dalyan on Saturday and one at the local center of Ortaca on Friday.

GETTING HERE AND AROUND
Dalyan is about 6 km (4 miles) southwest of the highway, and there are regular minibuses to the nearby town of Ortaca.

Sights

★ İztuzu Beach
BEACH—SIGHT | FAMILY | Unspoiled İztuzu Beach stretches for 8 km (5 miles), with the Mediterranean on one side and a

freshwater lagoon on the other. In June and July, *Caretta caretta* sea turtles lay their eggs here, which means that this is a conservation area and there are several rules in place so you don't disturb them; there's even a turtle hospital you can visit a short drive away. It gets crowded near the boat drop-off point, but walk a few hundred yards away and you'll have the beach to yourself. Regular boats and minibuses from Dalyan cost about 20 TL, so skip expensive tours or private rentals, unless you're venturing farther afield. Be aware that although you can catch the boat to the beach starting around 9:30 am, return trips don't begin until the early afternoon. **Amenities:** food and drink; parking; showers; toilets. **Best for:** swimming; walking. ⊠ *Dalyan ⊹ 12 km (8 miles) south of Dalyan.*

Kaunos

ARCHAEOLOGICAL SITE | Once a prosperous seaport (until silt from the river pushed the coast farther away), the ancient ruins at Kaunos date from the 4th century BC, and reflect a unique blend of Carian and Lycian influences. The site can be reached in 15 to 30 minutes by boat from Dalyan; alternately, you can find the *geçit* (a rowboat crossing) in the center of town, and then walk south for 30 minutes. Up from the ancient port is the agora, which has a restored fountain house and a ruined portico dotted with the foundation of statues. An old Roman street takes you up the hill, past the nice temple terrace, to a crumbling Byzantine basilica (look out for remains of black-and-white mosaics nearby), a massive Roman bath, and a well preserved semicircular theater that is cut into the hillside in the Greek style. There is a lovely, panoramic view of Iztuzu Beach from the ruined city walls. ⊠ *About 1 km (½ mile) southwest of Dalyan* 🖃 *12 TL.*

Lake Köyeceğiz

BODY OF WATER | **FAMILY** | An hour bus ride from Marmaris will take you to Lake Köyeceğiz and its refreshing, sulfurous mud baths. If you're staying in Dalyan, you'll find many tour companies at the riverside dock in the morning offering bird-watching or starlit boat trips to the tranquil lake, as well as trips to the bustling weekly market in the eponymous Köyceğiz village on Mondays.

🍴 Restaurants

Casa Nova

$$ | TURKISH | This pleasant open-air restaurant (formerly Dalyan La Vie), which occupies a prime spot on the river opposite the Lycian tombs, is one of the more upscale joints in town. There's a wide selection of appetizers and the usual array of Turkish mains, with lots of seafood as well as steak, chicken, and pasta. **Known for:** tenderloin steak; olivade sea bass; duck confit. 🖃 *Average*

main: *35 TL* ⊠ *Sağlık Sokak 5, Maraş Mahallesi* ☎ *252/284–5057* ⊕ *www. casanovadalyan.com.*

🏨 Hotels

Asur Hotel

$$ | HOTEL | With a large swimming pool and gardens overlooking the Dalyan River, this one-story property is a pretty upscale choice, yet a good value; accommodations are a mix of hotel rooms and apartment units with kitchens. **Pros:** complimentary bikes and boat trips to Iztuzu Beach; staff are friendly, helpful, and speak excellent English; wonderful views of the Lycian tombs. **Cons:** 1 km (½ mile) from center of town (10- to 15-minute walk); some stiff mattresses; some rooms on the small side. 🖃 *Rooms from: 300 TL* ⊠ *South edge of town, 116 Sok, No. 13 Ortaca* ☎ *252/284–3232* ⊕ *www.asurotel. com* 🕒 *Closed Nov.–Apr.* 🛏 *46 rooms* 🍴 *Breakfast.*

Dalyan Resort

$$$ | RESORT | This beautiful spot on a bend in the Dalyan River is a bit farther from the town center than most hotels, but is also more sophisticated. **Pros:** nice pool area; free Wi-Fi and shuttle boat to beach; friendly staff. **Cons:** upscale but not a lot of character; on the very edge of town; average breakfast. 🖃 *Rooms from: 470 TL* ⊠ *Kaunos Cad. 50* ☎ *252/284–5499* ⊕ *www.dalyanresort.com* 🛏 *100 rooms* 🍴 *Free Breakfast.*

★ Happy Caretta

$$ | B&B/INN | This modest, family-run hotel is in a shady garden on the banks of the Dalyan River, with breathtaking views of the ancient Lycian tombs from the large and comfortable riverside terrace, where you can enjoy a traditional breakfast or grilled fish supper in absolute tranquility. **Pros:** friendly service; nice dock area to swim with fish and the odd sea turtle; the best view of the iconic tombs in town. **Cons:** a bit hard to find;

rooms are very no-frills; no TV or mini-fridge in rooms. $ *Rooms from: 330 TL* ✉ *Kaunos Sokak, 26, Maraş District* ⚓ *Drive south down Dalyan River and look for signs to right* ☎ *252/284–2109* ⊕ *www.dalyanhappycaretta.com* ⤳ *14 rooms* ⦿ *Free Breakfast.*

Göcek

22 km (14 miles) east of Dalaman Airport on Rte. 400.

A 20-minute drive over the mountains from Dalaman Airport, Göcek is perfect for visitors who want to sample the grandeur of the Turquoise Coast but have little time to spare. This tranquil resort town offers gorgeous vistas of sea and mountains, easy access to the water, plus upmarket places to eat, sleep, and shop. Having avoided the excesses of package tourism and overdevelopment, it is focused on a pleasant, carless waterfront. Three marinas and an annual regatta make this a major center for Turkey's yachting world, and weekends see it awash with Istanbul *sosyete* (essentially the rich, frequently spoiled, and occasionally glamorous children of the upper classes). From Göcek, an hour's drive reaches the natural beauties of Dalyan, the sights around Fethiye/Ölüdeniz, or great Lycian sites like Tlos and Xanthos. There is only one private beach in Göcek itself, so hop on one of the several wooden tour boats that head out each morning to explore elsewhere. The best swimming and snorkeling are around the beaches or in the coves of the **Twelve Islands,** strung out like a necklace across the mouth of the bay.

Göcek is in prime Blue Cruise territory, so you can join a day cruise or rent a yacht or a *gulet* for as much time and money as you have to spare. The most popular anchorages include Tersane, Kapı Creek, Cleopatra's Bay, the obscure ruins at Lydae, Tomb Bay, or the lovely island of Katrancı.

GETTING HERE AND AROUND
The main highway passes immediately behind the town with exits to the east and west.

🍴 Restaurants

Can
$$ | SEAFOOD | This busy harborside fish restaurant is popular with Göcek natives and visitors alike and is considered a town institution. In summer, the seating extends out toward the waterfront, under tropical trees and with romantic views of the water. **Known for:** tuna with onion sauce and cheese; fish baked in salt; wild mountain mushrooms. $ *Average main: 45 TL* ✉ *Western edge of the Skopea Marina, across from the Migros store, Cumhuriyet Mahallesi* ☎ *252/645–1507* ☉ *Closed Dec.–Mar.*

Özcan
$$ | SEAFOOD | Cushioned bamboo chairs, an attentive waitstaff, and possibly the best grilled octopus you've ever tasted await you at Özcan, a fish restaurant on the wide esplanade that makes up Göcek's main public harbor. The wide range of starters includes unusual mushrooms from the mountains out back, fresh seaweed dishes, and squid in garlic, oil, and lemon. **Known for:** meze; garlic prawns; grilled red mullet. $ *Average main: 45 TL* ✉ *Middle of municipal yacht harbor, Cumhuriyet Mahallesi* ☎ *252/645–2593* ⊕ *www.ozcanrestaurantgocek.com.*

🛏 Hotels

The Bay Beach Club
$$$ | RESORT | FAMILY | This stylish resort right on gorgeous, secluded Günlüklü Beach is made up of wooden cabins under chestnut trees and offers all meals along with the room price. **Pros:** gorgeous waterfront cabins; lovely beach; very relaxing. **Cons:** isolated setting; limited dining options; expensive. $ *Rooms from: 1060 TL* ✉ *At Günlüklü Beach,*

Twelve islands are strung out across the mouth of Göcek Bay, offering excellent snorkeling and swimming.

Günlüklü Koyu ☎ 532/171–1215 🌐 www.thobaybeachclub.com 🕒 Closed Nov.–Mar. 🛏 47 cabins 🍴 Free Breakfast.

D-Resort Göcek

$$$$ | RESORT | FAMILY | This D-Resort outpost has a gorgeous private beach, and all the luxury and excellent service you'd expect from an international chain; that said, make sure you get one of the main floor rooms (attic ones have very low ceilings). **Pros:** central, but still secluded; stylish white-sand private beach; sleek facilities throughout. **Cons:** very pricey; rooms are pleasant but unexceptional, and many do not have views; beach a five-minute commute by buggy. [$] *Rooms from: 1560 TL ✉ Cumhuriyet District ☎ 252/661–0900 🌐 www.dresortgocek.com.tr 🕒 Closed Nov.–Apr 🛏 119 rooms 🍴 Free Breakfast.*

Hotel Forest Gate

$$ | HOTEL | This quiet cluster of white, two-story villas is a good base for exploring the area, but the 10-minute walk back from the main road is uneven and dark at night, making a car a good idea. **Pros:** friendly atmosphere; nice pool area; dinners are tasty and fresh. **Cons:** a bit out of the way; rather spartan furnishings; basic breakfast. [$] *Rooms from: 250 TL ✉ Boldibi Cad. No. 24, Cumhuriyet Mahallesi ☎ 252/645–2629 🌐 www.hotelforestgate.com 🛏 23 rooms 🍴 Free Breakfast.*

Villa DanLin

$$ | B&B/INN | On Göcek's main shopping street, this is a small hotel with rooms shielded from most noise, and an ideal location for access to the harbor, restaurants, and shops. **Pros:** central location near the harbor; family-run, with a friendly atmosphere; nice pool. **Cons:** rooms are nothing special; pool area is very nice but very small; some rooms on the small side. [$] *Rooms from: 250 TL ✉ Çarşı Içi ☎ 252/645–1521 🌐 www.villadanlin.com 🕒 Closed Oct.–May 🛏 13 rooms 🍴 Free Breakfast.*

Fethiye

50 km (31 miles) east of Dalaman Airport on Rte. 400.

This busy port city is a good base for exploring the ruins of ancient Lycia in the mountains that rise to the east. Fethiye was known in antiquity as Telmessos (not to be confused with Termessos, near Antalya) and was the principal port of Lycia from the Roman period onward. In front of the town hall is one of the finest of several tombs found throughout the city: it represents a two-story Lycian house, with reliefs of warriors on both sides of its lid.

The small original town was called Mekri and populated mainly by Greeks before the 1923 Greek-Turkish population exchange. It was renamed in 1934 for Fethi Bey, a famous Ottoman pilot. He was killed on the eve of the First World War when he crashed in the mountains of Lebanon while attempting a historic flight that was meant to link all the Middle Eastern provinces of the Ottoman Empire. Today's town is quite modern, having been substantially rebuilt after a 1957 earthquake. Strolling along the seafront promenade is pleasant, and scuba enthusiasts can choose between half a dozen dive boats that collect in the harbor. The harbor also has many yachts available for Blue Cruising. Fethiye is most fun on Tuesdays, when village folk flock in for the weekly market.

GETTING HERE AND AROUND

Fethiye's modern bus station is 1 km (½ mile) east of the center. Buses running east and west along the coast depart regularly, and several a day cross the mountains for Denizli and Pamukkale. Minibuses to Ölüdeniz, Göcek, Dalyan, and other nearby destinations leave from Akdeniz Caddesi, a few blocks west of the center; you may have to connect in Ortaca.

VISITOR INFORMATION

CONTACTS Fethiye Tourist Office ⊠ İskele Karşısı 1 (Fevzi Çakmak Cad. 9), Karagözler Mahallesi ☎ 252/614–1527.

👁 Sights

Ancient Theater of Telemessos (*Antik Tiyatro*)
ARCHAEOLOGICAL SITE | The main road around Fethiye's central harbor square also runs past the stage of the theater of Telmessos, a relatively recent chance rediscovery that gives a sense of history to the modern buildings all around. The rest of the ancient town remains under its urban tomb. The theater is undergoing long-term renovations and is closed to visitors for the time being. ⊠ *Fevzi Çakmak Cad., opposite the Yacht Habor.*

Fethiye Castle (*Fethiye Kalesi*)
ARCHAEOLOGICAL SITE | Along the crest of the hill overlooking the old town are the remains of the battlements of a castle; the foundations, which date back to antiquity, were later built up by the 12th-century crusaders, Knights of St. John (also known as the Knights Hospitaller), who also built the castle in Bodrum. It takes a good imagination to picture what a mighty fortress this must once have been. ⊠ *Kaya Cad.*

Fethiye Museum (*Fethiye Müzesi*)
MUSEUM | Fethiye has a relatively small but fairly modern museum with an excellent collection of artifacts from nearby sites, including sculptures from Tlos and the Fethiye theater, and stone sarcophagi. You'll also see the Letoon trilingual stela (a stone slab with Greek, Lycian, and Aramaic inscriptions), the mosaic from the Temple of Apollo, and a series of altars and stelae dedicated to the gods in thanks. Other displays include an interesting golden bowl with figures of bulls, a 19th-century Greek ship's figurehead, and an array of local handicrafts. ⊠ *Okul (505.) Sokak, just off Atatürk Cad.* ☎ *252/614–1150* 🎫 *Free.*

Continued on page 306

MEZE: MOUTHWATERING MORSELS

Prepare your taste buds for a Turkish culinary experience: tangy yogurt, pungent garlic, fresh herbs, smoky eggplant, marinated salads, and roasted vegetables await.

Whether you're sitting down for dinner along Turkey's coast, in one of Istanbul's historic neighborhoods, or somewhere in the untouristed southeast, your meal will almost certainly begin with meze—the assortment of small dishes that are the heart and soul of Turkish cuisine. Similar to the idea of tapas, meze are more than just a quick snack or an appetizer. For Turks, eating meze is often a meal in itself—a languorous repast made up of countless small plates and an ample supply of rakı, the anise-flavored liquor that is Turkey's national drink and the preferred accompaniment to meze.

Dolma

Eating meze is a centuries-old national tradition, influenced by Persian, Arab, and Greek cooking, and you'll find regional differences in what's offered. Dishes in the country's southeast have more of a Middle Eastern influence, while those in Istanbul and the Aegean area have more of a Greek flavor. What they have in common, though, is the Turkish belief that the meze experience is about more than eating and drinking—freewheeling conversation is an essential component. As one famous Turkish saying goes: "The best meze is good table talk."

WHAT'S ON THE MEZE MENU

A typical meze menu includes dozens of mostly meatless dishes, hot and cold, emphasizing freshness and seasonality. In Istanbul's *meyhanes*—rollicking, tavern-like restaurants that specialize in meze—servers arrive at your table with large trays piled high with small dishes. You choose whatever catches your eye.

Octopus salad

TASTES TO EXPECT

When it comes to meze, Turks tend to have a conservative palate. Meze meals, for example, often start with the simplest but most traditional dish of all—a piece of tangy feta cheese accompanied by a slice of sweet honeydew melon and a glass of rakı. Meze restaurants (with some notable exceptions) are not trying to outdo one another by inventing ever more creative dishes. Rather, they stick with tried and true meze that have become the classics of Turkish cooking. Here are some of the traditional meze you should be on the lookout for:

COLD (SOĞUK) MEZE

BAKLA EZMESİ—Dried fava beans that are cooked, mashed with garlic, olive oil, dill, and lemon juice, and turned into an earthy pâté.

BARBUNYA PİLAKİ—Barbunya beans (Roman or red beans), usually fresh from the pod, stewed in a garlicky tomato sauce.

ÇERKEZ TAVUĞU—A highlight of classical Turkish cooking, this dish consists of poached chicken that is ground with garlic and walnuts to make a deliciously enticing and flavorful dip.

DENİZ BÖRÜLCESİ—A wonderfully fresh-tasting dish made of samphire, a crunchy green that grows by the sea. It's cooked in olive oil and flavored with lemon juice.

ENGİNAR—Artichoke hearts stewed in olive oil with onion and carrot, served cold.

EZME—A salad of finely chopped tomatoes and onion, sometimes flavored with pleasantly astringent pomegranate molasses.

HAYDARİ—A dip made of thick and creamy strained yogurt, flavored with garlic and dill.

İMAM BAYILDI—Literally meaning "the imam swooned," this dish is one of Turkey's most famous: an eggplant is stuffed with onion, garlic, parsley, and tomato and stewed in olive oil.

KISIR—The Turkish version of tabbouleh, this is a tangy and somewhat spicy salad made out of bulgur wheat and red pepper paste.

LAKERDA—Turkey's take on lox, this is cured mackerel, sliced thick.

MİDYE DOLMASI—An Istanbul favorite sold by street vendors: mussels cooked with rice, pine nuts, currants, herbs, and spices and stuffed back into their shell.

PATLICAN SALATASI—An eggplant salad or dip, of which there are many variations (see the "Ubiquitous Eggplant" sidebar).

SEMİZOTU—When in season, purslane (a variety of green similar to watercress that's rich in vitamins and Omega-3 fatty acids) is mixed with yogurt to make a tangy salad.

YAPRAK SARMA—Grape leaves stuffed with rice, currants, and pine nuts.

ZEYTİNYAĞLI—Vegetables such as green beans and artichoke hearts that are stewed in olive oil and served cool or at room temperature. (Zeytinyağı, pronounced "zey-teen-yah," is the Turkish name for the oil.)

Kabaklı börek (filo pastries with zucchini).

THE UBIQUITOUS EGGPLANT

According to Turkish culinary lore, there are more than a thousand ways to cook eggplant (*patlican* in Turkish, pronounced "pat-li-jahn"). That may be an exaggeration, but you could certainly lose count of how many dishes feature the humble nightshade—it's even made into a jam! The vegetable certainly plays a starring role on the meze tray: cubes of fried eggplant come covered in a yogurt and tomato sauce; charcoal-roasted eggplant is turned into a smoky puree; and sun-dried eggplants are served stuffed with rice and herbs.

HOT (SICAK) MEZE

ARNAVUT CİĞERİ—Cubes of lamb's liver, fried with red pepper flakes.

BÖREK—Filo pastries, sometimes rolled up like cigars and stuffed with cheese, or layered over pastırma, which is spicy cured beef.

DOLMA OR SARMA—Stuffed grape leaves and other vegetables, such as peppers or cabbage, that are filled with a combination of rice, herbs, spices, and sometimes ground meat.

KALAMAR—Calamari rings batter-fried and served with an addictive sauce made of ground walnuts and garlic known as tarator.

KARİDES—Shrimp in a butter or tomato sauce, usually baked in a terra-cotta dish.

MÜCVER—Zucchini and herb fritters.

PAZI SARMA—Swiss chard stuffed with ground meat and rice, with yogurt on the side.

Fethiye Hammam

HOT SPRINGS | The 16th-century hammam is still in use and though it's a bit touristy, it is full of atmosphere, with 14 domes and six arches taking you back to the days of the old-fashioned Turkish bath. It's not the country's greatest spa experience, but it can be a fine way to scrub off the barnacles after a long voyage. They also offer facial, mani-pedis, and a popular rose oil massage. Feel free to wear your bathing suit, or use the *peştemal* (traditional hammam towel) they provide. ✉ *Hamam Sokak, No. 4, Paspatur* ☎ *252/614–9318* 🌐 *www.oldturkishbath.com* 🎟 *50 TL.*

★ **Lycian Rock Tombs** (*Amyntas Kaya Mezarları*)

ARCHAEOLOGICAL SITE | Sometimes called the "king's graveyard" (its Turkish name translates to such), these impressive ancient Lycian rock tombs are carved into the cliff that looms above town. These can be admired from a distance, but if you're keen to get a close look, follow the signs to Kaya Caddesi (literally "Rock Avenue") near the local bus station, and then climb the approximately 200 steps leading up to the rocks. Your effort will be well rewarded—particularly at dusk, when the cliffs take on a reddish glow. The largest and best-known is the Tomb of Amyntas, son of Hermepias (c. 350 BC), carved to resemble the facade of an Ionic temple, and presumably the burial place of a local ruler or nobleman. Inside are the slabs where corpses were laid out. ■ **TIP→ If you like Lycian tombs, but aren't keen to make the climb here, keep your eyes peeled for the ancient sarcophogi scattered throughout Fethiye.** ✉ *Follow the steps from Kaya Cad.* 🎟 *6 TL* ☞ *Be prepared for lots of stairs.*

🍴 Restaurants

Fethiye Fish Market

$$ | **SEAFOOD** | **FAMILY** | Those who are tempted by Turkey's fish markets but have nowhere to cook for themselves can head to Fethiye's lively local market area. For a small cover charge, several casual restaurants will cook your purchase, adding mezes and salads. **Known for:** grilled octopus; red snapper; mezes. [$] *Average main: 40 TL* ✉ *Just west of main market area, between Hükümet, Belediye, 96 and 97 Sts.*

Meğri Lokanta

$$ | **TURKISH** | **FAMILY** | The Meğris chain pretty much rules the restaurant market in Fethiye, but it's a well-deserved hierarchy because their food is consistently some of the best in town. This excellent, straightforward Turkish restaurant is on the western edge of the bazaar and favored by locals for its kebabs, *pide* Turkish pizza),and traditional casseroles. **Known for:** İskender kebap; pide; grilled sea bass. [$] *Average main: 35 TL* ✉ *Çarşı Cad., No. 30, Western edge of the bazaar* ☎ *252/614–4047* ⏲ *Closed Sun. in winter.*

Meğri Restaurant

$$ | **ECLECTIC** | **FAMILY** | In the center of the bazaar, the permanent part of this upscale restaurant has stone walls, high wood ceilings, and decorative kilims. In summer, most of the tables spill out into a large courtyard in the middle of the bazaar. **Known for:** arugula salad; lamb shish kebab; mushroom risotto. [$] *Average main: 35 TL* ✉ *40. Street (Türkocağı Str.), No. 10, Cumhuriyet Mahallesi* ☎ *252/614–4046* 🌐 *www.megrirestaurant.com.*

MOD Yacht Lounge

$$ | **INTERNATIONAL** | This glass-fronted, pleasingly modern café-restaurant on the harbor-front walkway has a chill nautical vibe and an unimpeded water view. In summer, dishes from its international menu can be enjoyed on the deck at tree-shaded tables. **Known for:** steak Parmesan; köfte (grilled meatballs); baked sea bass. [$] *Average main: 45 TL* ✉ *Ecesaray Marina, 1. Karagözler Mahallesi, Fevzi Çakmak Cad.* ☎ *252/614–3970* 🌐 *www.cafemod.net* ⏲ *Closed Dec.–Feb.*

Mozaik Bahçe

$$ | **TURKISH** | This restaurant in a backstreet garden, a stone's throw from the gauntlet of Fethiye's bazaar area, has been earning fans with its tranquil atmosphere and tasty dishes from eastern Turkey. Mains include *belen tava* (meat-and-vegetable casserole topped with cheese) and the Mozaik kebab with grilled chicken and lamb in a yogurt sauce. **Known for:** belen tava; Mozaik kebab; mixed grill. [$] *Average main: 35 TL* ✉ *Sokak 90/91* ✣ *Off Atatürk Cad., near the tour boat harbor* ☎ *252/614–4653* ⏲ *Closed Sun. and Nov.–May.*

Hotels

Ece Saray

$$$ | **HOTEL** | Part of the Ece Marina complex, this upscale option has a lovely location on the harbor front, meaning all of the large and tastefully decorated rooms have full sea views. **Pros:** right on the water; bright, large sea-view rooms with Ottoman-inspired decor; nice pool and recreation facilities. **Cons:** in need of some modernization; not in the center of town; sea but no beach. [$] *Rooms from: 400 TL* ✉ *Ece Marina, Karagözler* ☎ *252/612–5005* 🌐 *www.ecesaray.net* 🛏 *48 rooms* 🍴 *Free Breakfast.*

Villa Daffodil Hotel

$$ | **HOTEL** | If you're looking for a mid-size, mid-priced hotel, Villa Daffodil—on the quieter west end of Fethiye's waterfront—is comfy and pleasantly quirky, with a resident parrot and compelling photographs taken by the owner, a retired general. **Pros:** good value; nice rooms overlooking the water; friendly staff. **Cons:** a little out of town; some rooms are dark; the parrot is cute but ear-piercingly loud. [$] *Rooms from: 180 TL* ✉ *Fevzi Cakmak Cad. 139* ☎ *252/614–9595* 🌐 *www.villadaffodil.com* 🛏 *42 rooms* 🍴 *Free Breakfast.*

★ Yacht Classic

$$$ | **HOTEL** | Probably the best hotel east of the harbor, the medium-size Yacht Classic has been slowly moving upmarket with spacious and well-decorated rooms, though you need to ask for a sea view—most, but not all, rooms have one. **Pros:** luxurious waterfront pool area, complete with bar and beach; incredible design-oriented "water villas" for the utmost in luxury; many rooms have sea-view balconies, some with Jacuzzis. **Cons:** not in the center of town; international feel, without much local color; restaurant food is mediocre and quite pricey. [$] *Rooms from: 400 TL* ✉ *Karagözler Sokak, No. 24, just east of Ece Marinapro* ☎ *252/612–5067* 🌐 *www.yachtclassichotel.com* 🛏 *40 rooms* 🍴 *Free Breakfast.*

Nightlife

On weekends there are clubs off Hamam Caddesi in the center of Fethiye. Outside town, there is a strip of cheaper, less appealing hotels along Çaliş Beach that stretches west—this is where the package tours from northern Europe tend to stay and there are plenty of bars. It's a long way to go for a drink if you're staying in town, but the scene has an appeal for the younger crowd. During the week, nightclubs are busiest in Hisarönü, between Fethiye and Ölüdeniz.

Mango Bar

DANCE CLUBS | This small indoor dance club with live Turkish music some nights is a reliable favorite on Wednesday and weekend nights. Reservations are recommended. ✉ *45 Sok.* ☎ *252/614–4681.*

Activities

Boats and water taxis operating out of Fethiye offer a variety of tours to Göcek, the Twelve Islands, or Ölüdeniz. Itineraries are posted at the harbor, and there are generally people on hand to answer questions. Be sure to shop around, though, as packages vary widely, and some are essentially booze cruises. Standard boats, which charge about 50 TL per person with lunch, are large; smaller ones are generally worth the extra cost. If Ölüdeniz is your destination, be aware that windy weather can make for heavy waves. Most tours leave about 10 am, returning about 6 pm.

Kaya

10 km (7 miles) south of Fethiye; 6 km (4 miles) west of Ölüdeniz.

The valley behind Fethiye promises a cooler climate and evocative ruins that are decidedly different from their ancient counterparts on the Mediterranean coast. Levissi, as Kayaköy was then known, was a thriving Greek community until 1923, when the villagers were moved out in a compulsory population exchange that saw Greek Orthodox Christians living in Turkey evicted from their homes. Nowadays it's essentially an overgrown ghost town, with some charming settlements on the edges. Several hotels and open-air restaurants are scattered among the olive trees.

GETTING HERE AND AROUND

A dramatic, though potentially dangerous, route signposted from Fethiye runs directly over the hills, close to the Lycian tombs. An easier way to reach the village is to take the Ölüdeniz road as far as Hisarönü, and then make a right turn marked 3 km (2 miles) for Kaya. If you don't have a car or bike, there are regular dolmuşes from Fethiye.

Sights

Kayaköy

GHOST TOWN | Spread across three hills, the old Greek town of Levissi—called Kayaköy, or "stone village", by the Turks—is atmospheric and eerily quiet. It had a population of about 2,000 before residents of Greek origin were "sent home" to a motherland they had never known in 1923. Today you can wander through crumbling cube houses reminiscent of those in the Greek Islands, some with a touch of bright Mediterranean blue or red still visible on the walls. There are two large churches and many chapels, as well as several schools and a fountain house. From the chapel on the hill at the southwest corner, a path leads down to the remote beach of Cold Water Bay, a 30-minute walk. ✉ *Kaya* 🎟 *6 TL.*

Restaurants

Izela

$$ | INTERNATIONAL | FAMILY | Part of the Gunay's Garden villa complex, this tranquil spot in the far corner of Kayaköy village blends the best of Turkish and European cuisine, using homegrown ingredients as much as possible. There is a good range of largely organic starters; try the mixed meze plate to get a taste of everything. **Known for:** salmon in saffron sauce; baked aubergine; steak. [$] *Average main: 60 TL* ✉ *Gunay's Garden, Gumruk Sokak* ☎ *252/618–0073* 🌐 *www.gunaysgarden.com/izelaRestaurant.asp* 🕓 *Closed Nov.–Mar.*

★ Lebessos Wine House and Restaurant

$$$ | ECLECTIC | What was once the house of a prosperous Greek merchant is now a fine restaurant specializing in steak and an ultra-tender *lamb kleftiko* (lamb marinated in wine and slow-cooked in a 400-year-old oven). The wine cellar has more than 10,000 bottles, including a good selection of Turkish wines. **Known for:** steak; braised lamb; stuffed meatballs. [$] *Average main: 65 TL* ✉ *Kaya* ✣ *Near western ticket office* ☎ *536/484–7290* 🌐 *www.lebessos.com* 🕓 *Closed Mon. and Tues. in winter.*

Hotels

Gunay's Garden
$$$ | RENTAL | FAMILY | Half a dozen attractive stone villas are clustered around a pretty garden and pool at this self-catering property; spacious two- and three-bedroom options have full kitchens, multiple bathrooms, and comfortable terraces, ideal for kids. **Pros:** well-equipped villas arranged to maximize privacy; good on-site restaurant (Izela); views of Kayaköy from the villas and the grounds. **Cons:** popular with young families which may not be best for others; one-week stays preferred; a bit pricey during high season. *[$] Rooms from: 470 TL ✉ Gumruk Sokak ☎ 252/618–0033 🌐 www.gunaysgarden.com 🛏 6 villas 🍴 No meals.*

Ölüdeniz

60 km (38 miles) east of Dalaman Airport; 8 km (5 miles) southeast of Fethiye.

Little wonder Ölüdeniz appears on so many Turkish promotional posters. With a photogenic mountain and a fringe of fragrant evergreens behind it, this oh-so-blue, beach-rimmed lagoon really is picture-perfect. The same, unfortunately, cannot be said of the bland package-tourist town that serves it.

GETTING HERE AND AROUND

Ölüdeniz can be reached by day cruise from Fethiye as well as by dolmuş or car. If you're driving, one inland route is through Ovacık (it's the shorter option when coming from outside Fethiye); a prettier one leads past the ruined town of Kayaköy, climbing steeply from a point 1 km (½ mile) west of the harbor.

Sights

The water of Ölüdeniz is warm and the setting delightful, despite the crowds. The view is even more splendid from the air (this is one of Turkey's premier locations for paragliding). Travel agencies in town will organize Jeep safaris into the surrounding high mountain pastures and villages for about 80 TL a day, lunch included.

The Lycian Way starts in the hills above Ölüdeniz, and one of its most pleasant sections is the three- to five-day walk to Patara.

★ **Butterfly Valley** (*Kelebekler Vadisi*)
CANYON | Only a 14-minute drive from Ölüdeniz, Butterfly Valley is a favorite stop for boat trips (it's either that or a treacherous climb down a very steep hill), with its pretty beach and campgrounds. Those who brought their sneakers can enjoy a bracing climb up to a little waterfall. The canyon opens up at a lovely Mediterraean beach. Clear turquoise waters and lush nature attract a laid-back crowd, but it can get a bit overcrowded in high season. This has been a protected nature area since 1981, in order to preserve the natural habitat of the valley's eponymous butterflies, some 100 different species in all, including the Jersey Tiger. It was opened for tourism in 1981 in part to provide funds to support conservation areas, and there's been little commercial development since, though from April through November, campers are allowed to stay. If you don't take a larger excursion that includes multiple stops, there's a taxi boat service with scheduled service leaving from Ölüdeniz. *✉ Uzunyurt Köyü 🎫 Taxi boat 15 TL.*

★ **Ölüdeniz Natural Park**
BEACH—SIGHT | FAMILY | If you want to take a dip in the iconic sandbar that lies across the mouth of the lagoon, then you must first enter Ölüdeniz Natural Park. To do so, go down to the seafront, turn west, then left at the fork where you can see the toll booth; the charge is 20 TL per car or 7 TL per person on foot (kids are half price or free, depending on age). The setting is absolutely beautiful, which means you should expect a lot of crowds. Pretty much the entire pebbly beach is taken up by densely packed

lounge chairs and umbrellas, either of which can be rented for 10 TL. Just around the corner a concession rents out pedalos and kayaks for about 30 TL per hour. The sea gets deep quickly here and there are several diving platforms anchored a short swim out. **Amenities:** food and drink; parking; showers, toilets; water sports. **Best for:** swimming. ✉ *Ölüdeniz.*

🍴 Restaurants

Oyster Mediterranean Restaurant
$$ | **INTERNATIONAL** | This restaurant in the Oyster Residences, at the western edge of the strip of bars and eateries along the beach, probably has the best food in town. Putting a contemporary spin on Mediterranean staples, its menu features lots of seafood (including swordfish kebabs), as well as steaks and beautiful baked lamb. **Known for:** swordfish kebab; steak; baked lamb. [$] *Average main: 60 TL* ✉ *224 Sok., No. 1, Belcekiz Mevkii* ✥ *On water, 1 block east of main intersection* ☎ *252/617–0765* 🌐 *www.oysterresidences.com* 🕓 *Closed Nov.–Apr.*

🛏 Hotels

Meri Hotel
$$$ | **HOTEL** | Built in 1973, this hotel was the first—and last—to be allowed by the government to set up shop on the famed Ölüdeniz lagoon; built on a steep incline amid terraced gardens overlooking one of Turkey's most beautiful bays, the site is a delight. **Pros:** location, location, location; most rooms have balconies with gorgeous sea views; private beach on the famous (and famously crowded) lagoon. **Cons:** average rooms, last updated in 1975; daunting stairs; can be noisy. [$] *Rooms from: 470 TL* ✉ *Ölüdeniz lagoon* ☎ *252/617–0001* 🌐 *www.clubhotelmeri.com* 🕓 *Closed mid-Nov.–mid-Apr.* 🛏 *94 rooms* 🍽 *All-inclusive.*

Montana Pine Resort
$$$ | **RESORT** | It's not Montana, but this resort—located uphill from Ölüdeniz in neighboring Hisarönü—does have a splendid mountain setting and temperatures that seem refreshingly cool compared to the coast. **Pros:** daily shuttle service to Ölüdeniz beach; fun bar; many guests return every year. **Cons:** you'll have to walk the last 100 yards because outside vehicles aren't permitted; some rooms are a bit dated; some mattresses are too soft. [$] *Rooms from: 440 TL* ✉ *Asagi Yasdam Cad., 2, Hisarönü* ☎ *252/616–7108* 🌐 *www.montanapine.com* 🕓 *Closed Nov.–May* 🛏 *164 rooms* 🍽 *Free Breakfast.*

★ **Oyster Residences**
$$$ | **HOTEL** | Nestled among olive trees just off the beach, this elegant boutique hotel is a happy misfit in package-tourist-dominated Ölüdeniz. **Pros:** beautiful and unique decor; hotel restaurant is good, though expensive; tranquil and stylish. **Cons:** some evening noise from nearby bars; no kids under 14 are permitted; not all rooms have sea views. [$] *Rooms from: 435 TL* ✉ *224 Sok., No. 1, Belcekiz Mevkii* ✥ *By the water, 1 block east of main intersection* ☎ *252/617–0765* 🌐 *www.oysterresidences.com* 🛏 *31 rooms* 🍽 *Free Breakfast; Some meals.*

🍸 Nightlife

Buzz Beach Bar
BARS/PUBS | The white terrace of the Buzz Beach Bar offers gorgeous views of the moonlit beach while the courteous staff helps you cool down with frozen cocktails, fruit smoothies, and an eclectic (if rather pricey) international menu. ✉ *Ölüdeniz Beach* ☎ *252/617–0526* 🌐 *www.buzzbeachbar.com.*

Help Beach Lounge
BARS/PUBS | Chilled-out bar by night, and family-friendly eatery by day, the Help Beach Bar serves up live music, a

wide array of cocktails, and surprisingly good food (from schnitzel and nachos to more traditional Turkish options), under climbing vines, just opposite the beach from May through October. ✉ *Waterfront promenade, Belceğiz Mahallesi, Denizpark Cad., No. 5/C* ☎ *252/617–0650* 🌐 *www.helpbeachlounge.com* 🕒 *Closed Nov. 1–May 1.*

Activities

BOATING

A day out on a boat can be arranged by the skippers of Ölüdeniz Kooperatif, who work from a kiosk halfway between the main body of hotels and the beach. From May through November, their 15 boats take groups to places with catchy names like Blue Cove, Butterfly Valley, Aquarium Bay, St. Nicholas Island, Cold Water Spring, Camel Beach, and Turquoise Bay. Trips usually run from around 10 am to 6 pm and cost about 50 TL per person, with lunch included (cold drinks extra). It's a great way to see the area, though some fellow passengers may be more interested in beer than sightseeing.

PARAGLIDING

The first thing you'll notice in Ölüdeniz is people soaring through the sky; paragliding is a busy industry here and a major spectator sport. The launch point is about 1,700 yards up Mt. Baba, some 20 km (13 miles) by forest tracks from Ölüdeniz—tour operators will drive you up from town. Tourists flying tandem with a pilot (around 350 TL) generally stay up for 30 to 40 minutes before landing gently on the beach. Full training and internationally recognized certificates in solo piloting are also available. Most travel agencies can arrange a flight.

Sky Sports

FLYING/SKYDIVING/SOARING | A reputable company with an English-speaking staff, Sky Sports offers paragliding from $80 per flight. ✉ *Çarşı Cad., 8* ☎ *252/617–0511* 🌐 *www.skysports-turkey.com/en.*

Kabak

16 km (10 miles) south of Ölüdeniz; 29 km (18 miles) south of Fethiye.

If you like your beaches in deep coves, framed by towering cliffs and pine forests, without a deck chair or beach umbrella in sight, then you'll love Kabak. For years it was one of Turkey's best-kept secrets, attracting hippies and alternative types. These days, accommodations are multiplying, but it's still one of the quieter places along the coast.

GETTING HERE AND AROUND

Just before the Fethiye road reaches Ölüdeniz, there's a turn to the left—from here it's 25 km (15 miles) to Kabak. Regular dolmuş service is available from Fethiye and Ölüdeniz via the village of Faralya. The main road does not continue to the beach itself. A section of the Lycian Way starts behind Mama's Restaurant and drops to the beach in about 30 minutes—the less intrepid may find the path rough and steep in patches.

Hotels

★ Olive Garden

$$ | **B&B/INN** | Perched on a terrace just down from the main road, this friendly, family-run place has comfortable cabins with simple furnishings and private porches that overlook the valley and sea. **Pros:** beautiful views; fresh and tasty food; warm, friendly, helpful staff. **Cons:** no air-conditioning means cabins can get hot during day; steep, 20-minute walk to beach; pool can get crowded. [$] *Rooms from: 180 TL* ✉ *Faralya-Kabak Sokak, No. 37* ☎ *252/642–1083* 🌐 *www.olivegarden-kabak.com* 🕒 *Closed mid-Nov.–Mar.* 🛏 *14 cabins* 🍴 *Free Breakfast.*

Turan Hill Lounge

$$ | **RESORT** | Perched high enough above the beach to ensure lovely sea views, Turan was the first campsite in Kabak, and it offers several sleeping options, from luxury tents to full cabins with bathrooms and fans (but not air-conditioning). **Pros:** lush garden; organic food made with local ingredients; regular yoga retreats. **Cons:** difficult to access; tiny pool; not for everyone. [$] *Rooms from: 380 TL* ✉ *Uzunyurt Village Kabak Bay No. 46, Gelemis* ☎ *252/642–1227* 🌐 *www.turanhilllounge.com* ⏲ *Closed in winter* 🛏 *22 rooms* 🍴 *Free Breakfast.*

Tlos Ruins

22 km (14 miles) east of Fethiye.

A day expedition to Tlos, a spectacular ancient Lycian city high above the valley of the Xanthos River, can be arranged from any town on the coast from Göcek to Kaş.

GETTING HERE AND AROUND

Head east from Fethiye on D90/E400. After 20 km (12 miles), follow signs for Antalya via Korkuteli. Drive another 1.2 km (¾ mile). Just after the bridge, there is a right turn for Tlos and Saklıkent. After 8 km (5 miles) there is a left turn for Tlos, 2.2 km (1½ miles).

Sights

Saklıkent National Park (*Saklıkent Milli Parkı*)
NATURE SITE | **FAMILY** | If you continue south from Tlos, you'll reach this spectacular gorge. It's a popular spot for picnicking and a wonderful place to cool off on a hot summer's day; children especially love wading up through the icy stream at the bottom of a deep rock crevasse. The first section goes over a walkway above the torrent to a pleasant leafy tea garden, beyond which the adventurous can cross the glacial water and carry on up the canyon. The first 30 minutes are straightforward; then the wading gets deeper and the rock scrambles more difficult, so know your limits—and expect to get wet. The road here heads south to Çavdır, which is just across the highway from Xanthos. If you don't have your own car, plenty of tour operators offer day trips. ■ **TIP→ Make sure to bring water shoes for this adventure.** ✉ *Saklıkent Milli Parkı* ✥ *15 km (9 miles) south of Tlos* 🎟 *10 TL.*

Tlos Ruins (*Tlos Örenyeri*)
ARCHAEOLOGICAL SITE | From the acropolis of Tlos, you can glimpse the view of Xanthos Valley to the west—a rich agricultural area both in ancient times and today. Mountains cradle Tlos's Roman Theater, with an 18th-century Ottoman fortress at the summit. Below the fortress, off a narrow path, is a cluster of rock tombs. Note the relief here of Bellerophon, son of King Glaucus of Corinth, mounted on Pegasus, his winged steed. The monster he faces is the dreaded Chimera—a fire-breathing creature with a lion's head, goat's body, and serpent's tail. Beside the acropolis is a large flat agora, with seats on one side from which spectators watched footraces. ✉ *Fethiye* ✥ *From Fethiye take exit to Rte. 400 and follow local road east to Antalya where a yellow sign marks a right turn that leads southwest for 15 km (9 miles)* 🎟 *6 TL.*

Restaurants

Yakapark Trout Restaurant Café and Bar
FISH HATCHERY | **FAMILY** | Continue up the hill beyond Tlos to the nearby village of Yaka Köyü (it's signposted) and you'll reach the vast but peaceful Yakapark Restaurant, which has become an attraction in its own right. The enormous space seats up to 600 people, which helps keep the price down to an extremely reasonable 15 TL per portion of trout. On the site of a now-demolished windmill, it has its own trout farm, guaranteeing the freshest of fish. Water is everywhere here, gurgling around traditional Turkish wooden platforms where diners sit, and there is even a little channel in the bar where fish can swim around your chilled beer. Bring a bathing suit if you dare—the waters of the wading pool are so icy, owners promise a free drink to anyone

who can withstand them for five whole minutes. If you can manage for a full 15 minutes, your drink and entire meal are free. ⊠ *Yaka Köyü* ☎ *252/634–0036.*

Pınara

40 km (24 miles) southeast of Fethiye; 40 km (25 miles) northwest of Kalkan.

Pınara (which means "something round" in Lycian) is a romantic ruin around a great circular outcrop backed by high cliffs, reachable from most holiday spots in western Lycia.

GETTING HERE AND AROUND
From Fethiye take E90/D400 toward Kalkan for 47 km (30 miles), and then take the right turn marked for Pınara. From there it's a farther 6 km (4 miles) via the village of Minare.

 ## Sights

Pınara
ARCHAEOLOGICAL SITE | The ancient city of Pınara was probably founded as early as the 5th century BC, and it eventually became one of Lycia's most important cities. You need time and determination to explore though, as it's widely scattered, largely unexcavated, and overgrown with plane, fig, and olive trees. You can park in the village of Minare and make the half-hour hike up the clearly marked trail. At the top of a steep dirt track, the site steward will collect your admission and point you in the right direction—there are no descriptive signs or good maps.

The spectacular Greek theater, which has overlooked these peaceful hills and fields for thousands of years, is one of the country's finest. It's perfectly proportioned, and unlike that of most other theaters in Turkey, its stage building is still standing. The site also contains groups of rock tombs with unusual reliefs (one shows a cityscape) and a

cliff wall honeycombed with hundreds of crude rectangular "pigeonholes," which are believed to have been either tombs or food storage receptacles. ⊠ *Minare Köyü, Fethiye* ✛ *40 km (25 miles) north of Kalkan, look for sign on Rte. 400* ☎ *252/614–1150* 🖾 *Free.*

Letoon

63 km (39 miles) southeast of Fethiye; 17 km (11 miles) northwest of Kalkan.

This site was not a city but rather a religious center and political meeting point for the Lycian League: the world's first democratic federation. It's quite rural and can be reached on a day trip from western Lycia's main centers—Fethiye, Ölüdeniz, Kaş, or Kalkan. Plan to visit in the late afternoon, perhaps after a stop in nearby Xanthos, which administered the temples in ancient times.

GETTING HERE AND AROUND
There are several signposted routes including one from across the Xanthos bridge, 5 km (3 miles) away. You can continue past Letoon to the far western end of the Patara beach, about 6 km (4 miles) away. Occasional buses run to Kumluova from Fethiye.

Sights

Letoon
ARCHAEOLOGICAL SITE | Excavations have revealed three temples in Letoon. The first, closest to the parking area, dates from the 2nd century BC and was dedicated to Leto, the mother of Apollo and Artemis (hence the name); she was believed to have given birth to the twins here, while hiding from Zeus's jealous wife, Hera. The middle temple, the oldest, is dedicated to Artemis and dates from the 5th or 4th century BC. The last, dating from the 1st century BC, belongs to Apollo and contains a copy of a mosaic depicting a bow and arrow (a symbol of Artemis)

and a sun and lyre (Apollo's emblems). These are the three gods most closely associated with Lycia. Re-erecting some columns of the Temple of Leto has made the site more photogenic. There is also a well-preserved Roman theater here—look for the carvings of theatrical masks on the northern wall. The once-sacred pool, now filled with ducks and chirping frogs, lends atmosphere. About 10 km (6 miles) south of Letoön, the road continues to a beach. Across a rickety bridge at the river mouth are the ruins of an early Lycian fort called Pydnai. ✉ *17 km (11 miles) north of Kalkan on Rte. 400, just beyond Kumluova, Letoon Plaj Cad., Hürriyet Mahallesi, Fethiye* 🎫 *10 TL.*

Xanthos

61 km (48 miles) southeast of Fethiye; 17 km (10 miles) northwest of Kalkan on Rte. 400.

Xanthos, perhaps the greatest city of ancient Lycia, is famed for tombs rising on high, thick, rectangular pillars. It also earned the region a reputation for fierceness in battle. Determined not to be subjugated by superior forces, the men of Xanthos twice set fire to their own city—with their women and children inside—and fought to the death. The first occasion was against the Persians in 542 BC, the second against Brutus and the Romans in the 1st century BC. The site was excavated and stripped by the British in 1838, and most finds are now in London's British Museum; the remains, however, are worth inspecting. Allow at least three hours and expect some company. Unlike other Lycian cities, Xanthos is on the main tour-bus route.

GETTING HERE AND AROUND
Xanthos is a short distance off Route 400. Buses along the highway will stop at the adjacent town of Kınık. In summer there are frequent minibuses from Xanthos to Patara, Kalkan, and Kaş.

👁 Sights

★ Xanthos
ARCHAEOLOGICAL SITE | Start your exploration of this UNESCO World Heritage Site at the Roman-style theater, where inscriptions indicate that its restoration was funded by a wealthy Lycian named Opromoas of Rhodiapolis after the great earthquake of AD 141. Alongside the theater are two much-photographed pillar tombs. The more famous of the pair is called the Harpy Tomb—not after what's inside, but because of the half-bird, half-woman figures carved onto the north and south sides. This tomb has been dated to 470 BC; the reliefs are plaster casts of originals in the British Museum. The other tomb consists of a sarcophagus atop a pillar—a rather unusual arrangement. The pillar section is probably as old as the Harpy Tomb, while the sarcophagus was added later. On the side of the theater, opposite the Harpy Tomb and past the agora, is the Inscribed Pillar of Xanthos. Dating from about 400 BC, it is etched with 250 lines (written in both Greek and Lycian) that recount the heroic deeds of a champion wrestler and celebrated soldier named Kerei. Check out the large Byzantine basilica with its abstract mosaics before following the path uphill, where you'll find several sarcophagi, a good collection of rock-cut house tombs, and a welcome spot of shade. ✉ *17 km (10 miles) north of Kalkan, Asar Cad., Kınık Belediyesi* 🎫 *10 TL.*

Patara

70 km (44 miles) southeast of Fethiye; 20 km (13 miles) northwest of Kalkan off Rte. 400.

Patara was once Lycia's principal port. Cosmopolitan in its heyday—Hannibal, St. Paul, and the emperor Hadrian all visited, and St. Nicholas, the man who would be Santa Claus, is said to have

The Lycian Way

Until the 1950s, the only way to reach the Lycian coast was by boat or via bone-rattling trips through the mountains in antiquated motor vehicles. Even the main roads today date only from the 1970s, which is why this was the perfect place to establish Turkey's first and most famous long-distance trekking route, the Lycian Way.

The footpath, marked by red-and-white painted blazes, runs along the sea for 530 km (331 miles), following ancient Roman roads, and sometimes clambering up barely visible goat tracks to peaks that rise nearly 6,500 feet at Mt. Tahtalı (one of the many high mountains known in antiquity as Mt. Olympos). Upsides include breathtaking views, innumerable ancient ruins, and a chance to accept hospitality in villages little touched by tourism or time. The downside is that backpacks can be heavy and hills steep; and while most of the path is well marked, finding the trail can occasionally be difficult. If you lose it, go back to the last marker you saw—they're positioned 50 to 100 yards apart—and try again. Despite government support, the track has no legal status and is subject to adjustments due to road building, landslides, and fencing by landowners.

It would take a month to walk the Lycian Way from end to end, but there's a lot you can do without a tent. Because the trail crosses many towns and highways, it's easy to break it up into day hikes, and you can cover about half of it while staying in *pansiyons* that have sprung up along the way. Kate Clow, the Englishwoman who first designed and mapped the Lycian Way in 2000, recommends several popular walks near Olympos in her book *The Lycian Way* (the route's only guide and a source of good maps). The website ⊕ *www.cultureroutesinturkey.com*, which Clow founded, provides updates and detailed information. Several tour companies also offer guided trips along the trail (*see Tours in the Planning section of this chapter*).

The best times to walk are spring, when days are long and wildflowers are out, and autumn, when the seawater is warm and the weather cooler. Summer is too hot; in winter there may be some perfect days, but the weather is not reliable enough to make plans in advance.

been born here—the port eventually silted up. Dunes at the edge of the village are now part of one of Turkey's longest and completely unspoiled sand beaches. From here, too, runs one of the best sections of the Lycian Way, a three- to five-day walk to Ölüdeniz. Thanks to the ruins and the turtles that nest on the beach, new development was banned in the modern village, making it a quiet alternative to the bustle of nearby Kalkan. If you're craving exploration, arrange a horseback riding expedition on the shore with one of the tour operators clustered in the center of town.

GETTING HERE AND AROUND
The village is 3 km (2 miles) south of the highway; the ruins and beach are a farther 3 km (2 miles) along the same road. Main buses will drop you at the highway, and frequent minibuses run between the beach, village, and Kınık (Xanthos), Kalkan, and Kaş, spring through fall.

Sights

★ Patara Beach

BEACH—SIGHT | FAMILY | Beyond the ruins of Patara is a superb 11-km (7-mile) sweep of sand dunes, surely one of the finest beaches on the Turqoise Coast. Despite its popularity with Turkish families and tourists from Kalkan, you don't have to walk far to find some nice solitude here. Note that umbrellas should only be planted within 20 yards of the sea to prevent disturbing the nests of Caretta caretta turtles. In summer, be prepared for intense and unobstructed sun. **Amenities:** food and drink; parking (free); showers, toilets. **Best for**: walking; swimming. ✉ *Patara Plajı, Gelemis* 🎫 *5 TL.*

Ruins of Patara

ARCHAEOLOGICAL SITE | FAMILY | The ancient city of Patara, now being excavated by Antalya's Akdeniz University, is slowly emerging from the sands near Patara Beach. The heavy stones that make up the front of the monumental bathhouse are impressive, and a triple arch built by a Roman governor in AD 100 seems a tenth of its age. Beyond are two theaters, several churches, and an impressive section of a colonnaded street. Follow the path west and you'll see the recently discovered Roman lighthouse. Still waiting to be found is the Temple of Apollo; Herodotus wrote that its oracle worked only part-time, as Apollo spent summers away in Delos (probably to escape the heat). ✉ *Just off the eastern end of Patara Beach, Gelemis* 🎫 *20 TL.*

Hotels

Dardanos Hotel

$$ | HOTEL | One of the few older hotels in "no new development" Patara to have benefited from some remodeling, the Dardanos has well-decorated guest rooms (each with a balcony) that mix modern European style with traditional Turkish features. **Pros:** modern perks include air-conditioning and free Wi-Fi; excellent English spoken; central location. **Cons:** a five-minute drive from the beach; simple and homey, nothing fancy; bar is somewhat expensive. [$] *Rooms from: 250 TL* ✉ *Gelemis* ✣ *On the main side street in the middle of the village towards the river* ☎ *242/843–5151* 🌐 *www.pataradardanoshotel.com* 🕓 *Closed early Nov.–late Mar.* 🛏 *18 rooms* 🍴 *Free Breakfast.*

Hotel Patara Viewpoint

$$ | HOTEL | One of the larger hotels in Patara, the Viewpoint is run by a Turkish-English couple who are a good source of information on the area. **Pros:** friendly, knowledgeable hosts who speak excellent English; complimentary transportation to the beach; breezy hillside location. **Cons:** need to walk up the hill to reach it; a bit far from the beach; basic breakfast. [$] *Rooms from: 280 TL* ✉ *Gelemiş Sokak Gedik, No. 11, Gelemis* ☎ *242/843–5184* 🌐 *www.pataraview-point.com* 🕓 *Closed Nov.–Apr.* 🛏 *27 rooms* 🍴 *Free Breakfast.*

Kalkan

80 km (50 miles) southeast of Fethiye; 27 km (17 miles) west of Kaş, on Rte. 400.

Kalkan has two distinct sides: on the one hand, it has fine restaurants and excellent hotels to match its superb, steep views of the Mediterranean Sea. But prices have been scaled up for the many ex-pats that have moved here, and regulars complain that the recent explosion of foreign-owned vacation villas has changed the town's character for the worse. With only a small, rocky beach, a few narrow blocks of whitewashed stone houses, and not much archaeology of its own, Kalkan is trying hard to develop its tourism offerings. Despite its growing overexposure, it's still a decent base for touring the area and the surrounding sites.

GETTING HERE AND AROUND

The highway is immediately behind town, so getting here is straightforward. While public transportation is available from the Fethiye bus station, a private car or a (rather pricey) taxi is a faster and more comfortable option. If flying, Dalaman Airport is closer than Antalya Airport (about 90 minutes away, compared to three hours), and shuttles are available for around 50 TL one way

Sights

★ Kaputaş Beach

BEACH—SIGHT | **FAMILY** | Since neither Kaş or Kalkan have proper beaches, this pretty spot between the two is quite popular. Set in a narrow, steep-sided inlet, there are 186 stairs leading down to it. The position between dramatic cliffs is picturesque, though the beach itself is small and can get crowded in summer; arrive early so you can find a parking space. **Amenities:** food and drink; parking (free but limited); toilets. **Best for:** swimming. ✉ *Kalkan* ✣ *On the D400 highway, 6 km (4 miles) from Kalkan.*

Restaurants

Aubergine

$$$ | **TURKISH** | The adventurous menu at this harborfront eatery includes excellent pasta, salmon *en croute,* stuffed sea bass with bacon, extra large steaks, and occasionally wild boar shot in the mountains. The restaurant caters predominantly to the well-heeled British ex-pat crowd (hence the rather ambitious prices), and offers a nightly happy hour and a legendary party on New Year's Eve. **Known for:** salmon en croute; stuffed sea bass; steak. [$] *Average main: 70 TL* ✉ *Yaliboyu Mah. Kalkan Harbour No. 25* ☎ *242/844–3332.*

★ Gironda

$$$ | **MEDITERRANEAN** | This gourmet restaurant evokes an elegant villa, complete with sumptuous sofas and plaster-of-Paris statuary. The food—which alone merits a stay in Kalkan—is outstandingly fresh, and the dishes are well thought out. **Known for:** grilled red snapper; stuffed fillet of lamb; barbecued sea bass. [$] *Average main: 70 TL* ✉ *Yalıboyu Mahallesi, Hasanaltan Cad. No. 28* ☎ *242/844–1298* ⏲ *Closed Nov.–Apr. No lunch.*

Müpptela

$$ | **TURKISH** | Müpptela means "addicted," and after one visit to this excellent *meyhane* (grillhouse) you'll understand why. The mezes are excellent, and there is a wide variety of hot appetizers and grilled meat and kebab dishes. **Known for:** excellent mezes; grilled garlic sausage with halloumi and pistachio; Adana kebab. [$] *Average main: 35 TL* ✉ *Ilkokul Sokak. No 17, Kas* ☎ *537/051–2077* ⏲ *No lunch.*

Hotels

Happy Hotel

$$ | **HOTEL** | **FAMILY** | Despite the unimaginative concrete-block architecture, this well-run hotel set amid wild olive trees overlooking Kalamar Bay is a good value, and all but four of its large rooms feature balconies that provide stunning sea views. **Pros:** sizable suites; delightful sea views; free shuttle four times a day to central Kalkan. **Cons:** hilly walk into town takes 20 minutes; minimalistic decoration may feel bland; some furniture needs replacing. [$] *Rooms from: 250 TL* ✉ *Kalamar Koyu Akdeniz Cad. No. 35-41* ☎ *242/844–1133* 🌐 *www.happyhotel.com.tr* ⏲ *Closed early Nov.–mid-Apr.* 🛏 *50 rooms* 🍴 *Free Breakfast.*

Hotel Prat

$$ | **HOTEL** | **FAMILY** | While this concrete construction lacks personality, you can't beat the location: it's right on the harbor, and the three pools have superb views of the bay. **Pros:** central location; excursions can be arranged; nice pool. **Cons:** feels dated; hokey decor; basic breakfast.

$ Rooms from: 200 TL ⊠ Kalkan Harbor, Iskele Sokak, No. 3 🖀 242/844–3178 ⊕ www.hotelpirat.net ⤳ 136 rooms ⦿ Free Breakfast.

★ Hotel Villa Mahal

$$$$ | HOTEL | Clinging to a cliff face with a wraparound view of Kalkan Bay, this immaculate establishment is one of Turkey's most spectacular hotels, with a gorgeous pool that juts out into the air (making swimming feel like flying), a beach club at the bottom of the cliff, and a hotel boat that will take you five minutes across the bay to Kalkan Harbor for an evening in town. **Pros:** peaceful private beach offering many water sports; glamorously minimalist and stylish rooms and public areas; stunning location. **Cons:** isolated location; a long trek down to the beach; expensive, though with facilities this luxurious, it's arguably value for money. $ Rooms from: 1000 TL ⊠ Patara Evler Yani ✛ About 2 km (1 mile) east of Kalkan down and around a signposted road. Take care on precipitous last approach 🖀 242/844–3268 ⊕ www. villamahal.com ⊗ Closed Nov.–Apr. ⤳ 13 rooms ⦿ Free Breakfast.

Kaş

27 km (17 miles) southeast of Kalkan on Rte. 400; 180 km (112 miles) from Antalya via Korkuteli mountain road.

In the 1980s, Kaş, with its beautiful wide bay and its lovely view of the Greek island of Kastellorizo (Meis), was the main tourist destination on the Lycian coast. But it fell by the wayside because it lacked a real beach and A-list attractions. This has, fortunately, kept away the worst overdevelopment; now Kaş is being rediscovered, with regular visitors migrating from Kalkan. There are excellent hotels and restaurants, the location is relatively central, and the size is about right, making it a good stop on your way along the coast. Like Kalkan, Kaş is also

a good base for sightseeing in the area; you can easily hop down to Kaleköy (ancient Simena) and Kekova Island, or across the water to Kastellorizo.

GETTING HERE AND AROUND

Route 400 runs immediately above the town, and there are two turns with large "Şehir Merkezi" (city center) signs and tiny signs for "Kaş." As you enter, there are marked turns—right for the Çukurbağ Peninsula, left for the seafront hotels.

Meis Express has an office on Kaş's waterfront, with ferry departures at 10:20 am daily; afternoon trips, returning in the evening, are sometimes available. In either case, expect to pay about 140 TL for a return ticket.

CONTACTS Meis Express ⊠ *Tourist Boat Harbor* 🖀 *242/836–1725* ⊕ *www.meisexpress.com.*

VISITOR INFORMATION

CONTACTS Tourist Information Kaş ⊠ *The main square by the tour boat harbor, Cumhuriyet Meyd. 5* 🖀 *242/836–1238.*

◉ Sights

Ancient Theater of Kaş (*Antik Tiyatro Kaş*) **ARCHAEOLOGICAL SITE** | A few hundred yards west of Kaş's main square, a small, well-preserved antique theater sits amid the olive trees; superb ocean views make it particularly lovely at sunset. There are other ruins in town to explore as well: next to the district prefect's office, east of the harbor, is an old wooden barn of the type once universally used as granaries in Lycian villages—and still clearly modeled on old Lycian architectural forms. ⊠ *Necipbey Cad.*

★ Kastellorizo

ISLAND | **FAMILY** | The 20-minute boat ride to the Greek island of Kastellorizo (called Meis in Turkish) gives you a taste of Greece and lets you imagine what Kaş must have been like before the 1923 population exchange, when most residents were of Greek origin. Isolated

Did You Know?

Kapıtaş Beach, between Kaş and Kalkan, is dramatically set between the cliffs.

from the rest of its country, Kastellorizo has escaped major tourist development and maintains the charm of an island that time forgot. Attractions include a small 12th- to 16th-century crusader castle, notable for its crenellated gray-stone walls; a large blue cave with fine stalactites (speedboat trips can be arranged in Meis Harbor when you disembark); the 1835 church of St. Konstantine and Eleni, which reused granite columns taken from the Temple of Apollo at Letoon in Lycia (usually locked); and a mosque converted into a small museum, which recounts the island's tragic history. You can get a taste of the island in just an afternoon, but if you want more, overnight at one of the island's several hotels or *pansiyons* . ■ **TIP→ If you're day-tripping, don't be alarmed if the ferry operator wants to hold onto your passport when you disembark in Greece—they process the passports in batches, to speed things up. If you're not comfortable with this, just ask to have your passport stamped while you watch.** ✉ *Kastellorizon.*

★ Limanağzı
BEACH—SIGHT | This tiny bay across from the main harbor in Kaş is only accessible by boat (or by hiking), which makes it the perfect retreat from the bustle of the city center. With a small beach with rentable chairs and a small bar to purchase beverages, Limanağzı is a great spot for a casual swim during a long, relaxing day. You can also rent a canoe if you want to paddle around the bay. **Amenities:** food and drink. **Best for:** swimming, walking. ✉ *Kas* ✣ *Directly across the bay from town.*

Lycian Sarcophagus
ARCHAEOLOGICAL SITE | Kaş (know as Antiphellus in ancient times) has a few ruins, including a monumental sarcophagus with four regal lions' heads carved onto the lid. In 1842, a British naval officer counted more than 100 sarcophagi in Kaş; however, most have been destroyed over the years as locals nabbed the flat side pieces to use in new construction projects in the town. ✉ *Kas* ✣ *Walk up Ibrahim Serin Cad. from the square by the tour boat harbor.*

🍴 Restaurants

Bahçe & Bahçe Balık
$$ | **TURKISH** | A casual but stylish courtyard restaurant serving delightful Turkish dishes in a quiet garden setting, Bahçe is located just opposite Kaş's 4th-century-BC King's Tomb. The starters are very famous—especially tasty options are grated carrot with yogurt, mashed walnut, cold spinach, fish balls, and *arnavut ciğeri* (fried liver prepared with chopped nuts). **Known for:** grilled octopus; fried liver; good mezes. [$] *Average main: 60 TL* ✉ *Anıt Mezar Karşısı, No. 31* ☎ *242/836–2370.*

★ Smiley's
$$ | **TURKISH** | **FAMILY** | Located next to a 19th-century Ottoman house at the edge of the harbor, Smiley's has been an open secret among Turquoise Coast yachters since 1987. Relax in the fresh air beneath vines, flags, and fishing nets and enjoy a reasonably priced and generously portioned meal of some of the best kebabs and seafood in Kaş, as well as some of the friendliest service. **Known for:** good mezes; grilled calamari; chicken with almond sauce. [$] *Average main: 35 TL* ✉ *Liman Sokak, near the intersection with Süleyman Sandıkçı Sokak* ✣ *Yacht harbor entrance (left-hand side as you face the sea)* ☎ *555/356–1863.*

🛏 Hotels

Gardenia
$$ | **HOTEL** | The first thing you notice here is the art, acquired by the owner on his off-season trips to Asia and South America; it fills the lobby, expands up the stairs, and overflows into the rooms, setting the tone for this boutique hotel. **Pros:** stylish and artistic; fabulous sea

views from the roof terrace and front rooms; peaceful and sophisticated (no kids under age 12); generous buffet breakfast with fresh-squeezed orange juice and local honey. **Cons:** some rooms are small; no elevator and lots of stairs; you can only swim across the street from a platform (no beach). $ *Rooms from: 200 TL ✉ Hükmet Cad., No. 41 ☎ 242/836–2368 ⊕ www.gardeniahotel-kas.com ⊘ Closed mid-Nov.–Apr ⇆ 11 rooms ⦿ Free Breakfast.*

★ Hadrian Hotel

$$$$ | HOTEL | For secluded, romantic tranquility with a knockout view, come to this beautifully designed and immaculately kept waterfront hotel on the peninsula outside Kaş. **Pros:** gorgeous location and sea views; private beach; tranquil (no kids under 11 years old). **Cons:** located down a steep hill from the main road, so a rental car is needed for sightseeing; not in central Kaş; pricey, though luxurious. $ *Rooms from: 750 TL ✉ Doğan Kaşaroğlu, Cad. 10 ⊕ South side of Çukurbağ Peninsula, 4½ km (3 miles) from Kaş ☎ 242/836–2856 ⊕ www.hotelhadrian.com ⊘ Closed Nov. 1–Apr. 20 ⇆ 14 rooms ⦿ Free Breakfast.*

Medusa Hotel

$$ | HOTEL | Be sure to get a sea-view room at this modest but well-run hotel (one of the many that line the seafront road east of the harbor), which has a friendly and helpful staff. **Pros:** spectacular panorama view from the terrace and some rooms; generous breakfast buffet with heaps of local veggies and rose jam; peaceful, but only a five-minute walk to central Kaş. **Cons:** small rooms, not all with sea views; lots of stairs; very small pool. $ *Rooms from: 250 TL ✉ Hükümet Cad., No. 53, Küçükçakıl Mevkii, Andifli ☎ 242/836–1440 ⊕ www.medusahotels.com ⊘ Closed Nov.–Apr. ⇆ 37 rooms ⦿ Free Breakfast.*

▼ Nightlife

Echo Café & Bar

DANCE CLUBS | Both a disco and a live jazz venue, Echo is also probably the only club in the world with a 3rd-century-BC basement cistern carved out of solid rock (now laid out with tables, and quieter than upstairs). The cistern was discovered by chance a few decades ago when the building—originally a stable for camels—was being extended. ✉ *Uzun Çarsi Cad., on eastern edge of harbor ☎ 242/836–2047 ⊕ www.echocafebar.com.*

⚡ Activities

SCUBA DIVING

Bougainville Travel

SCUBA DIVING | If you really want to immerse yourself in history, Kaş is a good base for scuba excursions. A profusion of dive boats shows the growing demand for the area's rich underwater sights, though a lot of the water is Greek and off-limits. Bougainville Travel is your best bet for making arrangements, either in advance of your trip or on arrival. ✉ *Ibrahim Serin Cad. No. 10 ☎ 242/836–3737 ⊕ www.bougainville-turkey.com.*

Simena-Kaleköy and Kekova Sound

30 km (19 miles) east of Kaş.

Charming, rustic, waterside Kaleköy (sometimes known by its ancient name, Simena), Kekova Island just across the water, and the surrounding coastline are among the most enchanting spots in Turkey—especially when the reflection of the full moon slowly traces its way across Kekova Sound. Kekova Island stands slightly off a shore notched with little bays, whose many inlets create a series of lagoons. This area is famed for its "sunken city" and although swimming around the fragments of the partly submerged buildings is now banned, it is still an interesting place to explore.

The village of Üçağız, which has small *pansiyons* and waterside restaurants, is the base for many boat trips across the bay to the island. But even more delightful is the tiny, castle-crowned hamlet of Kaleköy (Simena), a 10-minute boat ride or half-hour walk away. Kaleköy is a concrete-free village that resembles a Greek island before development. It's a pleasing jumble of boxy houses built up a steep rocky crag alongside layers of history: Lycian tombs, a tiny Greek theater, and the medieval ruins of Simena Castle atop the rocky hill. You'll enjoy the place even more once the day-trippers have departed. There are now numerous basic *pansiyons*, which, while rather expensive for the quality of the rooms, have balconies or terraces with sublime views of Kekova Sound and the sunken city. All offer boat pickup from Üçağız. Reserve well in advance, in season.

GETTING HERE AND AROUND

Kekova Sound is a beautiful patch of water that begs to be explored by boat. Day trips leave from Kaş and Üçağız. Some boats come directly from Kaş while others bus their customers into Üçağız. Expect to pay around 130 TL. If driving, look for a turnoff from Route 400 signposted "Üçağız," 14 km (9 miles) east of Kaş. After 16 km (10 miles) you'll reach Çevreli, where there is a turn to Üçağız, a farther 3 km (2 miles) onward.

Sights

Aperlai & Apollonia

ARCHAEOLOGICAL SITE | West of Kekova Island are two small, infrequently visited ruins, linked together by a section of the Lycian Way; they make a good day trip or overnight excursion for those who want to get off the beaten track. Apollonia is a minor site on a small hill just southwest of the village of Sahil Kılınçlı on the Kaş–Üçağız road 7 km (4½ miles) south of the highway. You'll see a good range of ancient Lycian tombs, scattered east and north of the walled acropolis hill. There's also a small theater and a well-preserved church with views west over the coast toward Kaş. Back on the side road, look for the signed turnoff to the right, then walk two hours down the hill to the ruins of Aperlai on a pretty little inlet. The city walls here are impressively intact. Buildings inside them include a well-preserved church, houses, and a bath by the water, as well the sunken remains of the ancient port—which you can explore with a mask and snorkel from the nearby Hikers' Inn (formerly Purple House) *pansiyon*. Another three hours, first inland, and then along the water, will take you to Üçağız. Some boats will drop you at the inlet, and give you time to walk to Aperlai and back.

Hotels

Ankh Pansion

$$ | **B&B/INN** | This simple family establishment is the place to choose if you want to escape from the world and soak up the otherworldliness of Kekova Sound. **Pros:** more private than other places around; bright rooms, many with lovely views over Kekova Sound toward the "sunken city"; great location. **Cons:** rooms lack character; a bit pricey for what you get; some towels need replacing. [$] *Rooms from: 350 TL* ✉ *Üçağız Kale Köyü Demre, Kalkan* ✣ *Eastern side of village, follow signs through maze of streets* ☎ *242/874–2171* 🌐 *www.ankh-pansion.com* ⏲ *Closed Nov.–Apr.* 🛏 *12 rooms* 🍴 *Free Breakfast.*

Kale Pansiyon

$$ | **B&B/INN** | This intimate family-run hotel is in a pretty stone building on the eastern side of the waterfront with a small courtyard, a private swimming area, and a jetty with tables for a sunset dinner. **Pros:** central location; private beach area a short walk away; lovely wooden ceilings. **Cons:** ground-floor rooms have less of a view; rooms are on the plain side; a bit pricey for what you get. [$] *Rooms from: 350 TL* ✉ *Demre* ⚓ *Just east of the Sahil Pansiyon, follow the signs* ☎ *532/779–0476* ⊕ *www. kalepansiyon.com* 🍴 *10 rooms* ⧉ *Free Breakfast.*

Sahil Pansiyon

$$ | **B&B/INN** | This pint-sized place above a restaurant and general store can be found in the center of the Kaleköy waterfront, with bright, clean rooms that share a long balcony with a magnificent view of the boats from the nearby port. **Pros:** central location; great views; excursions can be arranged. **Cons:** less private than other hotels; sparse decor; a bit pricey for what you get. [$] *Rooms from: 350 TL* ✉ *Kaleköy waterfront, Kaleköy-Simena, Demre* ⚓ *Look for the general store* ☎ *242/874–2263* ⊕ *www.sahilpension. com* 🍴 *3 rooms* ⧉ *Free Breakfast.*

Demre (Kale)

37 km (23 miles) east of Kaş; 140 km (87 miles) southwest of Antalya on Rte. 400.

Demre (also referred to as Kale in Turkish) is where St. Nicholas, who later became known as Father Christmas, made his reputation as bishop of the Greco-Roman diocese of Myra in the first half of the 4th century. Among his good deeds, St. Nicholas is said to have carried out nocturnal visits to the houses of local children to leave gifts, including gold coins as dowries for poor village girls; if a window was closed, said the storytellers, he would drop the gifts down the chimney.

Demre was once one of the most important cities along the coast. An ancient theater and some rock-cut tombs offer proof, but its remains lie mostly under the concrete of the modern urban center and the large greenhouses that dominate the hillside to the north. Now primarily an agricultural region (it's known as the tomato capital of Turkey), tourists typically view Demre as a quick stopover on their trip along the coast.

GETTING HERE AND AROUND

Demre is right along Route 400. St. Nicholas Basilica is a few blocks off the highway, signposted "Noel Baba." The theater is about 1½ km (1 mile) farther north.

👁 Sights

Andriake

ARCHAEOLOGICAL SITE | The seaport of ancient Myra was a major stopover on the Egypt-to-Rome route that supplied most of Rome's wheat. St. Paul changed ships here on his journey to Rome in AD 60; and Hadrian built a huge granary on the site (it's hidden in the bushes south of the road just before you get to the modern port of Demre, and is also clearly visible from the Kaş-Demre road, just west of Demre, as you come around the last bend). Recent excavations found a synagogue in the same area. If you're willing to ford the waist-deep water of the creek, Üçağız is about a seven-hour walk on the Lycian Way with several pretty coastal sections. Continue on the rustic road to Demre's yacht harbor for modest snack bars, an enlivening sea breeze, and a glorious view over the water. ✉ *Demre* ⚓ *Western edge of Demre on the road leading to the yacht harbor (yat liman).*

Myra

ARCHAEOLOGICAL SITE | The monuments of ancient Myra—a large, very well-preserved Roman theater and a cliff face full of Lycian rock tombs—sit just north of Demre. The theater dates from the 2nd century AD and for a time hosted gladiator spectacles and wild animal hunts. In the cliffs to the left and above are some good reliefs—keep an eye out for a small one of a warrior. Up a stone ramp east of the theater, a section of Lycian Way leads to the acropolis, offering nice views over the theater and town. There are more tombs farther east. When you arrive to the site, you'll see plenty of vendors hawking Orthodox Christian votives to Russian tourists, to tie in with the nearby church of St. Nicholas. ✉ *Demre* ✥ *2 km (1 mile) north of Demre* 🎫 *30 TL.*

St. Nicholas Basilica

RELIGIOUS SITE | The grave of Myra's famous 4th-century bishop—St. Nicholas (aka Santa Claus)—quickly became a pilgrimage site shortly after his death. A church was built around his tomb in the 6th century but later destroyed in an Arab raid. In 1043, St. Nicholas Basilica was rebuilt with the aid of the Byzantine emperor Constantine IX and the empress Zoë; it was, in turn, heavily restored in the 19th century courtesy of Russian noblemen. (To this day, most visitors to the church are Russian.) It's difficult to distinguish between parts of original church and the restorations, although the bell tower and upper story are clearly late additions. The colorful frescos are very evocative, and reminiscent of the early churches of Cappadocia. The reputed sarcophagus of St. Nicholas is in the southernmost aisle; however, his remains were stolen and taken to Bari, Italy, in 1087, where the church of San Nicola di Bari was built to house them. A few bones remained, so the story goes, and these can be seen in the Antalya Museum. A service is (theoretically, at least) held in the church every year on December 6, the feast day of St. Nicholas. ✉ *Near the center of Demre, a few blocks from the main square, Demre* 🎫 *30 TL.*

Sura

ARCHAEOLOGICAL SITE | This was ancient Myra's most important pre-Christian holy site. Priests of Apollo would release fish into the sacred pool here, and then "read" the future from the movements. It still has Lycian tombs and a small acropolis, from which the temple of Apollo is visible in the overgrown valley below. ✉ *Demre* ✥ *Beside the turnoff to Kekova, a few hundred yards north of Andriake.*

🍴 Restaurants

Ipek Restaurant

$ | TURKISH | One of the best of the group of traditional Turkish *lokantas* around the church of St. Nicholas, Ipek doesn't look like much and the waiters can be surly, but excellent meat dishes make this the restaurant of choice for many. **Known for:** köfte (grilled meatballs); moussaka; chicken soup. [$] *Average main: 18 TL* ✉ *ilkokul 3. Sokak no. 4, Demre* ✥ *As you exit the church, turn left along the pedestrian street. Ipek is 100 yds down, on the left* ☎ *242/871–5150.*

Nur Pastaneleri

$ | TURKISH | FAMILY | It may look plain, but after paying your respects to St. Nick, retire here to enjoy arctic air-conditioning and a cold drink or tea accompanied by some of Turkey's freshest baklava, the diamond-cut honeyed pastry with nuts. Until early afternoon the café also serves *su böreği,* a salty pastry flavored with crumbly cheese. **Known for:** baklava; ice cream; su böreği (savory pastry with crumbly cheese). [$] *Average main: 10 TL* ✉ *As you exit St. Nicholas Basilica, walk south to the square; on your right is a modern shopping center; Nur Pastaneleri is on the corner, Kolcular Sokak, Demre* ☎ *242/871–6310.*

Finike and Arykanda

30 km (18 miles) east of Demre; 111 km (70 miles) southwest of Antalya on Rte. 400.

Finike is a good lunch stop or jumping-off point for Arykanda and the series of less glamorous Lycian sites that dot the citrus- and vegetable-growing coastal plain. This small port town is less touristy than other coastal communities—and more friendly, helpful, and inexpensive. It's not the most exciting place to stay (most foreign visitors are yachters, docking at the marina to replenish supplies), but if you

These Lycian rock tombs have been carved into the cliff side of the ancient city of Myra.

just want a decent bed for a night, it's the best option between Olympos and Kekova. Although its yacht marina also harbors many European boats, Finike, which makes most of its money from its acres of orange trees, seems to take their presence unfussily in stride. A colorful town market is held every Sunday; be sure to get some of the famous oranges, if they're in season.

GETTING HERE AND AROUND
Finike is right on the highway. The old road for Arykanda goes north from the major bend at the center of town, and soon crosses the river, where you can then join the new road. Drive 35 km (22 miles) toward Elmalı, and then watch for the Arykanda sign to the right, at a popular roadside market.

Sights

Arykanda
ARCHAEOLOGICAL SITE | FAMILY | The well-preserved walls and lovely location of Arykanda, high in a mountain valley above Finike, make this ancient Lycian town one of the most beautiful and least crowded archaeological sites on the Turquoise Coast. A parking area and easy-to-follow trail lead up to the acropolis, first passing a church and the monumental Roman baths (perhaps Turkey's best-preserved), with intact mosaic floors, standing walls, and windows framing the valley. The tombs, farther east along the trail, are more properly Roman rather than Lycian—it's worth the hike to see the carved gateway on the last one. At the top of the hills sit a sunken agora, or market, with arcades on three sides and an intimate odeon, or small concert hall, topped by a Greek-style theater that offers a breathtaking view of the valley and mountains often capped with snow. Even higher up is the town's stadium, or running track. Farther north is a second, long thin agora, with a small temple above it. From here the official trail scrambles down to some Roman villas, but you may find it easier to backtrack. Back toward the car park is a temple of Trajan with an ancient Roman

toilet underneath. ✉ *Finike* ✣ *30 km (19 miles) north of Finike on the Elmalı road* 🌐 *www.antalyamuzesi.gov.tr/en/arykanda-ruins* 🎫 *Free.*

Elmalı

MUSEUM | North of Arykanda, the mountain town of Elmalı is the center of the country's apple (*elma*) industry. Although a glimpse of traditional Turkey and the cool mountain air are the main draws, Elmalı is also known for its traditional, half-timber houses and the Ömer Pasha mosque (1602), which is one of the best Ottoman mosques in southern Turkey. Several important pre-classical sites have been excavated in the area, and a hoard of nearly 2,000 coins from the 5th century BC, called the "Treasure of the Century" was unearthed near here. Most finds are now in the Antalya Museum, but a small, free museum, Elmalı Müzes **i**, opened here in 2011. ✉ *60 km (37 miles) north of Arykanda, Eski Hükümet Cad. No. 89, Elmalı, Finike* ☎ *242/618–4442.*

🍴 Restaurants

Altın Sofra

$ | **TURKISH** | This restaurant in the marina is famed for lamb and lambs' liver, but it serves a full menu. There is a pleasant garden shaded by plane trees and acacias. **Known for:** mezes; grilled sea bass; lamb's liver. [$] *Average main: 20 TL* ✉ *Kale Mahallesi, Limaniçi No. 111, Finike* ✣ *Inside the yacht marina, 100 yds past the entrance* ☎ *242/855–1281.*

Olympos and Çıralı

Çıralı is 76.2 km (47 miles) east of Finike; 80.4 km (50 miles) southwest of Antalya from Rte. 400.

Olympos and Çıralı are places unique on the Turquoise Coast for their natural beauty, ancient ruins, low-rise development, and easygoing culture that embraces international backpackers, Turkish students, and European families. They are also next to some of the best day walks on the Lycian Way, though the Olympos ruins and beach are the main area attractions. Both are accessed via a secondary road, parallel to the highway. Olympos has a great deal of character but can be noisy and crowded in summer and offers limited accommodations. The area above the valley has better places to stay, but you'll have a short drive to the beach. Relaxed Çıralı is directly on the beach, which it shares with the Olympos archaeological site, located a short walk inland. It's the quietest option, with the best range of hotels and a more family-friendly atmosphere.

The ruins of the ancient city of Olympos, enshrouded in dense vegetation, have received little excavation and, as a result, are wonderfully atmospheric. Olympos was once a top-voting member of the 2nd-century-BC Lycian League, but most of the buildings viewable today date from Roman times. Roman-era construction started in earnest after officers—including the young Julius Caesar—crushed a two-year-long occupation of the city by pirates in about 70 BC.

GETTING HERE AND AROUND

Olympos is off Route 400, between Kumluca and Tekirova. There are signposted turns to Adrasan (9 km/6 miles), Olympos (12 km/7½ miles), and Çıralı (7 km/4½ miles). From Upper Olympos a second road connects to Adrasan. There is no direct road between Olympos and Çıralı, so if you are staying in town, it's best to take the short walk along the beach rather than the long, 21-km drive around the mountain that can take as long as 45 minutes. Buses traveling between Kaş and Antalya stop on the highway at the Olympos/Çıralı intersections, and minibuses take passengers down to the coast every hour until the evening. Minibus prices about 10 TL each way.

◉ Sights

★ Olympos

ARCHAEOLOGICAL SITE | FAMILY | The ruins are next to a river and the shade provided by the surrounding tall firs, flowering oleander bushes, and a mountain gorge means they are also delightfully cool in summer, the perfect time to explore. Many tombs are scattered around the ancient city. In the center of the northern half of the site is the large cathedral complex, once the main temple, which includes a much-photographed 18-foot-high gate, dedicated to Marcus Aurelius in AD 171 and mistakenly referred to by signs as a temple. Note how some walls around the site have clearly been rebuilt in later centuries with narrow arrow slits. At the beach entrance is a poetic inscription on a sarcophagus in memory of an ancient ship's captain, along with a carving of his beached boat—not that different from today's *gulets*. From here you can also climb to a small acropolis and some medieval fortifications where citizens in ancient times would keep a lookout for ships and pirates. The southern side of the ancient city is best reached by crossing the riverbed (sometimes dry in summer) by the land-side ticket office and heading east toward the beach along a well-beaten path that starts with a remarkable row of tombs. Farther along are shipping quays, warehouses, a gorgeously overgrown theater, some of which lie half-buried in what feels like the floor of a tropical jungle. Farther south along the beach are the walls of a medieval castle and church. ⌧ *Çıralı* ✥ *Olympos is best approached from Çıralı by walking along the beach; otherwise, it's a 21-km drive all the way around the mountain* ⛁ *20 TL.*

★ Olympos Beach

BEACH—SIGHT | FAMILY | This 5-km (3-mile) sweep of beach, with a line of fir trees behind it and a surrounding amphitheater of mountains (including the 8,000-foot peak of Mt. Olympos) is one of the wonders of Turkey. Although it has managed to escape the ravages of industrial tourism, there are several good beachfront restaurants where you can eat during the day or spend an evening. Note that Olympos and Çıralı are only separated by a short walk along the beach, but it's a long, 21-km drive around the mountain. The surface here consists mostly of smooth white and multicolor pebbles mixed with some light gray sand, so prepare to recline on a lounger rather than a beach towel. Keep an eye out for the nests of Caretta caretta turtles, who regularly lay their eggs on the beach. ∎TIP➔ If it's **crowded near Olympos, stroll up towards Çıralı, where you're likely to find a patch of beach all to yourself, even in high season.** **Amenities:** food and drink, parking (free); toilets. **Best for:** swimming; walking. ⌧ *Çıralı* ✥ *Between Olympos Archaeological Site and Çıralı.*

Chimaera

NATURE SITE | FAMILY | At the far end of Çıralı, an evening scramble up a sometimes steep path will bring you to the Chimaera, named after the ferocious fire breathing beast of legend. Flames can still be seen rising from cracks in the rock, apparently also burning the gas deep below, since they reignite even if covered. In times past, the flames were apparently even more vigorous, visible by sailors offshore, and the ruins of an ancient stone building can be seen near the flames. The Chimaera is inland from the far southern end of Çıralı; take either of the main roads to the end, and then head inland. If you're staying in Olympos it's a 7-km (5-mile) 90-minute walk, so you may want to drive or bike to the bottom of the hill, or take a tour, which most hotels in the area will arrange. You can see the flames in the day, but they're best at night. Bring a flashlight for all the stairs, since there's no lighting. In peak season, you'll need to choose between going as late as possible to avoid the crowds, or in daylight so you can see the pretty mountainside. ⊠ *Yanartaş, Çirali* ✛ *7 km (5 miles) outside Olympos* 🔁 *7 TL.*

 Restaurants

Karakuş

$$ | TURKISH | FAMILY | Nestled right on the beach, Karakuş is one of the best places for dinner and drinks in the entire area. The mezes and oven-fresh flatbread are delightful, and the beachfront scene is serene. **Known for:** great mezes; lamb shish kebab; grilled sea bass. 🟊 *Average main: 35 TL* ⊠ *Çıralı sk. No 546, Çirali* ☎ *242/825–7376* ⊕ *www.karakusrestaurantcirali.com.*

Hotels

★ Arcadia

$$$ | HOTEL | This spot has the prettiest bungalows in the area; at present six occupy a perfect position between the road and the beach, while five more sit across the road. **Pros:** well-equipped cabins with Ottoman-style wooden ceilings, AC, and Wi-Fi; friendly staff; gorgeous, tranquil setting. **Cons:** comparatively pricey; not all bungalows are on the beach side of the little road; some improvements could be made. 🟊 *Rooms from: 480 TL* ⊠ *Çirali* ✛ *At the far, southern end of main beachfront road* ☎ *242/825–7340* ⊕ *www.arcadiaholiday.com* 🕙 *Closed mid-Nov.–Mar; will open on request* 🔁 *11 bungalows* ⫦ *Free Breakfast.*

Daphne House

$$ | B&B/INN | This pleasant stone hotel with a friendly, alternative atmosphere perches on the edge of a pine forest. **Pros:** friendly, alternative vibe, and helpful owners; tranquil, rustic environment; delicious food, mostly vegetarian. **Cons:** some rooms are small, and accessed by a spiral staircase; 3 km (1 mile) from the beach; off the beaten path, though for some that is the appeal. 🟊 *Rooms from:*

350 TL ⊠ *Yazır Mah. Kilise Yakası Sokak, No. 36, Olympos, Çirali* ☎ *242/892–1133* ⊕ *www.daphneevi.com* 🕙 *Closed Nov.– Apr.* 🔁 *6 rooms* ⫦ *Free Breakfast.*

Myland Nature Hotel

$$ | HOTEL | This relaxed and friendly *pansiyon* is across from the water, about halfway along the beach road, and has a rather New Age vibe. **Pros:** good food; beautiful garden; rental bikes available; complimentary yoga workshops. **Cons:** cabins are nice but not exceptional; just across the street, rather than directly on the beach; no sea views. 🟊 *Rooms from: 335 TL* ⊠ *Halfway along main beachfront road, on left; 3rd hotel after the primary school, Çirali* ☎ *242/825–7044* ⊕ *www.mylandnature.com* 🕙 *Closed mid-Nov.– Mar.* 🔁 *13 cabins* ⫦ *Free Breakfast.*

Olympos Mitos

$$$ | HOTEL | This low-key but high-end hotel complex is one of the nicest places to stay in the neighborhood. **Pros:** emphasizes sustainability and "soft" tourism; relaxing; offers a range of activities. **Cons:** out of the way; a bit pricey; not for everyone. 🟊 *Rooms from: 450 TL* ⊠ *Kiliseyakası Mevkii, Olympos, Çirali* ✛ *As you descend from Rte. 400, look for sign down a dirt track about 500 yds before you reach a river ford and final turn for Olympos itself* ☎ *242/892–1158* ⊕ *www.olymposmitos.com* 🕙 *Closed Oct. 15–May 15* 🔁 *22 rooms* ⫦ *Free Breakfast.*

Olympos Lodge

$$$ | HOTEL | FAMILY | By far Çıralı's most luxurious (and expensive) option, Olympos Lodge is located on the beach right by the entrance to the Olympos archaeological site. **Pros:** fabulous location; bright, luxurious rooms; lovely grounds. **Cons:** nearby water is not in the best health; crowded beach; pricey. 🟊 *Rooms from: 960 TL* ⊠ *Çirali* ✛ *On the far western end of Olympos Beach* ☎ *242/825–7171* ⊕ *www.olymposlodge.com.tr* 🔁 *14 rooms* ⫦ *Free Breakfast.*

The mythical Chimaera (for which the flame at Olympos is named) was a fire-breathing monster with the body of a goat, the head of a lion, and the tail of a serpent.

Şaban Tree Houses

$ | **B&B/INN** | **FAMILY** | One of the older lodgings in the gorge, Şaban is popular among foreigners of all ages; Olympos regulars say it has the best food in the valley. **Pros:** friendly and comfortable; helpful staff speak excellent English; nightly campfires in the pleasant garden. **Cons:** can be noisy and crowded in summer; a bit of a walk to the beach; very hot in mid-summer. [$] *Rooms from: 120 TL* ✉ *Olympos Yazırköyü, Olympos, Çirali* ✣ *Near where the road crosses the dry stream* ☎ *507/007–6600* 🌐 *www.sabanpansion.com* 🛏 *60 rooms* 🍴 *Free Breakfast.*

Activities

ROCK-CLIMBING

Kadir's Tree Houses

CLIMBING/MOUNTAINEERING | **FAMILY** | Towering Mt. Olympos is one of Turkey's premier rock climbing destinations. Kadir's Tree Houses, a few hundred yards up from the main cluster of buildings in the valley, has a climbing center which provides support for new and experienced climbers, with short climbs on offer, as well as two-day courses for beginners and more experienced climbers. They also offer short diving excursions. ✉ *Olympos Kadir'in Ağaç Evleri, Olympos, Çıralı* ☎ *535/811–5683* 🌐 *www.olymposrockclimbing.com.*

Adrasan

16 km (10 miles) south of Olympos

A relaxed little town on a long beach, Adrasan is a world away from the flashy resort areas, so don't expect five-star hotels, gourmet restaurants, or tour buses—just a great stretch of rarely crowded beach, a slightly scruffy town, and some decent family-run *pansiyons.*

GETTING HERE AND AROUND

Boat tours that take you to swim in local coves set off each morning at about 10 am and cost about 50 TL, including lunch. A wonderful, mostly shaded day's walk along the Lycian Way will take you through forests over Mt. Musa to Olympos; another leads to the lighthouse at the point of the Tekke Peninsula; a third, more difficult route goes around the peninsula to the wonderful lighthouse at Cape Gelidonya and to the small beach town of Karaöz. Bring along the official Lycian Way guidebook (it comes with a map), adequate water, and preferably a guide for the often-lonely pathways. Note that there is limited public transport to Adrasan, so you're best off if you have a car.

 Restaurants

Chill House Lounge

$$ | **MEDITERRANEAN** | "Chill" is the perfect word to describe this relaxed spot. Popular with locals, its tables are mostly set out in the prime open area, toward the southern end of the beach. **Known for:** grilled salmon; calamari; bolognese pasta. $ *Average main: 30 TL ⊠ Main beach road, Deniz Mahallesi, Kumluca, Adrasan* ☎ *532/775–2618* ☉ *Closed Nov.–Apr.*

Hotels

Ceneviz Hotel and Restaurant

$$ | **HOTEL** | This hotel set slightly back from the beach has modest, clean rooms, some with a sea view. **Pros:** central location near the beach; green and tranquil environment; rooms well-lit. **Cons:** rooms are quite basic; no pool (though very close to beach); no TVs in rooms. $ *Rooms from: 250 TL ⊠ Deniz Mahallesi, Sahil Cad. No. 106, Halfway along Adrasan Beach, Adrasan* ☎ *242/883–1030* ⊕ *www.cenevizhotel. com* ☉ *Closed mid-Nov.–mid-Mar.* ➯ *16 rooms* ❍❋ *Free Breakfast.*

Ford Hotel

$$ | **HOTEL** | **FAMILY** | This Adrasan hotel sits between the sea and a mountain on a prime spot at the southern end of the beach; the two-story main building's decent-sized rooms are sparsely furnished yet still comfortable, and many

have a balcony and sea view. **Pros:** just off the beach; delightful pool and terrace, with gorgeous, panoramic views of the beach; family-friendly atmosphere. **Cons:** at the far end of town; decor is clean and well kept, but a little dated, without much "local color"; some rooms on the small side. $ *Rooms from: 250 TL ⊠ Sahil Cad. 220, far end of the beach, Adrasan* ☎ *242/883–1044* ⊕ *www.fordhotel.net* ☉ *Closed Nov.–Apr.* ➯ *31 rooms* ❍❋ *Free Breakfast.*

Otto Palace

$ | **B&B/INN** | **FAMILY** | This charming hotel, just inland from the beach, makes a friendly base in Adrasan, with large, airy rooms with dark wood furniture (some with Turkish tiles) in an Ottoman-style building and a nice outdoor pool and garden. **Pros:** pleasant modern building; good for trekkers and divers; friendly, helpful English-speaking owners. **Cons:** a short walk from the beach; closes early in season; no TVs in room. $ *Rooms from: 160 TL ⊠ Deniz Mah., 130 Sokak, Adrasan* ⊹ *350 yards from the beach* ☎ *242/883–1462* ⊕ *www.ottopalace.com* ☉ *Closed late Sept.–Apr.* ➯ *12 rooms* ❍❋ *Free Breakfast.*

Phaselis

31 km (19 miles) north of Olympos; 60 km (37 miles) southwest of Antalya on Rte. 400.

Majestically located at the edge of three small bays, the ruins of the ancient port city of Phaselis make an atmospheric stop along the Lycian coast.

GETTING HERE AND AROUND

The well-marked turnoff is a short distance north of Tekirova; from there to the ruins and beach is about 2 km (1¼ miles). A bus regularly runs from Tekirova as far as the ticket office, about halfway along this road.

Sights

Göynük Canyon

TRAIL | For a cool, memorable day hike, pack a picnic and trek up the Göynük Gorge. Drive north of Phaselis to the corner of the coast where Beldibi ends and Göynük begins, a point clearly marked by blue "city limits" signs at the bridge over a riverbed. Turn inland onto the unmarked tarmac and dirt track on the northern bank of the river and follow sporadic signs to the "wasserfall" into the gorge. When you no longer feel comfortable with the rockiness of the track, park by the side of the road and walk on up. Having a guide with you is handy but not essential—red-painted signs from a local café will keep you on the right path. Take note: when the drive-able road definitively ends, take the path up the left-hand gorge, following the main river, cross to the far banks, then back again about five minutes later and a forest track carved into the side of the mountain, not the steeper right-hand one. Nearly an hour from the last car park, the road turns into a path, and drops down to the river. You can take a refreshing swim where the cold, clear river flows through a long, deep crevasse carved by the water through the rock. Follow the rope and walk the first section of the canyon, with chilly waist-deep water. With good waterproof shoes you can continue up some small waterfalls and rocky ledges as far as you feel safe—just observe usual precautions like not canyoning after recent rain. ⊠ *At the end of Kanyon Yolu, just inland of Göynük, Tekirova* ✛ *12 km (7 miles) north of Kemer* 🖅 *6 TL.*

★ Phaselis Archaeological Site (*Phaselis Antik Kenti*)

ARCHAEOLOGICAL SITE | FAMILY | The ruins of Phaselis, the ancient port city majestically located at the edge of three smalls bays, are as romantic as the reputation of its ancient inhabitants was appalling. Demosthenes the Greek called them unsavory, and Roman statesman Cicero called them rapacious pirates. Since the first Greek colonists from Rhodes bought the land from a local shepherd in the 7th century BC for a load of dried fish, classical literature is replete with the expression "a present from the Phaselians," meaning a cheap gift. Still, the setting is beautiful and Alexander the Great spent a whole winter here before marching on to conquer the east. A broad main street, flanked by some remarkably well-preserved buildings, cuts through the half-standing walls of the Roman agora. At each end of this main street is a different bay, both with translucent water ideal for swimming. A small theater with trees growing among the seats has a divine view of Mt. Olympos, and fine sarcophagi are scattered throughout a necropolis in the pine woods that surround the three bays. The ruins are poetic and impressive, ideal for a picnic or a day at the beach, but weekends and high season days can be crowded and downright depressing when tour yachts from Antalya arrive with loudspeakers blaring. ⊠ *Antalya-Kumluca Yolu 57, Tekirova* ✛ *2 km (1 mile) north of Tekirova* ⊕ *www. muze.gov.tr/tr/muzeler/phaselis-orenyeri* 🖅 *30 TL.*

🛏 Hotels

Sundance Camp

$ | **B&B/INN** | This popular and eco-minded stopover for Lycian Way trekkers and arty types is on a lagoon with a private beach between Phaselis and the less attractive resort town of Tekirova. **Pros:** good food; idyllic, light-filled wooden cabins; tranquil environment. **Cons:** no pool or TV; somewhat isolated location; simple, basic furnishings. $ *Rooms from: 175 TL* ⊠ *Faselis Cad./1015 Sok. No. 62, Tekirova* ✛ *Between Phaselis and Tekirova, follow the signs to the "ecopark" and keep going* ☎ *538/293–3371* ⊕ *www. sundancecamp.com* 🛏 *27 bungalows* ⦿| *Free Breakfast.*

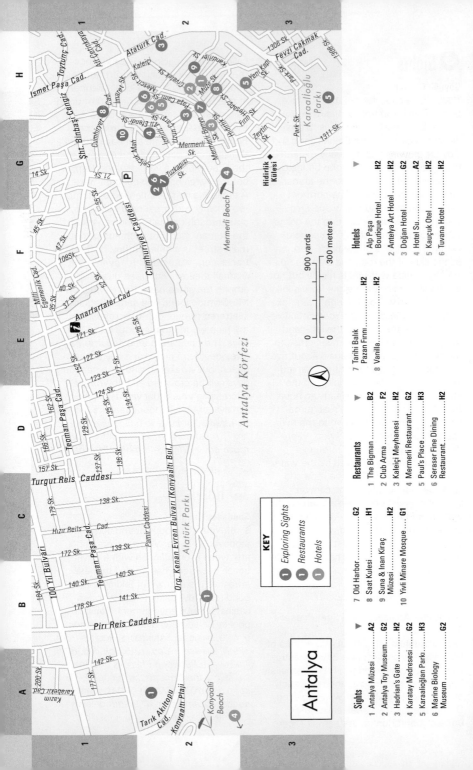

Antalya

KEY

- ⓵ Exploring Sights
- ⓵ Restaurants
- ⓵ Hotels

Sights

1. Antalya Müzesi A2
2. Antalya Toy Museum G2
3. Hadrian's Gate H2
4. Karatay Medresesi G2
5. Karaalioğlan Parkı H3
6. Marine Biology Museum G2
7. Old Harbor G2
8. Saat Kulesi H1
9. Suna & İnan Kıraç Müzesi H2
10. Yivli Minare Mosque G1

Restaurants

1. The Bigman B2
2. Club Arma F2
3. Kaleiçi Meyhanesi H2
4. Mermerli Restaurant G2
5. Paul's Place H3
6. Seraser Fine Dining Restaurant H2
7. Tarihi Balık Pazan Fırını H2
8. Vanilla H2

Hotels

1. Alp Paşa Boutique Hotel H2
2. Antelya Art Hotel H2
3. Doğan Hotel G2
4. Hotel Su A2
5. Kaucuk Otel H2
6. Tuvana Hotel H2

Antalya

298 km (185 miles) northeast of Fethiye.

Sophisticated Antalya is a definite tourist hub, and with a population approaching the 1-million mark, it's among Turkey's fastest growing cities. These days the international terminals of Antalya airport are busier even than those in Istanbul. Most visitors are on package tours, but Antalya is a popular destination among Turks, too. Enormous hotels east of the city help accommodate them; however, you can bed down in one of the restored mansions or *pansiyons* found in the atmospheric Kaleiçi quarter and hardly notice the big urban conglomeration all around. On the hilltop above the harbor are tea gardens and bars with views that extend south to the Bey Mountains and north to the Taurus Mountains.

GETTING HERE AND AROUND
The main bus station is north of the city, and there's a new tramline from there to the center. Buses going to Phaselis, Olympos, and the Lycian coast stop at a makeshift terminal opposite the Hotel Su, which is a much shorter taxi ride from the old city than the main station.

A ring road bypasses the inner city and joins with the roads southwest to Olympos and the Lycian coast or east to Side and Alanya. Another road heads north, signposted "Istanbul," and from this there is a left turn for Termessos and the mountain road to Fethiye. An older tram along the Antalya seafront, between Lara and the Antalya Museum, runs every half hour.

VISITOR INFORMATION
CONTACTS Antalya Tourist Office. ✉ *Head west from Saat Kulesi, and turn right onto Anafartlar Cad., the first major road, Anafartlar Cad. 31* ☎ *242/247–1747.*

◉ Sights

★ **Antalya Müzesi** (*Antalya Museum*)
MUSEUM | The province of Antalya has a rich collection of archaeological sites and their assembled finds means a first-rate collection at the Antalya Müzesi. The star is Perge, statues from which fill gallery after gallery here, including one just for the gods, from Aphrodite to Zeus. There are also Turkish crafts, costumes, prehistoric artifacts from the Carian Cave, and pre-classical statues from Elmalı, with bits of Byzantine iconography and some prehistoric fossils thrown in. One gallery has several fine Roman sarcophagi from the 2nd century AD, including a wonderful one illustrating the labors of a steadily aging Hercules. Upstairs are several coin hordes; the large one from Elmalı was recently returned to the museum after being smuggled to the United States. ■**TIP→ If you have the time, walk to the museum from the center of town along the clifftop promenade, which has a fine sea view.** ✉ *Konyaalti Cad., No. 1* ☎ *242/238–5689* ⊕ *www.muze.gov.tr/tr/muzeler/antalya-muzesi* 🎫 *30 TL.*

Antalya Toy Museum (Antalya Oyuncak Müzesi)
MUSEUM | FAMILY | With an international collection of nearly 3,000 toys dating from 1870 through 1980, this cheery little museum near the yacht harbor is a favorite with young families, and also organizes regular toy-making workshops. ✉ *İskele Cad., Yat Limanı, Kaleiçi* ✛ *Just off the yacht harbor* ☎ *242/248–4934* ⊕ *oyuncakmuzesi.antalya.bel.tr* 🎫 *5 TL.*

Hadrian's Gate
MEMORIAL | One way to enter the old town is via Hadrian's Gate, a short walk from the main Saat Kulesi intersection along pleasant palm-lined Atatürk Caddesi. The gate was constructed in honor of a visit by the Roman emperor in AD 130 and has three arches, each now restored, with coffered ceilings decorated with rosettes. Ruts in the marble road show

where carts once trundled through. From here, turn left onto a straight road that leads through town past Kesik Minare Camii to the Hıdırlık Külesi and the sea. ⊠ *Atatürk Cad.* ✛ *Eastern edge of the ancient town walls of Kaleiçi.*

Karatay Medresesi

BUILDING | Built in 1250 by a wealthy Seljuk official during the reign of Sultan Izzedin Keykavus II, this beautiful stone courtyard was once a *medrese*, or religious school. Follow a winding lane up from the old city's harbor, and enter through the towering carved archway into this haven of peace and quiet. Old men gather to practice traditional musical instruments, while onlookers sip tea from the simple, community-minded café. If you've overloaded on Antalya's more touristy side, this is the perfect antidote. ⊠ *Karadayı Sokak No. 3.*

Karaalioğlan Parkı

FAIRGROUND | FAMILY | Shady Karaalioğlan Parkı is a traditional green space with trees, grass, and benches, as well as a view of the Mediterranean, enlivened in summer by circus rides, and by a market during Ramadan. It also has a miniature wooden "apartment building" designed to shelter street cats and their kittens. At the northwest end is a stone tower, called **Hıdırlık Kulesi**, which dates from the 2nd century AD. At sunset, sip a drink at the Castle Café and Bar next door and enjoy an unforgettable panorama of the Bey Mountains across the water. ⊠ *Enter near the Hıdırlık Külesi at the end of Hesapçı Sokak, or via Park Sokak, on the southwestern edge of Kaleiçi.*

Marine Biology Museum (Deniz Biyologisi Müzesi)

MUSEUM | FAMILY | Just off the yacht harbor stands this small and eccentric nautical-themed collection of preserved sea creatures (mostly local), including the odd Damien Hirst-esque shark floating in formaldehyde, under spooky blue lights. It's part charming-local-natural-history-museum, and part aquarium-of-the-damned.

⊠ *Selçuk Mahallesi, İskele Cad. (eski PTT Binası), Kaleiçi Yat Limanı* ☎ *242/243– 2827* 🖰 *6 TL.*

Old Harbor

MARINA | FAMILY | Another way to enter the old city is via the Old Harbor, now overflowing with yachts, fishing vessels, and tourist-excursion boats; stroll up and take your pick, but be prepared for heftily inflated prices. If you're in a car, follow the signs to the *yat limanı* (yacht harbor) and you'll find a convenient, free parking lot behind the quaysides. From here you can head up any of the lanes leading north and east out of the harbor to get to the heart of the old town. Alternatively wander down from the Saat Kulesi, forking to the right past the T-shirt and perfume shops, until you reach the bottom. ⊠ *İskele Cad.*

Saat Kulesi

ARCHAEOLOGICAL SITE | At some point one of the city's Roman towers gained a clock and was dubbed the Saat Kulesi (Clock Tower). Several of the old town's cobbled lanes pass through the wall here. The area, also known as Kaleka-pısı (Castle Gate), serves as one of the interfaces between the old town and the new. ⊠ *At the junction of Uzun Çarşı Sokak and Cumhuriyet Cad., Kaleiçi* ☎ *242/242–4333.*

Suna & Inan Kiraç Müzesi

MUSEUM | Fifty yards inside Hadrian's gate, turn left for the Suna and Inan Kiraç Museum: a little oasis in a group of restored buildings with an unusual painted exterior that experts say reflects the way most Antalya houses looked in Ottoman times. The museum is part of a privately funded research institute and has an excellent library (accessible with special permission), plus a shop that sells a good range of guidebooks. The main display area has interesting pictures of Old Antalya and a couple of rooms with somewhat eccentric-looking but evocatively costumed mannequins that re-create Ottoman wedding scenes. The best part of the museum is the restored church in the garden, where there is a delightful display of historical kitsch. ✉ *Kocatepe Sok. 25, Barbaros Mahallesi* ☎ *242/243–4274* 🎫 *3 TL.*

Yivli Minare Mosque (*Fluted Minaret*)
RELIGIOUS SITE | A few dark blue and turquoise tiles still decorate the Yivli Minare, a graceful 13th-century cylinder erected by the Seljuk sultan Alaaddin Keykubat I; the imam once climbed its narrow steps five times daily to give the call to prayer. The adjoining mosque was built on the site of a Byzantine church, and fascinating traces can be seen if you step inside. Within the complex are two attractive *türbes* (tombs) and an 18th-century *tekke* (monastery), which once housed a community of whirling dervishes. The tekke is now used as an unremarkable art gallery. The *medrese* (theological school) adjacent to the Fluted Minaret has now been glassed in under a bus-station-style roof and is a tourist-oriented shopping center. It sells standard Turkish knickknacks (think pottery, copper work, carpets, and tiles) but prices are better than at most other resorts along the coast. ✉ *Cumhuriyet Cad., south side of Kalekapısı Meydanı.*

Beaches

Konyaaltı Beach
BEACH—SIGHT | **FAMILY** | For many Turks, Antalya is synonymous with the thick crowds of holidaymakers on Konyaaltı Beach, and the packed pebble strand is a hot, somewhat off-putting sight in high season. The city has worked hard to improve the quality of the beach experience though, with especially impressive results on the 1-km (½-mile) section starting after the museum and ending under the Su Hotel. The beach is largely divided up by concessions, each with its own restaurant, deck chairs, umbrellas, and showers. Energetic and often noisy, this is not the spot for a quiet, solitary swim. The city-run AntRay tram from just outside Kaleiçi will take you right to the beach, or you can take a cab. **Amenities**: food and drink; parking; showers; toilets; water sports. **Best for:** partiers; swimming; walking. ✉ *Konyaaltı Plajı, Akdeniz Blvd.*

Mermerli Beach
BEACH—SIGHT | **FAMILY** | If you didn't know that Mermerli Beach was there, you'd never guess it. This small strip of sand and pebbles outside the harbor wall is reached via the Mermerli Restaurant, halfway up the hill east of the harbor. If you're staying in Kaleiçi, this is the ideal way to escape the bustle. The admission price to this quiet oasis in the heart of town includes loungers and umbrellas. Lovely as it is, do be aware that the beach is accessible only by several flights of stairs. **Amenities**: food and drink; toilets. **Best for:** swimming. ✉ *Below Banyo Cad. 25, Kaleiçi* ☎ *242/248–5484* 🎫 *15 TL.*

🍴 Restaurants

The Bigman
$$ | **INTERNATIONAL** | Almost opposite the Antalya Museum but hidden a little down the hill towards the sea, this restaurant may well have the best view in town. Owned by an Antalyan former basketball player (aka the Big Man), it's a popular place for locals to come for a special meal. **Known for:** chicken Caesar salad; two-color ravioli; pepper steak. [$] *Average main: 35 TL* ✉ *Atatürk Parkı, Konyaaltı Cad.* ☎ *242/244–4636* 🌐 *www.thebigman.com.tr.*

Club Arma
$$$ | **INTERNATIONAL** | You can't miss this restaurant—it has a spectacular location halfway up the main road from the old harbor with a panoramic view of the old city and the sea. Inside, airy stone arches give it elegant style despite the fact that this was once the port's petroleum depot. **Known for:** octopus carpaccio; lobster; chestnut parfait. [$] *Average main: 65 TL* ✉ *Kaleiçi Yatlimanı 42* ☎ *242/244–9710* 🌐 *www.clubarma.com.tr.*

Kaleiçi Meyhanesi

$$ | TURKISH | Situated in the heart of Kaleiçi, this meyhane that bears the same name as its neighborhood serves up the best mezes in Antalya, as well as an array of hot appetizers and the freshest seafood. Great service in a spacious outdoor atmosphere. **Known for:** great mezes; hot Ayvalık cheese served in a clay pan; jumbo shrimp. $ *Average main: 40 TL* ⊠ *alıkpazari Sk. No 14.* ☎ *0545/639–3263.*

Mermerli Restaurant

$$ | TURKISH | At the eastern end of the harbor, the Mermerli has decent prices and a broad menu that includes fish, steak, pastas, burgers, Turkish grills, and all-day breakfasts. But the location is its best asset: a spacious, breezy terrace offers excellent views of the sea and the otherworldly looking mountains. **Known for:** grilled calamari; grilled octopus; entrecote steak. $ *Average main: 45 TL* ⊠ *Banyo Cad. 25, Kaleiçi* ☎ *242/248–5484* ⊕ *www.mermerlirestaurant.com.*

Paul's Place

$ | AMERICAN | FAMILY | A homey, peaceful retreat on the southern edge of the old city, St. Paul's Place is run by ex-pats and serves great coffee, fruit smoothies, homemade American cakes, and home-cooked lunches, notably Antalya's best grilled chicken salad. It's also one of the rare inexpensive eateries in central Antalya with distinctive and high-quality food. **Known for:** grilled chicken salad; carrot cake; pepper chicken soup. $ *Average main: 16 TL* ⊠ *Saint Paul Cultural Center, Yenikapı Sokak, No. 24, Kaleiçi* ☎ *242/244–6894* ⊕ *www.stpaulcc-turkey. com* ☾ *Closed weekends and last 2 wks of Aug. No dinner.*

★ Seraser Fine Dining Restaurant

$$$ | INTERNATIONAL | With fine food and excellent service, the stylish Seraser aspires to be the best restaurant in all of Turkey, and its inventive international menu certainly lifts it above other options in Antalya. This is considered a special-occasion restaurant, yet it's wonderfully relaxed and a decent value compared to its American counterparts. **Known for:** goat cheese and aubergine souffle; grouper; char-grilled lamb. $ *Average main: 65 TL* ⊠ *Karanlık Sok. 18* ☎ *242/247–6015* ⊕ *www.seraserrestaurant.com.*

Tarihi Balık Pazarı Fırını

$ | TURKISH | FAMILY | Every Turkish village has *a fırın*: a tasty, unpretentious bakery that churns out a daily bounty of cool puddings, flaky pastries, fresh bread, and sweets. The amazing thing about this one is that it's survived in the heart of touristy Kaleiçi—and with reasonable prices. **Known for:** spinach börek; milk pudding with figs and walnuts; baklava. $ *Average main: 6 TL* ⊠ *Balıkpazarı Sokak, Kaleiçi* ⊟ *No credit cards.*

★ Vanilla

$$$ | MODERN EUROPEAN | If you are kebabed out, this old city restaurant has some of the best contemporary cuisine on the coast and serves it in an appropriately stylish setting. The menu changes regularly, though it's basically modern European with a touch of Asia and includes items (like pork) that you don't see too often in Turkey. **Known for:** duck confit; prawn salad; steak. $ *Average main: 65 TL* ⊠ *Hesapçı Sok. 33* ☎ *242/247–6013* ⊕ *www.vanillaantalya.com.*

🛏 Hotels

Alp Paşa Boutique Hotel

$$ | HOTEL | FAMILY | This hotel—a mansion restored with a contemporary aesthetic—strikes a great balance between atmosphere and comfort, with tasteful rooms set around two shaded courtyards. **Pros:** stylish rooms; generous breakfasts; five-minute walk to Mermerli Beach and the marina; lovely, peaceful courtyard with pool. **Cons:** some rooms are small; mediocre and expensive food in the evenings; spotty Wi-Fi. $ *Rooms* *from: 350 TL ✉ Hesapçı Sokak, No. 30, Kaleiçi ☎ 242/247–5676 🌐 www.alppasa.com 🛏 106 rooms 🍴 Free Breakfast.*

Atelya Art Hotel

$$ | **HOTEL** | Inexpensive and friendly, this hotel has larger-than-usual lodgings and a good location in the Old Town, with many high-ceilinged rooms located in a 250-year-old Ottoman mansion. **Pros:** good value in a central location; rooms in the historic building are large and bright, with period furnishings and wooden ceilings; lots of character. **Cons:** some mild street noise; bathrooms are clean and functional, but on the small side; modern building is not as charming. [$] *Rooms from: 200 TL ✉ Civelek Sokak, No. 21, near Kesik Minare Mosque ☎ 242/241–6416 🌐 www.atelyahotel.com 🛏 28 rooms 🍴 Free Breakfast.*

Doğan Hotel

$$ | **HOTEL** | Every room is tastefully decorated in this family-run establishment, made up of three restored houses, with a pretty garden and pool. **Pros:** a short walk from the old harbor and Mermerli Beach; quiet, spacious garden area with a small, trickling waterfall and birdsong; very friendly staff. **Cons:** some rooms are a little dark; no elevator; some outdated furniture. [$] *Rooms from: 350 TL ✉ Mermerli Banyo Sok. 5 ☎ 242/247–4654 🌐 www.doganhotel.com 🛏 42 rooms 🍴 Free Breakfast.*

Hotel Su

$$$ | **HOTEL** | **FAMILY** | This boxy, all-white mother ship of a design hotel located on the beach is popular with the weekend crowd from Istanbul. **Pros:** funky, eclectic atmosphere; Konyaalti Beach is right on the doorstep; six on-site restaurants. **Cons:** not the coziest atmosphere; might make some travelers feel a bit trapped; on the expensive side. [$] *Rooms from: 560 TL ✉ Dumlupınar Bulvarı, Konyaaltı Korulugu Yanı ☎ 242/249–0700 🌐 www.hotelsu.com.tr 🛏 294 rooms 🍴 Free Breakfast.*

★ **Kauçuk Otel**

$$ | **HOTEL** | This small boutique hotel is made up of two houses that have been authentically restored with an eye to contemporary design. **Pros:** pleasant oasis in bustling Kaleiçi; spacious, historic rooms with modern amenities; lovely courtyard for lounging around the pool. **Cons:** some occasional street noise; pool is nice, but on the small side; spotty Wi-Fi. [$] *Rooms from: 450 TL ✉ Paşa Camii Sokak, No. 22 ☎ 242/244–2377 🌐 www.kaucukotel.com 🛏 10 rooms 🍴 Free Breakfast.*

Tuvana Hotel

$$$ | **HOTEL** | One of the classier options in Kaleiçi, this hotel is made up of four old houses and has comfortable lodgings, excellent service, and a wide range of facilities. **Pros:** great restaurant; traditional ambience; most rooms housed in a 300-year old Ottoman mansion. **Cons:** room sizes vary; decor is a bit bland; street noise in rooms. [$] *Rooms from: 503 TL ✉ Karanlık Sok. 18 ☎ 242/244–4054 🌐 www.tuvanahotel.com 🛏 45 rooms 🍴 Free Breakfast.*

Nightlife

Castle Café and Bar

BARS/PUBS | The perfect start to any evening out in Antalya starts by watching the sun set from the cliff-top Castle Café and Bar, next to the ancient Hıdırlık Kulesi. *✉ Hıdırlık Sokak 48/1 ☎ 242/242–6594.*

Performing Arts

Antalya Kültür Merkezi

ARTS CENTERS | Also known as AKM, the Antalya Kultur Merkezi is a cultural complex with an exhibition space and several theaters located in a cliff-top park about 3 km (2 miles) west of the city center. It hosts concerts year-round—look for flyers posted around the city—as well as the glitzy annual Golden Orange (Altın Portakal) film festival. *✉ Atatürk Kültür Parkı, 100 Yıl Bulvarı ☎ 242/238–5444.*

⚡ Activities

RAFTING

Rafting has become a major activity, with several agencies offering trips to various canyons; most will pick you up at your hotel. Another option is to drive your own vehicle to Köprülü Canyon. To avoid the crowds, get up to the water in the early morning before the package tourists are out of bed.

🛍 Shopping

Migros Shopping Center

SHOPPING CENTERS/MALLS | Set behind the Su Hotel, Antalya's fanciest mall has a large supermarket, eight cinemas, and a large food court, as well as 100 shops that represent both international brands (like Swatch, Lacoste, and Tommy Hilfiger) and Turkey's big clothing chains (including Mavi Jeans, LCW for children's clothes, Derimod for upmarket leathers, Bisse and Abbate for shirts, and Vakkorama and Boyner for general clothing). ⊠ *Arapsuyu Mahallesi, Atatürk Blv. No: 3* ⊕ *www. antalyamigros.com/en.*

★ Osmanlı Sultan Çarık

CLOTHING | Run by a helpful husband-and-wife team, this low-key little shop on the edge of Kaleiçi sells traditional, handmade Ottoman-style leather shoes and boots, as well as bags—all made here by the owner himself. In a city full of overpriced trinket shops, these are some of the most reasonably priced, beautiful, and unique souvenirs you could hope to find. Some shoes are made using only natural dyes, including pomegranate skins, which produce a deep crimson. ⊠ *Hesapçı Sok. 3/b, Barbaros Mahallesi, Kaleiçi* ☎ *242/247–1540* ⊕ *www.osmanlicarik.com.*

Termessos

37 km (23 miles) northwest of Antalya.

Writers in antiquity referred to Termessos as the Eagle's Nest, and when you visit the 4,500-foot-high site, you'll understand why. Seemingly impregnable, Termessos remained autonomous for much of its history and was quite wealthy by the 2nd century AD. Most of the ruins date from that period. A visit takes at least four hours, and there is no restaurant on-site, so pack water and lunch, and wear sturdy shoes.

GETTING HERE AND AROUND

Termessos is best reached by car. Alternately, tours can be arranged by agencies in Antalya, or you can catch any bus from the main bus station to Korkuteli and get off at the Termessos intersection where taxis usually wait; one way is around 50 TL.

⊙ Sights

Karain Cave

CAVE | Archaeological digs have proven that Karain Cave was inhabited as far back as the Paleolithic Age, making it one of the oldest settlements in Turkey. Later it seems to have become a religious center for a primitive civilization. Many of the Karain finds—stone implements, bones of people and animals, and fossilized remains, including those of hippopotamuses—are on display in Antalya Museum—but there is also a small museum on the edge of the high meadow where the cave is located. Part of the cave itself is electrically lighted and open to the public; this is a small site, however, and probably only worth stopping at if you have time after seeing Termessos. ⊠ *Karain Mağarası Örenyeri, Yağca Köyü, At the end of Yağca Köyü Yolu, off Karain Cad.* ☎ *6 TL.*

★ Termessos

ARCHAEOLOGICAL SITE | Over 1,000 feet above sea level, this compelling site is nestled inside the Mount Güllük-Termessos National Park, where golden eagles and fallow deer can sometimes be spotted. The attractions in Termessos start right by the parking area, with a monumental gate that's part of an ancient temple dedicated to the Emperor Hadrian. The steepness of the path that leads up to the craggy remains of the city walls soon makes it clear just why Alexander the Great declined to attack. Next, on your left, are a gymnasium, a colonnaded street, a bath complex built of dark gray stone blocks, and then, up and around, a 5,000-seat theater perched at the edge of a sheer cliff, which has one of the most spectacular settings in Turkey. From this staggering height you can see the sea, the Pamphylian plain, Mt. Solymus, and the occasional mountain goat or ibex. Farther around is the well-preserved bouleuterion (where the city council met), the very overgrown agora (market), and some huge underground cisterns. Termessos has one more wonder: several vast necropolises, with nearly 1,000 tombs scattered willy-nilly on a rocky hill. A signposted alternate route back to the parking lot takes you past several rock-cut tombs; another large collection of tombs can be accessed via a path from the ticket office. ⊠ *Güllük Dağı-Termessos Milli Parkı, Bayatbademleri Köyü* ✛ *Take E87 north toward Burdur, bear left at fork onto Rte. 350 toward Korkuteli and follow signs to Termessos* 🎫 *6 TL.*

Perge

22 km (14 miles) east of Antalya on Rte. 400.

Perge's biggest problem is that it suffers from comparison with its neighbors. It is, however, one of Turkey's best examples of a Roman city.

GETTING HERE AND AROUND

The ruins are well signposted 2 km (1½ miles) north of the small town of Aksu, 22 km (14 miles) east of Antalya on Route 400. There are frequent buses from Antalya Otogar to Aksu, but be prepared to make numerous stops along the way, and either take a taxi or walk from the village to the site itself.

◉ Sights

Perge Ruins (*Perge Örenyeri*)
ARCHAEOLOGICAL SITE | Although Perge isn't beautifully situated like Termessos or an A-list attraction like Aspendos, it is an ideal place to get an overall impression of a Roman city, and only a 25-minute drive from central Antalya. The first thing you'll see is a splendid theater, which has unfortunately been closed for repairs for years, but may be open by your visit. The stadium next door is however open and is one of the best preserved in the ancient world. The vaulted chambers under the stadium bleachers held shops (marble inscriptions record the proprietors' names and businesses).

The rest of the site is about 1 km (½ mile) north. After parking just outside the old city walls, you'll enter near sturdy 3rd-century-BC garrison towers. Directly ahead is a fine, long-colonnaded avenue, unique for the water channel that ran down its center, starting at a fountain at the far end. This street was trodden by St. Paul as he passed by on his way to Pisidian Antioch in the mountains. Beside the entrance is the old agora; the slender, sun-bleached columns lining the street once supported a covered porch filled with shops. Opposite is the well-preserved bathhouse, similar to the hammams still popular in the region today. Follow the main street to the end, and then climb the hill for a literal overview of the site. The rest of Perge is rather overgrown, but the keen-eyed can hunt down several churches and a gymnasium. ⊠ *Perge Yolu, just off Atatürk Cad., Barbaros Mahallesi, Aksu* ⊹ *22 km (14 miles) east of Antalya on Rte. 400* ☎ *242/247–7660* 🖃 *35 TL.*

Aspendos

49 km (31 miles) east of Antalya on Rte. 400.

Most experts agree that the theater in Aspendos is one of the best preserved in the world. A splendid Roman aqueduct that traverses the valley (another superior example of classical engineering) utilized the pressure of the water flowing from the mountains to supply the summit of the acropolis. The water tower dates from the 2nd century AD, and its stairway is still intact.

GETTING HERE AND AROUND

From Antalya, take Route 400 east and follow the yellow signs. There are frequent buses to the nearby town of Serik, but minibuses to Aspendos are rare.

👁 Sights

★ **Aspendos Archaeological Site** (*Aspendos Yolu*)

ARCHAEOLOGICAL SITE | Although there are many Roman theaters still standing, none are quite as perfect as the one at Aspendos, built by a local architect called Xenon during the reign of Emperor Marcus Aurelius (AD 161–180). It owes its current preservation to the fact that the Seljuk Turks repurposed it as a royal palace in the 13th century; traces of the distinctive Seljuk red-and-yellow paint work are still visible. In its heyday, it could hold 12,000 spectators and is most striking for the broad curve of seats, perfectly proportioned porticoes, and rich decoration. The Greeks liked open vistas behind their stages, but the Romans preferred enclosed spaces. The stage building you see today was once covered by an elaborate screen of marble columns, and its niches were filled with statues. The only extant relief on-site depicts Dionysus (Bacchus) watching over the theater. The acoustics are fine, and the theater continues to be used—for concerts and for the Antalya International Opera and Ballet Festival, held every June and July, rather than for wild-animal and gladiator spectacles as in Roman times. Most visitors just see the theater, but don't miss out on the rest of the site, which is located up a zigzagging trail behind it. The rewards are a tall Nymphaion (a sanctuary to the nymphs built around a fountain decorated with a marble dolphin) and the remains of a Byzantine basilica and market hall. You can also see, below in the plain, the stadium and the aqueduct which used an ingenious syphon system. ⊠ *Sarıabalı Köyü, Serik, Antalya* ⊹ *49 km (31 miles) east of Antalya* ☎ *242/247–7660* 🖃 *35 TL.*

Selge and Köprülü Kanyon

CANYON | FAMILY | Just east of Aspendos, a turnoff leads north to Köprülü Kanyon (a popular spot for white-water rafting) and the ruins of Selge. Just before Beşkonak (30 km/18 miles), the road splits and one branch crosses the river, passing the pleasant riverside Selge and Perge restaurants. After 10 km (6 miles), the two roads meet again at the start of the canyon proper—you'll drive over a remarkably well-preserved Roman bridge. There are dozens of raft operators on the river; the Selge and Perge restaurants have local rafting guides as well. From here you head another 15 km (9 miles) up a steep road through rock formations to the town of Zelve, the site of the Roman city of Selge. Just before you reach town, take the left turn and the impressive Roman theater will soon come into view. Most visitors are happy to clamber over the theater, but from the top you can see the ruins of the city itself on the hill opposite. The area is part of the St Paul's trail hike. If you'd

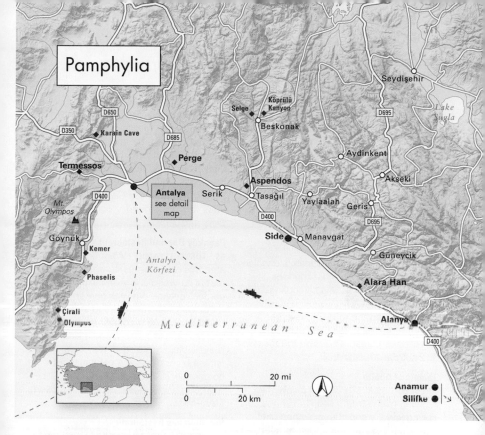

Pamphylia

Seydişehir

Köprülü
Kanyon
Selge
Beskonak

Lake
Suğla

D695

D650

D350

Karain Cave

D685

Aydinkent

Akseki

Perge

Termessos

Aspendos

Antalya
see detail
map

Serik

Tasağıl

Yaylaalah

Geris

D400

Mt.
Olympos

D400

Side

Manavgat

D695

Göynük

Kemer

Antalya
Körfezi

Güneycik

Phaselis

Alara Han

Çirali
Olympos

Mediterranean Sea

Alanya

D400

0   20 mi

0   20 km

Anamur

Silifke

---

like to explore with a local guide, call Adem Bahar (535/762–8116). ✉ Köprülü kanyon Milli Parki.

Side

75 km (47 miles) east of Antalya on Rte. 400.

Charter tour hotels crowded along this stretch of coast threaten to overshadow Side, but the city remains a delightful mix of ancient ruins and modern amenities. Sandy beaches border it on each side, with the ruins in the middle. Side, like Antalya or Alanya, offers all sorts of activities, from shopping and late-night dancing to kayaking in mountain canyons. It's also close to the major sites of Aspendos and Perge, and less than an hour from Antalya Airport. Like its bigger

Pamphylian sisters, Side is best visited out of the heat of high season (July and August). Even at peak times, though, most tourists stay in all-inclusive resorts and head home for dinner. This means that at night it's still possible to experience how Side felt in the 1960s, when the city was off the beaten track, and the likes of dancer Rudolf Nureyev and French intellectual Simone de Beauvoir were visitors.

GETTING HERE AND AROUND

Take the turnoff just west of Manavgat on Route 400—it's another 11 km (7 miles) into town. There's a large parking lot just outside the walls of ancient Side. Frequent buses come from Antalya and Alanya to Manavgat, and minibuses from Manavgat Otogar to Side run every few minutes, stopping at the same parking lot.

VISITOR INFORMATION Side Tourist Office. ✉ *1½ km (1 mile) north of the center on the main road, Side Cad., No. 3* ☎ *242/753–1265, 242/753–1265.*

👁 Sights

Side Müzesi (*Side Museum*)
MUSEUM | Across the street from the agora, the Side Müzesi is housed in a restored 5th- or 6th-century AD Roman bath. The collection of Roman statues is small but interesting; a gorgeous group of marble torsos includes the Three Graces, various cherubs, a brilliant satyr, and a bust of Emperor Hadrian, alongside the usual smattering of inscriptions, amphorae, columns, and sarcophagi, plus a Roman sundial. The sculpture garden behind the museum is larger than the museum itself and overlooks the Mediterranean. ✉ *Beside the theater* ☎ *242/753–1006* 🎫 *15 TL.*

Temple of Apollo
ARCHAEOLOGICAL SITE | If you follow the hustling main street filled with shops selling jewelry and cheap clothes until you reach the water and then turn left, you'll reach the picture-postcard ruins of Side's Roman Temple of Apollo, its gleaming white marble columns set off beautifully by the blue ocean behind it. Millions of visitors a year visit the sun god's ruined temple; come at first light to avoid the crush. Beside it lie the ruins of the temple of Apollo's half-sister Athena, goddess of wisdom and war. ✉ *At the end of Barbaros Cad., near the harbor.*

Theater
ARCHAEOLOGICAL SITE | Opposite the Side Museum is the city's large theater. It was rebuilt in the 2nd century, though the design is more Greek than Roman. There are views out over the agora, which is closed for excavations. ✉ *Just off Liman Cad., across from the Side Museum* 🎫 *30 TL.*

🍴 Restaurants

Orfoz
$$ | **INTERNATIONAL** | If you want to eat in the harbor area, many would say this is the best restaurant to choose. The tables are well spaced, the trees are shady, the service is good, and the food is excellent. **Known for:** garlic prawns; steak; sultan's meatballs. [$] *Average main: 50 TL* ✉ *Nar Sokak, No. 5, Liman Cad.* ☎ *242/753–1362* 🌐 *www.sideorfoz.com* 🕑 *Closed Dec. and Jan.*

Paşaköy Bar and Restaurant
$$ | **TURKISH** | **FAMILY** | What differentiates this pleasant restaurant from the rest is its weird and wonderfully kitsch garden, decked out with garden gnomes, mock-classical statuary, and stuffed animals. The grilled meat dishes are good, the waitstaff is friendly, and a kids' menu is available, as is a small play area. **Known for:** lamb chops; fillet steak; spaghetti bolognese. [$] *Average main: 40 TL* ✉ *Liman Cad. 98* ☎ *242/753–3622* 🕑 *Closed Dec.–May.*

Soundwaves Restaurant
$$ | **MEDITERRANEAN** | **FAMILY** | This open-air restaurant on a pedestrian walk overlooking the sea has a long and reliable reputation; it's run by the same management as the nearby Beach House Hotel. Specialties include fish baked in salt, garlic prawns, and (thanks to an Australian half-owner), a deep-fried seafood dish called Tasmanian Squid. **Known for:** fish baked in salt; garlic prawns; Tasmanian Squid. [$] *Average main: 35 TL* ✉ *Barbaros Cad., 28* ✣ *Next to the Beach House Hotel* ☎ *242/753–1607* 🕑 *Closed Dec.–Apr.*

🛏 Hotels

Barut Hotel Acanthus & Cennet
$$$$ | **RESORT** | This older four-story hotel—one of a large cluster of hotels on the beach, just west of central Side—is done in Mediterranean style, with whitewashed walls, dark-wood trim and

Did You Know?

The Roman theater of ancient Aspendos could seat an audience of more than 15,000 people.

terraces, a red-tile roof, and direct access to a fine sand beach. **Pros:** good beach location not too far from town; well run; good food. **Cons:** typical international package tourist resort; pricey; pool area can get crowded quickly. $ *Rooms from: 1100 TL* ✉ *Turgut Ozal Cad., No 35* ☎ *242/753–3050* ⊕ *www.baruthotels. com* ✄ *104 rooms* ⦿ *Free Breakfast.*

Beach House Hotel
$$ | HOTEL | FAMILY | If you want a few charmed days on the Side seafront, the Beach House, built on the grounds of a Byzantine villa, is a great place to book. **Pros:** friendly and helpful staff; great value; charming private beach only 10 yards away. **Cons:** not directly on the beach; may be past its prime; some small rooms. $ *Rooms from: 250 TL* ✉ *Barbaros Cad., No. 28* ☎ *242/753–1607* ⊕ *www.beachhouse-hotel.com* ⊘ *Closed Nov.–Apr.* ✄ *23 rooms* ⦿ *Free Breakfast.*

Doğa Pension
$ | B&B/INN | This pleasant *pansiyon* is in an old stone house a block from the beach; "doğa" means nature in Turkish, and you'll see this aesthetic reflected in the leafy garden and organic food prepared in the open kitchen. **Pros:** intimate; full of character and local flavor; good value. **Cons:** not right on the beach; rooms a bit basic; no parking. $ *Rooms from: 200 TL* ✉ *Lale Sok. 8* ☎ *242/753–6246* ⊕ *www.sidedoga.com* ⊘ *Closed Nov.–Mar.* ✄ *7 rooms* ⦿ *Free Breakfast.*

Kamer Motel
$$ | HOTEL | This modest, clean option in a quiet part of town has a great location on the eastern shore, with views of the sea and a private though rocky beach area. **Pros:** every room has a balcony with a lovely sea view; good value; good location. **Cons:** uninspired architecture and decor; beach is pretty, but quite rocky; some cramped showers. $ *Rooms from: 300 TL* ✉ *Barabaros Cad. No. 27* ☎ *242/753–1007* ⊕ *www.kamermotel. com* ✄ *16 rooms* ⦿ *Free Breakfast.*

▼ Nightlife

Royal Castle Pub
BARS/PUBS | The action begins after sunset at places like the Royal Castle Bar. Just in from the water on the southwest corner, its publike atmosphere and televised soccer games keep British patrons happy. There is also live music most evenings in season. Be warned, though: drink prices can be steep. ✉ *Turgut Reis Cad., 20 B* ☎ *242/753–4373.*

🏃 Activities

BOAT TRIPS
Boat trips along the Manavgat River can be arranged either from Side or from Manavgat (on Route 400). Prices vary widely depending on the length of the trip and whether food is provided. You should definitely bargain. Times often change, but a boat also usually leaves each morning about 9 am for Alanya: check the evening before at the sales desk in the middle of the Side harbor front. Boats stop to let you swim, and some arrange for activities such as jet-skiing, waterskiing, or parasailing; be warned, however, that not all operators are properly licensed or insured, and serious accidents have occurred.

JEEP SAFARIS
Jeep safaris are also popular and can be arranged from one of several travel agencies in Side.

Daily Trips Belek
TOUR—SPORTS | FAMILY | Based in Belek, near Antalya, Daily Trips Belek organizes jeep and quad safaris, rafting, and diving tours, with day trips starting at about 200 TL a head, including lunch. ✉ *Side Mh. Aquamare Sitesi No. 24 D: I-6, Belek* ☎ *507/214–8269 mobile, 242/453–5583 office* ⊕ *www.dailytripsbelek.com.*

Alara Han

*118 km (73 miles) east of Antalya; 43 km
(26 miles) east of Side.*

The Seljuk Turks fostered the prosperity
of their 11th- to 13th-century domains
with trade protected by a network of
kervansarays, or inns—also called *hans*
in Turkish. Alara Han is one of the best
surviving examples.

GETTING HERE AND AROUND

Turn north off Route 400 near the town
of Okurcular onto a local road signposted
"Alara Han." The site is 9 km (6 miles)
inland via the village of Ulugüney. There
is no public transport.

Sights

Alara Han

BUILDING | With its majestic vaulted interi-
or, Alara Han is among the most romantic
kervansarays (inns) in Turkey. Built on
the banks of the icy Alara River in the
early 13th century and now beautifully
restored, it has a fountain, prayer room,
unusual lamp stands carved into stone,
and lions' heads at the bases of the
arches. In summer, the inland countryside location also provides welcome
relief from the sweltering coast. If you're
feeling energetic, an unusual hand-carved
tunnel leads up to the Seljuk fortress
(Alara Kalesi) built on the crags above the
inn. A flashlight is essential to make the
climb. ⊠ *Alara* ✛ *Just outside the village
of Çakallar, on the banks of the Alara
River, 43 km (26 miles) east of Side.*

Alanya

135 km (84 miles) east of Side on Rte. 400.

Alanya is Turkey's hottest resort town—
literally. Temperatures here are higher
than almost anywhere else in Turkey,
averaging 106°F (27°C) in July and
August; the waves lapping the long

Mediterranean beaches that sweep
toward Alanya's great rock citadel are
only a degree or two cooler. This makes
high summer in Alanya heaven for
sun-starved, disco-loving, hard-drinking
northern Europeans but rather hellish for
anyone seeking a quiet holiday surrounded by nature. That said, Alanya is home
to one of Turkey's biggest year-round
expatriate communities, and in spring
and autumn it's a pleasantly warm and
inexpensive place to indulge in a few
days of easily accessible swimming,
historic sites, and good food.

Foreign influence has encouraged this
city to clean up its act. Former waste-
lands of concrete-block apartments are
now colorfully painted; Ottoman districts
around the harbor are well on the way to
being restored; and the eclectic jumble of
houses inside the magnificent red-walled
citadel contains an increasing number
of handsome boutique hotels. Other
improvements include the opening of a
microbrewery (Red Tower, which serves
what may be the best beer in Turkey) and
the debut of touch-screen bike rentals
around the city center.

Alanya is famed for its sandy beaches,
within walking distance of most hotels.
The best swimming place is known as
Cleopatra Beach—yet another accretion
to the fables surrounding Mark Antony's
courtship of the Egyptian queen—and its
yellow sands extend northwest from the
citadel. Boats can be hired from the harbor for relaxing day tours to caves around
the citadel and a view of the only surviving Seljuk naval arsenal. Alanya, called
Kalanaoros by the Byzantines, was captured by the sultan Alaaddin Keykubad
in 1221 and became the Turkish Seljuks'
first Mediterranean stronghold in their
centuries-long migration westward. Several amusing stories explain the Seljuk
sultan's conquest: one says he married
the commander's daughter, another that
he tied torches to the horns of thousands
of goats and drove them up the hill in the

dark of night, suggesting a great army was attacking. Most likely, he simply cut a deal. Once settled, he modestly renamed the place Alaiya, after himself, and built defensive walls to ensure he would never be dislodged. The Ottomans arrived in 1471, and gave it its current name, Alanya.

GETTING HERE AND AROUND

The highway passes around the city's northern outskirts. The castle marks the center of town, and there are two distinct clusters of hotels, shops, and restaurants on either side of it. There are frequent buses from Antalya and Side, and less frequent ones to Anamur and Adana. If you don't have a car, there is a bus to the summit where the castle sits, which allows you to walk up or down through the old city's residential area, starting or ending at the Kızıl Kule—it's a hot trek in summer, though.

VISITOR INFORMATION

CONTACTS Alanya Tourist Office.
✉ *Damlataş Cad. 81* ☎ *242/513–1240, 242/513–5436.*

 Sights

Alanya Arkeoloji Müzesi (*Alanya Archaeological Museum*)
MUSEUM | It's worth dropping by the small Alanya Archaeological Museum just to see the perfectly preserved Roman bronze statue of a gleaming, muscular Hercules from the 2nd century AD. There are also two nice mosaics, some interesting stone altars, and limestone ossuaries. Note the Ottoman Greek inscriptions in Karamanli—Turkish written with the Greek alphabet. ✉ *Hilmi Bağcı Cad., Saray Mahallesi* ☎ *242/513–1228* 🖾 *6 TL.*

★ **Alanya Castle** (*Alanya Kalesi*)
ARCHAEOLOGICAL SITE | FAMILY | Views of the splendid castle or *kale*, on a mighty crag surrounded on three sides by the sea, dominate all roads into Alanya. The crenellated outer walls are 6½ km

(about 4 miles) long and include 140 towers. The road pierces these outer walls through a modern break, dividing as it heads up the summit. One section leads to the **İç Kale** (inner fortress), the other to the **Ehmediye**; both have places to park. In the center of the castle are the remains of the original *bedestan* (bazaar); the erstwhile old shops are now rooms in the lackluster Bedestan Hotel. Along a road to the top of the promontory, a third wall and a ticket office defends the keep; inside are the ruins of a Byzantine church, with some 6th-century frescoes of the evangelists. Keykubad probably also had a palace here, although discoveries by the McGhee Center of Georgetown University indicates that in times of peace the Seljuk elite probably preferred their pleasure gardens and their hunting and equestrian sports on the well-watered plain below. Steps ascend to the battlement on the summit. A viewing platform is built on the spot where condemned prisoners and women convicted of adultery were once cast to their deaths. The ticket is also valid for the **Ehmediye**. Admire the ruined monastery down below but do not attempt to descend toward it—the mountainside is very treacherous. ✉ *Alanya* ☎ *242/512–3304* 🖾 *20 TL.*

★ **Cleopatra Beach** (*Kleopatra Plaji*)
BEACH—SIGHT | The crown jewel of Alanya is this beach that's right next to the city center. In fact, its main draw is its central location, making it one of the easiest to access, and wide array of activities available nearby. There are many beachside cafés and restaurants spread along the shore, and there are plenty of opportunities for water sports. **Amenities:** food and drink, parking (free), water sports. **Best for:** swimming, walking. ✉ *Ataturk Blvd.*

Kızıl Kule (*Red Tower*)
CASTLE/PALACE | A minor masterpiece of Mediterranean military architecture, the 100-foot-high Kızıl Kule was built by

the Seljuks in 1225 to defend Alanya's harbor and the nearby shipyard known as the tersane. Sophisticated technology for the time was imported in the form of an architect from Aleppo who was familiar with Crusader castle building. The octagonal redbrick structure includes finely judged angles of fire for archers manning the loopholes, cleverly designed stairs to cut attackers off, and a series of troughs to convey boiling tar and melted lead onto besieging forces. Nowadays the Red Tower's cool passages house the Ethnography Museum, usually less captivating than the view from the roof. A short walk south along the water—or along the castle walls, if you prefer—is the tersane, which is made up of five workshops, all under an arched roof. Ships could be pulled up under the vaulted stone arches for building or repairs, and the cover was likely also useful for storing war supplies. ⊠ *Eastern harbor at south end of İskele Cad.* ☜ *4 TL (6 TL with tersane).*

🍴 Restaurants

Flash
$$ | TURKISH | A few blocks north of the fray, Flash attracts more locals than tourists and survives on word of mouth. It's known for soups, steaks, kebabs, and *kiremit* (meat stew) cooked in a clay pot; they also make nice oven-fired *pide* and *lahmacun* (wafer-thin spiced-meat flatbread). **Known for:** Adana kebab; lamb shish kebab; kiremit stew. Ⓢ *Average main: 30 TL* ⊠ *Hacet Cad. 32/A* ☎ *242/511–4220* ⊕ *www.flashrestaurant. com.tr.*

Güverte Restaurant
$$ | TURKISH | This long-standing favorite promises a delightful view of the harbor and excellent traditional Turkish fare that's focused on fresh seafood. If you're lucky, they'll have *grida* (grouper) as a daily special; if not, try the fried squid with local *tarator* sauce—a mixture of yogurt, garlic, lemon, walnuts, olive oil, and bread.

Known for: grouper; grilled octopus; fried calamari. Ⓢ *Average main: 45 TL* ⊠ *Çarşı Mahallesi, İskele Cad. 70* ☎ *242/513– 4900* ⊕ *www.kaptanhotels.com.*

Red Tower Brewery Restaurant
$$ | TURKISH | This is one of Turkey's first microbreweries, and the beer here is some of the best you'll find in the country. Choices include a traditional pilsner and a dark Marzen ale. Ⓢ *Average main: 45 TL* ⊠ *İskele Cad. 80* ☎ *242/513–6664* ⊕ *www.redtowerbrewery.com.*

🛏 Hotels

Elysée Beach Hotel
$$ | HOTEL | FAMILY | This relatively quiet, clean, and modest hotel is right on Alanya's Cleopatra Beach, a short walk from the center of town and is particularly well suited for young families. **Pros:** prime beach location; relaxed feel; some rooms have views of the castle. **Cons:** few rooms have real sea views; impersonal; spotty Wi-Fi. Ⓢ *Rooms from: 220 TL* ⊠ *Saray Mah., Atatürk Cad. 145* ☎ *242/512–8791* ⊕ *www.elyseehotels. com* ⊘ *Closed mid-Dec.–Mar.* ⇌ *60 rooms* ⦿ *Free Breakfast.*

Grand Okan
$$ | HOTEL | The four-star Grand Okan is the slickest hotel on Cleopatra's Beach. **Pros:** own private section of beach; some sea views; relatively central. **Cons:** large, impersonal resort hotel; building is modern but not very aesthetically appealing; streetside rooms can be noisy. Ⓢ *Rooms from: 320 TL* ⊠ *Atatürk Cad., No. 39* ☎ *242/519–1637* ⊕ *www.grandokan.com* ⇌ *155 rooms* ⦿ *Free Breakfast.*

★ Lemon Villa
$$ | B&B/INN | An Ottoman building close to the Red Tower, the Lemon Villa was transformed into this intriguing boutique hotel, seamlessly combining traditional elements with a modern design aesthetic. **Pros:** beautiful rooms; lots of personal touches; close to city center. **Cons:** no views from the garden; lots of

stairs to climb; some rooms a bit small. $ *Rooms from: 300 TL* ✉ *Tophane Cad. 20* ☎ *242/513–4461* ⊕ *www.lemonvilla. com* ⌁ *9 rooms* ❖ *Free Breakfast.*

Villa Turca

$$ | B&B/INN | A restored mansion with a gorgeous shady terrace and an unbeatable view, Villa Turca offers some beautiful, refined rooms. **Pros:** wonderful terrace; unique rooms; romantic atmosphere with lots of character. **Cons:** a little far from the center; beach is a short walk away, down lots of stairs; spotty Wi-Fi. $ *Rooms from: 250 TL* ✉ *Kargi Sok. 7* ☎ *530/547– 4641* ⊕ *www.hotelvillaturka.com* ⌁ *10 rooms* ❖ *Free Breakfast.*

Nightlife

Summer Garden

DANCE CLUBS | Near the seafront on the road to Antalya, this hugely popular disco club and restaurant are part of the same sprawling complex. Two large bars among the palm trees have a dance floor cooled with outdoor air-conditioning (really!). Drinks start flowing at 11 pm, and the music doesn't stop until about 5 am. Free transport to/from Alanya is available for groups of five or more. ✉ *Konaklı Kasabasi, 10 km (6 miles) from downtown Alanya* ☎ *242/565–0059, 535/768–1326* ⊕ *www.summer-garden. com* ☉ *Closed mid-Nov.–mid-May.*

⚡ Activities

Alanya's main strand, Cleopatra Beach, remains relatively uncrowded except in the height of summer. It's also easy to reach other nearby beaches, coves, and caves by boat.

Legend has it that buccaneers kept their most fetching maidens at Korsanlar Mağarası (Pirates' Cave) and Aşıklar Mağarası (Lovers' Cave), two popular destinations for the tour boats that loiter in the harbor. The boats usually charge anywhere from 30 TL to 50 TL

per person for an excursion—it's usually better to go with a smaller boat. If you decide to rent your own (which you can do at the dock near the Kızıl Kule Tower), don't be afraid to bargain.

Anamur

130 km (80 miles) southeast of Alanya on Rte. 400.

Anamur is an uninspiring agricultural town, known throughout Turkey for its bananas. The ruins of ancient Anemurium and the dramatic Mamure Castle, however, give you a reason to stop. The roads both east and west of here are some of the windiest in Turkey. If you want to break up the journey, try one of the low-key waterfront resorts.

GETTING HERE AND AROUND

There are regular buses to Anamur, but they are much less frequent than on other stretches of coast. The highway passes through the center of town, where there is a turn to Anamur's seaside suburb of İskele. Anemurium and Mamure Kalesi, to the east and west respectively, are well signed.

◉ Sights

Anamur Müzesi (*Anamur Museum*)

MUSEUM | A small museum in the waterfront district of İskele displays finds from Anemurium and other nearby sites. The most interesting are the tomb mosaics and a bronze head of Athena. ✉ *Adnan Menderes Cad., No. 3, Yalıevler Mahallesi* ☎ *324/814–1677* 🎟 *Free.*

Anemurium

ARCHAEOLOGICAL SITE | Five kilometers (3 miles) before Anamur is the marked turnoff to ancient Anemurium. The extensive ruins here—mostly dating from the late Roman/early Byzantine period—are built mostly of durable Roman concrete, which makes them better preserved but less picturesque than the average stone ruins. Beside the entrance is a bath building, once part of a gymnasium. Beyond this is a small well-preserved theater, or odeon, opposite which sit the scant remains of a large theater. A second Roman bath building is easily the best preserved in the country, with even its great vaulted roof standing. Beside the road there are also numerous tombs, some with frescoes and mosaics. Anemurium, whose ancient name refers to the winds that often blow through the site, has long inspired the curiosity of foreign visitors; English archaeologist Francis Beaufort excavated here in the 19th century. At the end of the road there's a pebbly beach, where you can take a dip when you've finished, but no showers or other facilities. ⊠ *Anamurium Antik Kenti, at the end of Anamuryum Cad.* 🕾 *6 TL*

★ **Mamure Kalesi** (*Mamure Castle*)
CASTLE/PALACE | FAMILY | On the southeast edge of town the highway goes right past Mamure Kalesi—a spectacular castle with 39 towers, first constructed in Roman times to protect the city from seaborne raiders. It was expanded by the Seljuks, who captured it in the 13th century, and later rebuilt by the Karamanoğulları, who controlled this part of Anatolia after the Seljuk Empire collapsed. Note the inscription to the Karamanoğulları prince, İbrahim Bey II, dating from 1450. The place is so impressively preserved you'd think it was a modern reconstruction. ⊠ *7 km (4 miles) south of Anamur on the coastal road* 🕾 *Free*

🛌 Hotels

Ünlüselek Hotel
$$ | HOTEL | FAMILY | In Anamur's beachfront suburb of İskele, this older hotel has spacious guest rooms; all have sea-view balconies and most have been recently decorated, perhaps with excessive enthusiasm. **Pros:** waterfront location; plenty to keep you entertained, like a beach bar and live music every

night in season; very clean. **Cons:** decor verging on kitsch; on the pricey side for what it is; waterfront lounge/breakfast area a bit basic. $ *Rooms from: 380 TL* ⊠ *1620. Sokak, No. 12, Yalıevleri Mahallesi* 🕾 *324/814–2121* ⊕ *www.unluselek-hotelanamur.com* 🛏 *39 rooms* ❙❁❙ *Free Breakfast.*

Silifke

120 km (74 miles) east of Anamur on Rte. 400.

Lively, non-touristy Silifke is a small agricultural town beside the Göksu River that's dominated by the Byzantine castle, Silifke Kalesi. Traces of its long history are evident in the cave-church home of St. Thecla, one of St. Paul's most prominent disciples, a few minutes outside the village.

GETTING HERE AND AROUND
There are occasionally buses between Silifke and Anamur.

👁 Sights

Heaven and Hell
ARCHAEOLOGICAL SITE | An intriguing attraction that has been drawing visitors since before Roman times. Looking beyond a small café and ticket booth you'll see a completely enclosed valley that was created by an ancient subsidence, sort of a sinkhole. This is called the **Valley of Heaven**, or "Cennet Derisi." A five-minute walk takes you down to the peaceful valley floor and the well-preserved 5th-century AD Byzantine Church of the Virgin Mary. The path then descends into a huge, aircraft-hanger-like natural cavern, which may have been the site of a spring known among the ancients as the fountain of knowledge. Back up the stairs a short walk leads to the **Valley of Hell**, or "Cehennem Derisi," which is narrower, with walls too steep to enter, and deep enough for little sunlight to reach the bottom. A dark and gloomy

place, pagan, Christian, and Muslim sources all identify it as an entrance to hell. The road continues to a third cavern, the **Cave of Wishes**, "Dilek Mağarası": Romans picked crocuses here, and even today you may be met by villagers selling bunches of the little flowers. Down the hill from the highway, the village of Narlikuyu is a picturesque inlet dotted with fish restaurants. The site of ancient Corycos, it now has a small museum with an excellent mosaic depicting the "Three Graces." ⊠ *Hasanaliler Köyü, Narlıkuyu Beldesi* ✛ *Between Silifke and Kız Kalesı, turn north off Route 400 onto a local road signposted "Cennet ve Cehennem Derisi" and the sight is about 3 km (2 miles)* ▣ *18 TL.*

Seleukia Trachea
ARCHAEOLOGICAL SITE | Scattered through the village of Silifke in the vicinity of the castle, remains have been found indicating there was a settlement here as far back as the Bronze Age. Most of what can be seen today is from the Roman city known as Seleukeia Trachea, or Calycadnos Seleuceia and include Corinthian columns from the 2nd-century-AD Temple of Zeus, a stone bridge, and an ancient water cistern. A few kilometers out of the village, you'll find a basilica and tomb dedicated to St. Thecla, St. Paul's first convert and the first female Christian martyr. Most interesting is the cave church where Thecla lived—the Patriarchate in Istanbul now organizes services here occasionally. ⊠ *Silifke* ▣ *6 TL.*

Silifke Müzesi (*Silifke Museum*)
MUSEUM | Local finds, some dating as far back as the Bronze Age, are displayed in the small Silifke Müzesi, just out of the city center towards Anamur. The specimens of Roman jewelry are particularly lovely; there is also a folkloric exhibit. ⊠ *Malazgirt Bulvarı No. 29/A, Atik Mahallesi* ☎ *324/ 714–1019* ⊕ *www. silifkemuzesi.gov.tr.*

Uzuncaburç
ARCHAEOLOGICAL SITE | The small village of Uzuncaburç, in the mountains north of Silifke, makes a nice day trip. It's dotted with the ruins of Diocaesaria Olba, a town run by the priests of Zeus Olbios. Along the ancient main street you'll see a theater, a curious columned structure that once marked the main crossroads, a fountain, a temple of Tyche, and another temple dedicated to Zeus. This temple is one of the earliest surviving Corinthian-style buildings, whose score of upright columns make for an evocative sight. North of the temples is the impressive North Gate; to the northeast is a well-preserved five-story watchtower. The most straightforward road here is signposted from Silifke; after 6 km (4 miles) you'll pass ancient Imbriogon (Demircili), where there are four temple tombs. ⊠ *30 km (19 miles) north of Silifke.*

Kız Kalesı

22 km (14 miles) east of Silifke on Rte. 400.

This small town is easily the best place to stop on the long drive east of Alanya. Although a bit scruffy, it has a nice stretch of beach and a picture-perfect castle sitting just off the shore.

GETTING HERE AND AROUND
The town itself, between the highway and sea, is small and most hotels have frequent signs.

⊙ Sights

Kız Kalesi (*Maiden's Castle*)
MILITARY SITE | Just off the coast, an island—known to have been settled as early as the 4th century BC—is home to an evocative castle called Kız Kalesi. Several offshore castles in Turkey bear this same name, which is derived from a legend about a king, a princess, and a snake: the beautiful princess, apple of

The three Graces, or Charities, depicted in this mosaic are said to have linked arms to show that one kindness should lead to another.

her father's eye, had her fortune read by a wandering soothsayer who declared she would die of a snakebite. The king therefore sent her to a castle on a snake-free island. Destiny, however, can never be avoided, and the offending serpent was accidentally delivered in a basket of grapes sent as a gift from her father's palace. More prosaically, this particular castle was an important part of the row of defenses built and rebuilt over the centuries to stop invaders from Syria entering Anatolia via the coast route to Antalya. What you see dates mostly from the 11th century and was constructed by Byzantines to keep out Antioch-based Crusaders. Boatmen will offer to take you here, but hiring a paddleboat is the most popular way to explore. ⊠ *Just off the coast of Akdeniz.*

🛏 Hotels

★ Barbarossa Club & Hotel
$$ | **HOTEL** | **FAMILY** | This hotel boasts great views of the castle, its own section of beach, and attractive accommodations; guest rooms have tasteful contemporary furnishings and private balconies (most with sea views). **Pros:** modern well-equipped rooms; great location, with genuinely spectacular views of the castle and the sea; nice on-site restaurant. **Cons:** hotel building itself is rather dated; not all rooms have sea views; the only option available is half pension, which may not suit everyone. $ *Rooms from: 200 TL* ⊠ *Çetin Özyaran Cad., Akdeniz Mahallesi* ☎ *324/523–2364* ⊕ *www.barbarossaho-tel.com* ➫ *100 rooms* ⍾ *Free Breakfast.*

Tarsus

41 km (26 miles) southwest of Adana.

The dusty, provincial town of Tarsus is known as the place where St. Paul was born some 2,000 years ago. It has a broad range of Roman, Byzantine, and Turkish ruins, and effort is now being put into restoration. No individual site is exceptional, but taken collectively, they make Tarsus the most interesting stop between Kız Kalesi and Adana.

GETTING HERE AND AROUND

Route E90 passes along the southern edge of the city, so you need to take the old Adana Bulavarı into the center. Most of the frequent buses between Mersin and Adana stop here, but there is no actual bus station or luggage storage; buses stop just east of the Makam-ı Şerif Mosque.

Sights

Near the center of town, beside the tourist office, is an excavated section of Roman Road. North of here is a well in a small garden; it's traditionally identified as connected to the house of St. Paul, though the less pious may doubt it is worth the 6 TL entry fee. South of the well are some of Tarsus's best-preserved old houses, many of which are being restored.

Head east on the main road and you'll find the *Eski Cami* (literally "old mosque"), which was originally built as a church by the Armenians in 1102. Opposite Eski Cami is the 19th-century Makam-ı Şerif, which is said to have been erected over the grave of the Prophet Daniel. Nearby is the 16th-century Ulu Cami, or Great Mosque. To the south is the Church of St. Paul, a Greek-style edifice from the 19th century, now a small museum.

Gate of Cleopatra (*Kleopatra Kapisi*)
BUILDING | Near the main street is the monumental stone Gate of Cleopatra, which—despite the name—was likely built in the Byzantine period. It has made an impression on many visitors to the city, including the famous Ottoman traveler Evliya Çelebi. ✉ *Şht. Kerim Mahallesi.*

Kırkkaşık Bedesteni
BUILDING | Near the Great Mosque stands a covered bazaar dubbed Kırkkaşık, or "40 Spoons," which dates back to the 16th century. ✉ *Sayman Cad.*

Hotels

Elif Hatun Konağı
$$ | **B&B/INN** | This boutique hotel is as good a reason as any to stop in Tarsus; it occupies two restored mansions and has lots of character (picture wooden floors, Turkish carpets, and antique-style furnishings). **Pros:** beautiful, historic rooms, each with its own personality; spacious bathrooms; delightful courtyard. **Cons:** Tarsus is not the most interesting place to base your stay; not for everyone; cafe a bit pricey. [$] *Rooms from: 190 TL* ✉ *Tarihi Evler Sokak 31–33* ☎ *324/614–0807* 🌐 *www.elifhatunkonagi.com.tr* 🛏 *9 rooms* 🍴 *Free Breakfast.*

Adana

53 km (33 miles) northeast of Tarsus.

Adana is Turkey's fourth-largest city after Istanbul, Ankara, and İzmir. Being a commercial and industrial center, it is the least known to tourists; however, there are a few worthwhile attractions, if you happen to be passing through.

GETTING HERE AND AROUND

The main east–west road in Adana, Turhan Cemal Beriker Boulevard, divides the old and new city. There are frequent buses to Osmaniye and İskenderun. Adana also has its own airport, and you can fly here direct from many Turkish cities.

Both Yılan Kalesi and Toprakkale are beside Route E90, but there is no exit from the newer O50 tollway. Toprakkale guards the route south to İskenderun and Antakya. Karatepe is 30 km (19 miles) north of Osmaniye, which is 94 km (58 miles) east of Adana on the E90. Pass through Osmaniye, following signs for Kadirli, then the large signs for Karatepe. Alternately, from Kozan, there is a road, via Kadirli, to Karatepe.

Sights

Adana Archaeology Museum (*Adana Arkeoloji Müzesi*)
MUSEUM | Adana's archaeology museum has a small but nice collection of local finds. ✉ *Gazipaşa, Fuzuli Cad. No. 10* ☎ *322 /454–3857.*

Karatepe
ARCHAEOLOGICAL SITE | About 130 km (81 miles) northeast of Adana, Karatepe makes a (long) day trip from Adana or a worthwhile detour if you're heading to Antakya. Karatepe was a fortress founded in the 8th century by Asatiwatas, the ruler of the post-Hittite state of Adana. A short walk from the parking lot are two ancient gateways, where dozens of well-preserved carved stones (once the foundation of mud brick walls) have been left in place as an open-air museum. There is also a small indoor museum behind the ticket office. The area around the site is a beautiful national park, and you can picnic here or swim in the adjacent dam. It's best visited from Osmaniye, passing ancient Heiropolis-Kastabala, but a secondary road leads from Kozan past Kadirli, which has a well-preserved Byzantine church. ✉ *Karatepe Aslantaş Milli Parkı, Kadirli, Osmaniye.*

Sabancı Merkez Camii
RELIGIOUS SITE | Next door to the archaeology museum is the city's most prominent building and the largest mosque in Turkey, the Sabancı Merkez Camii. Completed in 1998, it is largely a copy of the 16th-century Selimıye Mosque of Edirne. ✉ *Reşatbey Mh.* 🌐 *www.sabancivakfi.org.*

Taş Köprü
BRIDGE/TUNNEL | Heading south along the river is another civic symbol, the impressively long Taş Köprü, or "stone bridge," built by the Emperor Hadrian in AD 125 and restored by later rulers. ✉ *Sinanpaşa Mh.*

Ulu Cami
RELIGIOUS SITE | One of the prettiest mosques in the country, the Ulu Camii is more Arabic than Turkish in style and its patterned stonework has been well restored. Behind the mosque is Adana's lively market area, with several other old mosques, including the Yağ Camii (Oil Mosque) on Alimunif Caddesi, built in 1501 and incorporating a Byzantine church. ✉ *Adana.*

Yılan Kalesi
CASTLE/PALACE | East of Adana, across the Çukurova Plain, there are many ancient remains, including several castles, mostly dating back to Armenian rulers of the 12th to 14th century AD. The easiest to reach, Yılan Kalesi, the "Castle of the Snake," sits conspicuously beside the old highway, 40 km (25 miles) east of town. There isn't a lot to see, but the walls are well preserved and the views of the fertile Çukurova Plain from the top are impressive. Farther east, just before Osmaniye and the turnoff to İskenderun, is a second Armenian Castle, Toprakkale; 70 km (45 miles) north of Yılan Kalesi, Kozan is another fine castle that was an important residence of the Armenian rulers of Cilicia. ✉ *Adana Ceyhan E-5 Karayolu, Ceyhan Merkez, Ceyhan.*

Restaurants

Ciğerci Memet Usta
$$ | **TURKISH** | Nestled in the old city near the clock tower, Ciğerci Memet Usta serves up some of the best kebabs in Adana, the country's reigning center for grilled meat. Try the speciality *ciğer* (grilled liver), the eponymous Adana kebab, and homeade şalgam (spicy pickled black carrot juice). **Known for:** grilled liver skewers; Adana kebab; şalgam. [$] *Average main: 25 TL* ✉ *Sk. no 5* ☎ *332/352–0008.*

Yüzevler

$$ | TURKISH | For most Turks dining in Adana means trying the Adana kebab, minced lamb slow charcoal-grilled on a long wide metal skewer. Everyone in town has an opinion on where to find the best one, but the traditional favorite is Yüzevler. $ *Average main: 30 TL* ✉ *64018 Sok. 25/A, Just off Ziyapaşa Bulvarı* ☎ *322/454–7513* ⊕ *www.yuzevler.com.tr.*

Hotels

Akkoç Butik Otel

$$ | HOTEL | This well-run midsize hotel isn't quite boutique, but it does a nice job of filling the gap between the city's two- and five-star accommodations. **Pros:** in the cool part of town; large rooms with nice decor; friendly staff. **Cons:** more of a business hotel; a bit bland; pretty basic breakfast. $ *Rooms from: 220 TL* ✉ *63005 Sok. 22* ☎ *322/459–1000* ⊕ *www.akkocotel.com* ➱ *30 rooms* ❶ *Free Breakfast.*

Hotel Bosnali

$$ | B&B/INN | Adana finally has a true boutique hotel—an intimate, well-run option occupying a restored, 19th-century mansion in the heart of the old city. **Pros:** central location on the west bank of the Seyhan River; Wi-Fi and valet parking are welcome amenities; rooftop terrace with great views. **Cons:** often booked out by tour groups; some noisy rooms; some dated furniture. $ *Rooms from: 200 TL* ✉ *Seyhan Cad. 29, Kayalıbağ Mahallesi* ☎ *322/359–8000* ⊕ *www.hotelbosnali. com* ➱ *12 rooms* ❶ *Free Breakfast.*

Antakya (Antioch)

191 km (118 miles) southeast of Adana.

Antakya—perhaps better known by its old name, Antioch—was founded in about 300 BC and quickly grew, thanks to its strategic location on the trade routes. Under the Romans, it became the empire's third most important city, surpassed only by Rome and Alexandria. Famed for its luxury and notorious for its depravity, Antioch was chosen by St. Paul as the objective of his first mission. The cave church in which he preached remains a pilgrimage site today, while stunning displays of mosaics in the Hatay Müzesi testify to the artistic achievements of the Roman era.

After enduring earthquakes and assorted raids, the city fell to Crusaders in 1098; then was nearly leveled by the Egyptians in 1268. A late addition to the Turkish Republic, Antakya was occupied by France after 1920 as part of its mandate over Syria, which still has an outstanding territorial claim on it. Though the city reverted to Turkey just before World War II, it still maintains a distinctive character. The people here are mostly bilingual, speaking both Turkish and a local dialect of Arabic. In the cobbled streets of the old quarter you can also hear Syriac (Aramaic), the language spoken by many of Turkey's Christians.

GETTING HERE AND AROUND

The old city, on the east bank of the River Orontes, is relatively compact. Senpiyer Kilisesi, north of the old city, is far enough to drive. There are frequent buses to Adana, Osmaniye, and Gaziantep, though sometimes you need to change in İskenderun. Turkish Airlines operates regular direct flights between Istanbul and Hatay Aiport.

SAFETY

Fascinating, welcoming, and culturally vibrant as it is, Antakya is located very close to the Syrian border. In more peaceful days, Aleppo was less than two hours away by car, and many local families regularly crossed the border to visit relatives on the other side. Impacts of the evolving political situation can be felt in the noticeable decrease in tourism in Antakya, and the increasing presence of Syrian refugees seeking safety on the Turkish side of the border. Although it's on the same coastline, Antakya is a world away from the European-style resorts farther north. Though the situation in Antakya was stable at the time of writing, please exercise utmost caution, and be sure to check both the news and the latest safety updates from the U.S. State Department before planning a trip to this area.

◉ Sights

Catholic Church of Antioch
RELIGIOUS SITE | The Catholic Church maintains its presence with a small sanctuary run by Capuchin monks. It is set in a garden on Kutlu sokak, several winding blocks in from the Sermaye Mosque. Enter its small courtyard from the side street. You may recognize the image of the church bell, with the mosque minaret behind—it's on tourist office brochures as a symbol of religious harmony. Services are usually held here every Sunday evening at 6:30; it may be a good idea to call ahead and confirm. ✉ *Kutlu Sok. 6, just off Kurtuluş Cad., Antakya* 🕾 *326/215–6703* ⊕ *www.anadolukatolik-kilisesi.org/antakya/en.*

Habib-i Neccar Cami
RELIGIOUS SITE | The River Orontes (*Asi* in Turkish) divides Antioch in two. In the old town you will find the Habib-i Neccar Cami, a mosque on Kurtuluş Caddesi, just south of St. Peter's. It's popularly dated from the 7th century and called Turkey's oldest mosque. More likely, a church of John the Baptist originally stood here, replacing a temple, and this was converted to a mosque, converted back to a church by the crusaders, then destroyed in 1268 by the Mamluk Sultan Baybars. He then had the current building constructed. It has since been much restored. A side chamber contains two sarcophagi, labeled as the prophet Jonah and John the Baptist, while downstairs are the tombs of "Habib-i Neccar," an otherwise unidentified early Christian martyr mentioned in the Koran, and "Sham'un al-Safa" (Simon the Loyal),

perhaps the Apostle Simon Peter. All presumably survive from the Byzantine Church, and with that pedigree could even be genuine. Between here and the river is the bazaar quarter, a real change of pace: the feel is more Syrian and Arab than Turkish. ✉ *Corner of Kurtuluş and Kemalpaşa Cad., Antakya.*

Harbiye
TOWN | Most mosaics at the Hatay Museum come from villas in Harbiye. Originally called Daphne, this beautiful gorge of laurel trees and tumbling waterfalls was said to have been chosen by the gods for the Judgment of Paris and contained one of the ancient world's most important shrines to the god Apollo. Mark Antony chose it as the venue for his ill-fated marriage to Cleopatra in 40 BC. Daphne was also a favorite resort for wealthy Antiochenes and developed such a reputation for licentiousness that it was put off-limits to the Roman army. Nothing ancient survives but it's still a popular escape and there are many open-air cafés and restaurants, all fairly similar, overlooking the river. ✉ *7 km (4 miles) south of Antakya on Rte. E91, Antakya.*

★ Hatay Arkeoloji Müzesi (*Hatay Museum*)
MUSEUM | Although little survives of old Antioch, the collection of mosaics (one of the largest in the world) here hints at the city's glorious past. Experts consider the dozens of Roman mosaics in the huge Hatay Archaeological Müzesi—portraying scenes from mythology and replete with figures such as Dionysus, Orpheus, Oceanus, and Thetis—to rank among the highest achievements of Roman art. ✉ *On the outskirts of the city, past the church of St. Peter, on the road to Reyhanlı, Antakya* 🕾 *326/225–1060* ⊕ *www. muze.gov.tr/tr/muzeler/hatay-arkeoloji-muzesi* 🎟 *20 TL.*

Senpiyer Kilisesi (*Church of St. Peter*)
RELIGIOUS SITE | On the northern edge of town is Senpiyer Kilisesi, or Saint Peter Church—a tiny cave high up on a cliff,

blackened by centuries of candle smoke and dripping with water seeping out of the rocks. According to tradition this is where the apostle secretly preached to his converts and where they first came to be called Christians. It is one of the oldest churches in existence; the facade you see, however, was added by the crusaders in the 11th to 12th century. The area around it was a cemetery in classical times, and there are numerous rock-cut tombs and tunnels. A path leads up to the giant carved face of Charon, the legendary boatman who took the dead across the River Styx. Adventurous visitors can follow the valley just south to view a large section of the Byzantine walls, which also served as a bridge and dam. The church was declared a site of pilgrimage by Pope Paul VI, and religious services are sometimes arranged for foreign tourists on Sunday evenings in June. ✉ *Off Kurtuluş Cad., well signposted, Antakya* 🌐 *www.muze.gov.tr/tr/muzeler/st-pierre-anit-muzesi* 🎫 *20 TL.*

Restaurants

Anadolu Restaurant
$$ | **TURKISH** | **FAMILY** | Although service can be a little slow and the modern roof over the garden is unattractive, locals still flock to this 100-year-old house–turned–library–turned–billiards hall–turned restaurant. While here, they dine on savory mezes, popular regional dishes such as *et şato* (minced meat with cheese) or *kağıt kebabı* (meat and vegetables wrapped in thin bread), and, for dessert, *künefe* (a roaringly popular—and intensely rich—pastry made with cheese and nuts). **Known for:** et şato (minced meat with cheese); kağıt kebabı (meat and vegetables wrapped in thin bread; künefe (rich pastry made with cheese and nuts). [$] *Average main: 25 TL* ✉ *Hürriyet Cad. 30/A, Antakya* ☎ *326/215–3335* 🌐 *www.anadolurestaurant.com.tr.*

Hatay Sultan Sofrası
$ | **TURKISH** | Tour groups often fill this restaurant at dinner for good reason: the food is both delicious and inexpensive. That combination makes it popular with locals at lunch; they also offer a nice, traditional Turkish breakfast. [$] *Average main: 18 TL* ✉ *İstiklal Cad., No. 20, Yeni Cami Mahallesi, Antakya* ☎ *326/213–8759* ⏲ *Closed Sun.*

Hotels

★ The Liwan Hotel
$$ | **HOTEL** | This stylish hotel in a restored 1920s mansion is easily the best of the new crop of boutique hotels in town, with its seamless blend of the traditional and the modern. **Pros:** excellent quality; a nice balance of authenticity and 21st-century comfort; good, central location. **Cons:** some noise from the bar, particularly on weekends; some small rooms; spotty Wi-Fi. [$] *Rooms from: 275 TL* ✉ *Silahlı Kuvvetler Cad., No. 5, Antakya* ☎ *326/215–7777* 🌐 *www.theliwanhotel.com* 🛏 *24 rooms* 🍴 *Free Breakfast.*

Saadet Grand Hotel
$$ | **HOTEL** | The modern Saadet Grand is a solid mid-range choice on the southern side of town. **Pros:** tasteful and new; good value; better-than-average English spoken. **Cons:** rooms lack character; a 15-minute walk into town; smoking allowed in some rooms. [$] *Rooms from: 180 TL* ✉ *Harbiye Cad., No. 101, Sümerler Mahallesi, Antakya* ☎ *326/444–3308* 🌐 *www.saadetgrandhotel.com* 🛏 *42 rooms* 🍴 *Free Breakfast; Some meals.*

Chapter 7

CAPPADOCIA AND CENTRAL TURKEY

Updated by
Kevin Mataraci

👁 Sights	🍴 Restaurants	🛏 Hotels	💼 Shopping	🍸 Nightlife
★★★★★	★★★★☆	★★★★★	★★★☆☆	★★☆☆☆

WELCOME TO CAPPADOCIA AND CENTRAL TURKEY

TOP REASONS TO GO

★ **Balloon over Cappadocia:** Dangling high above the spectacular terrain in a basket, you sail past ethereal rock cones and photogenic fairy chimneys.

★ **Explore underground cities:** Kaymaklı, Derinkuyu, and other vast, multistoried subterranean complexes once housed tens of thousands of inhabitants.

★ **Hike the valleys of Cappadocia:** Trails lead past fantastical rock formations and deposit you at cave entrances that open on ornately decorated churches.

★ **Luxuriate in a cave:** Some of Cappadocia's finest hotels are tucked into elaborately appointed caves, where soft lighting, plush beds, antique accents, and even Jacuzzis are common amenities.

★ **Peer into the past:** From the displays at Ankara's Museum of Anatolian Civilizations to Konya's Seljuk-era mosques, Central Turkey bears traces of the numerous cultures that have occupied it.

Central Turkey stretches across a vast, arid plateau, littered with the ruins of ancient civilizations, slashed by ravines in places and rising to the peaks of extinct volcanoes in others.

1 **Ürgüp.** Known for its charming, small hotels.

2 **Göreme.** The biggest city in Cappadocia is the most central location.

3 **Uçhisar.** Has some of the nicest hotels.

4 **Ortahisar.** A sleepy farming village.

5 **Avanos.** A center of Cappadocia pottery-making.

6 **Derinkuyu and Kaymaklı.** Cappadocia's famous underground cities.

7 **Ihlara Valley.** The lush valley offers wonderful hiking.

8 **Soğanlı Valleys.** Quiet and a bit off the beaten path.

9 **Niğde.** A small, quiet agricultural center.

10 **Konya.** A popular pilgrimage site, it's the spiritual home of the whirling dervishes.

11 **Ankara.** Turkey's capital and the best place to witness the legacy of Mustafa Kemal Atatürk.

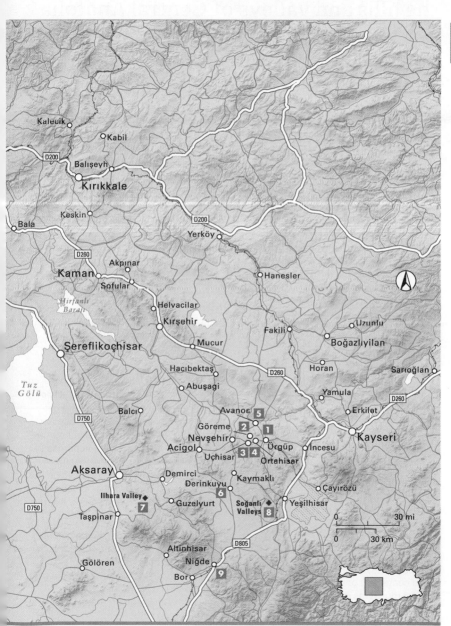

Some of the world's oldest known human habitations were established in the hills and valleys of Central Anatolia, but today the main attraction here is the magical panorama of Cappadocia, where wind and rain have shaped the area's soft volcanic rock into a kind of fairy-tale landscape.

In Cappadocia you'll discover incredible rock formations, spectacular valleys, ancient cave churches, and underground cities that reach many stories beneath the surface. The small towns of Ürgüp, Göreme, Uçhisar, and Ortahisar are good bases for exploring the region's otherworldly landscape. Whether hiking through the amazing terrain on foot, exploring underground passageways, or floating over the incredible landscape in a hot-air balloon, you'll find Cappadocia to be unlike any place you've ever been before.

Southwest of Cappadocia is Konya, home to the tomb of Rumi—the 13th-century founder of the whirling dervishes—and to a fascinating museum dedicated to him. Known as Turkey's most religiously conservative city, Konya is not a place for those looking for nightlife (alcohol can be difficult to find) or a sophisticated dining scene. But centuries-old mosques and religious seminaries lend historic character to Turkey's seventh-largest city.

The region's other major city is Ankara, Turkey's capital and second-largest metropolis. Though lacking the mystique of Cappadocia or Konya, this modern urban center has one of the best archaeological museums in the country and a handful of interesting historical sites, including a citadel that surrounds a picturesque neighborhood. Also in Ankara, the imposing mausoleum of Atatürk, founder of the Turkish Republic, provides visitors a great deal of insight into the modern Turkish psyche.

As you travel through the Turkish heartland, you'll see mostly agricultural regions—the province of Konya, with its vast plains where grains and other crops are grown, is known as the country's breadbasket—and encounter a slice of provincial life.

MAJOR REGIONS

The extraordinary landscape in **Cappadocia** is like a giant outdoor sculpture garden filled with elaborate pillars, needles, and cones. As if these natural phenomena weren't enticing enough, hundreds of caves conceal frescoed churches from the early days of Christianity. Included are Ürgüp, Göreme, Uçhisar, Ortahisar, Avanos, Derinkuyu and Kaymaklı, Ihlara Valley, Soğanlı Valleys, and Niğde.

A popular pilgrimage site, **Konya** contains the tomb of the 13th-century philosopher Rumi and is the spiritual home of the whirling dervishes. Medieval mosques enhance the city's holy feel. Nearby, Çatalhöyük ranks among the oldest known human settlements.

Ankara, Turkey's capital, is the best place to witness the enduring legacy of Mustafa Kemal Atatürk, founding father of the secular Turkish Republic.

Planning

WHEN TO GO

Much of Central Anatolia is blazing hot in summer and freezing cold in winter. The best time to visit is in the spring (May), before the crowds and heat arrive, or early fall (September or October), when the crowds are gone and winter hasn't yet descended.

DISCOUNTS AND DEALS

The Museum Pass Cappadocia allows single entry over a 72-hour period into many of Cappadocia's most popular attractions, including Göreme Open-Air Museum and the Dark Church, Zelve Open-Air Museum, Ihlara Valley, Derinkuyu underground city, Kaymaklı underground city, and Özkonak underground city. Priced at 110 TL (versus almost 200 TL if you pay each entry fee separately), it's a good deal if you plan on visiting most of the sights on your own rather than on guided tours, where entry fees are already included. Museum Pass holders can also avoid ticket lines and benefit from discounts at certain balloon companies, travel agencies, and other local businesses.

GETTING HERE AND AROUND
AIR TRAVEL

Air travel isn't much more expensive than bus travel, and flying to Central Anatolia saves a lot of time.

Several airlines operate direct flights from Istanbul to the city of Kayseri, about an hour's drive from the heart of Cappadocia. Pegasus and SunExpress each also operate several direct flights per week between İzmir and Kayseri; and, in summer, these two airlines generally operate one or two weekly flights from Antalya. Flying into the Nevşehir airport gets you closer to Cappadocian towns; however, flight times are more limited, particularly in winter. Nevşehir is served from Istanbul year-round by Turkish Airlines, its sub-brand Anadolu Jet, and Pegasus. In summer, there are also occasional flights between Nevşehir and Antalya on Anadolu Jet. Travel agencies can arrange a shuttle to take you from either airport to any hotel in the main towns for 25 TL–45 TL; most hotels also arrange pickups for guests.

Ankara's Esenboğa Airport is served by frequent flights from numerous Turkish cities, as well as direct flights from several European cities; Konya is served by frequent flights from Istanbul and near-daily flights from İzmir.

BUS TRAVEL

Cappadocia and Central Anatolia are well served by intercity buses, but the distances from other places you are likely to be visiting are long. The roughly 10-hour trip from Istanbul to Cappadocia costs about 120 TL, while fares from Ankara (4 to 5 hours) or Konya (3½ to 4 hours) are around 45 to 60 TL.

With the exception of Metro and Süha, most long-distance bus companies don't serve small towns of Cappadocia directly, so if you choose that mode of transport you may need to buy a ticket to Nevşehir and then transfer to a local bus. If you don't rent a car during your stay, you may end up passing through Nevşehir repeatedly, as it is the hub for local minibuses. Several daily minibuses also run between Avanos and Ürgüp, with a stop along the way in Göreme. Note that local buses tend to operate less frequently and/or keep shorter hours in winter.

CAR TRAVEL

Once you're here, renting a car is a good idea because you'll probably be traveling around a lot. Highways in Central Anatolia are generally well maintained and lead to all the major sights. Minor roads, however, may be rough and full of potholes. On narrow, winding roads, look out for oncoming trucks whose drivers often don't stay on their own side, and be especially careful at night, when farm vehicles without proper running lights and animals may be on rural roads.

There are good roads between Istanbul and the main cities of Anatolia: Ankara, Konya, and Kayseri. However, truck traffic on the main highway from Istanbul to Ankara, a distance of 454 km (281 miles), can be heavy. Two long stretches of toll road (*ücretli geçiş*) linking Istanbul and Ankara—E80 to beyond Düzce and E89 south from Gerede—provide some relief from the rigors of the other highways.

From Ankara, Konya is 261 km (162 miles) to the south, while Nevşehir—the gateway to Cappadocia—is 309 km (192 miles) to the southeast (via Aksaray).

You can also travel from Central Anatolia on major highways to the Mediterranean and Black Sea coasts: from Ankara, E90 (also known as Route 200) leads southwest toward Sivrihisar; continue southwest on E96 to Afyon, where you can pick up highways going south to Antalya or west to İzmir. Route E88/200 leads east out of Ankara and eventually connects with highways to the Black Sea coast.

TAXI TRAVEL
Taxis within Cappadocian towns aren't expensive, but fares for travel between them add up. Expect to pay close to 20 TL between Uçhisar and Göreme, around 40 TL from Göreme or Uçhisar to Ürgüp or Nevşehir, and 50 TL or more from Uçhisar or Nevşehir to Avanos. All taxis have meters, but you or the driver may prefer to negotiate a flat rate for longer trips.

TRAIN TRAVEL
Thanks to the 2014 launch of a long-awaited high-speed train, rail travel to Central Anatolia is now much faster: trains from Istanbul to Ankara take just under four hours and from Istanbul to Konya, just under four and a half. Until the railway track is extended into central Istanbul, however, passengers must board high-speed trains from the far-flung Pendik train station on the Asian side of the city, near Sabiha Gökçen Airport, which can only be reached by public buses or a taxi. Within the region, high-speed trains run regularly between Ankara and Konya. There is little to no train service to Cappadocia or between small towns in Central Anatolia.

HOTELS
Cappadocia is deservedly famous for its cave hotels—indeed, staying in one is a quintessential experience here. Carved out of soft tufa rock, they range from homey inns decorated in traditional style to high-end boutique properties with contemporary design and large hotels with luxurious furnishings. Some have been occupied for hundreds or even thousands of years, and original architectural details add authenticity. Most visitors find troglodyte lodgings absolutely charming, but bear in mind that they really are caves; some may have little natural light, low ceilings, and occasional falling dust. Cave hotels can also involve numerous interconnecting levels with nary an elevator in sight— that's part of the fun but it does require climbing. (Travelers with mobility issues are advised to contact a hotel before booking.) For those not wanting to stay in a cave, some hotels also have "stone rooms" built using traditional masonry techniques, often with beautiful vaulted ceilings and decorative carvings.

For the most part, hotels in Konya and Ankara don't come close to matching the atmosphere of Cappadocia's unique accommodations, but there are a few interesting boutique hotels and small inns to be found among the large international chains. *Hotel reviews have been shortened. For full information, visit Fodors.com.*

RESTAURANTS

Central Anatolia is the one region in Turkey that does not touch water, so fish has to be trucked or flown in. Be prepared for a lot of meat served in various permutations, including kebabs and stews. In Cappadocia, popular specialties include lamb roasted in a *tandır*, or underground pit, and meat cooked in a *testi*, a type of earthenware vessel. In Konya you'll see *etli ekmek* (flatbread topped with ground lamb and sometimes cheese) as well as local dishes, such as okra soup. Main courses in the region are often preceded by a delicious array of mezes—most notably warm hummus served with *pastırma* (Turkish pastrami), the local specialty.

In Cappadocia and Ankara, restaurants that cater to tourists serve beer, wine, and liquor, including *rakı*. In Konya and other conservative towns, however, alcohol can be quite difficult to find. The inhabitants of Cappadocia have been making wine for thousands of years, though the modern revival of the industry is still somewhat in its fledging stages. Of the local varietals, whites like the Emir tend to be better than reds, which include the Kalecık Karası. Vintners are also producing increasingly successful wines with grapes from other regions of Turkey, as well as foreign ones like Syrah and Cabernet Sauvignon. Whatever you eat and drink, you'll likely dine in atmospheric surroundings—restored *kervansarays* (old-fashioned inns), caves, Ottoman mansions, and garden patios. In some traditional restaurants you'll sit on cushions on the floor, and your meal might be accompanied by live music.

What it Costs in Turkish Lira

	$	$$	$$$	$$$$
RESTAURANTS				
	Under 15 TL	16 TL–30 TL	31 TL–50 TL	over 50 TL
HOTELS				
	Under $100	$101–$175	$176–$250	over $250

TOURS

In Cappadocia, consider joining a tour or hiring a private guide for at least one day. Guides know the terrain and can lead you to places you might not otherwise find (such as hidden rock churches), filling you in on fascinating details about the geology of the region and its early inhabitants. Most daily tours follow one of several broad itineraries, with slight variations: Göreme Open-Air Museum, Uçhisar castle, and nearby valleys; Ihlara Valley, Derinkuyu or Kaymaklı underground city, and scenic viewpoints; or the Soğanlı Valleys and nearby points of interest. A number of companies also lead half- or full-day hikes through scenic spots like Rose Valley. With the exception of very high-end agencies, expect to pay about €35 to €50 per person for a daylong group tour, depending on group size. Private tours typically cost at least twice as much, starting at around €100 per person for two people (there is usually a single supplement for one person). Hotels can make recommendations, or contact one of these companies directly.

Argeus

GUIDED TOURS | One of Cappadocia's best-regarded—and priciest—agencies, Argeus has 20 years of experience. It specializes in customized private tours but also organizes small-group day trips (maximum eight people), one- and multiday mountain biking trips, plus airport shuttles. There are no shopping stops on Argeus tours. ✉ *Ürgüp* ☎ *384/341–4688 in Ürgüp* ⊕ *www.*

argeus.com.tr ☞ Group tours from $110 per person, private tours from $155 per person (for 2).

HtR Travel

GUIDED TOURS | With more than 15 years of experience, HtR Travel runs daily sightseeing tours of Cappadocia (maximum 18 people) at reasonable rates. It also arranges private hiking and tailor-made sightseeing tours in the region, and the guides are excellent. ✉ *Ürgüp ☎ 384/341–5548 in Ürgüp ⊕ www. htrturkeytours.com ☞ Group tours from €40 per person; private tours from €225 (for two).*

Kirkit Voyage

ADVENTURE TOURS | Horseback riding, hiking, mountain biking, boating, camping, and other outdoor activities—both day trips or multiday excursions around the region—are the specialty of this agency, which also organizes sightseeing tours in Cappadocia, mainly on a private basis. ✉ *Avanos ☎ 384/511–3259 in Avanos ⊕ www.kirkit.com ☞ Group tours from €45 per person; private tours from €180 per person (for 2).*

Rock Valley Travel

GUIDED TOURS | In business for two decades, friendly, family-run Rock Valley Travel organizes private and small group day tours (maximum 12 people) as well as three-day trips to Mt. Nemrut and Urfa. The tours are good value and the guides are professional and personable. ✉ *Ürgüp ☎ 384/341–5819 in Ürgüp ⊕ www.rockvalleytravel.com ☞ Group tours from €45 per person; private tours from €180.*

★ Turkish Heritage Travel

GUIDED TOURS | This well-regarded company organizes cooking classes, grape-harvesting excursions (in season), village visits, and other unique outings aimed at introducing guests to authentic Turkish culture. Its knowledgeable, personal guides also lead more traditional group (maximum 15 people) and private tours of Cappadocia, including to off-the-beaten path destinations—and there are no shopping stops. ✉ *Uzundere Cad. 29, Göreme ☎ 384/271–2687 in Göreme ⊕ www.goreme.com ☞ Group tours from €35 per person, private tours from €120 per person (for 2).*

VISITOR INFORMATION

There are three government-run tourism information offices in the Cappadocia region. In the provincial capital of Nevşehir, one is inside the former governor's mansion (*Atatürk Bulvarı ☎ 384/213–3659; open daily 8–5 in summer; closed weekends in winter*), but it mainly provides maps and brochures; the other two, which are more oriented toward helping visitors, are in Ürgüp and Avanos *(see individual sections for details)*. Ankara also has three tourism offices—at the airport, the train station, and in Gençlik Parkı, the first of which keeps longer hours. Konya's visitor office is located behind the Mevlâna Museum; the multilingual staff are knowledgeable and helpful regarding all sorts of inquiries.

Ürgüp

300 km (180 miles) south of Ankara; 80 km (48 miles) west of Kayseri airport; 23 km (14 miles) east of Nevşehir.

Cappadocia comprises the triangle of land formed by the towns of Nevşehir to the west, Ürgüp to the east, and Avanos to the north. Inside this triangle is one of the most unusual natural landscapes you'll ever encounter.

Ürgüp is especially known these days for its charming small hotels, many of which are in restored cave houses and have views overlooking the town and the nearby cliffs. Some beautiful old mansions that were formerly owned by prominent local families—including Greeks, who were a significant presence in the area until the 1923

Greek-Turkish population exchange—
have also been converted into hotels.

Downtown Ürgüp is a somewhat tacky
jumble of buildings built up mostly for
the tourism industry, but you'll find
banks, ATMs, travel agencies, carpet
and souvenir shops, and even a Turkish
bath, along with a few low-key nightlife
venues. During the winter months, a
few hotels and restaurants in Ürgüp
close, which means somewhat reduced
options for travelers but a more tranquil
atmosphere.

GETTING HERE AND AROUND
Ürgüp is not quite as close to the sights
and scenic valleys as some other Cappadocian towns, so you may want to rent
a car. Minibuses run regularly between
Ürgüp and other towns in high season,
less frequently in low season.

Ürgüp has a larger population than
Göreme, Uçhisar, or other nearby
villages, and the town itself has several
distinct neighborhoods. From the Esbelli
neighborhood, where many small hotels
are located, it's a pleasant 10-minute
downhill stroll to the town center—you
may want to take a taxi when returning
at night to avoid the steep climb. To
reach Kayakapı Cave Suites, on a cliff
side overlooking the newer part of town,
you need a car or taxi.

VISITOR INFORMATION
CONTACTS Visitor Information. ✉ Atatürk
Blv. 37, inside park ☎ 384/341–4059.

Where to Base Yourself in Cappadocia

Göreme has lodgings ranging from backpacker digs to fancy rock-cut hotels, plus an array of travel services, and the area's only real nightlife. Proximity to the Göreme Open-Air Museum and scenic valleys makes it a logical choice if you don't have a car. The caveat is that it can be busy and overwhelmingly touristy.

Uçhisar, between Nevşehir and Göreme, sits high on a rock outcropping with incredible views of the surrounding valleys. It is central enough to be a good base if you have your own transport (or don't mind paying for taxis) and has a collection of mainly upscale hotels catering to visitors from around the world.

Ürgüp, being second only to Nevşehir in terms of size, has more of a "town" feel. It's a bit farther from the main attractions and lacks the delightful fairy chimneys of Göreme or Uçhisar, but Ürgüp does have a growing cluster of boutique cave and stone hotels that appeal to discerning vacationers.

Ortahisar, located just before Ürgüp when coming from Uçhisar, is a small, rather sleepy village that has only recently entered the tourism scene. It has a quainter, more authentic vibe than other towns, but there's not much in the way of services for visitors, and it's almost essential to have a car.

Sights

Turasan Winery

WINERY/DISTILLERY | Established in 1943, one of the region's largest wine producers has tastings in the factory store, as well as brief tours of the production facilities and cellars. Turasan, having substantially expanded and improved its range in recent years, makes wines from both local grape varieties (namely the white Emir and red Kalecik Karası) and foreign ones. Prices here are about 30% less than at a retail store. ✉ *Çimenli Mevkii, Tevfik Fikret Cad. 6A–B* ☎ *384/341–4961* 🌐 *www.turasan.com.tr* 🎫 *30 TL for vineyard/factory/cellar tour and 3 tastings.*

Restaurants

Old Greek House

$$$ | **TURKISH** | In the sleepy village of Mustafapaşa, about 5 km (3 miles) from Ürgüp, the charming Old Greek House serves delicious home-cooked specialties and decedant homemade desserts. Portions are generous, and the set menus are a genuine feast. **Known for:** great value prix-fixe menus; homemade baklava; decor including original, 250-year old furnishings. [$] *Average main: 40 TL* ✉ *Davutlu Mah. 12, Mustafapaşa* ☎ *384/353–5306* 🌐 *www.oldgreekhouserestaurant.com.*

Şömine

$$ | **TURKISH** | Right on Ürgüp's main square, this welcoming lair takes its name from the fireplace in the center that warms guests in winter; in summer, you can dine outside on the rooftop terrace. The menu focuses on regional specialties. **Known for:** cozy indoor seating; magnificant terrace view; selection of regional wines. [$] *Average main: 35 TL* ✉ *Cumhuriyet Meydanı 9* ☎ *384/341–8442.*

★ **Ziggy Cafe**

$$$ | **TURKISH** | The ambience at this Ürgüp favorite is especially inviting—picture attractive table arrangements, richly upholstered armchairs, wrought-iron lamps, and three open-air terraces with

sofalike seats and stone-topped tables. The contemporary, Mediterranean-inspired menu, moreover, is a refreshing change from the heavy, meat-based fare typical of Central Anatolia. **Known for:** hot and cold tasting menus; excellent service; elegant yet homey atmosphere. $ *Average main: 40 TL* ✉ *Yunak Mah., Tevfik Fikret Cad. 24* ☎ *384/341–7107* 🌐 *www.ziggycafe.com.*

Hotels

★ Esbelli Evi
$$ | B&B/INN | Carved into a rocky hillside, one of Cappadocia's longest-established cave hotels has spacious, comfortable, spotlessly clean accommodations—often with beautiful natural color banding in the volcanic-stone walls. **Pros:** extremely attentive staff; great for families; excellent value. **Cons:** closed in winter; longish walk to some rooms; lots of stairs. $ *Rooms from: €80* ✉ *Esbelli Mah., Dolay Sok. 8* ☎ *384/341–3395* 🌐 *www.esbelli.com* ⏲ *Closed Nov.–Apr.* 🛏 *13 rooms* 🍴 *Free Breakfast.*

Fresco Cave Suites and Mansions
$$ | HOTEL | Spread over three Ottoman mansions connected by courtyards and terraces, these appealing accommodations include both cave and non-cave rooms—a few have small original frescoes and painted floral mouldings. **Pros:** elegant rooms; atmospheric common areas, including a terrace with a good view; close to town center. **Cons:** rooms vary greatly in style and features; no elevator; staff's English could be better. $ *Rooms from: €80* ✉ *Musa Efendi Mah., Esat Ağa Sok. 15* ☎ *384/341–6660* 🌐 *www.frescomansions.com* 🛏 *17 rooms* 🍴 *Free Breakfast.*

Kayakapı Premium Caves
$$$ | HOTEL | This luxurious rock-cut resort-style hotel conveys a sense of the past through wooden floors and furnishings, rich Anatolian textiles, traditional low sofas, and accents like framed antique caftans. **Pros:** extremely spacious lodgings; good fitness and spa facilities; attentive service. **Cons:** hilltop location far from town center, not easily reachable on foot; restaurant rather underwhelming; little natural light in some cave rooms. $ *Rooms from: €150* ✉ *Kayakapı Mah., Kuşçular Sok. 43* ☎ *384/341–8877* 🌐 *www.kayakapi.com* 🛏 *43 rooms* 🍴 *Free Breakfast.*

★ Sacred House
$$$ | HOTEL | This luxurious, romantic hotel feels like a cross between a museum and a fairy tale and is one of Cappadocia's most unique accommodations. **Pros:** one-of-a-kind design and ambience; luxurious facilities; close to town center. **Cons:** no views from most rooms; heavy room decoration, with little natural light; not suitable for families with children. $ *Rooms from: €140* ✉ *Dutlu Cami Mah, Barbaros Hayrettin Sok. 25* ☎ *384/341–7102* 🌐 *www.sacredhouse.com.tr* 🛏 *21 rooms* 🍴 *Free Breakfast.*

★ Serinn House
$$ | B&B/INN | Sleek wood, designer furniture, sheepskin rugs on stone floors, and glass-enclosed showers give these cave accommodations looking onto a plant-heavy courtyard a true contemporary flair. **Pros:** sophisticated yet unpretentious; highly personal service; outstanding breakfast. **Cons:** closed in winter; longish walk from center of town; weak Wi-Fi in some areas. $ *Rooms from: $80* ✉ *Esbelli Mah., Esbelli Sok. 36* ☎ *384/341–6076* 🌐 *www.serinnhouse.com* ⏲ *Closed Nov.–Mar.* 🛏 *6 rooms* 🍴 *Free Breakfast*

★ SOTA Cappadocia
$$ | B&B/INN | Previously a private home, this sleek, modern design hotel was opened after owner Nil Tuncer spent nearly a decade in the area turning decent hotels into first-rate ones. **Pros:** bespoke tour-planning and exceptional service; delicious breakfast; lots of comfortable, quiet common areas with a view. **Cons:** uphill walk to get to hotel; lots of stairs; closed in winter. $ *Rooms*

from: €90 ✉ Burhankale 1 sk. no: 12 ☎ 384/341–5880 🌐 www.sotacappadocia.com 🛏 8 rooms 🍴 Free Breakfast.

Ürgüp Evi

$$ | B&B/INN | Poised atop a hill with wonderful views of Ürgüp and the surrounding scenery, this friendly guesthouse has large, rustic cave rooms with soft lighting, fireplaces, wooden floors with tribal rugs, and comfortable beds; many have a cozy outdoor sitting area in front. **Pros:** relaxed atmosphere; good for families; excellent views from several terraces. **Cons:** rather steep uphill walk to hotel; somewhat limited room amenities (no TVs); bathrooms a bit outdated. *[$] Rooms from: €55 ✉ Esbelli Mah. 54 ☎ 384/341–3173 🌐 www.urgupevi.com.tr 🛏 13 rooms 🍴 Free Breakfast.*

Göreme

10 km (6 miles) northeast of Nevşehir; 9 km (5½ miles) northwest of Ürgüp.

Bustling Göreme has the most options for hotels, dining, nightlife, shopping, and other commercial enterprises. Back in the early days of tourism in Cappadocia, the town was more or less inundated with backpackers, who still find inexpensive accommodations and laid-back bars and cafés. In recent years, though, a number of excellent midrange and higher-end hotels have opened, too. The main reason to come here is to see some of the most spectacular fairy chimney valleys in the region and the nearby Göreme and Zelve open-air museums, both UNESCO World Heritage sites and two must-sees in Cappadocia. The Göreme "museum," which tends to be packed with tourists, is a cluster of fairy chimneys famous for its impressive cave churches. Somewhat less crowded Zelve is a valley, which provides a glimpse into how people once lived in the rock-cut communities.

GETTING HERE AND AROUND

Small yet centrally located, Göreme is the most convenient base for exploring Cappadocia if you don't have a car. The Göreme Open-Air Museum is a pleasant 1½-km (1-mile) walk from the town; to get to Zelve, another 6 km (4 miles) past the Göreme museum, take a taxi, rent a scooter, or join a day tour.

Some of the area's most beautiful valleys and hiking trails begin just at the outskirts of Göreme. Although the town itself is somewhat hilly (like most of Cappadocia), it's compact and easily navigated on foot.

Sights

★ **Göreme Açık Hava Müzesi** *(Göreme Open-Air Museum)*

RELIGIOUS SITE | The open-air museum is a UNESCO World Heritage Site thanks to its spectacular landscape and amazing collection of cave churches decorated with elaborate Byzantine frescoes that were once part of a monastic complex. Within the museum is the 11th-century **Elmalı Kilise** (Church with the Apple), which has wonderfully preserved frescoes of biblical scenes and portraits of saints. The **Karanlık Church** (Dark Church) was extensively restored by UNESCO, and vividly colorful scenes, dominated by deep blues, decorate the walls and domed ceiling; the painting of Christ Pantocrator on the dome is particularly impressive (entrance to the church is an extra 15 TL). In the nearby **kitchen/refectory,** a huge dining table that could seat 50 is carved from the rock, and it's easy to imagine priests and members of the early Christian community here packing in for meals. The museum covers a large area with dozens of caves, nooks, and crannies to explore, almost all of them easily reachable on paved paths. *✉ About 1½ km (1 mile) southeast of Göreme town center ☎ 384/271–2167 🎫 45 TL.*

Zelve Açık Hava Müzesi (*Zelve Open-Air Museum*)
ARCHAEOLOGICAL SITE | Although the prizes at Göreme are the fresco-decorated churches, the outdoor museum at Zelve provides a fascinating look at how people lived in fairy chimney communities. Zelve was a center of Christian monastic life from the 9th through 13th century, and the town was inhabited until the early 1950s, when erosion and cracking caused slabs of rock to fall, forcing villagers to move out. The site is only about 2,145 feet long, but there's plenty to explore. The valley is made up of several uneven, naturally carved rows of fairy chimneys. These—and just about every spare rock face—shelter hundreds of dwellings that vary in size. Some are just simple cavelike openings and others are multistory houses with rooms on several floors linked by stairs carved deep inside the rocks. There's also a rock-cut mosque and several small churches. Certain structures have collapsed, leaving giant pieces of carved ceiling upside down on the ground. You can probably see the whole place in a little over an hour but could easily linger longer. ✉ *6 km (4 miles) northeast of Göreme Open-Air Museum, 3 km (2 miles) off the road to Avanos* ☎ *384/271–3535* 🎫 *15 TL.*

🍴 Restaurants

Orient Restaurant
$$ | TURKISH | The menu at this longtime Göreme restaurant is extensive and diverse. Typical mezes and grilled kebabs are served, in addition to a range of well-prepared steak and lamb options, chicken with spinach or a saffron sauce, and even pastas. **Known for:** meat dishes; generous portions; highly attentive service. [$] *Average main: 40 TL* ✉ *Adnan Menderes Cad. 3* ☎ *384/271–2346* 🌐 *www.orientrestaurant.net.*

★ **Pumpkin Restaurant**
$$$$ | TURKISH | This cozy venue is the place to come for simple home cooking, in the form of a reasonably priced four-course set menu cooked nightly by the owner and his team. Dinners come with soup, meze plate or salad, and a choice of two or three main courses (generally beef, lamb, or chicken; the vegetarian option can be somewhat basic), and a fruit/dessert plate. **Known for:** friendly and engaging service; open kitchen; homemade desserts. [$] *Average main: 100 TL* ✉ *İçeridere Sok. 7/A* ☎ *384/271–2066, 542/808–5050 mobile phone* ⏲ *No lunch.*

★ **Seten Restaurant**
$$$ | TURKISH | Housed in a magnificent old mansion at the top of Göreme's hotel hill, Seten provides a classy setting in which to enjoy a range of top-notch mezes and delicious mains. Standouts among the mezes include *imam bayıldı* (braised stuffed eggplant) and Circassian-style chicken. **Known for:** generous portions; luxurious atmosphere; views of Göreme. [$] *Average main: 58 TL* ✉ *Aydınlı Sok. 42, Aydınlı Mah.* ☎ *384/271–3025* 🌐 *www.setenrestaurant.com.*

🛏 Hotels

Anatolian Houses
$$ | HOTEL | Beautifully set among the fairy chimneys, this romantic retreat has junior and multiroom suites that are notable for their plush design—sometimes with traditional accents, sometimes more contemporary. **Pros:** luxurious, pampering atmosphere; extensive wellness facilities; well-decorated and comfortable common areas. **Cons:** service could be better; rooms can be warm and stuffy due to poor ventilation and no air-conditioning; Wi-Fi weak or nonexistent in many rooms. [$] *Rooms from: €55* ✉ *Gaferli Mah., Cevizler Sok. 32* ☎ *384/271–2463* 🌐 *www.anatolianhouses.com.tr* 🛏 *33 suites* 🍽 *Free Breakfast.*

Continued on page 380

Word of Mouth

"Nature is not the same everywhere. A day's hike took us to visit these natural phenomenons—a product of erosion over time."

—julzie49

ROCK OF AGES
UNEARTHING HOLY CAPPADOCIA

A fantasy come true, Cappadocia's phantasmagorical landscape of rock pinnacles, or "fairy chimneys," is one of Turkey's most otherworldly sights. A natural hideout—thanks to Mother Nature's chiseling tools of wind and water—the region became a sort of promised land for Anatolia's earliest Christians. Over the course of the 6th to 12th centuries, these early Cappadocian inhabitants incised the fantastic escarpments of Göreme and Zelve with a honeycomb of cave churches. Today you can trace the saga of the early Christians' religious faith by exploring this spectacular setting. As the first monks might have proclaimed: You have to believe it to see it!

Opposite: Cappadocia. Top: Göreme National Park

AN EARLY CHRISTIAN WONDERLAND

Remote and inaccessible, Cappadocia seemed custom-made for early Christian communities, whose members erected their churches in hollowed-out caves and expanded vast underground cities to hide from enemies and live reclusive monastic lives.

The story of Cappadocia begins more than ten million years ago, when three volcanoes began a geological symphony that dropped lava, mud, and ash over the region. Over eons, frequent eruptions of Mt. Erciyes, Mt. Hasan, and Mt. Melendiz covered considerable parts of the land with tufa—a porous rock layer formed of volcanic ash—over which lava spread at various stages of hardening.

Erosion by rain, snow, and wind created soaring stone "fairy chimneys," surrealistic shapes of cones, needles, pillars, and pyramids, not unlike the looming pinnacles of Arizona's Monument Valley. As time went on, earthquakes added valleys and rivers (mostly long-vanished) and slashed rifts into the fragile tufa. Depending on the variable consistency of the rock, the changes occurred more or less violently, with utterly fantastic results.

A REAL RUBBLE-ROUSER

Fast forward some millennia. Persecuted by authorities and often on the run from invading armies (Cappadocia was a frontier province), early Christians found the region's cliffs, rock pinnacles, and tufa caves ideal for the construction of their secluded colonies. Within a few hundred years of the death of Jesus, a regional bishopric had been established in nearby Kayseri (then Caesarea).

By the 4th century the number-one industry in the region was prayer, and the early recluses carved dwellings into Cappodocia's malleable stone, using simple tools. The ease of construction set a fashion that quickly led to the formation of anchorite colonies. These early monastic communities deftly combined the individuality of meditation with the communal work favored by St. Basil.

Above: Rock formations (chimneys) in the Göreme Valley

THE WORD MADE ROCK

The worship of God remained of uppermost importance here, and cave chapels and churches proliferated, especially throughout the Göreme Valley. When Arab raiders first swept through the region in the 7th and 8th centuries, large numbers of Christians sought refuge in rocky hide-outs and underground cities like Derinkuyu and Kaymaklı, which grew sufficiently large to house populations of up to 20,000 people.

After the Isaurian dynasty of Byzantine emperors repulsed the Arabs in 740, hollowed-out churches began to appear above ground. Reflecting contemporary Byzantine architectural styles, they were decorated with geometrical paintings. Following Empress Theodora's restoration of the use of holy imagery in the 9th century, churches were given increasingly ambitious frescoes. Many of these were painted in color schemes that rivaled the yellow, pink, and russet hues of their rock surroundings.

Top: Göreme Open-Air Museum.
Bottom: Rock homes, Göreme Valley

WHAT CREATED CAPPADOCIA'S "FAIRY CHIMNEYS"?

The volcanoes that formed Cappadocia are inactive now, but the most recent may have erupted just 8,000 years ago; Neolithic humans depicted the eruption in cave dwellings at Çatalhöyük (near present-day Konya). Nature continues to sculpt the landscape of Cappadocia. In the future, it is likely that some formations now visible will have turned to dust, and other forms will have been separated from the mountains, providing new experiences for tomorrow's travelers.

GÖREME: A ROCKBOUND HEAVEN

A UNESCO World Heritage Site, the Göreme Açık Hava Müzesi (Göreme Open-Air Museum) is a must-see for its amazing landscape and churches. These rock-hewn holy sanctuaries may be *in* the earth but they are not *of* it.

While Cappadocia is sprinkled with hundreds of cave churches—most built between the 10th and 12th centuries, though some as early as the 6th century—the best are found in the open-air museum at Göreme. Many Göreme churches are built in an inscribed Greek cross plan, a common Byzantine design, wherein all four arms of the church are equal in length.

The central dome almost always features a depiction of Christ Pantocrator ("Omnipotent"). Though dictated in part by Cappadocia's landscape, the small size and intimate feel of Göreme's rock-cut churches was also deliberate: the monastic community living here designed them not as houses of worship for the public but as chapels where members of the community could engage in solitary prayer and worship of specific saints.

EARTH AS ART

Most churches were commissioned by local donors who hired teams of professional artists—some local and some brought from as far away as Constantinople—to paint elaborate frescoes of scenes from the Old and New Testaments and the lives of the saints.

Visible in places where frescoes have peeled off, underlying geometric designs, crosses, and other symbols were painted directly onto the rock walls in red ochre. It is thought that these decorations were made when a church was first carved out of the rock, in order to consecrate the space. Sometime later, professional artists then painted their detailed frescoes on top of these designs. Note that the eyes of some of the figures have been scratched out, probably much later by Muslims who believed that visually representing human beings was blasphemous.

Above: Göreme Valley. Photo by yversace, Fodors.com member. Opposite: Elmalı Kilise (Church with the Apple).

TIPS FOR VISITING GÖREME

In summer, get an early start to beat the heat and the crowds, or go after 5 pm, when it's cooler and the crowds have thinned. The open-air museum covers a large area, with dozens of caves and crannies to explore, almost all of which are easily reachable on paved paths. Allow a good two hours to get the most out of your visit. Note that no photography of any kind is allowed inside the churches. ⊠ About 1.5 km (1 mi) southeast of Göreme town center. ☎ 384/271-2167 💷 45TL ⏱ Daily Apr.-Oct. 8-7, Nov.-Mar. 8-5, last entry 45 min. before closing.

WHAT TO SEE AT THE GÖREME OPEN-AIR MUSEUM

Fresco of St. George and St. Theodorus killing the dragon in Yılanlı Kilise.

1 Convent & Monastery. After you enter the site, you'll see a large chimney to your left: this housed a six-story convent, which had a kitchen and refectory on the lower levels and a chapel on the third; large millstones lay ready to block the narrow passages in times of danger. Opposite is a monastery with the same plan. Unfortunately, these structures were deemed unsafe and are closed to visitors.

2 Elmalı Kilise (Church with the Apple). Accessed through a tunnel, this 11th-century church has wonderfully preserved frescoes of biblical scenes and portraits of saints; red and gray tones predominate. There are an impressive nine domes: eight small and one large; the largest shows Christ Pantocrator "on His heavenly throne." You can see the red-ochre geometric designs and Maltese crosses where the frescoes have peeled off.

Elmalı Kilise (detail of fresco)

3 Barbara Şapeli (Chapel of St. Barbara). Above the Elmalı Kilise, this chapel has only a few frescoes, including Christ Pantocrator and St. Barbara. Far more interestingly, most of the chapel is decorated with red ochre symbols painted on the rock, including geometric designs and some unusual, almost whimsical, creatures.

4 Yılanlı Kilise (Snake Church/Church of St. Onuphrius). Small but intriguing, this church takes its Turkish name from the scene on the left wall depicting St. George slaying the dragon, which here—as in many Cappadocian churches—takes the form of a snake. More unusual is the story of St. Onuphrius, on the right wall of the church: the naked saint is depicted with both a beard and breasts. While the official story says that St. Onuphrius was a pious hermit who lived in Egypt, another version has it that the saint was a loose woman who repented, embraced Christianity, and was given a beard.

5 Refectory/Kitchen. You can still picture the huge rock-carved dining table here packed at mealtimes with priests. The table could seat 40 to 50 people; carved into the opposite wall are niches for wine making. There are several kitchens in Göreme, but this refectory (near the Yılanlı Kilise) is the largest.

6 Karanlık Kilise (Dark Church). Entrance to this church, which was extensively restored by UNESCO, costs an extra 8 TL, because of the exceptional group of frescoes. Vibrant scenes, dominated by deep blue colors, decorate the walls and domed ceiling; the frescoes have retained their brilliant colors due to the structure of the church, which lets in little light (hence the name). The frescoes show scenes from the Old and New Testaments; the Crucifixion scene is particularly intense.

7 Çarıklı Kilise (Church of the Sandal). Climb up a metal ladder to reach this church, named after the footprints (some might say indentations) on the floor below the Ascension fresco; some believe these to be casts of Jesus' own footprints. The beautiful frescoes in this 11th-century church have been restored

Çarıklı Kilise
(Church of the Sandal) **7**

Karanlık Kilise
(Dark Church) **6**

5

Yemekhane
(Refectory/Kitchen)

Azize Katerina Kilise
(St. Catherine Church)

Kızlar Manastırı
(Convent & Monastery)
1

Yılanlı Kilise
(Snake Church) **4**

Barbara Şapeli
(Chapel of St. Barbara) **3**

Tokalı Kilise
(Church with
the Buckle)
8

Aziz Basil Kilisesi
(St. Basil Church)

Elmalı Kilise
(Church with the Apple) **2**

and portray a similar narrative cycle to those in the Karanlık Kilise. Note also the geometric and floral patterns between the frescoes.

8 Tokalı Kilise (Church with the Buckle). Don't miss this church, across from the main museum area and a short way down the road toward Göreme (use the same entrance ticket). The oldest church in the open-air museum, and one of the largest and most impressive, it has high ceilings and brilliant blue colors. It's made up of an "Old Church" and a "New Church." The former was built in the early 10th century, and less than a century later it became the vaulted atrium of the "New Church," which was dug deeper into the rock; both sections have well-preserved frescoes depicting the life of Christ. This is the only church in Göreme in which the narrative scenes take place in chronological order. The church is to remain open while it undergoes restoration.

Left: Interior of Çarıklı Kilise, Christian frescoes dating from the 11th century AD.
Right: Murals from Tokalı Kilise

GREAT HIKES

One of the most rewarding walks from Göreme is through the **Rose Valley** (Güllüdere), where cave entrances lead to multistory, ornately decorated churches with columns that are two or three stories high. Roman graves, now unreachable, are adorned with Christian crosses and sit high upon eroded fairy chimneys. A hike through the valley often ends up at **Paşabağı**, a great monastic settlement of fairy chimneys. There are also spectacular hikes through **Love Valley** (Aşk Vadisi), perhaps named for the preponderance of phallus-like rock protrusions.

Though farther afield, the lush **Ihlara Valley** (see the section in this chapter) also hosts a wealth of rock-carved churches, which are an interesting contrast to those at Göreme because they were carved and decorated not by professional artists, as in Göreme, but by local monks living in the remote valley. The liturgical cycle depicted in the frescoes is somewhat abridged and the style more improvised. There are occasionally even spelling errors, such as in the Kokar Kilise, where the abbreviation of Jesus' name is misspelled with the Greek letters HC instead of IC.

ZELVE'S CAVE DWELLINGS

In typical Cappadocian fashion, humans improved on Nature's work to create Zelve, a village of rock-hewn houses that even Fred Flintstone would have envied.

While the prizes at Göreme are the fresco-decorated churches, the outdoor Zelve Açık Hava Müzesi (Zelve Open-Air Museum) provides a fascinating look at how people lived in fairy-chimney communities. Zelve was a center of Christian monastic life in the 9th through 13th centuries, and the town was inhabited until the early 1950s, when erosion and cracking began causing slabs of rock to fall and villagers were moved out of the hundreds of cave dwellings.

The site is only about 2,145 feet long, but there's plenty to explore. The valley is made up of several uneven, naturally carved rows of fairy chimneys. These and just about every spare rock face shelter hundreds of dwellings that vary in size—some are just simple cavelike openings and others are multistory houses with rooms on

several floors linked by stairs carved deep inside the rocks. There's also a rock-cut mosque and several small churches. Some of the structures have collapsed and giant pieces of carved ceiling lie upside down on the ground.

Be prepared to climb around, and definitely bring a flashlight or you won't be able to explore some of the most interesting and extensive dwellings. You can probably see the whole place in a little over an hour, but you could easily spend more time.

✉ 6 km (4 mi) northeast of the Göreme Open-Air Museum, 3 km (2 mi) off the road to Avanos.

☎ 384/271-3535

🎫 15TL

🕙 Daily, Apr.-Oct. 8-7, Nov.-Mar. 8-5, last entry 45 min. before closing.

Opposite: Rose Valley; above: Chimneys of Zelve, photo by dgunbug, Fodors.com member.

Aydınlı Cave House

$$ | **B&B/INN** | Mustafa Demirci converted his centuries-old family home into a picturesque guesthouse and has since taken over the place next door, too: both offer simple accommodations with wood and wrought-iron furniture, antique items, and travertine-lined bathrooms. **Pros:** wonderfully hospitable owner and staff; amazing views from breakfast area; extensive underground spa facility. **Cons:** lots of stairs to upper-level rooms and breakfast area; some bathrooms are a little tight; occasional street noise. [$] *Rooms from: €75* ✉ *Aydınlı Mah., Aydınlı Sok. 12* ☎ *384/271–2263* 🌐 *www.thecavehotel.com* 🛏 *14 rooms* 🍴 *Free Breakfast.*

Cappadocia Cave Suites

$$$ | **HOTEL** | Comfortable, elegantly designed rooms—most of which are quirkily shaped and carved from rock—combine antiques, old-fashioned wrought-iron beds, and folk-art spreads with modern conveniences like satellite flat-screen TVs, kettles for tea or coffee, and (in most cases) Jacuzzis. **Pros:** appealing ambiance; inviting public spaces with layout that allows for privacy; professionally run. **Cons:** lots of steps to reach some rooms and common areas; restaurant and reception area feel a little impersonal; size and amenities of rooms in the same category can vary. [$] *Rooms from: €120* ✉ *Gaferli Mah, Ünlü Sok. 19,.* ☎ *384/271–2800* 🌐 *www.cappadociacavesuites.com* 🛏 *36 rooms* 🍴 *Free Breakfast.*

★ **Kelebek Special Cave Hotel**

$$ | **HOTEL** | One of Göreme's longest-standing hotels—immensely popular for both its cozy atmosphere and personal service—Kelebek caters to travelers on different budgets, with accommodations ranging from small, somewhat basic cave rooms to spacious, antiques-filled cave and stone-built suites with bathtubs and fireplaces. **Pros:** good value; young, friendly feel; great views from the rooftop bar-restaurant. **Cons:** hotel is a long, rather steep walk up from town center; some lower-category rooms noisy due to proximity to common areas; some discrepancies in rooms of the same category. [$] *Rooms from: €70* ✉ *Aydınlı Mah., Yavuz Sok. 1* ☎ *384/271–2531* 🌐 *www.kelebekhotel.com* 🛏 *45 rooms* 🍴 *Free Breakfast.*

Kısmet Cave House

$ | **B&B/INN** | At this lovely family-run spot in a somewhat quieter part of Göreme, each carefully decorated room is named after a different flower, which features in colorful paintings and wooden furniture. **Pros:** very warm hospitality; inspired design; dinner can be served on request. **Cons:** rooms aren't so large; ground-floor ones can be a bit noisy; no views. [$] *Rooms from: €40* ✉ *Kağnı Yolu 9* ☎ *384/271–2416* 🌐 *www.kismetcavehouse.com* 🛏 *8 rooms* 🍴 *Free Breakfast.*

Koza Cave Hotel

$$$ | **B&B/INN** | Run by an exceptionally friendly local family, Koza Cave Hotel's charming cave rooms are centered around a small courtyard with amazing views from terraces on several different levels. **Pros:** warm, obliging hosts; character-filled rooms; highest terrace in Göreme. **Cons:** steep walk up from town; no doors (only curtains or archways) separate some rooms from bathrooms; lots of stairs. [$] *Rooms from: €150* ✉ *Aydınlı Mah., Çakmaklı Sok. 49* ☎ *384/271–2466* 🌐 *www.kozacavehotel.com* 🕒 *Closed Dec. and Jan. except for week of Christmas/New Year's* 🛏 *10 rooms* 🍴 *Free Breakfast.*

Sultan Cave Suites

$$ | **HOTEL** | High on one of Göreme's hills, this hotel has clean, comfortable cave and stone rooms that are simply decorated; wooden or stone floors are covered with kilims, wrought-iron beds are topped with embroidered spreads, and old-fashioned furnishings abound. **Pros:** good value; welcoming, professional

staff; some non-cave suites have balconies. **Cons:** steep uphill walk from town center; dim natural and artificial lighting in some cave rooms; some cave rooms can be stuffy. [$] *Rooms from: €90* ✉ *Aydınlı Mah., Aydınlı Sok. 40* ☎ *384/271–3023* 🌐 *www.sultancavesuites.com* 🛏 *30 rooms* 🍴 *Free Breakfast.*

Activities

HOT AIR BALLOONING

One of the most thrilling ways to appreciate Cappadocia's incredible landscape is from above. Hot-air balloon flights take off around sunrise (when the air is calmest) and last about 90 minutes. A skilled pilot can take you right into a valley, sailing through so that rock cones loom on either side, then climb the edge of a tall fairy chimney. The trip usually ends with a traditional champagne toast. Cappadocia is an ideal place for ballooning not only because of its spectacular scenery, but because the region's microclimate—with clement weather and around 250 flying days per year—makes it one of the world's safest ballooning destinations. Flights are run year-round, but April through November sees balmier temperatures and a lower probability of cancellation due to weather conditions.

Balloon companies have mushroomed here in recent years, and competition is intense. Nonetheless, it's recommended that you choose an outfit based on its reputation and safety record rather than price. The top-quality companies have the most experienced staff and also change their take-off locations on a daily basis according to wind currents, to ensure passengers see as much as possible on their flight. Due to restrictions on the number of balloons that can be in the air at a time, some companies run flights in two shifts; try to get a booking for the first flight of the day, as the later flights have a greater chance of weather-related cancellation. Companies suggest making your reservation as far in advance as possible. Double-check with the compnay to make sure that if your flight is canceled due to weather, you will be accommodated the following day.

All companies include hotel transfers, and most companies provide some sort of complimentary refreshments before taking off. Hotels and tour agencies in Cappadocia often make high commissions on bookings. You won't necessarily save anything by making your own arrangements, but many operators do give a small discount if you pay in cash.

Butterfly Balloons

BALLOONING | Small and personal, Butterfly Balloons has highly qualified pilots with American and European commercial pilot's licenses. Pilots have great rapport with passengers, who also benefit from generous legroom and outstanding service. ✉ *Uzun Dere cd 29* ☎ *384/271–3010* 🌐 *www.butterflyballoons.com* 🎫 *From €175.*

Cappadocia Voyager Balloons

BALLOONING | Run by experienced professionals, Cappadocia Voyager Balloons has certified pilots and newer balloons than some competitors. Four flight categories, based on capacity and duration, are available. ✉ *Avanos* ☎ *384/271–3030* 🌐 *www.voyagerballoons.com* 🎫 *From €160.*

Kapadokya Balloons

BALLOONING | The oldest and largest balloon company in Cappadocia, Kapadokya Balloons has been in business since 1991 and prides itself on its experienced team and professionalism. ✉ *Adnan Menderes Cd 14/a* ☎ *384/271–2442* 🌐 *www.kapadokyaballoons.com* 🎫 *From €175.*

Royal Balloon

BALLOONING | Working with some of the most experienced Turkish and foreign pilots in Cappadocia, Royal Balloon emphasizes boutique service and gives passengers a hot buffet breakfast. ✉ *Eski Bag Yolu Sk 2* ☎ *384/271–3300* 🌐 *www.royalballoon.com* 🎫 *From €160.*

Uçhisar

7 km (4 miles) east of Nevşehir; 3 km (2 miles) southwest of Göreme.

A lovely little town on a hill, built around a huge fairy chimney known as Uçhisar Castle, Uçhisar has some of the nicest places to stay in Cappadocia. There are carpet shops and trinket stalls near the base of the castle, but the town still feels calmer and a bit more residential than Göreme, with clustered stone houses overlooking the valleys. From here, it's easy to take off for a walk through Pigeon Valley (Güvercinlik Vadisi), so named for the birds the villagers traditionally raised in distinctive-looking cotes lodged in the walls of the valley.

GETTING HERE AND AROUND

Despite being fairly central, Uçhisar is less well served by minibuses than other nearby destinations; especially during the low season, it can be difficult getting to and from the town without a car. Once you're in Uçhisar, however, restaurants, hotels, and shops are conveniently located within walking distance of one another. The main attraction, Uçhisar Castle, is no more than a stone's throw from any hotel, and some hiking trails can be accessed from the edge of town.

Sights

★ **Uçhisar Kalesi** (*Uçhisar Castle*)
NATURE SITE | The highest fairy chimney in Cappadocia, Uçhisar Kalesi has the most spectacular views in the area, save a hot-air balloon. Called "Uçhisar castle" in Turkish, the giant rock outcrop was used as a fortress in the late Byzantine and early Ottoman periods, and later inhabited by the locals. The striking formation is riddled with rock-cut dwellings, giving it a Swiss-cheese look, but it was evacuated in the 1960s when erosion put everything in danger of collapse and the structure was declared a disaster zone (residents were moved to safer homes in the surrounding area). The top of Uçhisar Kalesi—reached by a steep climb on recently installed steps with good traction—is a beautiful spot to watch the sunset. On a clear day, you can see all the way to Mt. Erciyes, 57 km (36 miles) away. ✉ *Near center of town, Üçhisar* 🎟 *8 TL.*

Restaurants

Centre Restaurant
$$ | **TURKISH** | It's far from fancy, but this unpretentious local favorite tucked away just behind the town square is one of Uçhisar's best places for reliably good food at fairly reasonable prices. Though limited, the menu does not disappoint, with chef Hüseyin Örlü preparing staples like *çoban salatası* (shepherd's salad) that are well above average. **Known for:** generous portions; local crowds; relaxed, unrushed feel. [$] *Average main: 35 TL* ✉ *Belediye Parkı, Üçhisar* ☎ *384/219–3117.*

Seki Restaurant
$$$$ | **TURKISH** | The restaurant in Argos in Cappadocia hotel features contemporary adaptations of Turkish dishes that bring together local ingredients and international cooking techniques. Creative appetizers include traditional Turkish pastırma (beef pastrami) with goat cheese and melon sauce, while meat-heavy mains range from lamb loin with eggplant and plum sauce to beef cheek with rosemary. **Known for:** views of Pigeon Valley; best wine selection in Cappadocia; excellent service. [$] *Average main: 100 TL* ✉ *Argos in Cappadocia, Aşağı Mah. Kayabaşı Sok. 23, Üçhisar* ☎ *384/219–3130* 🌐 *www.seki.com.tr.*

Hotels

★ **Argos in Cappadocia**
$$$$ | **HOTEL** | Exceptional service, a spectacular location, and accommodations that meld sophisticated yet understated contemporary design with lovely local touches make Argos one of Cappadocia's

best hotels. **Pros:** inviting public spaces; first-rate service; magnificent views over Pigeon Valley. **Cons:** you won't want to leave; some cave rooms have little natural light or ventilation; hotel layout has many stairs and lots of twists and turns. [$] *Rooms from: €250* ✉ *Aşağı Mah. Kayabaşı Sok. 23, Üçhisar* ☎ *384/219–3130* 🌐 *www.argosincappadocia.com* 🛏 *51 rooms* 🍴 *Free Breakfast.*

★ Kale Konak Cave Hotel

$$$ | HOTEL | Occupying three old houses joined by a courtyard and underground tunnels, the delightful Kale Konak promises the friendly intimacy of a small guesthouse combined with the professional service of a larger hotel. **Pros:** central location just steps from Uçhisar Castle; splendid terrace views; accommodating owner and staff. **Cons:** few rooms have views; little natural light in cave rooms; maze of stairways and passageways require lots of climbing. [$] *Rooms from: €100* ✉ *Kale Sok. 9, Üçhisar* ☎ *384/219–2828* 🌐 *www.kalekonak.com* 🛏 *17 rooms* 🍴 *Free Breakfast.*

Les Maisons de Cappadoce

$$ | RENTAL | French architect Jacques Avizou has restored 16 houses—some carved out of caves, others built from local stone—to create one of the most beautiful places to stay in Cappadocia. **Pros:** lovely atmosphere; magnificent views; houses provide privacy and a less touristy experience. **Cons:** some studios are smallish; some lodgings are far from reception; bathrooms can be a bit basic. [$] *Rooms from: €80* ✉ *Cesme sk 1, Üçhisar* ☎ *384/219–2813* 🌐 *www.cappadoce.com* 🛏 *16 rooms* 🍴 *Free Breakfast.*

Museum Hotel

$$$$ | HOTEL | This cluster of cave and stone building accommodations connected by labyrinthine passages is a work of art; befitting the name, it is filled with the owner's impressive collection of antiques, ranging from metalwork to Ottoman caftans to carpets. **Pros:** authentic vintage decor; beautiful public areas and scenery; excellent restaurant. **Cons:** some cave rooms can be dark; bit of an uphill walk to get to Uçhisar castle and town center; lots of steps and narrow passageways to navigate. [$] *Rooms from: €350* ✉ *Tekelli Mah. 1, Üçhisar* ☎ *384/219–2220* 🌐 *www.museumhotel.com.tr* 🛏 *30 rooms* 🍴 *Free Breakfast.*

Sakli Konak Hotel

$$ | B&B/INN | This cozy, century-old house tucked away on a quiet street has six stone rooms, each with a story to tell and offering exceptional service and a great restaurant. **Pros:** huge and delicious breakfast; central location; excellent restaurant. **Cons:** limited common areas; no cave rooms; weak Wi-Fi in some areas. [$] *Rooms from: €60* ✉ *2 Karlik sk, Üçhisar* ☎ *530/568–1498* 🌐 *www.saklikonakhotel.com* 🛏 *8 rooms* 🍴 *Free Breakfast.*

Taşkonaklar

$$ | HOTEL | Five rock-cut homes sharing a grassy courtyard have been carefully restored to evoke an authentic sense of place while providing modern amenities. **Pros:** spectacular views overlooking Pigeon Valley; attractive rooms and courtyard garden; excellent breakfast. **Cons:** hotel somewhat lacking vibrancy; little natural light in cave rooms; maze of steps require lots of climbing. [$] *Rooms from: €110* ✉ *Gedik Sok. 8, Üçhisar* ☎ *384/219–3001* 🌐 *www.taskonaklar.com* 🛏 *23 rooms* 🍴 *Free Breakfast.*

Ortahisar

5 km (3 miles) southwest of Nevşehir; 6 km (4 miles) southeast of Ürgüp.

A rather sleepy farming village overlooking scenic Pancarlık Valley, Ortahisar was traditionally famous for its underground caves where fruit was stored. Although it has recently gotten into the tourism business, with the opening of a few small hotels and places to eat, Ortahisar is still a functioning village and retains a more pleasantly authentic atmosphere than most other area towns. Visitors tend to appreciate the off-the-beaten-path vibe but should be aware that dining options and other services for travelers are limited, and the place can feel a bit deserted at night. Ortahisar, meaning "middle fortress," is named after its main landmark, a large rock outcropping/fairy chimney that was once used as a fortress.

GETTING HERE AND AROUND

Aside from a minibus route that links Ortahisar with Ürgüp, transportation options are rather limited, so it's best to have a car here. Most tourist-oriented establishments are within walking distance of the castle.

Sights

Ortahisar Kalesi

NATURE SITE | Ortahisar's 282-foot "castle" is Cappadocia's tallest fairy chimney, though it appears lower than Uçhisar's because it is located in a slight depression rather than atop a hill. As in Uçhisar, the castle has been carved out into a honeycomb of rooms and tunnels. Formerly used both as a fortress and for dwellings, it has splendid views of the surrounding area. Getting to the top requires climbing up some extremely steep metal staircases and ladders. ✉ *Center of town* 🎫 *5 TL.*

Ortahisar Kültür Müzesi (*Ortahisar Culture Museum*)

MUSEUM | The region's only ethnographic museum showcases the traditional lifestyle and culture of Cappadocian villages. A dozen rooms house dioramas depicting local customs and scenes from daily life, such as a bride's henna party. Although small and funded privately, it has informative, well-written English texts plus an on-site restaurant. ✉ *Tepebaşı Meydanı 16* ☎ *384/343–3344* 🌐 *www.culturemuseum.com* 🎫 *7 TL.*

Hotels

★ Hezen Cave Hotel

$$ | HOTEL | This enchanting hotel has wonderful views of Ortahisar castle from several lovely terraces, tasteful cave rooms that are simple yet stylish, and down-to-earth service that makes guests feel right at home. **Pros:** delightful guest rooms and common spaces; welcoming staff; great views; delicious breakfasts. **Cons:** rather far from most sightseeing and dining options; steep, winding walk to get to hotel; many floors require lots of stairs to climb. [$] *Rooms from: $90* ✉ *Tahir Bey Sok. 87* ☎ *384/343–3005* 🌐 *www.hezenhotel.com* 🛏 *15 rooms* 🍴 *Free Breakfast.*

Avanos

17 km (11 miles) northeast of Nevşehir; 10 km (6 miles) north of Göreme; 12 km (7 miles) northeast of Uçhisar.

Avanos is a low-key town on the Kızılırmak (Red River), so named for the color of the clay that lines its banks, and is best known for its pottery made from this clay. A wobbly suspension footbridge crosses the river near the busy town square, and a couple of cafés are located on the waterfront (there are bridges for vehicles a short way up- and down-river). Artisans create designs inspired by Central Anatolian archaeological findings, particularly Hittite-style vessels and motifs; many also produce their own unique pieces, both functional and decorative. Pottery is a family affair, so in shops you'll see younger family members decorating pieces as their fathers and grandfathers operate the kick wheel. Almost all local potters give free demonstrations that showcase traditional techniques.

GETTING HERE AND AROUND

Though located somewhat farther afield from Cappadocia's main sights, Avanos is easy to reach if you have a car; minibuses also connect Avanos with other nearby towns. Most hotels, restaurants, shops, and businesses are along the northern bank of the river or just a short walk away.

VISITOR INFORMATION

CONTACTS Visitor Information. ✉ Atatürk Cad., Dr. Hacı Nuri Bey Konağı ☎ 384/511–4360.

🍴 Restaurants

Bizim Ev

$$ | TURKISH | This restored old stone house makes a pleasant setting for Bizim Ev ("Our House"), which attracts many tour groups with reliable food at reasonable prices. The menu includes a fairly standard array of mezes, grilled meats, and local trout, and portions are good. **Known for:** local wine selection; view of Cappadocia and the Kızılırmak River; Bostan Kebap. $ Average main: 35 TL ✉ Orta Mah., Baklacı Sok. 1 ☎ 384/511–5225 ⊕ www.bizim-ev.com.

🛍 Shopping

The ceramics shops are generally open seven days a week during tourist season, from 9 to around sundown, depending on business.

Avanos Çarşı Seramik (Chez Ferhat)

CERAMICS/GLASSWARE | Run by a cooperative of five artisans, Avanos Çarşı Seramik has an excellent array of functional and decorative ceramics, ranging from pieces with Hittite and Anatolian designs to the Kütahya and İznik styles more commonly seen in Western Turkey. Prices are negotiable. ✉ Atatürk Cad. 13–19, (across from post office) ☎ 384/511–4871.

Chez Galip

CERAMICS/GLASSWARE | The oldest, most famous, and by far the funkiest pottery shop in Avanos, Chez Galip is known not just for ceramics but also what its owner calls the world's largest collection of human hair—thousands upon thousands of locks are on display in Galip's downtown shop, near the post office (PTT). The pottery selection includes both typical styles and interesting freehand sculptural pieces. The production facilities, and a wider selection of pottery, are housed in a larger venue about 1½ km (1 mile) away on the other side of the river (Yeni Mah., Hasan Kalesi Mevkii 3). ✉ Fırın Sok., (across from PTT) ☎ 384/511–4577 ⊕ www.chezgalip.com.

Derinkuyu and Kaymaklı

Kaymaklı is 20 km (12 miles) south of Nevşehir; Derinkuyu is 9 km (6 miles) south of Kaymaklı.

The underground cities of Cappadocia have excited the imaginations of travelers since the Greek mercenary leader/historian Xenophon wrote about them in the 5th century BC. Hittite artifacts discovered in some suggest they may have been initially constructed a millennium before, but no one really knows for sure who dug the cities, or when, or why. The underground networks were certainly modified and probably also significantly expanded later by the early Christians who inhabited them. Some of these complexes are merely passages between different belowground dwellings. Others really deserve the title of "city": the largest, including Kaymaklı and Derinkuyu, have multiple levels and were equipped to house thousands of people for months at a time. The impermeable tufa, or porous rock, kept the insides of the cities dry, while ventilation shafts supplied air and interior wells provided water. Ground-level entrances were cleverly disguised, and in the event that invaders did make their way in, huge, round stones resembling millstones were used to block off different passageways and secure the city.

GETTING HERE AND AROUND

Kaymaklı and Derinkuyu are on Route 765 and can be reached by car or public minibus via Nevşehir. Travel time from Nevşehir is about a half-hour for Kaymaklı and an additional 10 minutes or so for Derinkuyu. If you visit the cities on your own, particularly during peak season, it's a good idea to get there as early in the day as possible, before the tour groups arrive, or in the late afternoon. There is little to no signage in the underground cities, so you may wish to hire a guide on-site, often available outside the entrances.

An easier and probably more time-efficient option is to join a day tour. These usually include a visit to one of the underground cities, where your guide helps you navigate the labyrinthine passageways and provide background that brings the place to life.

The underground cities can be challenging for those with claustrophobia or mobility issues. Visitors should wear good shoes and comfortable clothing.

◉ Sights

Derinkuyu

ARCHAEOLOGICAL SITE | Meaning "deep well," Derinkuyu is the deepest of the known underground cities that have been explored—eight floors are open to the public, though there may be many more. The subterranean labyrinth has stables, wineries, a chapel and baptismal pool, a school, scores of other interconnected rooms, and as many as 600 entrances and air ducts. You'll also see a ventilation shaft that plunges 180 feet from ground level. Claustrophobes, take note: spaces here are so tight that you'll have to walk doubled over for about 330 feet up and down steps in a sloping cave corridor. ☎ 384/381–3194 ☏ 35 TL.

Kaymaklı

ARCHAEOLOGICAL SITE | About 9 km (6 miles) north of Derinkuyu, Kaymaklı was discovered in 1950 and is thought to be the largest of Cappadocia's underground cities in square area, though fewer levels can be visited than at Derinkuyu. It's believed that many of the current homes in the area are connected to the tunnels, and the story goes that before parts of the underground city were closed off to the public, unsuspecting homeowners periodically found tourists popping up in their living rooms. The city extends below ground for eight levels, of which only four are currently open. Sloping corridors and steps connect the floors, with different areas used as stables, kitchens, wineries, and a church. The ceilings are low and can be difficult for tall visitors to navigate. ☎ 384/218–2500 ☏ 35 TL.

Ihlara Valley

82 km (51 miles) southwest of Nevşehir; 52 km (32 miles) west of Derinkuyu.

A verdant river canyon dotted with rock churches carved into the cliffs above, Ihlara Valley is a pleasant change of scenery from the arid terrain typically seen elsewhere in the region and the chance to see more of Cappadocia's rich artistic heritage. The valley, which can be explored with or without a guide, makes an easy day trip from the Avanos-Nevşehir-Ürgüp triangle.

GETTING HERE AND AROUND

If you're coming from Nevşehir, take Route 765 south to Derinkuyu, then head west on the winding road called Gülağaç-Derinkuyu Yolu. Alternatively, join a day tour that takes you to the most noteworthy rock churches and includes a stop for lunch at one of the restaurants inside the canyon—it's a good way to hit the highlights while leaving the driving to someone else.

Sights

★ Ihlara Valley

CANYON | The landscape changes dramatically when you head south through Cappadocia toward Ihlara: the dusty plains turn rich with vegetation along the Melendiz River, which has carved cliffs as high as 490 feet. Walking the entire valley takes the better part of a day, but if you just want to get a taste of it, the most interesting part is the middle section. A cluster of fresco-decorated churches are within walking distance of one another, including the Ağaçaltı (Under-a-Tree) church, Kokar (Fragrant) church, Yılanlı (Serpent) church, and the Church of St. George. Belisırma village, about 2 km (1 mile) north of the Ihlara Vadisi Turistik Tesisleri and roughly a three-hour walk from either end of the valley, has a handful of scenic restaurants, some of which have open-air cabanas built on stilts over the river—an idyllic place for a simple meal, accompanied by the relaxing sound of running water. Just outside the north end of the valley, Selime Monastery is a huge rock-cut complex with a chapel, two levels of rooms, and lots of nooks and crannies. ⊠ Ihlara Vadi Turistik Tesisleri, 2 km (1 mile) from Ihlara village ⛮ 30 TL.

Soğanlı Valleys

45 km (28 miles) southeast of Ürgüp.

The area of Cappadocia between Ürgüp and the Soğanlı Valleys was once considered to be off the beaten path. Though the sights are now well marked and guided tours are increasingly available, it is still often blissfully uncrowded, and remains almost totally uncommercialized.

GETTING HERE AND AROUND

About 9 km (6 miles) past the village of Güzelöz on Ürgüp Yolu, turn right onto Soğanlı Köyü Yolu and proceed about 3 km (2 miles) to the entrance to the Soğanlı Valleys.

The Keşlik Monastery and the archaeological site of Sobessos are both on the way from Ürgüp to the Soğanlı Valleys. From Ürgüp, take Ürgüp Yolu about 15 km (9 miles) to the village of Cemil; you will see signs for Keşlik Monastery about 2 km (1¼ miles) past the village on your right (west). Sobessos is about 6 km (4 miles) farther south on Ürgüp Yolu on the left (east), in the village of Şahinefendi.

There is almost no public transport to these areas, so you'll need to take your own car, hire a guide, or join a day tour.

◉ Sights

Keşlik Monastery

RELIGIOUS SITE | This small but interesting monastery complex has two main churches and a refectory carved out of rock. The Archangelos Church, thought to date to the 11th or 12th century, has extensive, but blackened, frescoes (a flashlight is essential), including one on the wall facing the entrance that shows the Archangel Michael fighting Lucifer in a landscape that strongly resembles Cappadocia. The walls and ceiling of the nearby Stefanos Church are covered with colorful, almost contemporary-looking floral and geometric designs dating to the 7th or 8th century. The monastery's ever-present caretaker, Cabir Coşkuner, speaks some English and is happy to guide visitors around. ⊠ 2 km (1 mile) south of Cemil village, off Ürgüp Yolu ⛮ 5 TL.

Sobessos

ARCHAEOLOGICAL SITE | Excavations of this 4th-century Roman town have been going on for about a decade. So far, the well-preserved remains of a Roman bathhouse and a meeting hall with an extensive mosaic floor have been uncovered, as well as a Byzantine church that was later built on top of the mosaics. A roof protects part of the site. There are catwalks and some limited explanatory panels for visitors. ⊠ Şahinefendi village ⛮ Free.

Soğanlı Valleys

CANYON | These two scenic wooded valleys that form a V-shape were home to a monastic community during Byzantine times, and there are hundreds of rock dwellings and churches cut into the cliffs. The northern, or "upper," valley (on the right-hand side), has most of the churches, while the southern, or "lower," valley is noteworthy for its many dovecotes. In the former, a path follows a little stream past enormous, house-size boulders and comes to churches including the Karabaş Kilisesi ("Church of the Black Head") and Yılanlı (Snake) Church, with extensive frescoes that have been badly damaged by graffiti. The two-story Kubbeli (Domed) Church has an unusual rock-cut cylindrical dome, reminiscent of medieval Armenian churches. If you're lucky enough to come on a day when there are no tour groups, you'll practically be on your own. Climb up the cliff face and you'll be rewarded with incredible views. ⊠ *Soğanlı Köyü Yolu* 🎫 *6 TL.*

Sultan Sazlığı Bird Sanctuary

NATURE PRESERVE | One of Turkey's most important bird sanctuaries, Sultan Sazlığı is a national park and Ramsar-protected wetland that's a 32-km (20-mile) drive from the turnoff for the Soğanlı Valleys. A total of 301 species have been observed here, including flamingos, spoonbills, buzzards, gray herons, lapwings, and great white egrets. There's no admission fee for the park, but first-timers are encouraged to hire a field guide to take them out by boat, jeep, or foot (depending on the water level in the marshes). ■TIP→ **Spring is the best time to visit—though, thanks to good rains in the last couple of years, birds can be seen year-round. Contact the guides who run Sultan Pansiyon in Ovaçiftlik village in advance to make arrangements.** ⊠ *Off Yahyalı Yolu, Ovaçiftlikköy* ✛ *From the turnoff for Soğanlı, head east 12 km (7½ miles) on Soğanlı Köyü Yolu to Yeşilhisar, turn south onto D805 (Kayseri-Niğde Yolu), and go about 9 km (5½ miles) before* turning left (east) onto Yahyalı Yolu. Continue until you see the left-hand turnoff for Ovaçiftlik village (Ovaçiftlik Köyü Yolu) 🕾 352/658–5549 for Sultan Pansiyon ⊕ www.sultanbirding.com 🎫 Free.

Niğde

85 km (53 miles) south of Nevşehir.

The small city of Niğde is primarily an agricultural center, and the few sights of interest, including the Niğde Museum, can be seen on a short excursion. In the 13th century, the city flourished under the Seljuks, who built the triple-domed Alaaddin Camii and the neighboring fortress. The Ak Medrese, dating to 1409, has stone carvings and a small museum and cultural center. A little ways out of town is Niğde's most important attraction, Eski Gümüşler Monastery.

GETTING HERE AND AROUND
Niğde and the Eski Gümüşler Monastery are best accessed by car via Route 765, but it's also possible to take a local bus from Nevşehir to Niğde and then a minibus to Eski Gümüşler from the terminal (Eski Terminal) in Niğde's town center; minibuses marked "Gümüşler" leave every 20 to 30 minutes during the day.

◉ Sights

Eski Gümüşler Manastiri (*Eski Gümüşler Monastery*)

ARCHAEOLOGICAL SITE | Some say the 11th-century Eski Gümüşler church inside this monastery complex has the only image of a smiling Virgin Mary in the world. Others say that this is due to an error made during the church's restoration. Whatever the case, the frescoes inside, though dark, are beautiful and amazingly preserved. When facing the alter of the church's main nave (the room on the right-hand side), look for the "smiling" Virgin is in a rock niche in the left-hand side. Parts of the monastery were carved as early as the 7th century but most of the frescoes are from around the 11th; they were later painted over by local Turkish Muslims, who considered the depiction of human beings idolatrous.

The monastery also contains a kitchen, rock-carved monks' chambers around the central courtyard, and two levels of underground rooms that may have been used in part as a water reservoir. The sign for the monastery is one of the first things you see as you approach Niğde; it's about 4 km (2½ miles) down the road from there. ⊠ 9 km (6 miles) northeast of downtown Niğde, east off Rte. 805, in village of Gümüşler 🖾 6 TL.

Niğde Müzesi (Niğde Museum)
MUSEUM | The small but nicely done Niğde Museum showcases a variety of finds from nearby archaeological sites dating mainly to the Early Bronze Age and Assyrian, Hittite, Greek, and Roman periods. On display are ceramics, metalwork, jewelry, stelae, and an extensive collection of coins. There are also five 10th- and 11th-century mummies—of an adult woman and four small children—found in a rock-cut church in the Ihlara Valley and elsewhere in Cappadocia. ⊠ Yukarı Kayabaşı Mah., Dışarı Cami Sok. 51100 ☎ 388/232–3390 🖾 6 TL.

Konya

261 km (162 miles) south of Ankara; 224 km (140 miles) southwest of Nevşehir.

Famous for its association with Rumi and the whirling dervishes, Konya has long attracted both religious pilgrims and travelers to the city's spiritual, even mystical, atmosphere. Its most important site is the Mevlâna complex, at once a secular museum with displays on dervish life and a mausoleum where the religious devotion the renowned Sufi philosopher inspires is immediately palpable. During the annual Mevlâna

Festival in December, Konya is transformed by an influx of followers—and other curious souls—who come from around the world to observe the anniversary of Rumi's death. The other main event is the International Mystic Music Festival in September.

The rest of the year, Konya is a quiet, rather provincial city; nevertheless, visitors can find evidence of its long and interesting history. Konya was the capital of the Seljuk Empire during much of the 12th and 13th centuries, and some notable medieval mosques and theological seminary buildings—now housing museums—showcase the characteristic architectural style of that period. You can probably see most city sights in a day. Going back further in time, the Neolithic archaeological site of Çatalhöyük, a UNESCO World Heritage Site, can be explored on a side trip.

Not surprisingly, Konya is known throughout Turkey as a religious and rather conservative city, where almost all of the restaurants are dry. Until recently, it catered mainly to domestic travelers, who still make up the overwhelming majority of visitors. But the last few years have seen the opening of several hotels and inns aimed more at foreign guests, and the museums typically have good signage in English. The Mevlâna Kültür Merkezi hosts a free sema (whirling dervish) performance every Saturday evening year-round, and free semas also take place in the garden of the Mevlâna Museum on Thursday evenings in summer.

GETTING HERE AND AROUND
Turkish Airlines, its low-cost sub-brand AnadoluJet, and Pegasus Airlines all run frequent daily flights from Istanbul to Konya; SunExpress has several flights a week to and from İzmir. Konya is also served by major bus companies, including Kamil Koç and Metro, as well as local firms Kontur and Özkaymak; all have offices downtown near the Mevlâna Museum.

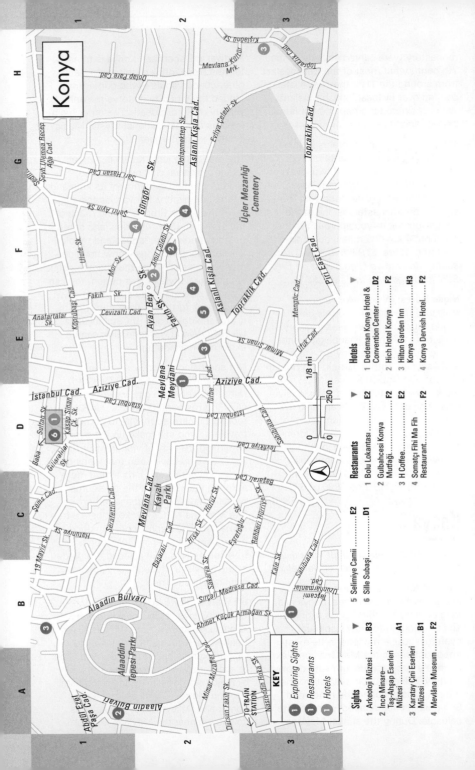

Konya

KEY

- **1** Exploring Sights
- **1** Restaurants
- **1** Hotels

Sights ▶
- Arkeoloji Müzesi **B3**
- İnce Minare–
  Taş-Ahşap Eserleri
  Müzesi **A1**
- Karatay Çini Eserleri
  Müzesi **B1**
- Mevlâna Museum **F2**
- Selimiye Camii **E2**
- Sille Subaşı **D1**

Restaurants ▶
1 Bolu Lokantası **E2**
2 Gulbahcesi Konya
  Mutfağı.........................**F2**
3 H Coffee........................**E2**
4 Somatçı Fihi Ma Fih
  Restaurant....................**F2**

Hotels ▶
1 Dedeman Konya Hotel &
  Convention Center.......**D2**
2 Hich Hotel Konya **F2**
3 Hilton Garden Inn
  Konya **H3**
4 Konya Dervish Hotel.....**F2**

Train travel time from Istanbul to Konya is just under 4½ hours via high-speed train; there are three trains daily in each direction, and tickets cost 86 TL one-way. A high-speed rail line also connects Ankara and Konya, with the ride lasting about 1¾ hours; trains run 10 times daily in each direction and a one-way economy-class ticket costs 31 TL.

Modern Konya is extremely spread out, but its tourist attractions are all concentrated in the city center near Alaaddin Tepesi (Alaaddin Hill). From the airport, 18 km (11 miles) to the northeast, Havaş shuttle buses make trips to the city center 25 minutes after the arrival of every flight (12 TL). Konya's bus terminal is about 15 km (9 miles) north of the city center; it's a 30-minute tram ride from the terminal to the Alaaddin tram stop downtown. The train station, 1½ km (1 mile) southwest of Alaaddin Tepesi, is only accessible by minibus or taxi. Taxis are relatively inexpensive for short distances downtown but can add up if you are going to the bus terminal or airport—a taxi from the Mevlâna area to the airport, for example, can run up to 50 or 60 TL.

CONTACTS Kontur. ☎ *332/265–0080 bus terminal ticket office, 532/444–4042 call center* ⊕ *www.kontur.com.tr.* **Metro.** ☎ *332/265–0040 bus terminal ticket office, 850/222–3455 call center* ⊕ *www.metroturizm.com.tr.* **Özkaymak.** ☎ *332/265–0160 bus terminal ticket office, 444–4206 call center* ⊕ *www. ozkaymak.com.tr.*

TOURS

Selene Tour
This agency runs tours in Konya—including Sufism-themed tours—and to nearby destinations; it can also help visitors make arrangements for attending the annual Mevlâna Festival. Owner Mete Horzum, a dervish himself, is knowledgeable about Konya, Rumi, and Sufism. ⊠ *Bostan Çelebi Sok. 15/1* ☎ *332/353–6745* ⊕ *www.selene.com.tr.*

VISITOR INFORMATION
The best time to visit Konya is during the annual Mevlâna Festival in mid-December, when the dervishes whirl and there are events dedicated to Rumi. The festival usually runs for 10 days, leading up to an intense finale on the night of December 17, the anniversary of Rumi's death. Tickets can be purchased through the Konya Culture and Tourism Office. It is wise to purchase tickets and make hotel reservations weeks or even months in advance, since thousands of people descend on the city for the festival and accommodations are limited. Do not miss a show of the whirling dervishes if you get a chance to see it. It's beautiful, entrancing, and unique. Rumi described dancing as such: "Dancing is when you rise above both worlds, tearing your heart to pieces and giving up your soul."

VISITOR INFORMATION Visitor Information. ⊠ *Aslanlı Kışla Cad. 5, behind Mevlâna Museum* ☎ *332/353–4021* ⊕ *www. konyakultur.gov.tr.*

◉ Sights

Some of Konya's most important historical sites were built by the Seljuks, members of a nomadic Turkic tribe that originated in Central Asia. The Seljuk Turks converted to Islam in the 10th century and began to push westward. They ruled a great swath of Anatolia from the late 11th through the beginning of the 14th century, making Konya their capital for much of that period. Seljuk architecture is similar to the Gothic architecture that was flourishing in Europe at the same time. Many of the mosques, fortresses, and kervansarays that brood over Turkish villages in the region were built in this style.

In addition to the Mosque of Selim, the city's most famous, a few mosques are located on or just off Mevlâna Caddesi between Konya's ancient acropolis, the Alaaddin Tepesi, and Mevlâna Meydanı. The graceful mosque crowning

The tomb of Mevlâna Celaleddin Rumi, the founder of the whirling dervishes, is Konya's most important site.

Alaaddin Tepesi is Alaaddin Camii, an early 13th-century mosque that was one of the most important for Seljuk Sultans, many of whom are entombed within the complex. The construction of **Şerafettin Camii** was begun by the Seljuks in the 13th century and completed by the Ottomans in 1636; the mosque features a dome painted in elaborate baroque Ottoman style and an intricately carved and decorated *mahfil*, the sultan's elevated platform. The **Şemsi Tebrizi Camii and Türbe,** north of Şerafettin Camii on the edge of a small public square, is dedicated to Mevlâna's mentor and friend and contains his mausoleum. Nearby is Konya's oldest mosque, the rather plain **İplikçi Camii** (*Thread-Dealer's Mosque*), dating from 1202. **Aziziye Camii** (*Sultan Abdül Aziz Mosque*), which dates from 1676 and was rebuilt in 1874–76, flanks the bazaar area. The light-filled mosque displays a combination of Ottoman and Rococo styles and is known for having windows that are larger than its doors.

Arkeoloji Müzesi (*Archaeology Museum*) **MUSEUM** | A magnificent **portal** marks the entrance to what was formerly the Sahip Ata complex, a group of structures dating from the late 13th century. A bit to the right is the small but interesting **Arkeoloji Müzesi** (Archaeology Museum), showcasing artifacts from a number of different periods. The most significant room has finds from the 7000 BC Neolithic site of Çatalhöyük, including pottery, jewelry, weapons and tools, and the remains of an infant burial; these are accompanied by quite informative explanations. There are also artifacts from the Bronze Age and Greek and Roman periods; the 3rd-century AD marble sarcophagus depicting the Twelve Labors of Hercules is outstanding. Around the left-hand corner from the Sahip Ata portal is the **Sahip Ata Müzesi** (Sahip Ata Museum), housed in the beautifully (but perhaps not that sensitively) restored dervish lodge of the mosque complex. Items on display include carved wooden doors from as early as the 13th century, ceramic fragments, calligraphic works and old Korans, and dervish accoutrements. It's free to visitors. ✉ *Sahibiata Cad* ☎ *332/351–3207* 🌐 *Free.*

İnce Minare–Taş-Ahşap Eserleri Müzesi
(Museum of Stone and Woodwork)
MUSEUM | The minaret of the 13th-century İnce Minare Medresesi, or "Seminary of the Slender Minaret," is bejeweled with glazed turquoise tiles. Unfortunately, due to a 1901 lightning strike, it is only half its original height. Also worth noting is the especially ornate Seljuk-style decoration of the beautiful stone entry portal. The building itself houses the small but well-done Museum of Stone and Woodwork, which displays a fine collection of tombstones and other inscribed stone fragments as well as elaborate wooden carvings dating from the 13th century. Highlights are the fascinating Persian-influenced Seljuk stone reliefs, which include double-headed eagles, winged angels, and strange creatures that are part human and part bird or beast. ✉ *Alaaddin Bul., west side of Alaaddın Tepesi* ☎ *332/351–3204* 🌐 *5 TL.*

Karatay Çini Eserleri Müzesi *(Karatay Museum or Ceramics Museum)*
MUSEUM | The Karatay Medresesi—a seminary founded in 1251 by Celaleddin Karatay, a Seljuk emir—is now home to Konya's small ceramics museum. The main attraction is the building itself, which is topped by a stunning dome lined with blue, black, and white tiles representing the starry heavens; in the vaulted corners below are stylized ceramic inscriptions of the names of the prophets. The frieze beneath the dome and the vaulted hall, or *eyvan*, at the end of the building, are just as dazzling. The emir's tomb is to the left of the main hall; other side rooms display smaller tile and ceramic works. Most impressive is a collection of rare figurative tiles from Kubadabad Palace in Beyşehir that show the Persian influence on Seljuk art. These include hunting scenes, people with distinctively Eastern features and clothing,

and figurines of animals and mythological creatures, all highlighted in rich shades of cobalt blue and turquoise. ✉ *Ankara Cad. at Alaaddin Bul.* ☎ *332/351–1914* 🌐 *6 TL.*

★ Mevlâna Museum
MUSEUM | When the Sufi mystic philosopher-poet Mevlâna Celaleddin Rumi died in 1273, he was buried in Konya beside his father and a great shrine was erected above them. Today, the museum is one of the most visited sites in Turkey, attracting more than 2 million people a year. The interior resembles that of a mosque, with its intricately painted domes, ornate chandeliers, and Islamic inscriptions on the walls. The main hall contains many dervish tombs, all of them with carved stone turbans wrapped in cloth atop the sarcophagi. The place is usually filled with Muslim pilgrims standing with their palms outward in prayer. Next to the mausoleum is a courtyard with a large *şadırvan*, or ablutions fountain, around which are rooms that formerly served as dervish cells. These have been turned into a museum, with each room illustrating a different aspect of life in the dervish brotherhood. A separate structure, the *matbah*, or kitchen, shows mannequins of dervishes engaged in the preparation and serving of food—activities that took on an almost ritual significance in the dervish hierarchy. ✉ *Off Mevlâna Meydanı* ☎ *332/351–1215* 🌐 *Free.*

Selimiye Camii *(Mosque of Selim)*
RELIGIOUS SITE | Sultan Selim II began this medium-size mosque just across from Rumi's tomb in 1558, when he was heir to the throne and governor of Konya. The structure, completed after he became sultan, is reminiscent of Fatih Camii in Istanbul, with soaring arches and windows surrounding the base of the dome. As of this writing, a restoration of the mosque is expected to be completed in early 2016. ✉ *Mevlâna Meyd, Opposite Mevlâna Museum.*

Continued on page 398

TURKEY'S
WHIRLING DERVISHES

Faith has many expressions. The Mevlevi dervishes' sema ritual may be the world's most mesmerizing.

As a means of attaining mystic union with God, the spinning "dance" of the whirling dervishes is considered one of the world's great spiritual rituals. A profound meditation in motion—this is no "Riverdance" theatrical spectacle—the sema ceremony of the Mevlevi dervishes is actually a form of worship. In breathtaking fashion, they whirl not to induce a trance but to symbolize how all things in the universe revolve, a belief expounded by the great 13th-century mystic Mevlâna Celaleddin Rumi, founder of the Mevlevi order. Buried in Konya, this hallowed figure espoused the use of dance as a surrender to the divine; he described it as such: "Dancing is when you rise above both worlds, tearing your heart to pieces and giving up your soul." As you may learn, there's nothing like a sema experience to add a spiritual spin to your visit to Turkey.

AROUND THE WHIRL

Extremely detailed and specific directions govern even the slightest pattern and gesture in the ritual dance of the whirling dervishes.

1 To help lift themselves into the spiritual realm, the *semazen* dancers are accompanied by musicians, who play the *ney* (reed flute) and the kettledrum, whose beating signals God's call to "be."

2 First dropping their black cloaks—to signify the shedding of earthly ties—the dervishes stand with their arms crossed over their chests, a posture that represents the number one, a symbol of God's unity. Their costumes are full of symbolism: the conical hat, or *sikke*, represents a tombstone, the jacket is the tomb itself, and the floor-length skirt, or *tennure*, a funerary shroud. The latter is hemmed with chain to allow it to rise with dramatic effect.

3 The dervishes' endless spinning—always right to left, counter-clockwise—symbolizes the rotation of the universe. To receive God's goodness, they keep their right hands extended to the sky; to channel God's beneficence to earth, their left hands point toward the ground.

4 The dervishes usually perform for four *selams*—or salutes—each to a separate musical movement. For the last, they are joined by their Sheikh Efendi—incarnating the figure of Rumi—who stands on a red sheepskin (oriented toward holy Mecca) to represent the channel of divine grace. At the climax, he and the *semazenbaşı* (dance master) join the others and whirl in their midst. At the finale, the dervishes put their cloaks back on—a symbol of return to the material world.

Above: The Sufi mystic, Mevlâna Celaleddin Rumi, inspired the whirl of the dervishes.

WHERE THE DERVISHES WHIRL

Ever since the days of the Ottoman sultans, the Mevlevi dervishes' semas have been wildly popular events. In Konya, the Mevlâna Cultural Center hosts free sema performances on Saturday evenings, but the best time to see the Mevlevi dervishes whirl is during the annual Mevlâna Festival, which runs every year for the week to 10 days leading up to December 17, the anniversary of Rumi's death. **Konya's Tourism Information Office** (tel. 332/353–4021), as well as local travel agencies, can help you find tickets and make hotel reservations for the festival; it is wise to book tickets as far in advance as possible. The dervishes have been assigned a special status as "Turkish folk dancers," and if you can't get to Konya during the festival or on a Saturday, you stand just as good a chance of seeing them in Istanbul.

Sille Subaşi

TOWN | The formerly Greek village of Sille can be visited as an excursion or detour on your way out of the city. In AD 327, St. Helena, mother of Constantine the Great, built a small church here; the Aya Elena (Hagia Helena) was extensively restored in the 19th century, and again in 2013, when it reopened as a museum. The recent restoration has preserved the beautiful frescoes, which date to the 1880s, and the gilt wooden iconostasis and pulpit *(free; Tues.–Sun. 9–6)*. In the hillside above town are some Cappadocia-style rock-cut chapels with badly deteriorated frescoes and graves carved out of the stone floors. Still a working village complete with crowing roosters and the smell of manure, Sille has recently become a popular destination for the cafés housed in old homes along the stream running through the center of town. To get to Sille by car, follow Yeni Sille Caddesi out of the city from where it begins near the Dedeman Hotel; or board city bus 64 in front of Alaaddin Camii. If you're heading out of Konya in the direction of Ankara, look for the fabulous Seljuk portal at the entrance to the Horozlu Han, a former kervansaray (now housing a restaurant) near the four-lane beginning of Route 715. ✣ *9 km (5½ miles) northwest of downtown Konya.*

🍴 Restaurants

Bolu Lokantası

$ | **TURKISH** | Don't expect to be wowed by the service or décor at Bolu; people come here for one thing only: etli ekmek, or literally "bread with meat." The Konya specialty is similar to *lahmacun,* a more common meat-topped Turkish flatbread, and consists of minced meat with spices on a long strip of *pide* bread and baked in a stone oven. White walls, white tables, and wooden chairs give Bolu somewhat of a cafeteria feel, but service is friendly and attentive, and though the place is crowded from open to close, waiters will always manage to find you a seat. **Known for:** etli ekmek; home-made ayran, a mint-flavored yogurt drink; crowds of locals. [$] *Average main: 13 TL* ✉ *Aziziye Cd. No: 27* ☎ *332/352–4533.*

Gülbahçesi Konya Mutfağı

$$ | **TURKISH** | The terrace of this restored mansion has one of the best views of the adjacent Mevlâna tomb complex. The menu contains largely regional dishes, and though the food isn't much above what you'll get elsewhere, the location goes a long way. **Known for:** Tirit, a layered concoction of cubed flatbread, yogurt, onions, and chopped lamb, drizzled with melted butter and sprinkled with parsley and ground sumac; unbeatable view of the Mevlana Museum; traditionally styled courtyard. [$] *Average main: 25 TL* ✉ *Eflaki Dede Sok. 3, Karatay* ☎ *332/353–0768* 🌐 *www.gulbahcesikonyamutfagi.com.*

Hi Coffee

$ | **CAFÉ** | Just across from Mevlâna Meydanı, Hi Coffee opened as the first Western-style coffee shop in downtown Konya, serving espresso, cappuccino, lattes, and filtered coffees from around the world in addition to teas and milkshakes. With a few tables inside and a handful more on the sidewalk outside, the tiny, hip venue provides a welcome dose of modern café culture amid Konya's historic sights. **Known for:** best espresso in Konya; views of Mevlana Square; English-speaking staff. [$] *Average main: 10 TL* ✉ *Aziziye Mah., Hendem Sait Çelebi Sok. 9/A* ☎ *332/352–4515.*

Somatçı Fihi Ma Fih Restaurant

$$ | **TURKISH** | By far the most unique restaurant in Konya, Somatçı is the project of a passionate local chef who spent several years recreating dervish cuisine from Rumi's time through historical and ethnographic research and a bit of improvisation. The menu features combinations not typically seen in modern Turkish cuisine; some dishes are downright unusual, but all are worth trying. **Known for:** badem helvası, a

Mevlâna Celaleddin Rumi

Turks tend to proudly embrace the philosopher and poet Rumi (full name: Jalal al-Din Muhammad Rumi), known in Turkish as "Mevlâna," as one of their own, though in reality he hailed from present-day Afghanistan and wrote his poetry in Persian. Born in the city of Balkh on September 30, 1207, he came to Konya in 1228, when it was a part of the Seljuk Empire. By that time the young Rumi had already been deeply influenced by mystic readings and had made the hajj to Mecca.

Rumi's transformative spiritual moment came in 1248, when his companion, Shams Tabrizi, a dervish who initiated Rumi into Islamic mysticism, mysteriously disappeared. Rumi's grief at his beloved friend's disappearance—suspected to be a murder—sparked a prodigious outpouring of verse, music, dance, and poetry. After years of searching for his friend and teacher, Rumi found himself in Damascus, where he had a revelation that the universe was one and each person could be his own holy universe. He exclaimed:

"Why should I seek? I am the same as he.

His essence speaks through me.

I have been looking for myself!"

For the rest of his life, Rumi attributed much of his own poetry to Shams, and in a way that would become

characteristic and controversial, mixed his love with his fellow man with his love for God and God's love for man. Rumi became known for his tolerance, his espousal of love, and his use of dance and song to reach spiritual enlightenment. Toward the end of his life, he spent 12 years dictating his masterwork, the *Masnavi*, to a companion. He died in 1273, and the Mevlevi order of dervishes, famous for their semas, or whirling ceremonies, was founded after his death.

The central theme of Rumi's philosophy is a longing for unity—of men, of the universe, with God and with God's spirit. Rumi believed in the use of music, poetry, and dancing as facilitators for reaching God and for focusing on the divine. Through ecstatic dancing, singing, or chanting, Sufi worshippers believed they could negate their bodies and vain selves, becoming empty vessels to be filled with love, the essence of the divine. In Rumi's poetry, he talks of God as one might a lover, and the ecstatic states reached through dancing and singing sometimes border on the erotic. In recent years, Rumi's legacy has been revived, ensuring that his timeless teachings endure. His epitaph suggests he would have been happy with that: "When we are dead, seek not our tomb in the earth, but find it in the hearts of men."

thick, melt-in-your mouth almond paste accented with rose oil; rose water; excellent service. $ *Average main: 25 TL* ✉ *Celel Sk. 9, Karatay* ☎ *332/351–6696* ⊕ *www.somatci.com.*

🛏 **Hotels**

Dedeman Konya Hotel & Convention Center
$$$ | **HOTEL** | The lobby of this 18-story tower in a busy commercial and residential area of Konya exudes opulence (though some may find it a bit overdone); rooms are spacious and nicely furnished, with all the amenities of a

first-rate business hotel. **Pros:** high-class service; multiple dining options; extensive fitness center. **Cons:** hotel is about 4 km (2½ miles) from Konya's tourist attractions; breakfast could be better; not accessible by public transportation. $ *Rooms from: €160* ⊠ *Özalan Mah., Yeni Sille Cad., Selçuklu* ☎ *332/221– 6600* ⊕ *www.dedeman.com* ⇱ *206 rooms* ⦙◯⦙ *Free Breakfast.*

★ **Hich Hotel**

$ | **HOTEL** | Konya's first true boutique hotel occupies a pair of nicely restored 19th-century houses across from the Mevlâna Museum. **Pros:** great value; refreshing, memorable room design; exceptional service. **Cons:** limited indoor public spaces; ground-floor rooms can be noisy; some rooms can feel a little cramped. $ *Rooms from: 300 TL* ⊠ *Celal Sok. 6, Karatay* ☎ *332/353–4424* ⊕ *www.hichhotel.com* ⇱ *13 rooms* ⦙◯⦙ *Free Breakfast.*

Hilton Garden Inn Konya

$ | **HOTEL** | The only international chain hotel in Konya's touristic center has large, comfortable, well-lit rooms with contemporary style—think dark leather headboards, plum-colored velvet armchairs, and silk screen prints of tulips. **Pros:** next to Mevlâna Cultural Center and close to sights; maintains reliable American-style hotel standards; small gym (rare in downtown Konya hotels). **Cons:** dull views of empty lots and a cemetery; lacks local flavor; weak Internet. $ *Rooms from: 600 TL* ⊠ *Kışlaönü Sok. 4, Karatay* ☎ *332/221–6000* ⊕ *www.hilton.com* ⇱ *228 rooms* ⦙◯⦙ *No meals.*

Konya Dervish Hotel

$ | **B&B/INN** | This family-run bed-and-breakfast is in a restored 200-year-old house on a quiet street, a short walk from the Mevlâna Museum. **Pros:** good value; warm, friendly owners; nice breakfast. **Cons:** no views of sights; bathrooms a bit tight; guests are asked to remove shoes and wear slippers throughout premises. $ *Rooms*

from: €80 ⊠ *Güngör Sok. 7, Karatay* ☎ *332/350–0842* ⊕ *www.dervishotel. com* ⇱ *7 rooms* ⦙◯⦙ *Free Breakfast.*

🎭 Performing Arts

Konya International Mystic Music Festival

FESTIVALS | Held annually from September 22 to 30, the Konya International Mystic Music Festival hosts free nightly performances of mystical music and dance at venues around the city. Performers come from as far away as India, Korea, and Mali, and have included big names on the world music scene, such as Zakir Hussain and Kayhan Kalhor. ⊠ *Konya* ⊕ *www.mistikmuzik.gov.tr.*

Mevlâna Festival

CULTURAL FESTIVALS | Each December, thousands of pilgrims from around the world descend on Konya for the Mevlâna Festival, which includes *sema* performances and other events commemorating Mevlâna Celaleddin Rumi. The program, which usually lasts about 10 days, culminates with an intense finale on the night of December 17—the anniversary of Rumi's death, considered his "wedding night" with God. Tickets can be purchased in advance through the website of the Konya Culture and Tourism Office, or contact a local travel agency, such as Selene Tour, to make arrangements. Be sure also to make hotel reservations well in advance, as accommodations are limited and fill up quickly. ⊠ *Konya* ☎ *332/353–4021 Konya tourism office* ⊕ *konyakultur.gov.tr.*

Mevlâna Kültür Merkezi (*Mevlâna Cultural Center*)

ARTS CENTERS | The huge, rather grandiose Mevlâna Cultural Center has a performance hall that seats 2,600; it hosts free sema (whirling dervish) performances every Saturday night at 7 pm. The center is also the venue for many of the events in the Mystical Music Festival in September (free) and the Mevlâna Festival in December (admission charged). Tickets for semas can be obtained at the center on the day of, while tickets for festival events can be arranged through travel agencies or the Konya tourism office. ⊠ *Aslanlı Kışla Cad., Karatay* ☎ *332/352–8111* ⊕ *www. mkm.gov.tr.*

🛍 Shopping

İkonium Atölye

TEXTILES/SEWING | Run by a Konya native and his American wife, İkonium is a studio and shop specializing in handmade felt textiles, a traditional local craft. The shop sells colorful felt hats, purses, and accessories; silk scarves embellished with felt; and other decorative items. All pieces are made on the premises, and the staff will gladly show visitors the felt production process. The owners' work has been showcased around the world, and the two occasionally run felt-making workshops. ⊠ *Aziziye Mah., Bostan Çelebi Sok. 12/A* ☎ *532/698–2824.*

★ Karavan Carpet

HOUSEHOLD ITEMS/FURNITURE | This six-floor store, on a street behind Mevlâna Caddesi, is a veritable treasure trove of collector-worthy rugs and antiques. The enormous stock includes pile upon pile of kilims and carpets—many of them vintage—plus an extensive collection of antique carved doors and architectural pieces sourced from across Anatolia. There are also copper items, some glassware and ceramics, traditional Turkish musical instruments, handicrafts, and other funky finds. ⊠ *Ayanbey Sok. 6/A* ☎ *332/351–0425* ⊕ *www.karavan-carpet.com.*

Konya's Bazaar

SHOPPING NEIGHBORHOODS | Just south of Mevlâna Caddesi and west of Aziziye Caddesi, Konya's traditional bazaar quarter was recently renovated and its pedestrian streets are now lined with nearly identical-looking merchants stocking an array of goods of interest mainly to locals, including jewelry, clothes, textiles, and household items. East of Aziziye Caddesi, the tiny alleyway known as Bostan Çelebi Sokak has so far escaped the face-lift and is home to several interesting shops selling carpets, antiques, and handicrafts. Farther down Aziziye near the intersection with Karaman Caddesi lies the Kadınlar Pazarı, an indoor food bazaar with vendors of spices, dried fruit and nuts, produce, cheeses, olives, and more. ⊠ *South of Mevlâna Cad. on either side of Aziziye Cad.* ⊘ *Closed Sun.*

Çatalhöyük

48 km (30 miles) southeast of Konya to Çumra, then 20 km (12 miles) north.

Dating to about 7400 BC, Çatalhöyük is the site of one of the oldest human settlements ever found and was added to the UNESCO World Heritage list in 2012. British archaeologist James Mellaart discovered the site in 1958 and initially excavated at least 160 buildings between 1961 and 1965, uncovering ancient wall paintings, some of the earliest known pottery, human burials, and countless artifacts. He theorized that female figurines and other finds pointed to the worship of a mother goddess by the site's prehistoric inhabitants. Although alternate theories have since been presented, the iconic figurines—many of which are displayed in the Museum of Anatolian Civilizations in Ankara—remain symbolic of Çatalhöyük. The excavations of the East Mound are protected by two open-air hangarlike structures. This is the older of the two mounds, and 18 settlement levels have been identified here; you can get a good sense of the different layers from the visitor areas at the top. The South Shelter covers the deepest excavations, begun by Mellaart and restarted in 1993 by Ian Hodder of Stanford University, while the North Shelter houses several excavation areas opened up by Hodder's team. A handful of illustrated explanatory panels explain what's what. The "Experimental House," near the entrance to the site, is a re-creation of a prehistoric Çatalhöyük adobe home. With murals on the walls and ceremonial animal skulls, it has been made to look as realistic as possible. The small visitors center is modern and very informative, with panels explaining the site and its significance; however, there are few artifacts on display, as most have been taken to either Ankara or the Archaeology Museum in Konya.

GETTING HERE AND AROUND

A round-trip taxi from Konya to Çatalhöyük costs around 200 TL, depending on your bargaining skills. Alternatively, you can take a minibus from Konya's downtown İlçe Terminali (aka Eski Garaj) to the town of Çumra (departing Konya roughly once an hour) and then a taxi to the site, for around 80 TL total. From the same terminal in Konya, minibuses labeled Küçükköy/Karkın go directly to the village where the site is located (about 10 TL each way). These typically depart Konya weekdays at noon and return from Küçükköy/Karkın around 3 pm Monday through Saturday, but it's wise to confirm times with Konya's tourism office so you don't get stranded in the village.

⊙ Sights

Çatalhöyük Archaeological Site

ARCHAEOLOGICAL SITE | The significance of this Neolithic archaeological site lies not just in its age but in the wealth of well-preserved art and artifacts found here, which shed light on humankind's transition to a sedentary, agricultural lifestyle. Thought to have been home to as many as 8,000 people at a time, Çatalhöyük was inhabited for more than 1,200 years, beginning in about 7,400 BC, with successive generations of residents erecting new mud-brick houses atop the old ones. The name Çatalhöyük actually means "forked mound," likely a reference to the two distinctive mounds—up to 69 feet high and separated by an indentation—which you can clearly see as you approach the site. Major excavations ended in early 2018, with minor excavations ongoing, but only a tiny fraction of the site has yet been excavated. ⊠ Küçükköy, near Çumra ☎ 332/452–5217 summer only ⊕ www.catalhoyuk.com ⊠ Free.

Ankara

261 km (162 miles) north of Konya; 454 km (281 miles) southeast of Istanbul.

In 1923, right after the War of Independence, Ankara was made the fledgling Turkish Republic's new capital—in part because it was a barren, dusty steppe city more or less in the middle of nowhere, and therefore considered to be secure. The city still feels that way somewhat, despite being the center of national political activity and home to more than 4 million residents. It doesn't come close to having the historical richness or vibrancy of Istanbul, yet Ankara does provide a sweeping overview of the history of this land, both ancient and modern. For proof, visit the Museum of Anatolian Civilizations, repository of the best archaeological treasures found in Turkey, and the Anıtkabir, Mustafa Kemal Atatürk's colossal mausoleum. Atatürk's larger-than-life persona and the impact he had on the country can be sensed more powerfully at the Anıtkabir than anywhere else in Turkey. Indeed, the capital city as a whole is permeated by the great man's fascinating and enduring legacy, and is nothing less than a monument to his overpowering will.

Though largely modern in appearance, Ankara is in fact an ancient settlement that was occupied successively by the Hittites and other Anatolian kingdoms, the Greeks, Romans, Byzantines, Seljuks, and the Ottomans. Glimpses of these layers of history can be seen in the Citadel and Ulus areas, where a few Roman ruins are haphazardly juxtaposed with Seljuk-era mosques, centuries-old Ottoman kervan-sarays, and nondescript modern buildings. The top of the ancient citadel offers excellent views of the city, and within the walls is a fascinating neighborhood.

Ankara is also a pleasantly green and easily navigable city, with restaurants, hotels, and shops that are increasingly diverse and cosmopolitan. This is at heart a government and college town, so you'll also find more relaxed attitudes here than in many other parts of Anatolia.

GETTING HERE AND AROUND

Staying at a hotel inside the citadel or in the surrounding neighborhood of Ulus gives you close proximity to almost all of Ankara's sights, and the citadel hotels, especially, are full of historic charm. Aside from a few restaurants, however, the old part of the city has little to offer in the way of nightlife and can feel somewhat deserted at night. The downtown neighborhoods of Kavaklıdere and Çankaya are bustling, with many fine restaurants, shops, and clubs—but you'll need to take a taxi or bus to reach the city's main attractions from these districts.

Ankara is served by all major bus companies—it's about a five-hour trip from Istanbul—but flying from Istanbul saves a lot of time and is not much more expensive. Two companies, Havaş and BelkoAir, run airport shuttles for 11 TL. Municipally owned BelkoAir shuttles pick up passengers in front of the terminal near flight arrivals and has several drop-off points in the city, including in Ulus and Kızılay; passengers can board shuttles going to the airport at the AŞTİ bus station, at Gama shopping center in Kızılay, at the train station, and in Ulus (19 Mayıs Stadium, B Gate). Privately owned Havaş shuttles run only between the airport and AŞTİ. Both companies operate shuttles in each direction approximately every 30 minutes during the day and about every hour at night.

By high-speed train, the journey from Istanbul to Ankara takes just under four hours; there are eight trains daily in each direction, and the fare is 71 TL one-way. High-speed trains from Ankara to Konya take just 1 hour and 45 minutes and run 10 times daily in each direction; a one-way economy-class ticket costs 31 TL.

Ankara is a big city with chaotic traffic, and you'll save yourself a lot of grief if you use public transportation rather than renting a car to get around. The main neighborhood encompassing the old part of the city is called Ulus; this is where most of the tourist attractions are, and it's quite compact and walkable.

Taxis are more expensive in Ankara than in Istanbul: a taxi from the airport, approximately 35 km (20 miles) from the city center, can cost you about 110 TL to the Ulus area, and 120 TL or more to Kızılay or Kavaklıdere, while a taxi from the Çankaya area to the citadel can cost as much as 30 TL. You can easily hail a cab in the city, or ask your hotel to call one.

There are two subway lines in Ankara: the metro, which runs north from Kızılay; and the Ankaray, which goes east–west from the AŞTİ bus station in the western suburbs, through Kızılay and on to Dikimevi in the east. It's easy to get downtown from Ankara's *otogar* (AŞTİ), which connects directly to the Ankaray. Take the Ankaray to the Kızılay stop and then transfer to the metro (using the same ticket) if you want to continue north to Ulus. The fare is 3 TL for a single-use ticket, or you can purchase a smart card for 6 TL, which discounts the fare to 2 TL per ride; trains run between approximately 6 am and midnight.

AIRPORT SHUTTLE CONTACTS BelkoAir.
☎ *444–9312 call center* ⊕ *www.belkoair. com.* **Havaş.** ☎ *212/444–0487 national call center* ⊕ *www.havas.com.tr.*

TRAIN CONTACTS Ankara train station.
✉ *Talatpaşa Bul. at Cumhuriyet Cad.*
☎ *444–8233 national call center.*

VISITOR INFORMATION

CONTACTS Visitor Information. ✉ *Main office, Gençlik Parkı İçi 10, (near Ulus metro station entrance), Ulus* ☎ *312/324–0101.*

⊙ Sights

★ **Anadolu Medeniyetleri Müzesi** (*Museum of Anatolian Civilizations*)

MUSEUM | The Museum of Anatolian Civilizations is a real gem, showcasing many of Turkey's best ancient treasures and providing excellent insight into the incredible amount of history that has played out here. Housed in a 15th-century *bedesten* (similar to a kervansaray), the museum covers every major civilization that has had a presence in Anatolia, going back more than 10 millennia. Highlights of the vast collection include finds dating back to 7000 BC—among them famous mother goddess figurines and wall paintings of animals and geometric patterns from the neolithic site of Çatalhöyük, one of the oldest human settlements ever discovered. Other items on display include clay cuneiform tablets—the earliest written records found in Anatolia—from the Assyrian trade colonies period, as well as a 13th-century BC bronze tablet (the only such bronze tablet found in Anatolia) recording a Hittite treaty. A significant collection of monumental stonework from around Anatolia, including well-preserved neo-Hittite reliefs depicting the epic of Gilgamesh, from the archaeological site of Karkamış (Kargamış) in Gaziantep, is on display in the central hall. ✉ *Gözcü Sokak 2* ☎ *312/324–3160* ⊕ *www.anadolumedeniyetlerimuzesi.gov.tr* 🎫 *30 TL.*

★ **Anıtkabir** (*Atatürk's Mausoleum*)

MEMORIAL | Atatürk's picture is on every single piece of Turkish currency, his visage hangs in just about every office and official building in the country, and his principles and ideas are the foundations of modern Turkish political thought. So his vast mausoleum, perched on a hilltop overlooking the capital city he built, is on a scale suitable to his stature in Turkey. A marble promenade flanked with Hittite-style lions leads to the imposing mausoleum, where a huge sarcophagus lies beyond a colonnade with inscriptions from his speeches and below a ceiling of brilliant gold mosaics. An adjoining museum contains personal belongings from the revered man's life, including his clothes, automobiles, and personal library. The corridors underneath the tomb house an in-depth exhibit on the 1919–22 War of Independence. To reach the mausoleum, you can take the metro to Tandoğan and walk up the long road that ascends from the main entrance at the northern end of the grounds. A quicker way is to take a taxi to the alternate entrance on Akdeniz Caddesi, on the southeast side. ✉ *Anıt Cad.* ⊹ *Alternative entrance on Akdeniz Cad.* ☎ *312/231–7975* ⊕ *www.anitkabir.tsk.tr* 🎫 *Free.*

Ankara Kalesi

HISTORIC SITE | Ankara's main historic sites are clustered around its ancient citadel (known as the Hisar or Kale in Turkish), high on a hill overlooking the city. Though the citadel's precise origins are not known, the inner and outer walls standing today are thought to have been built between the 7th and 9th century, during the Byzantine period. Although the modern city has grown up around the citadel, the area inside the walls has retained an almost villagelike atmosphere, an entire neighborhood with winding, cobblestoned streets and old houses built with timber and plaster. The municipality has recently cleaned up the entrance area, but some parts of the neighborhood inside the citadel remain fairly run-down. The easiest place to enter the citadel is from **Parmak Kapısı** (Finger Gate), also known as **Saat Kapısı** (Clock Gate), across from the Divan Çukurhan. Head toward the center, where you'll see the restored **Şark Kulesi** (Eastern Tower). Climb up the stone steps to the tower's upper ramparts for excellent panoramic views

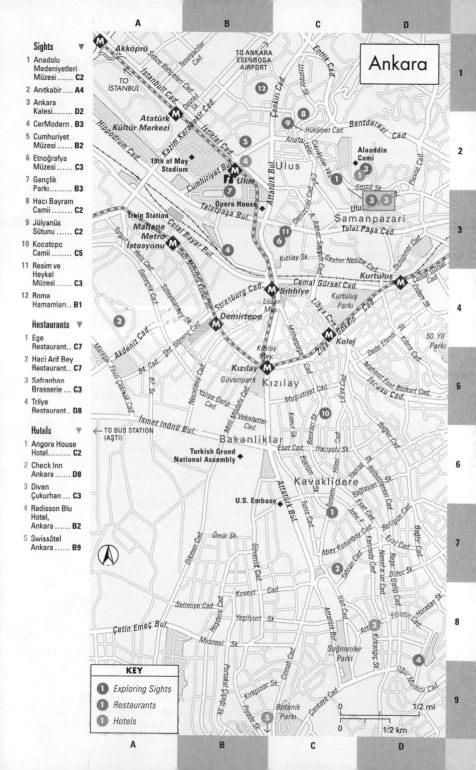

Ankara

KEY

1 *Exploring Sights*
1 *Restaurants*
1 *Hotels*

0 1/2 mi
0 1/2 km

of the city. ⊠ *Uphill from Museum of Anatolian Civilizations, Ulus.*

CerModern

MUSEUM | Ankara's first and only contemporary art museum is in a renovated former train maintenance depot not far from the train station. The space showcases both established international artists and up-and-coming local artists through well-conceived temporary exhibits (the museum has no permanent collection). The venue also hosts film screenings, concerts, and other events, and there's a hip café and small gift shop. ⊠ *Altınsoy Cad. 3* 🕾 *312/310–0000* ⊕ *www.cermodern.org* 🎫 *20 TL* ☾ *Closed Mon.*

Cumhuriyet Müzesi (*Museum of the Republic*)

MUSEUM | In Turkey's first parliament building, which now houses the Museum of the Republic, politicians debated principles and policies that would shape the Turkish Republic as a modern secular nation. The great hall where parliament convened from 1924 to 1960 is decorated in Seljuk and Ottoman styles, with an ornately inlaid wooden ceiling, enormous crystal chandelier, and a loggia-like gallery from which dignitaries addressed the assembly. The museum includes a small exhibit on the early years of the Republic; although signs are only in Turkish, a free—and very informative—English audio guide is available. ⊠ *Cumhuriyet Cad. 22, Ulus* 🕾 *312/310–5361* ⊕ *www.cumhuriyetmuzesi.gov.tr* 🎫 *6 TL.*

Etnoğrafya Müzesi (*Ethnography Museum*)

MUSEUM | Atatürk used this Ottoman Revival–style building as an office, and his body lay here for 15 years after his death while his enormous mausoleum was being built. This small museum mainly appeals to those interested in cultural artifacts. It houses a rich collection of Turkish carpets, folk costumes, weapons, Islamic calligraphy, and ceramics. The display of woodwork, which includes intricately carved doors, portals, *minbars*

(mosque pulpits), and Seljuk thrones—some pieces dating as far back as the 13th century—is especially impressive. ⊠ *Talatpaşa Cad. and Türkocağı Sok., Ulus* 🕾 *312/311–3007* ⊕ *www.etnografyamuzesi.gov.tr/en* 🎫 *10 TL.*

Gençlik Parkı

CITY PARK | The pleasant, well-tended Gençlik Parkı ("Youth Park"), though not large enough to make you forget you're in the middle of the city, is a nice place for a stroll. Plantings are manicured and a small man-made lake is surrounded by a partly trellised, partly tree-lined walkway. Ankara's main tourist information office is also in the park. ⊠ *Cumhuriyet Cad. and İstiklal Cad., Ulus.*

Hacı Bayram Camii (*Hacı Bayram Mosque*)

RELIGIOUS SITE | Dating to 1427, Hacı Bayram Camii is one of Ankara's most important mosques. Built mainly of brick, it is named after the revered founder of the Bayrami order of dervishes, Hacı Bayram, whose tomb is next to the minaret. A newer and showily decorated wing takes something away from the site's historic character. An attractive public square, with a fountain and landscaped flower beds, has also been built around the mosque in recent years. The location of Hacı Bayram Camii, practically abutting the ancient **Temple of Augustus and Rome**, indicates that this area has been a sacred site through the ages. Though it's in a rather sad state today, the temple, built 25–20 BC, is of great historical significance—inscribed in marble on its walls is the most complete Latin and Greek text of the *Res Gestae Divi Augusti*, in which Augustus, the first Roman emperor, lists his deeds. What's left of the structure is now largely supported by metal scaffolding, and it can only be viewed from a walkway that runs around it. ⊠ *Hacı Bayram Veli Cad., north of Hisarparkı Cad., Ulus.*

Jülyanüs Sütunu (*Column of Julian*)

ARCHAEOLOGICAL SITE | A stone's throw from the Temple of Augustus and Rome, in a small traffic circle surrounded by government buildings, is the Column of Julian. It commemorates a visit by Julian the Apostate (Rome's last pagan emperor), who passed through town in 362 en route to his death in battle with the Persians. The column, topped by a stork's nest, has 15 fluted drums and a Corinthian capital. A few steps away, in front of the Ankara Governorate, a section of Roman-era road has been excavated and covered with plexiglass. ✉ *Off Hükümet Cad., Ulus.*

Kocatepe Camii (*Kocatepe Mosque*)
RELIGIOUS SITE | It took 20 years to build this gigantic, elaborately decorated neo-Ottoman mosque in the center of Turkey's secular capital. Perched on an expansive raised platform, the illuminated edifice dominates the Ankara skyline at night and is one of the city's most prominent landmarks. The prestigious mosque is the site of most military and state funerals. ✉ *Dr. Mediha Eldem Sok. 67-89, Kizilay.*

Resim ve Heykel Müzesi (*Painting and Sculpture Museum*)
MUSEUM | These galleries, in an ornate marble building next door to the Ethnography Museum, display a vast number of works by late Ottoman and modern Turkish artists. With a few exceptions, most of the latter haven't earned international recognition, yet this collection provides an interesting glimpse into the way Turkey's artists have been influenced by Western trends over the last century and a half. Schools of art such as Impressionism and Abstract Expressionism are represented among the portraits, landscape paintings, sculptures, and other works on display. ✉ *Talatpaşa Cad. and Türkocağı Sok., Ulus* ☎ *312/310–2094* 🎫 *Free.*

Roma Hamamları (*Roman Baths*)
ARCHAEOLOGICAL SITE | You can't bathe at this 3rd-century complex just north of Ulus Square, but you can see how the Romans did. The large bath system featured a frigidarium, tepidarium, and caldarium (cold, warm, and hot rooms), as well as steam rooms that had raised floors. An illustration near the entrance shows the layout of the Roman city superimposed over a map of the modern area, indicating just how little of ancient Ancyra has been excavated. Also scattered around the open-air site are various stone fragments, some of which appear to be ancient gravestones, with Latin and Hebrew inscriptions. ✉ *Çankırı Cad. 54, Ulus* ☎ *312/310–7280* 🎫 *6 TL.*

🍴 Restaurants

Ege Restaurant
$$$ | **SEAFOOD** | This charming spot just off fashionable Tunalı Hilmi Caddesi specializes in nicely prepared Aegean-style mezes and seafood dishes (Ege is the Turkish name for the Aegean Sea), such as Cretan-style cubed cheese with herbs, or octopus with thyme. The design—painted wooden chairs, blue-and-white walls with seashore motifs, and maps of the region painted on the ceiling—transports you straight to the Aegean islands. **Known for:** Aegean design; sea bass fillet cooked in various styles; perfect spot for rakı. [$] *Average main: 60 TL* ✉ *Büklüm Sok. 54/B, Kavaklidere* ☎ *312/428–2717* 🌐 *www.egerestaurant.com.*

Haci Arif Bey Restaurant
$$ | **TURKISH** | Hidden in a courtyard on a quiet street in Kavaklidere, this restaurant offers a variety of Turkish dishes, with a clear emphasis on the cuisine of Gaziantep, home of many of the country's most beloved desserts. Meat and lamb are the stars of the menu, with varieties served wrapped in thin flatbread, covered in yogurt, or on a bed of grilled eggplant. **Known for:** personalized pide bread; künefe (a sweet, cheese-filled pastry); Ali Nazik dishes (smoked and spiced eggplant with lamb). [$] *Average main: 45 TL* ✉ *Guniz*

Meet the Hittites

Around 1800 BC a people called the Hittites, who like the Persians spoke an Indo-European language (unlike the Turks, whose language is Ural-Altaic), apparently entered Anatolia after crossing the Caucasus steppes beyond the Black Sea. They claimed the city of Hattuşa—with a fortress, temples, large administrative buildings, houses, cemeteries, and decorated gateways and courtyards—as their capital and soon began to build an empire. They worshipped a storm god and a sun goddess, and had a well-ordered society with written laws. At their height, they conquered Babylon and battled the Egyptian pharaohs. One of the most famous finds in Hattuşa is a copy of the Treaty of Kadesh (c. 1259 BC), signed between the Hittite and Egyptian empires after what might have been the largest chariot battle ever fought, involving some 5,000 chariots. The Hittites' reign came to an end after some 600 years, when tribes from the north sacked and burned Hattuşa in 1200 BC. The Phrygians then became the dominant people in the region.

What you can see today at Boğazkale (the modern-day Turkish name for Hattuşa) is mainly the foundations of buildings. Yazılıkaya, about 3 km (2 miles) to the east, is far more interesting. Yazılıkaya (meaning "inscribed rock" in Turkish) is thought to have served as Hattuşa's religious sanctuary. The walls here are covered with drawings of Hittite gods, goddesses, and kings from about 1200 BC. On the main shrine, 42 gods march from the left to meet 21 goddesses coming from the right. In the middle is the weather god Teshub with horns in his cap, and the sun goddess Hebat riding a leopard. It's thought that funeral rites for kings were performed here.

The Hittite cities are about 200 km (124 miles) northeast of Ankara, a two-hour drive. A guided trip from Ankara, however, will shed a great deal of light on what are often otherwise unintelligible piles of rocks arranged in squares.

sk 48/1, Kavaklidere ☎ *312/467–0067* 🌐 *www.haciarifbey.com.tr.*

Safranhan Brasserie
$$$ | **TURKISH** | Sitting just beneath Ankara Castle and with an incredible panorama of Ankara, this Turkish-style brasserie couples excellent food with first-rate service. An open kitchen gives way to an elegantly furnished dining room with floor-to-ceiling windows, but the views continue on the restaurant's large outdoor patio, where guests sit before white tablecloths and underneath oversized umbrellas. **Known for:** exceptional service; warm meze plate; Ankara tava. $ *Average main: 50 TL* ✉ *Divan Çukurhan Hotel, Gözcü Sk. 3/9, Ulus* ☎ *312/306–6424* 🌐 *www.divan.com.tr/Divan-Cukurhan/yeme-icme/safranhan-brasserie.*

Trilye Restaurant
$$$$ | **SEAFOOD** | Ankara may be landlocked, but Trilye serves such impressive fish and seafood dishes that you wouldn't know it. Opened more than a dozen years ago by Turkish food writer Süreyya Üzmez, the stylish restaurant has an extensive menu of creative mezes—such as prawn in avocado sauce, or marinated artichoke hearts with sesame seeds—and well-prepared main courses. **Known for:** Adana fish kebab; outstanding and knowledgable service; elegant decor. $ *Average main: 80 TL* ✉ *Hafta Sok.*

11/A-B, Kavaklidere ☎ *312/447–1200* 🌐 *www.trilye.com.tr.*

Hotels

Angora House Hotel

$ | **B&B/INN** | A beautifully restored 19th-century Ottoman house inside the walls of Ankara's ancient citadel has the feel of a private home—six charming rooms have original wood floors and ceilings, antique chandeliers, traditional textiles, and comfortable beds. **Pros:** good-size rooms; historic area; dedicated staff. **Cons:** neighborhood can be noisy; rather difficult for vehicles to reach and for taxis to find; bathrooms somewhat basic and showing age. [$] *Rooms from: €41* ✉ *Kale Kapısı Sok. 16, Hisar, Ulus, Ulus* ☎ *312/309–8380* 🌐 *www.angorahouse.com.tr* 🛏 *6 rooms* 🍴 *No meals.*

Check Inn Ankara

$ | **HOTEL** | In Ankara's bustling Kavaklıdere shopping and nightlife district, these recently opened accommodations have the personal feel of a small hotel with many of the amenities of a larger property. **Pros:** located in heart of trendy neighborhood; pleasant roof-terrace restaurant; fitness facilities. **Cons:** some rooms get a lot of noise; staff's English could be better; poor Wi-Fi in some locations. [$] *Rooms from: 280 TL* ✉ *Filistin Cad. 1, Kavaklidere* ☎ *312/474–4040* 🌐 *www.checkinnankara.com* 🛏 *33 rooms* 🍴 *Free Breakfast.*

★ **Divan Çukurhan**

$$ | **HOTEL** | In this gem of a hotel, elegant rooms in a restored 16th-century kervansaray at the edge of Ankara's citadel are decorated in different styles, such as Indochinese, Venetian, Tibetan, and Ottoman; some have citadel or city views, and all feature antique furniture and original works of art. **Pros:** unique historical atmosphere; personalized service; quiet, oasis-like rooms. **Cons:** atop a steep hill; no in-room minibar or fridge; poor Wi-Fi in some rooms. [$] *Rooms from: €92* ✉ *Necatibey Mah., Depo Sok. 3, Ulus* ☎ *312/306–6400* 🌐 *www.divan.com.tr* 🛏 *19 rooms* 🍴 *Free Breakfast.*

Radisson Blu Hotel, Ankara

$$ | **HOTEL** | The only international chain hotel in Ankara's historic Ulus district is somewhat lacking in flair but has comfortable rooms, with dark woods and muted, soothing turquoise, grays, and beiges. **Pros:** convenient location near major tourist attractions, and metro; exceptional customer service; excellent views from upper-floor rooms. **Cons:** overlooks a loud, busy expressway (to avoid street noise, request a back-facing room); bathrooms could be updated; area lacks options for evening and night life. [$] *Rooms from: €60* ✉ *İstiklal Cad. 20, Ulus* ☎ *312/310–4848* 🌐 *www.radissonblu.com* 🛏 *202 rooms* 🍴 *Free Breakfast.*

Swissôtel Ankara

$$ | **HOTEL** | A setting in the posh Çankaya district is part of the allure here, as are style and sophistication—rooms are elegantly designed in soothing colors; large bathrooms have deep tubs and separate rain showers; and an extensive wellness center includes a half-Olympic-size indoor pool, a beautiful hammam, sauna, full spa, and large fitness room. **Pros:** upscale yet relaxed; excellent service, dining options, and fitness facilities; exceptional and friendly service. **Cons:** in a residential neighborhood far from major sights and a short drive from nightlife; expensive food and drinks; some rooms need updating. [$] *Rooms from: €80* ✉ *Yıldızlıevler Mah. Jose Marti Cad. 2, Çankaya* ☎ *312/409–3000* 🌐 *www.swissotel.com* 🛏 *150 rooms* 🍴 *No meals.*

Nightlife

While Ankara may not contain the sprawling nightlife scene found in Istanbul, its residents value their free time, and certain areas of the city are packed on weekend nights until the early hours. The area known as Tunalı in Kavaklıdere consists of Tunali Hilmi Caddesi and some of its side streets from Kuğlu Park to John F. Kennedy Caddesi. Among the cafés, bars, and restaurants is where you will find much of Ankara's Western crowd on weekend nights, when nearly every establishment is full. The selections in Tunalı and the crowds they attract are varied, but most remain busy well after midnight. A few international chain cafés exist alongside local ones and mostly cater to families, who sit around a samovar while the children eat desserts and the adults smoke hookah. Among the restaurant selection in Tunalı are places specializing in burgers, durum, and pizza, but Turkish-style meyhanes dominate. Groups may spend as much as four or five hours at a mehyane, slowly working through their mezes and more than one bottle of rakı. Each has its own distinct style and specialties, and none has a defined closing hour. By 11 pm or midnight, most bars are filled up. Though there is a wide variety of themes among the bars in Tunalı, there is an emphasis on live music, which is generally available Thursday through Sunday nights and usually consist of jazz or contemporary Turkish hits.

👜 Shopping

Kavaklıdere

SHOPPING NEIGHBORHOODS | The upscale district of Kavaklıdere is home to an array of Turkish and international brands and designer labels, particularly along the lower end of the main drag, Tunalı Hilmi Caddesi, and its continuation, İran Caddesi. Just north of Kavaklıdere, the stretch of Atatürk Bulvarı heading toward Kızılay has more midrange shopping options. ✉ Ankara.

Samanpazarı

SHOPPING NEIGHBORHOODS | While the few shops inside Ankara's citadel are undeniably touristy, the strip just across from the citadel's main entrance, near the Divan Çukurhan hotel, has a handful of small boutiques selling jewelry, ceramics, handicrafts, and olive oil. From there, the area from Atpazarı Sokak down the hill toward Ulucanlar Caddesi has narrow, winding streets with shops selling antiques, handicrafts, carpets, metalwork, and other items. ✉ Ankara.

Chapter 8

THE BLACK SEA COAST AND LAKE VAN

Updated by
Paul Osterlund

⊙ Sights	🍴 Restaurants	🛏 Hotels	🛍 Shopping	🍸 Nightlife
★★★★★	★★★☆☆	★★★☆☆	★★☆☆☆	★★☆☆☆

WELCOME TO THE BLACK SEA COAST AND LAKE VAN

TOP REASONS TO GO

★ **Marvel at the ruins of Ani:** This dramatically situated ancient city was once the seat of a wealthy Armenian kingdom.

★ **Swim in Lake Van:** When visiting the monastery on the uninhabited island of Akdamar, take the opportunity to cool off in the startlingly blue water.

★ **Gaze at Mt. Ararat:** Take in the views of the iconic Mt. Ararat and explore the majestic Ishak Paşa Palace outside Doğubayazit.

★ **Glorious green in Çamlıhemşhin:** Behold the spectacular green mountain paradise of Çamlıhemşin.

★ **Indulge in Black Sea cuisine:** Turkey's Black Sea region boasts some of the country's most unique and rich culinary offerings.

For the visitor who makes it to Turkey's eastern regions, the rewards are plentiful: beautiful scenery, wild nature, and countless historic sites.

1 Trabzon. The largest city on the Black Sea coast is an ideal hub for exploring the region.

2 Sümela/Mereyemana. Sümela is the Black Sea coast's most famous monument, reopening in 2019 after a years-long renovation.

3 Çamlıhemşin. This majestic mountain town is nestled among some of the country's most splendid green backdrops.

4 Ayder. The cascading green flatlands are increasingly popular.

5 Kars. Kars is rich in history, culture, and cuisine—and near the Ani ruins.

6 Ani. The ruins of this millennium-old Armenian village are eerily breathtaking.

7 Mt. Ararat. The iconic Biblical mountain looms over Turkey's easternmost provinces.

8 Lake Van. Turkey's largest lake glistens with the presence of Akdamar Island.

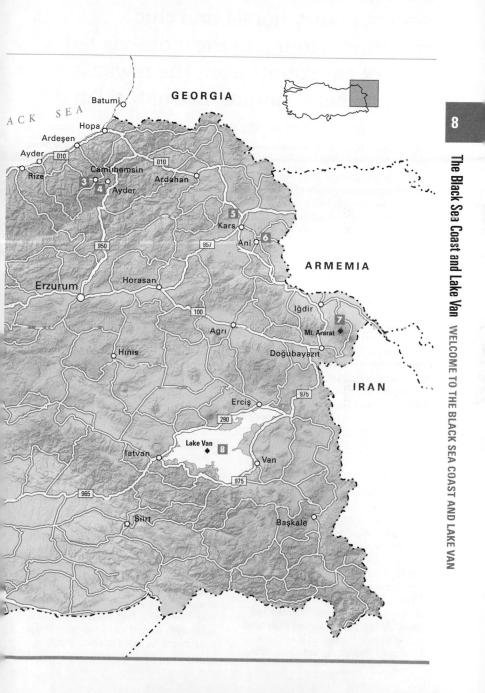

Eastern Turkey may not have the resorts, luxury hotels, and chic restaurants found in the more-visited parts of the country, but the rewards of travel here—impressive natural and man-made sites—are many.

Eastern Turkey offers much to the adventurous travelers who leave the more Europeanized resorts and cities of western Turkey behind. The landscape varies dramatically; in the north are the rocky beaches of the Black Sea, rising to lush, impossibly green foothills and soaring up to the snowcapped Kaçkar Mountains. As you head south, it changes once more into the stark highlands that lead to vast Lake Van and then again to the arid semi-desert borderlands of Syria, Iraq, and Iran. This southeastern region shows Turkey at its most Middle Eastern, where the call to prayer comes from intricately carved stone minarets and bazaars are filled with locals buying daily necessities rather than tourists buying souvenirs. Kurdish and Armenian histories are intertwined with Turkey's own history and this fascinating crossroads is littered with ancient history of much biblical significance.

Of all of Turkey's regions, the Black Sea coast least fits the bill of what most visitors imagine to be "Turkish." Instead of long, sandy beaches lined with resorts, the Black Sea's shores are rocky and backed by steep, lush mountains. And instead of sunny days, the area is often shrouded in mist. Culturally, the area has had as many Greek, Georgian, and Armenian influences as it has Ottoman and Turkish. Although less visited than other parts of Turkey, the region is also one of the most rewarding, with interesting destinations like the historic coastal town of Trabzon, the nearby monastery complex of Sümela, and the Kaçkar Mountains with 15,000-foot peaks towering over the area.

Turkey's east is a region filled with stark contrasts: dusty plains and soaring mountains, simple villages and bustling cities. Near Turkey's border with Armenia and Iran, this remote region is also filled with natural and man-made wonders and offers visitors the chance to see a part of Turkey that has yet to be invaded by the tourist hordes. Although this means that you may not find all the amenities and services available in western Turkey, the friendliness and hospitality of the area's predominantly Kurdish locals will very likely make up for it.

MAJOR REGIONS

The main destination on the Black Sea Coast is **Trabzon**, wedged between the Black Sea and the green mountains that rise behind it, and a city with a long historic pedigree that stretches back to Byzantine times, though today it's quite modern. It's a good base for visiting the fascinating (though defunct) Orthodox monastery complex of **Sümela, aka Mereyemana**, breathtakingly hidden in a narrow valley and clinging to the side of a steep cliff. At some point we may have to mention that Sümela's interior is currently closed for renovations and is expected to be open to visitors in May (or according to some accounts, August) 2019. Tour companies still take groups out there as it can still be observed from the outside. As you head toward the Georgian border, you will pass through Rize, Turkey's tea-growing capital, and later the village of **Çamlıhemşin** and the mountain village of **Ayder**.

The main destination in Turkey's far east is Lake Van. **Kars** is the gateway to this region, but many people come to visit **Ani**. Turkey's highest mountain is **Mt. Ararat**, but **Lake Van** is the main destination in eastern Anatolia.

Planning

WHEN TO GO
Spring and fall are generally the best times to visit these areas, with the exception of cities like Kars and Van, where summers are quite cool compared to the rest of Turkey.

GETTING HERE AND AROUND
Getting to eastern Turkey once meant grueling bus rides that sometimes took more than a day. The arrival of budget air travel has changed this dramatically, and several domestic airlines now crisscross Turkey. Many of the major cities in the region, including Trabzon and Van, have airports.

Most flights come from Istanbul or Ankara, but if you want to avoid these major cities, Sun Express Airlines has flights from several eastern cities to Izmir or Antalya.

You'll probably find that a rental car is the easiest way to take in the sights of eastern Turkey, allowing you to reach some of the more remote spots and explore at your leisure. Cars are readily available in most larger towns. You can also travel between major cities by bus, taking tours to sites like Sümela and Ani, but transport is usually by minibus rather than the more comfortable coaches found in western Turkey.

HOTELS
With some notable exceptions, the hotels in the east are basic, with little in the way of the luxuries you might find in Istanbul or along Turkey's Mediterranean coast. A few boutique hotels are beginning to pop up though, and most cities have at least one decent modern hotel catering to Turkish business travelers. It's advisable to book these well in advance, though there are always plenty of clean and comfortable budget options available.

Reviews have been shortened. For more information, visit Fodors.com.

What it Costs in Turkish Lira			
$	$$	$$$	$$$$
RESTAURANTS			
under 15 TL	16 TL–30 TL	31 TL–50 TL	over 50 TL
HOTELS			
under 150 TL	151 TL–300 TL	301 TL–500 TL	over 500 TL

RESTAURANTS
You won't find many fancy restaurants in this region, but eastern Turkey is the place for smaller eateries offering flavorful local cuisine and welcoming patrons. Food in the Black Sea area relies on dishes made with plenty of butter, rich yellow cheese, corn flour, and fish, especially *hamsi* (Black Sea anchovies). Although meat kebabs rule the rest of the east, most restaurants will also offer a variety of fresh salads and delicious vegetable dishes cooked in olive oil, along with stews and other ready-made hot dishes, which are usually meat-based.

SAFETY
During the 1980s and '90s, large parts of Turkey's east and southeast (but not the Black Sea area) were the scene of bitter fighting between the separatists of the Kurdistan Workers' Party (PKK) and Turkish security forces. The fighting subsided over the next decade, allowing tourism

in the region to get off the ground again. In 2012, the PKK declared a ceasefire, and there were several peace negotiations between the separatist organization and the Turkish government. This ended abruptly in July 2015 when the pro-Kurdish HDP (People's Democratic Party) failed to support the ruling party's attempts to implement an executive presidential system throughout Turkey. The PKK resumed its attacks on Turkish security personnel, declared self-rule in some cities and towns, and the Turkish state bombed PKK positions in northern Iraq. The situation in Turkey's predominantly Kurdish southeast has been complicated immeasurably by the conflict in Syria, which erupted in 2011. The rise of ISIS may give visitors to the border cities some cause for alarm, especially as the violence threatens to spill over the border in response to Turkish military attacks on both Kurdish and ISIS positions. In 2015, the Consulate General of the United States in Turkey was advising U.S. citizens to avoid areas in close proximity to the Syrian border while the U.K. Foreign and Commonwealth Office was advising against all travel within 10 km (6 miles) of the border, and all but essential travel to the areas of Sirnak, Mardin, Sanliurfa, Gaziantep, Kilis, and Hatay provinces as well as Siirt, Tunceli, and Hakkari provinces. Consequently, Fodor's has temporarily suspended our coverage of much of this region of the country. The situation is constantly evolving, so we recommend travelers interested in visiting the area to consult the United States security alerts before planning their trip.

That being said, the majority of visitors to the area do not run into any trouble, and are more likely to encounter friendly faces and warm hospitality. Most of the troubles exist between security forces and militants. The biggest security issues are predominantly in the Kurdish areas, while the northeast of Turkey and the Black Sea coast are considered perfectly safe.

TOURS

Tourism here is rather underdeveloped compared to the rest of the country, which makes options for organized tours limited. The main exceptions are tours from Trabzon to Sümela, Kars to Ani. Several companies can organize hiking expeditions in the Kaçkar Mountains. Usually you can find at least one tour guide in most major towns.

Trabzon

Trabzon has a spectacular location, perched on a hill overlooking the sea, with lush green mountains behind it. Once the capital of the empire founded in 1204 by Alexius Comnenus, grandson of a Byzantine emperor, the city was famed for its golden towers and glittering mosaics. Today's Trabzon seems far removed from that imperial past: the city is bustling and modern, with a busy port, crowded streets, and seemingly little to distinguish it from many other provincial Turkish towns. It only takes a little digging though, to get under the modern surface. Byzantine-era churches, such as the lovely Aya Sofya, a smaller version of the similarly named church in Istanbul, can be found not far from modern apartment buildings. Meanwhile, the city's old town with its Ottoman-era houses, pedestrian-only streets, and lively bazaar are a nice break from the concrete and crowds.

GETTING HERE AND AROUND

There are several daily flights to Trabzon from Istanbul, and at least one a day from Ankara, İzmir, and Antalya. Fares are competitive, so check with the different airlines to see who has the best.

You can drive or take a bus to Trabzon, but it's a long way from other Turkish cities you may be visiting—1,071 km (665 miles) from Istanbul, 744 km (462 miles) from Ankara, and 591 km (367 miles)

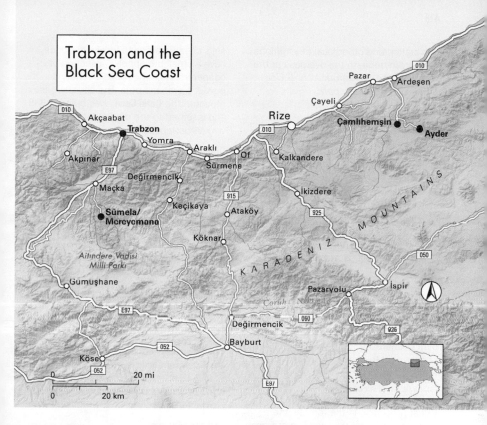

Trabzon and the Black Sea Coast

from Kayseri. You're better off flying and renting a car when you arrive.

Bus services between towns run frequently and are inexpensive. One of the most reliable and frequent services is run by Ulusoy, which has an office just off Trabzon's main square, Atatürk Alanı. Along with Metro Turizm, they also have daily tours to Sumela.

Renting a car, though, is the most convenient way of getting around the Black Sea region, and allows you to explore the mountains more easily. Avis has an office in downtown Trabzon, as well as one at the airport. There are also several local companies around Trabzon's Atatürk Alanı.

TOURS

Eyce Tours

GUIDED TOURS | Besides offering multiple-day trips around the region, Eyce also offers daily tours to the Sumela Monastery and to the Georgian city of Batumi. ✉ *Taksim İşhanı Sok. 11* ⚓ *Opposite the Sağıroğlu Hotel* ☎ *462/326–6367* ⊕ *www. eycetours.com* ☞ *From 50 TL.*

◉ Sights

Atatürk Alanı (*Taksim Meydanı*)

PLAZA | The heart of Trabzon's social activity is its pleasing central square, Atatürk Alanı, also known as simply Meydan. In Byzantine and Ottoman times, the camel caravans assembled here before heading across the mountains. Today the square is full of shady tea gardens and surrounded by restaurants and most of the city's hotels. Regular minibuses headed for the bus station and other local destinations leave from beneath the overpass at the southern end. ⊠ *Atatürk Alanı* ✛ *Up İskele Cad. from the port.*

Atatürk Köşkü
MUSEUM | Trabzon's wealthy citizens once retreated to villas in the hills above town. Greek banker Konstantin Kabayanidis built this attractive white gingerbread house, set in a small forest with nice views of the city below, and Atatürk stayed here in 1924, 1930, and 1937. Much of the original furniture remains in place. ⊠ *Soğuksu Cad.* ✛ *7 km (4 miles) southwest of Trabzon's central square* ☎ *462/231–0028* 🎟 *10 TL.*

Aya Sofya (*Church of the Holy Wisdom, or St. Sophia*)
RELIGIOUS SITE | Trabzon's best-known Byzantine monument is this well-preserved 13th-century church sitting on a bluff overlooking the Black Sea that was converted into a mosque in Ottoman times. The highlights are the wonderful Byzantine frescoes housed in the west porch: technicolor angels on the ceiling, Christ preaching in the Temple, the Annunciation, and the wedding at Cana— all executed in a style that shows strong Italian influences. Often overlooked is the graffiti of ships, carved into the outside of the apse by sailors for good luck. A shaded tea garden near the entrance is a popular place for breakfast. It was officially reopened as a mosque in 2013, but as images are forbidden in mosques, visitors are ushered into a section of the building from which a fraction of the frescoes can be glimpsed above large sheets of cloth. ⊠ *Kayakmeydan Cad.* ☎ *462/223–3043* 🎟 *Free.*

Bazaar
MARKET | The pedestrian-only Kunduracılar Caddesi leads into the maze of the covered bazaar, which includes a 16th-century *bedestan,* or covered market, that has been restored and now houses several cafés and some gift shops selling unremarkable trinkets. The bazaar largely sells cheap clothes to locals, but does have a small but appealing section of coppersmiths, who make a variety of bowls, trays, and pots. The city's largest mosque, the **Çarşi Cami**, was built in 1839 and is joined to the market by an archway. ⊠ *Just past Cumhuriyet Cad.*

Citadel
MILITARY SITE | Trabzon's Byzantine-era citadel was built on part of a hill formed by two ravines, and while not much is left of the building's former glory, the soaring outside walls and massive columns are still impressive (restored after the Ottoman conquest in 1461) and a testament to the fact that no army ever took Trabzon by force, though many tried. The only remaining part of the interior is the 10th-century church of **Panagia Chrysokephalos** (the Virgin of the Golden Head), which was the city's cathedral and where many of its rulers were married, crowned, and buried. The Ottomans converted it into a mosque, the **Ortahisar Camii,** in the 15th century. ⊠ *Kale Cad.* ✛ *From Hükümet Cad. (off Maraş Cad.), follow Tabakhane Bridge over gorge, turn left.*

Trabzon Museum
MUSEUM | The main attraction of the Trabzon Museum is the building itself, a 1910 mansion built for a local Greek banker. The grand rooms of the main floor have been restored and filled with period furniture. The basement holds a small collection of archaeological finds from the Trabzon region, while upstairs you'll find a collection devoted to local people and their culture. ⊠ *Zeytinlik Cad. 10* ☎ *462/326–0748* 🎟 *6 TL.*

🍽 Restaurants

Çardak Pide
$ | TURKISH | An always busy casual restaurant, Çardak serves as a bustling tribute to the Black Sea *pide* (stone-baked dough with savory toppings), which come smothered in an obscene amount of melted butter. The *kavurmalı* version

topped with slow-cooked chunks of lamb are especially recommended. **Known for:** kavurmalı pide; döner kebab; kıymalı pide (with minced ground beef). $ *Average main: 20 TL* ⊠ *Uzun Sok. 4* ☎ *462/321–7676* ⊕ *www.cardakpide.com.*

Cemil Usta
$$ | TURKISH | In an old stone building on the north side of Atatürk Alanı, you'll find this place serving a mix of seafood and local dishes like *akçaabat köfte* (the local meatball specialty) and *kuymak* (fondue made of cheese and cornmeal). Grab a seat street-side or on the long balcony upstairs, which makes this a great spot for watching the square on a summer evening. **Known for:** akçaabat köfte; kuymak; hazelnut baklava. $ *Average main: 25 TL* ⊠ *Atatürk Alanı 6* ☎ *462/321–6161* ⊕ *www.cemilusta.com.tr.*

Fevzi Hoca
$$ | SEAFOOD | There's no menu here at Trabzon's most serious seafood restaurant; you'll simply be shown the fish available—when in season this includes Trabzon's local obsession, hamsi (anchovies)—and you get to choose how you want your fish to be cooked. The restaurant is decorated with photos of famous Turks dining on the premises, a hint of just how popular it is. **Known for:** hamsi; grilled sea bass; akçaabat köfte. $ *Average main: 40 TL* ⊠ *Salacık Mahallesi 61300* ☎ *462/326–5444* ⊕ *www.fevzihoca.com.tr.*

Kebabci Ahmet Usta
$ | TURKISH | This sleek modern dining room on lively pedestrian Uzun Sokak is a busy local favorite. It offers all the standard kebabs and *pides*, plus a few rarer dishes such as *talaş kebabı* (lamb wrapped in pastry) and *orman kebabı* (stewed lamb with vegetables). **Known for:** talaş kebabı; orman kebabı; kuymak. $ *Average main: 25 TL* ⊠ *Uzun Sok. 56* ☎ *462/326–5666* ⊕ *www.ahmetusta.com.tr.*

Black Sea Specialties 🍴

Size isn't everything, as the miniscule *hamsi* (Black Sea anchovy) proves. It is often called the "Prince of the Black Sea" fish, and from the end of fall to the beginning of spring, it's found in an almost endless variety of dishes: fried in a coating of cornmeal, served in a fragrant pilaf, baked into bread, or thrown into an omelet. Also worth trying are *muhlama* and kuymak (types of cheese fondue), *laz böreği* (a dessert made from a thin pastry and a custard-like filling), and honey made in the high mountain villages of the Kaçkars.

★ Tarihi Kalkanoğlu Pilavcısı
$ | TURKISH | This charming restaurant is all dark wood and nostalgia, and specializes in buttery rice with either slow-cooked lamb or *kuru fasülye* (white beans in a tomato sauce). Wash it down with a frothy *ayran* (salty yogurt drink) or the house speciality: a sweet, refreshing drink made from sun-dried apricots. **Known for:** buttery rice with slow-cooked lamb; buttery rice with white beans and tomato sauce; ayran (salty yogurt drink). $ *Average main: 20 TL* ⊠ *Tophane Sok. 3* ☎ *462/321–3086* ▭ *No credit cards.*

🛏 Hotels

Horon Hotel
$$ | HOTEL | The best thing about this hotel one block off the main square are the spacious rooms, friendly service, and rooftop restaurant where you can enjoy breakfast overlooking the sea. **Pros:** central location; friendly English-speaking staff; parking and valet service are a blessing. **Cons:** a little pricey for what you get; breakfast could be better; some

rooms a bit small. $ *Rooms from: 190 TL* ✉ *Sıramağazalar Cad. 125* ☎ *462/326–6455* ⊕ *www.hotelhoron.com* ⟿ *44 rooms* ⏐◎⏐ *Free Breakfast.*

Hotel Nur

$ | **HOTEL** | One of Trabzon's best budget options, the rooms are spotless (though small), with some overlooking the main square. **Pros:** overlooks the town square; helpful English-speaking staff; cheap rates. **Cons:** call to prayer from the neighboring mosque is deafeningly loud; some rooms smell like smoke; some rooms a bit small. $ *Rooms from: 150 TL* ✉ *Cami Sok. 15* ☎ *462/323–0445* ⟿ *20 rooms* ⏐◎⏐ *Free Breakfast.*

Zorlu Grand Hotel

$$$ | **HOTEL** | Trabzon's fanciest hotel offers large, elegant, and comfortably furnished rooms and a courteous and professional staff. **Pros:** central location; extensive facilities; luxury spa. **Cons:** expensive additional spa services; some rooms overlook busy streets while others face interior courtyard; some outdated furniture/facilities. $ *Rooms from: 450 TL* ✉ *Maraş Cad. 9* ☎ *462/326–8400* ⊕ *www.zorlugrand.com* ⟿ *157 rooms* ⏐◎⏐ *Free Breakfast.*

Sumela/Mereyemana

47 km (29 miles) south of Trabzon.

The Sumela Monastery (also known as the Monastery of the Virgin Mary (and *Mereyemana* or *Sümela Manastırı* in Turkish) is a spectacular and unforgettable sight, perched some 820 feet above the valley floor and often lost in the clouds. The monastery has been undergoing a major renovation and has been closed to the public; it is expected to reopen by mid-2019.

GETTING HERE AND AROUND

Many companies in Trabazon offer day trips to Sumela, usually for about 50 TL, which can be arranged through your

Turkish Nuts and Tea 🍴

Agricultural life on the Black Sea is dominated by two crops: hazelnuts and tea. Near Rize, the hills are covered in row after row of tea plants. Every spring, more than 200,000 tons of tea are harvested in the area. Turkey is also the globe's leading producer of hazelnuts, responsible for more than 80% of the world's supply. Fresh off the tree and still in their shell, they are easy to find in late summer and early fall.

hotel. Alternatively, if you don't require a guide, it's possible to visit the Monastery by public transport with daily trips organized by both Ulusoy and Metro bus companies. If you are driving, take Route 885 to Maçka, then head east on the road to Altındere National Park.

CONTACTS Ulusoy. ✉ *Taksim Cad., Trabzon* ☎ *462/321–1281.*

👁 Sights

★ **Sumela Monastery**

RELIGIOUS SITE | In a dramatic valley and clinging to the side of a sheer cliff, the Sumela Monastery is stunning to behold. Orthodox monks founded the retreat in the 5th century, living in clifftop caves surrounding a shrine that housed a miraculous icon of the Virgin Mary painted by St. Luke. The labyrinth of courtyards, corridors, and chapels date from the time of Emperor Alexius III of Trebizond, who was crowned here in 1340—the monastery continued under the Sultans, remaining until the Greeks were expelled from Turkey in 1922. Although the icon and other treasures have been removed, extensive frescoes done between the 14th and 18th century remain. Though sections

The hike up to the breathtaking Sumela Monastery makes for a worthy day trip.

have been chipped away or scribbled over with graffiti, they are impressive nonetheless in their depictions of Old and New Testament images—look for an Arab-looking Jesus, an almost African Virgin, and a scene of Adam and Eve, expelled from Eden, taking up a plough. The first, lower, parking lot is beside the river and Sumela Restaurant. From there a well-worn trail to the monastery is a rigorous 40-minute uphill hike. Farther on is a second, upper parking lot, at the level of the monastery, a 15-minute walk away on a level path. Most organized day excursions from Trabzon drop you at the upper lot and collect you from the lower one. The monastery has been undergoing renovation but is expected to reopen in mid-2019. ✉ *Altındere National Park, Maçka* ☎ *462/326–0748* 🎫 *25 TL.*

🍴 Restaurants

Sümer Restaurant

$$ | TURKISH | These wooden gazebos set on the edge of a small river are a fine spot to have lunch or dinner after visiting Sumela, a 15-minute drive away. There is a wide selection of mezes, along with regional specialties such as *tereyağlı alabalık,* trout baked in butter, and *kaygana,* an omelet made with Black Sea anchovies. **Known for:** mezes; baked trout; kaygana (omelet with Black Sea anchovies). [$] *Average main: 22 TL* ✉ *Maçka Sümela Manastırı Yolu, Maçka* ☎ *462/512–1581.*

Çamlıhemşin

124 km (77 miles) northeast of Trabzon; 22 km (14 miles) south of Ardeşen.

The small village of Çamlıhemşin, at the junction of two rushing rivers, serves mainly as a gateway to mountain valleys above, particularly to the village of Ayder. Yet this is a pleasant and quiet overnight stop before heading up into the Kaçkars. There's not much to do here other than look out on the green mountains and listen to the river flowing by.

GETTING HERE AND AROUND

You will probably want to make the excursion to Çamlıhemşin by car, the only real way to explore the villages and valleys. Follow the coast east from Trabzon to Ardeşen, then head inland to Çamlıhemşin on a well-marked road. If traveling by bus you have to change in Pazar.

🍴 Restaurants

Yeşil Vadi Cafe and Restaurant

$ | TURKISH | Perched on the corner of a bridge overlooking the thundering Fırtına River, this smart restaurant serves as a great lunch stop before heading farther into the mountains. It serves local specialties with delicious desserts including laz böreği (thin pastry layers filled with custard) and a type of helva made with corn flour. **Known for:** laz böreği (custard-filled pastry layers); mıhlama (buttery cheese fondue); trout. $ *Average main: 22 TL* ⊠ *İnönü Cad.* ✦ *On the corner, just before you turn left on the Ayder road* ☎ *464/65–17282* ⊕ *www. yesilvadicaferestaurant.com.*

🛏 Hotels

★ Puli Mini Otel

$$ | B&B/INN | Earthy and arty, traditional and modern, with lots of exposed timber, this beautiful 80-year-old chestnut building beside the river brings a different experience to the area, with six surprisingly stylish rooms with touches like cute wooden bathroom cabinets and funky stone bowl basins. **Pros:** cool and intimate; good for visiting both the Fırtına Valley and Ayder; riverside rooms have pleasant river sound. **Cons:** traffic noise in some rooms; small bathrooms; a bit pricey for what you get. $ *Rooms from: 400 TL* ⊠ *İnönü Cad. 35* ☎ *464/651–7497* ⊕ *puliminiotel.com.tr* ⇶ *6 rooms* ⏐◎⏐ *Free Breakfast.*

Do You Speak Turkish? 👁

These areas are less touristy and finding English speakers can sometimes be a challenge, though tourist offices and most hotels will usually have someone on staff who speaks at least some basic English. In a pinch, try gesturing and using just a few key English words, but it's a good idea to take a Turkish phrase book with you on visits to this region.

Ayder

90 km (56 miles) northeast of Rize; 17 km (11 miles) southeast of Çamlıhemşin on a well-marked road.

At 4,000 feet and surrounded by snowcapped mountains and tumbling waterfalls, the mountain village of Ayder, with its wooden chalets and wandering cows, can seem like a piece of Switzerland transported to Turkey. Once a sleepy *yayla*, a high-pasture village where locals live in the summer, Ayder has become a popular destination for Turkish tourists and, increasingly, foreign ones. Although a few years ago the village's bucolic nature was threatened by overdevelopment, local laws have now ordered all building to be done in the local style, with wooden exteriors and peaked roofs. Summer weekend crowds can fill the small village to capacity, but the setting is still beautiful. The village is also an excellent base for day hikes or extended treks in the Kaçkars and for visiting some of the less accessible yaylas in the region to see a way of life that has changed little over the centuries.

The easiest yayla to visit from Ayder is Yukarı Kavron, about 10 km (6 miles) from the village along a dirt road. A collection of squat stone houses, it's set on a high plateau surrounded by gorgeous mountains. There are several nice hikes leading out of the village. There is regular minivan service in the morning out of Ayder to the yayla, although it's best to check with your hotel or *pansiyon* about the exact schedule.

Ayder has a grassy main square that during the summer frequently plays host to festivals celebrating local Hemşin culture. Locals in traditional dress (for women this includes the colorful red, orange, or gold head scarves that many still wear) play music on a version of the bagpipe (known as the *tulum*) and dance together holding hands in a line or semicircle, known as *horon* dancing. The shoulder shimmying that is a key part of this dance represents the sliver of the famous Black Sea anchovy.

 Sights

★ Ayder Hot Springs

HOT SPRINGS | Ayder is also known for its *kaplıcaları* (hot springs), reputed to cure all types of ailments. Whether this is true or not, the springs, housed in a modern, marble-lined building near the village's mosque, are good for a relaxing soak after a day of hiking. There's a large pool to splash around in and a hammam area where you can give yourself a good scrub. There are separate facilities for men and women, as well as private rooms for couples that want to bathe together. ⊠ *Ayder* ☎ *464/657–2102* ➵ *10 TL, 40 TL for a private room.*

Restaurants

Ayder Sofrası

$ | **TURKISH** | In good weather, the place to sit is the stone-lined terrace with wooden picnic tables that look over the mountains and the waterfall. The kitchen turns out trout and local dishes such as stuffed cabbage and *turşu kavurması* (roast pickled vegetables), as well as meat

options, and serves an open buffet breakfast every day. **Known for:** trout; stuffed cabbage; turşu kavurması. $ *Average main: 22 TL* ⊠ *Haşimoğlu Otel* ✛ *Next to the hot springs* ☎ *464/657–2037* ⊕ *www. hasimogluotel.com.*

Hotels

Kardelen Bungalows

$$ | **B&B/INN** | Run by the affable Nadir and his family, this *pansiyon* is a little way up the hill, away from the crowds, and offers a number of environmentally friendly Swiss-style wooden bungalows. **Pros:** away from the crowds; good regional food; reasonable rates. **Cons:** accommodation is quite basic; no TV in rooms, though for many that is the point; not for everyone. $ *Rooms from: 250 TL* ⊠ *Kalegon Mevkii* ☎ *464/657–2107* ➵ *6 bungalows* ❍ *Free Breakfast.*

Kuşpuni Dağ Evi

$$ | **B&B/INN** | On the edge of a green field, this wooden chalet has large, comfortable rooms, and colorful rugs and kilims in the hallways that add a homey feel. **Pros:** beautiful terrace with wonderful views; owners are helpful in arranging excursions; more peaceful than other pansiyons. **Cons:** small shower cabinets; low ceilings; thin walls. $ *Rooms from: 240 TL* ⊠ *Yukarı Ambarlik* ☎ *464/657– 2052* ➵ *15 rooms* ❍ *Free Breakfast.*

Natura Lodge

$$ | **B&B/INN** | Some of the front rooms at this basic inn have wonderful views, and the staff is extremely knowledgeable about outdoor activities in the area; an on-premises agency arranges water rafting and guided hikes. **Pros:** trekking advice available; alcohol served; friendly staff. **Cons:** lacks personal family-pansiyon style of other places; showers are not enclosed; Wi-Fi spotty in some rooms. $ *Rooms from: 200 TL* ⊠ *On left as you go up the hill, just past springs* ☎ *464/657–2035* ⊕ *www.naturaotel.com* ➵ *21 rooms* ❍ *Free Breakfast.*

🏃 Activities

There are lots of hiking opportunities in the area, but most involve serious uphill sections. Well signposted from Ayder is the route to Hazindak, a collection of pretty wooden chalets on a ridge, which is a strenuous climb of around three hours. **Yukarı Kavron** is the best jumping-off point if you want to trek to the top of the highest point in the rugged Kaçkar range. At the 3,937 meters, the summit of **Kaçkar Dağı** offers stark, sweeping views of rocky peaks and alpine lakes. Although it's covered with ice and snow much of the year, the summit can be reached in a single day during a short window of time in late summer without technical equipment, though you should hire a guide. There's regularly scheduled minivan service from Ayder to Yukarı Kavron. Most pansiyons in Ayder can help you set up a day trip to the mountain.

Kars

The setting for Turkish novelist Orhan Pamuk's somber novel *Snow*, Kars is a rustic and foreboding city set on a 5,740-foot plateau and forever at the mercy of the winds. Not far from Turkey's border with Armenia and Georgia, it looks like the frontier town it is; since 1064, Kars has been besieged over and over, by various sundry invaders from the Akkoyunlu to the Mongol warriors of Tamerlane. In the 19th century alone, it was attacked three times by Czarist armies from Russia who remained in power until 1920. The Russian influence is still obvious in many buildings.

With its tree-lined streets and low European-style buildings, Kars feels different from other Turkish cities. It can be surprisingly relaxed, has a reputation as a liberal and secular-minded outpost, and certainly has more bars and licensed restaurants than other towns in the conservative east. Attempts to develop a ski industry and lifting restrictions on visiting the ancient city of Ani—previously a closed military zone—has meant that more tourists are coming through the area, giving locals the incentive to upgrade what Kars has to offer.

GETTING HERE AND AROUND

The iconic Eastern Express runs between the capital of Ankara and makes its final stop in Kars about 24 hours later. The scenic route has become wildly popular over the years among young Turkish travelers and tour agencies have followed suit by buying up large quantities of tickets and selling them at a premium, but as of late 2018 they are easy to obtain from the website of the Turkish State Railways (there's an English-language option).

The Kars airport is 6 km (4 miles) outside town. Turkish Airlines, Atlas Jet, and Pegasus have regular flights from Istanbul to Kars and SunExpress flies from İzmir to Kars.

There are daily buses from Istanbul and Ankara to cities in the east, but it's a long trip (22 hours from Istanbul, 18 from Ankara) and not much cheaper than flying. Kars is the end of the line for Turkey's train network, but while the scenery from Sivas is spectacular, the trip is brutally slow, taking 38 hours or more from Istanbul via Ankara. If you are planning on limiting your explorations outside Kars to Ani, you can arrange a tour or take a taxi. Otherwise, you will want to rent a car to visit outlying sights.

CONTACTS Turkish State Railway (*TCDD*). ⊕ *ebilet.tcddtasimacilik.gov.tr.*

TOURS

Celil Ersözoğlu

GUIDED TOURS | The tourist industry may not be very developed in Kars, but Celil Ersözoğlu is a good choice if you want someone to show you a bit more. With perfect English, he arranges transport to Ani most days in the summer and

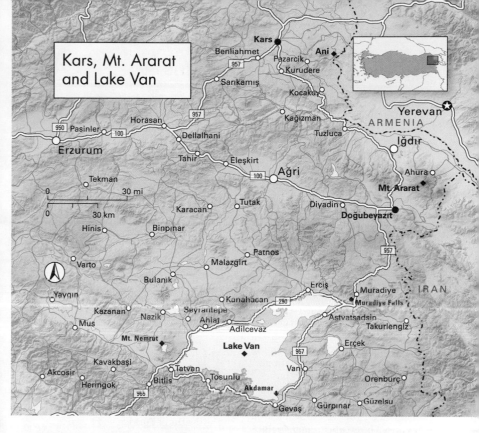

Kars, Mt. Ararat and Lake Van

can organize private trips to some of the Armenian and Georgian monuments in the area. He often knows when visitors are in the area, and will probably find you before you find him. ☎ 532/226–3966 ✉ celilani@hotmail.com.

VISITOR INFORMATION

CONTACTS Visitor Information. ⊠ Hakim Ali Rıza Arslan Sok. 15 ☎ 474/212–2179.

👁 Sights

Kars Kalesi (*Kars Castle*)

CASTLE/PALACE | The town's castle looms over the area from its high, rocky vantage point. Though it dates from the 10th century, in 1386 Tamerlane swept violently through the region and razed the original structure, and most surviving fortifications were commissioned by Lala Mustafa Paşa in 1579. The castle has

gone through some restoration in recent years and the panoramic views of Kars merit the 10-minute walk uphill. There's a large café/restaurant where you can enjoy a reasonably priced lunch or a drink with an impressive view. ⊠ Kale Cad.

Kars Museum (*Kars Müzesi*)

MUSEUM | This museum has a lot of pre-classical pottery, as well as the beautiful doors of an Armenian church. Also of note are photographs and finds from the excavations at Ani. Located near the train station on the eastern edge of town, it's a long walk from the center and a little difficult to find—you may want to take a taxi. Easily missed outside is the railway carriage where Ottoman General Kazım Karabekir signed the treaty of Kars with the Soviet Union, settling today's border. ⊠ 485 Cumhuriyet Cad. ☎ 474/212–2387.

Spotlight on the Armenians 👁

Historically, Armenians have been an integral part of the ethnic mix in Turkey's east, although today very few remain in the region. What happened to them is a topic of sensitive debate in Turkey.

There were various Armenian kingdoms in the region starting in the 3rd century BC and lasting until almost the 11th century AD. After that, the Armenians—who adopted Christianity in AD 301—became the subjects of a succession of rulers, from the Byzantines, to the Persians, and finally the Ottomans. Armenians became the bankers and traders of the Ottoman Empire and ended up living throughout the Ottoman world, with Istanbul eventually becoming one of their main cultural centers. Armenians were legendary builders and many fine examples of their buildings survive, while their influence can also be seen in Seljuk architecture. The great Ottoman architect Sinan was born to an Armenian family and in the 19th century the Armenian Balyan family were the sultan's official architects, designing Istanbul's Dolmabahçe Palace among many other important buildings.

During World War I, when the Ottomans came under attack by Russia and the other Allied powers, some Armenians in the east saw this as a chance for independence and rose up in revolt. The Ottoman Turks, afraid of how much land would be left to them in an empire filled with Greeks, Armenians, and Arabs, deported the entire Armenian population of Anatolia on foot across the mountains into the deserts of Syria and Iraq, a process that led to significant deaths and suffering. Many did not arrive, and Armenian survivors and U.S. consular staff reported massacres. The Armenians claim that hundreds of thousands (some claim even 1.5 million) perished and have been trying to have the events of the time recognized as genocide. The Turks, while admitting that large numbers of Armenians died at the time, say this was the result of war and disease, which also cost the lives of many others living in the region—the deaths of Turkish and Kurdish villagers in revenge attacks are often cited as examples. It remains a highly sensitive topic, but Armenian culture has sprouted in the region in recent years, with an annual Armenian service in the Akdamar Church and the restoration of Diyarbakır's abandoned Armenian cathedral.

Kümbet Cami (*Church of the Apostles*)
RELIGIOUS SITE | Located at the foot of the hill by Kars River, this was originally built in the 10th century as the Armenian Church of the Twelve Apostles. You can still make out the Apostles on the exterior of the drum-shape cupola. Since 1998, the building has served as a mosque, with the entrance on the far side. ✉ *Kale Cad.* ⚓ *At the foot of the castle.*

Taş Köprü
BRIDGE/TUNNEL | The area between the castle and the Church of the Apostles was the heart of Kars prior to its Russian occupation, but only a few early constructions survive. The most notable is the Taş Köprü, which means "the Stone Bridge," of Seljuk origin, dating from the 1400s and built of volcanic rock. On either side of the bridge are several mostly abandoned hammams and timber and stone

houses; you'll also find the restored 300-year-old home of famed poet Nemik Kemal that is now a cultural center with a slightly bizarre collection of miniature Turkish buildings in the garden. The rest of the area is somewhat neglected, though local authorities occasionally attempt to rejuvenate the area. ✉ *Kars.*

🍴 Restaurants

Ani Ocakbaşı
$$ | **TURKISH** | As the name implies—*ocakbaşı* means "by the hearth"—the emphasis here is on grilled meats: the usual kebabs, plus the Black Sea meatball specialty, *akçaabat köfte.* The kitchen also prepares some local stews, but usually only at lunchtime. Vegetarian options, including delicious fresh mezes, are also available. **Known for:** akçaabat köfte; ali nazik (kebab with eggplant in yogurt); boiled lamb shank. [$] *Average main: 24 TL* ✉ *Kazım Paşa Cad. 128* ☎ *474/212–0423.*

Fatih Döner Pide ve Lahmacun Salonu
$ | **TURKISH** | This restaurant does exactly what its name suggests: serves up tasty döner kebabs, *pide* topped with the usual range of meat and cheese, and crispy lahmacun (baked dough topped with ground meat, fresh parsley, and a squeeze of lemon). Try a *mercimek* (lentil) soup to start (ask for *az posiyon* to get a small bowl). **Known for:** döner kebab; lahmacun (baked flatbread topped with mincemeat); lentil soup. [$] *Average main: 15 TL* ✉ *Kazım Paşa Cad. No. 87* ☎ *474/212–5552.*

Kamer Cafe and Restaurant
$ | **INTERNATIONAL** | One of Kars's better restaurants is set in an old Russian building, where old tiles blend with modern decor, and an open kitchen fills one end. The menu features a decent mix of Western, Turkish, and local dishes. **Known for:** dumplings in garlic yogurt; roast goose; steak with onion sauce. [$] *Average main: 20 TL* ✉ *Halitpaşa Cad. 41* ☎ *543/617–6611.*

Local food 🍴

Along Halitpaşa Caddesi are a number of inviting shops dedicated to the Kars specialty *eski kaşar*, an aged yellow cheese with a taste similar to Italian pecorino. Many shops also sell local honey, and you can also do as the locals do and stop by in the morning for a takeout breakfast of delicious *bal kaymak*—honey with the Turkish version of clotted cream.

Ocakbaşı Restoran
$ | **TURKISH** | The kebabs here are simple and tasty, and embroidered curtains, rust-color tablecloths, and waiters in shiny vests add a bit of atmosphere to the cave-like space. Try the ali nazik kebab (grilled meat served on a cheesy eggplant puree) or the *Ejder kebab,* pieces of grilled meat, cheese, parsley, sesame, and egg yolk in a calzone like wrapping. **Known for:** Ali Nazik kebab; Ejder kebab; Kars goose. [$] *Average main: 22 TL* ✉ *Atatürk Cad. 276* ☎ *474/212–0056.*

🛏 Hotels

Güngören Hotel
$ | **HOTEL** | Although decorated in a questionably outdated fashion, this former budget hotel is now one of the better mid-range options in town. **Pros:** friendly service; quiet street; reasonable rates. **Cons:** no great views; rooms vary in quality; some smoking rooms. [$] *Rooms from: 160 TL* ✉ *Halit Paşa Cad. 2, corner of Millet Sok.* ☎ *474/212–6767* 🌐 *www.gungoren-hotel.com* 🛏 *34 rooms* 🍴 *Free Breakfast.*

Hotel Cheltikov
$$ | **HOTEL** | A spacious boutique hotel with plenty of character, Cheltikov is located in a restored 19th-century Russian mansion that oozes historical charm. **Pros:** quiet location; beautiful historical building; excellent value. **Cons:**

a little out of town; no alcohol served; pricier than other Kars options, but the building/setting is lovely. $ *Rooms from: 420 TL ✉ Şehit Hulusi Aytekin Cad. 63 ☎ 474/212–0036 ⊕ www.hotelcheltikov. com ➟ 27 rooms* ⦿ *Free Breakfast.*

★ Kar's Otel
$$$ | HOTEL | This wonderfully restored late 19th-century Russian-built mansion is extremely stylish, with a cool, minimalist white-and-gray color scheme, original art on the walls depicting monuments in Kars, and comfortable rooms furnished with contemporary flair. **Pros:** plush and modern rooms; a warm welcome after a day of skiing or sightseeing; housed in a beautiful old Russian building. **Cons:** top-floor rooms can get hot; small extra charges for tea/coffee; pricey. $ *Rooms from: 620 TL ✉ Halitpaşa Cad. 79 ☎ 474/212–1616 ⊕ www.karsotel.com ➟ 8 rooms* ⦿ *Free Breakfast.*

Nightlife

Barış Türkü Bar
BARS/PUBS | Kars is not a party town, and there's not much alcohol to be found here. If you want a drink, Barış Club is one of your better options, and there's often live music. Set in a restored historical mansion, it's popular with students, and therefore busy during term time and closed for the summer. ✉ *Atatürk Cad. 33* ☎ *473/233–0702.*

Ani

42 km (26 miles) east of Kars.

Most visitors to this remote area of Turkey come to pay a visit to the haunting Ani, one of the country's most important historical sites. Once the capital of an Armenian kingdom that ruled the area more than a thousand years ago (the walls were erected in AD 972), Ani is today more like a ghost town, filled with ruins of churches and palaces that still

manage to evoke the city's former glory. Its location, at the edge of a windswept gorge with snowcapped mountains in the background and grassy fields stretching out to the horizon, only adds to Ani's mystique. The city's mighty walls, which stretch for more than 8,200 feet and are 32 feet tall, protects the third side. Today a small village called Ocaklı also occupies the site.

GETTING HERE AND AROUND
Take the provincial Kars Yolu road (Route 36–07) from Kars. Alternatively you should be able to haggle with a taxi driver to pay around 150 to get here, including a waiting time of 2½ hours.

⦿ Sights

★ Ruins of Ani
ARCHAEOLOGICAL SITE | Scarcely a half dozen churches remain of the medieval Armenian capital of Ani, all in various states of disrepair, but, even so, the sprawling site is breathtaking—crumbling majesty amid stark, sweeping countryside, tiny Kurdish settlements, and fields of wildflowers. There is a haunted, yet strangely meditative, feeling at the site, with an open-air museum holding what are considered some of the finest examples of religious architecture of its period. You enter through the **Aslan Kapısı** (Lion's Gate), one of three principal portals. Highlights include the circular **Church of the Redeemer,** built 1035 but hit by lightning in the 1950s, slicing it neatly in half, leaving a surrealistic representation of an Armenian church with the rubble of its former half in the foreground. In the gorge is the striking **Kusanatz** (Convent of the Three Virgins), on a rocky outcrop. At the center of the site is the former cathedral, built in 1001 by the architect Trdat. Already staggering in size, it was once topped by a large dome that fell in an earthquake in 1319. A short distance away is the **Menüçehir Camii,** which clings to the heights overlooking the Arpaçay River. The walls offer sweeping views

out over the rock-cut village which dates back thousands of years. You will then pass the foundations of the massive round **Church of King Gagik,** another of Trdat's designs. Finally, the over-restored **Seljuk Palace** is an imposing reminder of when the city was conquered by the Seljuks in 1064. ⊠ *Ocakli* 🖼 *10 TL.*

Doğubeyazıt and Mt. Ararat

192 km (119 miles) southeast of Kars.

The scrappy frontier town of Doğubeyazıt (doh- oo-bay-yah-zuht) is a good base from which to enjoy views of Turkey's highest and most famous mountain, the majestic Mt. Ararat (Ağrı Dağı). Not far from the Iranian border, the place seems neglected, if not downright forgotten, with dusty streets and crumbling buildings. But the pace here is laid-back and the locals are friendly. You'll share the town with sheep and travelers bringing in contraband cigarettes and other cheap goods from Iran. There aren't many carpet and kilim shops here compared to tourist spots in western Turkey, so you can wander the main street, Çarşı Caddesi, without being bothered too much. A day is more than enough time to spend here, catching an early visit to the sites around Mt. Ararat and then the İshak Paşa Sarayı at sunset.

GETTING HERE AND AROUND
Doğubeyazıt is best reached via bus from Kars or Erzurum, the closest cities with airports. If you wish to climb Mt. Ararat, you'll need to make arrangments through a tour operator since climbing permits are required.

TOURS
Tour offices in Doğubeyazıt tend to go in and out of business every week, so if you need a guide, you're best off asking at your hotel and/or getting recommendations from other travelers. However,

there are some established and reputable tour companies that offer pre-organized Mt. Ararat treks. If you just want a glimpse of Araerat, then you can certainly arrange that through a local operator.

Middle Earth Travel
ADVENTURE TOURS | Although based in Cappadocia, Middle Earth Travel is a respected tour agency with a great deal of experience in trekking tours. It runs an eight-day, seven-night climb of Mt. Ararat. ☎ *384/271–2559* ⊕ *www.middleearthtravel.com* 🖼 *From €960.*

Tamzara
WALKING TOURS | Based in Istanbul, Tamzara offers climbing tours of Ararat (four to nine days) and cultural tours in eastern Turkey, and can offer advice on travel and getting climbing permits. ⊠ *Yeniçarsı Cd. 36* ☎ *212/251–9864 in Istanbul* ⊕ *www.tamzaratur.com* 🖼 *From 1675 TL.*

◉ Sights

İshak Paşa Sarayı (*İshak Paşa Palace*) **CASTLE/PALACE** | Other than to catch a glimpse of Mt. Ararat, the main reason to visit Doğubeyazıt is the enchanting İshak Paşa Sarayı, in the mountains southeast of town. The fortified palace was built in the late 18th century by local potentate Çolak Abdi Paşa and his son İshak. The interior of the building features ornate stonework, a fantastic mixture of Armenian, Persian, and classical Ottoman styles, but the once gold-plated doors were carted off by Russian troops in 1917 and are now in St. Petersburg's Hermitage Museum. Like Istanbul's Topkapı, the palace is divided into three areas: the first courtyard, open to all; the second courtyard, which holds the mosque and meeting rooms once used by the Paşa and other important personages; and the third courtyard, an inner sanctum housing the massive kitchen and the harem. Note how most rooms are small and equipped with their own hearths for the long cold winters. Visit in the morning or late afternoon, when the sun casts a deep orange glow over the palace. A renovation has placed a discordant, modern glass roof over portions of the site. You can clamber up to the fortress on a rough trail that starts next to the mosque; look for the two Uratian figures carved in the rock. Above the palace are a few Kurdish mud-brick houses. Taxis from Doğubeyazit cost around 30 TL one way, though they can also wait for an hour for an extra 10 to 20 TL. ⊠ *Dogubayazit* ✛ *6 km (4 miles) southeast of town on road to Göller* 🚗 *6 TL.*

★ **Mt. Ararat** (*Ağrı Dağı*)
MOUNTAIN—SIGHT | The region's most famous mountain is actually an extinct volcano covered with snow even in summer and soaring dramatically 16,850 feet above the arid plateau and dominating the landscape. According to Genesis, after the Great Flood, "the waters were dried up from off the earth; and Noah removed the covering of the ark, and looked, and behold, the face of the ground was dry." The survivors, as the story goes, had just landed on top of Mt. Ararat. Many other ancient sources—Chaldean, Babylonian, Chinese, Assyrian—also tell of an all-destroying flood and of one man who heroically escaped its consequences. The truth is that people have been searching for the actual ark since medieval times, and nothing has ever been found. The mountain can be easily viewed from Doğubeyazit, although actually climbing it requires a permit that can only be obtained by a licensed agency and usually takes at least a few days to acquire. Be prepared for a lot of walking on gravel, and be forewarned that the summit is often shrouded in clouds. Local tour offices will take you on a day trip that includes a visit to a village at the base of the mountain, which is the closest you can get to Ararat without a permit. ⊠ *Mt. Ararat, Dogubayazit.*

🍴 Restaurants

Murat Camping
$ | TURKISH | Despite the rustic name (there is a small campground on the premises), this large space with an outdoor terrace on a hillside just below the İshak Paşa Sarayı, is Doğubeyazit's only option for a big night out. It might not be the best meal of your life, but the views of Doğubeyazit and the surrounding mountains are commanding. **Known for:** kebabs; meze; rakı available. $ *Average main: 20 TL* ⊠ *Dogubayazit* ✛ *On road up to İshak Paşa Palace, just before it* ☎ *472/312–0367.*

🛏 Hotels

Ararat Hotel
$ | HOTEL | This hotel, popular with Mt. Ararat climbers, is geared towards backpackers, but tries harder than most places in town, making it your best option in the area. **Pros:** family-run; some English spoken; can organize tours. **Cons:** basic rooms; a bit run-down; basic breakfast. $ *Rooms from: 120 TL* ⊠ *Belediye Cad. 16, Dogubayazit* ☎ *472/312–4988* 🛏 *48 rooms* 🍴 *Free Breakfast.*

Tehran Boutique Hotel
$ | HOTEL | Since opening in 2015, this hotel has seriously upped the game of Doğubeyazit's accommodation options with friendly service, stylish modern decor, and comfortably spacious rooms. **Pros:** helpful English-speaking staff; alcohol available; large bathrooms. **Cons:** no air-conditioning; on a busy street. $ *Rooms from: 160 TL* ⊠ *Büyük Ağrı Cad. 72, Dogubayazit* ☎ *472/312–0195* ⊕ *www.tehranboutiquehotel.com* 🛏 *24 rooms* 🍴 *Free Breakfast.*

Lake Van

Lake Van is 171 km (106 miles) from Doğubeyazıt, continuing past Muradiye to the town of Van.

Van is the commercial center of Eastern Anatolia, and modern streets are lined with shops both modern and traditional and choked with traffic. There's a definite sense of bustle to the town, with restaurants and cafés filled with young people, many of them students from the local university. With its collection of rather uniform-looking and ugly cement buildings, what Van really lacks is a sense of history, which should not be surprising. The Van of today dates back to the early 20th century, when it was rebuilt some 5 km (3 miles) farther inland from Lake Van after being destroyed in battles with the Armenians and Russians during World War I. *Eski Van,* or Old Van, first appears in history 3,000 years ago, when it was the site of the Urartian capital of Tushpa, whose formidable fortress—built on a steep cliff rising from the lakeshore—dominated the countryside. What remains of Eski Van, in a grassy area near the lake, is a melancholy jumble of foundations still surrounded by its old walls. It's possible to make out two mosques, an Armenian church, and some *hans* (old-fashioned inns).

GETTING HERE AND AROUND

Turkish Airlines, Pegasus, and Atlas Jet have regular flights from Istanbul and SunExpress flies to Van from İzmir and Antalya. The airport is on the south of the city, on the road to Akdamar and Tatvan. A taxi from the airport to the city center costs around 30 TL. If you intend to hire a car, Europcar, Avis, and other companies have offices at the airport, although it's best to reserve a vehicle in advance. The airport and city center are just off the main highway that skirts the southern portion of Lake Van. If you're traveling by car, Van is 176 km (110 miles) south of Doğubeyazıt on D975.

TOURS

Ayanis

GUIDED TOURS | Based in Van's city center, Ayanis organizes day tours to Akdamar, Nemrut Crater Lake, and even İshak Paşa Palace for groups of 8 to 15 people. ⊠ *Cumhuriyet Cad., Van* ✛ *Under the City Hall* ☎ *432/222–0222* ⊕ *www.ayanis. com.tr* ✆ *From 90 TL.*

VISITOR INFORMATION

CONTACTS Visitor Information. ⊠ *Cumhuriyet Cad. 105, Just south of Fevzi Çakmak Cad., Van* ☎ *432/216–2530.*

Sights

Ahlat

ARCHAEOLOGICAL SITE | Situated on Lake Van's north shore 42 km (26 miles) northeast of Tatvan, the small town of Ahlat was once an important bridge from East to West. Now the remains of Seljuk and Ottoman mosques, tombs, and fortresses are the main focus of the otherwise shabby town that exists today. It's particularly famous for its medieval cemetery and its impressive collection of monumental *türbe* (tombs). A small museum on the sprawling site contains a collection of Uratian metalwork and pottery. ✛ *Northwestern shore of Lake Van.*

★ Akdamar

ISLAND | On the tranquil, uninhabited islet of Akdamar, among the wild olive and almond trees, stand the scant remains of a monastery that include the truly splendid **Church of the Holy Cross.** Built in AD 921 by an Armenian king, Gagik Artsruni of Vaspurakan, the compound was originally part of a palace, but was later converted to a monastery. Incredible high-relief carvings on the exterior make the church one of the most enchanting spots in Turkey. Much of the Old Testament is depicted here: look for Adam and Eve, David and Goliath, and Jonah and the whale. Along the top is a frieze of running animals; another frieze shows a vineyard where laborers work the fields and women dance with bears; and, of course, King Gagik, almost hidden above the entrance, is depicted, offering his church to Christ. The monastery operated until WWI, and since 2010 annual religious services have been allowed, usually in early September. There are a handful of small cafés and gift shops on the island, and a few coves that offer the opportunity to swim in the alkaline lake. One of the most charming things about the island may be the large number of grey rabbits scampering about. To reach Akdamar from Van, take a minibus (9 TL) or follow Route 300 to Gevaş, which is about 20 miles away. Just past Gevaş, you'll see ferries waiting at the well-marked landing to collect the required number of passengers—between 10 and 15—for the 20-minute ride. Normally it costs 15 TL per person but if there aren't enough passengers the round-trip is around 150 TL. Boats return to the mainland hourly until 6 pm. ⊠ Van ✛ Rte. 300, 56 km (35 miles) west of Van ⛴ 15 TL.

Çarpanak Island

ISLAND | Aside from Akdamar, there are several other small islands on Lake Van, with their own Armenian churches. While none are quite as glorious as Akdamar, the most interesting is Çarpanak Island, north of Van, often visited in combination with Adır Island. If you have the time and money, it can make a nice excursion where you'll likely to have the whole island to yourself. You need to hire a whole boat to visit, which costs around 150 or 250 TL. ⊠ Van.

Lake Van (Van Gölü)

BODY OF WATER | Turkey's largest and most unusual lake consists of 3,738 square km (1,443 square miles) of startlingly blue water surrounded by mighty volcanic cones, at an elevation of 5,659 feet. The lake was formed when a volcano blew its top and blocked the course of a river, leaving the water with no natural outlet; as a result the lake is highly alkaline and full of sulfides and mineral salts, six times saltier than the ocean. Lake Van's only marine life is a small member of the carp family, the İnci kefalı, which has somehow adapted to the saline environment. Intermittent daily ferries ply the route between Van and Tatvan, taking around four hours and costing just 10 TL, but without fixed departure times. Recreational water sports are limited, and beaches along the rocky shores are few and far between. Swimming in the soft water is pleasant, but try not to swallow any—it tastes terrible. If you're in the mood for a dip, your best bet is to do so when visiting the nearby island of Akdamar, from the lake's south shore. Alternatively, if you head northeast from Van on the Doğubeyazit road, you can stop at the little holiday camp located on the lake's edge just past the farming village of Çolpan. Soft drinks, barbecued food, sunbeds, and basic rooms are all available. ⊠ Van.

Mt. Nemrut

MOUNTAIN—SIGHT | Across the lake from Van is one of Turkey's loveliest natural wonders, the beautiful and rarely visited crater lakes of Mt. Nemrut (Nemrut Krater Gölü, which should not be confused with the more famous Mt. Nemrut farther west). From Tatvan, 146 km (91 miles) west of Van, a rutted road leads up the mountain to the 10,000-foot-high rim of what was once a mighty volcano. From the rim of the crater, you can see down to the two lakes below—a smaller swimmable one fed by hot springs and larger and much colder one. A loose dirt road leads down to the lakes, where very simple tea stands are set up. The inside of the crater has an otherworldly feel to it, with its own ecosystem: stands of short, stunted trees and scrubby bushes, birds and turtles, and cool breezes. It's only open after the snow melts in May/June until the winter begins again in November. After this time, it's possible to visit a small ski resort located halfway up the mountainside, with a chairlift that takes visitors to the summit. ⊠ Van.

The Armenian Church of Holy Cross, on the uninhabited islet of Akdamar, is a work of art, inside and out.

Van Kalesi (*Van Castle*)

CASTLE/PALACE | Steps—considerably fewer than the 1,000 claimed in local tourist handouts—ascend to Van Kalesi, the sprawling Urartian fortress on the outskirts of town. A path branches right to Urartian tombs in the sheer south rock face; an impressive cuneiform inscription here honors King Xerxes, whose Persian troops occupied the fortress early in the 5th century BC (look for the red metal fence on the southeast side). ■ TIP→ **You may need to pay a local a tip to show you these.** The crumbling ramparts are still impressive (more so than the parts that have been heavily restored), but as is often true in these parts, it's the view—sweeping across the lake and mountains—that makes the steep climb worthwhile. A taxi from the new town should cost no more than 30 TL one way. Cheaper *dolmuş* (shared taxis) depart regularly from the north end of Cumhuriyet Caddesi and are marked "Kale." ⊠ *Van Kalesi, Van* 🖼 *6 TL.*

🍴 Restaurants

Van breakfasts are famed throughout Turkey for their epic proportions as much as their delectable components. Served meze style, there's a huge array of small dishes best shared among several people: there's usually a variety of locally made cheeses (the popular local *otlu peyniri* is a salty white cheese studded with a type of wild garlic), eggs served several ways (fried, with *sucuk*, a garlic sausage, or with *kavurma*, slow-cooked chunks of meat), olives, tomatoes, jams, and, most importantly, *kaymak*, a delicious clotted cream that's eaten on bread with honey. Unlike in the west of Turkey, there are usually some typically Kurdish dishes like *kavut* (toasted ground wheat with honey and walnuts) and *cacık*, which is made with strained yogurt, garlic, and parsley. The city has many small restaurants that serve breakfast all day, but the best ones are along Kahvaltı Sokak, parallel to Cumhuriyet Caddesi; *kahvaltı* is the Turkish word for breakfast.

Grand Deniz Turizm

$ | **TURKISH** | A pebbly lakeside beach set with plastic tables is a good spot for lunch or dinner after a visit to Akdamar. The food, which includes local dishes such as kebabs and trout baked in a terra-cotta dish, is delicious. **Known for:** baked trout; grilled chicken wings; Adana kebab. [$] *Average main: 20 TL* ✉ *Van-Tatvan Karayolu Km 40, Gevas* ☎ *432/612–4038.*

Kervansaray

$ | **TURKISH** | Hidden up some unassuming stairs on the west side of Cumhuriyet Cadessi, this popular kebab place is a little bit more refined than the competition around town and has excellent food to boot. There's a broad range of typical kebabs, plus a few more unusual choices here, such as the *kaşarlı sarma beyti,* ground meat and cheese in a tomato sauce–covered wrap. **Known for:** kaşarlı sarma beyti; döner kebab; lahmacun. [$] *Average main: 20 TL* ✉ *Cumhuriyet Cad. 119, Van* ☎ *432/215–9482.*

Hotels

Büyük Urartu

$ | **HOTEL** | This established lodging option a little out of the center of Van makes an attempt at character with reproductions of Urartian art on the walls throughout and gold-embroidered bedspreads and floral wallpaper in the small but pleasant guest rooms. **Pros:** 24-hour room service and information desk; good café; friendly staff. **Cons:** popular with tour groups; some rooms in the back face brick walls and are dark; some noisy rooms. [$] *Rooms from: 160 TL* ✉ *Cumhuriyet Cad. 60, Van* ☎ *432/212–0660* 🌐 *www.buyukurartuotel.com* 🛏 *75 rooms* 🍴 *Free Breakfast.*

Hotel Dosco

$ | **HOTEL** | **FAMILY** | This newer hotel on the northern fringe of Van's city center offers clean facilities at reasonable rates, as well as friendly staff and guides that can be hired for the area sights. **Pros:** friendly staff; clean, spacious rooms; reasonable prices. **Cons:** some smoky rooms; married couples must show marriage certificate and unmarried couples not allowed; area is a bit run-down. [$] *Rooms from: 140 TL* ✉ *Koçbey Cd. 29, Van* ☎ *0432/214–6065* 🌐 *www.doscohotel.com* 🛏 *55 rooms* 🍴 *Free Breakfast.*

Nightlife

Hinar Bar

BARS/PUBS | Tucked down a side street not far from the junction of Cumhuriyet Caddesi and Fevzi Çakmak Caddesi, this place is a nice gem in the Vanbar scene. As long as you don't mind the smoky atmosphere, it's a great place to spend the evening people-watching the liberal intelligentsia of Van while enjoying some cold beers and warm bar snacks. ✉ *Yüzbaşıoğlu 1. Sok* ✣ *Off Maraş Cad.* ☎ *532/325–2447.*

Janya Bar and Şarap Evi

MUSIC CLUBS | This fourth-floor bar focuses on wine and has live music most nights, with performances leaning towards Turkish pop and rock, and some more traditional sounds thrown in. It can be a little noisy for a decent conversation, but still a fun place to soak up the atmosphere. Alternatively, take a seat next to the window and watch the nonstop hustle and bustle of the city. ✉ *Bozbay İş Merkezi, Cumhuriyet Cad., Van.*

Index

440

W

X

Y

Z

442

Photo Credits

Front Cover: Koraysa / Shutterstock [Description: Galata Tower, Karaköy quarter of Istanbul, Turkey.] Back cover, from left to right: Antony McAulay/Shutterstock; Turkey Ministry of Culture & Tourism; muharremz/Shutterstock. Spine: Sailorr/ Shutterstock. Interior, from left to right: DoreenD (1). Mikel Bilbao / age fotostock (2-3). Sailorr/Shutterstock (5). Chapter 1: Experience Turkey: DoreenD (8-9). Ig0rzh | Dreamstime.com (10-11). Kostyantyn Mikhyeyev | Dreamstime.com (11). Beats1 | Dreamstime.com (11). Oksana Saman | Dreamstime.com (12). Olga Savina/Shutterstock (12). muratart/Shutterstock (12). Orlok/Shutterstock (12). epic_images/Shutterstock (13). Lals stock/Shutterstock (13). Hakan Can Yalcin | Dreamstime.com (14). Softdreams | Dreamstime.com (14). Prometheus72/shutterstock (14). Nina Hilitukha | Dreamstime. com (14). Thrithot/shutterstock (15). gvictoria/shutterstock (16). piotreknik/Shutterstock (16). saaton/Shutterstock (16). Sonerbakir | Dreamstime.com (16). muratart/shutterstock (17). Evren Kalinbacak | Dreamstime.com (17). Kemal Mardin/ Shutterstock (18). Nazile Keskin | Dreamstime.com (18). IgorZh/shutterstock (18). Boris Stroujko/Shutterstock (19). Olena Tur/Shutterstock (19). Svitlana Tereshchenko | Dreamstime.com (22). Deniz | Dreamstime.com (22). Batuhan Gencosmanoglu/Shutterstock (22). Yuliia Kononenko | Dreamstime.com (22). Mehmet Cetin/Shutterstock (22). Esin Deniz/Shutterstock (23). Alp Aksoy/Shutterstock (23). Esin Deniz/Shutterstock (23). Ali Haydar/Shutterstock (23). Ozmedia | Dreamstime. com (23). Fedor Selivanov/Shutterstock (24). Fedor Selivanov/Shutterstock (24). Kirlikedi/Shutterstock (24). Ravital/ Shutterstock (24). Cristi Popescu/Shutterstock (25). park1688/Shutterstock (25). Shuo Wang | Dreamstime.com (25). Zehra Başak | Dreamstime.com (25). Andrew Mayovskyy/Shutterstock (26). Romas_Photo/Shutterstock (26). tolgaildun/ Shutterstock (26). Nejdet Duzen/Shutterstock (27). Evgenii Proskuriakov | Dreamstime.com (27). Sylvain Grandadam (33). Images&Stories / Alamy (34). Klaus-Peter Simon (34). Andreas Praefcke (34). joearena99 (35). Robert Harding Picture Library Ltd / Alamy (35). Interfoto Pressebildagentur / Alamy (36). PixAchi/Shutterstock (36). wikipedia.org (37). Hazlan Abdul Hakim/iStockphoto (37). Peter M. Wilson / Alamy (37). wikipedia.org (37). Yogesh Brahmbhatt/National Maritime Museum, Greenwich, London. Caird Fund., via Wikimedia Commons, Public Domain (38). wikipedia.org (38). wikipedia. org (39). jonbwe (39). Chapter 3: Istanbul: Xantana | Dreamstime.com (71). Ozimician | Dreamstime.com (74). 2008 Pinguino Kolb/Flickr, [CC BY-ND 2.0] (75). sila/Flickr, [CC BY-ND 2.0] (75). Michele Falzone / age fotostock (94). wikipedia. org (96). wikipedia.org (96). Mediamix photo/Shutterstock (97). dundanim/Shutterstock (97). Erik Lam/iStockphoto (97). Gryffindor / wikipedia.org (98). Imcflorida (98). David Pedre/iStockphoto (98). murat $en/iStockphoto (98). ImagesStories / Alamy (99). Earl Eliason/iStockphoto (99). Robert Harding Picture Library Ltd / Alamy (99). Art Kowalsky / Alamy (99). Dennis Cox / Alamy (100). Alex Segre / Alamy (100). Sibel A Roberts/iStockphoto (100). danilo donadoni / age fotostock (101). Images&Stories / Alamy (101). Images&Stories / Alamy (101). queenmab225 (112). Superstock/age fotostock (119). Alaskan Dude/Flickr, [CC BY-ND 2.0] (129). DavidHonlPhoto.com (133). Dennis Cox / age fotostock (136). Jason Keith Heydorn/Shutterstock (136). TimTheSaxMan (137). Vladimir Melnik/Shutterstock (139). Orhan/Shutterstock (140). Alvaro Leiva (140). ukrphoto/Shutterstock (140). Jonbwe (140). Johnny Lye/Shutterstock (141). rj lerich/Shutterstock (141). suzdale (141). David Sutherland / Alamy (142). steve estvanik/Shutterstock (142). steve estvanik/Shutterstock (142). steve estvanik/Shutterstock (142). Gavin Hellier / Alamy (143). Jose Enrique Molina (144). suzdale (145). Wikimedia. org (145). Chapter 4: The Sea of Marmara and The North Aegean: Peter Horree / Alamy (169). Bruno Morandi / age fotostock (183). Carlos Chavez/iStockphoto (189). Sadık Güleç/iStockphoto (197). Alaskan Dude/Flickr (204). Chapter 5: The Central and Southern Aegean Coast: muratart/Shutterstock (207). eerkun (218). Jose Fuste Raga / age fotostock (238). IML Image Group Ltd / Alamy (240). Fan (241). Kitkatcrazy (242). Turkey Ministry of Culture & Tourism (242). Nikater (242). S-F / Shutterstock (144-145). Turkey Ministry of Culture & Tourism (245). Marie-Lan Nguyen/Wikimedia Commons (246). Wikipedia.org (246). Connors Bros./Shutterstock (247). Dennis Cox / Alamy (247). Michael Harder / Alamy (247). Emei | Dreamstime.com (251). Tulay Over/iStockphoto (267). Chapter 6: The Turquoise Coast: Demetrio Carrasco / age fotostock (279). John Picken/Flickr, [CC BY-ND 2.0] (282). TurkeyShoot / Alamy (283). yusuf anil akduygu/iStockphoto (283). Efe Cem/Shutterstock (301). Konstantin Kopachinskii | Dreamstime.com (303). Dominic Whiting / Alamy (303). canvaspix / Shutterstock (304). Bon Appetit / Alamy (305). Deniz Ünlüsü/Shutterstock (305). Nejdet Duzen/Shutterstock (319). K.Jakubowska/Shutterstock (325). Simon Podgorsek/iStockphoto (329). ismail hayri ordu/iStockphoto (343). Turkey Ministry of Culture & Tourism (351). Chapter 7: Cappadocia and Central Turkey: Turkey Ministry of Culture & Tourism (357). julzie49 (370). photolibrary.com (371). Walter Bibikow/age fotostock (372). Karsten Dörre / wikipedia.org (373). Travelscape Images / Alamy (373). yversace (374). Blaine Harrington III / Alamy (375). Tolo Balaguer / photolibrary (376). Tolo Balaguer / photolibrary (376). photolibrary.com (377). photolibrary.com (377). Turkey Ministry of Culture & Tourism (377). Turkey Ministry of Culture & Tourism (378). dgunbug (379). Suronin | Dreamstime.com (392). Bruno Morandi / age fotostock (396). Bruno Morandi / age fotostock (397). Chapter 8: The Black Sea Coast and Lake Van: Shutterstock (411). Asafta | Dreamstime.com (421). Mark Grigorian/Flickr, [CC BY-ND 2.0] (433). About Our Writers: All photos are courtesy of the authors.

Notes

Notes

Notes

Notes

Fodor's ESSENTIAL TURKEY

Editorial: Douglas Stallings, *Editorial Director;* Margaret Kelly, Jacinta O'Halloran, Amanda Sadlowski, *Senior Editors;* Kayla Becker, Alexis Kelly, Teddy Minford, Rachael Roth, *Editors;* Jeremy Tarr, *Fodors.com Editorial Director;* Rachael Levitt, *Fodors.com Managing Editor*

Design: Tina Malaney, *Design and Production Director;* Jessica Gonzalez, *Graphic Designer;* Mariana Tabares, *Design & Production Intern*

Production: Jennifer DePrima, *Editorial Production Manager;* Carrie Parker, *Senior Production Editor;* Elyse Rozelle, *Production Editor;* Jackson Pranica, *Editorial Production Assistant*

Maps: Rebecca Baer, *Senior Map Editor;* David Lindroth, Mark Stroud (Moon Street Cartography), *Cartographers*

Photography: Jill Krueger, *Director of Photo;* Namrata Aggarwal, Ashok Kumar, Carl Yu, *Photo Editors;* Rebecca Rimmer, *Photo Intern*

Business & Operations: Chuck Hoover, *Chief Marketing Officer;* Robert Ames, *General Manager;* Stephen Horowitz, *Director of Business Development and Revenue Operations;* Tara McCrillis, *Director of Publishing Operations*

Public Relations and Marketing: Joe Ewaskiw, *Senior Director Communications & Public Relations;* Esther Su, *Senior Marketing Manager;* Ryan Garcia, Thomas Talarico, Miranda Villalobos, *Marketing Specialists*

Technology: Jon Atkinson, *Director of Technology;* Rudresh Teotia, *Lead Developer;* Jacob Ashpis, *Content Operations Manager*

Writers: Jennifer Hattam, Kevin Mataraci, Katie Nawdorny, Paul Osterlund

Editor: Douglas Stallings

Production Editor: Jennifer DePrima

1st Edition

ISBN 978-1-64097-140-0

ISSN 2640–6314

Library of Congress Control Number 2018914624

SPECIAL SALES
This book is available at special discounts for bulk purchases for sales promotions or premiums. For more information, e-mail SpecialMarkets@fodors.com.

PRINTED IN THE UNITED STATES OF AMERICA

10 9 8 7 6 5 4 3 2 1

About Our Writers

Jennifer Hattam is a freelance journalist who has been based in Istanbul since 2008 and has traveled extensively in Turkey and around the region. She writes about environmental, social and urban issues, as well as art, food and travel. Find her work at ⊕ *www.jenniferhattam.com* or follow her on Twitter @TheTurkishLife. She updated Experience Turkey and Travel Smart.

Kevin Mataraci is a writer and editor who divides his time between San Francisco and Istanbul. He updated The Sea of Marmara & the North Aegean and Cappadocia & Central Turkey.

Katie Nadworny is an Istanbul-based freelance writer who specializes in travel, art, and the intersection of politics and culture, with a focus on Eastern Europe and the Middle East. She is a contributor to *Cornucopia Magazine*, a bi-annual glossy for connoisseurs of Turkey, and her work has appeared in *National Geographic, The Daily Beast, The Guardian, The Independent,* and *BBC Travel,* among other places. She updated Istanbul.

Paul Benjamin Osterlund is an Istanbul-based freelance journalist and writer. He updated The Turquoise Coast and The Black Sea Coast & Lake Van.